THE COMPLETE BOOK OF

MONEY SECRETS

THE COMPLETE BOOK OF
MONEY
SECRETS

Reader's Digest

The Reader's Digest Association
(Canada) Ltd., Montreal

PROJECT STAFF

Project Editor
Robert Ronald

Senior Editor
Andrew Byers

Designer
Cécile Germain

Copy Editor
Gilles Humbert

Production Manager
Holger Lorenzen

Production Coordinator
Susan Wong

Editorial Administrator
Elizabeth Eastman

Consulting Editor
Gordon Pape

Books and Home Entertainment

Vice President
Deirdre Gilbert

Art Director
John McGuffie

ISBN 0–88850–758–5

Address comments about *The Complete Book of Money Secrets* to:
    Editor, Books and Home Entertainment
    c/o Customer Service, Reader's Digest
    1125 Stanley Street, Montreal, Quebec H3B 5H5

For information about this and other Reader's Digest products, or
to request a catalog, please call our 24-hour Customer Service hotline at
1-800-465-0780.

You can also visit us on the World Wide Web at
http://www.readersdigest.ca

Printed in Canada
03 04 05 / 5 4 3 2 1

NOTE TO OUR READERS

Reader's Digest publishes the advice of expert authorities in many fields. But the use of a book is not a substitute for legal, accounting or other professional services. Consult a competent professional for answers to your specific questions.

ABOUT THIS BOOK

Do you ever get the feeling that other people know how to handle their money better than you do? That there's information to help you manage your money, but you don't know how to get it?

Help is here. *The Complete Book of Money Secrets* provides all the practical information you need to help you deal with banks, plan for retirement, pay for an education, buy or sell your home, start or run a business, grow your money and more.

At your fingertips are 14 clearly organized chapters containing more than 700 easy-to-read entries of financial advice from top Canadian and American experts in every money-related field—advice you can use every day.

The Complete Book of Money Secrets also helps you keep your hard-earned money by avoiding extra bank fees, cutting excessive insurance premiums and reducing your federal and provincial tax bills.

You'll find tips and advice from some of Canada's best-known financial experts: Evelyn Jacks on tax savings, Murray Baker on paying for university, Bruce Cohen on pension plans, Sally Praskey and Helena Moncrieff on insurance, G. Pierce Newman on estate planning, Howard Turk on home ownership and many others.

Concise, easy-to-understand articles take the mystery out of shrewd investing and the mishaps out of retirement planning. Straightforward language eases the doubts of financial decision-making. You'll learn how to make your money work harder, go further and grow faster.

With top-notch advice at your fingertips, this book can help you get a sharper financial edge, and give you the peace of mind you deserve.

—Gordon Pape, consulting editor

CONTENTS

Business Tactics

Shelters

3 Dealing With the CCRA

Cutting Through Red Tape

Audits

4 For Businesspeople Only

5 Dealing With Banks, Credit & Debt

6 Holding the Line on Medical Costs

7 Friends, Family & Your Money

8 Financing an Education

9 Retirement Planning

10 Insurance Tactics & Strategies

Life Insurance

13 Real Estate Strategies

14 Buying & Selling a House, Condo or Co-op

Before Buying a Home

Financing a Home

Home Improvements

Smart Money Management

1

The Most Common Mistakes in Personal Financial Planning

More families should note Ben Franklin's observation that "in this world nothing is certain but death and taxes." Many intelligent people don't know how to achieve their life goals, provide for their families or prepare for the death of the main income earner.

Take full control of your life—before you begin to invest. Of the many errors families make in money management, 12 are repeated constantly:

● **Only one family member is involved in financial affairs.** One spouse should have ultimate responsibility for decision making, but both should be involved in financial planning with accountants and lawyers.

Bonus: Goals are more easily met if both partners pull in the same direction.

● **Life goals are not on paper.** Write down your goals, attach a dollar amount to them and weigh their relative importance.

● **There is no family budget.** Budget carefully, so you know what you're spending. It's easier to change what you spend than what you earn.

● **The family has no excess liability (umbrella) insurance.** This type of coverage provides extra protection against lawsuits if someone is injured on your property, in your car, by a mis-struck golf ball, etc. Acquiring this type of insurance could be one of the wisest investments you ever make.

● **The contents of your home are not insured up to their replacement value.** To maintain your standard of living, buy replacement-cost coverage. Discuss exceptions with your insurance agent.

● **There is insufficient liquidity to handle emergencies or opportunities.** Create a war chest. Have emergency funds available equal to three to six months of spending money. Use your budget to arrive at an exact figure.

● **Tax reduction is not a goal.** People devote too much attention to reducing taxes when they should be concentrating on accumulating wealth.

● **Employee benefits are poorly understood.** Maximize your contributions to group RRSPs with corporate matching, if this benefit is available where you work. They are the best tax-deferral mechanisms among voluntary retirement programs.

Also, make sure your group disability plan is adequate. Check for inflation protection, partial disability coverage, lifetime benefits and "own occupation" definition of disability—all of which most plans exclude. You can purchase a residual wrap policy that fills in some of the holes.

● **Investments are not diversified.** Buy non-specialty mutual funds (e.g., index funds). They are a relatively inexpensive way to play the market while making your first significant investment diversified.

● **A general-practice attorney drafts the family's wills.** Consult an estate-planning specialist, especially if your life insurance and death benefits equal $500,000—or more.

● **No tax projections are made.** Know the tax "weather" so you can better decide which "investment clothes" to wear. Read the financial pages regularly and consult with professionals.

● **Income earners do not have disability insurance.** Know your disability coverage needs and seek adequate protection. It is well worth your time and effort to do so. Most agents do not push this type of policy (because it's hard to explain the importance of it or because the commissions are lower than those on whole life insurance).

Generally, you should get as much disability coverage as the insurance company will let you have. Disability differs from life insurance in that companies are reluctant to sell you so much coverage that you would have no incentive to return to work.

Source: Charles Haines, president, Haines Financial Advisors.

How to Apply Sophisticated Financial Techniques to Personal Finances

When finances become complicated, they often become clouded as well. When you're dealing with a variety of assets, investments and income sources, it

> " **Tax reduction is not a goal. People devote too much attention to reducing taxes when they should be concentrating on accumulating wealth.** "

can be hard to focus clearly on how well things are really going for you financially.

The wizards who run the financial affairs of large corporations have developed analytical tools to deal with this problem by providing clear answers in crucial areas. These tools are just as useful for diagnosing your personal financial health.

In order to get valid and useful figures, you must begin with accurate data. A net worth statement, a cash-flow analysis and a taxable income statement should contain all the numbers you need. Simply plug the appropriate figures into the formulas given below.

These tools should help you put your personal financial picture in perspective, but keep in mind that, unlike a business, there are no "objective" guidelines to follow in shaping your personal financial future. Only you can accurately assess the weight you give to factors of personal circumstance.

For example, Joe in Alberta with a taxable income in 2001 of $110,000 would have had a marginal tax rate (federal and provincial) of 39%. This is the percentage of each investment dollar he is paying in taxes on any interest income earned. At present, Joe has $100,000 in a taxable money-market fund earning 5% ($5,000 annual income). The after-tax return is 3.05%

$$\frac{[\$5,000 \times (1 - 0.39)] + 0}{\$100,000}$$

Joe then uses this figure and compares it with tax-advantaged yields from bank preferred shares to determine which has a better after-tax return. He uses a 4.5% gross yield on the preferreds. The tax rate on dividends in Alberta in 2001 for someone in his bracket was 24.08%.

Using the same formula, Joe finds that, although he is earning fewer gross dollars than in the money market fund ($4,500 versus $5,000) the after-tax return on the preferred shares is actually higher, at 3.42%, thanks to the effect of the dividend tax credit. He is better off putting his $100,000 into the preferreds, even though their before-tax yield is less.

The same person has monthly expenses of $6,000 and his expense coverage ratio is:

$$\frac{\$100,000}{\$6,000} = 16.7 \text{ months}$$

TOOL	FORMULA	WHAT IT SHOWS
Liquidity ratio	$\dfrac{\text{LIQUID ASSETS}}{\text{CURRENT LIABILITIES}}$	Are liquid assets sufficient to meet short-term obligations?
Expense coverage ratio	$\dfrac{\text{LIQUID ASSETS}}{\text{MONTHLY EXPENSES}}$	How many months' expenses will your liquid assets cover?
Debt ratio	$\dfrac{\text{TOTAL ASSETS}}{\text{TOTAL DEBT}}$	How aggressive is your balance sheet?
Working assets ratio	$\dfrac{\text{INVESTMENT ASSETS}}{\text{TOTAL ASSETS}}$	How much of your net worth is working for you?
Marginal tax rate	TAX RATE PAID ON YOUR LAST EARNED DOLLAR	What percentage of each additional dollar will go for taxes?
Work ratio	$\dfrac{\text{EARNED INCOME}}{\text{TOTAL INCOME}}$	How dependent are you on your job to meet income needs?
Fixed expenses as percentage of total income	$\dfrac{\text{FIXED EXPENSES}}{\text{TOTAL INCOME}}$	How much of your income goes to cover expenses over which you have no control?

After-tax return on investment assets (see formula below).

$$\frac{[\text{taxable investment income} \times (1 - \text{marginal tax rate})] + \text{nontaxable income}}{\text{total investment assets}}$$

This should highlight to him or her that he or she is being overly conservative and can invest the funds (within his or her risk tolerance) at a higher return.

Note: Many financial advisers use a rule of thumb of keeping enough liquid funds to cover six months' expenses. Since many factors, including your disability coverage and your attitude, must be taken into account, be careful of rules of thumb.

Source: *Joyce A. Streithorst, CFP, is manager of personal financing for Joel Isaacson & Co.*

A Net Worth Calculation

Calculating your net worth is the basic method of determining if you're getting ahead or falling behind in the struggle for financial health. Those who like to keep close tabs on their progress may want to do this frequently; most ought to do it annually. January is a convenient time, since you receive year-end statements and have to do much of this work for your taxes anyway. Hopefully, each year will show you are closer to financial independence.

Assets

Item 1: **Cash.** Total the contents of your chequing and savings accounts, money-market funds, and certificates of deposit.

Item 2: **Nonincome-producing assets.** These include the value of your home, vacation home (if you have one and don't rent it out for part of the year), jewelry, automobiles, home furnishings, art.

Item 3: **Insurance.** Determine the cash value of all insurance policies. If you haven't checked recently, it is definitely a good idea to write to your insurers and find out.

Item 4: **Investments.** Check the current value of your stocks and bonds, any rental properties, real estate partnerships, oil and gas partnerships (which may have no current value), gold and silver (and other personal commodities), company stock options, personal collections (stamps, coins, antiques, etc.), notes receivable, and the book value of your business.

Item 5: **Retirement assets.** Add in RRSP, CPP/QPP, pension and profit-sharing plans, any deferred compensation, and company savings plans.

Be sure to count only the amount you could take from your company if you left tomorrow.

Liabilities

Liabilities include mortgages, bank loans, credit card and any other trade debit balances, and notes due.

Total the assets and liabilities. Subtract the latter from the former. The result is your net worth—the

HOW MUCH OF YOUR WEALTH SHOULD BE KEPT LIQUID?

Determining the best size of liquid monetary reserves (chequing account, savings account, money-market funds) is largely a matter of psychology: What do you feel comfortable with?

Remember that the purpose of keeping liquid assets is to avoid having to disturb your long-term investments in the event you need money. In fact, cash reserves are seen by many people as an emergency hedge. What fewer people see is that you can hold a larger amount as an opportunity reserve, making it easy to take advantage of investment opportunities that come along.

With this in mind, figure that adequate liquid reserves should be a minimum of three months' expenses— not income. When adding up your liquid assets, you may want to include your guaranteed investment certificates, which could be liquidated prior to maturity with the loss of only part of the interest. The possibility of borrowing against the value of your life insurance is another plus.

Source: *Alexandra Armstrong, CFP, president of the independent financial-planning firm Armstrong, Welch and MacIntyre, Inc., 1155 Connecticut Ave. NW, Washington, DC 20036.*

Cash Flow

Positive cash flow is what counts. You can be getting rich on paper and still not be able to meet your bills—unless you have a positive cash flow. Fortunately, it is not difficult to make a reasonably accurate annual projection of where you stand.

Step 1

Itemize every source of income you have. This will include base salary, any bonuses, commissions, self-employment income, CPP/QPP payments, Old Age Security and pension or other retirement income (if any). Add to that any capital gains you anticipate for the year. Add any interest, dividend, trust fund or other investment income.

Step 2

Figure your yearly expenses. The following spending schedule should cover all of most people's categories of expenditure. If you have others, you can add more headings. The schedule includes this year and next so you can record the past and plan for the future. This way you can avoid the emergency expense—because you will have planned for it. Total your expenses and subtract from income. If you come up with a positive number, congratulations—you are accumulating wealth. If the bottom line comes up negative, it's time to trim some of your voluntary (nonfixed) expenditures. *Suggestion:* Consider your retirement contributions and annual investments as expenses to include.

Annual Spending Schedule

These annual figures are for the current year. If you expect next year's expenditures or deductions to vary greatly, indicate them in the second column.

Source: *Alexandra Armstrong, CFP, president, Armstrong, Welch and MacIntyre, Inc.*

	THIS YEAR	NEXT YEAR
Food/groceries		
Clothing		
Mortgage payment(s)		
Utilities		
Telephone		
Dry cleaner, drugstore, hairdresser		
New household purchases		
Real estate taxes		
Auto maintenance (gas, repairs, etc.)		
Transportation (cabs, bus, etc.)		
Car payments		
Entertainment		
Club dues		
Vacation trips, camp		
Domestic help		
Child care (deductible)		
Home maintenance		
Yard/pool maintenance		
Subscriptions/books		
Gifts/birthdays, etc.		
Medical expenses (not reimbursed)		
Insurance premiums		
—Life		
—Disability		
—Medical		
—Auto		
—Personal liability		
Alimony		
Child support		
Regular allotments to savings		
Retirement contributions		
Stock purchase plans		
Personal property taxes		
Charitable contributions		
Unreimbursed business expenses		
Tax preparation fees		
Education		
Legal fees		
Federal estimated tax payments		
Provincial/local estimated tax payments		
Other—Source:		

figure that can help you estimate when to retire with adequate finances or the progress you are making to increase your wealth.

Source: *Alexandra Armstrong, CFP, president of the independent financial-planning firm Armstrong, Welch and MacIntyre, Inc.*

A Plan to Double Your Wealth

The concept of doubling your wealth has little meaning without a specific time frame. If you have any income-producing investments, they will eventually double your wealth without your having to do anything. But doubling your wealth within a target time period calls for some planning.

If invested capital remains constant, the return on investment needed to accomplish your goal can be figured by the "rule of 72": Divide the number 72 by the number of years within which you aim to double your worth. The resulting number is the percentage you must earn on invested capital. Doubling in 10 years will require investments to yield 7.2%; in five years, 14.4%; in two years, 36%.

To find out if your current investment portfolio is producing up to your expectations, do a careful review. Consider liquidating poorly performing investments and reinvesting the capital. A good rule of thumb in deciding whether to keep or sell an investment is: "If I had the cash, would I make this investment now?"

A good wealth-building portfolio is diversified and balanced. A good balance would be about one-third in stocks, one-third in income-producing real estate, one-third in "other" (which includes bonds, annuities and precious metals).

Regardless of how well balanced your portfolio is, your wealth will grow far more rapidly if you augment it with a regular and ongoing program of new investment. This will require some self-education in investment matters to help you work more effectively with your financial adviser. Careful investigation of each new asset prior to purchase greatly reduces your risk. Emphasize updates, too: Regular review of your portfolio on at least an annual basis will indicate how well your plan is working or if there is a need for review.

Source: *Alexandra Armstrong, CFP, president of the independent financial-planning firm Armstrong, Welch and MacIntyre, Inc.*

Finding a Financial Planner

Most successful people are too busy being successful to spend any serious time analyzing their financial situation, establishing goals and structuring and executing a financial plan that will enable them to achieve these goals. That is what a good financial planner should be able to do—alleviate the time burden on the very people who have the least amount of time to spare.

What to Expect

Financial-planning firms assume responsibility for coordinating your financial affairs—balance your investments, manage your taxes, plan for retirement, plan your estate and, above all, protect your assets. What they will require of you is that you take an inventory of your assets and gather every conceivable kind of financial paper. Once you've provided the necessary information, a planner will analyze your financial profile and issue a comprehensive plan for achieving your major financial objectives. The plan will make recommendations and organize follow-through.

You should receive periodic reports of your financial condition to help you adjust your decisions over time. With a good financial planner, there is no such thing as "one size fits all." A quality planning firm will help you develop the perspective needed to make intelligent financial choices.

What to Look For

Over the past several years, it seems everyone has become a "financial planner." That can make your search a little tricky, but looking for the following characteristics should provide some help.

Professional expertise: Credentials are important. The best credentials in the field are the Registered Financial Planner (RFP) and the Certified Financial Planner (CFP) designations. Some attorneys and accountants also specialize in financial planning.

Resources: Financial planners should work closely with other professionals—attorneys, accountants, tax experts, investment specialists—to cover all of the important financial-planning areas for the client. State-of-the-art computer facilities are almost essential to the firm's ability to work out the tax and other consequences of various planning proposals. Also, a reliable network of contacts throughout major financial circles is an important asset.

Range of offerings: A financial-planning firm should be licensed to offer securities, limited partnerships and insurance—a full range of products to support the plans and strategies of all its clients.

Affiliation with a major institution: Many financial institutions, including banks and investment houses, are now offering financial planning in the same manner that life insurance companies have been doing for many years. A company with a strong long-term reputation can be your best guarantee of superior service.

Source: *Randy Breidbart, J.D., former regional director, Mutual Benefit Financial Service Co., 633 Third Ave., New York, NY 10017.*

Choosing the Best Financial Planner

A sound professional relationship with a financial planner is vital in today's increasingly complex financial world. A financial planner will help you analyze your current financial situation, define your financial goals, develop a specific plan to achieve those goals and implement the plan.

The first step in choosing a financial planner is familiarizing yourself with the field in general. Read. Talk to knowledgeable friends and professionals. Furthermore, you will be better able to evaluate the quality of service you are receiving.

The next step is to begin interviewing planners. If you need help in getting names, obtain references from friends or other financial advisers whom you trust. Other possible sources: The *Financial Planners Standards Council* (www.cfp-ca.org) and the *Canadian Association of Financial Planners (CAFP)* (www.cafp.org).

Interview a number of practitioners over the telephone. You will soon get a feel for the ones who are likely to be suitable for you. Plan to narrow your choices to three or four and schedule an interview with each. In the interview, you will want to inquire about professional credentials, scope of services, areas of specialization and compensation (fees and/or commissions). Feeling comfortable and confident with your choice of planner is very important.

Checklist: Interviewing Financial Planners

When interviewing a prospective financial planner, make sure to cover these vital points:

✔ **Experience.** Three years' track record as a professional financial planner should be considered a minimum. A related background in brokerage, accounting, insurance, etc., is a plus.

✔ **Credentials.** CFP (Certified Financial Planner) credentials indicate extensive education. Registered Financial Planner (RFP) status (maintained by the Canadian Association of Financial Planners) indicates experience as well as expertise.

✔ **Support.** Make sure your planner has full computer services and adequate support staff. A solo practitioner is at a distinct disadvantage today. Many planners are teaming up to offer broader, better service.

✔ **Clients.** How many and what type? Favor a planner who has clients like you. A planner with more than 150 clients is spread too thin, unless he or she has adequate staff to service them. Also find out how many of them renew each year. A 75% client-renewal rate is minimum.

✔ **Reviews.** Are ongoing reviews provided to make the plan current? How does the planner keep clients up-to-date? A regular newsletter and periodic seminars are customary.

✔ **Fees.** Don't expect a personalized plan for less than about $1,500. Fees can go up to many times this figure, consistent with the complexity of your particular situation. Ask beforehand.

✔ **Trust.** Be sure you are comfortable with this person. Trust is an essential factor in producing meaningful results.

Source: *Alexandra Armstrong, CFP, president of the independent financial-planning firm Armstrong, Welch and MacIntyre, Inc., 1155 Connecticut Ave. NW, Washington, DC 20036.*

Credentials

Two types of certification are available to financial-planning professionals, and they indicate rigorous courses of professional training. The Certified Financial Planner (CFP) designation is awarded to those who successfully complete the comprehensive six-part curriculum of the Canadian Institute of Financial Planning (CIFP), based in Toronto (www.cifp.ca). The Registered Financial Planner (RFP) designation is awarded by the Canadian Association of Financial Planners, following successful completion of its program.

Both certifications include adherence to a strict code of ethics. The CFP also indicates commitment to a plan of continuing education due to the changing nature of many areas of finance, including investments, insurance and taxes. Planners who offer investment advice must be registered with their provincial or territorial securities commission.

Continuing educational activities should be on the roster of interview questions. Many organizations sponsor major continuing-education programs in financial planning: The Canadian Securities Institute (CSI), the CAFP and the CIFP. All three issue certificates for programs successfully completed.

Scope of Services

Does this planner develop a plan that is reviewed and updated periodically? Is there continual contact between the planner and the client as investment opportunities arise? How specific is the advice offered? Does your planner suggest investments that may be appropriate for you? What is the planner's role in actually purchasing investments?

Different levels of service may be appropriate to your needs, depending on the size and the activity of your portfolio, your degree of personal involvement, your work situation, etc. For example, many people have done a fine basic job of structuring their investments and may simply need some overall strategic advice or merely the peace of mind that comes from confirmation of the value of their efforts.

Areas of Specialization

Look for a planner who serves clients whose needs are similar to yours. A financial planner who claims to be an expert in many fields should be regarded with some skepticism. A competent planner should have working relationships with other financial-services professionals and be willing to work with the financial advisers you are already using.

Compensation

Find out how much the services are going to cost. On what basis is the planner compensated? Hourly fee? Commissions on financial products sold? Or a combination of the two? The advice of a fee-only planner is generally free from any conflict of interest. When working with a commission-compensated planner, make sure that a variety of financial instruments and products is being offered, not just the ones on which the planner stands to make the largest commission. Investigate the fee-and-commission alternative—it may provide a flexible solution for both parties.

A final qualification is personal compatibility. Your financial planner should be someone whose philosophy and background you respect and with whom you feel comfortable. Clients who have selected carefully can be rewarded with a financial-planning partnership well suited to meeting their personal goals.

Source: Jan Walsh, MBA, academic associate at the College for Financial Planning, 9725 E. Hampden Ave., Denver, CO 80231. A Certified Financial Planner, she is a member of the ICFP and IAFP and is on the board of directors of the Rocky Mountain Chapter of the IAFP.

Make an Asset Inventory

If something should happen to you, would your family know where your important papers and assets are? Here's an inventory form that will make this job easier. Give copies to your spouse, perhaps another relative outside your home, any outside executor and your attorney. It will make their jobs easier—and you might locate some neglected assets. Keep blank copies of the form on hand and update your inventory when significant changes take place.

If you have a fireproof lockbox at home that holds your important (nonnegotiable) papers, it is a good place to store your asset inventory. Your spouse (or whomever you designate) should know where this box is and should have access to it. You could also put a copy of the inventory in your safe-deposit box.

Source: Alexandra Armstrong, CFP, president of the independent financial-planning firm Armstrong, Welch and MacIntyre, Inc.

ASSET INVENTORY

For _____

Social Insurance number _____

Employer _____

IMPORTANT NAMES, ADDRESSES AND PHONE NUMBERS

Lawyer _____

Accountant _____

Stockbroker _____

Insurance agent _____

Date prepared _____

Copies given to _____

_____

_____

_____

MY VALUABLE PAPERS AND ASSETS ARE STORED IN THESE LOCATIONS:

A. Residence (address and where to look)

_____

_____

B. Safe-deposit box (bank and address)

_____

_____

C. Office (address)

_____

D. _____

E. _____

F. _____

_____

ITEM	LOCATION	A	B	C	D	E	F
1. Estate Planning							
My will (original)							
My will (copy)							
Powers of attorney							
My burial instructions							
Cemetery plot deed							
Spouse's will (original)							
Spouse's will (copy)							
Spouse's burial instructions							
Document appointing children's guardian							
Handwritten list of special bequests							
Safe combination, business							
Safe combination, home							
Trust agreements							
Life insurance, group							
Life insurance, individual							
2. Insurance							
Other death benefits							
Property and casualty insurance							
Health insurance policy							
Home owners insurance policy							
Car insurance policy							
3. Business							
Employment contracts							
Partnership agreements							

ITEM	LOCATION	A	B	C	D	E	F
4. Financial							
List of chequing and savings accounts							
Bank statements, canceled cheques							
List of credit cards							
Guaranteed investment certificates							
Cheque books							
Savings passbooks							
Record of investment securities							
Brokerage account record							
Stock certificates							
Mutual fund shares							
Bonds							
Other securities							
Corporate retirement plan							
RRSP/RRIF							
Annuity contracts							
Stock option plan							
Stock purchase plan							
Profit-sharing plan							
Income tax returns							
5. Real Estate							
Titles and deeds to real estate and land							
Rental property records							
Notes & other loan agreements including mortgages							
6. Possessions							
List of stored and loaned valuable possessions							
Auto ownership records							
Boat ownership records							
7. Personal Records							
Birth certificates							
Citizenship papers							
My adoption papers							
Military discharge papers							
Marriage certificates							
Children's birth certificates							
Children's adoption papers							
Divorce/separation records							
Names and addresses of relatives and friends							
Listing of professional memberships							
Listing of fraternal organization memberships							
Other:							

How to Handle Financial Paperwork

Here's a quick quiz. Do you honestly know…

- **Where all your important financial papers are?**
- **How long to keep those papers?**
- **Which papers should be stored where?**

Most people would answer "no" to these questions. Any "no" answer should indicate that it is time to go through all your important papers and records and get them organized.

Start by dedicating a file drawer or small file cabinet to your financial records. Anything less than that will prove to be inadequate over time.

Keep one section of the file cabinet or drawer for files that you will have to handle often during the year. Keep another section for files that will hold permanent information.

Getting Started

Next, go through the records you currently keep…file by file, envelope by envelope, paper stack by paper stack. Follow these rules on what to keep and where to keep it:

Current records: Files you have to update regularly. Keep these files in your home file drawer or cabinet.

- **Auto insurance.** Policy, claim forms, records of claims filed and paid.
- **Bank statements.** Use separate files in which to keep chequing, savings, guaranteed investment certificates.
- **Charge accounts.** Have one file for each creditor. File bills and records of payments.
- **Credit cards.** File statements and records of payment. Also keep a readily available list of credit card numbers and the phone number to call if a card is lost or stolen.
- **Health insurance.** Policies, benefits explanations, claim forms, records of claims filed and paid.
- **Home insurance.** Home or apartment insurance, fire insurance, umbrella liability policies.
- **Mortgage statements.** Keep records of statements and evidence of payment.

> **"Long-term records:** Keep a separate folder for each year. By law you should keep all tax records for at least six years—tax returns and all backups. Be safe…keep them for seven years. In fact, keep copies of your actual returns indefinitely.**"**

- **Personal loan agreements.** Keep records of payments on all loans you owe to others…and of all loans others owe to you.
- **Retirement accounts.** Keep separate files for RRSPs, CPPs, non-registered plans, profit-sharing and stock-option plans and pension statements.
- **Stockbroker statements.** Keep records of all purchases and sales.

Long-term records: Files you have to handle rarely. Keep these at home or, when indicated, in a safe-deposit box at the bank.

Caution: Keep valuables and vital papers in a safe-deposit box, but don't overdo it. The box may be sealed when you die, so wills, cemetery deeds and life insurance policies kept there may be inaccessible just when they are needed the most, unless you have taken steps before your death to give the trustee of your estate access to your safe-deposit box.

Be sure your trustee knows where the box can be located, where the key is and what you keep in the box.

- **Life insurance.** Current policies and copies of the summary statements highlighting the terms of the policy. *Also useful:* List each policy by name of insurance company and policy number. It is usually possible to make a claim with only this information, without the policy itself. Throw out policies you have canceled.
- **Will.** File copies of the current will. Keep a copy at home in an accessible location. You can keep originals in your safe-deposit box and/or with your lawyer.
- **Living will.** Give copies to family members or close friends, your attorney and others who should know your wishes. Remember to keep one copy accessible at home.
- **Power of attorney.** Copies of power of attorney forms giving you power over others' accounts or giving others power over your own accounts. Whoever holds your power of attorney should have a copy. So should your attorney.

● **Durable power of attorney** for health care or health care proxy. Leave copies to the individuals mentioned above.

● **Social Insurance cards.** Photocopy each family member's Social Insurance card. Keep originals in a safe-deposit box.

● **Birth certificates.** Make copies for each family member. Keep the originals in your safe-deposit box.

● **Marriage,** separation, divorce and prenuptial agreements, adoption papers. Keep in your safe-deposit box.

● **Military discharge papers.** Keep in your safe-deposit box.

● **Real estate.** Keep deeds and title insurance in your safe-deposit box.

● **Trust agreements.** For trusts you set up or of which you are the beneficiary. Originals should be kept in a safe-deposit box. Leave copies with your lawyer and trustees.

● **Partnership agreements.** Keep in your safe-deposit box.

● **Burial arrangements.** Include cemetery deeds and instructions. Give copies to family members or friends who will have to make arrangements.

Tax Records

As these are so important, keep them separately:

Current records: Mark a file folder with the year for all tax-related information for that year.

When cheques are returned with your bank statement, segregate your cheques that are important in preparation of your taxes. Make photocopies, and keep the originals together with each bank statement.

Long-term records: Keep a separate folder for each year. By law you should keep all tax records for at least six years—tax returns and all backups. Be safe and keep them for seven years. In fact, keep copies of your actual returns indefinitely. Just throw out the backup after seven years.

Keeping on Top

At the end of each year, go through each current file. Save annual summary statements… all current insurance policies and outstanding loans…all claims and other matters that are still pending…all documents necessary for your taxes and for establishing the value of the assets you own.

Source: Alexandra Armstrong, CFP, president of the independent financial-planning firm Armstrong, Welch and MacIntyre, Inc., 1155 Connecticut Ave. NW, Washington, DC 20036.

For any year in which you buy or sell real estate, keep the tax returns and backup to the transaction. Keep the returns and backup, too, for any major renovations to the property. You will need this information in order to establish the cost basis, on which any capital gain will be figured.

Assets That You Own

● **Stocks and other securities.** Keep confirmation statements from your stockbroker when you purchase any stock until seven years after you sell it. You need this to establish your cost and selling price for tax purposes.

● **Mutual funds.** The monthly statement summarizes all transactions—shares purchased and sold—during that period. Subsequent monthly statements may recapitulate this data from the beginning of the year. If so, throw out the previous months' statements and keep only the most current one.

Keep each annual statement from the fund that summarizes the year's activities…basically forever. You will need the information to figure out your cost basis when you sell shares.

Source: Alexandra Armstrong, CFP, president of the independent financial-planning firm Armstrong, Welch and MacIntyre, Inc., 1155 Connecticut Ave. NW, Washington, DC 20036.

Protect Your Assets From Personal Financial Crisis

These days, most professionals and businesspeople can easily and unexpectedly find themselves embroiled in a financial conflict that could cost them most of their assets: Doctors, lawyers and other professionals sued for malpractice or misconduct; business owners who must fight liability suits; anyone dealing with whopping medical bills to cover a long-term illness that requires care not covered by provincial health plans; people who can't get enough insurance or can't afford to pay for the coverage they need.

In this escalating crisis, the best self-defense is to get assets out of your name far in advance of any trouble with creditors. Although judges don't look kindly on people who transfer their assets in order to defraud creditors, the longer the time between a transfer and a court judgment, the less likely the transfer will be deemed fraudulent. Once you're involved in a suit or have been dunned by creditors, a transfer may be considered fraudulent and can be reversed if successfully attacked by creditors. The provinces and the government of Canada do provide for different legislation whereby creditors can attack transactions and reverse them, but where an individual can also show a bona fide purpose, the creditors might not be successful. *Example:* An individual transfers assets to a trust which has the effect of protecting the assets from creditors; however, the individual can show that the transfer was done to effect true estate planning objectives.

> "Umbrella liability... which protects... above and beyond the limits of your home owners and automobile insurance...is the best...bargain there is, costing about $100 a year for each $1 million in additional coverage."

Caution: Don't overdo it. If you impoverish yourself, the transfers won't stand up in court as estate and tax-planning measures, and you'll run into serious financial difficulties even if never sued.

Effective Strategies

● **Setting up a "personal family holding company" lets you keep control** of your assets while transferring ownership of most of them out of your name. *How it works:* An individual transfers his or her assets to a corporation and takes back preferred shares having a locked-in value of the assets and the rest of the family would have growth shares of the company. The preferred shares taken back would provide that they lose 50% of their value if owned by a third party (i.e., not a family member). If he or she is sued, creditors can only take preferred

shares, with a depreciated value, which isn't very useful. In many cases, creditors will be willing to settle for much less than originally demanded if it's in a more liquid form (cash, publicly traded stocks, bonds, etc.).

Tax implications: The transfer of the assets to a Canadian taxable corporation can be done on a rollover basis under section 85 of the Income Tax Act. Under these circumstances, tax is not paid then, but deferred until such time as the company disposes of the assets.

● **Giving away assets to family members is effective,** as long as the giveaways aren't used to defraud someone. *Guidelines:* A gift must be given well in advance of credit difficulties, and the receiver has to exercise control over the gift—and be able to prove it—not merely serve as a front.

Drawbacks: Possible gift tax and complete loss of control over the assets you give away. In the event of a falling-out with the receiver (such as a divorce), you may regret the gift.

Alternative: Transfer assets into either an irrevocable or a discretionary trust, with your heirs and yourself as beneficiaries. You, along with two other persons, can be trustees. Then at a future date, assets can be transferred to you as the trustees will have discretion to distribute to whichever beneficiaries they want. (*Note:* You need two other trustees because if there is the possibility that you can have a veto on distributions, and you are a beneficiary, then the trust will be a reversionary trust and will lose most of its tax advantages.)

Advantages: With both types of trusts, you can give assets to family members even if you can't trust them to manage the assets wisely. With a discretionary trust, the assets are returned to you at some date in the future (assuming at least one other trustee is in agreement).

Trap: Once back in your name, the assets are again fair game for creditors.

● **Company pension plans are one of the easiest ways to sequester funds from your creditors.** If you don't have access to the funds, neither does anyone else. However, creditors can attach distributions. Unprotected are retirement plans in which you do have access to the money, such as RRSPs.

● **Gift-leasebacks can be used to give property to an individual,** trust or corporation, which then leases it back to you for your use, but not for your control.

● **Life insurance policy cash values can't be touched by creditors.** In common-law provinces (i.e., all provinces, except for Quebec), while a designation in favor of a spouse, child, grandchild or parent of the insured is in effect, the rights of the insured in the contract are exempt from seizure. In Quebec, the policy will be exempt from creditors if the beneficiary is the spouse or an ascendant or descendant of the policyholder.

Trap 1: Investment-advantaged insurances, such as single premium annuities, may not be protected.

Trap 2: Proceeds of life insurance that are payable to a named beneficiary are not subject to claims of creditors of the insured, but the creditors of the beneficiary may come after him or her. If there is such a danger, you can provide that the life insurance proceeds are payable to a life insurance trust, which pays out periodically to certain beneficiaries.

Less Effective Strategies

● **Joint ownership.** In most provinces, judges will trace assets held jointly to see which party contributed to them and then determine the portion that can be attached by creditors. Avoid moving your assets into a joint bank or brokerage account with someone who contributes little or nothing. You might, however, be slightly better off with assets in joint ownership than in your own name because getting assets from a joint account requires extra legal proceedings that might encourage creditors to settle for a lesser amount. *Danger:* Having assets in joint ownership may also be problematic if the other joint owner also is subject to creditor claims.

● **Power-of-attorney accounts.** Transferring your assets to an account in a relative's name is better than leaving them in your own name, but it's certainly not safe. A judge will probably rule that the account is de facto yours.

● **Home ownership.** Unlike the United States, where many states offer some degree of protection against creditors for family homes, the entire value of a principal residence can be subject to creditors' claims in Canada.

After the Fact

Once you've been sued by a creditor, there's little you can do to protect your assets. *Bad idea:* To liquidate your assets for cash, gold coins or precious gems and hide them in a cookie jar or foreign bank. Such schemes are illegal and dangerous.

What can happen: The court can dig into your financial records—as far back as it wants to go. If the records show that you once had $1 million and now have nothing, you'll be asked, under oath, what happened to it. Refuse to tell, and you're on your way to jail for contempt of court. Lie and get caught, and you've perjured yourself into jail.

Strong defense: You might be able to substantially limit damage to your finances by setting up a variation on the family personal holding company described previously. The holding company now owns your assets, and the transfer is unlikely to be considered fraudulent because you didn't really give away your assets—you exchanged them for something of equal fair market value (the preferred stock). And that's all creditors can get from you. That might be all it takes to convince the creditors to settle for less.

Sources: Attorneys Mark N. Kaplan, partner, Skadden, Arps, Slate, Meagher & Flom, New York, NY, and Peter J. Strauss, senior partner, Strauss & Wolf, New York, NY; Samantha Prasad, associate, Minden Gross Grafstein & Greenstein LLP, Toronto, Ont.

More on Protecting Your Hard-Earned Assets

Insurance

● *Mistake:* **Not having an umbrella liability policy.** It protects you against liability above and beyond the limits of your home owners and automobile insurance policies (which usually carry a maximum limit of $2 million in Canada). This is the best insurance bargain there is, costing about $100 a year for each $1 million in additional coverage. Yet an amazing number of people don't have it.

● *Mistake:* **Not having disability insurance coverage.** At any given age, there's a much greater chance of becoming disabled than of dying. *Example:* At age 42, you're four times as likely to be disabled as to die before age 65. If you have no disability

SAVINGS ARE COMING BACK INTO STYLE

Canada has one of the lowest savings rates in the world, placing us at the bottom of the list of industrialized nations. We save less than 4% of our income each year, compared with 10% in Germany and 11% in Japan.

In the short run, our penchant to spend rather than save isn't all negative. High consumer spending ultimately translates into a growing economy. However, over time, a low savings rate means less money is available for businesses to borrow and to invest in new plants and equipment. That means a decrease in the amount of capital goods made each year. When a nation's capital creation declines, so does its standard of living.

Who's to blame? The baby boomers—those in their thirties and forties, who make up the largest component of our population. They are spending like crazy and saving next to nothing. With their rising salaries and easy credit, most are spending beyond their means and digging into debt.

Problem: Many baby boomers are not planning for the future. Most don't even know what it will take to achieve their most basic goals: buying a home, sending their kids to college, retiring without depending on other people or the government for assistance.

Typical Example

Bob and Helen have a combined salary of $50,000 and two children ages 7 and 10. They have no savings and no debt, and they want to send their children to $10,000-per-year colleges. Bob and Helen figure that if they save 5% of their income, they will have plenty for retirement.

Harsh reality: When retirement time rolls around, Bob and Helen will be $31,000 in debt.

The situation is far from hopeless. By making some small adjustments, Bob and Helen can get themselves back on sound financial footing.

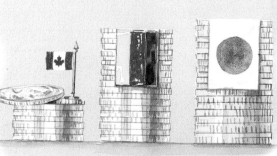

● **First, they must take steps to reduce the educational expenses for their children.** By choosing less expensive schools, taking out student loans, and sending the children to work during the summer, Bob and Helen can scale back anticipated college costs from $10,000 per year to $3,000. If they save the difference and invest it at a modest after-tax rate of 3% (after inflation), they will have accumulated a net worth of $70,000 by retirement time.

● **By selling the rarely used boat and trailer** (nonearning assets) for $10,000 and investing the money, they can boost their retirement nest egg to $94,000.

● **If they can manage to save 10% of their income rather than only 5%,** their net worth will go up to $207,000.

● **If they put some of their savings into safe stocks,** increasing their real after-tax return from 3% to 5%, their net worth at retirement will increase to $293,000.

Although these steps are small, it takes planning and discipline to execute them effectively.

The Sooner, the Better

The earlier you start, the easier it is to save what you need for retirement. The magic of compound interest makes smaller savings grow faster over long periods of time.

Example: Let's say your goal is to have $500,000 by the time you retire. If you start saving at age 20, you will have to put away only $650 a year at a 10% average return to reach your goal by 65. If you don't start until you are 35, you will need to put away $2,750 per year. At 50, you will have to save $14,000 per year. And at 55, you will need to save a whopping $27,500 per year.

Prediction

In the next 5 to 10 years, many people will realize that they're going to come up short at retirement. They will then change their habits dramatically.

For the past two decades, we have been enjoying the present by sacrificing the future. The time has come to start sacrificing in the present so we can enjoy the future. This is what Japan did after World War II, and it's one of the major reasons that it became the world's second-largest economy.

Source: John Rutledge, Ph.D., chairman and president, Rutledge & Company, Inc., Greenwich, CT.

coverage and do lose the ability to earn a living, you and your family will have no choice but to live off of your assets—as long as they last.

Trap: In selecting a disability policy, be careful about the definition of disability. You want to be covered if you can't do your regular job.

A good noncancelable, guaranteed renewable policy will be expensive—about $1,980 a year for a 35-year-old lawyer to replace 60% of a $100,000 annual income for life—somewhat less so if you elect a longer waiting period than the standard 90 days. The insurance proceeds are generally nontaxable.

● *Mistake:* **Inadequate malpractice insurance.** If you're in a business or profession with a high risk of malpractice liability, take out adequate malpractice protection.

Caution: Home owners and umbrella liability policies do not cover malpractice, so separate insurance is needed.

Important: Read fine print carefully. Legal costs of malpractice defense can be huge. Some policies include legal costs in the maximum amount they will pay. Others don't limit payment for legal costs, so they will actually cover much more.

For best protection with all types of insurance, remember that higher deductibles usually go along with higher limits of insurance protection to keep the costs in perspective. Your aim should be to protect your assets on the high end. Pick a high-deductible, high-limit policy over a lower deductible with a lower limit. *Example:* $500 deductible with a limit of $1 million, rather than a $100 deductible with a limit of $300,000.

Business Complications

● *Mistake:* **Not putting major assets in the name of the spouse who's at less risk.** It's best to do it now, before a claim arises. Courts can simply set the transfer aside if it was made after the cause of action.

> "In today's litigious society, anyone can be sued. And once sued, anyone can get hit with a judgment that strips away assets. But with foresight and nimble footwork, you can shield your assests from predators, incluing the Canada Customs and Revenue Agency, former spouses, creditors and legal opportunists."

Divorce trap: In a divorce, most provinces now mandate equitable distribution of assets, so, in theory, title to assets doesn't matter. Tactically, however, before a judge finally rules, the person who owns the assets has control, can pay lawyers, and generally has the upper hand.

Important: Don't operate as an unincorporated business when it can be avoided. Use a limited partnership. Since many complainants name all shareholders when suing, this is not foolproof, but it can help if the complainant is not able to prove that you had any personal involvement or responsibility.

The safest way to protect your home is to transfer title to the lower-risk spouse. Owning the house together as tenants-in-common provides some measure of protection because creditors can't force the noncreditor spouse out.

Caution: When transferring to the lower-risk spouse, be careful because a transfer at less than fair market value can be subject to attack by creditors. The rules differ in every province, so check with a local lawyer.

● **Use different legal entities for different projects.** If your business operates in a building that you also own, for example, put the building in a separate corporation or a limited partnership properly formed under provincial law. If you own several rental properties, put each in a separate legal entity so that if one has a legal problem, the others won't be lost.

Trap: If you're held personally liable, all properties in which you own stock/partnership interests may be at risk. To minimize your liability, avoid signing anything personally—that is, in your own name. Always sign in the corporate name, as an officer of the corporation (XYZ Corporation, by John Doe, president) and be sure to follow all corporate formalities in tax filings, minutes of board meetings, etc., or the courts may not respect the corporation as a legal entity and the limited liability it offers.

● **Separate assets from liabilities in arranging business entities.** *Example:* A manufacturing plant (which entails all kinds of risk) should be separated from other assets. *Helpful:* A limited partnership could own the real estate and lease it to the manufacturing corporation. Another person—such as a trustee for your child—could own the trade name and license it to the manufacturing company. Thus, a lawsuit filed against the manufacturer might not reach the real estate or trade name assets, which would be insulated from creditors.

Sources: *Martin M. Shenkman, MBA, CPA, and attorney-at-law, Teaneck, NJ. He is the author of 14 books on tax and financial matters, the latest of which is* The Estate Planning Guide, *John Wiley & Sons; Samantha Prasad, associate, Minden Gross Grafstein & Greenstein LLP, Toronto, Ont.*

Keep Your Wealth Safe From a Lawsuit

In today's litigious society, anyone can be sued. And once sued, anyone can get hit with a judgment that strips away assets.

But with foresight and nimble footwork, you can shield your assets from predators, including the Canada Customs and Revenue Agency (CCRA), former spouses, creditors and legal opportunists.

If you think you're at risk of being sued, consult an attorney who specializes in asset protection. Each province's laws are different, and what is legal and advisable depends on individual facts and circumstances. But here are four successful judgment-proofing techniques to discuss with your attorney:

● **Go abroad.** The surest protection is to move your assets out of reach of Canadian courts. Look for banks or financial institutions in countries that offer secrecy, low or no taxes for foreigners, financial asset protection trust laws and political stability.

Current favorites: Bahamas, Cayman Islands.

Warning: The new proposed section 94.1 of the Income Tax Act, scheduled to come into effect in 2003, will affect offshore trusts. The new legislation basically provides that where a Canadian resident contributes property to a nonresident trust, the contributor, nonresident trust and certain Canadian resident beneficiaries of the trust may all become liable to pay Canadian tax on the worldwide income of the trust.

● **Buy insurance and annuities.** Every province offers significant protection of insurance policies from creditors. This may also include segregated funds held in registered plans, like RRSPs. If the RRSP is held with a life insurance company, it is potentially eligible for protection against creditors under applicable insurance legislation as it may be considered to be a life insurance contract. Therefore, moving money from bank and brokerage accounts into insurance and insurance-sponsored RRSPs will often lawsuit-proof those assets. Swiss annuities are fully protected from creditor claims after one year's ownership pursuant to Swiss law.

Even when provinces offer total insurance protection, the exemption may not extend to claims from the CCRA. Lawyers feel there still remains a question as to whether or not the CCRA could defeat creditor protection legislation as it relates to life insurance. To be on the safe side, you may be able to protect your holdings from the CCRA by having an irrevocable life insurance trust own the insurance policies. When a life insurance trust owns the insurance policies, any funds payable to the trust should be exempt from creditors, including the CCRA.

● **Set up a family limited partnership.** While there is no specific legal entity in Canada called a family limited partnership, there is nothing to prevent a limited partnership being set up with a husband and wife as the limited partners. A limited partnership is a legal entity to which you can transfer assets. Spouses can serve as general partners and control the assets. The assets can be owned by trusts to provide an additional layer of protection.

This approach gives you control over your assets while offering strong creditor protection and an opportunity for creative estate planning and reduced estate taxes.

● **Use irrevocable trusts.** Irrevocable trusts offer asset protection because the trust owns the assets—not you. Among the types of trusts your attorney may recommend are charitable remainder trusts, insurance trusts and foreign-based trusts.

The very nature of an irrevocable trust is that it cannot be rescinded or modified and that you lose control of the assets, so be 100% sure of what you are doing before you act.

Living trusts, while an excellent way to avoid

WHAT GOES ON SALE WHEN
Here is a month-by-month schedule for dedicated bargain hunters.

January

After-Christmas sales
Appliances
Baby carriages
Books
Carpets and rugs
China and glassware
Christmas cards
Costume jewelry
Furniture
Furs
Lingerie
Men's overcoats
Pocketbooks
Preinventory sales
Shoes
Toys
White goods (sheets, towels, etc.)

February

Air conditioners
Art supplies
Bedding
Cars (used)
Curtains
Furniture
Glassware and china
Housewares
Lamps
Men's apparel
Radios, TV sets and stereos
Silverware
Sportswear and equipment
Storm windows
Toys

March

Boys' and girls' shoes
Garden supplies
Housewares

Ice skates
Infants' clothing
Laundry equipment
Luggage
Ski equipment

April

Fabrics
Hosiery
Lingerie
Painting supplies
Women's shoes

May

Handbags
Housecoats
Household linens
Jewelry
Luggage
Mother's Day specials
Outdoor furniture
Rugs
Shoes
Sportswear
Tires and auto accessories
TV sets

June

Bathing suits
Bedding
Boys' clothing
Fabrics
Father's Day specials
Floor coverings
Lingerie, sleepwear and hosiery
Men's clothing
Women's shoes

July

Air conditioners and other appliances
Bathing suits

Children's clothes
Electronic equipment
Fuel
Furniture
Handbags
Lingerie and sleepwear
Luggage
Men's shirts
Men's shoes
Rugs
Sportswear
Summer clothes
Summer sports equipment

August

Back-to-school specials
Carpeting
Cosmetics
Curtains and drapes
Electric fans and air conditioners
Furniture
Furs
Men's coats
Silver
Tires
White goods
Women's coats

September

Bicycles
Cars (outgoing models)
china and glassware
Fabrics
Fall fashions
Garden equipment
Hardware
Lamps
Paints

October

Cars (outgoing models)
china and glassware
Fall/winter clothing
Fishing equipment
Furniture
Lingerie and hosiery
Major appliances
School supplies
Silver
Storewide clearances
Women's coats

November

Blankets and quilts
Boys' suits and coats
Cars (used)
Lingerie
Major appliances
Men's suits and coats
Shoes
White goods
Winter clothing

December

Blankets and quilts
Cards, gifts, toys (after Christmas)
Cars (used)
Children's clothes
Christmas promotions
Coats and hats
Men's furnishings
Resort and cruise wear
Shoes

probate, are generally revocable and useless for asset protection.

Sources: *Samantha Prasad, associate, Minden Gross Grafstein & Greenstein LLP, Toronto, Ont.; Dr. Arnold S. Goldstein, president, The Garrett Group, 384 Military Trail, Deerfield Beach, FL 33442.*

A Shopper's Guide to Bargaining

Bargaining will not turn you into a social outcast. Before you can negotiate, you have to get over this attitude. All shopkeepers see when you walk in is dollar signs. If you are willing to spend, they will probably be willing to make a deal. They know that everybody is trying to save money.

Bargaining is a business transaction. You are not trying to cheat the merchant or get something for nothing. You are trying to agree on a fair price. You expect to negotiate for a house or a car—why not for a refrigerator or a winter coat?

You have a right to bargain, particularly in small stores that don't discount. *Reason:* Department stores, which won't bargain as a rule, mark up prices 100%–150% to cover high overhead costs. Small stores should charge lower prices because their costs are less.

The Savvy Approach

Set yourself a price limit for a particular item before you approach the storekeepers. Be prepared to walk out if they don't meet your limit. (You can always change your mind later.) Make them believe you really won't buy unless they come down.

● **Be discreet in your negotiations.** If other customers can overhear your dickering, the shop owner must stay firm.

● **Shop at off-hours.** You will have more luck if business is slow.

● **Look for unmarked merchandise.** If there is no price tag, you are invited to bargain.

Tactics That Work

● **Negotiate with cash.** In a store that takes credit cards, request a discount for paying in cash.

● **Buy in quantity.** A customer who is committed to a number of purchases has more bargaining power. When everything is picked out, approach the owner and suggest a total price about 20% less than the actual total. Or, if you are buying more than one of an item, offer to pay full price on the first one if the owner will give you a break on the others. Storekeeper's alternative: You spent $500 on clothing and asked for a better price. The owner couldn't charge you less but threw in a belt priced at $35 as a bonus.

● **Look for flawed merchandise.** This is the only acceptable bargaining point in department stores, but it also can save you money in small shops. If there's a spot, a split seam, or a missing button, estimate what it would cost to have the garment fixed commercially, and ask for a discount based on that figure. *Variation:* You find a chipped hair dryer. When you ask for a discount, the manager says he or she will return it to the manufacturer and find you an undamaged one. Your reply: "Sell it to me for a little less and save yourself the trouble."

WHAT SUPERMARKETS DON'T TELL YOU

Supermarkets usually place the most expensive items at eye level, where they are more likely to be selected on impulse. *Suggestion:* Take a look at the entire group of products before deciding on a purchase, unless you have a strong preference for a specific brand. Generic items can offer real savings, but quality varies widely.

Best bets: All brands of products like household disinfectants usually contain some of the same ingredients. Canadian law does not require their makers to list all ingredients.

Trap: National brands may be cheaper than generic brands when on sale, so comparison shop.

● **Adapt your haggling to the realities of the situation.** A true discount house has a low profit margin and depends on volume to make its money. Don't ask for more than 5% off in such a store. A boutique that charges what the traffic will bear has more leeway. Start by asking for 25% off, and dicker from there.

● **Buy at the end of the season,** when new stock is being put out. Offer to buy older goods at a discount. *In neighborhood stores:* Push the local television or appliance dealer to give you a break to ensure that you will make your future purchases in the community.

Source: Sharon Dunn Greene, coauthor of The Lower East Side Shopping Guide.

Get Out Your Scissors

When is the best time to hunt for coupons in newspapers, magazines, store circulars, etc.? Coupon clipping is most profitable in the months of June and October. Next best: May, September and November. Poorest months: July and December (but even then, you can still save).

Source: The Frugal Shopper *by Marion Joyce, Perigee Books.*

Catch-22 for Consumers

A new big-ticket appliance doesn't work, and no one will be home to wait for the serviceman. Nor is the retailer usually obligated to take it back (because the manufacturer must be given a chance to make repairs). *What to do:* At the time of the sale, get the seller to accept a carefully worded statement, written on the receipt, that if for any reason the buyer is not satisfied, the appliance may be returned or exchanged. This

will be done at the seller's (or buyer's) expense, within a certain number of days and/or on a weekend (or whatever time is convenient for the buyer). The statement becomes part of a binding contract.

Source: Dan Brecher, Esq., 230 Park Ave., New York, NY 10017.

Telephone Company Secrets

A network interface is a special telephone jack that allows you to determine which wires are faulty when your phone goes dead—outside wires, which the

WHAT AUTOMAKERS WON'T TELL YOU

A well-kept secret of the automobile industry is the existence of "informal" warranties. *How they work:* When a significant number of new-model cars are reported to have the same mechanical problem, the manufacturer may inform sales offices and car dealers that it will cover the cost of repair beyond the standard warranty.

Problem: Neither manufacturers nor dealers publicize these warranties.

Solution: If your car has a malfunction that may be covered under one of these warranties, write to the Center for Auto Safety, an auto-complaint clearinghouse that tracks corporate memoranda, bulletins to

sales offices and dealers, and car-owner complaints to deduce which components are likely to fall under informal warranties. They can be reached at 1825 Connecticut Ave. NW, Suite 330, Washington, DC 20009-5708, (202) 328-7700, or through their website at www.autosafety.org.

Tell the center the automobile's year, model and problem, and it will send you pertinent information. If the malfunctioning part is covered, speak with the dealer's service manager; if he or she won't fix the problem, contact the factory's regional office and ask a representative to mediate.

Last resort: Take the dealer to small-claims court or seek arbitration through the Better Business Bureau. You'll have a good chance of winning, if you're armed with documentation.

Source: Robert Dewey of the vehicle safety division, Center for Auto Safety.

phone company must repair at no cost, or inside, which the phone company may charge to repair. If you want to install your own network interface, consider buying the materials at a telephone-supply store such as Radio Shack. If your phone repairman installs it, you must purchase the materials from him. *Tip:* To avoid charges for the visit, have the repairman install the interface when he is at your house doing other phone work.

You can repair an internal problem yourself or you can have an electrician do the job, which is often cheaper than using the phone company's work.

> " **Get as much information as possible about a car before you sit down with the salesperson. Collect brochures—dealers don't usually keep them on display because they want you to approach the salespeople—and read consumer magazines that rate automobiles.** "

Source: *Carl Oppedahl, New York City lawyer and author of* The Telephone Book, *Weber Systems, Inc.*

How to Buy a Car Without Getting Taken for a Ride

Just Any Dealership Won't Do

There's more to buying a car than price. Where you buy it counts, too. Take the time to evaluate different dealerships. Pay a visit to a few and walk around the showrooms. When a salesperson comes up to you—and one will—say, "I'm just looking around. I'll come to you when I'm ready." Don't let any of them intimidate you.

Walk through the service area and sit down. Stay for about a half hour. *Observe:*

- **Is it orderly and run efficiently?**
- **Is the manager there and working?**
- **Are the customers treated with respect?**

Proceed into the service lot and look at the license plate frames. In a good dealership, you'll see frames from competing dealerships, too.

Don't choose a dealership that's out of the way. The salespeople know that they have just one chance to make a sale, and they can lean hard on you. Also avoid multifranchise dealerships. Too many people run different parts of the operation, causing confusion in service.

Choose your salespeople, don't let them choose you. Speak with several. *Be sure to ask the following questions:*

- **How long have you been at this dealership?** (The longer, the better.)
- **Where else have you worked? For how long?**
- **May I have the name and number of a recent customer?** (Follow up with a phone call.) If there's a lot of turnover, the dealership is likely unstable.

Trap: Looking for a salesperson who's a member of your ethnic group because you think you'll get special treatment. You won't, and you'll be letting your guard down.

Knowledge Is Power

Educate yourself. Get as much information as possible about a car before you sit down with the salesperson. Collect brochures—dealers don't usually keep them on display because they want you to approach the salespeople—and read consumer magazines that rate automobiles.

Don't let salespeople woo you into trusting them with their "impressive" knowledge of a car. That's how they try to establish authority and take control of the sale.

Know the competition, too. If you say that you are considering a competing brand, the salesperson will knock it as much as possible and be very convincing if you are uninformed.

Know What You Want

If you're not completely certain about the vehicle you want, you could easily end up with what the salesperson wants to sell you—the most expensive model, with the most extravagant options, at the highest price.

Once you show serious intentions of buying, the

salesperson will offer you a test drive, during which he or she will talk glowingly about the car to get you to take mental ownership of it. Be aware that he or she is seducing you. Resist.

Trap: Negotiating to buy when you're tired of shopping. Salespeople are attracted to this kind of customer like bees to honey. They know that if they promise you what you've been looking for—whether they have it or not—you'll probably buy on the spot. Buy only in an energetic mood.

Few salespeople ask idle questions. Seemingly irrelevant questions are actually attempts to find out about your lifestyle, income, driving habits, etc. Avoid answering these questions.

Unscrupulous Tricks

Options are where dealers make their money.

Common tactic: The dealer says, "Sorry, but all the cars arrive with power windows. If you don't want them, I'll have to make a special order. It could take months." *Result:* You may pay for an option that you don't want. If you stand firm, the dealer will work something out—he or she wants the sale.

Another trick: Cars for the lot are ordered without carpeting, and customers are told that carpeting is extra, when it's really a standard option. Read the dealer's brochure carefully. It lists every standard option and every extra.

Also make sure every option has the car's name on it: That means the dealership is responsible if something breaks. For example, Honda uses Alpine brand radios, but Honda's name is on the faceplate—which means Honda is responsible for any repairs.

To get the best price for a new car, first check the range of prices from several different dealerships, and write them down. When you're at the first one, don't let the salesperson know this is your first stop. When he or she asks what other dealers have quoted,

say, "Why don't you give me your best deal and we'll take it from there."

Read the sticker carefully. DAP stands for dealer added profit. The term "locator cost" means the dealer located the car. "Procurement cost" means the dealer procured the car. All these charges are negotiable.

Take particular note of a common price-padding tactic: A prep fee of $100 or more (which might be whatever the dealership thinks it can get away with). The cost of preparing your car for delivery is already included in the manufacturer's sticker price.

Salespersons' trick: Constantly consulting with the manager and pretending that they're really on your side. They aren't—all the sales staff is working on commission.

Don't shop for a price by phone, because salespeople will quote anything just to get you to come into the dealership. Be sure to shop for financing in advance so you'll know a good deal when you hear one. Don't believe salespeople who claim that they can get you good insurance rates—they can't.

Trap: Accepting a trade-in price for your old car that you know is too high. The dealership will make up the difference on the price of the new car.

Being "Turned Over"

Don't let yourself get "turned over." If a salesperson feels that he is not in control of the sale, he'll say that he's going on a coffee break and will "turn you over" to another salesperson.

In a high-pressure operation, this sort of treatment could happen to you three or four times, until they wear you down. *How to resist:* Go out for a walk, have a cup of coffee at a nearby diner, say that you need to think about it. Get away from the salespeople so you can think clearly.

> "To get the best price for a new car, first check the range of prices from several different dealerships, and write them down. When you're at the first one, don't let the salesperson know this is your first stop. When he or she asks what other dealers have quoted, say, 'Why don't you give me your best deal and we'll take it from there.'"

Now You Own It

When the deed is done, inspect your new car thoroughly before you leave the dealership. Make sure everything in the vehicle is working correctly.

Final dirty trick: The car was dented in transport, so the dealer parks it close to a wall to hide the damage—which greets you when you arrive home.

Source: *Two veteran car salesmen who asked to remain anonymous.*

Cheaper, Better, Faster Flying

Over 80% of all airline tickets are currently purchased at discounted fares, but because the fare system is so confusing, most travelers are still paying too much for air travel. Because the fare maze is so confusing, most companies channel their travel planning through a professional travel agent.

Common problem: Many of the agencies are too ill-equipped or too ill-staffed to find you the lowest fare.

Trap: While many of the travel agencies use computerized systems to book clients at the lowest fare available at the time of making a reservation, the airlines' computers are programmed to sell the greatest number of seats at the highest fares. They release cheap seats close to flight time if they haven't sold them at higher fares.

Recommendation: Use only travel agents that contract with one of the preticketing audit services. These services monitor travel agency bookings and check fares once every 12 or 24 hours. As cheaper seats become available, they automatically change your reservation to reflect the lower rate.

Even computerized, preassigned seating and issuing of boarding passes don't eliminate the problem of overbooking. Although the airlines are accurate in

Vacation With Tax-Advantaged Income

You can pay for your vacation with tax-advantaged income simply by renting out your home while you're away. The rental income itself isn't tax-free, but if you have a reasonable expectation of making profit from renting, you are entitled to deduct a pro rata share of household expenses.

Source: *Evelyn Jacks, president, Evelyn Jacks Productions, Inc. and best-selling author,* Tax Secrets for Tough Times *and* Make Sure It's Deductible, *published by McGraw Hill Ryerson.*

predicting the percentage of no-shows, all flights are routinely overbooked. *Most likely people to be bumped from a flight:* Late arrivals.

Source: *Harold Seligman, president, Management Alternatives, Inc., a travel consulting firm to major American companies, Box 8119, Stamford, CT 06905.*

How to Travel Free

There are hundreds of budget guides that tell you how to cut costs on trips. Many of these books contain low-cost travel tips, but they don't give you the ultimate scoop on no-cost travel. Instead of traveling cheap, you could be enjoying the benefits of traveling free of charge—from transportation by air—or sea—to hotel accommodations, meals and entertainment. Most free travel requires no special skills, credentials or contacts. And it can be just as luxurious—and often more pleasurable—than the most expensive paid vacation.

Complimentary Cruises

Cruise lines generally offer a free passage to anyone who recruits 10 to 15 paying passengers. (Many airlines also offer similar deals.) If you can't lure that many customers, you can get a prorated reduction on your fare.

You can also cruise free as an expert in a pertinent subject. Historians, anthropologists, naturalists and ornithologists are in especially high demand. Your job on the cruise would be to present a series of lectures and to be available for informal questioning. It helps to have a Ph.D. (or at least a Master's degree) and to have published articles on the subject. But an affable personality and a willingness to share your knowledge with others can stretch your credentials. After your first cruise in this capacity, a good reference will ease your way to similar employment on other lines.

Free cruises are available to doctors and nurses

who are willing to be on 24-hour call (a salary is an added inducement), to athletic directors who can organize recreational activities, to musicians and entertainers willing to perform and to cosmetologists who can barter their services.

There is also a strong demand for "hosts"—distinguished single gentlemen who are usually 55 years old and up. They serve by dining and dancing with the many unattached older women taking these vacation cruises. "Hosts" are required to fill out an application and be interviewed for the job. One of the prerequisites for such shipboard employment is to be an expert in social ballroom dancing.

Free Foreign Tours

Enlist enough people and get a whole trip—long or short—free. Some travel agencies recruit teachers, who receive a free trip if they bring six students. With 12 or more students, the teacher's spouse also travels free. The same deal is available to anyone willing to organize a special-interest tour. An auto-racing fan might lead a group to Le Mans in France; an opera aficionado might arrange a trip to the famous La Scala in Milan. Similar trips focus on photography, architecture, theater, music, golf or wine-tasting. The group leader sets the itinerary, chooses lodgings, and arranges for side trips. Travel experience and linguistic skills are usually helpful, but not absolutely essential.

Source: *Robert William Kirk, author of* You Can Travel Free, *Pelican Publishing Co.*

Ticket Savvy

Some supersaver fares are low enough that even if you can't stay as long as their requirements (usually seven days), you will save by buying two round-trip tickets—one from your home to your destination for the day you want to leave and one from your destination to your home for the day you want to

return. The total may be less than the regular round-trip fare.

Source: *Your Money and Your Life* by Robert Z. Aliber, Basic Books.

Testing for Loaded Dice

Fill a tall glass with water, drop each dice in gently. Repeat several times, with a different number on top each time. If the dice turns when sinking so that the same two or three numbers always show up, it's loaded. *Less obvious test:* Hold dice loosely between thumb and forefinger at diagonally opposite corners. Loaded dice will pivot when the weighted side is on top. The movement is unmistakable.

Win Bigger and Cut Your Losses

There are two kinds of odds you've got to beat to have a successful day at the casinos. Numerical odds for each game are set by the casinos, and you have little chance of controlling them. All you can do is play the games and bet the combinations that offer the best odds.

Odds are based on a branch of mathematics known as probability. It is used in all aspects of our lives: weather, science, genetics, medicine, business, stocks, insurance. Within gambling, the question becomes, what are the house odds? For example, a double-zero roulette wheel significantly changes the odds of winning at the game.

Behavioral odds, however, are what really give the casinos the winning edge. Few casino visitors are practiced or skilled enough to make the best bets every time. The casinos count on most players making the same dumb mistakes over and over again. When the house holds, say, a 2% edge in a particular game, that is just the numerical edge and tells only part of the story. The behavioral edge is much, much greater.

Players can turn the behavioral edge to their advantage. Professional gamblers know how, and so do casino insiders.

Biggest edge: All casinos aren't alike in the odds they offer, and there can even be important differences among neighboring tables in the same house. In Nevada, for example, the odds in the casinos vary widely from one house to another—more than they do in the gambling establishments in Atlantic City, New Jersey.

In Canada, charity casinos offer better odds than the large government-owned casinos. But many Canadian charities, most notably the nationwide food banks, have refused to accept gambling money for ethical reasons.

Gambling in Las Vegas

In Las Vegas, the best deals are usually found in the smaller casinos located in the Fremont Street downtown area, away from the city's fabled Strip.

In Vegas craps, steer clear of the "Big 6" and "Big 8" sucker bets. The odds might look attractive, but an identical wager of place bets on the 6 or 8 gives a higher payoff. *Better:* Look for craps tables that offer triple odds bets after the come-out roll. This shaves the casino edge to well under 1%.

On the Vegas Strip, the best place to play blackjack allows you to double down on a 9, as well as on 10 and 11. All Strip casinos stymie card counters, however, by dealing players' cards face down. The less you can see, the less you can count.

Downtown Vegas rules are less strict than those on the Strip. Some houses allow for six-card Charlies, where the player wins by taking six cards totaling 21 or less.

If you can count cards: Look for a two-deck game with player cards dealt faceup. The rules in any given casino can—and do—change frequently. You're allowed to ask about the details before you sit down.

Variations to avoid: "Double exposure" is a game in which player and dealer cards are dealt faceup. *Trade-off:* The house wins all ties, instead of having to push the bet to the next hand. Overall, the odds are worse than in conventional blackjack.

> "All casinos aren't alike in the odds they offer, and there can even be important differences among neighboring tables in the same house. In Nevada, for example, the odds in the casinos vary widely from one another..."

Another Nevada variation of this game is mini baccarat, played at conventional blackjack tables. It attracts many players because of the low $2 minimum bet.

Drawback: Some Las Vegas casinos take out a minimum 25¢ commission on bets on the banker. On a $2 wager, that is a 12.5% built-in loss, as compared to the traditional house edge of 5%. If you like the game, find a Vegas casino that plays it with four, rather than eight, decks. The fewer the decks, the better the odds when betting the player position. In Nevada poker games, you're playing against the house.

Problem: High-stakes poker attracts pros, hustlers and cheats.

Safest: Stick to $5-limit games.

Playing slots: Vegas rules are most chaotic for slot machines. In Atlantic City, all machines must return at least 83% of the amount wagered, and a few return even more than 83%. But in Nevada, one machine might pay back 99% while the one right next to it pays back only 60%. The bettor's problem is that it's impossible to identify the hot machines. Their placement is the casino's most private and closely guarded secret.

Atlantic City

Among Atlantic City's casinos, the variations are narrower than they are in Vegas, but they can still be worked for or against you.

Look for a single-zero roulette game instead of one that uses a wheel with two zeros. Since the house always wins when the roulette ball lands on 0 or 00, a single-zero game halves the house edge.

In blackjack or baccarat, seek games with the lowest minimum bets.

If you are a slot player, stick to the so-called progressive slot machines, because the jackpots can build indefinitely. The best casino for slots in Atlantic City offers both liberal payoffs and coupons to exchange for prizes or hotel discounts.

Source: Lee Pantano, a professional gambler, teacher and consultant.

Taxing Your Winnings

You pay no tax on winnings in a Canadian casino. Although all winnings are theoretically taxable in the United States, in practice the first $1,199 are not taxed. You pay tax on a win of $1,200 or more. In this case, it pays to stay at home if you're going to gamble.

How to Spot a Card Cheat

One gambling survey indicates that cheating takes place in 10% of card games. *How to protect yourself:*

- **When shuffling cards,** never take them entirely off the table, either for the riffle or for squaring the deck.
- **Get into the habit of cutting the cards** at least once during the shuffle by pulling out the bottom half and slapping it onto the top.
- **Sit with your back against the wall.**
- **If you suspect marked cards, riffle the deck and watch the design on the back.** If the cards are marked, some lines in the design will move like an animated cartoon. In an honest deck, the design will stand absolutely still. The player to suspect: the one who keeps his eyes glued to the backs of the cards—especially the hole card in stud poker and the top card of the deck in gin rummy.

Source: *John Scarne's* Newsletter.

Tricks That Casinos Use to Take Your Money

The casino is a place of glitz and glamour. Many people get caught up in the excitement. When this happens it is easy to get carried away and gamble more than you should. This is exactly what the casinos want you to do. Casinos are a business. Their primary business is separating you from your money and making you think you're having fun while they do it. They do this in a few ways.

- **They convert your cash into chips at the tables.** You find yourself looking at the chips and seeing red and green tokens. You lose the sense that this is really money. This leads to over betting.
- **Dollar slot players use tokens for the machines.** Once again these lose their value. If you were using silver dollars you would hesitate a little more before randomly dropping them into machines.
- **They supply you with free drinks while you are playing.** Nothing like a few cocktails to loosen up the inhibitions!
- **The pace of the casino is fast.** The dealers try to deal at lightning speed. They have dollar bill receptors in the slot machines so you can keep hitting the spin button as fast as you can.

Keep these subtle ploys in mind while you are in the casino. Counteract them by slowing down. Hand feed coins into the machines if you are playing slots. Take a second to make sure you are playing your hand correctly at the tables. Pay attention to your bets on the craps table and, if you do drink while playing, use moderation.

> "There is no system that can beat a game of pure chance. One of the biggest myths about gambling is that games of luck can be beaten by methods of varying bet size to manipulate the odds. There are plenty of charlatans promising systems that can beat games of luck like roulette, craps and even the lottery. Most systems trade a lot of small wins for a few huge losses. In the long run, it is impossible to beat the house at games of chance."

Ten Rules for New Gamblers

- **Expect to lose.** The odds almost always favor the casino. If losing money upsets you, then you shouldn't play at all.
- **Don't rely on hunches.** Always make the mathematically best decision. On the player's side is the unlimited use of ESP and other psychic powers. The casinos have mathematical odds on their side.
- **Although you will lose money,** in the short term your winnings will go up and down like a roller

SAVING MONEY WITH COUPONS

Most of us pay more than we should for groceries, household products and other goods and services. The biggest mistake we make is failing to take full advantage of cents-off coupons, refund offers, two-for-one deals and other money-saving offers. With more than 300 billion coupons issued annually, fewer than 8 billion are redeemed each year. *Reasons:* Many shoppers are too embarrassed to present coupons to checkout clerks. Others are not aware, or uninterested in the available deals, or feel that clipping coupons is too time-consuming.

Today, however, more consumers are looking to cut weekly costs and stay on a budget. There are several ways to clip coupons and save up to 25% on your supermarket bill. *Helpful suggestions:*

● **Set up a system.** Spend a few minutes each week looking over newspaper inserts and other likely sources of coupons. Clip the ones you think you might use and toss them into a shoe box, then separate them by category. Mark each grouping of coupons with its own labeled note card. Be as general or as specific as you like with your categories.

Just prior to each trip to the grocery store, review your shopping list. Transfer the coupons you plan to use from the storage box to an envelope labeled unused. Take this envelope and a second, empty one (labeled used) along to the store. As you toss each item on your list into your shopping cart, transfer its coupon from the first envelope to the second.

● **Be choosy.** Coupons should be used to buy only two types of products—those you use regularly and those you'd like to try. Don't let coupons entice you to buy products you neither need nor truly want. Don't be trapped

by brand loyalty. Buy whatever brand for which you have coupons.

● **Accumulate as many coupons as possible.** Today coupons are available from a wide variety of sources, including product labels and cartons, supermarket ads, inserts in your Sunday newspaper and displays placed along supermarket shelves. Coupons are also distributed directly through the mail, on airline flights and at movie theaters.

● **Save unused coupons.** Take them along to the supermarket. *Reason:* Some markets maintain informal coupon-exchange bins where customers can exchange coupons they don't want for those they do.

● **Join a coupon-exchange club.** There are several large clubs to choose from, all offering the same basic service. *How they work:* Upon joining, members fill out a form specifying which products they use. Periodically, members mail in coupons they don't need and the club mails back coupons they do.

● **Shop at "coupon-friendly" supermarkets.** Some markets accept coupons only grudgingly. Others not only accept them, but will give you twice their face value.

● **Use coupons in conjunction with other savings offers.** When reading through your local newspaper's supermarket ads, watch for "double plays"— items discounted by both coupons and special sale prices. *Even better:* Triple plays. These occur when prices are reduced not only by coupons and specials, but also by a mail-in refund offer.

To keep track of the thousands of refunds being offered at any given time, there are now refunding newsletters. They not only list all the offers, but also detail the often byzantine regulations governing how to obtain the refunds.

● **Bank your savings.** Because coupons net you only a few dollars each time you shop, it's easy to squander the money you saved by using them.

Solution: Put your coupon savings in a savings account. Decide on a particular item to save for. Don't dip into the account until you've accumulated enough to make the purchase.

Source: *Linda Bowman, devoted coupon clipper and the author of six books on money-saving hints, including* Free Food...& More, *Probus Publishing Corp.*

coaster. Regardless of how good you are, your bankroll will make large swings in the short run. You should expect this. Following correct strategy is more beneficial to long-term play.

● **In general, the harder a game is to understand,** the smaller the house edge is. Your best bets are the more complicated games of blackjack, craps, baccarat, and video poker—always assuming you play them wisely. Your worst bets are the simple games of pure chance such as keno, roulette and the wheel of fortune.

● **Don't gamble with anything but entertainment money.** Treat gambling as entertainment, not a source for revenue. So bet enough to make it interesting but not so much that it would hurt if you lost.

● **Don't hedge your bets.** Don't take insurance in blackjack and never make the any 7 or any craps bet in craps. In gambling it makes good business sense to not insure risks you can deal with yourself. If you are afraid to lose then you are betting too much to begin with.

● **There is no system that can beat a game of pure chance.** One of the biggest myths about gambling is that games of luck can be beaten by methods of varying bet size to manipulate the odds. There are plenty of charlatans promising systems that can beat games of luck like roulette, craps and even the lottery. Most systems trade a lot of small wins for a few huge losses. In the long run, it is impossible to beat the house at games of chance.

● **It pays to shop around for the best possible playing conditions.** In many games, especially blackjack and video poker, rules can vary from one casino to another and one province to another.

Know what rules are favorable to the player and seek them out.

● **Avoid the side bets and gimmicks.** Good examples of side bets to ignore are those in Caribbean stud poker and Let It Ride. Mathematically, the house edge is huge.

● **Have fun.** Gambling is a recreational activity. Enjoyable in moderation, it can also be disastrous in excess. If you lose the ability to walk away from the table or machine at will, then you shouldn't play at all.

If you find that you're having a problem with gambling, get some assistance. Websites such as www.problemgambling.ca offer plenty of information and support for gamblers who have taken their hobby too far.

Source: Compiled by Kendrew Pape from various sources.

The Truth About Provincial Lotteries

Provincial lotteries are one of the worst bets around. The official website of the Ontario Lottery and Gaming Corporation reports that only 49.5% of the money wagered was returned as prizes in the fiscal year 1999–2000. In fact, considering the lotteries' deferred-payment schedules (a $1 million prize is awarded as $50,000 a year for 20 years), the payout could be less than 25%.

Comparisons: In the United States, video lottery terminals generally pay out 80% to 90%. In Atlantic City or Nevada, the payout in roulette is about 94%.

Sources: The Wall Street Journal; www.winalot.com, Ontario Lottery and Gaming Corporation website.

Enjoy a Day at the Races Without Going Broke

The aim of a day at the track should be to enjoy every race while controlling your losses.

● **When betting,** begin with the choices of the "morning line." The "morning line"—the prediction of the odds that each horse will go off at and of likely winners—is done by a track official who assigns odds to the horses in the morning. Handicapping is also done by bettors in the course of the day (which causes the odds to change). One-third of the favorites chosen by handicappers win their races.

● **Decide on the amount of money you are willing to lose.** Set aside one-fifth of it for entertainment betting. The rest should be spent on serious betting.

● **Avoid the temptation to increase bets when losing in order to catch up.** Also avoid the trap of betting more when winning to try to make a killing.

● **To control spending,** bet just 20% of your remaining capital each time you bet, whether your capital goes up or down.

● **For fun betting,** choose horses by name, jockey, appearance or any means you wish. You may get lucky and win 1 out of 10 bets this way.

● **For serious betting,** pick the appropriate races to bet on. Always eliminate maiden races, two-year-old races and races where it's indicated that the horses chosen won no race but their maiden race.

● **To pick the two or three likeliest winners in the race,** check handicappers' choices in local newspapers, tip sheets sold at the track or the *Daily Racing Form,* a publication most handicappers use.

Look especially for handicappers who predict in great detail how the race will be run, and those who tell you the front-runners and the come-from-behind horse as well as the outcome.

Also consult popular websites like www.racingpicks.com.

● **Late scratches** (the elimination of contenders) can dramatically change the projected script of a race. If one of the two predicted front-runners is scratched, the remaining front-runner's chance is increased.

● **Rain.** The *Daily Racing Form* lists "mudders" (horses that have a history of doing well in the rain) with each horse's lifetime wet-track record. As the track is progressively softened by rain, the chances of mudders improve.

● **Shifts in odds.** Lengthening (higher) odds on a horse can increase your chance of a good return. Observe the physical condition of your horse during the viewing ritual, when the horses are paraded at the rear of the track just before each race.

Protecting Your Home and Family

Request a security audit from your local police. Have your children fingerprinted by the local police. Keep fingerprints on file at home in case the children are ever missing. Some experts say that children should be fingerprinted regularly until the age of seven, when their hands are completely developed.

Also: Borrow a metal engraver—available at many police stations—to place a traceable identification number on your valuables, in case they are ever stolen. Use a digital camera to record and update an index of your possessions.

Source: Ladies' Home Journal.

You can place several types of bets:
● **To win.** Pays only if the horse comes in first.
● **To place.** Pays if the horse comes in first or second.
● **To show.** Pays if the horse comes in first, second or third. A combination of bets, such as a win and a place or a win and a show, increases your chances of a payoff. But the return will be smaller.

Source: The late Peter Shaw, cultural critic, historian and college professor.

Picking Harness Winners

Harness racing is far easier to handicap than thoroughbred ("flat") racing: The bettor has fewer variables to take into consideration.

Harness races are almost always at a mile and on the dirt. The fields are more manageable, with rarely more than nine entries. And, since the horses carry no weight on their backs, there are no weight differences for which to compensate. (Thanks to the laws of physics, the sulky pulled by the horse actually adds momentum, rather than drag.)

Standardbred harness horses are calmer, tougher and more dependable than thoroughbreds. The favorites win more often than thoroughbred favorites—about 36% of the time. Still, most bettors are chronic losers, in part because they ignore the most important betting factors.

Post Position

Most decisive of all is post position, especially on short half-mile or five-eighths-mile tracks. The nearer the rail, the less distance the horse must travel, both at the start and around a turn. The horse in the number one post (at the far inside) has a tremendous advantage. Since he's already at the rail, he doesn't need to spend energy to get there. Even if he doesn't make the lead, he will likely be close enough to make a move in the stretch.

Conversely, if a horse draws an outside post (number six or higher), the driver will have to either "park" outside other horses while contending for the lead or take back to the rear. Later on, he may be boxed in with no racing room. To mount a stretch drive, he will have to return outside, losing at least one and a half lengths around the final turn. And given the width of the other sulkies, there may be no convenient holes to burst through. All in all, it's tough to catch the leader.

Post positions are also a key to interpreting past performances. *Example:* In his last outing, your pick raced from the eight post and finished a distant sixth. But in the race before that, starting from the one post, he led the way and won handily. If he's returning to an inside post, you can expect the horse to improve, perhaps at good odds.

The Driver

The other underrated factor: The driver's ability. Every track has a few leading drivers; check their names in your program and remember them. Steer clear of any drivers who fail to win at least 10% of their starts. And you should never bet on a novice or provisional driver.

Positive sign: A switch from a trainer-driver to a leading full-time driver. This often means the trainer believes the horse is now at his best, ready to win.

> " Cash, vacations, houses, cars, electronic equipment, cameras and much, much more are the dream prizes that keep millions of North Americans doggedly filling out entry blanks for contests. More than $100 million in prize money and goods are dispensed annually through an estimated 500 promotional competitions and drawings. "

But even the best driver can't help a slow starter from an outside post. Check each race—carefully consult the track program—for horses with good early speed.

There are no Silky Sullivans in harness racing—no champions who consistently come from last place to take the purse. You'll find that the winner is usually among the first four horses at the half mile.

Pluses and Minuses

In weighing past performances, the horse's time in the final quarter-mile is more revealing than his overall time. *Most promising:* A fast final quarter (under 31 seconds) following a fast first half-mile.

It's also positive if the horse:

● **Won his last race** (unless he won by a small margin that was less than the last time).

● **Is going off at lower odds than in his last race.**

● **Raced steadily last time while parked** (indicated by a small "o" in the program) for one or more calls. ("Parked" means outside one or more other horses.)

But don't bet heavily if the horse:

● **Is moving up steeply in class** (signified by purse money or claiming price).

● **Hasn't been in a race for more than two weeks.**

● **Seems clearly superior in the program** but is going off at odds of 5–2 or greater. (The horse's handlers don't think he can win.)

● **Broke stride in his last race** (check in your track program).

● **Has pinned ears** (the horse's ears are back flat against his head) or is nervous or sweating in pre-race warmups.

Source: *Don Valliere, manager of the Ontario Jockey Club's track in Fort Erie, and author of* Betting Winners: A Guide for the Harness Fan, *Gambling Book Club Press.*

Provincial Lottery Winning Strategy

When playing a lottery, it's a good idea to choose at least one number higher than 31. *Reason:* Many lottery players use number combinations based on birthdays, anniversaries and other dates. Since this group concentrates on numbers of 31 or lower, a winning combination with one or more higher numbers will likely be shared by fewer people.

Source: Dr. Jim Maxwell, American Mathematics Society.

Contest Winner's Secrets of Success

Cash, vacations, houses, cars, electronic equipment, cameras and much, much more are the dream prizes that keep millions of North Americans doggedly filling out entry blanks for contests. More than $100 million in prize money and goods are dispensed annually through an estimated 500 promotional competitions and drawings.

Dedicated hobbyists know that there is an advantage of a planned approach to overcome the heavy odds against each entrant. *Winning strategies:*

● **Use your talents.** If you can write, cook or take photographs, put your energy into entering contests. They take skill, so fewer people are likely to compete—improving your chances. Photography contests have the fewest average entries.

● **Follow the rules precisely.** If the instructions say to print your name, don't write it in longhand. If a piece of paper of specified length and width is called for, measure your entry exactly. The slightest variation can disqualify you.

● **Enter often.** Always be on the lookout for new contests to enter. *Sources:* Magazines, newspapers, radio, television, store shelves and bulletin boards.

● **Make multiple entries, if they are permitted.** The more entries you send in, the more you tip the odds in your favor.

● **Spread out your entries over the duration of the contest**—one a week for five weeks, for example. When the volume of entries is big enough, they will be delivered to the judges in a number of different sacks. The theory is that judges will pick entries from each sack, and your chances will go up if you have an entry in each of the several different mailbags.

● **Stay informed.** Join a local contest club or subscribe to a contest newsletter. Either source will help you to learn contest traps, problems and solutions. They'll alert you, too, to new competitions.

● **Be selective.** Be sure the prizes are appropriate for you. If you don't live near the water, winning an expensive boat could be a headache (Some contests offer cash equivalents, but not all do.)

● **Some contests ask you to enclose some proof of purchase** or a plain piece of paper with a product name or number written on it. Many people assume that a real proof of purchase will improve their chances of winning. *Fact:* In a survey, more than half the winners of major prizes reported that they had not bought the sponsor's product.

Source: Rich Henderson and Ann Faith, coeditors of **Contest** **Newsletter,** *Danbury, CT.*

Long-Distance Phone Savings

Here's yet another benefit of the Internet: you can save money on telephone calls. With Internet Protocol (IP) Telephony, phone calls are transmitted digitally via cyberspace; all you need is a phone. (Some companies may require an Internet account.) Calls are cheaper largely because IP Telephony providers don't have to contribute to a universal phone service fund.

Savings: You get the best deal on international calls—at least 50% cheaper than with traditional phone companies. Some IP Telephony providers offer unlimited international calling for a low fixed monthly rate.

Drawbacks: Voice transmission with IP Telephony is still sometimes quirky. Also, Internet phone companies may soon have to pay domestic industry access fees, which would then be passed on to customers.

IP telephony carriers: Orbit 416-814-4402/ www.orbitcanada.com; Net2Phone www.net2phone. com; Delta Three 1-888-335-8230/www.deltathree. com.

Note: To stay competitive, most major long-distance providers such as AT&T and Sprint plan to offer IP Telephony service, too.

Tax Tactics, Strategies & Opportunities

2

Nine Big Loopholes

In Canada, the Department of Finance is constantly trying to eliminate planning strategies that it perceives as abusive, or which circumvents the intent of tax law. However, despite legislation to curb overly aggressive action through the years, there are still a number of tax loopholes open to you. Here are nine common tax preferences to consider:

1. RRSP—*The* deduction for the average working person. RRSP contributions can put taxpayers in lower tax brackets and increase both refundable and nonrefundable tax credits. Under current and foreseeable tax trends we expect personal taxes to drop in the short term—largely due to indexing of tax brackets, tax credits and clawback zones. Therefore, every dollar invested in an RRSP sooner rather than later will bring larger marginal tax gains. Your RRSP investment can also be leveraged to help you meet multiple financial objectives: first, reap double-digit returns in tax savings immediately; and invest that money wisely to pay down nondeductible debt, make deposits to your child's education savings plan or buy life insurance. Or you can plan to further increase your personal wealth by tax-free withdrawals from the RRSP under the Lifelong Learning Plan and/or Home Buyers' Plan, which can help you fund your education or home-buying needs. But note, in these latter cases, RRSP funds may not be withdrawn on a tax-free basis until a minimum 90-day investment period is met.

2. Income-shifting loophole. Plan to shift income to young children or their stay-at-home parent so it will be taxed at a lower rate. Each Canadian taxpayer can earn taxable income up to their Basic Personal Amount completely tax-free—that's over $600 a month. However, tax treatment will depend on the source of the principal. Unfortunately, the government's attribution rules force the reporting of earnings from principal transferred to low-income earners back to the return of the transferor. There are, however, a few exceptions to these rules. In the case of minor children, interest and dividend income is attributed back to the higher-income earner, while capital gains are not. When money is transferred to a lower-income spouse, unfortunately, interest, dividends and capital gains resulting from reinvestment are attributed back to the higher earner. This can be circumvented when spouses draw up bona fide investment loans and ensure that interest on that loan is actually paid once a year within 30 days of the calendar year-end. Further, small-business owners can consider paying salary or wages to a spouse or minor children who work in the small business, and make sure that own-source income from part-time jobs is strictly invested. All resulting investment earnings are then taxed in the hands of the spouse or minor child. Earnings on deposits of Canada Child Tax Benefits are also fully taxed to the spouse or minor child, provided the funds are deposited in an "untainted account." Note also that a new "Tax on Split Income" will apply at the top marginal rates to dividends flowing through to a business owner's minor children, so it's best to save those distributions for adult children. *Strategy:* Put enough assets in your low-earning spouse or minor children's names to give each enough taxable employment or properly attributed investment income a year to meet the level of the Basic Personal Amount.

3. Capital loss application loophole. Capital losses are fully deductible against other capital gains of the current year, the immediately preceding three years or any capital gains on dispositions occurring in the future. *Strategy:* Be sure to record all capital losses in your "carryover" pool to ensure their use to recover taxes paid in the past or payable in the future.

4. Income diversification loophole. Owners of small business corporations with accumulated retained earnings that are not needed in the company can pay out dividends, which are taxed at a top federal/provincial combined rate of approximately 30%. However, provincial tax rates and brackets vary from province to province, which could boost the total tax bill. *Strategy:* Diversify income and time its realization by declaring dividends from your small business corporation.

5. Tax-free compensation loophole. Even better than paying dividends to owner/managers are tax-free fringe benefits (such as private health insurance plans, education assistance for the family of those who are working in remote work sites, discounts on merchandise and subsidized meals, and certain moving expenses). The corporation can deduct the costs while you as an owner-employee are not taxed on these fringe benefits. *Strategy:* Plan compensation to maximize both cash and benefit payments.

6. Bunching or "carry-over" loophole. Sometimes, you can win tax-savings points by "bunching" certain nonrefundable tax credits together for a better claim over several years. For example, you could bunch together your charitable donations over a maximum period of five years, claiming them all in one for a better claim. As a minimum, make sure you bunch charities to exceed the $200 mark, as you'll qualify for a higher write-off rate. Other credits susceptible to bunching: medical expenses, moving expenses, tuition and education amounts, and for proprietorships, capital cost allowances. *Strategy:* Group expenses together over a period of years for a better average tax result.

7. Alimony deduction loophole. Alimony payments continue to be deductible by the spouse who pays it and taxable to the spouse who receives it. There are no minimum or maximum payments. However, payments should be planned so that an amount equal at least to the recipient's basic personal amount plus RRSP contribution deductions are paid. The amounts will then be tax-free to the recipient, while the deductible payments reduce the net income of the payer. *Strategy:* Make tax planning an integral part of your divorce agreement.

8. Rental property loophole. All rentals are treated as a "passive" investment or "income from property," for tax purposes even though there are operational costs associated with the investment. Some of those operational costs are subject to restricted tax treatment. For example, the capital cost allowance (CCA) deduction claims for the revenue property assets cannot be used to create or increase an operational loss. Aside from that, the CCA can be claimed at the taxpayer's option, so be sure to "save" this deduction for a year in which net income is higher. If taxable income persists after the application of the CCA deduction, consider splitting that income between spouses. This is only possible, however, if spouses can prove their own-source investment in the property. To avoid attribution of income or losses, the higher-income earner may loan funds to the lower-income earner to acquire a partial (or full) interest on the property. Provided that the interest is actually paid within 30 days of the calendar year, income and capital consequences on a future disposition can be split with the spouse, according to his or her ownership share. *Strategy:* Use optional deductions, like capital cost allowances and their restrictions, to your advantage in reducing net rental income and the loopholes in the attribution rules to split future income and capital gains with your spouse.

9. Recover gold in prior-filed returns. If you discover errors or omissions on prior-filed tax returns, you can ask for an adjustment. The tax department will do so for most returns according to the following provisions:

● **Most federal provisions:** back to 1985.

● **GST provisions:** back to 1991.

● **Most provincial provisions:** current year and two years back.

● **Capital cost allowance revisions:** within 90 days of receipt of the notice of assessment.

In some cases, you can reap tax refunds in the thousands of dollars, if you have become aware of a provision that was missed over the last decade and a half.

Source: Excerpted from Personal Tax Update Seminars *by Evelyn Jacks Productions, Inc., Winnipeg, Man.*

Personal Tax Breaks You Can Use

Every year, federal and provincial departments of finance tinker with the tax law, but recently important personal tax breaks have been enhanced. Here are some breaks you may be able to use. Discuss these with your tax adviser:

● **Win with bracket indexing.** Canadians stand to gain tax savings each and every year in the future as their tax brackets, personal amounts, refundable tax credits and clawback zones are indexed for inflation. This presents the opposite phenomenon of "bracket creep," the hidden taxes that had characterized our tax system through much of the '90s. Rather than being bumped into a higher tax bracket by inflation, many Canadians now find themselves pleasantly placed in a lower tax bracket due to inflation adjustments. Ask your tax adviser to identify those savings each year; then invest that new money.

● **New tax brackets and rates.** The new millennium brought with it reduced federal tax rates for all taxpayers and significant reductions for those with incomes under $100,000. The results of these changes are illustrated below. Keep in mind that tax brackets will be annually adjusted for inflation and that these tax rates will increase once provincial tax consequences are added to the equation.

Benefit from CCRA Mistakes

The CCRA's Fairness Package allows taxpayers to appeal to a special "Fairness Committee" to have interest or penalties canceled if they result from a delay in processing by the CCRA or errors in public documents, or delays in providing information to the taxpayer. Further, if the CCRA provides you with erroneous information you may appeal for removal of the interest and penalties. Unfortunately, the correct amount of taxes assessed are always payable.

FEDERAL TAX BRACKETS AND RATES 2002	
TAXABLE INCOME	FEDERAL TAX RATES
$0 to $7,634	0%
$7,635 to $31,677	16%
$31,678 to $63,354	22%
$63,355 to $103,000	26%
Over $103,000	29%

● **Provincial budget changes.** The calculation of provincial taxes has been "de-linked" from the federal tax system. Under the new Tax on Income (TONI) system, the provinces can develop their own tax brackets and rates as well as increase or supplement non-refundable tax credits, providing only that they extend at least the same tax credits as the federal government. Also, both levels of government must use the same definition of taxable income.

As a result, there are some significant tax variations between the provinces. But it is important to note that these differences can rise and fall with different income levels and family structures. That is, at the time of writing, taxpayers at the lowest tax

bracket currently fared better in Ontario than in Alberta; whereas the highest income earners kept more of their earnings when they lived in Alberta.

It is therefore important for Canadians to understand in their personal planning that they are taxed for the whole year in their province of residence as at December 31. Time your move according to the best provincial tax rate structure, especially if you move late in the year.

● **New spousal definitions and amounts.** The Spousal Amount is a special nonrefundable tax credit for those who support a spouse or common-law partner. Also, same-sex partners are now recognized for tax purposes, and so a series of new tax terms has been implemented. "Spouse" now applies only to heterosexual couples who are legally married. All others in conjugal relationships will be considered to be "common-law partners" if the certain criteria are met:

● **The couple has lived in a conjugal relationship** for a continuous period of 12 months during the year or a prior year, and are living together at the end of the year, or

● **The partners live together** at the end of the year and are the natural or adoptive parents of child they have together.

When couples meet the criteria, tax-free zones increase for the family unit, family net income is taken into account for the purposes of claiming refundable tax credits, spousal RRSP contributions can be made and the attribution rules will apply.

● **New nonrefundable tax credits.** Most taxpayers miss out on important nonrefundable tax credits that can reduce the federal and provincial taxes payable significantly over a period of years. Personal amounts increase the "tax-free zone" available to families experiencing different life circumstances, like illness, support of disabled adults, students, or their favorite charities. Indexing and budget enhancements have recently increased these amounts significantly, as outlined in the chart below. But keep in mind that indexing of these amounts will continue as time goes by.

● **New eligibility for federal refundable tax credits.** More families now qualify for the federal refundable tax credits: the Canada Child Tax Benefits (CCTB), and the Goods and Services Tax Credit (GSTC). Refundable tax credits are sent out to you whether or not you are taxable. Both spouses simply have to file a tax return to report your family's net income. In the case of the CCTB, a monthly payment results, depending on net income level and number of children. The GSTC is sent quarterly and both credits are paid on a "benefit year" cycle: from July of one year to June of another. This allows the tax department time to assess your eligibility based on the filing

of your tax return. Clawbacks of the full amount of the credits can begin at family net income levels of about $34,000. Often higher-income-earning families can create at least partial credits by making RRSP contributions, which reduce net income.

● **New, lower capital gains inclusion rates.** Starting with transactions occurring after Oct. 17, 2000, the capital gains inclusion rate for tax purposes has been reduced to 50%, which is good news for investors and those experiencing temporary cash flow problems. If you must tap your savings, generate the lowest possible taxable income with your tax-efficient withdrawal choices. Taking money out of your non-registered equities makes more sense than generating a full income inclusion by cashing in RRSP funds.

● **Capital gains tax rollovers.** A tax-free rollover allows individual small-business owners who sell their firms to defer the tax on capital gains from eligible small-business investments, if they reinvest in another eligible small business. This is good news for entrepreneurs who like to keep on growing new businesses.

TAXPAYER PROFILE	APPROXIMATE AMOUNTS	APPROXIMATE REAL DOLLAR VALUE USING AVERAGE FEDERAL/PROVINCIAL RATES
Seniors:		
Age amount	$3,800	$990
Clawback begins at individual net income of	$28,000	
The sick and disabled and their caregivers:		
Amount for infirm dependent adult	$3,600	$935
Clawback begins at individual net income of	$5,000	
Caregiver amount for in-home care of adult	$3,600	$935
Clawback begins at individual net income of	$12,500	
Pension income amount (for certain pension receipts)	$1,000	$260
Disability amounts for adults	$6,400	$1,665
Supplemental amount for minors	$3,600	$935
Allowable child care and attendant care before clawback	$2,200	
Education amounts for full-time students (not indexed)	$400 a month	$105 a month
Education amounts for part-time students (not indexed)	$120 a month	$31 a month
Medical expense net income ceiling	$1,750	
(expenses must exceed 3% of net income to a maximum of this figure)		
Charitable donations (amounts up to $200)	26%	$52 on $200
Charitable donations (amounts over $200)	39% to over 46%	Depends on province of residence

● **New deduction for mechanics' tools.** Starting in 2002, those individuals who are enrolled in an educational program leading to a designation as a licensed motor vehicle mechanic may deduct the cost of tools acquired against the income made in their employment as an apprentice. If those costs exceed income, the amounts can be carried forward to a subsequent tax year. The deduction will be limited to the total cost of the tools and ancillary equipment required for the apprenticeship and the greater of $1,000 or 5% of the individual's income for the year from the apprenticeship.

The cost of the tools will be reduced by the deduction received in the year and this will be used as the cost base of the tools. Later, that adjusted cost base will be used to compute further tax consequences on disposition.

● **Gains on the sale of your home remain tax-free.** This tax-exempt rule applies to one home per family unit only. These rules now apply to same-sex couples, whose conjugal relationship is now recognized for tax purposes.

● **Gifts and inheritances aren't taxable income to the recipient.** The recipient simply pays tax on the unsheltered earnings on the subsequent reinvestment. For that reason, some of those inheritances should be invested into tax-sheltered vehicles—like registered retirement savings plans, registered education savings plans or universal life insurance policies. For the remaining unsheltered funds, consider tax-efficient investments that generate tax-preferred income like capital gains or dividends.

● **Property that you inherit gets a "stepped-up value."** Widows/widowers have the option of receiving inherited property from a deceased loved one at its fair market value at date of death, rather than its original adjusted cost base, if that saves the couple more money now. Otherwise, the property is transferred to surviving spouses at adjusted cost base on a "tax-free rollover." Property inherited by other family members is generally transferred at fair market value, except in some transfers of farm property. This causes immediate tax consequences on the final returns filed for the deceased, but provides you with the benefit of paying taxes yourself only on the accrued values from time of inheritance. *Example:* You inherit your mother's diamond ring, which was originally purchased for $1,000.

At her death, the value of the ring has appreciated to $6,000. If you sell the ring for $8,000, you have to pay tax only on your gain of $2,000—that is, the difference between its value at your mother's death and the selling price.

● **Interest and dividends earned by your existing** sheltered investments continue to be tax deferred. These investments include the following: registered retirement savings plans, registered education savings plans, registered retirement income funds, registered pension plans and investments within universal life insurance policies.

Source: Personal Tax Update Seminars *by Evelyn Jacks Productions, Inc. Winnipeg, Man.*

More Tax-Exempt Income Sources

● **Life insurance proceeds** that you receive as a result of the death of the insured.

● **Cash-value buildup of life insurance policies** and most deferred annuities.

● **Employer-paid tuition** for courses of benefit to the employer.

● **Employer-paid counseling** for mental or physical health or reemployment or retirement.

● **Employer-paid memberships to recreational facilities** including social or athletic clubs.

● **Employer-paid premiums under private health services plans.**

● **Sale of one personal residence or vacation property** if this property qualifies as your tax-exempt principal residence.

● **Scholarships and fellowships** in amounts up to $3,000 if your studies otherwise qualify for the education amounts.

Common Tax Deductions

● **Registered pension plan contributions through your employment.**

● **RRSP contributions; based on RRSP contribution room.**

● **Annual union and professional dues.**

● **Child care expenses.**

● **Attendant care expenses.**

● **Business investment losses.**

● **Moving expenses.**

● **Support payments based on agreements made before May 1, 1997.**

- **Carrying charges.**
- **Employment expenses,** including auto and home office expenses, providing a declaration of employment conditions signed by the employer is available.
  - **Cleric's residence deduction.**
  - **Employee home relocation loan deduction.**
  - **Stock option and shares deductions.**
  - **Noncapital losses of other years.**
  - **Net capital losses of other years.**
  - **Capital gains deduction.**
  - **Northern residents deduction.**

Common Federal Nonrefundable Tax Credits

- **Basic personal amount.**
- **Age amount.**
- **Spouse or common-law partner amount.**
- **Amount for infirm dependents age 18** or older.
- **CPP or QPP contributions** through employment and on self-employment earnings.
  - **Employment insurance premiums.**
  - **Pension income amount.**
  - **Caregiver amount.**
  - **Disability amount and disability amount** transferred from a dependent.
  - **Interest paid on student loans.**
  - **Tuition and education amounts** for yourself or transferred from a child.
  - **Amounts transferred from spouse or** common-law partner.
  - **Medical expense.**
  - **Charitable donations.**

Source: Personal Tax Update Seminars *by Evelyn Jacks Productions, Inc., Winnipeg, Man.*

New Laws That Help Taxpayers

Interest Offsets

When taxpayers are late in making tax payments to the government, they will be charged interest and a premium of 4% above the Treasury Bill rate for the last quarter. However, when the tax department is late in processing your refund, they will pay you interest, but only after 45 days have elapsed from the receipt of your tax return, and then at a rate that exceeds the Treasury Bill rate by only 2%. It is now possible for the interest you may owe on a prior year's return to be offset by any tax refund interest that the tax department owes you. These new rules will apply to tax refund interest accrued or payable after 1999.

Checklist: Before Sending in Your Return

Check to make sure you've completed everything on this list. A slipup can cause delays and inconvenience. Moreover, every time you draw attention to your return, you increase the chance of audit.

✓ **Does your name, address and Social Insurance Number (SIN) appear on page 1?** If you used the CCRA address label, be sure you have made any necessary corrections.

✓ **Have you put your SIN on every document** to be sent to the CCRA?

✓ **Are all T-Slips attached?**

✓ **Are all other necessary forms and schedules attached?**

✓ **Have you checked and rechecked your arithmetic?**

✓ **Are all required forms signed and dated?**

✓ **If you owe money, is your cheque or money order attached to the return?** Have you written your SIN and the year on the cheque?

✓ **Is the return addressed to the correct CCRA office?**

✓ **Have you affixed the correct postage?**

✓ **Have you made a copy of the return for your own records?**

✓ **Have you stored all supporting documentation** that is not required to be sent in with the return, in a safe place, properly sorted and labeled?

How to Recover Your Legal Fees From the CCRA

If the tax department has taken an unreasonable position that pushed you into spending money on legal fees to defend yourself, you may be able to recoup them on your tax return. Accounting and legal costs incurred in appealing tax reassessments, or decisions surrounding Employment Insurance or Canada Pension Plan benefits are deductible.

In addition, those who pay legal fees to collect late alimony or taxable maintenance payments are eligible to deduct them. So are those who fight for a retiring allowance or pension benefits.

Catch: There may be a limit to the recovery of legal fees in the battle for severance: the deduction for the fees will be reduced by any amount of severance transferred to an RRSP.

Penalties for Breach of Confidentiality

The information you file with your tax return is held in strictest confidence and must not be communicated to any third party by the employees of the tax department. There are heavy fines in place should that happen: a maximum fine of $5,000 and/or imprisonment of up to one year. The same penalties will apply if your Social Insurance Number is disclosed without your authorization.

Third-Party Penalties

Your tax preparer or financial planner must not knowingly, or in circumstances amounting to gross negligence, make false statements or omissions on your tax return. Should this happen, civil penalties of not less than $1,000 will be assessed. This includes "culpable conduct" for misrepresentation in planning arrangements or participation in the making of false statements on behalf of another person.

Source: *Evelyn Jacks, president, Evelyn Jacks Productions, Inc. and best-selling author,* Tax Secrets for Tough Times *and* Make Sure It's Deductible, *published by McGraw-Hill Ryerson.*

What Do You Need From a Tax Preparer?

Aside from the first requirement—honesty—and the second—competence—what do you look for in a tax preparer? The answer depends on your specific tax preparation and planning needs, but usually boils down to one basic concept: peace of mind.

The Options

For most taxpayers, the tax department itself can supply some appropriate help. Its many instructional booklets are useful, though they may take the tax collector's side in arguable matters. The booklets cover subjects from record-keeping requirements to moving expenses, from deductions for employees and the self-employed to tax information for home buyers, seniors, students, the disabled or those who give money and goods to charity. The tax department also answers questions over the telephone, in person or by mail—millions make inquiries every year. There are even volunteer programs located in malls and other public places each tax season. The tax department's website is also a wonderful resource from which you can print most forms and publications and review the latest news releases.

A step up from free tax advice are commercial tax preparers. They will use the proper forms and fill out your return based on the information you give them, and file your return either on paper or electronically. It's usually all done correctly, the accuracy is usually guaranteed and fees are relatively expensive, but it is possible that the service is not sophisticated enough for your specific needs. You may need to do some shopping around to tap into the best tax preparation and tax planning solution.

You may have heard of an independent tax practitioner who has been helpful to a colleague. That's not a bad way to find tax help, if you remember that ability and experience vary greatly. Determine the professional qualifications of the preparer, and whether that person regularly keeps up with the federal and provincial tax changes as well as recent outcomes at the court level.

Professional accountants differ in their services to their clients. Only a small percentage are tax experts. However an accounting office can provide a more diversified service, including person, corporate and trust tax assistance, as well as financial planning, estate planning and business succession services. Most professionals will also represent you in case of dispute with the tax department.

GETTING THE MOST FROM YOUR TAX PREPARER

Familiarize yourself with the tax law. There are many tax-preparation guides on the market, and the CCRA itself provides plenty of free basic filing information, both in paper and on their website.

Organize your materials. Don't show up with a briefcase full of tax-related paperwork that you expect him or her to sort out—unless you'd like to really pay a lot of money for the work. Remember, if your preparer has to muddle through the papers, it will cut into the time that should be spent on figuring out the best tax strategy.

Bring the right information to the meeting. Once you have organized your records, bring the necessary information, such as:

● **Past tax returns.** Bring old returns. It will give your new preparer valuable information about your tax history—and he or she can review your prior files to see if you missed any tax breaks in those years.

● **Tax information slips and statements.** Bring all your information slips received in the mail including all T4, T5, T4A(OAS), T4A(P), T4RSP, T$RIF, T4E, T5007, T508 and T3 slips. Also bring along any statements that show income and proceeds from security transactions. Don't forget offsetting deduction receipts for employment expenses and carrying charges like safety deposit boxes.

● **Expense diary.** This will help your preparer determine the deductibility of your expenses for auto costs, home office or coin expenditures like phone or parking. He or she will also be able to tell you if it meets the stringent record-keeping requirements of the CCRA. If it's not in good enough shape for use on this year's return, your preparer should be able to advise you about making it audit-proof for next year's return.

● **Canceled cheques.** Bring all your cheques, even those not written for deductible items. Your accountant may find some deductions that you didn't know about, including expenses paid for medical costs, tuition and education costs, moving expenses and child care. Some mixed use expenditures may trigger deductions—for example, costs of a new car.

● **Preparer worksheets.** Many firms send out detailed worksheets for you to fill out long before your actual appointment. Bring that worksheet with you, and be sure you have filled it out with scrupulous care.

Never jump to tax conclusions. Many taxpayers don't mention some financial matters to their accountant because they have already made a decision on its tax status. Taxpayers often reach the wrong conclusions and lose out on deductions. Tell your preparer everything, and let him or her make the decision.

● **Get a tax projection.** Ask your preparer to look at next year's taxes while he or she is doing your return. You'll see early in the year where you stand, and you'll know what to expect. Also, number one goal is to make sure you don't overpay your taxes during the year through excess tax withholding or overpayments of quarterly tax instalments.

● **Stay in contact during the year.** Always contact your tax adviser before a major personal, career or financial decision takes place to check out any tax consequences.

Source: Personal Tax Update Seminars *by Evelyn Jacks Productions, Inc., and Evelyn Jacks, best-selling author,* Tax Secrets in Tough Times *and* Make Sure It's Deductible, *published by McGraw-Hill Ryerson, 300 Water Street, Whitby, ON L1N 9B6.*

The Interview

Interview any tax adviser before signing on for service. Come armed with a list of tax questions you need to have answered to judge whether the prospective tax adviser is up-to-date, can communicate, and in general whether he or she is willing to help you with tax planning as well as tax preparation. Here's a sample of such a list:

1. What are the latest tax changes that will apply to my family/business operations this year?

2. What is the tax rate I will pay on each source of income I earn in the coming year?

3. What tax provisions should I be carrying forward from previous filing years?

4. What are the latest tax changes for our family unit to take advantage of?

5. How can our family members split income and transfer deductions and credits this year?

6. What are the retirement savings strategies we should be working toward?

7. How can we plan new investments outside our registered accounts to increase tax-deferred income sources?

8. How can we reduce tax withholding/tax installment payments this year?

9. How should asset acquisitions and dispositions be timed to make the most tax sense?

10. What audit-proofing procedures should we be putting in place this year?

Remember, taking a longer term view to your taxation affairs will reap financial benefits with the potential to multiply significantly over time. ***Catch:*** If a preparer asks you to sign a blank return, guarantees a refund, won't quote exact fees, doesn't itemize services to be provided, doesn't ask for receipt verification for your income and expense claims, won't stand behind his or her work, has no strategy for the occurrence of mistakes, won't represent you in case of audit, doesn't provide copies of your return, closes down for long periods after the tax season without a forwarding number, is unavailable for post-assessment audit service, refuses to sign the return as preparer, or fails to communicate with you to your liking, look elsewhere.

Source: Make Sure It's Deductible *by Evelyn Jacks, published by McGraw-Hill Ryerson, 300 Water Street, Whitby, ON L1N 9B6.*

How to Pick the Shrewdest Tax Adviser

The shrewdest tax adviser (preparer, practitioner, accountant, etc.) is the one who can minimize your overall expenditures for taxes (your tax bill plus his or her bill plus any expenses connected with audits, etc.) over a period of years. Therefore, it is important to find someone who is interested in having a long-term relationship with you and your family. This close relationship can save you thousands of dollars of time, and is most effective when tax planning and tax preparation activities are approached in tandem.

The first requirement in finding the most astute tax adviser is to understand what specific services you need and whether the adviser offers them. Then, in addition to being prompt, courteous, diligent, organized, thorough and well versed in new developments, the best tax adviser will be focused on helping you make the most tax efficient decisions in your personal life, with your investments and in your career. That person will be educational, inquisitive, innovative and sensitive to your situation, temperament and outlook.

The relationship will be personal as well as professional, so plan to devote as much time and effort as necessary to make it work to your advantage. It will pay off. The most effective procedure is to first solicit recommendations and referrals from friends and business acquaintances whose business acumen you respect, and to follow up with interviews.

Here's a checklist of points to consider.

● **Technical competence.** Is this person able to field most of your questions with ease and confidence? If he or she has to grope for answers or look everything up in a book, you can conclude that knowledge is weak in areas of importance to you. If, on the other hand, you find yourself being told about new developments in tax laws in your areas of interest, consider this person to be a strong candidate.

● **Organization and interview depth.** Does this tax professional provide an organized worksheet prior to the interview to help you gather your materials effectively and efficiently? Does this person offer advice on record-keeping procedures that speeds and clarifies your work together? Go through your chequebook register, discuss your investments with you, pore through your records and receipts for overlooked deductions?

● **Comprehensive analysis.** In the initial interview, a top-notch tax adviser will do all of the following: review your financial activities for their tax impact; review your three prior years' returns, looking for tax breaks you might have missed; spend time discussing ways to cut your tax bill for the coming year. The only way to save on taxes is by year-round planning. This is what you pay a tax adviser for. If your adviser isn't inclined to probe, ask questions, and offer advice, you should consider a change to someone more diligent. Filling in the forms should not be all you are paying for.

● **Audit compatibility.** While we would all love to pay the lowest possible tax bill and never be audited, the fact is that to save tax dollars, you must take aggressive positions on your financial dealings—which makes it much more likely your returns are going to be audited. If you want to cut your audit risk, you must take a more conservative approach. You can't have it both ways. What's important is that you and your adviser agree on your audit tolerance.

● **Audit representation.** Will this professional represent you at an audit? Will there be an extra fee for this? Will he or she be able to strongly argue the positions you took on your return, especially where the tax law isn't clear?

● **Support network.** Is the tax adviser in question a member of a firm that includes specialists/experts in various tax fields, attorneys, accountants? Such support personnel will ensure that you receive a more comprehensive service.

● **Silent partner.** Even the shrewdest tax adviser is only as strong and effective as his or her silent partner—you, the client. To get the most from your tax advice, you must take an active role—the more active the better. If you are careful to bring to your adviser's attention any potential out-of-the-way deductions, present your records in an organized way, make sure records are complete at interview time, keep your expert informed about changes in essential personal and financial matters, and make your own tax education an ongoing concern, your relationship with any tax adviser you choose will be that much more fruitful.

Source: *Paul N. Strassels, a tax-law specialist, Money Matters, Inc., Box 195, Burke, VA 22015.*

Action Plan for Finding a Tax Adviser

To find your trusted tax adviser, follow these steps:

● **Seek referrals.** Ask your friends and business associates for referrals; check out the yellow pages and chamber of commerce or board of trade in your area for the names of well-respected tax advisers.

● **Expertise and services needed.** Find out what level of expertise you need: commercial tax preparation, accounting and auditing, corporate as well as personal returns, trust returns and estate planning.

● **Reputation and experience.** Interview at least three professionals in your area. This can include independents, partners in a partnership, financial institutions, and so on. It's best to include one from every group to get the best overview of potential service, quality and price. You will receive a broad sampling of services and fees and, most important, an opportunity to judge the effectiveness of communications with you.

● **Ask questions.** Come to the interview prepared to ask at least your top three taxation concerns.

● **Listen well.** When you ask questions, note how the answers are communicated. Can you learn from this person? Is he or she interested in you and your business? The last thing you need is to feel intimidated or unclear about the way your concerns were addressed. You are looking for peace of mind and a professional partner for the future of your business and personal affairs.

● **Find out about service.** Ask about fees, guarantee of service, billing practices, errors or omissions insurance, size of organizations, additional services provided. What happens when errors occur?

● **Integrated services.** Ask about the professional's ability to interact with others: lawyers, financial planners, insurance advisers and so on, should you need these services.

● **Make the decision.** Choose the adviser you are most comfortable with.

● **Give a trial.** Ask the adviser to complete a small job to see if there is integrity behind the quality of the work, the ability to meet deadlines and to work with you on follow-up procedures.

● **Review the accuracy of the work.** Listen and learn as the adviser explains the results of the work.

Source: Make Sure It's Deductible *by Evelyn Jacks, published by McGraw-Hill Ryerson, 300 Water Street, Whitby, ON L1N 9B6.*

The CCRA's Current Hot Topics

The best way to head off unwanted problems with the tax department is to know in advance what areas on your return are likely to get the most scrutiny. Here's a list of the CCRA's current hot topics and the steps that you can take to handle them and avoid a tax dispute before troubles arise.

Who's an audit risk? The CCRA must ensure that a level playing field exists for all taxpayers and so is particularly concerned that income is not understated, and deductions or credits are not overstated. Under Canada's self-assessment system, it is every taxpayer's legal right and duty to arrange his or her affairs within the framework of the law so as to pay the least amount of tax possible. With this right comes the "burden of proof"; that is, the taxpayer must have records to prove both income and expense claims.

Those who receive income sources reported on slips (T4's, T5's, etc.) have lower audit risks because the CCRA does receive a copy of these and can match your reporting—or non-reporting—very accurately. But especially if income is self-reported, or many discretionary, receipt-based deductions or credits are claimed, taxpayers must be prepared to show books and records. You must have the ability to verify income of all types—cash, barter or in kind—and receipts, logs and other documentation is required to prove that all expenses claimed to reduce income is both reasonable and, in the case of the self-employed, incurred to earn income with a reasonable expectation of profit.

The CCRA will tend, therefore, to audit the following common income sources and discretionary deductions and credits like those listed below, because they must rely on you to self-assess:

Income
- Self-reported capital gains and losses.
- Rental property income.
- Net partnership income.
- Alimony or support payments received.
- Self-employment.

Deductions
- Child care expenses.
- Attendant care expenses.
- Business investment losses.
- Moving expenses.
- Alimony or support payments.
- Employment expenses, including the board and lodging claims of long-distance transport drivers or the sales expenses of employed commissioned salespeople.

Nonrefundable Tax Credits
- Caregiver amount.
- Disability amount.
- Interest amount on student loans.
- Medical expenses.
- Charitable donations.

In addition, the CCRA launches special investigative projects into "high risk" industries where a high incidence of tax fraud is suspected. Those who report (or underreport) income from tips in the services sector, independent couriers, subcontractors, and those in home renovation or car repair are often scrutinized.

What to do: When a discrepancy is found, you'll receive a computer-generated, mailed notice from the CCRA. Be sure to make a copy of the notice, assess whether you can understand it and agree or disagree with it. If it is relatively straightforward (i.e., send in your medical expenses to support your claim), make a copy of all receipts for your files and then send the originals in. If it is not straightforward, seek assistance from a qualified tax adviser immediately. That professional can take steps to preserve your appeal rights by filing a notice of objection and can request extensions to any time deadlines the CCRA wants you to meet in replying to the letter.

Source: *Evelyn Jacks, president, Evelyn Jacks Productions, Inc. and best-selling author,* Tax Secrets for Tough Times *and* Make Sure It's Deductible, *published by McGraw-Hill Ryerson.*

How to Get More Time to File

Most taxpayers must file a tax return by April 30 of the year following the tax year in question. Unincorporated small-business owners have until June 15 to file their returns without a late filing penalty, but there is a catch: If you owe money to the tax department, the interest clock starts ticking as of May 1. So it pays to file by April 30 just in case.

If you need extra time to prepare your tax return, you can get it automatically, if you can prove there is hardship involved. Under the CCRA's "Fairness Provisions" the tax department has the authority to waive penalties and interest if the taxpayer has suffered a hardship beyond his or her control due to illness, death in the family, natural disasters, etc.

In the case of audit, extension requests for the purposes of gathering information are usually granted, provided the time line is reasonable. However, don't push your luck here . . . once you've asked for an extension, be sure to meet it.

Never file a late return. If you owe money to the CCRA, the late filing penalty is 5% of the unpaid taxes, plus interest, which is compounded daily at a rate 4% higher than the last quarter's treasury bill rate. That's expensive. And late filing penalties can increase if you are a multiple-year offender!

If the tax department owes you money on the other hand, late filing is just as foolish. You are continuing to provide an interest-free loan to the government—money that likely could be put to better use in your own hands.

Source: *Evelyn Jacks, president, Evelyn Jacks Productions, Inc. and best-selling author,* Tax Secrets for Tough Times *and* Make Sure It's Deductible, *published by McGraw-Hill Ryerson.*

Consequences of Noncompliance

An audit request is to be taken seriously (resist the urge to hide the letter under the cutlery tray) and if your first impulse is to procrastinate, your potential liability can quickly multiply out of control. The penalties involved can also be eye-opening, as revealed in the chart below.

PENALTIES FOR NONCOMPLIANCE TO AN AUDIT REQUEST	
Circumstance	**Penalty**
Failure to file a return on time	5% of unpaid taxes plus 1% per month up to a maximum of 12 months from filing due date, which is June 15 for unincorporated small businesses
Subsequent failure to file on time within a three-year period	10% of unpaid taxes plus 2% per month to a maximum of 20 months from filing due date
Failure to provide information on a required form	$100 for each failure
Failure to provide Social Insurance Number	$100 for each failure unless the card is applied for within 15 days of the request
Failure to provide information with regard to foreign-held property	$500 per month for a maximum of 24 months; $1,000 a month for a maximum of 24 months if there is a failure to respond to a demand to file plus an additional penalty of 5% of the value of the property transferred or loan to a foreign trust or the cost of the foreign property where failure to file exceeds 24 months
Gross negligence: false statement or omission of information in the return	50% of tax on understated income with a minimum $100 penalty
False statements or omissions with regard to foreign properties	5% of the value of the property, minimum of $24,000
Late or insufficient installments	50% of interest payable exceeding $1,000 or 25% of interest payable if no installments were made, whichever is greater
Tax evasion	50% to 200% of tax sought to be evaded and imprisonment for up to five years
Failure to deduct or remit source deductions	10% of amount not withheld, or remitted
Second such failure in same year	20% of amount not withheld or remitted if this was done knowingly or through gross negligence.

Source: Make Sure It's Deductible *by Evelyn Jacks, published by McGraw-Hill Ryerson, 300 Water Street, Whitby, ON L1N 9B6.*

Big Tax Refund? You've Done Something Wrong

If you received a fat tax refund this year, don't feel too happy about it. It means you overpaid your estimated taxes or had too much withheld from your salary. In effect, you made an interest-free loan to the government, when you could have been using the money for yourself—for example, by putting it in an interest-paying bank account.

Trap: The CCRA can withhold all or part of your refund to offset a tax liability, a debt to a government agency (for instance, a student loan) or unpaid child support.

What to do: File a new Form TD1 to reduce the amount withheld from your salary. If you pay estimated tax, reduce your quarterly payments by filing Form T1033 Calculation of Installment Payments. And, if you have special deductions that will reduce your income and increase your refund at year-end—like child care expenses, RRSP contributions, or employment expenses—you can reduce your tax withholding by filing Form T1213 Request to Reduce Tax Deductions at Source, with supporting documentation.

Caution: Don't overdo it. You may be hit with interest charges and a request to increase quarterly installment payments if your estimations of taxes payable fall short.

Tax Refunds: The Second Time Around

It's not too late to get a cash refund for errors or omissions made on prior filed returns, by filing Form T1-ADJ-01 with the CCRA. Take the time to review old tax returns to see if you overlooked anything that may lead to getting money back. The time limit for amending your original tax return is variable: for provincial provisions amendments are limited to the current tax year and two prior years.

> "As you fill out your return this year, perhaps you will remember deductions that you should have taken in the past. If you forgot to claim an item to which you were entitled, consider amending that year's return. The most commonly missed tax deductions include the safety-deposit box, employment and moving expenses."

For most federal provisions, adjustments can be made all the way back to 1985.

Caution: Filing an amended return may invite the CCRA to take a second look at your original return. If there is anything on it that you think may not pass this additional scrutiny, you should be wary about amending. On the other hand, if you will get back a significantly larger refund by amending, or you know the tax department can't challenge anything on the original return, it may be worth the risk.

What You Can Amend

The most common oversights that eventually lead to an additional refund upon adjustment include the following:

● **Filing the wrong form.** Short-form or Internet filers might have been able to file a long form (the T1 General) and get the benefit of a lower tax bill. But you are not stuck with your original choice. Perhaps you used one of the short forms because you were in a last-minute rush to file the return, or you thought the T1 General was too difficult. If you file on the T1 General this year but filed a short form for the past two years, check your earlier returns to see if you should have used the long form. No matter what your original reason for filing a shorter form, it is worth taking the time now to see how much you would save by filing the only form that makes reference to all your tax deductions and credits.

● **Overlooking deductions.** As you fill out your return this year, perhaps you will remember deductions that you should have taken in the past. If you forgot to claim an item to which you were entitled, consider amending that year's return. The most commonly missed tax deductions include the safety-deposit box, employment and moving expenses.

● **Overlooking credits.** Taxpayers often forget or miscalculate certain nonrefundable tax credits.

Carefully review the following items on your past tax returns:

- **Caregiver amount.**
- **Disability amount.**
- **Interest amount on student loans.**
- **Medical expenses.**
- **Charitable donations.**

Other Common Errors

- **Missed GST rebates** on union or professional dues.
- **Missed deduction for premiums** paid through employment for wage loss replacement plans.
- **Missed claims** for brokerage fees.
- **Missed deductions for safety-deposit box.**
- **Lost RRSP receipts.**
- **Missed or erroneous claims** for child care expenses.
- **Missed or erroneous claims** for moving expenses.
- **Failure to record capital losses.**
- **Failure to claim amount** for an eligible dependent when marital status changes.
- **Missed disability, caregiver and medical expense claims,** especially nursing home fees.
- **Failure to carry forward** unclaimed charitable donations.
- **Failure to transfer unused amounts from spouse** including the age, pension income, disability and tuition and education amounts.
- **Failure to transfer** tuition and education amounts from child.

Form T1-ADJ has space in which to properly identify yourself, the tax year in question and the details of your adjustment. It will allow you to record your income, deductions and credits as you reported them on your original return and then the changes you want to make for those amounts.

Important: When you're making amendments, always include explanations for the changes you are making and supply any supporting documentation. Keep a copy of everything for your own files. You must not calculate the new tax on the corrected amount; the CCRA will do this for you and send out a notice of reassessment once they are done. Check the results over carefully and compare them to your own calculations (or that of your tax adviser).

On the form, be sure to state all possible grounds for your adjustment. However, if you or your tax adviser believe the dispute is more than just a simple adjustment and may reach an appeal or court level, you will have to file a notice of objection to preserve all of your appeal rights.

Simple and Straightforward Amendments

- **Changes of very small dollar amounts** that are easily supported with receipts (i.e., safety-deposit box deduction).
- **Mathematical changes.**
- **Claims for disability amounts,** medical expenses and other nonrefundable tax credits.
- **Missed T4 slips** or receipts for registered retirement savings plan contributions.

Riskier Amendments

- **Any change that has huge dollar consequences** on your return (i.e., very large charitable donations or capital losses).
- **Additional deductions** contributing to losses from business activity.
- **Reclassifying ordinary income** to capital gain.
- **Claiming large carrying charges** like interest costs.
- **Adjustments to claims** for revenue properties.
- **Adjustment to farm losses** when there is another source of income.

Where to send it: Mail the amended return to the Tax Services Office nearest to where you now live. If you moved during the year, mail it to the service center at your new address.

Caution: When you amend your federal tax return, your provincial tax liability from that year will be affected, too.

How Long Should Tax File Documents Be Kept?

- **Normally, tax returns and the supporting documents** should be kept for six years from the day the return for that taxation year is filed.
- **Where there is an objection or appeal:** until that appeal or the time to appeal is over.
- **If the Minister demands it, indefinitely.**

A person may request that records be destroyed

at an earlier date, but will generally initiate an audit.

Be sure to put canceled cheques and supporting documents into boxes or envelopes, marked clearly with the tax year and the discard date and put it on the top shelf of your highest closet (or the next safest place in your house). You'll only need this material if you are audited. Returns should be kept in an accessible file drawer.

Source: *Evelyn Jacks, president, Evelyn Jacks Productions, Inc. and best-selling author,* Tax Secrets for Tough Times *and* Make Sure It's Deductible, *published by McGraw-Hill Ryerson.*

Free Information From the CCRA

The CCRA publishes a wealth of material on virtually every subject taxpayers have to grapple with. The publications are all free for the asking. The CCRA updates its general tax guides every year. They are indispensable.

Most Helpful

- P102 Support Payments
- P110 Paying Your Income Taxes by Installment
- P113 Gifts and Income Tax
- P119 When You Retire
- P151 Canadian Residents Going Down South
- RC4064 Information Concerning People with Disabilities
- RC4110 Employee or Self-Employed?
- T4037 Capital Gains
- T4040 RRSPs and Other Registered Plans for Retirement
- T4044 Employment Expenses

Interpretation Bulletins

The following publications contain in-depth explanations of a wide variety of tax-related subjects. Among the publications are:

- Accounting fees IT-99
- Adjusted cost base of capital property . . IT-456

TAX-FREE INCOME CHECKLIST

The CCRA isn't allowed to put the bite on every dollar that finds its way into a taxpayer's pocket. The following is a list of what's exempt from taxation:

- **Gain on the sale of your home.**
- **Gifts you receive.** Any tax on income or capital gains is payable by the person who makes the gift.
- **Money you borrow.** Normally, borrowing is not a taxable transaction, but it could have tax consequences. For example, interest costs incurred for the purpose of earning income from a business or property may be deductible. Interest received from the CCRA may be taxable.

- **Severance rollovers.** No tax is payable on a lump-sum amount that is received upon job termination if the money is transferred to an RRSP according to service and time-related eligibility rules and within 60 days after the end of the year.
- **Inheritances of property.** Beneficiaries don't pay income tax on an inheritance. Moreover, you would usually inherit property at its fair market value, thereby providing you with the "stepped-up value" to use as your adjusted cost base, in the case of assets which have appreciated over time. If you are the spouse, an amount between the adjusted cost base and fair market value can be chosen as the deceased's proceeds of disposition and your adjusted cost base. It is important to get some help with this to minimize tax on the final return(s) of the deceased as well as to plan to mini-

mize the beneficiary's tax exposure in the future.
- **Life insurance proceeds.** The beneficiary gets the full amount income-tax-free.
- **Property settlements between spouses in divorce or separation proceedings.** There is generally no tax at the time property is transferred.
- **Child-support payments.** They are tax-free to the recipient. Alimony payments to a spouse or ex-spouse, however, are taxable to the recipient.
- **Money recovered in lawsuits for personal injury awards.**
- **Workers' Compensation payments.** They are reported as income and serve to reduce refundable tax credits, but are not taxable.
- **Disability payments from accident and health insurance plans.** The payments are tax-free if you paid for the insurance, but taxable if your

- Age tax credit IT-513
- Attribution rules IT-511
- Auto expenses IT-478, IT-521, IT-522
- Convention expenses IT-131
- Deduction for travel expenses IT-522
- Farm property transfers to child IT-268
- Gambling profits IT-334
- Medical expenses IT-519
- Rental properties IT-434
- Transfer of property on divorce IT-325

All of these documents are available on the CCRA website: www.ccra-adrc.gc.ca.

Don't Pay More Than the Law Demands

Under our system of self-assessment, it is every Canadian taxpayer's legal right and duty to arrange affairs, within the framework of the law, so as to pay the least amount of tax possible. Resolve to pay the correct amount of taxes for your situation, and not one dime more. Here are some tips to keep your taxes as low as possible under the tax law we have today.

● **Be aggressive both in setting strategies that save taxes and in preparing your return.** Too many people deny themselves the full tax breaks they're entitled to because they're afraid they will be audited. They take overly conservative positions on their returns and scale back unusually large deductions that they think—often erroneously—the CCRA will disallow. In effect, these people are auditing themselves. The CCRA may never get a chance to review the item.

Better way: Take the full tax preference available to you—provided it is applicable to your circumstance, and in the case of "grey areas" that it follows the intent of the law, is reasonable under the circumstances and can be backed with proper documentation—no matter how high it is in relation to your income. Always bear in mind that many tax provisions

employer paid any of the premiums. In that case any portion of the premiums that you paid can be deducted when wage loss replacement benefits are received.

● **Income tax refunds.** Note, however, that any interest the CCRA pays you on a late refund is taxable.

● **"Like-kind" property exchanges**—swaps of certain small-business corporation shares are tax-free if the properties are of similar nature and acquired within a certain time frame. Other replacement properties subject to tax deferral rules include eligible capital property, depreciable property that has been involuntarily disposed of, and land and building used in a business.

● **Room and board.** If you rent your home, there will be no tax reporting if there is no reasonable expectation of profit.

● **Dependents' wages.** Dependent children and spouses can earn up to

the basic personal amounts on a completely tax-free basis.

● **Scholarship Income.** The first $3,000 of income received under a scholarship, fellowship or bursary is tax-exempt if the student otherwise qualifies for the education amount.

● **Kids' investment income.** Dependent children can receive up to $1,200 a month of capital gains income without paying taxes.

● **Fringe benefits from your employer.** Examples: health insurance, pension contributions, certain child and dependent care, supper money, gifts, awards, memberhips to recreational clubs, etc.

● **Meals and lodging,** if furnished by your employer for the employer's convenience—for example, to enable the employee to remain at the workplace.

TAX SHELTERING A WINDFALL

Want to bet on a sure thing? Let's say you do so and you win, then it's certain that you'll want to keep as much as you can of that windfall. In Canada, if you're lucky enough to be a winner at the racetrack and in the casino, your winning bet is definitely going be a sure thing, because it is completely tax-free. That's right, if you buy a lottery ticket, or bet on a horse, and win, those winnings are not subject to tax here.

American rules: If, however, you take your gambling habit to the United States and win there, the Internal Revenue Service (IRS) will take its share, even though you're not a U.S. resident. You may be able to recover some or all of that withholding tax, however, by filing a U.S. tax return for non-resident aliens (Form 1040NR). Be sure to get an ITIN number from the IRS. For information about your ITIN number and to obtain your tax forms, call the IRS in Philadelphia at (215) 516-2000, or go to their website: www.irs.gov.

You can use your gambling losses to reduce taxes on your winnings. So always keep a log of your winners and losers! If you still have net profits from gambling, you'll get a refund if the withholding taxes that you paid exceed the actual taxes payable on the profits.

Damage awards: Damages received for a personal injury award will not be subject to tax reporting. Further, if the recipient is under the age of 21, income earned on the investment of the award is also not taxable.

are applied over a period of years—like capital cost allowance or business losses for example.

Therefore, missing out on some discretionary deductions today could affect the taxes you pay in the future. Don't audit yourself—let the CCRA do it.

● **Buy a home, and then a vacation home.** Every Canadian householder can own one tax-exempt principal residence. Gains on second residences are taxable at the time of disposition, but properly managed, it's possible to earn tax-free income by renting that property out to others. If you rent a vacation home, you get no tax break from it, and you could miss out on accruing tax-deferred equity. But when you buy a vacation dwelling, the carrying charges—mortgage interest and property taxes, as well as cost of repairs, insurance and other operating expenses—can be deductible if there is a reasonable expectation of profit from your revenue property.

● **Hire the best tax preparer and planner you can find.** Don't let the fee stop you from getting sound professional advice. To save taxes over the long term, you need a tax specialist who can guide you through your financial transactions. Most tax professionals will save you far more money than they will charge you.

● **Buy deferred savings plans—like RRSPs or RESPs—or universal life insurance.** Earnings on your investment in these products accumulate tax-deferred until you are ready to cash them in. And these investments can pay a relatively high return, depending on your asset allocation strategies. With a deferred annuity, you have a choice of taking out the money you have invested (plus earnings) in a lump sum or in a series of payments over a number of years. If you don't cash in your universal life policy, your beneficiary will receive the proceeds free of income tax.

Caution: Consider that all distributions from deferred annuities are taxed as ordinary income. Moreover, there may be steep transaction costs (commissions and fees) and most companies charge penalties for early withdrawal. Fees and penalty structures vary widely, so it's important to shop around for the best deal.

● **Make the maximum contribution to your company's registered pension plan (RPP).**

In this case, earnings on your investment are tax-deferred—and you get the equivalent of a deduction for the contribution, since you don't pay tax on the salary that goes into the plan. That's a great return for your money.

● **Keep a diary of all tax-deductible expenses.** If you are self-employed, be sure to keep an auto distance log and a hard copy of all business expenditures, including the details of your travel and entertainment expenses. Don't forget to keep a log of cash expenses such as coin car washes, phone and parking costs. As an employee, you should also keep track of business expenses for which your company doesn't reimburse you.

● **Create your own proprietorship.** Form a business and create partially deductible expenses from otherwise personal outlays. It's important to claim only the "business portion" of these expenses, which will be generally allowable if your business has a reasonable expectation of profit.

● **Invest in rental real estate.** A house or small apartment building is something that you actively manage. If your write-offs for operating costs like insurance, repairs, interest, taxes, etc., exceed the rent, you can deduct losses against your salary and other taxable income. However, you may not create or increase a rental loss by claiming capital cost allowances on the assets.

● **Let family members inherit assets that have appreciated in value.** If you dispose of taxable assets before you die, the full increase in value will be taxed in your hands. This may be to your advantage if (a) you have a buyer who is willing to pay you the right price or (b) you think the market value of the asset will be higher upon your death, or if you want to use up capital losses you have been accruing. But if you let your spouse inherit the property, he or she can receive it at any amount between its adjusted cost base and fair market value, thereby maximizing planning opportunities.

● **Minimize your AMT liability.** Find out now whether you are going to be subject to the Alternative Minimum Tax (AMT) this year. If you are, plan to defer income and accelerate deductions. If you were subject to the AMT in the past, but are not now, remember you can offset regular taxes this year by AMT paid in the last seven years.

The Tricky Alternative Minimum Tax

A hidden danger that may unexpectedly increase the tax bills of high-income individuals is the Alternative Minimum Tax (AMT). This tax applies primarily to those with large tax-shelter losses or unusually large capital gains. Most upper-income individuals, who take advantage of existing tax preferences, will have to think about how to avoid falling into the AMT trap when devising year-ahead tax-planning strategies.

Dangers:

The AMT requires that the following tax preferences—otherwise legitimately calculated as part of the regular tax calculations—must be added back into income for taxation under the AMT.

● **The exempt portion of taxable capital gains** (except from foreclosures or disposition of eligible capital property).

● **Capital cost allowance (CCA)** claimed on certified films, video tapes.

● **CCA-created losses in partnerships,** farm and restricted operations and other business operations.

● **Losses resulting from CCA** and carrying charges claimed on rental and leasing property.

● **Certain carrying charges and losses claimed** on limited partnerships and other tax shelters.

● **Losses created by claiming specific resource expenses** and depletion allowances on resource properties.

Relief:

● **A $40,000 exemption is allowed,** so if the tax preference being tested for AMT purposes is less than this, no AMT is payable.

● **If regular taxes on the AMT-eligible amounts** is greater than the AMT, no AMT is payable.

● **Those with significant capital gains** to add to otherwise high income of the year may wish to defer generating a taxable disposition into the next tax year, if AMT can be avoided. This calculation is very complicated and should be performed and interpreted by an experienced tax professional.

● **The form used in claiming the AMT** or in applying an AMT carryover to offset regular taxes in the seven years in the future is Form T691.

Source: *Evelyn Jacks, president, Evelyn Jacks Productions, Inc. and best-selling author,* Tax Secrets for Tough Times *and* Make Sure It's Deductible, *published by McGraw-Hill Ryerson.*

Frequently Overlooked Deductions by Investors

- **Safety-deposit box fees.**
- **Interest costs** paid to purchase a Canada Savings Bond on a payroll deduction plan.
- **Costs of borrowing** against cash values in life insurance policies, provided the loan is used for investment in non-registered accounts.
- **Interest benefit** from a low- or no-interest bearing loan, provided the proceeds of the loan were used to fund non-registered investments.
- **Accounting fees** paid to calculate tax consequences of your investment portfolio.
- **Brokerage fees, legal, advertising or appraisal costs** incurred to sell taxable assets. These costs are not written off in full as carrying charges, but rather, reduce capital gains or increase capital losses.
- **Travel expenses** to check on income-producing revenue property, providing there is more than one.
- **Fees paid for mortgage** on purchase or improvement of revenue properties.

Frequently Overlooked Deductions by Proprietors

- **Gifts and promotional expenses.**
- **Meals and entertainment** (only 50% of the full amount of meals, drinks, tips, etc., are deductible).
- **Expenses related to seminars attended for business purposes.** Deductible items include registration fees, travel, lodging and 50% of the cost of meals. *Caution:* Only two conventions per year may be deducted by the self-employed.
- **Legal and accounting fees.**
- **Financing costs like banking service charges** and annual fees on credit cards used for business.
- **The cost of telephone,** cell phone, postage, office supplies, home office costs and automobile operation (trips to and from business appointments, or professional advisers).
- **Books, magazines and newsletters** on investment, financial or tax matters, that are business-related, including appropriate daily papers, if self-employed.
- **Cost of hiring your family members** to work in your business, provided their compensation costs are reasonable and paid at a rate that a stranger would be paid, and the work was actually done.

- **Insurance and storage charges** for merchandise held as inventory of a business.
- **A portion of health insurance** for the self-employed.
- **Deductible items on December credit card statement,** even if paid in the following year, include medical expenses, charitable contributions and miscellaneous business expenses.
- **Capital cost allowance** on the undepreciated cost of capital assets.

Source: Evelyn Jacks, president, Evelyn Jacks Productions, Inc. and best-selling author, Tax Secrets for Tough Times *and* Make Sure It's Deductible, *published by McGraw-Hill Ryerson.*

Easy Tests for Dependency

It's not easy to find a place to claim a tax break for minor children on your return. That's because there generally is none—tax preferences for the care of minor children come in the form of the Canada Child Tax Benefit (CCTB) and are based on net family income; that is, the net income of one or both supporting individuals in the family. Otherwise, specific provisions for children are limited claims for child care expenses, attendant care costs in some cases and medical expenses. In cases of severe disability, a disability tax credit may be claimable.

Nonrefundable tax credits, on the other hand, are available for supporting individuals who have spouses or common-law partners and/or who support infirm, dependent adults. These credits are based on the spouse's net income (Line 236 of the tax return).

Trap: Many taxpayers use "Gross Income" in assessing whether a spouse or adult dependent may be claimed. Use "Net Income."

Note: You can reduce gross income with deductions like RRSP contributions, union dues, childcare, employment and moving expenses, etc., in order to create a claim for the higher-income earner.

To be claimed as a dependent for income tax purposes, a person must meet certain criteria.

The dependent must be related to you or be a member of your household by blood, marriage or adoption or you must be that person's legal guardian in the case of minors. The individual must fall within one of the following categories:

- **Child, grandchild, adopted child, stepchild.**
- **Brother, sister, half brother, stepbrother.**
- **Parent, grandparent, but not foster parent.**
- **Stepfather, stepmother.**
- **Brother or sister of your father or mother.**
- **Son or daughter of your brother or sister** (nephew or niece).
- **Father-in-law, mother-in-law, etc.**

In general, the dependent must live with you in a household maintained by you. However, absences due to nursing home or hospital stays or temporary absences like vacations, or going away to school are allowed.

A foster child is not claimed as a dependent, nor is the social assistance income received for his or her care reported for tax purposes.

When parents are separated or divorced, the non-refundable/refundable tax credit generally goes to the parent who has custody of the child. In case of joint custody, the parties must agree on who makes the claim or neither will receive it. The single parent will qualify for the "amount for eligible dependent"—a claim equal in tax benefit to the amount for dependent spouse or common-law partner—if the child is under 19 and income-eligible.

Also lucrative: When marital status changes, individuals can apply to have their income position adjusted for the purposes of receiving the refundable CCTB. This usually means that more money will be available on a monthly basis, as the credit will be based on the income of the single parent, rather than the combined income of both parents. Parents lose their CCTB when the child turns 19. Otherwise, the income of the child does not affect the CCTB received.

Tax Breaks on Canadian Securities

Taxpayers who invest in Canadian securities within their non-registered accounts have a number of "tax efficiencies" going for them:

Equities: Those who hold assets with the potential to appreciate in value, like stocks, bonds, mutual funds, revenue properties or certain personal properties have the opportunity of producing "tax-preferred" income in the form of capital gains.

Tax-Deferred Income Checklist

Deferring taxation of a portion of your income until a year in which your income will be lower can save you a bundle on your tax bill. Here's a list of the kinds of income eligible for deferral—starting with the one that no one should overlook.

✔ **Income from an RRSP, RESP, RRIF** or profit-sharing plan is tax-deferred until time of withdrawal.

✔ **Interest on deferred annuities** is tax-deferred until you "annuitize" (start to receive annuity payments).

✔ **Income from the exercise of incentive stock option plans** is tax-deferred until the stock is sold.

✔ **Capital appreciation** is tax-deferred up to the point when you sell.

- **Capital gains are only generated on disposition of the asset.** This means that any increases in the adjusted cost base of the asset need not be reported for tax purposes while the asset is being held.
- **Once a disposition occurs,** only 50% of the capital gain is included in income.
- **If the asset being disposed of is a qualified farm property or small business corporation,** resulting gains may qualify for the $500,000 lifetime capital gains exemption.

Note: When the asset is disposed of at a value under its adjusted cost base, a capital loss results. Capital losses are subject to special rules:

1. In the case of personal use properties, like homes or personal vacation properties, there is no write-off for the loss in value.

2. Losses on listed personal properties—art, jewelry, stamp collections and other precious collectibles—can only be used to offset other listed personal property gains.

3. The adjusted cost base of both of the property classes above is deemed to be $1,000 to eliminate small transactions.

4. Most other capital dispositions resulting in loss are treated as follows: the loss may only be used to offset capital gains in the year in which the sale or disposition takes place, or if there are no capital gains (or unapplied losses left over) in that year they can be carried back to offset capital gains of the previous three years or carried forward to offset gains of the future—indefinitely. Upon the death of the taxpayer, unapplied capital loss balances can offset other income in the year of death or the immediately preceding year; however, those loss balances must first be reduced by any capital gains deduction used in the past.

5. In the case of losses from investments in a small business corporation, unapplied balances may be used to offset other income in the current year, the three prior years or seven years in the future, after which unapplied balances are treated as normal capital losses.

Dividends: Dividends that are declared on the investment in Canadian equities are also subject to special tax treatment. The income is first grossed up and then resulting taxes are reduced through a "dividend tax credit," which results in a lower tax rate than that applied to interest income.

Unfortunately, the taxes applied to interest earnings are the most severe, particularly because they are payable even on the accrued earnings on compounding investments—the tax department gets paid even before you get the money! Therefore, astute investors and their advisors will aim to diversify their investment holdings to minimize market risk and look for the best tax efficiencies to minimize tax erosion.

Source: *Evelyn Jacks, president, Evelyn Jacks Productions, Inc. and best-selling author,* Tax Secrets for Tough Times *and* Make Sure It's Deductible, *published by McGraw-Hill Ryerson.*

Sales Tax Can Add Up— to Savings

● **Win with refundable sales tax credits.** Sales taxes paid on personal purchases are not deductible. They are absolutely off-limits—but there are ways to recoup your sales taxes on nondiscretionary income by filing a tax return.

Every Canadian resident, age 19 and older, may apply for the federal Goods and Services Tax Credit (GSTC) simply by filing a tax return. This quarterly payment, based on your family net income on Line 236 of the tax return, is paid fully when income is around $35,000 or less and partially thereafter. Its size depends on different factors, including whether you are a single parent, single or married, or living in a conjugal relationship. A single person may qualify for a maximum credit of about $200 annually.

Certain provinces also have refundable sales tax credits to offset the costs of provincial sales taxes on nondiscretionary income.

So it's important that everyone—even those with no earnings—file a tax return to receive the GSTC; providing they are income and age-eligible.

● **The GST/HST (goods and services tax/ harmonized sales tax) rebate.** Taxpayers who claim union dues or professional dues on Line 212 or employment expenses on Line 229 may receive a refundable tax rebate on Line 457 of the tax return for GST/HST paid on those tax-deductible items. The rebate is included in taxable income, however, in the year it is received.

● **Sales taxes for proprietors.** Those who operate a small unincorporated business will be allowed to include in their operational or capital expenses any federal or provincial sales taxes they paid for those business expenditures. However, if they elect to become a "GST/HST Registrant," which is optional if gross sales are under $30,000 and mandatory if over this amount, they will be able to receive a refund of any GST/HST paid that exceeds GST/HST collected on their GST-taxable sales.

Source: *Evelyn Jacks, president, Evelyn Jacks Productions, Inc. and best-selling author,* Tax Secrets for Tough Times *and* Make Sure It's Deductible, *published by McGraw-Hill Ryerson.*

Loopholes for Working Families

Very few working families take advantage of all the possible tax breaks. But loopholes are there—for spouses who have separate jobs or businesses, and for those working together in a family business.

The Advantages of a Family-Owned Small Business Corporation

A small business corporation is defined to be a Canadian-controlled private corporation in which all or substantially all of the assets (90% or more) are used in an active business or carried on primarily in Canada by the corporation. The shares must not have been owned by any person or partnership other than the individual or a person or partnership related to him or her throughout the 24 months immediately preceding the disposition. During the holding period, more than 50% of the fair market value of the corporation's assets must have been used in an active business. Finally, if the taxpayer disposes of shares of a small business corporation, some of which do not meet the holding requirement, the shares are deemed to be disposed of in the order in which they were acquired.

This is all significant information because when the shares of a small business corporation are disposed of, the shareholders may offset any capital gains with the $500,000 capital gains exemption (CGE). One exemption per lifetime is available to every individual.

When setting up a qualifying small business corporation, it is important to give thought to the ownership of the shares, asset transfer provisions and compensation packages. The initiative is complicated and requires significant planning. However, Tables 1 and 2 make an important point: the use of the $500,000 capital gains exemption can help qualifying small business owners accumulate serious wealth. Both tables show the capital gains exemptions in the cases of a single shareholder and two shareholders, using the hypothetical examples of Thomas and his wife Pat.

TABLE 1: SOLE SHAREHOLDER USES CGE

Tax provision	Calculation
Proceeds of disposition	$2,000,000
Adjusted cost base	$1
Capital gain	$1,999,999
Taxable gain (½)	$999,999
Less capital gains deduction (½ x $500,000)	$250,000
Net taxable gain	$749,999
Taxes payable at 46%*	$345,000

*Consult with advisers for accurate calculation for your province of residence.

Table 1 illustrates how the tax liability would have been calculated if Thomas had been the sole shareholder of his small business corporation when he decided to sell it. This calculation assumes no prior use of the capital gains exemption.

Now, let's assume that Thomas and his wife Pat were each shareholders of this small business corporation at the time of its sale. Table 2 shows how each could split the gain and use their capital gains exemptions, if available:

TABLE 2: CAPITAL GAINS SPLIT WITH TWO SHAREHOLDERS

Tax provision	Thomas	Pat
Proceeds of disposition	$1,000,000	$1,000,000
Adjusted cost base	$1	$1
Capital gain	$999,999	$999,999
Taxable gain (½)	$499,999	$499,999
Less capital gains deduction (½ x $500,000)	$250,000	$250,000
Net taxable gain	$249,999	$249,999
Taxes payable at 46%*	$115,000	$115,000

*Consult with advisers for accurate calculation for your province of residence.

Table 2 shows Thomas and his wife Pat pocketing $115,000 more in tax savings. They would have kept more of the $2 million if each of their adult children had also owned shares in this small business corporation. Therefore, it pays to set up your business in anticipation of future windfalls.

Ask your tax adviser about any alternative minimum tax implications and about the special new provisions that allow for a capital gains tax deferral when a replacement company is acquired after the sale of the former one.

Before starting any small business venture, it's worth it to spend a little money getting the right tax advice. Be sure to ask your adviser about the best time to transfer assets from a proprietorship to a corporation, the timing of such an event and the structure of the shareholders' agreements and family members' compensation structures.

Source: Evelyn Jacks, president, Evelyn Jacks Productions, Inc. and best-selling author, Tax Secrets for Tough Times and Make Sure It's Deductible, published by McGraw-Hill Ryerson.

Tax Advantages of a Family Business

The following tax-savings tips are important to those who wish to open a proprietorship or small business corporation within the family:

1. Start-ups. There can be tax advantages in operating the business as a sole proprietorship, rather than a corporation, upon start-up. That's because any start-up losses incurred in the proprietorship are considered to be "noncapital losses" that can be used to offset other income of the current year. If an unapplied loss balance remains, it can be used to offset other income of the prior three years or for seven years in the future, after which time the loss expires. It is important to show the tax department that the losses are reasonable under the circumstances and were incurred to earn income from an active business with a reasonable expectation of profit.

2. Spousal bliss. You can hire your spouse as an employee. The wages or salary paid, which is deductible by the business, provides a good path to family income splitting. Income is created in your spouse's hands for reinvestment purposes—free of attribution. RRSP contribution room (limit) is created in his or her hands to accumulate retirement savings on a tax-deferred basis—instrumental for future retirement income splitting and capital formation.

Caution: Some of the tax savings benefits of family income splitting through a small business have recently been eroded with the cost of funding the Canada Pension Plan (CPP). The premiums (both employer and employee portions) must be funded by the business for each family member that is employed by it, and the costs of doing so has been rising significantly. Those CPP obligations should be factored into any income-splitting projections being undertaken.

3. Hire your children. Instead of giving them nondeductible allowances, find real work for your children to do in your business. Help pay their education costs by hiring them while they are going to college. Give them jobs doing market research for your business, product testing, marketing, telephone sales, inventory management, etc. Pay them reasonable salaries and deduct the salaries as a business expense. Remember that you don't pay Canada Pension Plan premiums on wages paid to a child who is under 18. Also, a dependent can earn around $600 each month on a tax-free basis, while building RRSP contribution room (18% of earnings). This can really build into an important tax saver once the child goes to university or later when he or she is taxable and needs an additional tax deduction.

4. Business travel. Write off working vacations with your spouse. The extra cost of taking your spouse along on a business trip isn't ordinarily deductible. But when the spouse is an employee of the business, it's much easier to make the case that his or her services are essential to the overall business purpose of the trip.

5. Make costs of running your home deductible. Clear away a separate space in your home for a home office and then deduct your utility costs, insurance, property taxes, interest on your mortgage, cleaning costs and maintenance and repairs. You'll have to account for personal use by measuring out what amount of space is used solely for business purposes, comparing that to the total living space in the home, and then prorating all the expenses to reflect only the business portion of the costs. The home workspace must be used to earn business income on a regular basis, and be the regular meeting place for clients, or the principal place of business. Home workspace expenses cannot create or increase a loss from the operations. If this happens, reduce net income to zero and carry forward the balance of the expenses for use in reducing business income in a future year.

6. Family medical insurance. Since 1997, proprietors have been allowed to deduct from business income any premiums paid to a private health plan for themselves, their family and their employees. The business income must be the main source of income on the return, premiums must be made to an authorized plan supplier and they cannot again be claimed as a medical expense. The deduction is subject to annual limits of $1,500 for each adult and $750 for minors who work in the business and may be disallowed completely if the owner does not pay premiums on behalf of other employees.

7. Avoiding probate. You can avoid the hassle and expense of probate upon your death by establishing one or more trusts during your lifetime, to hold some or all of the shares in your company. You may also wish to set up an "estate freeze" to crystallize the value of your company today, thereby limiting your personal tax exposure and passing the liability for tax on future growth to the next generation. This may also be a good way to use up your $500,000 capital gains exemption and create the possibility for future taxes on accrued equity to be offset by the exemptions available to other family members. Be sure to speak to your tax adviser about these planning options.

Working Couples and Child Care

You may be eligible for the child-care expense deduction even if your spouse doesn't work. Usually, child-care costs must be deducted by the person with the lower net income, provided that person has qualifying "earned income": salary and wages, profits from self-employment, training allowances, scholarships, bursaries or disability pension from the CPP. In the case of the higher income earner, he or she may deduct the amounts, however, only in the following circumstances and conditions:

● **The lower earner** was a full-time or part-time student, was incapable of caring for the children because of physical or mental infirmity or was confined to a prison or correctional institute for at least two weeks.

● **The couple was separated** for at least 90 days in the year but reconciled within the first 60 days after the tax year.

Trap: If you hire baby-sitters, you must pay source deductions like CPP, Employment Insurance and income taxes for them, and issue a T4 Slip at the end of the year. Be sure to adjust your income tax withholding at source or through quarterly installment remittances to take into account anticipated child-care expenses. You'll want to generate more after-tax cash to help you pay these expenses throughout the year.

When an Employer Gives Noncash Gifts

An employer may gift his or her employee on a tax-free basis a noncash gift of up to $500 in any tax year, including birthday and wedding gifts.

Also, child-care expenses can reduce Canada Child Tax Benefits and Disability Tax Credits in some cases, so be sure to get some professional help if these circumstances apply to you.

Source: *Evelyn Jacks, president, Evelyn Jacks Productions, Inc.*

Divorce Is Never an Easy Matter

Tax issues may be the last thing on a couple's mind when they experience marital difficulties. But ignoring them can cause serious repercussions. It is important for couples involved in a matrimonial dispute to seek the advice of a knowledgeable tax professional before they break up. *Here are some points to consider:*

Alimony or maintenance for former spouse or common-law partner. Payments made by a taxpayer to a former spouse will be deductible to the payer and taxable to the recipient. They must be paid according to a court order or written separation agreement and on a periodic basis. The taxable amounts received qualify as earned income for RRSP purposes. Lump-sum payments are neither deductible nor taxable.

Timing in the year of divorce or separation. The amount for spouse or common-law partner is claimed by the higher-income earner and based on the lower earner's net income. When a couple separates during the year, but reconciles before the end of the year, the couple is consider married or living common law for tax purposes for the whole year. Therefore, net income of the whole year is considered when claiming this credit. This is also true if the period of separation was for less than 90 days. If the relationship is permanently broken and the separation has exceeded 90 days, the amount for spouse or common-law partner can be claimed in the year of the breakdown, but only if no tax-deductible claim is made for spousal support.

Tip: Break up early in the year, as net income of the spouse is based on income up to the date of separation only.

Child support. Payments are not deductible by the parent who pays them, nor are they taxable to the parent who receives them, if they were made as a result of new or revised agreements after April 30, 1997. Under old agreements in existence prior to May 1, 1997, payments are still deductible to the payer and taxable to the recipient.

Credits for dependents. The parent who has custody of the children is the one entitled to claim the child for the purposes of the Canada Child Tax Benefit and the amount for an eligible dependent (formerly known as the equivalent-to-spouse amount). In cases of joint custody, the parents must agree who will claim the refundable and nonrefundable credits for the children. The amount for an eligible dependent is not available to the person who is making nondeductible child support payments. Also, in the year a couple reconciles, that nonrefundable credit will be available to the parent who had custody of the child before reconciliation, provided the other spouse does not claim the amount for spouse or common-law partner.

Family home. Under a property settlement, a spouse who receives title to the marital residence that had been in the other spouse's name can sell the home immediately and reap any gains that have accrued on the property on a completely tax-free basis. Other personal property and RRSP deposits are rolled over on a tax-free basis to avoid tax liabilities at the time of separation or divorce. However, in the case of taxable assets, it is possible for couples to choose fair market value (FMV) as the proceeds of disposition, if this is to their mutual tax advantage.

Legal fees. The portion of a divorce lawyer's fee that is for tax advice or obtaining taxable alimony is not deductible. Only fees paid to enforce the right to payment previously established can be deducted on the tax return.

Alimony and the Taxman

Basic tax principles to keep in mind:

A property settlement made after a divorce is not tax deductible, but alimony payments are fully deductible. If you're paying alimony, know the rules:

1. Payments must be required by a decree of divorce, separation or support, or by a written separation agreement or order by a competent tribunal. They cannot be voluntary payments.

2. The parties had to be separated and living apart during the time the payments are made and throughout the rest of the taxation year.

3. The payments are made to the spouse or common-law partner or a third party for the maintenance of the spouse.

4. The payments are made on a periodic basis. If the ex-husband deducts the alimony, the wife must declare it as income. However, because the amount qualifies as earned income for RRSP purposes, taxes on the alimony can be reduced with an RRSP contribution. Child support paid pursuant to agreements created or changed after April 30, 1997, lump-sum payments, the spouse's legal fees, premiums on life insurance policies owned by the husband—all these are not deductible by the spouse paying them. And they need not be reported as income by the spouse who receives the payments.

It's essential to prepare carefully several alternative plans for the division of property and income maintenance to keep the most money in the hands of family members. Here are some tips:

● **Transfer of assets.** To maximize long-term wealth and your accumulation efforts throughout the period of the union, transfer assets held within the family unit as tax efficiently as possible. Determine the fair market value (FMV) on the date of deemed disposition due to marriage breakdown, and decide whether the taxable asset should be transferred at its adjusted cost base or its FMV at the time of transfer. You may wish to use FMV if it is worth less today than it will be in the future, or if the taxpayer's income is lower today than it is expected to be in the future. Resulting capital losses could then be used to reduce income taxes paid on capital gains in the prior three years or sometime in the future. However, remember the recipient spouse will have to pay capital gains taxes in the future based on a stepped-down value.

● **Retirement income provisions.** RRSP accumulations can be transferred tax-free between spouses and common-law partners upon the breakdown of the marriage or relationship. Use Form T2220, relating to the transfer of RRSP or RRIF arising from marriage breakdown, to do so. Most agreements call for a division to all pension credits earned during the marriage or relationship. The parties should also agree to structure some of the alimony payments in the form of contributions to an RRSP and, possibly, a labor-sponsored investment fund (LSIF) to maximize tax-deferred income sources.

● **Post-separation income generation.** Calculate the "tax-free zone"—that is, your spouse's basic personal amount, plus any additional deductions (like RRSP contributions) and nonrefundable tax credits he or she is eligible for. The minimum taxable spousal amount payable should be based on this number, thereby structuring an annual tax-free income for the recipient. That same amount would be tax deductible, however, to the payer. Should payments exceed these minimums, taxes would need to be taken into account and assistance with quarterly installment payments to the tax department may need to be negotiated. Reinvested assets held outside of registered plans should be invested to maximize tax deferral and growth.

● **Minimize nondeductible debt.** Remember, legal fees to obtain a divorce are not deductible. Working within a conciliatory atmosphere will result in a big financial win for each family member.

Source: Evelyn Jacks, president, Evelyn Jacks Productions, Inc. and best-selling author, Tax Secrets for Tough Times *and* Make Sure It's Deductible, *published by McGraw-Hill Ryerson.*

How to File as a Unified Household—Even When You're Not

1. **In contemplating separation, define pre- and post-tax positions.** To understand the impact of separation on a family's after-tax financial position, review existing tax burdens to properly compare tax costs and cash flow after separation.

2. **The progressivity of the tax system can work in separated families' favors.** Separation brings about income splitting, which can be advantageous under our progressive tax system. That is, the same income transferred to a lower-earning spouse or common-law partner can reap higher after-tax rewards.

3. **Provisions for family fairness and equity can also reap tax rewards.** Low-income families are supplemented in their living standards with certain "tax-free zones"—nonrefundable tax credits— and certain social benefit payments—refundable tax credits. These provisions can increase after-tax results by thousands of dollars annually for a separated family.

4. **The tax-free zone for single parents.** It is approximately $14,000. A single parent can claim a basic personal amount of approximately $7,600 and an amount for eligible dependent for one child in the amount of approximately $6,500, allowing for a tax-free zone of around $14,000 or close to $1,200 a month. This should be taken into account in planning taxable spousal support payments. In fact, couples can create an "inflation-adjusted raise" for the recipient of the support payments by linking the payments amounts to the nonrefundable tax credits available each year.

5. **Spousal support is taxable but creates RRSP contribution room.** By contributing 18% of taxable spousal support received, lower-income earners can top up their retirement savings, and reduce net income for the purposes of calculating GST Credits and Child Tax Benefits.

6. **Multiply RRSP tax savings with an LSFTC.** If the RRSP contribution is invested in a labor-sponsored investment fund, a further tax credit can be created federally and in most provinces. This tax credit can be reinvested in next year's RRSP contribution, or fund children's education savings or life insurance premiums for the single parent.

7. **Spousal support payments are tax deductible if periodic.** This can save tax dollars—the higher the payer's income, the greater the saving— but the deduction will reduce RRSP contribution room. Those resulting tax savings can be used to fund RESP or other education savings for the children or the payer's own RRSP accumulations.

8. **Child support payments are not taxable or deductible.** This is true if the separation agreement was negotiated after April 30, 1997, or old agreements were revised by mutual election to be treated as nontaxable or deductible. Otherwise, payments for agreements in effect prior to May 1, 1997, will still be taxable to the recipient and deductible to the payer.

9. **Income attribution ends after separation.** Assets that were transferred to the spouse during the conjugal relationship were subject to income attribution, except under very specific instances (i.e., when a spousal RRSP contribution is made,

when a bona fide loan is drawn up or if the principal is invested to earn business profits). However, after separation, that income is properly taxed to the transferee, providing both parties make an election to agree to this.

10. Capital property of the failed relationship. It can be transferred at adjusted cost base (ACB) or fair market value (FMV). It is possible to divide the property of the failed union by transferring it at either its ACB (in which case there are no immediate tax consequences) or at its FMV (in which case certain tax consequences can bring an immediate tax advantage). These options require careful review before agreements for separation and transfer of assets can be finalized.

11. RRSP and RRIF accumulations. They are transferred on a tax-free basis. By using Form T2220, registered assets can be split and transferred without tax consequences. Even the three-year holding rules for spousal RRSP accumulations can be avoided upon relationship breakdown.

12. Lower-income earners can now claim child-care expenses. When a couple is in a conjugal relationship for tax purposes, the child-care expenses paid for care of children while parents work must be claimed by the person with the lower net income, except in very specific circumstances. After separation, each parent can claim their own child-care expenses, until they begin cohabiting with another partner.

13. Time separation to maximize the spouse or common-law partner amount. Because this lucrative credit is based on the spouse's or common-law partner's net income prior to separation, make the break in early January if possible, to win more tax savings.

14. Calculate Canada Child Tax Benefits (CTB) receivable before and after separation.

Most couples find that when one spouse has little or no income, the CTB can provide significant support on a tax-free basis, now that it is calculated on that lower earner's net income only.

15. Immediate adjustments to CTB and GSTC are possible. The new net income should be disclosed to the CCRA immediately after separation so the benefits from the Canada Child Tax Benefit and Goods and Services Tax Credit can be based on that lower net income and, therefore, begin immediately.

16. Payments from U.S. residents for child support are not taxable. Provisions within the U.S.-Canada Tax Treaty have provided a special tax break since 1985 for recipients of child support from U.S.-resident payers. Those receipts are not taxable. They must be reported as child support in Canadian funds for the purposes of increasing net income on

Appreciated Securities: Shifting Capital Gains

Give appreciated securities to your parents instead of after-tax cash if you are supporting them. There are no attribution rules to worry about in this transaction, providing this is not purely a tax-avoidance scheme. They can cash in the securities and pay tax at lower rates on their other income. *Caution:* A large gain could push your parents into a higher bracket, that may match yours, or worse, cause a clawback of their Old Age Security Benefits. Prepare several preliminary tax calculations to determine the best level of capital gains income to be received with a view to maximizing their other eligible provisions on the return, or get some professional help.

the Canadian return (thereby reducing refundable tax credits and other provisions based on net income), but a deduction may be taken on Line 256.

17. Minimize nondeductible expenditures on legal fees. Always think of your separated family's legacy first. Legal fees to obtain a separation or divorce are not deductible. Spend your money shoring up RRSPs, RESPs or other non-registered investments for the benefit of the family, instead.

18. Remember: Tax consequences on reconciliation. When couples reconcile within 60 days of year-end, child-care expenses are deducted according to rules in effect for married or common-law unions for the whole year. However, the amount for eligible dependent (formerly equivalent-to-spouse amount) may be claimed by one parent even if the couple reconciled before year-end, if all other criteria for making the claim were met.

Source: Tax Secrets for Tough Times, by Evelyn Jacks, published by McGraw-Hill Ryerson, 300 Water Street, Whitby, ON L1N 9B6.

Checklist of Tax Tips for Retirees

● Age credit: If you turned age 65 during the year, you may qualify for the age credit, but this may be clawed back, depending on your net-income level.

● Report your income from Old Age Security, then calculate a possible clawback of your pension starting in July. That's the beginning of the new "benefit year" based on the assessed net income tax position of the prior year. This calculation is called the "Deduction for Repayment of Social Benefits."

● Canada Pension Plan benefits are taxable to the recipient. Be sure to split those benefits between spouses by asking for an assignment of the benefits in equal amounts to each.

● Claim the $1,000 pension income amount to offset periodic superannuation or private pension benefits or for those over 64 or in receipt of benefits due to a spouse's death, RRSP or RRIF withdrawals.

● Transfer lucrative nonrefundable tax credits from the lower-income earner to the higher: the age amount, the disability amount, the tuition and education amount or the pension income amount.

● Claim the disability amount for yourself or a spouse or other dependent with a prolonged and severe medical or physical infirmity that markedly restricts daily living activities.

● Maximize medical expenses claimable on the tax return, including dental work, glasses, hearing aids and their batteries, wheelchairs, nursing home fees, etc.

● Group and claim charitable donations on one return for a maximum benefit.

● Continue to make spousal RRSP contributions until the end of the year in which your spouse reaches age 69, as long as you have RRSP contribution room.

● Make a final spousal RRSP contribution to reduce income on the final return of the deceased.

● Move to a low-tax province, like Ontario, before year-end to minimize taxes and quarterly installment payments. You are taxed in the province of residence as of December 31 in the tax year.

● Downsize your home. You can exclude a capital gain from the sale of your principal residence. You don't have to buy another home to get this benefit, and you can use the money for reinvestment or to achieve your retirement dreams in other ways.

● Give inheritances during your lifetime. This is particularly important if you are sitting on large RRSP accumulations and expect that these will be taxed at a higher rate on your final return than while you are living.

● Review insurance policies on each family member's life, and shore up tax-deferred investments in those policies as a way to deal with tax liabilities upon death or to provide for children and grandchildren.

● Prepare estate and business succession plans with the assistance of your legal and accounting advisers.

● Establish trusts to shift income to family members who are in lower tax brackets.

Source: Evelyn Jacks, president, Evelyn Jacks Productions, Inc.

Paying Your Child a Tax-Deductible Allowance

Paying your children to work in your business is a good way of providing tax-deductible allowances. A child with no other income can earn up to approximately $7,500 tax-free.

Bonus: Your children's wages are exempt from Canada Pension Plan premiums until they turn 18. When it comes to Employment Insurance (EI) premiums, however, you are required to make deductions and remittances for all employees, regardless of age, unless they are substantial shareholders. Employment of an individual connected to the employer by blood, marriage, common-law partnership or adoption is not insurable, and therefore not subject to premiums, unless a similar employment contract would have been negotiated with someone unrelated. Given the audit-proofing criteria above, this means that EI premiums will be required in most cases.

Caution: Keep very good records of the type of work they do, the hours they put in and how they are paid. The mere fact that you pay wages to your children won't trigger an audit. Their pay is lumped in with wages of other employees on your return. But if you are audited for some other reason, the CCRA is likely to question this expense. Be prepared to show the pay was reasonable for work actually done and for compensation similar to that which would have been paid to a stranger.

Source: *Evelyn Jacks, president, Evelyn Jacks Productions, Inc.*

How the CCRA Helps With Child-Care Bills

Here are tips on child-care expense deductions:

● **Eligible taxpayers.** Child-care expenses may be claimed by parents who must pay another individual to care for their children so that they may earn income from employment or self-employment or so that they may attend school either full or part time.

● **Eligible dependents.** Expenses are deductible for the care of dependent children who were under the age of 16 (at any time during the year) or who are physically or mentally infirm. An eligible child must be your child, your spouse or common-law partner's child or a child who was dependent on you or your spouse (or partner). If the child is not your child or your spouse's or partner's child, the child's net income must be less than the basic personal amount ($7,412 in 2001).

● **Eligible baby-sitters.** Expenses actually paid to a Canadian resident or paid to a nonresident for services outside Canada to a resident or deemed resident of Canada. Baby-sitters may be related to you, but if they are, the sitter must be over age 17. Payments made to a parent of the child or to a supporting person are not deductible.

● **Earned income definition.** The child-care deduction is limited to two-thirds of "earned income." Earned income includes:

1. Salaries and wages.

2. Net profits from self-employment.

3. Training allowances, the taxable portion of scholarships, bursaries, fellowships and research grants.

4. Disability pensions under CPP or QPP.

● **Special rule for students.** In addition to the limitations for all taxpayers, students have the following limitations on their claims.

Full-time students' claims for child-care expenses are limited to:

1. $100 for each child age 7 to 16 for which the disability amount cannot be claimed, plus

2. $175 per child under 7 for which the disability amount cannot be claimed, plus

3. $250 per disabled child times the number of weeks of full-time attendance.

Part-time students are limited to:

1. $100 for each child age 7 to 16 for which the disability amount cannot be claimed, plus

2. $175 per child under 7 for which the disability amount cannot be claimed, plus

3. $250 per disabled child times the number of months of part-time attendance.

● **Maximum claim.** The maximum claim for child-care expenses is the least of the following:

1. Eligible child-care expenses paid to eligible child-care providers.

2. Two-thirds of earned income.

3. The following limits: $4,000 per child aged 7 to 16 for which the disability amount cannot be claimed, plus $7,000 for each child under 7 for which the disability amount cannot be claimed, plus $10,000 for each disabled child.

● **Marginal benefits.** Child-care expenses create a deduction which reduces net income and will affect the following refundable and nonrefundable credits:

1. Age amount.

2. Spousal amount.

3. Amount for infirm dependent adults.

4. Caregiver amount.

● **Amounts transferred from spouse.**

1. Medical expenses.

2. Charitable donations.

3. Canada Child Tax Benefits.

4. Goods and Services Tax Credits.

5. Provincial Refundable Tax Credits.

6. Old Age Security clawbacks.

7. Employment Insurance Benefits clawbacks.

● **Eligible expenditures.** The following expenses may be claimed:

1. Baby-sitting costs.

2. Day-care costs.

3. Costs of a live-in nanny.

Tax Breaks for the Handicapped

Handicapped taxpayers who receive transportation to and from work, or the services of an attendant while on the job, can receive those benefits on a tax-free basis.

In addition, those who suffer from severe and prolonged disabilities that markedly affect their basic daily living activities—or their supporting individuals—may claim a disability tax credit. Medical expense deductions include the 20% of the cost of modifying a van to accommodate a disabled person to a maximum of $5,000, and the costs of modifying a home and its driveway to better accommodate the mobility requirements of a disabled person.

4. Lodging paid at boarding schools, day camps, day sports camps and overnight camps to a maximum of $100 per week for each child aged 7 to 16 for which the disability amount cannot be claimed, plus $175 per week per child under 7 for which the disability amount cannot be claimed, plus $250 per week for each disabled child.

Source: Tax Secrets for Tough Times, *by Evelyn Jacks, published by McGraw-Hill Ryerson, 300 Water Street, Whitby, ON L1N 9B6.*

The CCRA Can Help With Tuition Bills

Special institutions. The cost involved in sending your child to a special school because he or she is mentally or physically handicapped or has special behavioral problems, or other challenges, can be deductible as a medical expense if the school has the resources to relieve the handicap.

Private schools. Tuition fees paid for private schooling at a primary or secondary level are not tax deductible, although sometimes fees paid to a religious school have a charitable component to them. That portion of the fees considered to be a donation can be claimed if proper receipting is available.

Post-secondary schools. There are several tax breaks for students of universities, colleges or other institutes of higher learning leading to a diploma or a degree, including the following:

● **Credit for interest paid on student loans.** Interest paid on student loans granted under the Canada Student Loans Act or a provincial statute that governs the granting of financial assistance to students can be claimed in the current year, or if the student is not taxable, the claim can be made within a five-year period in the future to offset other income.

● **Tuition fees.** Students can claim the costs of tuition fees to reduce their taxes, but only if the amounts are over $100 and the student is at least 16 years old. If the student is under 16, the courses taken must lead to a degree or other post-secondary diploma. The student may also claim fees paid for courses certified by Human Resources Development Canada, provided they furnished occupational skills.

Caution: The cost of books will not be deductible unless they are a part of a correspondence course.

● **Education amount.** This monthly allowance, in the form of a nonrefundable tax credit, has recently been increased to $400 a month for full-time students and $120 a month for part-time students. Even those who receive scholarships, fellowships, bursaries or other prizes can claim this amount.

● **Transfers of tuition and education amounts.** A supporting individual, usually a parent, may transfer and use up to $5,000 of the student's tuition and education amount on his or her return, if the student is not taxable. Otherwise the student may choose to carry forward unused tuition and education credits to offset other income of a tax year in the future.

● **Bursaries, scholarships, fellowships.** The first $3,000 of such income is tax exempt, provided the courses in question otherwise qualify for the education amount.

Tax Planning for Students

● **Save all Canada Child Tax Benefits** in an untainted account in the name of your child. Resulting investment earnings of any type on this source are taxed to the child, not to the parents.

MORE TAX HELP FOR TUITION BILLS

NEW TAX BREAKS FOR EDUCATION ASSISTANCE PLAN

Use new tax incentives to pay for or save for college. New tax breaks starting in 1998 can be used to defray the costs of higher education.

● *Education tax credits for higher education.* Claim $400 for each month the student is in full-time attendance and $120 a month for each month in part-time attendance at a post-secondary institution or in a private vocational school which teaches occupational skills.

● *Registered Education Savings Plans (RESPs).* You can save for a child's education on a tax-advantaged basis by contributing up to $4,000 annually to an RESP for the benefit of a child. Most plans will terminate after 25 years, although under family plans younger siblings can replace older siblings who do not go on to become students. In the case of children under age 18, the federal government will contribute 20% of the annual contribution to a maximum of $400 as a tax-free Canada Education Savings Grant. RESP contributions are not deductible, but income earned on the funds accumulates on a tax-deferred basis. Those earnings are later taxed in the hands of the student if that person attends a qualifying educational program at a post-secondary level.

● *Deduct interest on student loans.* You may be able to deduct an interest on student loans under the Canada Student Loans Act, the Canada Student Financial Assistance Act or through a provincial law that grants financial assistance to students. Family loans or personal loans taken at a local bank, or lines of credit will not qualify. The credits, if unused can be carried forward for use in up to five taxation years in the future.

● **Invest in a Registered Education Savings Plan for your child.** You receive a "sweetener" from the government: 20% of your investment to a maximum of $400 annually, defer taxes on any earnings in the plan, and then have the student report the earnings when he or she starts post-secondary school. This is a good tax-deferral and income-splitting technique.

● **File tax returns even if your child is not taxable.** Baby-sitting, lawn care, part-time work at the local hamburger joint, part-time work in your small business—all economic activities by your minor children should be reported on the tax return even if the child is not taxable. The reason? Create RRSP contribution room! Then, later when the child becomes taxable, the unused RRSP contribution room can be used up and the resulting RRSP deductions will reap tax benefits for the child—and possibly for you— if you become eligible to transfer unused tuition and education tax credits to your own return.

● **Take advantage of the Lifelong Learning Plan.** Those with RRSP accumulations can make tax-free withdrawals of up to $10,000 per year (maximum $20,000 over four years) under the Lifelong Learning Plan to fund full-time training or higher education. Withdrawals must be repaid within a 10-year period to remain tax-free.

● **Fund your adult child's tax-exempt principal residence.** Purchase an off-campus house or condo for your college-age child to live in. There are two ways of handling this:

1. Treating the house as your child's principal residence. This purchase will provide your child with a free place to live. Moreover, when your child finishes school, the house will have most likely appreciated in value. The tax-exempt capital gain will set your child up for his or her future with some equity for reinvestment purposes.

2. Treating the house as your rental property. The rules are more complex, but will allow you to write off costs like mortgage interest, insurance, property taxes, maintenance and repairs, as long as there is a profit motive. Net operational losses can be used to reduce your other income of the year. You should consider this strategy only after discussing it with your tax adviser, as start-up costs must be properly documented.

Trap: Minor children must pay taxes, referred to as "the kiddie tax," at the highest marginal rates on income received by way of dividends or shareholder benefits, either directly or through a trust or partnership, if that money comes from a corporation controlled by a relative. Therefore, it is better to fund university-bound children or grandchildren by hiring them to work in the family business rather than to provide them with dividend income, unless they are already reporting income taxed at the top marginal rates.

Source: Personal Tax Update Seminars *by Evelyn Jacks, president, Evelyn Jacks Productions, Inc. and best-selling author,* Tax Secrets for Tough Times *and* Make Sure It's Deductible, *published by McGraw-Hill Ryerson.*

Tax Advantages of Personal Bankruptcy or Insolvency

Insolvency or bankruptcy are never good news, but certain tax preferences can soften the blow of the losses. Here are some tips:

Debt forgiveness—mortgage foreclosure and conditional sales repossessions. When a debt is forgiven, the debtor must report the amount forgiven as income. This could generate a capital gain for unsuspecting taxpayers, who were not bankrupt at the time debts were forgiven. Subsequent repayment of the debt is classified as a capital loss if related to non-depreciable property. In other cases, repayment is eligible for an income deduction.

Absolute bankruptcy discharges. When the taxpayer is bankrupt, the entire principal amount owed to a creditor is canceled, and therefore there is no forgiven amount. Bankrupts who receive an absolute discharge which cancels all debt, will, however, have to face the following consequences:

● You may not carry forward any tax losses accumulated prior to the discharge.

● You may not deduct any minimum tax carry-forward amounts.

● You may not carry forward unused tuition and education credits of prior years.

● You may not claim charitable donation carry-forwards.

Debt forgiveness when there is no bankruptcy. A "forgiven amount" does have tax conse-quences to those who are not bankrupt. Such forgiven amounts are reduced by any amounts paid at the time the debt is settled, any amounts included in the income of an employee or shareholder on debt forgiveness, or any amounts included in income of the debtor. The forgiven amounts are then applied:

● To reduce any loss carryovers.

● To reduce the capital cost of depreciable property and the adjusted cost base of capital property.

● Remaining balances are added to the debtor's income in accordance with the capital gains inclusion rate for the year (currently 50%).

These rules are complicated and require the assistance of a qualified tax professional.

Taxes owing. Unpaid federal and provincial income taxes are canceled in bankruptcy, but not premiums payable to the Canada Pension Plan.

Tax refunds. Tax refunds are payable to the trustee in bankruptcy, not to the individual who files for bankruptcy. *Loophole:* Taxpayers who expect to file for bankruptcy in the next tax year should ensure that only the correct amount of tax is being paid throughout the year through source deductions and quarterly installment payments. This will ensure no refund is due when the return is filed.

Claim tax losses due to insolvent investments. If you have made a guarantee on a business loan that is not repaid to you or invested in shares of companies that are now worthless, claim a capital loss on your tax return in the year in which the insolvency occurs. This is allowable if the investment was made with the intent to earn income (loans of a personal nonbusiness or investment natures cannot be written off). If the investment was made in a small business corporation, the loss may be classified as a business investment loss, which can be used to offset other income of the year.

Source: Evelyn Jacks, president, Evelyn Jacks Productions, Inc.

Charitable Giving: Good News

Charitable donations can provide taxpayers of all income brackets with a tax break, but it is important to understand three basic rules:

1. The write-off for charitable donations comes in two tiers: the federal tax credit is 17% on the first $200 given in the year and 29% on amounts over this. When you add the provincial component, the combined tax benefits of the credit is approximately 26% and 46% (this will differ slightly depending on your province of residence).

2. Spouses may use each other's charitable donations, so it's best to group them together to get the family's claim over $200.

3. Charitable donations can be carried forward five years, so if you don't have $200 in donations this year, consider saving them for a future year when the $200 threshold can be exceeded or if you are not taxable this year and know that the credit will give you a bigger tax savings benefit in the future.

Taxpayers often accelerate their donations at year-end, so that they can get their tax benefits sooner: if you wait until January of the new year to give, you'll have to also wait an additional 15 months or so until next year's tax return is assessed.

Also, charitable donations may not exceed 75% of your net income (100% in the year of death or the immediately preceding year). Therefore, if the donation is a single bequest that is particularly large in one year, carry the claim forward for tax savings benefits over several tax years and claim it on the return of the person with the highest income.

Big-Dollar Deductions When You Give Shares

Investors may give eligible securities or eligible stock options to their favorite charities. When they do so, there is a deemed disposition of the shares for tax purposes. However, there is a special tax break for this type of disposition: only one half of the normal income inclusion rate will apply to this transaction. This provides a lucrative incentive, too, for investors. Eligible securities include publicly traded shares, mutual funds, bonds, bills, warrants and futures listed on a prescribed stock exchange, interests in segregated fund trusts.

Source: Evelyn Jacks, president, Evelyn Jacks Productions, Inc.

Giving Doesn't Have to Hurt

The easiest way to make a charitable donation is by cash or cheque. To be deductible, your donation must be made to a registered charity and your receipt must bear that charity's registration number. You can also give money or property to governments and their agencies, registered national arts service organizations, or even to the federal Debt Services and Reduction Account for application directly to Canada's public debt. Donations are also allowed to certain prescribed universities outside Canada, provided they have received donations from the federal government, and to registered Canadian amateur athletic associations.

But other kinds of gifts to public charities may accomplish the same objectives at less cost:

Gifts of life insurance. Taxpayers may give a life insurance policy as a gift, and claim a tax write-off for the amount of the cash surrender value, plus any dividends and interest accumulated. The policy, however, must be signed over to the charity absolutely and the charity must be the registered beneficiary. No rights or benefits of any kind can be received by the donor.

If the taxpayer is also paying the premiums on the policy that is being donated, through his or her cash donations to the charity, those amounts will qualify for the charitable donation credit as well.

If you assign an existing life policy to a charity, there is a deemed disposition for tax purposes, which is equal to the cash surrender value plus any accumulated dividends. Be sure to get some help with the tax consequences from a qualified adviser before you make the donation.

Donations of ecologically sensitive land. Donations of this type of property, which is important to Canada's environmental heritage for conservation and protection, must be certified to define its value by the Minister of the Environment and the beneficiary must be a Canadian municipality or registered charity whose primary mission is conservation. Such gifts also qualify for the reduced capital gains inclusion rate on deemed disposition as donations of certain publicly traded shares; that is, one half of the normal rates.

Donations of cultural property. Before throwing out those old professional letters or books, etchings, or sculptures, examine them carefully. You may be sitting on a national treasure, the value of which can be certified by the Cultural Property Export Review Board. If you donate those treasures to a designated institution or public authority, they'll provide you with a tax credit receipt. There is no tax on any capital gain reported when you give this type of property, but capital losses can be applied in the normal manner.

Donations by artists. Gifts of the inventory of an artist have two consequences: a disposition of inventory at an amount between its inventory value (which could be nil) and its fair market value; and a charitable donations credit for the same value. If the gift is made to a designated institution or public authority, and is certified as a cultural property, there is generally no income inclusion (which is deemed to be at cost), but the artist will receive the receipt for the charitable donation.

Source: Personal Tax Update Seminars *by Evelyn Jacks, president, Evelyn Jacks Productions, Inc. and best-selling author,* Tax Secrets for Tough Times *and* Make Sure It's Deductible, *published by McGraw-Hill Ryerson.*

Making the Most of Medical Deductions

You can only deduct medical expenses that exceed 3% of your net income, but that restriction ends once an indexed threshold is reached (approximately $1,750, subject to indexing each year). Most people miss out on claiming common medical expenses every year. The basic rule is that you can claim unreimbursed costs you incur for prescribed medical treatments or drugs as well as certain specified devices that allow you to resume normal living activities or help you to live with a disability. Plan ahead to take advantage of as many medical expenses as possible.

Medical expenses are claimed in the best 12-month period ending in the tax year and a taxpayer may claim expenses incurred for self, a child, grandchild,

parent, grandparent, brother, sister, uncle, aunt, niece or nephew if that person is dependent upon the taxpayer for support sometime during the year. That person must also be a resident of Canada. Medical support will, however, be allowed if your spouse or children are not resident in Canada. In addition, either spouse can make a claim for medical expenses. Generally the claim is made on the return of the person with the lower net (but taxable) income, to minimize the effect of the 3% limitation.

Medical-Related Education Costs

Costs of special schooling for children with medical problems may qualify as medical expenses in these specific instances: care in a detoxification clinic or other treatment center for drug addicts; cost of schooling for those with behavioral or attendance problems or dyslexia. In addition, the costs of training to care for a disabled relative are claimable, as are the costs of training a seeing-eye or hearing-ear dog, and the costs of transporting the animal to the training school.

Cost of respite care: After 1996, up to $10,000 may be claimed in costs incurred for respite care provided to those who give care to disabled relatives in their home. Care given in a nursing home is also claimable as are the expenses of hiring a full-time attendant to care for the patient in his or her home.

Source: Personal Tax Update Seminars *by Evelyn Jacks.*

The Best Tax Shelter: Your Home

The best tax shelter you'll ever have may be your own home. While the major costs of carrying a house as an investment—mortgage interest and property taxes—are not tax-deductible, unless you are using that home partially in your small business or employment pursuits, the appreciation in the property's value qualifies for a complete tax exemption. Other personal residences are taxable; however, you have the option to choose the one that has appreciated the most in value as your tax-exempt property, provided you lived in each property at least some time during the year.

COMMON MEDICAL EXPENSES

Medical Practitioners

- acupuncturist
- audiologist (after Feb. 18, 1997)
- chiropodist (or podiatrist)
- chiropractor
- Christian Science practitioner
- dental hygienist
- dentist
- dietitian
- medical doctor
- medical practitioner
- naturopath
- nurse, including a practical nurse whose full-time occupation is nursing as well as a Christian Science nurse
- occupational therapist who is a member of the Canadian Association of Occupational Therapists
- optometrist
- osteopath
- pharmacist
- physiotherapist
- psychoanalyst who is a member of the Canadian Institute of Psychoanalysis or a member of the Quebec Association of Jungian Psychoanalysts
- psychologist
- qualified speech-language pathologist or audiologist
- speech-language pathologist
- therapeutist (or therapist)

Treatments

- alterations to the home for disabled persons
- ambulance fees
- attendant or nursing home care
- caregiver training
- eyeglasses
- guide dogs
- lab tests
- lip reading or sign language training
- medical and dental services
- moving expenses for a disabled person to a more suitable dwelling
- nursing home care
- prescribed drugs
- private health plan premiums
- sign language services
- therapy for a disabled patient
- transplant costs
- transportation
- travel expenses
- tutoring services for a patient with a learning disability or mental impairment
- van for wheelchair

Devices

- aid to hearing
- artificial eye
- artificial kidney machine
- artificial limb
- brace for a limb
- crutches
- ileostomy or colostomy pad
- iron lung
- laryngeal speaking aid
- rocking bed for poliomyelitis victims
- spinal brace
- truss for a hernia
- wheelchair

Source: Tax Secrets for Tough Times, by Evelyn Jacks, published by McGraw-Hill Ryerson, 300 Water Street, Whitby, ON L1B 9B6.

Following are some other ways to use the investment in your home to increase wealth:

● **Convert nondeductible interest payments into deductible interest.** To decrease interest that is not deductible, consider using the equity in your home to back an investment loan. The resulting interest on that loan is tax-deductible, provided there is a potential for the earning of income from the property.

● **Have a boarder help you with mortgage payments.** You may rent out a portion of your home and, provided there is a profit motive and that rent is charged at fair market value, you will be able to deduct from that rental income the costs of mortgage interest, insurance, taxes, maintenance, and repairs and other expenses based on the portion of the home that is rented. However, be careful not to claim capital cost allowance on the property. This will wipe out your tax exempt status on that portion of the property.

● **Rentals to family members may not be reportable.** If you charge your child board and lodging and it can be shown that they do not cover operational costs (in other words that there is no profit motive), the CCRA will not require reporting of this income, as no losses would be deductible. However, once your family boarding house shows a profit or a reasonable expectation of profit, it is required that those profits be reported.

MEDICAL DEDUCTIONS FOR HOMEOWNERS

You may be able to deduct at least part of the cost of capital improvements you make to your home for medical reasons. Of course, you must be able to prove that you have a valid medical reason for making the improvement. Your deduction will be limited to the cost of the improvement which allows you to gain better access to the home or to be more mobile or functional within the home minus any rebates or reimbursements received. Moreover, you can only deduct that portion of your total medical expenses for the year that exceeds 3% of your net income.

Examples of deductible medical home improvements:

● **Half the cost of central air-conditioning** installed when a member of the family suffers from a respiratory ailment, provided this is prescribed by a medical practitioner, up to a maximum of $1,000.

● **A swimming pool or whirlpool installed** after a doctor advises special therapy for an illness or handicap and public facilities are not accessible.

● **Reasonable costs to alter a driveway** to allow a disabled person greater access to a car, van or bus.

● **Write off the costs of the property as a business expense.** The same general rules apply if a portion of your home is used as a workspace to see clients in your small business or if that workspace is your exclusive place of business. You may also write off home workspace costs if you are an employee who is required to work out of the home. In that case, you may not write off the costs of mortgage interest, insurance or property taxes. Employed commission salespeople may claim insurance and property taxes but not mortgage interest. Again, you should be careful not to claim capital cost allowance on the property, as this will wipe out your tax exempt status on that portion of the property used in the business or employment pursuit.

Source: Personal Tax Update Seminars by Evelyn Jacks.

Tax Loopholes for Executives

One of the major income tax problems facing salaried executives is that they have to pay taxes on their salaries as they are earned, and that income must be added to income in full. Generally, executives will be better off financially if a portion of those taxes can be deferred until a later date, but there is no opportunity to do so if the source of the compensation is salary, even if the employee opts to participate in a funded or unfunded salary deferral arrangement. In those cases, accrued income must be reported in the year the taxpayer receives any benefit.

If your employer will cooperate, there are various methods to structure compensation arrangements that will minimize their tax impact. These involve the use of noncash compensation arrangements. Remember cash must be included in income in the year received, but this is not always the rule for noncash compensation, as described below:

● **Employee stock option plans.** Changes announced on Feb. 28, 2000, put in place a series of rules that allow those employees who receive options to acquire stock of a publicly traded company as part of their compensation, to defer any employment benefit stemming from this transaction to the year he or she disposes of the security. To qualify for this deferral, it must be a qualifying acquisition and the amount of the deferred benefit must not exceed $100,000 per year. The year in which the deferral is elected is based on when the options vest (first become available for exercise) with the taxpayer, and on the fair market value (FMV) of the securities. When a taxpayer acquires several qualifying securities at the same time, they are deemed to have been acquired in the order that the options were granted.

Other complicated rules should be discussed with a tax adviser. For example:

1. The employee must file an election to defer the benefits of the option with the grantor (employer) and to record the deferral for tax purposes. This is done through Form T1212, which must be filed with the individual's tax return annually.

2. The securities for which taxable benefits are deferred are deemed not to be identical for the purpose of cost averaging. Therefore, they can easily be identified for the purposes of an order of disposition.

3. The order of disposition of properties on which a deferral is possible is unique: they can only be considered disposed of after identical properties for which no deferral is possible. Once those properties on which no deferral is possible have been disposed of, properties on which a deferral is possible are disposed of in the order in which they were acquired.

4. An exception occurs on a "quick flip"—when a taxpayer disposes of a security acquired under an option agreement within 30 days of acquiring it.

5. When the securities are disposed of, a taxable benefit must be reported in income. An offsetting deduction is then applied on the tax return, in an amount to mirror the capital gains inclusion rate.

6. As well as the employment benefit, the taxpayer may be required to include in income the capital gain or loss arising from the disposition of the security.

7. Amounts received as compensation for stock option rights which cease to be exercisable in accordance with terms of the option agreement are taxable.

Source: Evelyn Jacks, president, Evelyn Jacks Productions, Inc. and best-selling author, Tax Secrets for Tough Times *and* Make Sure It's Deductible, *published by McGraw-Hill Ryerson.*

Tax-Free Benefits

Be sure to negotiate for the following tax-free benefits from employment:

● **Death benefits received by the family** of an employee—up to $10,000 may be exempt from income for payments made for unused sick benefits or other service recognition.

● **Employer-provided meals through expense accounts** that is used when traveling or entertaining business clients.

● **Employer-provided lodging for business travel.**

● **Employer-provided entertainment for business purposes.**

● **Discounts on merchandise and commissions on sales.** If the employee buys merchandise at a discount from the retail firm he or she works in or buys an insurance policy for his or her own personal benefit, resulting discounts are not taxable, nor is the resulting commission on the policy taxable, if the salesperson is required to make the premium payments.

● **Subsidized meals.** When the employee buys low-cost meals at an employer-provided cafeteria or restaurant, there is no taxable benefit if a reasonable cost-covering charge is paid.

● **Uniforms and special clothing.** When a special employer-provided uniform must be worn, including footwear for safety, costs of the clothing are not taxable, nor employer-paid laundry bills on these items.

● **Transportation to the job.** If your employer picks you up and brings you to work and back for security or other reasons, the cost of transportation is not considered to be a taxable benefit. This is different from a transportation allowance, which is used to get back and forth from the place of employment. Such amounts are taxable as an employment benefit.

● **Recreational facilities**. Employees may use recreational facilities supplied by the employer—for example, gyms and exercise rooms, golf courses or shuffleboards—without incurring a taxable benefit. Memberships to recreational and social clubs may also be received tax-free.

● **Moving expenses.** If the employer requires an employee to move to take a position in a different city, moving expenses paid to relocate the employee and his or her family are not considered to be a taxable benefit. This includes compensation for losses on the sale of the family home or guarantees on receipt of the fair market value of the home; whether or not this is received, unless the home is sold to someone the taxpayer is not dealing with at arm's length (i.e., a relative). The maximum tax-free compensation is computed as one-half the amount paid that exceeds $15,000.

● **Premiums under private health services plans.** Employer-paid contributions to a private health service plan are not taxable to the employee, although the employee will want premiums for long-term disability included as a taxable benefit so that resulting benefits received in the future are considered tax-free.

● **Employee counseling services.** When the employer pays for counseling in respect of retirement, reemployment or mental or physical health for the employee or someone who is related to the employee, including drug or alcohol abuse, stress management and job placement, the amounts are received on a tax-free basis.

● **Other tax-free benefits include payments** by the employer for professional membership fees, transportation passes, reasonable traveling allowances, certain travel expenses of university teachers, noncash gifts in the amount of $500 and tuition fees paid for courses taken by the employee if those courses are for the benefit of the employer.

● **Taxable benefits.** While the following benefits paid for by the employer are taxable, it is better to receive these than having to earn the money, pay the tax and then buy the goods or services yourself:

1. **Employer-provided vehicles.**
2. **Holidays, prizes and awards.**

VACATION PROPERTIES

Vacation properties owned by Canadians can have several interesting tax consequences whether they are used for personal enjoyment or rented during the ownership period and upon disposition.

If used solely for personal enjoyment, the costs of repairing the property will not be deductible, however if those costs improve the useful life of the property, they are added to the capital cost base. This will later reduce any capital gain resulting from the sale of the property if it is classified as a taxable residence. So be sure to keep careful records of all such expenses.

An exempt principal residence is one upon which no tax is paid on appreciated value upon disposition. Before 1982, a Canadian family could own two tax-exempt principal residences, one in the name of each spouse. Since 1982, only one per household is allowed.

The principal residence election can be made for any personal residence, including vacation properties, provided the taxpayer and/or his family inhabited the property at some time during the year—even if that's only for a long weekend.

Obviously, one would elect the property that has appreciated the most in value as the exempt property, but other factors include the length of the exemption time (pre-1982 and number of years after 1982 in which the status is elected), the amount of appreciation, the sales price or fair market value upon disposition, and whether or not a capital gains election has been previously made on the property. Use Form T2091 to figure it all out.

If used as a rental property, the income received must be reported; however, net losses resulting from the application of operational expenses will not be allowed unless there is a reasonable expectation of profit from the enterprise. In other words, rental income will be reduced to zero only in those cases. If the expenses exceed the rental income, you won't be able to deduct the difference from your other income.

Trap: Do not use the deduction of capital cost allowance to increase or create a loss. In general, capital cost allowance should not be claimed on a property that may be elected to be the principal residence, as such a claim will knock out the property's tax-exempt status.

Note: Losses on personal residences are considered to be personal—not deductible against other gains of the year, prior years or gains of the future. The status of any property being rented should therefore be carefully considered. If you can show a reasonable potential for profit, this property should perhaps be considered as a revenue property instead, to preserve the right to claim capital losses in the future. Discuss this with your tax adviser.

3. Interest-free or low-interest loans. The benefit is deductible as a carrying charge, by the way, if the loan is used for the purposes of earning income from property investments or a business.

4. Low-rent or rent-free housing.

5. Tuition fees paid for courses taken for personal (not business) benefits.

Source: Personal Tax Update Seminars by Evelyn Jacks Productions, Inc., Winnipeg, Man. Evelyn Jacks is the best-selling author of Tax Secrets for Tough Times and Make Sure It's Deductible, published by McGraw-Hill Ryerson.

Deductions for Executives and Other Employees

Those who earn salary only may deduct the following out-of-pocket business-related expenses on their personal tax return:

- **Accounting and legal fees,** not including income tax preparation.
- **Motor vehicle expenses including capital cost allowance (CCA),** interest or leasing costs, as well as operating costs.
- **Traveling expenses, including rail,** air, bus or other travel costs.
- **Meals, tips and hotel costs providing the excursion** is for at least 12 hours away from the taxpayer's metropolitan area. Meals and tips are subject to a 50% restriction.
- **Costs of parking** (but generally not at the place of employment).
- **Supplies used directly in the work** (stationery, maps, etc.).
- **Salaries paid to your assistant** (including spouses or children if fair market value is paid for work actually performed).
- **Office rent or certain home office expenses,** described below:

Employees who earn their living negotiating contracts for their employers or selling on commission may claim expenses for travel and sales if they are required to pay their own expenses and regularly perform their duties away from their employer's place of business.

In addition, expenses are claimable only if the employee is not in receipt of a tax-free travel allowance. Deductible travel expenses include:

1. Automobile-related operating expenses like gas, oil, repairs.

2. Automobile-related fixed costs like licenses, insurance, capital cost allowance, interest and leasing. The latter three expenses are limited to annual maximums. At the time that this book was being prepared, those maximums were:

- **For CCA:** $30,000 plus GST and PST.
- **For interest:** $300 a month.
- **For leasing costs:** $800 a month plus GST and PST.

3. The cost of air, bus, rail, taxi or other transportation which takes the employee outside the employer's metropolitan area.

4. When travel expenses only are claimed, the amounts may exceed commissions earned and excess expenses over this may be used to offset other income of the year.

Deductible sales expenses include:

- **Promotional expenses.**
- **Entertainment** (subject to the 50% restriction).
- **Travel and auto.**
- **Home office.**

Note: Those who claim "sales expenses" may not claim expenses that exceed commissions earned in the calendar year.

Trap: Employees are not allowed to make a claim for capital expenditures with the exception of the purchase of vehicles, musical instruments or aircraft. Therefore, it is a wise tax-planning move to lease computers, cell phones or other kinds of equipment.

Tip: Employees who claim employment expenses may receive a cash rebate of any GST paid on these expenses. Form GST/HST 370 must be completed. Many employees have missed this provision in the past. The amounts can be recovered by filing an adjustment back to the inception of the GST: 1991 (HST: 1997).

Documentation: All employees who claim employment expenses must complete Form T2200 Declaration of Conditions of Employment for each year in which tax-deductible expenses are claimed. They should also have this document signed by their employers.

Source: Tax Secrets for Tough Times, by Evelyn Jacks, published by McGraw-Hill Ryerson, 300 Water Street, Whitby, ON L1N 9B6.

Bigger and Better Business Deductions on Personal Tax Returns

Deducting a Company Car and Chauffeur

The use of a company car can be a valuable fringe benefit. The expenses of the car, including depreciation, are deductible by the employee provided that the employee is not receiving a tax-free travel allowance. Expenses are deductible if the employee is ordinarily required to carry his or her duties out away from the employer's place of business and is responsible for paying all of the costs of operating the vehicle.

An auto distance log must be kept to record both business and personal driving throughout the year. Then a fraction of the overall distance, based on the total business distance driven compared to the total distance driven, is used to prorate all expenses. They break down into two groups:

● **Operating expenses.** This includes gas, oil, tires, insurance, auto club memberships, maintenance and repairs, car washes, license fees.

● **Fixed expenses.** Leasing costs (to a maximum of $800 a month plus taxes), capital cost allowance (based on capital cost of the vehicle that may not exceed $30,000 plus taxes) and interest costs of $300 a month, based on rules in effect at the time of writing. These maximums apply to "passenger" or luxury vehicles that are placed in a separate class for CCA purposes (Class 10.1) and are subject to special rules on disposition.

Don't forget to claim the GST rebate for any GST included in your tax-deductible expenses. This rebate must be included in income in the year received.

The cost of the chauffeur will be deductible if it is reasonable under the circumstances, and incurred to earn income.

However, you can't deduct expenses of looking for a new job in a new trade or business, even if you get the job.

> "If less than 90% of the trip was for business purposes, you would be wise to audit-proof yourself by allocating expenses according to the appropriate business/personal-use ratio."

Deducting Vacation Costs as a Business Expense

Combining a tax-deductible business trip with a short vacation, perhaps with family, can be quite attractive. It is important to keep expense categories straight, since different tests apply for deductibility.

You can deduct the cost of traveling for business or professional purposes if you are self-employed. But you must be able to show that the primary purpose of the trip was business. This does not mean that you cannot combine business with pleasure, only that the primary purpose must be business.

The best way to satisfy the taxman is to prove that more than 90% of your time at the destination was spent on business. In that case, your transportation expenses are fully deductible as will your hotel, ground transportation, and meal and entertainment expenses at your destination (subject to the normal 50% restriction).

If less than 90% of the trip was for business purposes, you would be wise to audit-proof yourself by allocating expenses according to the appropriate business/personal-use ratio.

Do not count on deducting the full cost of a trip with your spouse, unless that spouse is a partner in the business, an employee who is required to be there for business purposes or if your spouse's presence is required for business purposes. If your spouse attends with you, but on a personal basis only, you can still deduct the full amount of what it would cost you to attend alone at the single-room hotel rate, for instance. You can deduct the full cost of services where your spouse's presence does not boost the charge, say, for the taxi from the airport or if you rent a car and drive to the meeting site. If you fly or take the train, only your ticket is deductible.

Convention Expenses and Training Expenses

Only two conventions a year may be deducted by those who are proprietors. The deductions will be questioned on a tax audit if they are taken offshore, in a resort or before or after a personal vacation. No costs can be deducted for days in which no training was held. However, the tax department will generally allow the taxpayer to deduct costs relating to the day of arrival and departure and any weekends. Where the cost of the convention includes meals and entertainment, $50 a day will be deemed to be the portion of costs related to this, and this is the amount to which the 50% restriction will be applied.

Training expenses or seminars may be fully deductible, even if multiple sessions are attended during the year. Training courses generally do not have a formal members' meeting, but rather feature study sessions that can include testing and certification for credit.

Four Ways to Beat the "Only 50% of a Business Meal Is Deductible" Rule

Company dining rooms, employee cafeterias and other "eating facilities" operated by an employer for employees are not subject to the 50% rule if the facility is located on the business premises of the employer, brings in revenue that normally equals or exceeds its direct operating costs and does not discriminate in favor of highly compensated employees.

Company parties. The 50% rule does not apply to certain traditional employer-paid social or recreational activities that are primarily for the benefit of the employees. Holiday parties and annual summer outings continue to be fully deductible, but there is a limit of six such parties per year.

Meals en route. Taxpayers are allowed to fully deduct the cost of meals and beverages served on planes, trains or buses. This is important these days when meal/beverage services on discount airlines must be paid for by passengers.

Reimbursement angle. Employees are not subject to the 50% rule if their company reimburses them for

Better Than a Raise

Negotiate for tax-free perks of employment in addition to cash. This can include:

● **Membership to a recreational club.**

● **A $10,000 death benefit in recognition** of your service with the company.

● **An annual $500 noncash gift for your birthday.**

● **Tuition fees for courses** you'd like to take to improve your performance and enhance your career.

● **Counseling services** for health or retirement or reemployment.

● **Premiums for private health services plans** (however, ask that long-term disability plan premiums be taxed back to you to ensure that any resulting wage loss replacement benefits are nontaxable).

business meal and entertainment expenses. It's the company that's subject to the rule—the company must limit the amount of deduction it claims on its tax return to 50% of the amount given to the employee.

Bottom line: The tax law restriction for meals and entertainment costs has no adverse effect for an employee on an expense account who is reimbursed in full for business meal and entertainment costs. It may be more desirable to have your employer reimburse you than for you to receive an expense allowance and deduct meal and entertainment expenses on your own return, where they will be limited to 50%.

Source: *Evelyn Jacks, president, Evelyn Jacks Productions, Inc. and best-selling author.*

Imaginative Travel Deductions

Traveling for Education

Traveling costs to educational seminars are still deductible if you are in the trade or business that is the subject of the seminar. Also, the full amount of the training costs will be deductible if it is for the maintenance, updating or upgrading of an existing skill.

However, if the training is "capital" in nature, leading to a diploma, professional qualification or similar certificate (i.e., training by a medical doctor to become a specialist), and a lasting benefit to the taxpayer, the costs will be scheduled in the cumulative eligible capital account and written off over time.

Note to investors: The cost of attending a general seminar on how to improve your dealings with your financial adviser or broker is not deductible, even if you have many investments. But stockbrokers who attend the same seminar would be entitled to a deduction because that's their trade or business.

Caution: Teachers cannot deduct the cost of foreign travel to enhance their general understanding of the culture and language of that country.

Traveling for Medical Reasons

If you must travel for medical reasons, you can deduct the cost of getting there, provided the medical procedures or treatment you seek are not available in your home town, and that they are prescribed by your doctor. The medical services must be at least 80 kilometers away and costs incurred for the patient and one attendant, if required, are deductible as a medical expense credit.

Actual costs of gas, oil, hotel and meals may be claimed, if they supported by receipts and an auto log, if you used your car. An alternative "simplified calculation" is possible. No receipts are required. The taxpayer may multiply the number of kilometers driven by a prescribed rate per kilometer, which differs in each province but averages around 36 cents at the time of writing.

Source: Personal Tax Update Seminars *by Evelyn Jacks.*

A Sideline Business: A Good Tax Shelter

A sideline business can be a very good tax shelter. With it you can generate large paper losses, claim deductions for the business use of personal expenditures and shift income to your low-tax-bracket minor children. Here's how a sideline business can be used to get big tax-shelter-type deductions.

Income Splitting

You can claim the cost of paying your family members to work in your business—and then deduct those costs to reduce your own income, provided that your family member actually did work that:

- you would have hired a stranger to do,

- was paid at a rate you would have paid the stranger, or

- was actually paid to the family member.

Be sure to take source deductions from the pay like you would for any other employee, and issue a T4 Slip at year-end or a separation slip when the family member/employee stops working for you.

What Qualifies As a Business

A part-time activity can easily qualify as a business enterprise. The only requirement is that you operate your activity with the objective of making a profit, and that expenditures made are reasonable and incurred to earn income. You don't actually have to make a profit during the year, and start-up losses are

COMMUTING COSTS CAN BE DEDUCTIBLE

Most taxpayers know that driving to and from work is not tax deductible. However, there are certain exceptions to that rule. For example, if you are required to use your own car in performing your duties as a commission sales employee or as a self-employed person, driving to your regular place of work will be considered personal driving. However, if you first stop off to see a client, pick up the mail, buy supplies for the business, do your business banking, etc., that trip has a business purpose and is deductible. So plan to write off the majority of your driving by arranging your affairs to take advantage of all tax provisions. In the morning, arrange to pick up your mail at a location that's on your way to work; arrange breakfast meetings with your clients. In the evening, do your business banking and pick up supplies on the way home. Or, meet your client for a late afternoon meeting that's close to your home. Only the short distance from there to your home is considered personal driving.

DEDUCTION CHECKLIST FOR BUSINESS OWNERS

More than ever, the best source of tax breaks is running your own business. *Business owners' tax advantages:*

● **Fully deductible business expenses.** For the self-employed, business expenses that are operational in nature—advertising, promotion, banking charges, interest costs, professional fees, salary and wages, rent, consulting fees, etc.—are deductible in full directly from gross income.

● **Full home-office expense write-off.** If you run a business from your home and meet certain requirements, you may deduct not only a portion of property taxes and mortgage interest, but also a percentage of depreciation, utilities, insurance, repairs, and any other costs of maintaining the home workspace, according to the percentage obtained when you divide the total square area of the office by the total living area in the home. Your home-office deductions may be restricted; that is, they cannot be used to increase or create a business loss. However, you can carry over any unused deductions and take them in future years, when you have income from the business.

● **Tax-deferred retirement savings.** Qualified retirement plans offer business owners an opportunity to save for their retirement on a tax-deductible basis. These kinds of plans include RRSPs and registered pension plans, as well as employee profit sharing plans.

● **Family income splitting.** By hiring your kids, you can create "own-source" income in their hands which may be invested. Resulting earnings on those investments are taxed to the child. In the meantime, their wages are deductible business expenses. And, provided their income is not taxable (generally this means less than the basic personal amount), you may still claim certain deductions for them (i.e., child-care expenses for a child 16 and under) as well as certain nonrefundable credits (medical expenses and tuition/education credit transfers).

Bonus: Children under 18 who work for a parent are exempt from paying the Canada Pension Plan.

Caution: Kids must perform actual services for reasonable compensation, that is actually paid to them through a regular payroll or on a consulting basis. Phony jobs and inflated wages don't stand up to the CCRA's scrutiny.

● **Hiring your spouse.** Aside from paying your spouse a deductible salary or wage for work actually performed in your company, he or she may participate in any perks or benefit plans that you have for other employees (registered pension plans, group health benefits, up to $500 annually in noncash gifts, etc.). In most cases, he or she may also qualify for deductible RRSP contributions, if prior tax returns have been filed, he or she is age-eligible and RRSP contribution room has been created. Finally, if your spouse accompanies you on a business trip as an assistant or colleague, you may be able to

deductible against other income if you can show the business has actually started.

When did the business start? According to the tax department, they are looking for three indicators:

● Some significant activity that forms a regular part of the income-earning process starts.

● A specific concept of the type of business activity that will be carried on is evident.

● An organizational structure exists to show this is an ongoing enterprise.

Next, you have to prove that your business is not just a hobby. This can be trickier, especially if your hobby turns into a business. It is therefore really important to keep a daily record of activities that have a business purpose, and a budget that shows expected earnings as time goes by.

Big-Dollar Deductions

While taxpayers who are employed or who have only passive investment income sources are limited to only a few itemized deductions with which to offset their income, those who manage their own sideline business may be able to claim big-loss deductions to offset other income of the year, the previous three years or up to seven years in the future.

Important: Tax losses do not always mean cash losses. Items such as capital cost allowance on cars, equipment and other income-producing assets can

write off travel expenses for both of you.

● **Timing income.** If you use the cash accounting method, available only to small cash-based proprietorships or farming operations, you can defer income from one year into the next. It is not necessary to report accrued income; only that which is actually received in the year. Likewise accrued expenses cannot be deducted—only those which are actually paid in the year.

● **More deductible transportation expenses.** Going to work and coming home are nondeductible commutation expenses. If you work out of your home, you're already at your place of business when you get up in the morning. If you have a home office but you have to travel, most business-related travel costs are deductible.

● **Fully deductible casualty losses.** Business casualty losses (from fire, theft, accident, natural disaster, etc.) may be written off in full against business income; however, losses relating to depreciable property will result in involuntary dispositions.

● **Full write-offs for bad debts.** Bad business debts may be deducted in full in the year in which they become uncollectible. This deduction can include amounts which were reported as accrued income last year, but which failed to materialize, or in the case of uncollectible loans, you extended to another, the loss is considered to be a capital loss or an allowable business loss with an insolvent small business corporation.

● **Operating losses.** If your business loses money—as many firms do during the early stages—you may write off the loss against your other income of the year. If the loss exceeds income, you may carry back the excess and apply it to income earned in the previous three years to get a refund for those years. If there's still any excess loss, you may still carry it forward for the next seven years.

result in deductible tax losses while the business is earning a cash-flow profit. Capital cost allowance is always claimed at the taxpayer's option, so it is possible to "save" a deduction for CCA to a future year when income may be higher.

Beware: The tax department will quickly disallow losses when the business is not your chief source of income and you cannot show that over a reasonable period of time your sideline business will be profitable.

Profit Motive
The assessment of whether or not your business has a profit motive is subjective. You have to have a strong position to counter the assertion of a tax audit that there is no profit motive. The courts have taken the following into consideration:

● **You operate in a businesslike manner** and keep accurate books and records.

● **You institute new operating procedures** to correct past business practices that resulted in losses.

● **You act professionally.** Show that you hired or consulted with recognized experts in the field, and that you followed their advice.

● **You made a serious effort.** Show that you hired qualified people to run your day-to-day operation. Remember, no rule says you must devote 40 hours a week to your sideline business.

HOW TO HOLD ON TO MEAL AND ENTERTAINMENT DEDUCTIONS

Meal and entertainment deductions have been drastically altered by tax changes over the years. In most cases you can only deduct 50% of the cost (rather than 100%). Also, the rules of proof are stricter. It's essential to comply with these rules or the whole deduction could be lost.

Substantiation: There is a specific checklist of information you must have for all business meals and entertainment costs. Be prepared to prove:

- **The amount of the expenditure.**
- **The time, date and place of the expenditure.**
- **The nature of the business discussion,** and the business reason for the expense or the nature of the business benefit to be derived as a result of the expense.
- **Identification of the people who participated in the business discussion.**

- **There is a profit potential.** Even if your business continually produces losses, you can still prove a profit motive by showing that assets you have acquired are expected to produce income.
- **You have had past successes.** It may help establish a profit motive if you show that in the past you were successfully involved in your current activity.
- **You have the training and experience** to be successful at the business.
- **You have detailed and reasonable budgets** and business plans for the future.
- **Your business would be profitable but** for the

paper losses you have claimed due to your investment in capital assets.

Remember: Each business is assessed on a case-by-case basis and there is no set time limit to achieving profitability.

Source: Evelyn Jacks, president, Evelyn Jacks Productions, Inc. and best-selling author, Tax Secrets for Tough Times *and* Make Sure It's Deductible, *published by McGraw-Hill Ryerson.*

Doing Business

The tax department will look for tangible indications that you have really embarked on a business enterprise. Some examples of activities that can help you prove this:

- Register your business name. Use business cards and stationery.
- Set up a business bank account and credit cards (annual fees and interest/carrying costs are then fully deductible).
- Get a separate business line and telephone.
- Take out a company listing in the Yellow Pages.
- Keep a log of the business contacts you've seen during the year.
- Advertise.
- Send promotions to prospective customers.
- Buy a computer, printer and fax machine.
- Hire at least some part-time help, or have work done by independent consultants.
- Set up a website and e-mail address.

Tougher Questions

The tax department may argue that, since you had other sources of income and could afford to lose money, you could not have had a profit motive.

Defense: Nobody goes into business expecting to lose money. Even with your tax deductions, you would have been better off had you done nothing and never started the venture in the first place.

Businesses that involve horse racing, farming, car racing and antiques are particularly vulnerable to audit, as there is a strong likelihood that there is a personal pleasure component. Know the following:

In Canada, windfall income is not subject to tax, unless you operate a gambling establishment or are a professional gambler.

There are special rules for hobby farmers which restrict losses claimable to $8,750 annually (the first $2,500 plus 50% of the next $12,500).

Profits on the occasional sale of listed personal properties—like antiques—may be subject to capital treatment—which means that only 50% of the gains on the sale are taxable. However, if the taxpayer is clearly in the business of buying and selling antiques, the venture is likely considered to be business in nature if the transactions are frequent and the taxpayer has special knowledge.

Special Advice for the Self-Employed and Moonlighters

Those already in business for themselves know that the tax department can be a force to be reckoned with—and those just starting out will soon learn it. The tax department's role is to be an overseer, to ensure that Canadian businesses compete in a level playing field, and that those with like circumstances pay similar amounts of taxes. It cannot be ignored. Mistakes are costly from the point of view of both time and money. Even if your accountant makes the mistake on your return, you still pay—and late filing penalties and interest charges can accumulate to be more expensive than the tax bill itself. To avoid audit trouble:

Keep separate bank accounts and separate credit cards for business transactions. This will simplify record-keeping.

Note: It is inevitable that there will be some cross-flow of funds between business and personal accounts. Pay special attention to documenting this flow of funds. Without adequate documentation, the tax department may suspect, and may allege, additional unreported and taxable business income.

Additional advice: Keep a diary keyed to your business credit card use and all cash expenditures for business.

● **Have separate equipment,** etc., for business use. If the nature of your business requires that you make and receive business calls at home, install a separate telephone for that purpose. If you drive a significant distance on business, keep a separate automobile for that purpose. If your business requires that you do substantial work at home, set aside a room or area of your home as an office. Furnish the area exclusively with office furniture, equipment and business materials, and use it exclusively for business purposes.

● **Know your tax responsibilities.** Even if you leave the matter of taxes largely to your accountant and bookkeeper, take the time and trouble to educate yourself on the subject. The penalties for gross negligence are prohibitively high. You cannot claim a defense when there is willful blindness. Learn your personal responsibility for income tax, corporate tax, sales taxes and installment tax payments. Be sure to have some understanding of your responsibility in the area of source deductions, and try to be aware of provincial tax implications.

Helpful: Guide to Business Income published by the CCRA.

● **Keep good records.** Your accountant has primary responsibility to provide you with a system that clearly and properly reflects your business income and transactions. A simple method of record-keeping that works is one that is organized to reflect tax return items line by line. For example, if you are a sole proprietorship, set up your accounts according to the line items on Form T2124. Mark your cheques, credit-card receipts and diary entries with the appropriate type of expense or line number.

Note: Computer records are acceptable as long as certain controls are in place to protect the integrity of these records. Also, when entertaining or buying promotional gifts, cards or other acknowledgments to give to employees or clients, always mark your receipts with that person's name, the occasion and revenue source.

For more complex and/or active business enterprises, you would be wise to rely on the expertise of a reputable accountant familiar with your type of business. Expect your accountant to set up a record-keeping system, give business advice and represent you at the tax department if necessary. That person can also help you set up GST registrations and source remittance registrations. The tax department will provide you with a single business number that will identify your business for all of these purposes.

Source: *Evelyn Jacks, president, Evelyn Jacks Productions, Inc. and best-selling author,* Tax Secrets for Tough Times *and* Make Sure It's Deductible, *published by McGraw-Hill Ryerson.*

Escaping the Penalties

We have previously outlined the various penalties a taxpayer may be subject to for noncompliance. However, there are also numerous ways to avoid a penalty:

● **Increase withholding.** If it looks like your tax payments will fall short, increase quarterly installment payments. Or ask your employer to withhold more. Withheld taxes are presumed to be paid equally throughout the year so larger installment payments late in the year can be applied retroactively to wipe out any interest charges on earlier underpayments.

● **Penalty exception.** You can rely on an annualization safe harbor. If most of your income is derived late in the year, you can take advantage of the "annualization" rules, but you'll probably need an accountant to make the calculations.

● **Pay something.** Even if you can't pay the whole tax bill, contact the collection department and arrange to make monthly payments you can afford. Interest will be charged but you can show yourself to be a "model filing citizen" despite your current cash-flow hardship—something that can really work in your favor should you ever suffer a severe hardship.

● **Fairness provisions.** The CCRA has the ability to waive penalties and interest charges in cases where the taxpayer has undergone a severe hardship (personal illness, death of a family member, natural disaster, etc.). Simply write a letter to the Fairness Committee outlining your circumstances and ask for a review to waive penalties and interest.

Source: *Evelyn Jacks, president, Evelyn Jacks Productions, Inc. and best-selling author,* Tax Secrets for Tough Times *and* Make Sure It's Deductible, *published by McGraw-Hill Ryerson.*

A Great Tax Shelter That Isn't a Tax Shelter

If you own your business, you can take advantage of certain tax strategies to substantially improve your cash flow and the quality of your life. For example, you can have your business start a medical reim-

THE HOME OFFICE

Using a part of your home in your business may enable you to deduct certain expenses if you satisfy specific tests. To take this deduction, that portion of your home must be used exclusively and regularly:

● **As the principal place of business** for any trade or business in which you engage, or

● **As a place to regularly meet** or deal with your trade or business; or clients.

Exclusive use means that you must use that specific part of your home only for the purpose of carrying on your trade or business. Any personal use in that space will prevent you from claiming the deduction. Regular use means that you use the exclusive business part of your home on a con-tinuing basis, not just occasionally. (However, your home office is treated as a principal place of business if it is used for substantial managerial or administrative activities such as paying bills, ordering supplies, and scheduling appointments and there is no other fixed location for these activities.)

As an employee, you must be using your home as a requirement by your employer in addition to satisfying these three tests. Just being helpful to your work will not qualify you for a home office deduction.

To deduct the expenses for the business use of your home office, the use must be connected with an active trade or business that has a reasonable expectation of profit. If you use part of your home to carry on personal investment activities, not as a broker or dealer, expenses cannot be deducted since you are not in that trade or business.

The allowable deductions attributable to the business use of the home may not create or increase a loss from that business. Excess expenses that are not deductible may be carried forward and applied to income in the following year.

bursement plan for employees. Rationale: The only medical expenses you can deduct on your personal tax return are those that exceed 3% of net income. But if your company sets up a group health benefits plan, the premiums may be deductible as a business expense (subject to some limitations if you hire family members).

Salary Versus Dividends

If you own a small business corporation, you can diversify the type of income you draw out of it, thereby averaging your tax bills downward. You can take salary, which will help you to create RRSP contribution room, or dividends that are after-tax distributions of profits in the company to its shareholders and are taxed at lower rates on your personal return.

Salaries are taxed only once, in your hands. The company will receive a deduction for the amount paid. Salary also creates RRSP contribution room, the prerequisite for funding your tax-sheltered retirement savings through an RRSP.

You should try to draw enough salary to maximize your RRSP contribution room every year, and then make the contribution and take the deduction.

In the case of dividend income, the company has already paid taxes on the company's profits. When the dividend is flowed out to you, the shareholder, a lower marginal tax rate is applied to dividend income. Taken together, however, both levels of tax can be more expensive than taking only salary or bonuses. This depends on your province of residence and the level of other taxable income received in the year. Obviously, the more of your total compensation you take in salary, or as a bonus, the better, in those instances.

If you are going to take a dividend out of your company, try to do so in January, rather than the end of the current tax year, so as to defer the reporting of the dividend until the following tax season.

Source: Evelyn Jacks, president, Evelyn Jacks Productions, Inc.

Tax Havens, Residency and Taxes

"Tax haven" is probably one of the most misunderstood terms in investment jargon. Despite the visions it conjures up of tax-free investments and avoidance of a host of other taxes, so-called "tax havens" have relatively little potential for tax savings for Canadian residents. Nor do they offer (in any meaningful way) much-vaunted privacy or confidentiality of business records. But they do offer some real benefits to investors.

A tax haven is not a type of investment (like a tax shelter). It is a political jurisdiction: a state or nation in which the local government has elected not to levy taxes—on income, inheritance, property, etc. Tax-free status, however, exists only in that particular jurisdiction.

Canadian residents with accounts, investments, trusts or other business structures in tax havens still pay income tax on all earnings derived from them. That's because if you are a resident of Canada, you are required to pay taxes on your world income in Canadian funds. Nonresidents are only required to pay tax in Canada on Canadian-source employment, investment or self-employment income, or on taxable Canadian property (property held in Canada, upon which the Canadian government has reserved the right to tax accrued gains after the taxpayer left the country).

Whether or not you are a resident of Canada is assessed on a case-by-case basis, but generally revolves around whether a person continues to have significant family, residential, social and economic ties to Canada. Temporary absences generally do not eliminate Canadian resident status, and if the taxpayer does not establish significant residential ties elsewhere, he or she can be deemed to still be a resident of Canada. Intent at the time of departure is also important: those who sever ties permanently are required to report a deemed disposition of all taxable assets and pay tax or post security for the tax on their final Canadian return.

A tax haven is not a means to privacy. Although your investments are confidential in most jurisdictions, you will have to keep evidence of those investments in personal records. No matter how or where your records are maintained, any privacy to be gained from a tax haven ceases as soon as they are found. The only way to achieve total privacy would be to keep no records—in which case it wouldn't matter where your investments were located.

Investors, then, should remember these rules when evaluating a tax haven opportunity:

● **Do not invest just because the asset is located in a tax haven.** Your income is still taxable in Canada as long as you are a Canadian who is ordinarily resident in the country, a deemed or factual resident.

● **Examine the opportunity**—not its location—for tax advantages.

● **Do not buy or establish a business structure in a tax haven jurisdiction,** unless you have the exceptional business skills and have sought in advance the professional guidance necessary to operate it.

● **Privacy is not a sufficient reason for investing in a tax haven.**

● **If the investment wouldn't be an attractive one in Canada,** then its location in a tax haven jurisdiction usually will hold no advantage for you.

> "Taxpayers who are "passive" or non-active investors in certain types of investments may be limited in the amount of money that can be written off for tax purposes, in the case of losses."

Source: *Evelyn Jacks, president, Evelyn Jacks Productions, Inc. and best-selling author,* Tax Secrets for Tough Times *and* Make Sure It's Deductible, *published by McGraw-Hill Ryerson.*

Escaping Limits on Investment Losses

Taxpayers who are "passive" or non-active investors in certain types of investments may be limited in the amount of money that can be written off for tax purposes, in the case of losses. This includes the following:

● **Limited partnerships.** Taxpayers who invest money as non-active partners of a limited partnership are restricted to their "at risk amount" in determining how much of their losses can be written off against other income. Portions of the losses that are not deductible are eligible for an indefinite carryforward so they can be applied to a year in which there is income from the property, or to tax consequences from increased investments in the partnership.

● **Rental properties.** A rental loss cannot be increased or created by claiming capital cost allowance; this deduction can only be used to reduce the rental income to zero.

● **Interest costs.** The cost of borrowing money to make passive investments will be tax-deductible and used to offset all other income in the year. However, this will not apply to investments that earn capital gains only. There must be evidence that interest, dividends, foreign income, rents or royalties will be earned. In the case of investment in equities (stocks, mutual funds), there must be a reasonable expectation that the dividends will be declared at some time in the future for the interest costs to be deductible.

● **Situations arising in tough times.** When times are tough, unusual losses may arise from circumstances that are completely beyond an individual's control. Some interesting tax breaks can result, including the following:

● **Uncollectible debts.** When it becomes clear that a debt will be uncollectible, the creditor may elect a deemed disposition and consider the debt to be disposed of at the end of the tax year. The proceeds are considered to be nil in that case and it is deemed that the debt is reacquired immediately after the disposition at a value of nil. A capital loss will generally result. This treatment will only be allowed, however, if it can be shown that the debt was acquired for the purposes of earning income.

● **Losses arising on loans.** Those taxpayers who find that loans they have extended to other people cannot be repaid may be subject to varying tax treatment, depending on the purpose of the loan.

If the loss arises from a loan that was noninterest bearing or that bore interest at a rate below commercial or prescribed rates, losses will generally not be deductible unless the loan was made for bona fide business purpose.

● **When guarantees must be fulfilled.** Capital losses may be deducted in cases where a guarantor must pay the obligation, again if it can be established there was a bona fide expectation that income would be earned from the transaction.

● **Shares of insolvent public corporations.** When a public corporation goes bankrupt, shareholders are deemed to have disposed of their shares in the company as of the end of the year for proceeds equal to nil, which results in the reporting of a capital loss. However, if there is a sale of the shares later, proceeds will have to be reported, using an adjusted cost base of nil. As a result, there will have to be a reporting of a capital gain at that time. This tax treatment is possible even if the corporation is not formally bankrupt, but simply insolvent.

● **Shares of insolvent small business corporations.** Insolvency of a small business corporation which results in losses due to uncollectible debt, guarantees paid or worthless shares will also qualify for a deemed disposition at a value of nil.

However, the resulting loss is considered to be a business investment loss (BIL), a portion of which is deductible against all other income of the year on Line 217 of the return. The deductible amount is based on the capital gains inclusion rate in effect at the time of disposition.

This deduction reduces net income, which in turn can increase benefits from refundable and non-refundable tax credits. Excess BIL can be carried back and applied against income of the previous three years, or carried forward and applied to income in the next six years.

Excess losses become normal capital losses in the seventh year, which can only be used to offset capital gains in the future.

To qualify for this special tax treatment the assets of the private small business corporation must have met certain criteria, including the following:

1. Substantially all of the assets must have been used in an active business in Canada.

2. This definition must have been met within the 12-month period before insolvency or bankruptcy.

3. In the case of losses due to the payment of a guarantee, the debt is not required to be repaid within 12 months of insolvency, but called within that period.

4. BILs must be reduced by any capital gains deduction claims in the past. When this rule is applied, disallowed amounts become normal capital losses.

● **Interest costs on assets of diminished value.** For interest costs to be deductible as a carrying charge on Line 221, there must be the potential for income from property (interest, dividends, rents, royalties or other income, but not including capital gains).

Special rules introduced in 1993 allow for the continuation of interest deductibility on outstanding loans where the income-producing source no longer exists (i.e., when there has been a significant decline in the value of the property). The portion that has been lost is "deemed" to continue to be used for income-producing purposes. This ensures that interest on the loan will continue to be deductible.

Source: Personal Tax Update Seminars *by Evelyn Jacks.*

Best of the Legal Tax Shelters

Most of the old-style tax shelters have passed into history—but there are still safe and legal ways to avoid or defer taxes.

Buy Your Own Home Tax-Free

If you have RRSP accumulations, you can tap into that capital to buy one of the best tax shelters—a tax-exempt principal residence—by withdrawing some of that money on a completely tax-free basis. Here are the rules:

● You have to be a first-time home buyer. This can include someone who has previously owned a home, but not in the year of withdrawal or any of the four preceding calendar years.

● You cannot withdraw more than $20,000. However, each spouse can make a withdrawal from their own RRSP to buy a home, so that a couple could conceivably withdraw $40,000 for these purposes between them.

● You cannot deduct and then withdraw funds contributed to an RRSP less than 90 days before the withdrawal.

● In general, all the funds withdrawn must be received in the same calendar year and Form T1036 must be used to make the withdrawal.

● You must have entered into a written agreement to acquire a home before applying to withdraw the funds, but may not have acquired it earlier than 30 days before receiving the withdrawals.

● You must use the funds to buy a home no later than October 1 of the year following the withdrawal.

● Withdrawals must be repaid equally within a 15-year period. These repayments must begin at least 60 days after the end of the second year following the first withdrawal. If the repayments are not made, the amount due is added to your income and is fully taxable. If you wish, you can repay the money at a faster. *Other ways to avoid or defer income include the following:*

Assets Held Outside Registered Funds

● **Hold capital gains producing assets** rather than interest-earning ones. Interest must be reported annually even if it is being earned on a compounding basis and not actually paid. Increases in the value of capital assets, on the other hand, need not be reported until disposition.

● **Capital gains.** Sell assets early in the next year rather than late this year to defer capital gains into the following tax year.

● **Capital loss.** Sell losers at the end of the current tax year if you have capital gains to offset, or if you'd like to offset capital gains that occurred in one of the prior three years.

● **Dividends.** Declare dividends from your small business corporation early in the new year to defer taxes to next year, unless you expect income to be much higher next year.

● **Buy labor-sponsored investment funds (LSIFs)** to receive federal (and in some jurisdictions, provincial) tax credits.

● **Fund universal life insurance policies** with tax savings from RRSPs or LSIFs and accumulate further tax-deferred income in those plans.

● **Turn nondeductible interest into deductible interest.** Average back into a bull market by arranging for an investment loan, backed by your home equity (always speak to your financial adviser about any risk you take and whether that fits into your financial planning goals, objectives and risk-tolerance levels).

● **Split and diversify income with your spouse.** Loan money to your spouse or common-law partner and have him or her invest the funds so that income will be taxed on that person's return. This will stay onside with the taxman if the loan bears interest at the prescribed rate and your spouse actually pays that interest to you within 30 days after the end of the calendar year. You'll have to report that interest as income on your return.

Try to have the lower-earning spouse receive income sources that are taxed more heavily—like interest—so

that your investments are diversified from a family unit, rather than individual, perspective.

Assets Held Within Registered Funds

● Always file a tax return to receive any refundable tax credits and tax refunds you are entitled to promptly, and to create RRSP contribution room.

● Always maximize your RRSP contribution room.

● Use RRSP tax savings to fund registered education savings plans (RESPs) for your children or grandchildren, and receive the Canada Education Savings Grant.

● Make an LSIF investment with some of the money within the self-directed RRSP and use the resulting tax credits to fund education savings or investments in disability or life insurance policies.

● Identify your tax savings from registered investments each year and invest them faithfully.

● Never overpay tax withholding at source or quarterly tax installments.

More Shelters

It's not necessary to resort to complicated or expensive shelter investments to reduce taxes.

Simpler strategies:

● **Maximize deductible interest.** Structure debt financing with a tax viewpoint. For example, if you intend to buy a car for personal use only and also wish to make a stock market investment, pay cash for the car and borrow for the investment. That makes your interest costs deductible. If you have a business, you can borrow to meet business costs—such as equipment purchases—while maintaining the amount of cash available for personal expenditures.

● **Also be vigilant about credit-card debt.** Pay it off quickly, if it's not deductible. If you must use credit, do so for business purposes only, so that the exorbitant fees and interest charges are deductible.

● **Home-based business.** A business run from your home—even as a sideline—offers major tax breaks. A sideline activity can also pay off personally by promoting professional advancement or a career change. *How to take advantage of this situation:*

1. Try out a new line of work by freelancing through a sideline, without risking a sudden career change.

2. Sideline consulting can help you network to gain valuable contacts.

● **Tax breaks.** Legitimate business expenses can be deductible even if they exceed your business income. Therefore, if you incur a loss during your business start-up, you can deduct it against other income, such as salary. And if your current operating losses exceed this year's income, the unapplied losses can be carried back and applied against income of the prior three years. *You may be able to deduct the following:*

● **Salaries paid to family members who work for you.** Canada Pension Plan premiums are *not* owed on salary paid to a child under age 18.

If a child receiving a salary is in a low tax bracket, the family's overall tax bill may be reduced. Remember that children can receive about $600 a month tax-free; more if they have RRSP contribution room.

Caution: Be sure the amount of salary is reasonable for the work done.

● **Home office,** including the cost of utilities, insurance, maintenance property taxes, interest and rent or depreciation.

To qualify for a deduction, the home office must be used exclusively for business purposes and be the principal place where you conduct the business, or a place where you meet clients or customers regularly.

To support business status for a home-based activity, you must demonstrate a genuine profit motive for engaging in it. You don't actually have to make a profit. The department recognizes that legitimate businesses suffer losses. But you must conduct the activity in a businesslike manner consistent with the goal of earning a profit—by keeping good books and records, a diary of business activities, a business chequing account, etc.

● **Make retirement plan contributions early.** Most people think of the deduction they get for a retirement plan contribution as its major tax benefit. But over the long run, tax deferral on the plan's compound investment returns may be even more valuable. Take advantage of this by making plan contributions as

> "Most people think of the deduction they get for a retirement plan contribution as its major tax benefit. But over the long run, tax deferral on the plan's compound investment returns may be even more valuable."

early in the year as possible instead of waiting until the last minute.

● **Withdraw tax-sheltered funds on a tax-efficient basis.** Remember that when tax-sheltered RRSP contributions are withdrawn, the full amount of the withdrawal must be added to income. Therefore, it is wise to split withdrawals over two taxation years, if possible (take half in December and half in January), and to make the withdrawal in a year of low earnings.

This works, for example, when a mother takes leave to stay home with her small child and withdraws some RRSP savings to tide the family over until she works again. Also, seniors should withdraw RRSP accumulations in the low-earner's hands first, if possible. Finally, if the rate of tax on unused RRSP accumulations will be higher after death of the second surviving spouse, consider withdrawing more while living. Generally, in that case, all savings must be added back into income on the final return of the deceased.

● **Make gifts to low-tax-bracket family members.** Attribution-free gifts can be made to your adult children or retired parents; provided that you record accrued increases in value of the property and income earned up to the date of transfer. By giving income-producing properties to family members who are in low (or zero) tax brackets, you can shift income into their tax brackets and reduce the family's overall tax bill. However, tax consequences for the donor may result if the gift is given to minor children, who reinvest it and produce investment earnings. To avoid the attribution rules in this case, the earnings must be in the form of capital gains income. Interest and dividends unfortunately are attributed back to the original owner and taxed in his or her hands. When money or other assets are transferred to a spouse, most earnings will be attributed back to the donor, unless business profits result from the reinvesting of the funds, or a bona fide loan is drawn up with payment of interest to the donor at least 30 days after the end of the year.

Source: Evelyn Jacks, president, Evelyn Jacks Productions, Inc.

Compensation Loopholes

The compensation package you get from your employer may include some form of deferred compensation whereby money is put away for you but is not available until some time in the future. This form of compensation boosts your pay and offers significant tax advantages.

Loopholes

Your employer contributes money to a retirement plan on your behalf, or to a deferred profit sharing plan, the money accumulates, together with earnings thereon, on a tax-deferred basis. You don't pay a current tax on the contribution or on the interest the money earns. No tax is due until you receive a distribution of money from the plan. Other benefits arising out of employment that are tax-free to the employee include an employer's contribution to:

- **Group sickness and accident insurance.**
- **Supplemental unemployment benefit plan.**
- **Noncash awards for employee suggestions.**

It's possible to reap some great rewards for being an exemplary thinker in your organization; however, if the award is received in cash, it's taxable. The employer is allowed to give two noncash awards in the value of up to $500 as an award, prize or for birthday, wedding or other special occasion gifts without assessing a taxable benefit to you.

Other work-related, employer-paid benefits that can be received by the employee on a tax-free basis include the following payments by the employer:

- **A plan whose sole purpose is to provide education** to improve the work skills of the employees.
- **Reasonable traveling allowances** (those based on a per-kilometer log of travel for employment purposes).
- **Traveling allowances received by part-time teachers** or professors who must travel to designated post-secondary institutions that are at least 80 kilometers away from the employee's residence, using the shortest route available.
- **Allowances received to send an employee's children** away to school because the work location is not near a suitable school, are not taxable. This can include transportation and tuition-fee payments.
- **Parking costs paid for by the employer.**

- **Employer-provided child care.**
- **Employer-provided computers.**
- **Employer-provided cell phone use.**
- **Disability-related employment benefits.** The cost of transportation, parking or a personal attendant for a disabled employee are not taxable to that employee.

Other perks of employment are taxable, but may provide for an interesting elevation in your standard of living:

- **Forgiveness of employee debt.** When a loan provided to an employee by the employer is forgiven, the amount forgiven is added to the employee's income. However, you as the employee have still had access to the funds in the meantime—and perhaps have written off the value of the employment benefit as a carrying charge if the loan was used for investment purposes. Therefore, this results in the deferral of income from employment into the future.
- **Employer-provided vehicle.** A company car that is leased or purchased for use by the employee generates a taxable benefit to that employee; however, that benefit may be reduced if personal use is less than 10% or 12,000 kilometers per year.
- **Frequent-flyer points.** When an employee earns frequent-flyer points traveling for his or her employer, any points used for personal travel will become taxable at the time they are used. However, the value used is the lowest equivalent ticket price for the flights in question. So with the advent of "discount carriers," the tax on this benefit can be quite minimal.

How to Pass Your RRSP on to Your Spouse and Children

Withdrawals from an RRSP are taxable whenever money is taken out of them during your lifetime. Therefore, it is important to assess the best time to make those withdrawals.

If you don't need the money, you can opt to continue to accrue the principal and earnings on a tax-deferred basis until the end of the year in which you reach the age of 69. The accumulations must then be converted to either a registered retirement income fund (RRIF) or an annuity to provide for taxable withdrawals.

DIRECT ROLLOVERS OF SEVERANCE PAYMENTS

In addition to the normal RRSP contribution limit (room), taxpayers in receipt of severance or job termination payments may transfer certain amounts of those payments to an RRSP to defer taxes. The direct transfers will not generate the requirement to report the income and offsetting deductions, and no tax withholding is required. However, if the amounts are paid out in cash during the year, the taxpayer does have until 60 days after the year-end to make the allowable RRSP contribution and receive an off-setting deduction to the income that will have to be reported. Any taxes withheld during the year would also be reported as a credit at that time.

If possible, try to negotiate a direct rollover of qualifying amounts before accepting the severance package. Qualifying retiring allowances for an RRSP rollover are the lesser or the following:

● **The amount received.**

● **The total of the following:**

1. For the period prior to 1989. $3,500 per year of service. However, this is reduced to $2,000 for each year in which the employer's contributions to a pension plan or deferred profit-sharing plan for the employee vested in that employee.

2. For the period from 1988 to 1996, $2,000 per year of service.

3. After 1996, no rollovers are allowed on any service.

When the annuitant dies and leaves a spouse or other qualified dependent (which could be a minor child), the amounts may be rolled over to that person on a tax-free basis. Amounts withdrawn by the survivor beneficiary are taxable. If that person then later dies with accumulations in the plan, the remaining amounts are fully taxable before distribution to other beneficiaries.

Those who are single and know that their tax rate on the accumulations will be higher upon death than it is on smaller amounts of income withdrawn now, should consider withdrawing funds and paying the tax during their lifetimes. The amounts can be reinvested in non-registered investments or given to relatives as an "early inheritance." Reinvestment in those relatives' hands may result in earnings taxed at lower rates. Or if the relatives themselves have RRSP contribution room, the amounts will serve as a continuing tax shelter.

So the best way to fund an RRSP for your spouse or child, or to transfer your RRSP accumulations to that person, during your lifetime or at death is to consider the following:

● **Give new tax-paid money to the dependent to be used to buy their own RRSPs.** They must, however, have the required earned income to do so.

● **Make an RRSP contribution in the name of a spouse.** It is possible to make such an RRSP contribution—which has significant income-splitting advantages—but in this case withdrawals will come back to haunt you if they are made within three years of the last spousal contribution. If the time limit is met, or if the spouse uses the accumulations to create a registered retirement income fund (RRIF), subsequent withdrawals will be taxed in his or her hands.

Note: In the case of the RRIF, the withdrawals cannot exceed the "minimum amount" requirement during the three-year restricted period or the attribution rules will be invoked.

● **Plan for a tax-free rollover of your RRSP/RRIF.** Accumulations to your spouse or qualifying dependent upon your death and designate the beneficiaries both in the plan and in your will.

Source: Evelyn Jacks, president, Evelyn Jacks Productions, Inc. and best-selling author, Tax Secrets for Tough Times *and* Make Sure It's Deductible, *published by McGraw-Hill Ryerson.*

Dealing With the CCRA

3

What the CCRA Already Knows About You

Canadian residents must report income from all sources in Canadian funds on their tax returns. For most individual taxpayers, this income includes cash, barter and receivables acquired from January 1 to December 31. Keep this fundamental requirement in mind as you read this chapter.

The Canada Customs and Revenue Agency (CCRA) gets certain income information from third parties and matches this to you in its computers. Stay a step ahead and avoid tax refund processing delays by carefully reporting on your tax return all of your income, including what the CCRA already knows about you. (You should receive from the third parties—employers, financial institutions, etc.— copies of all the information that they send to the tax department. Generally, where investment amounts are less than $50, you will not receive a slip, but you'll still have to report the income.) *What the CCRA knows, and how:*

● **Your employment income.** The CCRA knows, of course, if you have employment income. An employer must report this payment to the income and employment benefits to CCRA on the T4 Slip. Total income will include taxable benefits and other details required to complete your return. For example, it will tell how much of your income was from commissions, which will be your reminder to deduct offsetting expenses elsewhere on the return. Also included on this slip is information that will generate nonrefundable tax credits for medical expenses (private health insurance premiums) or charitable donations, deductions for union dues, carrying charges (from low- or no-interest loans used for non-registered investment purposes), moving expenses, employment expenses, as well as northern-residence deductions, stock options and shares deductions, or home relocation deductions. Remember to claim the GST/HST rebate for any tax-deductible employment expenses including union dues.

● **Your company pension, retirement, annuity and other income** (including scholarships, fellowships and bursaries) listed on a T4A slip.

● **Your public pension benefits from the Canada Pension Plan** listed on Form T4(A)P, including retirement, survivor, death, disability and orphan benefits.

● **Your Old Age Security benefits listed on the T4A(OAS).**

● **Your withdrawals from RRSPs listed on Form T4RSP.**

● **Your withdrawals from RRIFs listed on Form T4RIF.**

● **Your investment income listed on T3 and T5 slips.** These slips are issued if amounts earned in the non-registered accounts are $50 or more.

Important: Make sure the reports you receive agree with your records.

Trap: Interest income must be reported to the CCRA even though you have not received it yet. The annual accrual method of reporting income must be used for all compounding investments, such as CSBs, CPBs, GICs and strip bonds, which means that every year the amount earned by the investment must be reported as taxable income. This is true even if you do not receive a T slip like a T3, T5 or T600 from the financial institution, which must issue the slips only if interest exceeds $50. You must use money from other sources to pay the tax on that accrued income. However, when the investment matures, only the interest for that final year is reported. Therefore, over the course of the investment, the income and its tax consequences are averaged.

● **Your employment insurance benefits listed on Form T4E.**

● **Your social benefits, like worker's compensation or social assistance, listed on Form T5007.**

● **Your statement of securities transactions on Form T5008.**

● **Your partnership income listed on Form T5013.**

● **Your Canada Savings Bonds interest on Form T600.**

● **Your subcontracting income on construction jobs on Form T5018 titled Information of Contract Payments**

● **Tax-refund income.** The CCRA will report interest that has been credited to you while you wait for a tax refund. Because this amount is shown on your notice of assessment and is taxable to you, be sure to remember to claim it as interest income. Starting with the tax years after 1999, the CCRA will offset any interest it owes you with interest you owe them from a previous year's assessment and send you the

Tax Return Completion Checklist

In dealings with the CCRA, no news is good news. More precisely, in this case, no mail is good news.

Every time the CCRA sends a letter to a taxpayer, it means that someone within the agency has taken another look at the return in question. Every look taken increases the chance that "problems" will come to light (if they haven't already). There are a number of simple steps you can take to minimize the risk of ongoing activity with your tax return.

✔ **Before filing, make sure your return is complete.** Check to see that all necessary forms and schedules are present and accounted for. This includes any and all attachments. For example, if you donate common stock to a charitable organization, you must attach certain information regarding the gift. Attach all supporting documents to your return securely. Missing pages generate correspondence.

✔ **Make sure the return is accurate.** Check, double-check and recheck all arithmetic. Failing to do this is the most common source of tax-filing errors.

✔ **Make sure your reporting is consistent with the information the CCRA receives.** For example, if you have invested in BCE and Royal Bank stock through XYZ Brokerage, your return should list dividends paid to you by XYZ, not BCE or Royal Bank, because the CCRA will receive a reporting slip from XYZ.

✔ **Double-check to see that the return is signed in all the required places and by all necessary parties.**

✔ **Finally, file your return on time.** By all means request an extension if you need one, otherwise mail your return well before the deadline. In the event you must file at the last minute, use registered mail or courier delivery in order to have evidence of timely filing.

net amount, if any, which is reported as income by you.

Tax break: Gambling winnings or other windfall income is not subject to tax in Canada.

Other Income the CCRA Knows About

- **Distributions from pension and profit-sharing plans.**
- **Tax shelter participation.**
- **Income from your small business based on your GST remittances.**
- **Subcontracting income from a construction site.**

Source: Tax Update Seminars by Evelyn Jacks, Evelyn Jacks Productions, Inc., Winnipeg, Man.

Unanswered Questions and Incorrect Returns Can Cause Problems

It always pays to file a tax return that is as complete and audit-proof as possible and it is most important to hang on to all supporting documentation. Income tax returns which invoke unanswered questions may prompt a request for more information from the tax department. Fortunately, the statute of limitations for audit requests by the CCRA is limited to three years—the current filing year and two years back—except when CCRA suspects fraud, in which case they can go as far back as the record retention rules require. That means you are required to hang on to your tax records for six years from the year in which you receive your notice of assessment for a particular tax year. You may, however, be required to hang on to your tax records longer than this, if required by the minister responsible for the CCRA.

Most unanswered questions simply require the submission of receipts or clarifications to your claims. However, incomplete or incorrect returns can delay refunds, result in interest charges and call attention to your return. If a question doesn't seem to apply to you (i.e., "Do you have any foreign bank accounts?"), just answer "no"—but do answer all requests from the CCRA for further information promptly. Never procrastinate or bury the letter in panic. Things can only get worse if you do.

When Is It Safe to Ignore Your Tax-Filing Deadline?

The short answer to this question: Never. There are many reasons you should always file a tax return every year, on time.

Most Canadians are required to file a tax return by April 30, for the tax year ending December 31 the year before. If you have a balance due on April 30, filing late will result in a penalty of 5% of the unpaid amount plus 1% per month for a period of 12 months. Repeat offenders are almost guaranteed to pay more if they fail to file on time again within a three-year period: 10% of the unpaid amounts, plus 2% per month for up to 20 months. In fact, for most tax-filing delinquents, the interest and penalties can add up to be a much bigger problem than the taxes over a period of time. Interest compounds and accrues daily at a rate that is four percentage points higher than the rate paid on Canada Treasury bills for the previous quarter.

Those who report income or losses from an unincorporated small business may file by June 15 without fearing a late filing penalty. (This is unwise, however, if you owe money to the tax department when you do file, because interest will be charged from May 1st onward in those cases.)

Other reasons to file on time:

● **You get your refund faster.** And if the CCRA actually owes you money, you won't earn any interest on the amount until 45 days after you file the return. The taxman is smart, though . . . the department tries to get the return processed before this deadline. This means that if you file two years late and the department owes you a refund of $3,000, you'll receive no interest on the overpayment you made if the return is processed within 45 days of your filing date. Why give the tax department an interest-free loan?

TRACKING DOWN YOUR REFUND

If it has been at least 10 weeks since you filed your tax return and you still haven't received your refund, you can do something about it.

Step 1: Get out the copy you kept of your tax return. Be sure you know your Social Insurance Number, your filing status, the exact amount of the refund you claimed and the service center to which you sent your return.

Step 2: Call the CCRA's automated refund-information service to find out the current status of your refund. Use the number for your area listed in the Tax Guide (1-800-959-8281). This has automated responses 24 hours a day or agents from 8:15 a.m. to 5:00 p.m. During February to April, agents are available until 10:00 p.m. and on Saturdays, from 9:00 a.m. to 1:00 p.m.

You may also access information about your refund, GSTC and Canada Child Tax Benefit on the Internet. Go to T.I.P.S. (http://www.ccra-adrc.gc.ca/eservices/tipsonline/menu-e.html).

Step 3: If there's still a problem, drop down to the local tax services office or write to the CCRA tax service center where you filed your return. Include your name, address, Social Insurance Number, the tax year involved and an explanation of your problem. Keep copies of the letters.

Step 4: If you've done all of the above and still haven't received your refund, it's time to call the CCRA's Problems Resolution Office (PRO).

The telephone number of the local PRO can be obtained from the local CCRA district office. To get help from the PRO, you must show that you first tried to resolve your problem through normal channels. Have a record of the names of the CCRA representatives you've talked with, along with copies of all your correspondence with the CCRA. Shortly after a PRO officer is assigned to your case, you'll get either your refund or a full explanation of what's holding it up.

● **Filing may qualify you for refundable tax credits.** Even if you have no taxable income, it could pay to file a tax return to receive refundable tax credits throughout the year. This includes two from the federal government: the Canada Child Tax Benefit (CCTB) and the Goods and Services Tax Credit (GSTC). There are also refundable tax credits available in some provinces.

● **You will preserve tax breaks for use in other tax years.** It is important to record capital and non-capital losses, unused RRSP contributions, moving expenses, unused home workspace expenses, unused capital cost allowances, charitable donations, medical expenses, tuition and education credits and student loan interest amounts for use in "carryover years." It is possible that some of these provisions may be applied back to recover refunds of taxes in the prior three years (this is the case for capital and noncapital losses) or carried forward to offset income in the future.

● **You will avoid unexpected late filing penalties.** It may turn out that you miscalculated, and actually owe taxes instead of having a refund coming. In that case, you'll be charged penalties and interest for late filing.

● **You preserve your options under the "Fairness Provisions."** If you suffer a severe hardship in the future, you may have to file your tax return late. Such hardships include serious illness, death in your immediate family, or the catastrophic impact of a natural disaster. In these circumstances, you may apply for leniency from the CCRA under its "Fairness Package." The committee that reviews your request may grant you an extension for filing and/or waive penalties and interest. Moreover, it will take into account whether you have otherwise been a model tax-filing citizen.

● **You will avoid gross negligence and tax-evasion penalties.** Procrastinators beware: don't push your luck with the CCRA.

● **If the CCRA concludes that you are willfully refusing to file a return,** you may be hit with further penalties. Those who are found to be grossly negligent face additional penalties of 50% of the unpaid tax, plus the late-filing penalty and the interest that continues to compound and accrue. Tax evaders face penalties of up to 200% of the unpaid tax, plus all the

other penalties and interest and/or jail time. So, if you owe, pay the tax. It's much cheaper to file on time, and causes a lot less stress.

Source: *Evelyn Jacks, president, Evelyn Jacks Productions, Inc. and best-selling author of* Tax Secrets for Tough Times *and* Make Sure It's Deductible.

What You Can Do to Eliminate Late-Filing Penalties

Penalties for filing your tax return late without getting a valid extension may be forgiven by the CCRA if you can show that you had reasonable cause for filing late.

Although the CCRA is not required to waive late-filing penalties, it may do so when convinced that the late filing was not the taxpayer's fault. Among the excuses the CCRA may accept as cause for late filing:

● **Death or serious illness** of the taxpayer or a member of his or her immediate family that results in an inability to file taxes.

● **Unavoidable absence of the taxpayer.**

● **Destruction of records** in a fire, natural disaster, or other casualty.

● **Delay or mistakes caused by erroneous information** given the taxpayer by the CCRA.

● **A timely request for needed tax forms** or an adjustment to your return wasn't answered on a timely basis by the CCRA.

● **The return was filed on time but was sent to the wrong CCRA service center.**

Bottom line: You have a relatively good chance of avoiding a late-filing penalty and/or interest charges if you can convince the CCRA that the delay was not your fault, and you have otherwise been a model tax-filing citizen.

Excuses That Worked

Taxfilers have avoided penalties and interest charges successfully in the following instances:

● **When the CCRA took too long to process** a request to include a missed T5 slip in income.

● **When the CCRA sent out the wrong form** requested by the taxpayer.

● **When a farm bankruptcy,** resulting from illness of the farmer and a subsequent seizure and sale of farm assets, caused a capital gain due to foreclosure.

● **When a taxpayer was duped by a dishonest tax accountant** and could show he took all steps to file on time, inform himself of his filing obligations and correct errors made by the accountant on the return when he found out about them.

● **When the taxpayer suffered a major depression** and couldn't file due to his mental incapacity.

● **When the taxpayer faced the death of her spouse** and couldn't file on time because of his terminal illness.

Source: Evelyn Jacks, president, Evelyn Jacks Productions, Inc. and author of Tax Secrets for Tough Times and Make Sure It's Deductible.

> " Suppose you discover, about a year after filing your return, that you omitted a sizable deduction or credit. You immediately file an adjustment request and claim for a refund, only to find out that this triggers an audit. The good news is that your claim will likely be allowed in full by the auditor, assuming you have the supporting documentation and your circumstances fit the eligibility criteria. "

What Happens When Your Tax Professional Forgets to File?

If you sign your tax return in time, and for some reason your tax advisor doesn't file it on time, who's responsible? You are. It's your responsibility to see that the return is filed and on time. Even though it's your advisor's fault, you pay the penalty and the interest. So, make sure you deal with an advisor that has a written guarantee of service to cover your costs in those cases.

Never Let the CCRA Apply a Refund to Another Year's Tax Bill

The CCRA can use your current year's tax refund to offset taxes you owe in a prior year, or if you are delinquent in making child support payments, your refund can be reallocated to your ex-spouse for those purposes. So be sure you stay current with

your obligations, but if you aren't, don't commit your refund for other purposes.

Avoid Tax Refunds If You Can

Don't use your tax refund as a long-term savings strategy! Plan your affairs all year long so as to pay only the correct amount of tax and not a cent more. Maximize your RRSP deductions, minimize source deductions and quarterly installments, and make your money work directly for you, not the taxman.

Unclaimed Tax Refunds

The CCRA is sitting on millions of dollars in unclaimed tax refunds, and some of that money may be yours or belong to a member of your family. This money is sometimes left unclaimed because the addresses listed under taxpayers' social insurance numbers are wrong or out of date. As a result, income tax refunds, Canada Child Tax Benefits and GST credit cheques are returned to the government. Be sure to claim them promptly! Those most likely to be affected: Anyone who has moved during the year; a surviving spouse who filed a joint return now qualifies for the GST credit; those who marry after filing their tax returns and change their names and addresses without giving notice to the CCRA; and those taxpayers who have just become separated or divorced and moved out of province. Individuals recently separated or divorced qualify for refundable tax credits for the first time because of revised net income levels. These refunds can be initiated immediately upon the change of marital status.

Suggestion: If you move, or someone dies in your family, notify the CCRA immediately to report your change of address and marital status. This will ensure you receive all the tax benefits available throughout the year.

Can a Taxpayer Penalize the CCRA for Lateness?

Question: I filed my tax return in February and got a refund in May—but no interest. Does the government owe me interest on the money?

Answer: No, the government must only pay interest to you if it sends your refund later than 45 days after the date the return was due—April 30—not 45 days from the date you filed it. But if it doesn't get the refund out by June 15, it has to pay interest all the way back to April 30.

Source: Personal Tax Update Seminars *by Evelyn Jacks, president, Evelyn Jacks Productions, Inc. and author of Canadian best-sellers* Tax Secrets for Tough Times *and* Make Sure It's Deductible, *published by McGraw-Hill Ryerson, Whitby, ON L1N 9B6.*

Best Time to File for a Refund

Suppose you discover, about a year after filing your return, that you omitted a sizable deduction or credit. You immediately file an adjustment request and claim for a refund, only to find out that this triggers an audit. The good news is that your claim will likely be allowed in full by the auditor, assuming you have the supporting documentation and your circumstances fit the eligibility criteria. The bad news is that during the audit the auditor may probe through other areas of your return and request more information. If your proof of claim is weak, you could end up owing the CCRA additional tax and interest.

So it always makes sense to review prior filed returns for errors or omissions. You can adjust most federal provisions all the way back to 1985 and recover your missed tax preferences. And if you find that you mistakenly overstated deductions or understated income, be sure and let the CCRA know. Voluntary compliance will ensure you aren't charged with gross negligence or tax-evasion penalties.

Problem for the CCRA: The limitation period that applies to the department for reassessment of your tax-filing claims is relatively short: generally, it is the current year and the two immediately prior years. The department can go back further if they suspect fraud, but because you are only required to keep tax records for six years from the date your return was assessed or reassessed, there is a limit to the taxman's reach.

How to Answer When the CCRA Writes

The CCRA sends out thousands of notices demanding more information and/or more money to taxpayers each year. By responding shrewdly to such notices, taxpayers can often reduce the amount they owe—and sometimes pay nothing.

Keys to success:

● **Never blindly pay what the notice claims you owe without checking the facts.** Never assume that the bill is correct just because it came from the CCRA. It's imperative that you review the notice, line by line, and understand how the tax department arrived at each figure. Only after you do this will you be in a position to respond effectively. It is possible that the CCRA is wrong.

● **Always ask that penalties be excused.** It can't hurt to file an appeal for fairness if you have suffered a severe personal hardship that resulted in tax-filing delinquency. Or, if you are the subject of interpretation of a "grey area," you can file an appeal with the chief of appeals at the tax services office with a notice of objection. You may wish to get some professional help with this.

To get penalties dropped: You must show there was "reasonable cause" (that is, a good excuse) for your alleged misdeed such as misreporting income, filing late, paying late, etc. *Encouraging news:* Most taxes in dispute are settled with the CCRA before the matter goes to court.

If You Receive a Notice

● **Answer promptly**—within one week of the day that you receive the notice—regardless of the deadline specified (usually 30 days out). *Reason:* The earlier you respond to the notice, the less likely is the possibility that you will receive computer-generated follow-up notices and that correspondence between you and the CCRA will cross in the mail. Ask for an extension in supplying the information required if you can't do this in 30 days. Most such requests are granted. (*Editor's note:* If you don't understand the notice, you may contact the CCRA by phone. In such cases, it's probably best for you to obtain professional help beforehand.)

● **Keep your letter succinct.** Just stick to the facts. *Reason:* Brevity and directness increase the chances that the matter will be settled quickly and not turn into a full-scale investigation.

● **Back up your response with documentation.** For instance, if you are claiming that you already paid the amount of tax that the CCRA says you owe, attach a photocopy of your canceled cheque (both sides) proving the tax payment. Always keep copies of all documents sent in to the CCRA.

● **Mail your response by registered mail,** return receipt requested. Keep the receipt in case the CCRA "loses" your letter. Or, if you drop the information off at the tax department, get the receiving clerk to provide you with a receipt.

Shrewd Answers

Types of CCRA notices and letters of response:

● **Penalty notices** for filing a tax return late, paying taxes late or failing to pay the correct amount of estimated taxes.

Address to: The Fairness Committee at the CCRA. The complete address for the tax-services office closest to you can be found on the CCRA website (www.ccra-adrc.gc.ca/contact/tso-e.html).

Sample response:

To Whom It May Concern:

Re: Taxpayer's name, SIN and the tax year in question:

I am in receipt of your notice of assessment (or reassessment) dated April 26, a copy of which is enclosed. This states that a late-filing penalty has been assessed in the amount of $561. I would like you to consider, as outlined under the Fairness Package, waiving that penalty and any accrued interest charges, given that I believe that reasonable cause exists.

Although I had obtained an extension that permitted me to file my tax return up until October 15, it was impossible to obtain the information needed to complete my return until the middle of November. During this time, my husband suffered an

aneurism and passed away two weeks later. As a result, I have been dealing with the funeral and other details in the aftermath of this shock. However, I have compiled the information and now submit it to you on November 20. The missing information was a business statement that reflects the amount of income I earned as a partner in ABC limited partnership. Unfortunately, I had forgotten about this investment and failed to include it in my income when I originally filed the return. In addition, while searching for this documentation, I realized that I had not filed for carrying charges and medical expenses for the tax year in question and, therefore, request that these items be included in the reassessment.

Because the late filing was caused by circumstances beyond my control, I hope that you will waive the late-filing penalty and interest.

● **You-owe-us-more-tax notices,** which indicate that you made a mathematical error on your return, or that the CCRA did not give you credit for tax withheld or for estimated tax payments.

Address to: The Tax Services Office.

Sample response:

To Whom It May Concern:

Re: Taxpayer's name, SIN and the tax year in question:

I am in receipt of your May 12 notice of assessment, a copy of which is enclosed. This indicates you have no record of my tax return.

Enclosed is a copy of my return, which was filed on or about April 15, 2002. Also enclosed is a copy of both sides of my canceled cheque for the balance of tax paid with that return.

Please process the return and reverse any interest that may have resulted from the misplacement of this return at your office.

● **Unreported-income notices that demand additional tax,** interest and a penalty because—the CCRA claims—income paid to you was not reported on your return.
Address to: The Tax Services Office.

To Whom It May Concern:

Re: Taxpayer's name, SIN and the tax year in question:

I am in receipt of your May 3 notice of reassessment, a copy of which is attached. Please be advised that your notice of reassessment is incorrect.

Enclosed is a copy of a corrected T5 slip issued by XYZ bank indicating $3,124 of taxable interest. The information previously furnished was incorrect.

Please correct your records.

● **No-return notices that indicate that the CCRA has missed** giving you credit for installment payments made.
Address to: The Tax Services Office.

To Whom It May Concern:

Re: Taxpayer's name, SIN and the tax year in question:

Enclosed is a copy of your notice dated May 15, which indicates an amount due of $300.

Your notice fails to give me credit for estimated tax payments that I made during the past year. Enclosed are photocopies of both sides of my canceled cheques for payment of estimated tax. Accordingly, no money is owed.

Thank you for your prompt attention to this matter.

How to Avoid Getting a Notice

Some provisions on the tax return receive more preassessment attention than others. To avoid getting a notice from the tax department, it is wisest to give an accurate account of amounts when reporting claims, charges and expenses. Here are some examples of these provisions that the taxman will scrutinize:

● **Unreported amounts** employment and/or investment income T slips.

● **Carrying charges** that are higher than those claimed in the past.

● **Moving expenses.**

● **Child-care expenses.**

● **Large amounts** for medical expenses.

● **Large operating losses** from a small business.

● **Auto expenses.**

● **Home office expenses.**

● **Business investment losses.**

How to Answer Notices About Unreported Income

The CCRA mails millions of computer-generated notices of reassessment to taxpayers whose returns fail to show investment income such as dividends or interest income. Be aware the CCRA will discover the oversight through banks and financial institutions which also report on such earnings. In such cases, taxpayers will get a notice showing a recalculated tax on this income, plus interest charges.

How should taxpayers handle such notices? What can they learn from these notices that will help in preparing future returns? Here's the procedure:

Step 1: Study the notice carefully and define the problem. Discover precisely which item, or items, of income the CCRA says you did not report.

Step 2: Review the copy of your return and the relevant T slips. Determine whether the CCRA notice is right or wrong. Never automatically write out a cheque for the amount the CCRA says you owe. The notice could be dead wrong—many are.

Step 3: Answer the notice, in writing, within the time limit given—usually 30 days. Write to the CCRA service office at the address given in the notice.

● **If the CCRA is right,** and you did accidentally fail to report an item of income, pay the tax and interest. If for some reason a gross negligence penalty was assessed (this would be unusual), request that the penalty and interest thereon be waived.

CCRA Service Office
City, Province
Attention: Fairness Committee
      Re: Taxpayer's name, SIN and the tax
year in question
To Whom It May Concern:
      In response to your notice, a copy of which is attached, you will find enclosed a cheque payable to Receiver General for Canada in the amount of $x, consisting of tax of $y and interest of $z.
      The item in question was inadvertently omitted from our return as filed under the following circumstances:
(Describe the circumstances that were out of your control.)
      It is contended that this constitutes reasonable cause for the inadvertent omission of this item. It is respectfully requested that the negligence penalty assessed in your notice be abated.

● **Either you did not report the income,** or the notice is wrong. Review the notice and your return to discover the cause of the discrepancy. One of several things may have happened, and the CCRA may not have the correct information. Or, the T slips may

have been right, but you reported the income incorrectly. You can correct such oversights as follows:

Sample response:

To Whom It May Concern:
      In response to your notice, a copy of which is enclosed, I am submitting the following in explanation of the alleged omissions.
      1. The dividend of $1,200 reported on my return as being received from General Motors should have been reported as being received from my broker. A copy of my Schedule 3 and supporting documentation is enclosed.
(Circle the item where it appears on your Schedule 3 to show that you reported it.)

Lesson: Report dividends from stock held by your broker as received from the broker, not from the company. That's how the T5 slip will show them.

      2. The dividend of $40 from ABC Funds was reported as interest income of $40 from ABC. It should have been reported as a dividend. A copy of my Schedule 4 is enclosed. *(Circle the item.)*

Lesson: Report the income as it is reported to the CCRA on the fund's T3 or T5 slip. If no slip was received because the amount was under $50, contact the mutual fund company or your broker to determine the correct income classification.

      3. Interest of $600 from XYZ bank was on an account owned jointly by myself and my brother. I properly reported only one half of the interest—$300, as we both equally contributed principal to the account. A copy of my Schedule 4 is enclosed.
Lesson: Report interest from a joint account as follows: "Interest, XYZ bank, $600, less amount reported by others, $300. Net amount: $300."

      4. Interest of $500 from XYZ bank was reported on my return as $100, per the amended T5 slip, a copy of which is enclosed.

Lesson: Review all T5s when you receive them. Immediately request corrected copies of any that are wrong. Report the correct information on your return, and include the amended slip in your documentation. If the CCRA doesn't pick up the correction, you'll have it in your files should you need it.

5. Interest of $2,140 from DEF bank was nontaxable income to the recipient—a minor child who received the principal as part of a personal injury award.

How to end the letter:

If there are any further questions, please contact me.

● **If you get a second notice that seems to have ignored your letter:**

Sample response:

To Whom It May Concern:

In response to your notice dated March 28, we received a similar notice dated February 23. We answered that notice with the enclosed letter. It would appear that our response was not received in time to prevent the second request for payment from being issued. *(Enclose photocopies of both notices and a copy of your original letter.)*

Please adjust your records.

Source: Evelyn Jacks, president, Evelyn Jacks Productions, Inc. and best-selling author of Tax Secrets for Tough Times and Make Sure It's Deductible.

Some Excuses That Work and Some That Don't

Taxpayers who face penalties for misfiling returns or misreporting income will do the best they can to come up with a good explanation. Some excuses work—others don't.

Some Excuses That Work With the CCRA

● **Reliance on misleading advice** from a CCRA employee or publication. If the advice came from an employee, you must show that it was his or her job to advise taxpayers correctly and that you provided him or her with all the facts.

● **Misleading advice from a tax professional can excuse a mistake,** if you fully disclosed the facts to this adviser. You must also show that he or she was a competent professional, experienced in tax matters.

● **Lost or unavailable records will excuse a mistake,** if the loss wasn't the taxpayer's fault and a genuine attempt is made to recover or reconstruct the records.

● **Severe hardship, including incapacity of a key person,** can be a legitimate excuse. *Examples:* Serious illness of the taxpayer or a death in his or her immediate family.

Some Excuses That Don't Work With the CCRA

● **Pleading ignorance** or misunderstanding of the law generally does not excuse a mistake that appears on your tax return.

● **Someone else slipped up.** You are personally responsible for filing your tax return correctly. You can't delegate that responsibility to anyone else. Therefore, if your accountant or lawyer files late, you pay the penalty.

● **Personal problems don't carry much weight with the CCRA.** For example, don't expect to avoid a penalty by pleading severe emotional strain that was brought on by overspending or lack of budgeting on your part.

Source: Tax Update Seminars by Evelyn Jacks, president, Evelyn Jacks Productions, Inc. and best-selling author of Tax Secrets for Tough Times and Make Sure It's Deductible, published by McGraw-Hill Ryerson, Whitby, ON L1N 9B6.

Methods of Appeal

Most taxpayers don't understand their appeal options when they receive a CCRA notice of assessment or reassessment. (You will find these options summarized in the chart on the next page.)

How to Take Advantage of CCRA Mistakes

The tax department can make mistakes on a reassessment of your tax return if they don't know all the facts, or if its employee(s) have erred. In that case, the reassessment will be reversed and the taxpayer should end up in the same position as if the return was filed correctly in the first place.

The CCRA, however, has substantial powers under the Income Tax Act, especially as it relates to the returns of the self-employed. The following sections of the act give this power:

● **Under Section 152(7),** the CCRA has the legal power not to accept your tax return as filed and may make its own assessment of the amount it believes you owe.

● **Section 152(8)** makes the assumption that the CCRA is correct in its assessments, unless those assessments are challenged by the taxpayer.

● **Under Section 18(1) (a) and (h)** the CCRA may question whether an outlay was made to incur income from a business or property, and whether the expenses were really personal or living expenses of the taxpayer.

It is, therefore, important for all taxpayers to understand that they, not the CCRA, bear the "burden of proof." However, if the CCRA alleges fraud, the burden shifts to the tax department to prove that there was intent to defraud the government and commit a crime.

● **How to meet the burden of proof.** To win a tax audit, the taxpayer must not only have the

METHOD OF APPEAL	BASIC PARAMETERS
1. Informal objection	When you perceive a mistake has been made in the initial assessment of your return, have your tax adviser write to the CCRA to request an adjustment. If the CCRA refuses to make the adjustment, and you still believe they are incorrect, contact your tax professional immediately to discuss further options.
2. Notice of objection	This is a formal objection to the chief of appeals at the local tax services office. It must be filed within one year after the taxpayer's filing due date or 90 days after the day of the mailing of the notice of assessment, whichever is later. You may indicate in this notice that you wish to appeal directly to the Tax Court of Canada.
3. Appeals to the Tax Court of Canada	An appeal may be made after the minister has confirmed the assessment or reassessed, or within 90 days after the service of a notice of objection to which no reply has been received. This court has an informal procedure, for federal taxes in dispute of $12,000 or less, and a general procedure for amounts over this, which requires the services of a lawyer. This court may dispose of the appeal by either dismissing it or allowing it in whole or part.
4. Appeals to Federal Court of Appeal	If you have lost an appeal at the tax court level, you have—under informal procedures—30 days from the date the decision was mailed to you or your representative to appeal to the federal court. A lost case under the general procedure may be appealed to the federal court within 30 days from the date on which the judge signs the decision. The months of July and August are omitted; so if the decision date was June 30, the taxpayer would have until September 30 to file the appeal.
5. Appeals to the Supreme Court of Canada	Appeals to the Supreme Court of Canada require the granting of permission to hear the appeal by the supreme court itself. The taxpayer has 60 days from the date of the judgement at the Federal Court of Appeal to file an application. The month of August is left out.

Source: Make Sure It's Deductible, *by Evelyn Jacks, published by McGraw-Hill Ryerson, Whitby, ON L1N 9B6.*

documentation to support all claims, but also be prepared to justify why the return was correct as filed. When the test of "reasonableness" must be met for expenses or losses claimed, be sure to show how income will result from the present expenditures, and why expenses claimed were reasonable under the circumstances. It is easier to do so if you keep an ongoing and detailed business journal that complements your formal budgets and marketing plans.

When taxes remain in dispute after negotiations with an auditor, you should know the following:

Garnishee Orders

The CCRA can't garnishee your wages for taxes owing if taxes are "in dispute." Therefore, it always pays to file a formal notice of objection promptly if you disagree with your assessment or reassessment. You will preserve your appeal rights in the future if you and the tax auditor must agree to disagree.

Defects in Liens

Before the CCRA can put a lien on your property, it must follow the collection procedure set down in the tax law. *Checklist of possible defects in tax liens:*

● **You can prove** that you did not receive a notice of the assessment as well as a demand for payment.

● **The notice and demand** weren't sent to your last known address.

● **The CCRA didn't begin the necessary collection proceedings** within the three-year limitation period they are allowed.

Every Taxpayer's Dream: Catching the CCRA in a Mistake

All in all, the CCRA's accuracy rate on an audit is good. But the CCRA is far from infallible. In many cases, its approach has been to shoot first and ask questions later.

Some areas of CCRA attack:

● **Disallowed items.** A legitimate deduction may be disallowed with no elaboration simply because it was screened out by the CCRA's auditor according to general internal guidelines not available to the public. This, however, may not apply to your situation.

Defense: Your best move is to immediately write to the tax service center, explaining in detail why the disallowed item is deductible.

● **Mistaken information returns.** The reporting of interest and dividends by banks and brokerage companies is not always right. *The CCRA approach:* The information return is correct and the taxpayer is wrong. This is puzzling because the taxpayer generally knows how much money he or she has or should have. However, if the interest and dividends you declare are less than what is reported on the information return, the CCRA will invariably reassess in favor of the information on the slip and assess more tax. *Defense:* If you come up with figures different from those on the information returns, be prepared to defend your numbers with copies of bank and brokerage account statements. Do your homework in advance and ask the bank or brokerage to issue an amended slip immediately. You'll need it to convince the CCRA that you are right and the institution was wrong.

The following are some of the common mistakes:

● **Misplaced installment payments.** You get a letter from the CCRA saying your estimated payments don't show up on its computers.

Essential: Send in photocopies of both sides of canceled cheques used to make installment payments.

● **No return filed.** Sometimes the CCRA may say it has no record that you filed a return at all.

Precaution: Some people like to send tax returns electronically, through the Internet or by telefile; others use registered mail. All of these methods provide proof of filing. If you drop off a return at the tax office, obtain a receipt. If you receive a notice that no return was submitted, send in a copy of your receipt along with a photocopy of the return (you should always make one) to comply with CCRA's request to file. Indicate on which date you filed the original return.

● **Interest errors.** It's easy for the CCRA to make a mistake in calculating interest on deficiencies and refunds or when interest is to be reversed. The question of when interest on a deficiency ends is governed by very complex rules. *Defense:* Ask for details on the calculation of the interest owing.

Getting Help

● **Phone lines.** Many taxpayers experience frustration with "canned tips" and automated phone responses that do not apply to their particular circumstances. Worse, CCRA phone auditors are usually seasonal help with knowledge levels that may not suit the complexity of the question you need answered.

Solution: You often get what you pay for. Free help lines may not provide you with the right solution to your tax problem. And, if you subsequently file your return based on the advice you received over the phone, and that advice was wrong, you're still responsible for the mistake on your return. Seek professional help if you don't know how to properly fill out your tax return. Free over-the-phone advice may seem helpful in the short term, but professional help can be a worthwhile investment.

● **Problem resolution.** If you haven't received your tax refund in a reasonable time and can't get any action from the CCRA Tax Services Office, you can take the matter to the CCRA's Problems Resolution Office (PRO). This section of the CCRA is staffed with people whose job is to cut through CCRA red tape.

Problems resolution officers, however, are not advocates for the taxpayer. They're expediters. Their job is to understand the problem, and get the right people to act. The PRO won't fight the battle for you, but can assist in obtaining the right solution.

However, you may wish to run your problem past a tax professional first, to ensure you don't miss any appeal deadlines while you are waiting for a resolution.

● **CCRA forms and publications**. Don't blindly rely on instructions given in CCRA forms and publications. The tax laws are so complicated that the government itself makes mistakes in its own publications and/or in applying the laws and their policies to your very unique situation. CCRA information booklets and information bulletins and circulars are often outdated. It takes a while for the booklets to catch up with changes in the law. On debatable issues, CCRA instructions almost always take the government's side of the case. So, it is very important for taxpayers and their advisers to be up to date on the most current tax laws and proposals for the future to ensure the CCRA does not assess the tax return on prior year rules, and takes into account the intent of the law over a period of years.

Remember: There are many ways to file your return to ensure it is mathematically correct. However, your goal is to file it to the best benefit of the family unit as a whole over a period of time.

How to Get the CCRA to Solve Your Tax Problems

The safest way to play the CCRA game is to stay onside with the law and not to draw attention to your situation. The less contact you have, the better. But there comes a time for almost all taxpayers when they have to communicate with the CCRA. *How to safely handle some typical predicaments:*

● **The CCRA doesn't send your refund.** Wait at least six weeks from the date you filed your return. If you still haven't received your refund, get the CCRA to check its status. Call the CCRA's automated refund-information number (look in the Blue pages of your phone book under Government of Canada).

● **The CCRA's answers to your questions are incorrect.** Any taxpayer who has tried, knows it can be frustrating to call the CCRA. The numbers are often busy, the wait for call answering by an employee is long, they are often unprepared to answer your question or give you a wrong answer, or worse, you get into "voice mail jail" which makes it impossible to speak to a living human being.

Suggestion: If you're having trouble getting through, use the CCRA's website for technical information and to obtain guides, booklets and tax forms. You can also make your request in writing if you are prepared to wait for an answer. This will likely increase your chances of getting a response that is correct for your situation.

● **Formal rulings.** You may also request a formal ruling in cases where large sums of money are at stake and are subject to gray areas in the law. There is an hourly charge for this ruling which amounts to $100, plus GST, for the first 10 hours and $155 per hour for subsequent time charges, with a minimum deposit of $535.00 required. According to technical bulletin IC 70-6, the purposes of these rulings are to promote voluntary compliance, uniformity and self-assessment by provided certainty for proposed transactions. Bulletin IC 70-6 can be found on the CCRA website or at any tax-services office.

HOW TO CUT THROUGH CCRA RED TAPE

The frustration of getting a problem straightened out at the Canada Customs and Revenue Agency is enough to make most taxpayers despair. But don't give up if you get bogged down in the bureaucracy—when the regular channels of communication have broken down, there remains a way of cutting through the CCRA red tape.

Where to Turn

The CCRA Problems Resolution Office (PRO) was created so taxpayers would have somewhere to turn when the system failed. It is the one

office at the CCRA where your problem will not be overlooked.

PRO Prerequisites

Before the PRO will take your case, you must have attempted to solve the problem through the normal CCRA channels without success. Be ready to explain to the CCRA what you have already done to try to solve your case. You must have allowed sufficient time for the CCRA to act on your problem through its regular channels. Depending on the type of problem you have, there are different prerequisites for getting a case accepted at the PRO. (*Note:* PRO prerequisites are spelled out in CCRA publication 883, titled *Problem Resolution,* which you can obtain by calling 1-800-959-8281 or visiting the following website: http://www.ccra-adrc.gc.ca/ eservices/tipsonline/infotax/ mess883-e.html.)

More Problems

● **You can't pay your tax bill.** Contact the collection division at your local CCRA office before April 30. It's possible to work out an installment plan. Interest will be charged in these cases, but at least you'll avoid wage garnishment or liens on your property.

Secrets of Getting Fast Action in the Audit Process

● **Use your Declaration of Taxpayer Rights.** Sometimes it's necessary to fight fire with fire. There are rare situations when a CCRA auditor will use his or her position to intimidate a taxpayer or the taxpayer's representative. In these cases, it pays to know your taxpayer rights.

The Declaration of Taxpayer Rights ensures fair treatment in dealings with the taxman, including:

● **The right to information.** Access to full, accurate and timely information about the Income Tax Act.

● **The right of impartiality.** An impartial determination of the law by department staff who must seek to collect only the correct amount of tax.

● **The right of courtesy and consideration.**

● **The presumption of honesty,** unless there is evidence to the contrary.

● **The right to privacy and confidentiality.**

● **The right to independent review.** However, you must file a timely notice of objection to begin this review process.

● **The right to an impartial hearing before payment.** Taxpayers may withhold payment (or stop liens or wage garnishment) while taxes are is dispute. Exceptions are when your appeals are frivolous or where collection is in jeopardy.

● **The right to bilingual services.**

● **The right to every benefit allowed by law.**

This last right is most important. Canadian taxpayers are entitled to arrange their affairs within the framework of the law so as to pay the least amount of taxes possible. It is also your right to expect the government to administer tax law consistently.

Secrets of Getting Fast Action From the CCRA

Be assertive about your position, with a professional. Making waves at the CCRA is sometimes an effective way to move an audit case along. While the majority of employees at the CCRA are professional, courteous and helpful, the hardest part of dealing with an initial auditor is understanding and speaking the tax lingo and effectively explaining the gray areas—why certain expenses should be considered reasonable under the circumstances, for example.

If you suspect an employee is being biased, unfair, going on a "fishing expedition," or taking too long to complete the audit, particularly if you know you will be subject to interest charges, obtain assistance from an experienced tax adviser and ask that person to speak to the auditor and/or his or her supervisor. You'll need to provide written consent to the professional to speak to the tax department on your behalf. Generally, this is done by signing the department's consent form T1013.

Audit Strategies

Remember it is possible for you and your adviser to have your own "audit strategy" in place to counter the tax department's. Always ensure that you and your tax adviser go into an audit battle with some deft weapons of your own:

● **Tell the story of the evolution of your business.** Yesterday, today and tomorrow, which will show this is a commercial venture—not a hobby—with a reasonable expectation of profit over time.

● **Make full use of your appeal rights.**

● **Come to the audit interview armed with precedents** set in similar cases by the courts.

● **Summarize the tax law of the day,** current tax law and future tax proposals.

The auditor has the benefit of hindsight; something no small-business person has in his or her journey to profitability. Few people go into business to lose money. However, an auditor's position to disallow deductions or losses can often be successfully thwarted by the vision—backed by strong business plans and strategies—of the self-employed taxpayer.

Personality Clashes

A tax dispute is almost always a very emotional experience for the taxpayer. This is especially true in cases where the small-business owner has struggled for years to make his or her business venture work. There's a lot of blood, sweat and tears behind every business success story, and to have those efforts questioned during an audit can appear to be unfair.

That is why it usually pays to hire a professional who can deal with the facts and speak the same language as the auditor. Allow your adviser to have access to all pertinent documents, and any verbal communication you think may be pertinent. Working as your advocate, the experienced tax adviser can explain the rationale behind your business decisions in the past, spot errors, omissions and opportunities in the auditor's position and in your prior filings.

However, if you are on your own and you feel you've been treated unfairly by lower-level CCRA employees, file a notice of objection to the reassessment of taxes immediately upon receipt of the notice. There's a good chance the chief of appeals, who takes a fresh approach to the situation, will attempt to accommodate you. Most disputes are settled at this level.

> "There's a good chance the chief of appeals, who takes a fresh approach to the situation, will attempt to accommodate you."

Speak to the Right Person

Finding the right person at the CCRA to solve your problem is often the biggest challenge. Many taxpayer difficulties occur at the regional service centers where tax returns and tax payments are processed. Fortunately, the CCRA includes the name and telephone number of an employee you can contact on all notices sent to you if you need to speak to someone about your return. Otherwise, contact the problem resolution officer at your tax-services office.

Reduce Audit Risk

You may have the impression that the CCRA computers are quite sophisticated and that the department's audit program is as well. Well, you're right. However, an effective audit program is in everyone's best interest to ensure a level playing field for each and every taxpayer.

It bears repeating that at all times it is your legal right and duty to arrange your affairs within the framework of the law so as to pay the least amount of tax possible. Tax avoidance is not a crime.

However, when you circumvent the intent of the law, or when your financial arrangements have no bona fide business purpose other than the avoidance of tax, they can be ignored by the tax department under their General Anti-Avoidance Rules (GAAR).

Tax evasion, on the other hand, is a crime. It is the deliberate understatement of income or

CCRA AUDIT TRIGGERS

If you know what makes the CCRA decide to audit your return, you should be able to avoid audits entirely, right? Well, yes and no.

There are certainly some provisions that will cause a higher likelihood of audit including the following:

- Self-employment losses
- Rental losses
- Farming losses
- Business investment losses
- High capital losses
- High limited-partnership losses
- High losses from other years
- High RRSP deductions
- High carrying-charges
- Employment expenses, including claims for board and lodging by long-distance truck drivers
- Moving expenses
- Child-care expenses
- Alimony or support deductions
- Northern-residence deductions
- Caregiver amounts
- Disability amounts
- Interest on student-loan amounts
- Tuition and education amounts and transfers
- Medical expenses
- Charitable donations
- Political contributions
- Employee GST rebate

However, the CCRA also uses audit projects, special screening, informants, secondary files and other leads in their audit activities.

Most provocative for a potential tax audit:

- Unusually large deductions in relation to income.
- Unusually large refunds (which you should avoid anyway, unless you enjoy subsidizing the government with interest-free loans).
- Missing forms or schedules.

Discrepancies, including:

- Reporting the sale of a dividend-paying stock, but failing to report any dividend income.
- Reporting the installment sale of property, but failing to report interest income.
- Married couples claiming the same deductions.
- Unmarried couples filing separately and claiming refundable tax credits despite the fact that they live in a common-law partnership.

The higher your income and the more complex your return, the greater the likelihood that you'll be audited.

Other factors that could lead to an audit:

- A taxpayer's past history with the CCRA. Some taxpayers may be audited regularly, particularly if a tax deficiency has been found in the first audit year.
- In any given year, the CCRA will target certain types of businesses and financial dealings for intensified audit activity (for example, large corporations, small proprietorships, investors in abusive tax shelters, etc.).

Trap: The CCRA maintains a list of unscrupulous tax return preparers and audits a much higher proportion of returns prepared by these persons.

Sources: Evelyn Jacks, president, Evelyn Jacks Productions, Inc. and best-selling author of Tax Secrets for Tough Times and Make Sure It's Deductible. Also, Michael H. Frankel, partner in the international public accounting and consulting firm of KPMG Peat Marwick, LLP, and director of the firm's Washington National Tax Office. The author of many publications, Frankel has lectured at several tax conferences and has been widely quoted in the newspapers.

overstatement of deductions, or fraudulent declaration of circumstances to create or enhance refundable tax credits.

For example, if a contractor is hired to renovate your basement and quotes a very advantageous ask-price, the contractor can be charged with tax evasion if he does not declare that income on his return. This "underground economy" makes it impossible for the honest contractor, who pays his or her fair share of taxes, to quote competitively for your work, which in turn undermines our whole self-assessment system of taxation.

Proprietors. To avoid the risk of audit, small-business owners should carefully report all income received—cash, cheque, credit card, or barter—and document this with bank deposits to an account that does not commingle with personal funds.

Next, it is important to avoid the following errors in reporting tax-deductible items:

● **Categorize each deduction.** Don't place deductions under headings such as miscellaneous or sundry. A large "miscellaneous" deduction begs the question: "What's this?" Remember, a good tax auditor is a curious tax auditor. Your role is to satisfy that curiosity with proper documentation, and the breakout of your expenditures.

● **Keep an auto log.** A surefire way to lose money on a tax audit is to fail to track your business driving during the year. There is only one way to claim automobile expenses for a vehicle that is used both for business and personal driving: to keep a distance log. Record total driving of the year and what distances of that total driving were of a business nature. The total business driving over total driving for the year creates the fraction used in prorating all expenses of the auto's use.

Remember that driving to and from your place of work is considered to be personal driving. In the case of those who work out of a home workspace, driving from the home to pick up supplies, meet a client, get the mail, make a deposit, etc., all make up business travel in the eyes of the taxman. Driving from the home office to pick up milk or the kids for dinner, however, is considered personal.

It pays to keep a well-documented log. Most taxpayers find they have been underclaiming their auto expenses when they start keeping the log.

● **Log your cash expenditures.** You'd be surprised to see how lucrative it is to keep a log of unreceipted expenses—coin phone calls, coin parking, coin car washes, cash tips paid to bellhops and other service personnel. Simply keep a record of those expenditures as they happen and their deduction will be perfectly legitimate despite the fact that they are unreceipted.

● **Watch your CCA claims.** Capital cost allowance (CCA)—the deduction allowed for the cost of the wear and tear on income-producing assets—is usually claimed as a percentage of capital cost on a declining balance basis. But it is always claimed at the taxpayer's option. Small-business owners often claim CCA in error when income of the year does not exceed all the personal deductions and credits available. So try to save it for use in a year of higher income by claiming only what's needed to get down to the level of your "tax-free zone" this year. CCA claims are also tricky to adjust because the adjustment must be made within 90 days of receipt of the notice of assessment or reassessment. *Tip:* If you've missed the adjustment deadline, find a small item you may have missed claiming—like your safety-deposit box or medical expenses—to reopen the tax year and then make your CCA correction.

● **Employees.** Employment expenses claimed must be supported by receipts and an employer-signed Form T2200 "Declaration of Conditions of Employment." These expenses are often audited, however, so it might be a good idea to negotiate an employment contract that limits your exposure to self-paid expenses in pursuing the duties of your office or employment. Try to have as many of those expenses as possible reimbursed by your employer rather than paying for the expenses first and then deducting the costs on your return. It's better money-management for you and reduces your audit-risk.

CCRA Hit List

The CCRA will audit certain tax-filing groups they find to be at high risk for tax-filing irregularities. Among the groups recently targeted:

● **Home-renovation contractors.**
● **Auto mechanics.**
● **Home jewelry and cleaning-product sellers.**

- **Couriers.**
- **Long-distance truck drivers.**
- **Doctors and dentists.**

Items CCRA auditors will look for include:

- **Dubious promotional expenses.** If the same four people take turns having lunch together once a week and take turns picking up the tab, a close examination of diaries and logbooks will show this, and the auditor may question whether the expenses are really personal in nature.

- **Chits without names.** To claim entertainment and meal expenses, it is important to note the name of the person being entertained and the business purpose right on the chit. Those who stoop to pick up liquor receipts on the floor of the store at Christmas time will find the expense will be disallowed even though there is hard copy. This is another example of a crime: tax evasion through the overstatement of expenses that were not paid for by the taxpayer.

- **Travel expenses.** Commissioned salespeople who have poorly documented travel expenses are at risk here. For employees, business travel must take them out of their home base for at least 12 hours before personal meals can be claimed.

- **Questionable tax shelters.** Those with high incomes, including medical professionals and airline pilots, may have a tendency to invest in questionable tax shelters. Be sure to get professional and independent tax advice before making the investment to ensure it passes all audit scrutiny.

- **Cost of supplies.** Employees such as television personalities or flight attendants should be very careful in claiming unreimbursed costs of supplies that are used up in their employment activities. For example, the cost of hair styling or cosmetics generally is not deductible if it would be normally worn in day-to-day activities. Heavy theater makeup would be allowable. Some try to deduct pantyhose, nail polish and similar items that the courts have repeatedly ruled are per-

If a CCRA Agent Comes to Your Door

The CCRA can issue instructions to serve notice by phone, mail or in person to taxpayers or third parties who are acquainted with the taxpayer, to produce any information or any document within a reasonable time (generally 30 days). It is required that books and records be kept at your place of business, so auditors may generally enter to inspect any such records. It is customary that notification occurs before the visit. It is within your rights to ask that requests for additional information be put in writing, which will result in a requirement to provide information and documents. Those who fail to provide the required information can be fined an amount of not less than $1,000 and not more than $25,000 or both the fine and imprisonment of up to 12 months.

sonal rather than business expenses. Legitimate supply costs include maps bought by a real-estate salesperson, air time used on a cell phone (but not the cost of the phone itself), ballet slippers used by a ballerina, paper supplies of an employed writer, etc.

- **Executives.** Be prepared to explain your carrying charges for interest expenses on loans taken for investment purposes. Also, make sure you file Form T1212 to defer your stock option benefits if you received them after February 2000 and in amounts under $100,000.

- **Home workspace deductions.** Auditors can pounce on returns claiming home workspace deductions if the taxpayer is also provided with an office by the employer elsewhere. The office must be the sole place of work or used on a regular and continuous basis to see clients in order to be deductible.

- **Training seminars.** The self-employed can only claim two conferences per year. However, training seminars are not limited provided there is evidence that they maintain or update the employee's required knowledge. Auditors are especially wary of educational-expense deductions by the employed or self-employed that turn out to be vacations in disguise.

- **Tips of service industry employees.** Don't get caught pocketing your tips without reporting them if you work as a waitress/waiter, cabdriver, bellhop, etc. Anyone in an occupation where tips are a significant factor is likely to get a closer look from the CCRA. Remember, it is easy for the department to audit a restaurant, establish gross income receipts, and allocate 15% of this to every employee who has worked there. If they find that you have allocated nothing on your return, while another employee has allocated tips according to a properly kept log, you're in tax audit trouble. Remember, such audits generally span three taxation years. It's not unusual for waiters and waitresses who fail to report their tips to be in for thousands and thousands of dollars of unpaid tax, penalties and interest charges. Ouch!

● **Allocate personal components.** If you're a grocery store owner who writes off the cost of inventory as an expense, be sure to keep a log of any items taken for personal consumption. The same is true of a farmer who takes food from the farming operation for the family, a contractor who uses materials to build his family's deck or swimming pool or the cosmetics saleslady who uses her own products. Keep a log, add back into income the value of those items taken for personal consumption and avoid audit grief.

When It's Smart to Ask for a Tax Audit

Well, not often, but here are some thoughts on taxpayer-initiated actions that can trigger a tax audit:

● **When you want permission to destroy records** earlier than the six years from the date of receipt of notice of assessment or reassessment.

● **When someone dies,** the executor will want to request a clearance certificate and this may trigger an audit before the deceased's final return can be permanently closed. However, the executor will want to request this to ensure there are no liabilities that he or she will be personally responsible for in the future.

How to Protect Yourself

Knowing what to do if you receive notification of a CCRA office audit makes all the difference in whether or not you survive it. *Crucial things to remember:*

● **Read the notice thoroughly.** It tells you which items are being questioned and what you should bring to the audit. Sometimes the CCRA is just questioning one or two items on your return. If you have the records and the items are allowable, simply show that proof at the audit.

● **Respond to the notice promptly.** If you ignore it, the CCRA may automatically adjust your bill—in its favor. You usually have 30 days from the date of the notice to answer. You may also miss the opportunity to preserve your appeal rights. So, get on it immediately.

● **Prepare carefully.** Review the return for the year to be audited, and gather your evidence and documentation from your files.

● **Avoid a second appearance at the CCRA office.** Best time for an audit: In the morning, so the auditor can finish your case and start the next one.

● **Bring only relevant material to the audit.** If you include extra items of proof about other matters on your return, you open yourself to the danger of an expansion of the audit. Your auditor probably won't be interested in anything beyond matters requested unless you bring up something new. Just deal with the items at hand as quickly and in the most organized way that you can. Where appropriate, provide calculator tapes of cheques or invoices that show grand totals agreeing with the line items on your return.

● **Ask for additional requests in writing.** If the auditor requests any additional information at the audit, ask for this in writing. The strategy is that you only give the auditor what he or she wants—no more.

● **Don't give the CCRA the only copy of receipts or proofs.** The CCRA is notorious for misplacing paperwork. Make a photocopy of everything you need, and then give the originals to the auditor.

● **Replace any lost records right away if it's possible.** Get a copy or statement from the original source verifying the deductions in question. *Example:* If your medical bills are being questioned and you've lost your receipts, ask your doctor/pharmacist/naturopath/dentist for copies of them or a statement of what you paid for the year in question.

● **Be cooperative.** Courteous treatment works both ways. The CCRA auditor is only doing his or her job. Starting the whole process with a surly attitude will work against you, making the auditor less willing to compromise on gray areas. Your courtesy may mean a more favorable decision.

● **Avoid arguments with an unreasonable auditor.** You may be confronted by an auditor who is discourteous or just plain unreasonable. Ask to see the auditor's supervisor if you feel you are being mistreated. You should also ask to speak to a supervisor if you and the auditor reach an impasse on proposed disallowances. Discuss the situation with the supervisor calmly.

TYPES OF CCRA AUDITS

There are several different types of audits:

● **Office audit.** The CCRA sends you a letter asking you to come in for an audit. The items in question are listed, and you are asked to bring in substantiation for these items.

● **Field audit.** The CCRA conducts this audit at *your* home or office. This is the main audit tool used by CCRA and you will be contacted in advance for a convenient time. This is a detailed examination of your books and records and can involve a team of auditors. The auditor will identify himself or herself formally and discuss the nature of the business with the taxpayer and/or receive a tour of the premises. It pays to have everything in order before the auditor arrives to conclude the audit as fast as possible. The auditor will decide what records need to be examined and what audit techniques will be used and could ask for journals, ledgers, bank account records, invoices, shipping and receiving records, sales accounts, contracts and agreements, inventory records, minute books, etc.

When income records appear to be inconsistent with the taxpayer's lifestyle (low income, but travels regularly and owns an expensive car), a net-worth assessment is prepared to determine the level of income the auditor believes is more akin to lifestyle than what was reported on the return.

● **Correspondence audit.** You are asked to mail information or proof, or to sign a form and mail it back if you agree with the CCRA's conclusions. These audits often result from the CCRA's computer-matching program. Read the letter very carefully, and make sure it refers to the correct Social Insurance Number. Also overview the effects of changes on your return to other family members' returns. The CCRA frequently makes mistakes. Don't agree to anything until you are satisfied that the CCRA is correct.

Source: Evelyn Jacks, president, Evelyn Jacks Productions, Inc. and best-selling author of Tax Secrets for Tough Times.

Better strategy: Hire a tax professional to make progress. Restarting the process can often pay off as old hostilities are discarded and a new working relationship is developed in your best interests.

● **Don't give in to pressure.** Get professional tax assistance if the audit is too overwhelming. If the auditor is obstinate about a deduction to which you are sure you are entitled, and you are sure there are no other questionable items on your return, don't give up. Rather, stop the action and tell the auditor you would rather wait until your tax professional can be present. If you have any doubts, ask your professional to attend the first CCRA interview.

● **Don't volunteer any information.** Otherwise, the auditor may introduce a whole new line of questions about another item on your return.

● **Always be truthful.** Lying or giving misleading information to the auditor can result in penalties. If you find yourself in a sticky situation that you can't handle (that is, the auditor uses an indirect method and claims you have omitted income), terminate the audit right then and there. Bring in an experienced tax professional. Also, there is the question of trust. If the CCRA auditor sees that you are a truthful person in general, he or she is more likely to accept your explanations of deductions.

Another plus for truth: The auditor could be testing you by asking questions to which he or she already knows the answers.

● **Know your appeal rights.** Although in general it's better to get your tax liability settled at the audit level, you don't have to accept an auditor's decision.

You are entitled to a conference with the CCRA Appeals Division if you think the auditor has made a mistake. If no agreement is reached with the Appeals Division, you can go to court.

After the Examination

Once the examination is complete, the auditor has four options: agree that the return was correct as filed, find an overpayment, find additional refundable tax credits or propose additional taxes. If the auditor proposes a deficiency, there is often an opportunity to negotiate. On legal matters, the auditor is bound by specific CCRA rules and regulations, but some deductions are discretionary. Your powers of persuasion may help you arrive at a compromise proposal. If not, be sure to understand the auditor's position fully so that you can go on a successful counterattack on appeal.

Before you make the decision to disagree, work the numbers carefully. What will it cost in professional fees to go on to the appeals level? Also consider the fact that, on an appeal, the CCRA can dispute any item on a return, not just those already scrutinized. Thus, if there is an undiscovered issue that you know about, but the CCRA has not raised, it may be to your advantage to settle.

Source: Evelyn Jacks, president, Evelyn Jacks Productions, Inc.

Preparing to Face the Auditor

Before facing the CCRA auditor yourself, the most productive way to spend your time and energy is in gathering and organizing documentation of your deductions and exclusions.

The process includes preparation of schedules and worksheets that lead the auditor through a logical path of verification. Be organized and make sure all of his or her questions are answered. The audit may simply be short and sweet in those cases.

If you anticipate disputes over certain deductions and exclusions, a valuable added weapon is a memorandum from your accountant. *It should contain:*

● **A statement that shows you understand the law involved** and CCRA's assessment policies.

● **A corroborating statement on how and why you fit the particular provision in question,** or how specific circumstances warrant the position taken on the return.

● **Citations of recent relevant court cases.**

Preparation Is the Key to Winning a Case

The weaker the case, the better the preparation and presentation must be. Always present your case as attractively as possible. Organize the material in a binder, complete with a cover, table of contents and index tabs. Address every negative point the CCRA could raise and reach a favorable conclusion to those points whenever possible. Make your presentation to the CCRA in person—literally read your material out loud, cover to cover, to the CCRA auditor.

Ask for additional requests in writing, and promise to give the requested documents at another time.

What to Do If You Haven't Kept Good Records

Under the law, a taxpayer has the burden of proving his or her income or deductions. If you haven't kept good records, get duplicate receipts from the people to whom you paid money.

Alternatives: Sworn affidavits, copies of canceled cheques from your bank (although the latter can be refused by the CCRA). It is important to have actual receipts. Under CCRA guidelines, auditors generally will give you adequate time to come up with proof if they believe you're making a good-faith effort to cooperate, and will allow for extension requests in most cases if you require this.

Most auditors will allow only what you can substantiate under the circumstances. However, be prepared to explain your lack of records, and how you have corrected your past ways. *Example:* "I realize I didn't keep an auto log for the tax years in question, but as you can see I am keeping one now and this is reflective of my business/personal driving patterns over the years."

Records You Should Have

Certain discretionary deductions are a common CCRA target. Here's the information you'll need to support your numbers.

Medical expenses:

- All receipts for unreimbursed amounts including doctor and dentist bills.
- Cost of eye glasses, contact lenses, hearing aids and their batteries.
- Copies of prescriptions and their costs.
- Doctor's letter describing the illness and treatment to justify travel costs.
- Copies of premium invoices and policies to prove medical insurance coverage.
- Copies of cheques to claim group health care premiums.

Taxes:

- Copies of federal and provincial tax calculations, including all schedules and worksheets.
- Tax bills and receipts (property tax).
- Tax installment payments to the CCRA.

Interest:

- Copies of promissory notes.
- Mortgage amortization tables.
- Copies of personal lines of credit and their connection to investments in non-registered accounts.
- Interest paid to you by the CCRA.
- Copies of earnings from foreign countries.

Donations:

- Receipts from the organization that prove the amount of the eligible donation. This must include an official registration number on the receipt.
- Appraisals or other proof of value if the property is ecologically or culturally significant.

Casualty losses:

- Police and fire department reports.
- Description of property and proof of ownership.
- Appraisals to establish value.
- Itemized list of stolen/destroyed items.
- Documented insurance recovery.

Note: Personal injury awards are not taxable. Property losses will be reported on capital cost allowance statements.

When and Why You May Need Your Accountant

Whenever taxes are in dispute, it is a good idea to call your accountant—especially if the CCRA is proposing a sizable adjustment of the monies that you owe. Ask your accountant to call the CCRA and handle the audit for you.

By insulating yourself from the CCRA's auditor in this way, you can't say the wrong things. Also, your accountant will gain more time to think about answers to complex questions, since he or she will have to get more information from you and then get back to the auditor. *Point:* Weigh the cost of bringing in your accountant against the amount of any potential tax assessment. If the tax is relatively small, it may not be worth it to pay for an accountant.

Legal and accounting costs incurred to appeal a tax assessment or reassessment are tax deductible.

Source: Thomas LoCicero, senior tax manager and executive tax-planning specialist.

Professional fees:

- Invoices or letters itemizing services and detailing percentage of tax-deductible work.

Second-Best Evidence

Just because you can't prove something to the CCRA auditor during the audit interview doesn't mean that you should pay more tax right then and there. Taxpayers often show up for audits with inadequate proof of their deductions. The auditor's initial reaction is to disallow the deduction, in the belief that the taxpayer would have brought the complete documentation if it existed. *Strategy:* Ask the auditor to tell you what he or she would accept as satisfactory documentation. If the auditor demands proof you can't obtain, negotiate for a second-best proof that you can get. For example, you can't find receipts to match canceled cheques, but you know you can get duplicates—if you have more time. In this case, get the auditor to agree to an extension time, during which you can get duplicates. Or, if you didn't keep an auto distance log, required to legitimize auto expense claims, ask the auditor if you can go back over your calendar to estimate the business distance traveled during the year based on your appointments, your estimated trips to banks, suppliers or mail outlets, etc. Usually the auditor will accept this as reasonable second-best proof.

Source: Evelyn Jacks, president, Evelyn Jacks Productions, Inc. and best-selling author of Tax Secrets for Tough Times.

Fighting a Bank Deposit Analysis

A routine audit procedure is a bank deposit analysis. Deposits in a taxpayer's accounts are added up and then compared with the amount of income reported on the tax return. What if you don't think that a particular deposit was income, but you can't remember the source? Ask your bank to supply you with a copy of the cheque that was deposited. Most banks keep these records for several years, but in storage. It may cost you a retrieval fee and some time. The person who wrote the cheque can also furnish you with an affidavit explaining the reason for issuing the cheque. However, it is much better to file an audit-proof return up front. *Audit-proofing tips:* Never commingle personal and business bank accounts. Be sure to set up a separate account for the business and use separate credit cards for

---

DOCUMENTATION CHECKLIST

INCOME SOURCES

Employment
T4
Commissions
Research grants
Directors fees

Public pension
OAS
CPP Retirement
CPP Disability
CPP Death

Private pensions
Superannuation
RRSP
RRIF

Foreign pensions
USA
Germany
Other

Employment insurance benefits
Under $48,750
Over $48,750

Taxable dividends
T3 and T5 slips

Interest income
T3 and T5 slips
Any self-reported amounts

Rental income
Gross
Net
Capital assets
Support payments: gross, taxable
(Include separation agreement)

Capital gains
Proceeds of disposition
ACB details
Expense detail

Partnership income or losses
Statements/T slips

Other income
Scholarships
RESP
Death benefits

Self-employment
Gross
Net
Capital assets

Tax-exempt benefits
Worker's compensation
Social assistance
Supplements

TRANSFERABLE PROVISIONS

From spouse
Moving expenses (if spouse has income at new location)
Dividend tax credit
Age amount
Pension income amount
Disability amount
Tuition/education amount
Medical expenses
Charitable donations
Political contributions

From child
Disability amount
Tuition/education amount
Medical expenses

PROVISIONS AVAILABLE FOR MULTI-YEAR CARRYOVERS

Self-employed & some commission sales agents
Undeducted home office expenses
● Carry forward until net income is reported
Undeducted CCA balances
● Until asset is disposed of

All taxpayers
Undeducted RRSP contributions
● Indefinitely to offset future income, assuming RRSP room
Undeducted moving expenses
● Year following the move
Undeducted medical expenses
● Best-12-month period ending in the tax year
Undeducted donations
● 5-year carryover
Minimum taxes paid
● 7 years forward for application against regular taxes
Capital losses
● 3 years back; forward indefinitely
Noncapital losses
● 3 years back; 7 years forward

Source: Tax Secrets for Tough Times, by Evelyn Jacks, published by McGraw-Hill Ryerson, 300 Water Street, Whitby, ON L1N 9B6.

business and personal use. Always use duplicate deposit sheets that provide room for the itemization of the cheque and a copy for both you and the bank.

Remember, cash and barter transactions are considered to be income as well as cheque receipts, and invoicing must be taken into account by all taxpayers using the accrual method of accounting. That means income is reported when it is earned and expenses are reported when they are incurred.

Audit-Proof Your Personal and Business Affairs

Every day Canadian business people are contemplating a variety of business transactions and asking themselves "Will it be deductible?" How does one intelligently make the correct judgment call? This can be a real concern for many taxpayers, and legitimately so.

That is because Canada's Income Tax Act alone does not provide the guidance fully required to assess the way Canadians file their returns. There are, in addition, a number of filing policies enacted by the CCRA, and these policies, together with the law encoded in the act itself, are open to a variety of subjective interpretations by both sides.

What's more, the Income Tax Act grants to the CCRA a number of arbitrary powers. In fact, under Section 152(7), the CCRA has the right to change your tax return if they don't agree with the way you've filed it. These powers allow the CCRA to change your income figures, your deductions or your credits prior to the expiration of your reassessment period, which is normally three years. Your tax-filing fate, therefore, can rest with an auditor who perceives

your tax and personal affairs quite differently than you do. It is often very difficult to say in advance whether your business expense will ultimately be deductible or not.

For some, this is scary stuff. These gray areas of interpretation by two opposing parties could be seen to be somewhat weighted in favor of the taxman. Does the audit process itself lead to inequality in the ultimate tax assessment of two taxpayers with like enterprises and income levels? Do those who get audited pay more tax than those who don't?

These are all legitimate questions. In a recent report, titled *Compliance: From Vision to Strategy,* the CCRA admitted that it is the complexity, particularly the "gray" areas in tax law and tax planning, that are the most problematic for taxpayers and tax auditors alike. These gray areas have resulted in too many expensive court challenges. Therefore, tax filers should be aware of the following rules:

● **Under Section 18(1) (a) and (h),** the CCRA may question whether an expenditure was made to incur income from a business or property, and

How Long Should You Keep Your Tax Records?

Always keep tax records for six years past the end of the tax year in question. However, remember you may go all the way back to 1985 to request adjustments to most provisions for errors and omissions. You should also carefully take into consideration any carryover provisions like:

● Capital cost allowances
● Home office expenses
● Moving expenses
● RRSP carryforward room and undeducted contributions
● Prior year's losses (capital and noncapital)
● Medical expenses
● Charitable donations
● Tuition and education amounts
● Student loan interest
● Labor-sponsored funds tax credits
● Minimum taxes paid in the past seven years

Sometimes it pays to keep those records in the closet for a number of years!

whether the expenses were, in fact, personal or living expenses of the taxpayer.

● **Under Section 152(7),** the CCRA has the power not to accept your tax return as filed and may make its own assessment of the amount of tax it believes you owe.

● **Section 152(8)** makes the assumption that the CCRA is correct in its assessments, unless those assessments are challenged by the taxpayer. Therefore, the burden of proof is on the taxpayer to disprove CCRA's assessment.

● **The taxpayer and his or her adviser should be aware of tax law** and its changes over a period of years in order to determine the best final outcome for the audit.

That burden of proof is your best weapon against a subjective judgment from the CCRA. It presents an opportunity for you to explain your business motives, and therefore to exercise your full legal rights under the Income Tax Act. Because nobody knows your business and its potential in the future as well as you do, you have a distinct advantage

AT THE AUDIT— WHEN TO TALK AND WHEN TO KEEP QUIET

If you've decided to handle a CCRA audit yourself, the sound policy is to make as little sound as possible. You never can tell when some thoughtless remark will draw the auditor's attention to something you want ignored.

The first step in keeping quiet is preparation. Prior to the audit, try to think of all the questions you might be asked. Go over them in your head until you're satisfied with your answers. Do not plan to lie.

During the audit itself, be on guard for seemingly innocent questions or other conversational gambits that pry into your family affairs or lifestyle.

For example, the "innocent" question, "How old are your children?,"

clearly has nothing to do with the business at hand. Moreover, if you're not fully on your guard, you might find yourself responding, "Well, one is 9 and the other is 11. The 11-year-old goes to private school, and boy, is that expensive!"

While questions about your upcoming vacation plans may make pleasant conversation, they can have no possible relevance to the issues at hand. But your answers are likely to be quite revealing about your lifestyle.

Also be on the lookout for trick questions. An example might be, "How many kilometers is your trip to work each day?" Here the auditor may be looking to disallow some of your travel costs as nondeductible commuting expenses.

For questions that do legitimately relate to the audit process, take all the time you need to think through your answers. It is prudent to say no more than the minimum required to answer

the question. In other words, supply only requested information. The auditor can always ask for more information if you haven't provided enough.

Finally, and most important, do not, under any circumstances, answer an incriminating question. If the auditor asks, "Did you report all of your income?" for example, what do you say? If you have reported all your income, you can, of course, say "yes." If you haven't and you lie (by saying "yes"), you face even more trouble. But you don't have to say either. One evasion tactic is to pose a counterquestion: "What makes you think I haven't declared all my income?" (*Editor's note:* The CCRA may ask this question only if there is a reasonable indication that there is a likelihood of unreported income.)

If you can't deter the auditor and you find yourself being backed into a corner, you can always terminate the audit. This is your right. You can invoke it at any time. Simply tell the auditor you need the assistance of your lawyer or tax professional. Flight may go against all your instincts, but conceding the opening skirmish still gives you a chance of winning the war.

Source: *Mark A. Levinson, tax manager, Edward Isaacs & Co.*

going into a tax audit. You have the opportunity to control the outcome.

When you combine the expert knowledge you have of your business vision for today and tomorrow, with tax-filing compliance and the tax expertise of your financial advisers, the result should be audit-proof tax returns that reduce your overall tax costs over the period of years in which you run your business. It is critical, though, that the audit strategy that both you and your advisers will employ is decided upon at the time your tax returns are being filed. This is the key to winning a tax audit.

Source: Make Sure It's Deductible, *by Evelyn Jacks.*

Beware of Net Worth Assessments

If the CCRA has a reasonable indication that there is a likelihood of unreported income, it will reconstruct a taxpayer's income by estimating his or her cost of living. The CCRA does this by adding up all living expenses paid for throughout the year, then adding an amount it feels is reasonable for other living expenses it assumes have been paid for with cash. This is called a "net worth assessment." *Tip:* Make sure to pay for personal expenses such as food, medical expenses, automobile costs, mortgage payments, and credit-card payments by cheque, or if you are using electronic banking, print a copy of transactions. This should head off an auditor's contention that you had "hidden" living expenses.

How to Handle a CCRA Auditor

Prepare meticulously for the audit. Gather all your receipts for the deductions the CCRA has questioned. Draw up a detailed list of receipt on a sheet of paper. Also, meticulously reconstruct cash expenditures for which you don't have receipts. Explain exactly how and when you made those expenditures. By presenting your case in factual detail, you

> " If the CCRA has a reasonable indication that there is a likelihood of unreported income, it will reconstruct a taxpayer's income by estimating his or her cost of living. "

establish your credibility. And credibility is everything at an audit. It will be easier for the auditor to allow non-documented items if you can show him or her that you kept some receipts, that you made an effort to comply with CCRA rules and regulations, and that you've reconstructed, as best you could, your cash outlays.

How to Handle a Tax Auditor

I. Initial Audit Assessment Steps

1. Be sure to act immediately upon receipt of the audit notification. Go to see your tax adviser, with all the records you can find for all the tax years being audited.

2. Determine key dates to be met: The deadline for filing a notice of objection, for example, is the first milestone. Determine whether this document should be filed, and when.

3. Have your adviser request an extension from the CCRA, in order to pull together the documents required. This will take some of the pressure off, and allow you to continue with your normal income-producing activities while you put together the tax audit case. But from here on in, do not miss any agreed-upon dates or tasks in dealing with the CCRA.

4. Identify the problem areas in your position, like missing receipts or logbooks, as well as the subjective issues: no reasonable expectation of profit or the accuracy of the auditor's net worth assessment.

5. Identify the problem areas in the CCRA's position, including misinterpretation of the actual facts, errors in assumptions made, omissions of facts in making the assumptions and so on.

6. Anticipate your outcomes: Quantify your upside and your downside. *Your upside would be one of two things:*

● **No changes are made to the return.**

● **You uncover a tax-filing method,** provision, or new receipts that have been previously missed, and use these to actually have your taxes decreased for the year.

Your downside could be one of three things:

● **Taxes are increased because source documents for write-offs are missing.**

● **Taxes are increased because tax losses are disallowed.**

● **Taxes are increased because income reported is adjusted upward.**

Put numbers to these circumstances to analyze your financial risk factor before you file your return.

7. Identify the tax provisions that were new for the tax year in question. This will ensure you took advantage of them all, and understand their carryover potential. Keep a list of these in your tax files.

8. Establish your tax audit action plan.

9. Set aside the time to work with your tax adviser in putting together the appeal.

10. Be prepared to go back and look through old files, recover duplicate receipts, create auto logs from the information in your daily business journal, etc. A tax audit will require your personal resources of time and money.

II. Tax Audit Action Plan

1. File the notice of objection only when all the documentation has been gathered.

2. Organize your evidence: the documents that support your tax return as filed, any other additional documents, a listing of all relevant facts in your case to support your filing position, and a listing of facts that will answer the CCRA's assumptions. It would be a good idea for all of these facts and answers to be organized in such a manner that they can be referred to quickly and often. A tabular numbering system, set out at the start of the process, generally saves everyone a lot of time.

3. A taxpayer is within his or her rights to ask the CCRA to disclose the facts behind all of their

findings, and the exact provision in the law that supports these facts.

4. It is important to stick to the facts at all times. You and your tax adviser must separate emotion from fact to win the case. Embellishment that is not supported by fact can sink your case and, besides, is probably unnecessary. Remember that you have more facts than the CCRA does, because you know the truth: what actions were taken in the past and why, and what potential there is for the business for the future. Judges understand that you did not have the benefit of hindsight when you acted as you did.

5. Neither you nor your advisers should express personal opinions within your written materials or at the audit interview. Simply say: "Our position is the following. . ." This response will keep your presentation at a high level of professionalism.

6. Correspond with the CCRA in writing throughout the audit. For example, ask the CCRA to put any requests for additional information in writing.

7. Identify your weaknesses at the outset. If you don't have an auto log, say so. Often, the auditor will allow the taxpayer to go back and look through any documentation that will show a business driving pattern, and submit a summary of this. Another strategy that sometimes will work is to start keeping an auto log immediately, even if this is throughout the audit period. A long shot, it will at least give the auditor a trend to observe.

8. Identify any tax provisions you may have missed in that tax year, or prior years. This is a good idea at any time, as you always want to be in a position to recover missed provisions. You can, of course, open prior-filed returns all the way back to 1985 for most provisions. In fact, it may pay to find a reason to do this to assist in your audit position. For example, if you missed claiming your safety-deposit box fees, prepare an adjustment to your prior-filed returns to claim these. You will have 90 days from

> " **Meet with your adviser before the interview with the auditor and overview the materials and the strategy once more. This is a good rehearsal for your adviser, who may have some last-minute questions. What you are hoping for is that you have communicated the story of your business.** "

the date on the notice of reassessment to open up claims for capital cost allowances elsewhere on the return. This could reduce your net income, CPP liability, tax liability, perhaps even create or increase your spouse's claims for the spousal amount, and so on.

III. Your Adviser and the Auditor
Generally, once all the information is gathered, the taxpayer's adviser will meet with the auditor to impart the information and have a discussion about the file. It is not generally a good idea for the taxpayer to participate in this process. Consider the following:

1. Meet with your adviser before the interview with the auditor and overview the materials and the strategy once more. This is a good rehearsal for your adviser, who may have some last-minute questions. What you are hoping for is that you have communicated the story of your business, your intent for its future and why the tax return should be accepted as originally filed. Because you will have all of these facts in writing, you should have peace of mind and confidence in your adviser to represent you with all the details you feel are important to express to the auditor.

2. The adviser should begin the presentation of the materials with a solid overview of the essence of the

A LOOK AT TAX LITIGATION AND APPEALS PROCEDURES

Is it a good or a bad idea to appeal a CCRA decision? The following list of steps in the appeals process will help answer the questions you'll have when the CCRA contacts you.

● **Changes to return filed on notice of assessment.** If those changes made by the CCRA are incorrect, you have the right to write a letter explaining why the return should not have been changed. Always review this notice carefully and keep it in a safe place. There is a "grace period" of 20 days after receipt of the notice of assessment or reassessment, in which to pay your tax bill without interest charges.

Notice of objection. If you want to preserve your appeal rights, always file a notice of objection one year from the filing due date or within 90 days after receiving the notice of assessment or reassessment, whichever is later.

● **Audit.** If the CCRA questions or

takes exception to any portion of your tax return, you will be notified of an examination or audit, to be held either "in the field" (on your premises) or in the local CCRA offices. Following the conclusion of the audit, you will receive a notification of the tax service's findings and proposed adjustments. The letter of notification gives you 30 days in which to accept or appeal an auditort's decision.

● **CCRA appeal.** A CCRA conference at the appellate level is initiated by filing a notice of objection to the chief of appeals. Most disputes are settled at this level.

● **Tax Court of Canada.** An appeal to this court is initiated by filing a written notice of appeal within 90 days from the date of the CCRA's response to your notice of objection. The majority

of cases are held under the informal procedures (that is, if the disputed amount is under $12,000 or losses in dispute are under $24,000). The formal or general procedure hears cases with disputes involving sums greater than this.

● **The Federal Court of Canada.** The next avenue of appeal is the federal court. Taxpayers must be represented by a lawyer at this level.

● **The Supreme Court of Canada.** This is the final court of appeal in the country. Your case would have to be very serious and involve a large amount of money to get to this level, and it will only be heard if the supreme court agrees to consider it. There is no requirement that the court accept a case.

133

taxpayer's position, and what information is enclosed to support this position. It is important that this information is assembled so that the auditor can review it easily.

3. Once the facts of the position and the supporting documents are identified, the adviser should proceed to explain how these items relate to the way the tax return was actually filed. It is at this time that new provisions to be included should be identified, or prior errors on returns should be corrected.

4. The adviser has the opportunity to gather additional information needed by the auditor to come to his or her conclusions about the file. Therefore, if the adviser doesn't know the answer to the question, or the auditor needs additional information, this should be written down, and confirmed with the auditor—in writing—as the pieces of information required to satisfy the process.

5. The adviser then should clearly articulate the conclusion the taxpayer wishes to see, including the details of specific provisions (additions or deletions) and how they should be filed. With regard to subjective conclusions, the adviser should be prepared to stand firm on the reasons why the return was filed the way it was, and in the case of tax losses why the taxpayer is within his right to believe his assumption of reasonable expectation of profit from the venture. The adviser may cite previous cases that address the theory of the law, present information about changes in the tax law that apply to the taxpayer, as well as the documents that support the future growth of the business.

6. Remember that the case of Johns Manville Canada Inc. established that where there is reasonable doubt, the case should be resolved in favor of the taxpayer. This is especially true if the law is ambiguous or uncertain. In the end, the judge of a dispute must look to the Income Tax Act for guidance in coming to a decision. If it can be shown that the taxpayer attempted to comply with the law as it stands (without the benefit of hindsight at the time

> "If you incur damages resulting from a normal risk of your business operations, a deduction for the costs, including interest payments or wrongful dismissal payments, will normally be allowed as fully deductible."

his or her actions were taken) and that the law does support the taxpayer's position, the CCRA's subjective interpretation of the act is the weaker position.

Tips for worse-case scenario: If it's a downside you are facing, you'll need to pull some rabbits out of a hat to pay the tax bills—reviewing prior-filed returns for errors or omissions is a good way to find new money. Also, you can negotiate installment payments over time with the collection department at the CCRA.

Source: Make Sure It's Deductible, *by Evelyn Jack, president of Evelyn Jacks Productions, Inc., published by McGraw-Hill Ryerson, Whitby, ON L1N 9B6.*

Special Audit Problems

Accounting and Legal Fees
The key pitfall taxpayers run into here is that they write off accounting and legal fees in full in cases where they really relate to capital transactions. The CCRA has issued a technical bulletin (IT-99R5) to address certain specific cases when legal or accounting fees will be deductible. They will be 100% deductible when paid in normal business activities, such as preparing contracts, collecting trade debts, preparing minutes of directors' meetings, conducting appeals for sales or property tax assessments, and so on. They may even be deductible in defense of a charge of performance of illegal activities, depending on the relationship of the conduct to the income-earning activities. Fees for preparing income tax returns and assistance in preparing an appeal on assessment of income taxes, interest or penalties, CPP or EI premiums will be deductible, as will the costs of preparing advance tax rulings.

However, when legal and accounting fees are incurred on the acquisition of capital property, they are normally included in the cost of the property, or as an outlay or expense in the case of dispositions of capital property.

Legal fees surrounding successful corporate acquisitions will be treated as capital expenses added to the cost base of the shares acquired. Legal and accounting fees incurred in an abortive attempt to acquire shares would normally not be deductible at all unless the taxpayer can demonstrate that he or she intended to make the business a part of a similar business already operated by the taxpayer. (See CCRA forms IT-143 and IT-259.)

Convention Expenses

This is a real problem area for taxpayers at audit time. First, self-employed taxpayers may claim the costs of only two conventions a year provided that they were held by a business or professional organization. While you need not be a member of the organization, you must have had an income-earning purpose related to your business in attending the convention. In addition, the CCRA's technical bulletin IT-131R2 explains another little-known requirement: that the convention be "held at a location that may reasonably be regarded as consistent with the territorial scope of the organization." A good example of this would be an ocean cruise held by a Canadian organization. Therefore, taxpayers must be cautioned to choose their convention locations wisely—remember that only two per year are deductible in the first place—and ensure they can prove that attending a convention in another country is directly related to their business or profession.

Damages and Settlements Paid

If you incur damages resulting from a normal risk of your business operations, a deduction for the costs, including interest payments or wrongful dismissal payments, will normally be allowed as fully deductible, unless the damages are on account of capital, in which case they would be classified as "eligible capital property." In such cases, three-quarters of the value of the damages are scheduled in the cumulative eligible capital account, and may be deducted at a rate of 7% of that value per year.

Noncompetition Agreements

Here's a "dark horse" for any business owner who sells his or her company in the future and agrees to work under an employment contract that includes a noncompetition clause. Any such payment received in exchange for the agreement not to compete can be classified as an "eligible capital expenditure" which means that only 50% will be subject to tax.

Health Care Premiums

For tax years after 1997, the tax department will allow you to deduct from your business income any premiums paid to a private health plan on behalf of yourself, your employees and your spouse or children. For these premiums to be deductible, you must meet certain criteria:

● **Your income from the business** in the current or preceding year must exceed 50% of your income for the year and your other income must not exceed $10,000.

● **Premiums are paid** to a government-authorized private health services plan.

● **The premiums are not claimed** as a medical expense by anyone else.

● **The deduction depends on several criteria** including how many qualifying (nonfamily) employees are insured and for what part of the year.

The deduction is either the lowest amount that is or would be paid for nonfamily members or:

● **An annual dollar maximum of $1,500** for yourself and each adult family member covered by the plan plus

● **$750 for each family member** who is under 18 years of age at the beginning of the fiscal year.

Note: If you do not pay the premiums for any employee covered by the plan, the limit for yourself is zero. If the period of coverage is less than one year, the amounts are prorated. Where you have no non-arm's-length employees, you are limited to the dollar maximums described above.

Hospitality

In another detailed technical bulletin (IT-518R), the CCRA has summarized their position with regard to the deductibility of food, beverages and entertainment.

The 50% Restriction

Reasonable amounts may be deducted, if incurred to earn income from a business or property. The total costs must, however, be restricted to 50% of the amounts actually paid or payable.

Note that the following activities will qualify as entertainment subject to the 50% rules:

- **Tickets to theater, concerts, athletic events.**
- **Private boxes at sporting events.**
- **Cost of a cruise.**
- **Admission to a fashion show.**
- **Hospitality suites.**
- **Entertaining at athletic or sporting clubs.**
- **Entertaining while on vacation.**
- **Cost of taxes, gratuities and cover charges.**
- **Cost of security escorts.**
- **Cost of escorts or tour guides.**

The 50% limitation does apply to taxes and tips left, as well as to restaurant gift certificates purchased as a gift for your client.

The 50% limitation will not apply to the computation of other provisions on the tax return, including:

- **Moving expenses claim using Form T1M.**
- **Child-care expenses claim using Form T778.**
- **Medical expenses claim.**

Other Exceptions to the 50% Rule

The small-business owner must be aware of several exceptions to the 50% restriction that will result in 100% claims on his or her statement of business activities. These exceptions include:

- **The hospitality business.** The cost of food, beverages or entertainment provided in the ordinary course of business, in which the business provides food, beverages or entertainment to others in return for compensation, is exempt from the 50% rule. Restaurants, hotels and airlines, therefore, are all exempt from the 50% restriction on food, beverages or entertainment provided to their customers.
- **The food & beverage business.** If you're in the food, beverage or entertainment business, the cost of promotional samples is 100% deductible. However, any time you take someone out for a business meal, the costs will be subject to the 50% rules.
- **Registered charities.** The 50% restriction will not apply if the food, beverages or entertainment are for a fund-raising event to primarily benefit a charity. The 50% rule will apply to the price of admission to an event that is part of the regular activities of the charity. For instance, Morena invites her client, Gustav, to

the annual fund-raising dinner of the Manitoba Theatre for Young People. The expenses in that case are not subject to the 50% rules. Next week, she will be giving Gustav tickets to the group's five new plays to be held over the next seven months. The cost of those tickets is subject to the 50% rule.

- **Consultant's billings.** If your work for a company requires travel, and if the costs of meals are billed to the client and reimbursed to you, you are able to fully deduct those meal expenses, as the reimbursement would be included in your income.
- **Meals at conferences.** Where an all-inclusive fee is paid, entitling the participant to food, beverages and/or entertainment, an amount of $50 is allocated for each day to be the amount that's subject to the 50% restriction. All other costs will be fully deductible.
- **Beverages en route.** You can fully deduct the cost of any meals and beverages served or entertainment provided on planes, trains or buses (but not ships, boats or ferries). So, keep a log of those expenditures, as receipts are normally not available, and the CCRA will allow a reasonable amount as your claim.
- **Employer-sponsored events.** When you entertain your staff, you'll be able to avoid the 50% limitation on food, beverages and entertainment, provided that these are generally available to all employees at a particular place and enjoyed by them, like a Christmas party. After Feb. 24, 1998, such events are limited to six per year.
- **Employer-operated restaurants or cafeterias.** In this case, the costs of food and beverages are not subject to the 50% rule, but subsidized meals do present a taxable benefit to the employees. Restricted facilities like an executive lounge or dining room are always subject to the 50% limitation.

Fines and Penalties

Taxpayers often want to know if they can write off parking tickets and speeding tickets incurred while in pursuit of business income. In general, judicial and statutory fines and penalties are not deductible. However, certain exceptions to the rules exist, according the CCRA's technical bulletin, IT-104R2, if the following tests are met:

- **The fine or penalty was laid out** for the purpose of earning income.

- **Allowing the deduction would not be contrary** to public policy.
- **Incurring the type of fine or penalty received is a normal risk** of carrying on business, even though due care is exercised. In general, the violation is inevitable and beyond the control of the taxpayer and/or his or her employees.
- **The offense does not result from negligence,** ignorance or deliberate disobedience of the law and does not endanger the public.
- **It is not a capital outlay** and not incurred to earn tax-exempt income.

What this tells us is that a courier may face the inevitability of receiving parking tickets while on the job, which likely will be tax deductible.

The bulletin clearly points out that pollution and speeding offenses will not be deductible under any circumstances. Other notable nondeductible amounts are fines and penalties levied by professional organizations against their members.

Interest Costs

Interest costs on money borrowed at a reasonable interest rate to earn income from a business or property will generally be deductible. However, interest expenses will not be deductible in the following cases:

- **The loan is interest-free** or the interest costs payable are not reasonable.
- **The money is not used directly in the pursuit** of income from a business with a reasonable expectation of profit.

Note: Income from property does not include capital gains accruals. Therefore, income in the form of dividends, rents or interest must be present for interest deductibility on all loans used to acquire capital properties.

Capitalizing Interest Costs

Many business owners are unaware of the election to capitalize the cost of borrowed money used to acquire depreciable property. This election can be made for the current year and the three immediately preceding years, and for one, some or all of the properties acquired. It can also be made for all the money borrowed or some of it. An election under Section 21(1) or (3) of the Income Tax Act must be made

and submitted with the tax return each year to opt for the treatment. The amount of the interest is simply added to the capital cost of the property and written off as part of the CCA claim each year. Using this method, you can effectively move your interest deduction to future years when you have a higher income level. Look at IT-121R3 for more details.

Source: Make Sure It's Deductible, *by Evelyn Jacks, president, Evelyn Jacks Productions, Inc., published by McGraw-Hill Ryerson, Whitby, ON L1N 9B6*

Other Special Audit Problems

- **Business audits.** If your business is being audited, meet your auditor at a CCRA office or your accountant's office, not at your home or your place of business. The latter is not a good idea. You don't want the auditor to see your standard of living or run the risk that an employee will say something to the auditor that could hurt you.
- **Unreported income.** If the CCRA has some basis for believing you failed to report income, an auditor may ask "Have you reported all your income?" Never answer this or other potentially embarrassing questions with a lie. Deliberately failing to report all your income is a crime. So is lying to a CCRA employee. To avoid incriminating yourself, deflect the question with, "Why do you want to know that?" or "I believe so, but I can go back over all the transactions again to double-check the accuracy and let you know." The question may not come up again.

How to Beat the CCRA at Its Own Game

Section 231.1 of the Income Tax Act covers the taxpayer's obligations regarding a tax audit. This section also gives the CCRA the right to request and examine the taxpayers income and expense documentation and other records, including a GST review when an income tax audit is initiated.

The CCRA has a special pamphlet available to overview what you can expect in a tax audit (RC4188—*What you should know about audits*). It is normal practice for the department to allow 30 days to respond to its audit requests, but reasonable time extensions may be allowed.

What the CCRA Cannot Do

● **Home entry.** It is important to note that an auditor may not enter your home without your consent unless he or she has a warrant to do so. A warrant will only be issued by a judge if that judge is satisfied that such entry is necessary for enforcement of the provisions of the Income Tax Act.

● **Fishing expeditions.** The CCRA must not impose on any third party the requirement to provide information or any documents on another third party unless such a right is obtained from a judge. The judge cannot issue such a right unless it is reasonable to expect that the taxpayer being inspected will fail to comply.

What the CCRA Can Do

● **Copies of documents seized.** The auditor has the right to make copies of all documents seized for use in court proceedings.

● **What taxpayers cannot do.** Taxpayers may not physically or otherwise interfere with or molest an official doing his or her job in a tax audit or collections proceeding and must do everything to cooperate with that official.

When to Negotiate, When to Litigate

Unless you are prepared to cave in to the judgment of the auditor on every issue, any tax audit is likely to be a negotiation. In disputes with the CCRA, the outcome of the controversy depends not only upon the nature of the items at issue, but also upon the level at which settlement is reached.

Where to Negotiate

Generally, a taxpayer's chance for success at negotiating questionable items is directly proportional to the bureaucratic level at which settlement is achieved. Your chance of success is lowest at the lowest level—the audit. Since the function of the CCRA is to raise revenue, it's no surprise that auditors do not readily concede a deduction or exclude an item of income subject to debate.

The taxpayer's position and outlook improve somewhat, however, at the appeals level, where the case is reviewed for technical propriety and where arguments involving your individual circumstances and/or precedent (such as litigation on similar issues, advanced rulings, or announced policy of the CCRA, etc.) may become the focal point of the discussion. The majority of appeals are successfully negotiated to a conclusion at this level.

If the controversy is sufficiently serious, in terms of both the nature of the item and the dollar amount, proceeding to the court level may be considered. However, the taxpayer's chances for success diminish substantially here: The CCRA wins most court cases. *To proceed to the court level, you must preserve all appeal rights:*

● **Notice of objection.** The time for objecting to a current-year assessment is one year from the filing due date or within 90 days after the mailing of a notice of assessment, whichever is later. An extension may be granted or a taxpayer may appeal directly for an extension to the tax court.

● **Tax Court of Canada.** A written notice of appeal must be filed with the registrar of the Tax Court of Canada within 90 days of the CCRA's formal response to your notice of objection. The court hears appeals under two types of procedures:

1. The informal procedure. This is suitable for those who owe federal taxes and penalties in amounts less than $12,000 or losses in dispute of $24,000 or less. Taxpayers may either represent themselves or have a representative do this. Judgments made at this level will not be precedent-setting and appeals on questions of law may be made to the Federal Court of Appeal.

2. The general procedure. This is suitable for amounts in dispute above the $12,000 and $24,000 ceilings described above. Again, representation can be made by either the taxpayer or his or her representative and the procedure is much more formal.

● **Federal Court of Canada.** At this level, taxpayers who appeal must either pay full amounts owing or provide acceptable security for those amounts. Legal representation is necessary and certain strict time guidelines must be met.

● **Supreme Court of Canada.** This is the final court of appeal.

Source: *Taxation seminars of Evelyn Jacks Productions, Inc., a national firm based in Winnipeg, Man.*

Who Should Represent You?

We all applaud harassed taxpayers who defend themselves in court against the CCRA. But such cases are few and far between. At the prelitigation stages, however, the situation is different.

Many reasonably sophisticated taxpayers can adequately represent themselves across the table from an examining auditor, or even at the appeals level—and win. In many instances, only the person who must eventually sign the cheque to pay the tax deficiency (if any) can bring to bear the requisite amount of enthusiasm to press his or her point.

On the other hand, representation by a specialist (an attorney, accountant or other tax professional) adds much to prospects for a successful outcome:

● **The representative can be expected to have an adequate grasp** of the technical aspects of your case and the terminology required to communicate properly with the auditor.

● **A professional tax specialist is generally more objective** and less likely to be distracted by emotional considerations, discussing only the facts at issue, and never volunteering more than the necessary amount of information.

● **A representative acting in the absence of the taxpayer** offers extra negotiating space. The representative may tentatively agree with a settlement offer but will have to confer with his or her client, thus buying additional time to evaluate the proposal.

If a situation is serious enough to litigate, it is also serious enough to justify the cost of a representative who is informed, and up-to-date on past and current tax law and policy.

Note: Keep in mind that a representative need not be present at the outset. A taxpayer is not obligated to agree to the CCRA settlement offer at the initial meeting. A specialist may be brought in later. This strategy may be advisable if you detect a losing situation during or after the initial confrontation.

Sources: *Richard D. Lehmbeck and Henry J. Murphy, partners in KPMG Peat Marwick, LLP.*

How to Win the Fight After You Lose the Audit

Taxpayers who disagree with an auditor's findings can appeal the decision both within the CCRA and beyond—to the courts. The end of the audit may, if you choose, just be the beginning of your fight with the CCRA.

Round One

Actually, it's the CCRA that really starts the fight—with what is called its 30-day letter. It contains a copy of the audit report showing the examiner's proposed adjustments to your tax bill. You have 30 days to respond or request an extension.

Important: Never ignore a 30-day letter.

Best: Try to settle the case without going to court. It's quicker and much cheaper.

How to get to the CCRA appeals office: Send a notice of objection. This will move your case from the audit division to the CCRA appeals office. *Advantages:* The hearings officers at the appeals office have more authority to settle a case than CCRA auditors do. They can use their discretion to judge by the facts and circumstances of the case what the chances are of each side winning in court. Their mandate is to work toward a settlement of the case before court proceedings begin. This is your best chance for a negotiated settlement.

If you haven't hired a tax professional to help you up to this point, now is the time. He or she will assist you with information that must be well organized at the appeals level. Your arguments, reasons and justifications must also be as compelling.

Your tax adviser will know what the best legal arguments are in support of your case. He or she will also know what information to include in your notice of objection. This should include:

● **A statement that you want to appeal** the findings of the examiner to the appeals office.

● **Your name and address** and Social Insurance number.

● **The tax year(s) in question.**

● **The date and reference number** from the letter transmitting the proposed adjustments and findings you are protesting.

● **An itemized schedule** of the adjustments with which you do not agree.

● **A statement of facts** supporting your position in any contested factual issue.

● **A statement outlining the law,** policy or other authority on which you rely.

Appeals Conference

You will be notified by the CCRA when the appeals conference will take place. This can take several weeks to arrange. However, the chief of appeals has only 90 days from receipt of your notice of objection to render a decision about your file, so you'll likely find the turnaround time to be quick.

While you can represent yourself at the conference with the chief of appeals, it's a better idea to be represented by a professional qualified to practice before the CCRA. Such experts have experience in presenting your side of the issue to the CCRA.

There is a very high rate of settling cases at this point. Usually the cases that aren't settled involve issues upon which the CCRA has decided it isn't going to compromise, such as abusive tax shelter cases. On these issues, the CCRA usually wants to test the cases in court in order to set a precedent for the future. *Advantages of settling at this point:* Court proceedings are costly and time consuming, and should be conducted with legal counsel.

Continuing the Fight

If you can't reach agreement with the CCRA at the appeals level, you don't have to give up. You have the option of fighting it out in court. You have 90 days from the date of the chief of appeals' formal response to your notice of objection to file a notice of appeal with the registrar of the tax court.

Important: Never ignore a notice from the chief of appeals—or fail to consider your options for further appeal within the 90-day period. If you do ignore it, the CCRA will automatically make an assessment and bill you for what it thinks you owe. You will forever give up your right to argue your case in Tax Court. In Tax Court, you don't have to pay the tax until the trial is over.

Appealing CCRA-Audit Conclusions

The best forum to fight in, after the audit or examiner level, is the CCRA's own Appeals Division. There, taxpayers who disagree with the CCRA audit conclusions and who can document their position with sound facts have a good chance of getting at least part of what they're asking for, without going to court.

An appeal to the chief of appeals is handled by highly trained CCRA personnel called appeals officers. It is the appeals officers' job to settle cases—to see that they don't go to court—while still getting the most they can for the government.

Unlike auditors, who are bound by the regulations and rulings of the CCRA, the appeals officer is entitled to consider the hazards of litigation. That is, the chance that the government might lose in court if it litigates a case. If the officer feels that the government has a weak position on the facts, or there are cases in the taxpayer's jurisdiction against the government, odds are that he or she will concede or agree to a settlement.

The officer has a great deal of leeway. It is possible for a taxpayer to horse-trade and negotiate on individual items with conferees.

Some issues that are not likely to be settled at the audit level, but that taxpayers have a good chance of resolving at appeal, are:

● **Cash expenditures that the auditor has disallowed** for lack of documentation, where those expenditures are common in the taxpayer's business. An appeals officer may allow these based on a reasonable explanation by the taxpayer.

● **Travel and entertainment deductions** that are disallowed because the taxpayer does not have all the support the tax law requires. These disallowances can normally be settled on appeal if the amounts are reasonable.

● **Business/personal use of property.** For example, a taxpayer uses his car in business 75% of the time. But the auditor says he hasn't supported his deduction. If the taxpayer can show that he normally uses his car in business, and provides evidence that shows normal business/personal use over a period of time, an appeal should be successful.

Issues surrounding reasonable expectation of profit. One of the most contested areas of dispute is an auditor's disallowance of business losses because he or she arbitrarily determines there is no reasonable expectation of profit from the business in the audit period. Taxpayers usually win if they can prove with business journals, business plans, and evidence of future contracts/commercial activities that they are conducting a business that will be viable in the future.

Caution: Despite the above, do not go up through the appeal process on a lark, hoping for the best outcome. Prepare a decent, solid case based on the law, jurisprudence and taxation policy. Get sound professional advice. The appeals officers are technically competent, professional people. They are not likely to let anything slip by them.

Do not expect to get 100% of what you ask for. If several issues are taken to appeal, be prepared to concede some as part of the give-and-take negotiations.

Cases that involve questions of fact rather than law have the best chance of being settled because facts lend themselves to compromise. On legal issues, there's less room for negotiation. For every six cases the taxpayer can come up with in support of a legal position, the appeals officer will have six for the government. If there's a standoff, the officer will have no choice but to resolve on the principle of hazards of litigation.

The best approach in dealing with an appeals officer (or an auditor, for that matter) is to give as much factual background as possible. Point out where the auditor was wrong or why the auditor's interpretation of the facts was incorrect in your case. Support that position with facts. What prevails is a strong factual presentation, and meticulous organization, forcefully argued.

Sources: David E. Lipson, tax expert; and Evelyn Jacks, president, Evelyn Jacks Productions, Inc., a national firm based in Winnipeg, Man.

If You're Out of the Country

A tax court petition usually has to be filed within 90 days after the taxpayer receives a notice of deficiency. But what if you were out of the country when the CCRA mailed the notice? Taxpayers who are out

> "If you can't reach agreement with the CCRA at the appeals level, you don't have to give up. You have the option of fighting it out in court. You have 90 days from the date of the chief of appeals' formal response to your notice of objection to file a notice of appeal with the registrar of the tax court."

of the country when the notice is mailed may request an extension in writing under the Income Tax Act Subsection 166.2(1) to (4), and 167(1).

Getting the Government to Pay Your Legal Fees

The Federal Court of Canada has the power to award legal costs to either the taxpayer or the tax department, regardless of who wins the dispute. Legal fees paid but unreimbursed may be claimed as a deduction on the tax return.

When Not to Trust a Bill You Get From the CCRA

After the appeals process and particularly when the taxpayer has won his or her appeal partially, it is important to have interest charges adjusted all the way back to the start of the dispute. This extra interest can be several hundred, if not thousand, dollars more than you should pay.

What to do: Carefully check interest charges before paying the deficiency bill. Pay the tax you owe and the interest that you determine to be correct. Clearly explain in an accompanying letter how you arrived at your figures, including a detailed computation of the correct interest charges.

Interest is calculated based on a prescribed rate, compounded daily on the unpaid amounts from the time they first become due. The prescribed rate is calculated every quarter using the rate of government of Canada bills that mature three months after their date of issue plus 4% more. Since the 1998 that rate has hovered in the 9% range.

Note: For most taxpayers whose files are in dispute over a long period of time, the taxes owed are the least of their problems. Often interest and penalties are substantially higher. It pays to settle any tax bill promptly to stop interest charges from accruing.

How to Stop the Interest Clock

One way to prevent interest charges is to make payment while taxes are in dispute and then have a refund issued by the CCRA if you win. The CCRA will then have to pay interest to you on amounts they owe. However, this will be at the Treasury bill rate plus only 2%.

Sources: *Evelyn Jacks, president, Evelyn Jacks Productions, Inc., author of* Make Sure It's Deductible *and* Tax Secrets for Tough Times, *published by McGraw-Hill Ryerson, Whitby, ON L1N 9B6; and Peter A. Weitsen, a former tax auditor.*

What Do You Do If You Can't Pay Your Taxes?

Can the CCRA put you in jail because you owe it money and have failed to pay, even though the debt has been outstanding for years? The answer is no, unless you fraudulently conceal your assets or otherwise conspire to cheat the government out of its money. No crime has been committed merely because you cannot afford to pay your taxes.

The best way to approach the situation of having fallen behind in the payment of taxes is to respond immediately to all notices sent to you requesting payment. Make every attempt to speak to someone at the CCRA and follow up the conversation with a confirmation letter. The CCRA must give you an installment agreement to pay your liability according to the scope of your assets and your ability to pay.

The best time to try to get the CCRA to offer you an installment agreement is at the beginning of the collection process. If you have ignored CCRA attempts to work out an arrangement and it is now at your door with a garnishment order or other asset seizure process, it may be too late to negotiate an installment plan.

> **"One way to prevent interest charges is to make payment while taxes are in dispute and then have a refund issued by the CCRA if you win. The CCRA will then have to pay interest to you on amounts they owe. However, this will be at the Treasury bill rate plus only 2%."**

Advantage of Informal Payment Arrangements

Entering into an informal arrangement to pay your tax over a number of months may be the way to buy extra time from the CCRA.

If your financial statement shows that you own assets, the CCRA will generally request that you sell them. One way you can avoid this is by gathering enough money together to pay the tax bill without having to sell or liquidate assets you would rather keep. Often it is less expensive, for example, to pay the tax bill from a line of credit or loan at the bank that is backed by your assets. You should avoid cashing in RRSPs to pay a tax bill, as that will only compound your tax miseries with a further income inclusion.

Suggestion: Tell the revenue officer that you will pay a percentage of the bill immediately and the balance in equal payments over two or three months. This gesture will be viewed favorably as a solid attempt to deal with the situation as quickly as possible, and it may be easier to negotiate a longer period for the remaining payments.

Buying Time

Just because a case has been assigned to the Collection Division, it does not necessarily mean that collection activity will begin right away. In a great many cases, enforcement action will not start until after the taxpayer has failed to respond to a series of letters from the Collection Division requesting payment.

Even after personal contact has been made by a revenue officer, it is still possible to squeeze out a few more months before you are in serious jeopardy of losing your house and business. The way you can really get in trouble with the CCRA is to completely ignore the Collection Division. Sooner or later, time will run out.

Negotiating a Settlement When You Owe Money

The first step in negotiating a settlement of taxes owed is to discuss what you think you can afford to pay on a monthly basis. The CCRA will then determine whether this is acceptable and may ask for a current financial statement.

The CCRA will be interested in knowing how much money you receive each month, how much is spent, and where. The CCRA is more inclined to go along with a part-payment offer if it feels confident there is money available to make the agreement work.

If you have assets and no income, the CCRA can ask you to liquidate those assets voluntarily before they begin seizing them. It is always to your advantage to maintain control over the sale of your assets.

The Fairness Provisions

The CCRA has the power to be lenient in three key areas of compliance, and this could help you beat expensive charges. The department may:

1. Accept late, amended or revoked elections.

2. Cancel and waive interest and penalties in cases of hardship.

3. Refund overpaid taxes beyond the normal three-year period for assessment.

This is all outlined in Information Circular 92-3. Your past tax-filing habits will have a bearing on whether or not these requests are granted and so it really pays to be a model tax-filing citizen when you need relief.

Ask the CCRA to Remove a Late-Filing Penalty

The CCRA will assess a late-filing penalty of 5% of the unpaid taxes owing at April 30 plus 1% per month (up to a maximum of 12 months) of the unpaid tax if your income tax return is filed late. If the tax department has issued a demand to file in any of the preceding three years, you will have to pay 10% of taxes unpaid plus 2% of the unpaid tax per month for a maximum of 20 months. Repeat offenders are not viewed favorably. However, under the Fairness Provisions, the CCRA may be willing to abate the penalty if you can establish reasonable cause for the late filing. Being physically or emotionally incapacitated at the time your tax return was due is generally considered reasonable cause. *Another approach:* Take the position that your late filing was an isolated event in an otherwise perfect record of compliance—you always file on time. And appeal to the CCRA that the imposition of a late-filing penalty will cause you to suffer an unnecessary financial hardship.

Tax Fraud: Who Gets Caught?

Some individuals are subject to more scrutiny than the general population. They include: executives claiming employment expenses, certain investors and investment promoters, farmers, doctors and other high-income professionals, home renovators, auto mechanics, subcontractors in the construction industry, direct salespeople, self-employed couriers and other small-business owners.

However, tax fraud is also common amongst certain lower-income groups who attempt to receive higher refundable tax credits by providing misinformation about income levels, number of dependents and marital status.

Tax evasion or fraud will result if there was willful or intentional failure to file, understatement of income or claiming of fraudulent deductions. The onus of proof is on the CCRA to show there was willful intent to defraud the government.

The penalty for tax evasion is not less than 50% and not more than 200% of the tax sought to be evaded or both the fine and imprisonment for up to five years in some cases.

The government now has also put into place a new offense for taxpayers who try to obtain or increase a refund or tax credit through fraud.

Third-Party Penalties

Individuals (including partnerships) who, after June 29, 2000, participate in planning and/or valuation activities that lead to the reduction, avoidance or deferral of taxes, are subject to civil penalties under

Section 163.2. This section defines "culpable conduct," which is subject to penalties, as conduct that:

- **Is tantamount to intentional conduct.**
- **Shows an indifference as to whether the Income Tax Act is complied with.**
- **Shows a willful, reckless or wanton disregard of the law.**

These are the penalties levied under this section:

- *Circumstance:* Misrepresentation in tax-planning arrangements if made at the time of the planning or valuation activity. *Penalty:* $1,000 or the total that the person is entitled to receive from the planning or valuation activity; whichever is more.

- *Circumstance:* Misrepresentation in tax-planning arrangements if not made at the time of the planning activity. *Penalty:* $1,000.

- *Circumstance:* Participating in misrepresentation. *Penalty:* Greater of $1,000 and lesser of

1. The penalty for which the taxpayer would be liable if that person made the statement and knew it to be false, or

2. The total of $100,000 and the amount that the person is entitled to receive from the planning or valuation activity.

How the CCRA Gets Inside Information

The audit process itself is based on the number of estimated returns filed by each taxpayer "grouping"— employees, self-employed, investors, etc.—and the degree of noncompliance within those various groups is determined based on the results of previous audits.

Within each taxpayer grouping, detailed information about the taxpayer's occupation or business, gross income, net income and other relevant information is compiled, compared and analyzed.

> "You are inviting a "net worth assessment" if your bank deposits far exceed your income. That is a sign, or badge, of fraud to a CCRA auditor. Or if someone drives a new Mercedes and wears pure-silk suits—but reports only $15,000 in income—he or she is driving and wearing badges of fraud."

Computer matching makes all of this much easier these days, allowing for instant sorting of groups of taxpayers and their filing patterns. Sophisticated comparisons can be made of current and prior-year data and how taxpayers engaged in similar businesses or occupations report their earnings and deductions. From this analysis, lists of returns for potential audit are generated.

Other common forms of return selection for audit purposes include:

- **Audit projects.** This is where a particular group of taxpayers is tested to see whether there is any noncompliance in the group. In that case, all of its members (i.e., all long-distance truck drivers claiming meal expenses) may be summoned for audit on a local, regional or national basis.

- **Leads.** Tax files are selected for audit as a result of leads from other files, other audits or from outside sources including informers. It is not uncommon, for example, for jilted lovers and ex-spouses to volunteer information to the CCRA.

- **Secondary files.** On occasion, files are sometimes selected for audit because they are associated with another file that is being audited. This could happen, for example, if a restaurant is being audited and subsequently all its waiters and waitresses receive a letter to test whether they reported their tips.

Audit Tips and Traps

Distances driven for business or employment purposes can be easily established by the auditor if you do not have an auto log. The auditor can ask to see car repair bills, even though you used the CCRA allowed-per-kilometer deduction and didn't itemize car expenses. *Reason:* Repair bills often show the odometer reading on the car being serviced. By comparing readings at various dates, the auditor gets an idea of how far the car has been driven. For example, suppose a bill in January 2002 showed an odometer reading of 15,000 kilometers and a December 2002 bill showed only 30,000 kilometers. A taxpayer would have a hard time claiming a deduction for 75,000 kilometers driven during the year.

Informant Danger

If a friend, relative or employer turns on you, steals your personal financial records, and delivers them to the CCRA, there's nothing you can do to keep the CCRA from using them against you.

> "Distances driven for business or employment purposes can be established by the auditor if you do not have an auto log. The auditor can ask to see car repair bills, even though you used the CCRA allowed-per-kilometer deduction."

Badges of Fraud

You are inviting a "net worth assessment" if your bank deposits far exceed your income. That is a sign, or badge, of fraud to a CCRA auditor. Or if someone drives a new Mercedes and wears pure-silk suits—but reports only $15,000 in income—he or she is driving and wearing badges of fraud. Anything indicating a lifestyle beyond apparent means, or any sudden, substantial increase in net worth (assets less liabilities) is a badge of fraud that could attract audit attention.

However, frequently, there are honest reasons for these conditions. Included are inheritance, borrowing, successful investments, appreciation of assets, and nontaxable windfalls, such as an award of damages in a lawsuit or even winning of a lottery!

Best defense: Think like the CCRA. Anticipate questions. Keep good records. Prepare cost of living statements and net worth statements periodically and compare them with those of prior years. Be sure you can explain large bank deposits and sudden increases in your net worth.

Warning: If you ever find yourself being questioned by a CCRA special auditor (criminal investigator), hire a qualified accountant and/or tax lawyer for professional assistance. This is a sign that the CCRA is serious about possible fraud.

Source: *Evelyn Jacks, president, Evelyn Jacks Productions, Inc.*

What the CCRA Is Really Looking For

In Canada there is a very high level of compliance—approximately 95% of all taxpayers voluntarily file tax returns. Our system of self-assessment is effective, and Canadians are generally interested and supportive of audit activity to ensure fairness and a level playing field in the economy.

The CCRA states that the primary purpose of audit activities is to monitor and maintain our self-assessment system.

Canadians are required to keep tax records by law to determine the taxes they properly must pay. These records must be kept for a minimum of six years from the last day of the tax year to which the records relate.

Destruction of tax records without permission is a serious matter. If this is done to evade taxes, the taxpayer can be prosecuted. You can request permission to destroy records sooner, but this will generally invite a tax audit.

All CCRA enforcement personnel—auditors, revenue auditors, special auditors, revenue officers and estate tax attorneys—are trained to detect possible fraud by taxpayers. The prize they're all looking for is substantial unreported income, overstated deductions or fraudulently obtained tax credits. Prosecution for tax fraud can be the result of such findings.

For Businesspeople Only

4

What Should Be in Your Employment Contract?

Movement from job to job has become today's prevailing career strategy. One result of this change has been the development of increasingly complex employment contracts aimed at helping companies hold on to and motivate managers, and at protecting executives' benefits and even their jobs.

Who Benefits From a Contract?

Employment contracts offer advantages and disadvantages to both employer and executive, but overall, a well-rounded agreement favors the interests of the employee. Here are the pros and cons.

Disadvantages to employer:

● **Generally, employers don't like employment contracts for managers,** since they limit the freedom to fire employees at will. The cost to an employer of terminating the contractual relationship can be steep, measured in terms of severance payments.

● **Employers resent broad use of employment contracts** because they establish precedents.

● **Employers fear that executives protected** by contracts may not show the desired amount of drive.

Advantages to employer:

● **A contract locks in the executive for the life** of the agreement at the terms specified.

● **Annual bargaining and divisiveness over salary** and bonuses are eliminated.

● **Contracts may protect the employer** and contain a covenant that the employee will not compete for a specified period after leaving the organization.

● **The employee's use of confidential or secret information** (important in certain industries: fashion, high technology, etc.) may be barred.

Disadvantages to employee:

● **The employee is tied to the company for the life of the contract** (although if another company wants the employee badly enough, it will offer compensation for the loss in the form of up-front bonuses, enhanced benefits, accelerated vesting in the pension plan, etc.).

> "Employers resent broad use of employment contracts because they establish precedents, [and they fear] that executives protected by contracts may not show the desired amount of drive."

● **Noncompete clauses may be enforced,** although courts tend to look askance at these provisions if they are too restrictive of the employee's ability to earn his or her livelihood.

Typical Contract Elements

● **Term.** This clause spells out when the contract is to begin and end. Most employment agreements run three to five years.

● **Duties.** Description of the job and status. This is important, as it would be the basis of any employer's claim of termination "for cause." It is often very general, but it should be specific.

● **Compensation.** The focal point of most agreements. Usually spells out minimum salary without limitation on the upside amount, and includes bonuses, stock options, etc.

● **Vacation.** How long each year, whether it can be accrued and the availability of payment in lieu of vacation.

● **Benefits.** Life and health insurance, retirement plans, etc. Can include one-time relocation expenses; can call for an up-front bonus for signing the contract, for example.

● **Place of performance.** Spells out where the employee will be performing his or her duties (corporate headquarters, subsidiary or field offices, city, province and country).

● **Termination.** Under what circumstances parties can discontinue the agreement.

● **Severance.** What compensation is due an executive upon firing. May include special provisions (e.g., "golden parachute" package, triggered automatically in the event of a change of ownership).

● **In event of death.** Can provide that the "fruits of the agreement" are assured for the employee's heirs if he or she dies and for those persons entitled to receive them if the employee is incapacitated.

● **Disability provision.** Can specify that disability of the employee does not constitute breach of the contract.

● **Options of perks.** For example, an expense account (standard), limousine, club membership,

Your Perk Shopping List

The following is a list of perks commonly offered to valued executives by Canadian corporations.

Perks are special by nature, and you might think of one or two more you'd like—and that are appropriate to your situation. Remember, when negotiating for perks, that the most important ones permit the accumulation of wealth. They allow you to build for the future rather than just live off your paycheck.

✔ Signing bonuses (usually 10% to 15% of base salary).
✔ Deferred compensation plans.
✔ Discounts on products or services.
✔ Educational programs.
✔ Employment contracts.
✔ Large expense account.
✔ Health club membership.
✔ Entertainment allowances.
✔ Incentive stock options.
✔ Group life insurance.
✔ Added life, health and disability benefits.
✔ Loans or mortgages at low or no interest.
✔ Luncheon club memberships.
✔ Lavish offices.
✔ Special parking privileges.
✔ Personal computers.
✔ Personal financial, legal and tax services.
✔ Preretirement counseling.
✔ Private secretaries.
✔ Resort or convention accommodations.
✔ Supplemental retirement plans.
✔ Severance payment plans.
✔ Tickets to theater or sports events.
✔ First-class travel.
✔ Extra vacation time.
✔ Use of company aircraft.
✔ Executive apartments and suites.
✔ Company-provided cars (with or without chauffeurs).
✔ Country club memberships.

Source: Andrew Sherwood, founder, chairman and CEO of the nation's largest full-service human resources management consulting firm, Goodrich & Sherwood Company, 521 Fifth Ave., New York, NY 10017.

financial counseling, consulting provisions, noncompete provision, arbitration clause, purchase of old and/or new residence.

● **Amendments.** Provide for continuing the agreement unchanged for an additional period.

● **Mutual assent.** The best practice is for both parties of the employment contract to sign the document.

Source: Sandra E. Rapoport, attorney and managing consultant with William M. Mercer-Meidinger, Inc., 1211 Avenue of the Americas, New York, NY 10036. Her specialty is consulting to management on labor and employment relations, including reductions-in-force, communications strategy during labor negotiations, executive compensation, employment contracts and equal employment planning.

Salary Negotiating Tactics

Negotiating salary with a prospective employer is, and probably always will be, the most awkward phase of the hiring process. Keep in mind, however, that you will probably never again have as good an opportunity to get what you want from your employer. As in any negotiation, you cannot hope to succeed unless you know what you want and what you can realistically hope to get.

Proven Strategies

The single most important bargaining tactic is to hold off the salary discussion until you know you have the job. *Explanation:* Once you are offered the job, it usually means that other candidates have been disregarded. Most companies don't pursue runner-up applicants if their primary choice turns them down. The company wants *you,* and that gives you an advantage when the question of money comes up.

If the prospective employer raises the salary question early in the interview process, do your best to evade the issue. A good way to handle this is to mention your current salary, then add, "I'm really more interested in the career opportunities for me here."

Once you've been offered the job (and assuming you've been able to delay the salary question), present your salary demands with confidence. After all, you're the one they've chosen.

Trap: Don't blow your new job by asking for the moon. There has to be some give and take on both sides of the desk. Going for every last nickel can only create resentment and an adversarial atmosphere, which is not what you want when starting a new position.

If you and your new employer reach a true standoff on the salary question, and you're unemployed, try this novel approach: Make your employer an offer he or she can't refuse. Offer to work for a month at the minimum wage. At the end of the month, your boss has the option either to fire you or to give you the salary you are asking for. Chances are the firm won't take you up on your offer to work at the minimum wage, and may agree to your initial salary demands.

Source: *Robert Half, founder of Robert Half International, Inc., and Accountemps (Box 3000, Menlo Park, CA 94025), employment specialists in the financial, accounting and information-systems fields. His most recent book is* Finding, Hiring and Keeping the Best Employees, *John Wiley & Sons.*

Raising the Odds in Salary Negotiations

Most executives pride themselves on their negotiating skills in complex, high-pressure bargaining sessions. Yet it is not unusual for normally polished performers to falter badly when the issue being negotiated is as basic and personal as pay or status.

The temptation to hire a proxy to represent you in raise negotiations can be almost overwhelming. Unfortunately, this is one situation in which no one can do the job as effectively as you can. In fact, the mere presence of a third-party representative will usually create an adversarial situation.

Basic Strategies

If you dread salary discussions, you'll find that by applying business strategies to raise negotiations, you can turn a negative prospect into a positive outcome. The basics of these strategies never change.

● **Be fully informed in advance on the details of your own desired result** and on the nuances of the situation of the other party.

● **Ensure the strength of your position before you begin;** you cannot negotiate from weakness.

● **Apply the same rules you would use in a business situation:** Both parties must perceive and achieve benefits; avoid cornering the other party or being cornered—ultimatums are a mistake.

Two Realities

Getting the raise or title you want involves taking a very close look at two realities. First, you. What do you do best? What do you enjoy doing most? What do you want to learn to do? Under what conditions do you wish to work? What are you aiming for in the company—or outside of it?

Second, the reality of your company and the position you hold in it. How is your company positioned in the market? What is its need for new products? How important is service to the buyer? Is the company in a field with growth opportunity?

What is the importance of your present function to the profitability of the company? (In the case of a not-for-profit, what is your role in the value of its service?) How is your boss positioned politically in the organization?

When there's a good match between the needs and wants of both parties, the probability of raises and promotions rises dramatically. Successful negotiations therefore rest on informing yourself of these two realities in advance.

Swing Into Action

Make the first move. Rarely do people get the best opportunities by waiting to be asked—initiate an appraisal discussion. Propose a new product or service, with an appropriate raise and change in title for you incorporated in the proposal. Volunteer your services if you can help meet a need expressed by the company.

Present your proposal with company politics in mind. Know who is politically disposed to accept or reject you and your ideas. Peers who may feel threatened, or superiors who may be displaced, should be sidestepped. The party with whom you negotiate must be able to see the overall benefit of your actions.

Always begin negotiations orally, rather than with written communiqués. This will enable you to test reactions, modify your proposal, if necessary, and follow it up in writing. Since timing is extremely important, a conversation will aid your judgment. Then persevere. One turndown doesn't mean a permanent no.

Alternative Rewards

Consider a performance-based raise or bonus. If resources for an early monetary reward seem scarce, don't overlook the long-term monetary value of a more elevated title should you choose to leave the company. At least get that. You can also arrange for other rewards, such as time off, a better working space, etc. If you know in advance what you want, you'll be able to present your case as to how these rewards are appropriate to your responsibilities.

Be wary of asking your superior for more than the situation warrants, however. It may be tempting or even easy to do this if you appear indispensable to a project, but ultimately you will suffer for it.

Finally, be willing and prepared to move out of your present organization if your needs aren't met over time. If you don't see yourself as able to move, you can't negotiate as a free agent.

Source: Nella G. Barkley, president and founding member, Crystal-Barkley Corporation, 152 Madison Ave., New York, NY 10016. She was formerly a private consultant to industry and nonprofit organizations on management planning and start-up projects. She has completed the Advanced Management Program at Harvard University's School of Business Administration.

Alternatives to a Straight Salary

Tax-favored fringe benefits can reduce the after-tax cost of compensation to both the company and its employees. Review the company's compensation program to make sure it is making the best use of fringe benefits.

No Special-Break Perks

Perks that don't receive favorable treatment under the Income Tax Act often can be provided to employees in a manner that provides tax benefits for both the employees and the company.

That's because even when an item provided by the company is *taxable* to an employee, the cost of the tax may be *much less* than the expense the employee would incur to buy the same item using his or her own money.

Also, the company may be able to *deduct* the cost of the benefit as a compensation expense even if the item would not be deductible by the individual. The deduction reduces the item's cost, and the savings can be shared with the employee so both parties can come out ahead.

Both the company and the employee may do well by arranging a compensation package that pays less in salary and more in benefits—even if the benefits are fully taxable.

Taxable benefits that may be provided include:
● **Investment counseling.**
● **Legal counseling.**
● **Electronic equipment**—car phones, computers, fax machines, etc.
● **Entertainment.**
● **Insurance.**
● **Interest-free loans** are another often overlooked, but potentially advantageous, benefit. An employee who receives an interest-free loan from the business has income in the amount of the unpaid interest, an imputed figure set quarterly by the Canada Customs and Revenue Agency (CCRA)—but again, paying the resulting tax may be a lot less costly than paying the interest itself.

Caution: Shareholders taking loans from the business must make sure that the CCRA won't view the loans as disguised taxable income. To avoid this, repay any shareholder loans by the end of the corporate tax year.

Tax Benefits

Of course, even better than taxable benefits are benefits that are *tax-free* and *tax-favored*. *Consider the following opportunities:*
● **Discounts on merchandise.** If your employer has a standard practice of selling merchandise to employees at a discount, this is not normally regarded as taxable benefits. However, the good must not be sold at less than the employer's cost, unless old or soiled.
● **Commissions on certain sales.** A commission received by a sales employee on merchandise acquired for his or her personal use is not taxable. Similarly, where a life insurance salesperson acquires a life insurance policy, a commission received by the salesperson on that policy is not taxable provided he or she owns that policy and is obligated to make the required premium payments.

● **Subsidized meals.** Subsidized meals are not considered to be a taxable benefit provided you pay a reasonable charge for them. The CCRA describes a reasonable charge as "one that covers the cost of food, its preparation and service."

● **Uniforms and special clothing.** An employee who is supplied with a uniform or with special clothing (including safety footwear) designed for protection from the hazards of the employment is not regarded as receiving a taxable benefit. The cost of laundering or dry cleaning such clothing is also tax-free.

● **Subsidized school services.** If you live in a remote area, an employer may provide free or subsidized school services for children of the employees.

● **Transportation to the job.** Employers sometimes find it expedient to provide vehicles for transporting their employees from pick-up points to the location of the employment at which, for security or other reasons, public and private vehicles are not welcome or not practical. There is no taxable benefit in such cases. *Exception:* Any reimbursement or allowance paid to the employee for transportation to work must be included in income.

● **Recreational facilities.** This can be a very attractive tax-free perk. If your employer offers recreational facilities such as exercise rooms, swimming pools, gymnasiums, tennis or squash courts, golf courses, shuffleboard courts, etc., free of charge or at a nominal fee, there is no tax payable. As well, if your employer pays the fees required for you to be a member of a social or athletic club, there's no taxable benefit involved as long as it can be shown that the membership was principally for the employer's advantage rather than the employee's. There's no limit on the cost, which is why senior executives try to negotiate memberships in top clubs as part of their package.

● **Moving costs.** If you have to move to take a new job or are transferred by the company, your employer can pick up the tab and you won't pay anything.

● **Premiums under private health services plans.** Your employer can pay for your share of the premiums paid to a private health services plan without any tax implications to you. Also, any benefits paid to you from the plan aren't taxable. This is one of the most common tax-free perks used by businesses.

● **Employee counseling services.** Your employer can provide certain counseling services to you without attracting tax. These include services relating to an employee's mental or physical health (or that of a relative) and services arising from reemployment or retirement. The CCRA specifically states that such services as tobacco, drug or alcohol counseling, stress management counseling, and job placement and retirement counseling qualify under this rule.

● **Professional membership fees.** If your company pays professional membership fees on your behalf, it's tax-free as long as the employer is the primary beneficiary. The CCRA says that when the professional association is related to an employee's duties, and membership is a requirement of employment, the non-taxable rule applies.

● **Gifts.** Your boss can give you a gift worth less than $100 tax-free. However, this can only be done once a year, unless you get married, in which case a second gift is allowed.

● **Parties.** You can attend a party thrown by your employer, including Christmas parties, without being dinged for a taxable benefit as long as the event is open to everyone in the organization and the cost per person is reasonable. The CCRA uses a guideline of $100 per person.

● **Vacations.** You can get your employer to pick up part of the tab for a vacation trip without incurring a taxable benefit. It works like this. Suppose your employer sends you to attend a convention on the company's behalf. That's tax-free. If you then extend the trip to take some personal time relaxing, and pick up the tab for that yourself, no taxable benefit arises. In effect, you received your air fare free.

● **Education expenses.** If your company pays for you to continue your education and the course(s) primarily benefited the employer, the benefit is tax-free to you. However, if you are the main beneficiary of the program and/or it's not an arm's-length relationship (such as in a small family firm), then the cost of the course must be included in income.

Source: Gordon Pape, with reference to Canada Customs and Revenue Agency Bulletin IT-470R.

Executive Pension Planning

Tax laws have a big impact on executive pension planning—both in terms of the cost of qualified retirement programs to the company and by reducing the amount of benefits that top executives can claim through such programs.

However, there are alternatives to conventional pension programs that a company and its executives can use that may provide greater benefits.

The Basics

There are four basic kinds of retirement programs:

● **Defined benefit pension plans.** With these, an employee receives a specified annual pension payment, usually equal to a percentage of his or her salary. Usually both the employer and the employee make contributions to the plan, however there is no law that requires this to be the case. Some senior executives negotiate arrangements whereby the company picks up the entire pension contribution tab. The payments are tax-deductible to the corporation but tax-free to the executive. *Result:* An employee can be sure of what his or her pension will be, relative to final salary, at retirement age.

● **Defined contribution pension plans.** These are also known as money purchase plans. In this case, there is no guarantee as to the amount of the pension that will be paid. The contributions are invested and the payments at retirement are determined by the returns earned by the pension pool over time. *Result:* An employee could end up with a lower than anticipated pension if the investments perform poorly.

● **Group RRSPs (registered retirement savings plans).** These are similar to money purchase plans in the way in which they're funded and managed. Again, the end value of the plan will depend on a combination of contributions and growth rate, and the actual pension that will be paid cannot be predicted with accuracy until you're close to retirement.

However, there are some major differences between a money purchase pension plan and a group RRSP. In fact, technically, there is no such thing as a group RRSP. Every RRSP is registered in the name of an individual. A group plan simply involves bundling many individual plans together under the same set of rules.

For most people, the group RRSP is a better choice than a money purchase plan because it provides greater flexibility. For example, you can withdraw money from a group RRSP if you need it for a cash emergency. You can't do that with a money pur-

chase plan, which is owned collectively by all the participants. Also, you have more options at retirement. With a money purchase plan, you can only choose between an annuity and a life income fund (LIF). A group RRSP allows you to open a registered retirement income fund (RRIF), which has fewer constraints than an LIF, or buy an annuity, or even take the money in a lump-sum payment if you prefer.

Employers also prefer the group RRSP approach because it doesn't fall under the pension regulations, which means they aren't obliged to file all sorts of returns. Less paperwork means more efficiency.

● **Deferred profit-sharing plans.** These programs are designed to allow employees to participate in the profits of a company for retirement purposes. They operate in a similar way to money purchase plans, but the employer contribution limit is only half as much. No employee contributions are allowed.

Limits and Restrictions

Qualified retirement plans cannot make contributions or provide benefits over limits set by law.

● **Private pension plan limits.** There is a limit on the amount contributable to a private pension plan, and on the maximum allowable payments. These were put into place to avoid the possibility of companies using tax-deductible contributions to fund outrageously high benefits for some employees. The pension cap is calculated by multiplying $1,722.22 by your years of service in the plan. This figure has been in place for many years, however it is scheduled to be indexed to increases in the average national wage beginning in 2005. To illustrate how it works, if you have 20 years of service, your maximum annual pension in your first year of retirement is $34,444.40 (20 x $1,722.22). Your pension may exceed these limits in subsequent years if your plan provides for indexing. Rules allowed for indexing up to 4% a year or the increase in the consumer price index (CPI), whichever is greater. The pension cap itself is not indexed to inflation, so more retiring Canadians find they are bumping up against the ceiling each year.

● **Contribution limits.** The maximum annual contribution that can be made to a money purchase plan or a group RRSP is 18% of earned income to a maximum of $13,500 (scheduled to rise to $14,500 in 2004 and $15,500 in 2005). The maximum allowed for a deferred profit-sharing plan is 18% of your remuneration to a limit of $6,750 in 2002, $7,250 in 2003, and $7,750 in 2004.

Alternatives

● **Retirement compensation arrangements (RCAs).** These are arrangements under which the company agrees to provide benefits to key executives on an individual basis. These plans are not subject to the pension cap and contribution limits that apply to registered pension plans. And since a plan can be designed to meet an executive's specific needs, it's likely to be more valuable to him or her.

Some pitfalls:

Contributions are tax-deductible but are subject to a 50% refundable withholding tax, which is returned to the employer when payments are made and included in the employee's income.

There is also a 50% withholding tax (again refundable) on income earned by investments within the plan. This has the effect of eliminating tax-sheltered compound growth.

HOW TO GET FIRED PROFITABLY

Anyone can get fired. This risk is an integral part of work life. Like any other normal risk, it should be factored into your own long-range life and career plans and reduced to manageable proportions by intelligent planning. In combination with a little assertiveness, realistic planning allows you to turn a potential disaster into a positive opportunity.

Preparing for risk allows you to be alert to any early warning signs. And, unlikely as it may sound, reading the handwriting on the wall early gives you a substantial measure of control over the progress of events. Most important, it gives you time to make preparations to move smoothly on to another—and better—job or into your own business. (*Note:* Don't concentrate all your attention on finding a new job; take whatever time is necessary to familiarize yourself with company policy on termination and with your rights under the law.)

Making a Forceful Exit

You have picked up warning signs and have begun your preparations. Here's an approach that may well turn the situation to your advantage: Preempt the decision by arranging a meeting and calmly asserting that you have read the signs and would like to make things easier for all concerned by asking for your own dismissal—under certain terms, of course—thus saving emotional wear and tear on all sides.

It does not take as much courage to do this as you might think—just hard-headed realism. In some cases, the reaction may be quite surprising. The impression you create by being very professional about the situation may stimulate your superior to revise earlier opinions of you. Once in a while this can lead to a real opening in which you can (if you wish) offer your own proposal as to how you could serve that same employer far better in a position much more to your liking. Your proposal might just be accepted—it has happened.

If, instead, your proposed self-dismissal is accepted, these are terms you should negotiate for (as needed):

● **Use of your office for several months.**

● **Full severance pay.**

● **Use of corporate "outplacement."**

● **Secretarial and other support help.**

● **Opportunities to meet other potential employers.**

● **Permanent or temporary use of your car or other perks.**

● **A recommendation** (specific

form to be mutually agreed upon).

You may not win on every point, but you will probably win on a significant number. Realize that corporations will go to surprising lengths to avoid the unpleasantness associated with terminating highly placed employees—and make this work for you.

Source: *The late John C. Crystal, founder of Crystal-Barkley Corporation, 152 Madison Ave., New York, NY 10016.*

An employee may make contributions to the RCA, but they are subject to the same tax rules.

Warning: If you're considering an RCA, make sure the money is held in a separate trust account and does not form part of the employer's general liabilities. This will protect the assets in the event of a corporate bankruptcy.

● **Individual pension plans (IPPs).** These were originally created as a method by which owner-managers and high-income executives could plan for their retirement years in situations where an ordinary pension plan did not exist and it was impractical to create one. By setting up an IPP, a person could create a defined-benefit pension plan specifically tailored to his or her needs. The level of retirement income would be guaranteed, indexing could be included and, if desired, the company could pick up all the (tax-deductible) contributions. The plan beneficiary didn't need to put in one cent.

IPPS also carried another advantage: you could contribute more to them than to an RRSP. That was because the rules allowed for additional funding of the pension plan to ensure that the benefits could be paid. So the company could get a larger tax deduction than the owner-manager could claim as an individual. In cases where the corporate and the personal entity were, in effect, one and the same, the advantages were obvious: more tax relief, plus a larger pool of tax-sheltered assets.

However, in the 1995 and 1996 budgets, the federal government imposed highly restrictive rules on the use of IPPs. As a result, they only make sense in certain cases. But for those who fall into the right category, they can still be useful. The accounting firm of PricewaterhouseCoopers now only recommends such plans to people who are 56 or older and have incomes of at least $70,000 a year. The maximum income an individual can have that qualifies for a pension benefit is $86,111 a year. Any income beyond that cannot be funded from a tax-assisted pension plan (in other words, contributions to fund a pension beyond that level are not deductible). If you think an IPP may be right for you, discuss the pros and cons with an accounting firm or pension consultant who is knowledgeable about these plans.

Source: Retiring Wealthy in the 21st Century, *by Gordon Pape (Prentice Hall Canada).*

Borrowing Against Your Retirement Plan

Technically, you may not borrow money against the assets held within a registered plan, including your personal RRSP. If you do, you're supposed to include the value of the assets you have pledged as security in your taxable income for that year. However, you are not required to take the money out of the plan.

There's a way around this rule, however. If you have a self-directed RRSP, use a technique called "substitution." If you have securities outside the RRSP (such as a guaranteed investment certificate), swap them for cash within the plan rather than using them for loan collateral. There are no tax implications involved as long as the market value of the asset going into the plan is equal to the cash being withdrawn. The net effect is to make the RRSP your personal banker. By substituting securities for cash in your RRSP, you are, in effect, providing yourself with an interest-free loan.

Source: Gordon Pape's Buyer's Guide to RRSPs, *by Gordon Pape and David Tafler (Prentice Hall Canada).*

When an Employment Agreement Goes Sour

You have a written employment agreement. At the time the contract was signed, everything was rosy. Neither party thought the termination provisions of the contract would come into play. But now the relationship has gone sour. What do you do?

● **Review your employment contract.** Some people make the mistake of merely looking over the severance clause, which specifies what the company must pay if the employer terminates the agreement. Look instead for loopholes the employer might use to withhold severance pay or force you into a bad bargaining position. The key lies in the "for cause" provision, which describes the conditions under which you can be held in violation of the contract, making it unnecessary for the employer to pay you anything.

● **Fulfill the contract provisions meticulously.** Your job is in jeopardy. Do not give the employer any pretext for refusing your severance pay. Follow the terms of the agreement in detail. Work a full day. Make all meetings. Don't violate any company policy, major or trivial.

● **Collect proof.** Build a file that gives evidence of your service to the company: Appreciative memos, reports, documents showing you have achieved goals, etc.—whatever you can get that shows the employer has recognized your worth to the organization. Then, if told you've been doing a poor job, produce the evidence.

● **Request an evaluation of your work.** Go on record as giving your boss a chance to criticize your work. Send a memo reviewing your progress on a particular project. Add something like, "As I see it, this fulfills all the conditions of the assignment, and substantially achieves the stated goals." The worst that can happen is that your employer disagrees. If your document is accepted, actively or tacitly, you have evidence that you've been doing a reasonably good job.

None of this is calculated to keep your head from rolling. But it can help you get the full severance pay and benefits called for in your contract.

Planning for the Worst

If you're lucky enough to be reading this before the crunch and you don't have a contract, ask for one. This may be easier than you think—if the company values your work and wants to keep you around. Negotiate a good severance agreement and a tight "for cause" provision. Some such provisions are drawn so broadly as to cover almost anything: " 'For cause' shall mean failure to carry out assigned duties…"

Make this provision in your contract as narrow and specific as possible—e.g., "The company may terminate this agreement for cause in the event of gross, repeated and demonstrable failure to carry out reasonable instructions, if such failure is not remediated within a reasonable time after written notice…"

Also include a clause that submits disagreements over the contract to binding arbitration. This will keep you from being forced to negotiate your severance under the threat of a long and costly lawsuit.

An employment contract can be the best protection against being fired with minimum severance. It is much better to have a strong contract than to try to make up for weaknesses in the contract when the agreement goes sour—or to have no contract at all.

Source: *John Tarrant, 167 S. Compo Rd., Westport, CT 06880, author of more than a dozen business books, including* Perks and Parachutes—Negotiating Your Executive Employment Contract; Drucker: The Man Who Invented the Corporate Society; *and* How to Negotiate a Raise.

Do What You Really Want to Do

It's never too late to do what you want. The biggest barrier is not age, but fear. As one woman who went back to college in her 80s said, "I'm going to be 88 in five years no matter what I do—so I might as well do what I want to!"

Getting Ready: First Steps

Few of us embrace change with open arms—but we can gear ourselves up to make the most of it by taking some important preparatory steps:

● **Be willing to be a beginner.** One of the defining characteristics of change is that we don't know what's coming next or how to handle it when it happens. Instead of getting upset by this fact, *get curious.*

Let go of your preconceptions, especially those about your capabilities and limitations.

When your life is changing, you will not know exactly what to do. Let uncertainty keep you open to a variety of exciting possibilities.

● **Spend time with yourself.** Build into your life—every day, if possible—some kind of uninterrupted time to reflect, to acknowledge frustrations, to celebrate victories—and to dream. You'll need this emotional compass to steer by as you advance toward your goals.

● **Recognize the gifts of age.** Far from holding you back, age can propel you toward what you want. No matter what you've done with your life, you can't reach midlife without accumulating a great deal of knowledge, experience and understanding of the world.

This information and wisdom puts you well ahead of younger people who may have aspirations but lack perspective.

How to Change a Job or Career After 40

When you're in your twenties, changing jobs within the same field, or even changing to another field, is relatively easy. But it gets progressively more difficult after 40. The first thing that an over-40 job changer is questioned about is his or her track record at work.

Employment agencies and personnel people will tell you that your experience and credentials are not easily transferable. So, if you stay away from the conventional system, you'll have a better chance for success.

Understanding the Realities

The usual reaction of people who are trying to change careers or jobs is simply to keep trying. If 1,000 résumés don't work, they send out 3,000. By the time they realize that this isn't getting results, they're in a syndrome of rejection and depression. And once they are in that self-defeating cycle, it's extremely difficult to escape. *A better approach:*

● **Don't even think about looking for a job** through employment agencies or personnel departments, sending résumés or answering newspaper ads. Decide beforehand to forget that route.

● **Think of yourself as a product that you have to market.** If you've been in management, you've been trained and are experienced in analyzing your company's problems. This is the time to use those abilities in analyzing your own situation.

Marketing Yourself

● **Do research and development on yourself.** You must figure out who you are, what your skills are, and what you really want to do most. This should include considerations such as where you want to live and intermediate goals versus long-term goals. See yourself as a whole person with skills, interests, and goals that may have nothing to do with your past employment. Be specific. A vague goal such as "I'd like to be a teacher" is meaningless. "I want to teach music at the high-school level in Vancouver" is much better.

● **Do market research for yourself.** Find out exactly who would be interested in the product you're selling—yourself. *How to do this:* Talk with people to find out what's available in your area of interest. Don't look for a job. Simply survey the situation and find out what the needs are. This takes the pressure off, and enables you to make valuable contacts.

● **Meet with contacts.** Personal and business contacts are all-important. You'll make some contacts while surveying your interest area. But don't hesitate to survey friends, relatives or current business associates.

● **Go with your heart.** Radiate enthusiasm about your goal. A positive attitude is crucial and comes only from doing what you really want to do, not what you think you should do, or what seems sensible, or what someone else wants you to do. If your proposal turns you on, it will have the same effect on your potential buyers.

● **Go to the right person with your proposal.** Approach the person who has the power to accept or reject it. Find this person through your contacts. *Example:* A 42-year-old graphic artist was interested in getting into the television field but had no TV experience. She talked with a number of people in various aspects of television and found there was a need for artists to do on-screen computer graphics and animation. One broadcasting company was hiring artists who had taken a particular manufacturer's three-day course. She took the course and got the job. She's now making triple her previous salary.

● **Make them an offer they can't refuse.** Figure out not only what you can contribute but also the best method of reaching your potential market with a strong sales message. *Helpful:* The business proposal. Work up a proposal identifying a need in a particular area. Then outline and explain how you think it can be filled by using your services.

Source: The late John C. Crystal, founder of Crystal-Barkley Corporation, 152 Madison Ave., New York, NY 10016.

Own-Business Basics

Launch a new business only after you have formulated a complete business plan. The plan should include careful projections of your monthly cash needs and available income for the first three to five years. Rarely does a new enterprise produce a fluid cash flow early on.

Questions to answer first:

● **Is the money to be invested** in the new business money that you can afford to lose?

● **Will you be able to get another job** and build another career if the new venture fails?

● **Can you afford to replace the insurance** coverage you may have now as an employee?

● **Do you need a bank loan to start?** If so, would you be wise to apply for it before you quit your present job?

Source: Edward Mendlowitz, partner, Mendlowitz Weitsen, 2 Penn Plaza, New York, NY 10121.

Start a Business on a Shoestring

Shoestring businesses aren't limited to small ventures tucked away in the dusty corner of someone's garage. Many are capitalized at hundreds of thousands of dollars. They're called "shoestring" because the owner has invested little—if any—of his or her own cash.

Shoestring businesses are more a state of mind than a modus operandi. They work only if the owner is willing to adhere to the One-tenth Principle. Starting a business with one-tenth of the required capital demands that you exert 10 times the effort.

Planning Comes First

Don't fall into the trap of thinking that the smaller a business, the less risk involved. Starting too small is actually more of a risk than starting too big. If you're starting a service business, microscopic beginnings might work. But new retail and manufacturing ventures require some more capital to begin—and enough to generate profits.

Careful planning and well-researched start-up costs are the keys to attracting financing. *Helpful:* Visit the Online Small Business Workshop at the Canada Business Service Centres website (http://www.cbsc.org/osbw/workshop.html). It's invaluable in explaining all the aspects of a business start-up and in pinpointing frequently overlooked items. The Cash Flow Worksheet in Session Four is especially useful in identifying sources of revenues and costs.

Once you've identified costs, the next crucial step is figuring out how to slash them. Don't emulate the small journal publisher who struggled in his plush $66,000-a-year offices when a $10,000 facility would have sufficed—and would have produced profits instead of red ink.

If your shoestring business does require extensive quarters, however, look for retail basement space or space in a large, older home (if zoning laws permit). Both are usually priced well below conventional commercial property.

Retail businesses must focus on location. These businesses need immediate cash flow, and that means a high-traffic, high-rent location. *Avoid:* low-rent space that will force you to plow rent savings into advertising to attract customers. *Better:* Negoti-ate with the landlord to pay partial rent early in the lease and a higher rent later when cash flow is likely to be more substantial. Or, negotiate to pass renovation costs on to the landlord. Remember that a landlord who pays for your carpets and air-conditioning is going to charge a higher rent. But this can save you as much as $100,000 in initial costs.

Equipment bargains are next on the shoestringer's cost-slashing list. In fact, it should be part of every entrepreneur's game plan to scour auctions, equipment supply houses, classified ads, bankruptcy sales, and trade journals for secondhand equipment.

Nothing Down...The Smart Way

One-hundred-percent financing is plentiful—if you know where to look. Although banks and acceptance companies aren't prime lending sources for shoestring businesses, they'll usually consider full financing on bargain-priced equipment with established collateral value. And equipment sellers may be more interested in unloading unneeded equipment than in getting immediate cash.

Manufacturer financing can also be arranged. *Trade-off:* Manufacturers' lending standards are more lenient than those of banks, but you'll have to pay two or three percentage points more.

Leasing is often a wiser choice than buying, especially for motor vehicles, computers, carpets and cash registers. *Rule of thumb:* If it will last more than five years, buy. If it will wear out or become obsolete within five years, lease whenever possible. *Inside idea:* Whether buying or leasing, negotiate with the equipment manufacturer for a 30- to 60-day trial run. If you've planned well, your business should be generating enough cash flow to complete the buy or lease agreement by the end of the trial. If this isn't the case, you can return the equipment at no charge.

Look to suppliers for financial support. If your business looks like it will do well in the future, small suppliers might offer price breaks or better terms. *Example:* A small enterprising baked-goods manufacturer convinced his flour supplier to buy $40,000 of baking equipment for him against $800,000 in flour purchases over four years. The deal amounted to nothing-down equipment and a 5% discount for the baker, and a long-term customer for the supplier.

If you can't offer good collateral to a lender, you'll have to look to nontraditional financing sources.

Best bets: friends, relatives, high-tax-bracket investors.

Source: Arnold S. Goldstein, partner, Meyer, Goldstein, Chyten and Kosberg, Chestnut Hill, MA.

Use RRSP Money to Start Your Own Business

Employee Getum has "had it" working for his employer. He feels he is being overworked and underpaid, at his annual salary of $50,000. He wants out now. He has built up $100,000 in his RRSP over the years and decides to use that money to start out on his own, reasoning that the best pension plan is a successful business of your own. Getum finds out the tax bite on the $100,000, if distributed this year, would be $45,000 because the money would be taxed at the top marginal rate in his province. He needs $60,000 to finance his new business, although not all at once. There are steps to reduce the tax bite on the RRSP withdrawal and use more of it for the business.

HOW TO MAKE MONEY AS A CONSULTANT

At one time or another, most executives consider selling their expertise on their own, as consultants. The majority are at least moderately successful, but many fail. Most commonly, they overestimate the salability of their services and underestimate the effort needed to sell them.

How to find out if your service will sell: There is no fail-safe method. A talk with several potential clients will tell you if you are headed in the right direction. The big sellers: services that help companies keep up with change, whether it is in technology, marketing, personnel relations or other areas that business needs to know about to stay successful.

Pitfalls for New Consultants

● **Not realizing that consultants,** especially new ones, spend more time selling their services than performing them.

● **Wasting time on unproductive prospects.**

● **Choosing too broad a field** in which to consult.

● **Not learning to talk the client's language.** This is vital because many consultants sell a specialized service with its own vocabulary to an equally specialized customer who uses a totally different language.

Example: A computer expert who is hired to automate market research for a diaper maker.

New consultants are also faced with the temptation to sell their services cheaply at first in order to build up a good track record. Do not underprice. Clients are reluctant to establish a good working relationship with a bargain-basement consultant. And without that, the job is likely to be a failure.

It is also unnecessary to hire a public relations firm at the outset because a PR campaign will not have a track record to promote. Using a part-time PR could be helpful, however, in planning a credentials brochure.

To sell their services, successful consultants:

● **Maintain pressure** by keeping in touch with clients and prospects.

● **Master such sales and marketing methods** as the art of writing letters, making convincing phone calls and developing presentations.

● **Start at the top,** contacting the chief executives of the Report on Business Top 1000 companies (see the *R.O.B. Magazine* or go to http://top1000.robmagazine.com for detailed information). Send individually typed letters and follow up with phone calls.

Source: Charles Moldenhauer, vice president, Lefkowith, Inc., marketing and corporate communications consultants, New York, NY.

The steps are as follows:

1. Getum makes a minimum withdrawal from the RRSP, say $10,000, to provide the capital to form a new corporation, Go-Getum Co. The tax on this withdrawal would be $3,000–$4,000, depending on where he lives; say $3,500 on average.

2. Getum provides his services to Go-Getum Co. without drawing a salary for the next three years. Instead, he uses profits generated within the company to provide self-financing. He makes annual withdrawals from the RRSP of $30,000 a year to live on. He can do this and maintain his standard of living because many of his expenses have been eliminated since he runs the business from home. These include commuting costs, maintaining a wardrobe for office wear, lunches out, etc. His annual tax bill on the RRSP withdrawals will be around $5,000. Total tax on the $100,000 will therefore work out to about $18,500 instead of the $45,000 he would have to pay on a lump sum withdrawal had he collapsed the plan when he quit his job.

3. Once Go-Getum Co. is operating with a comfortable profit margin, it sets up an individual pension plan (IPP) for Getum. The contributions to the plan are tax-deductible. In time, the value of the plan exceeds that of the RRSP he cashed in to provide the seed financing.

Source: Tom Slee, CFA, CGA, a financial consultant and tax specialist. He can be contacted at TSlee10659@aol.com.

The Basics of Using Other People's Money

Other than your own pockets, where do you go for business financing? Trends in the popularity of different types of financing vary from year to year, but the sources all fall into two categories: *debt* and *equity*. The following summary covers a few of these sources, along with their respective criteria.

S *mart Investing*

Putting your money where your business plan is makes you likely to get backing for that plan. Venture capitalists look favorably on managers who make significant investments (relative to their personal wealth) in their own companies.

Source: Financing and Managing Fast-Growth Companies by Teledyne, Inc., co-founder George Kozmetsky, Lexington Books.

Debt

● **Banks.** Short- or long-term, secured or unsecured, bank loans are the traditional form of financing for all types of business needs. Banks typically make lending decisions based on a company's operating history and potential cash flow. They analyze the past few years' financial statements, requesting that they be audited, reviewed or compiled, and examine projected cash flow, income statements and balance sheets for the next few years. Banks look at a number of key financial ratios, including receivables and inventory turnover, liquidity, debt/equity and profit margins. Their emphasis is on historic trends of the business and comparable industry averages.

The banking industry has shown greater interest in recent years, making financing available for small- and medium-sized businesses, and most banks have been actively promoting these services in print and television ads, as well as providing Internet-based resources.

● **Insurance companies, trust companies, credit unions.** These aren't as high profile as the big banks, but these financial institutions are also useful borrowing sources. Credit unions in small communities will often be especially helpful to local companies.

● **Commercial credit and acceptance companies, venture capital loan companies.** Small businesses that are just starting up or with less stable operating histories can turn to these types of companies for funding. They offer many of the same forms of asset-based lending as banks, but focus more on a company's collateral than its operating record or potential profits, and are often willing to lend to less stable businesses. The cost of these loans typically is higher than that of bank loans, because of the greater risk assumed and the cost of monitoring the collateral. However, the true differential may not be as great as it appears, once all the hidden costs of bank loans (compensating balances, commitment and other fees, prepayment penalties, etc.) are factored in.

● **Canada Small Business Financing (CSBF) Program.** This federal plan is designed to help small businesses (revenues not in excess of $5 million) to obtain loan financing of up to $250,000. The loans are partially insured by the federal government but are made directly by a qualified lender (chartered banks, caisses populaires, Alberta Treasury Branches, most credit unions, many trust, loan and insurance companies). For details, go to the Canada Business Service Centres website at http://www.cbsc.org or write to National Secretariat, Canada Business Service Centres, Industry Canada, 235 Queen Street, Ottawa, Ont. K1A 0H5. Fax: 613-954-5463.

● **The Micro Business Program.** This is a financing program for very small, innovative businesses that is sponsored by the Business Development Bank of Canada (BDC). The program combines personalized management support with term financing of up to $50,000 for existing businesses and up to $25,000 for start-ups. It also offers two years of follow-up mentoring and management support. For details, go to http://www.bdc.ca or contact a branch of the Business Development Bank in your province.

● **The Student Business Loans Program.** The Business Development Bank also sponsors other financing plans designed for specific situations. This one is administered on behalf of Human Resources Development Canada (HRDC). Interest-free loans of up to $3,000 are available for business start-ups initiated by students in Canada. The financing can be used for start-up and operating costs, and is available through the BDC on a first-come, first-served basis as projects are approved.

● **Young Entrepreneur Financing Program.** Another BDC plan, this one is designed to give start-up entrepreneurs between the ages of 18 and 34 a solid foundation to build a new business. Term financing of up to $25,000 and 50 hours of tailor-made business management support help are available to entrepreneurs with commercially viable business proposals and excellent potential get their businesses off the ground. As with all these plans, contact the BDC for more information.

Equity

● **Venture capital.** Unlike sources of debt financing, venture capitalists place less emphasis on a company's stable financial track record—financial history and projects are important, but secondary to management, market and product. Venture capitalists are more inclined to look for medium-term payoff from a new venture's management-team strength, identification of a strong market need and ability to satisfy that need with a unique product.

You can find a list of venture finance companies that operate in Canada by going to the website of the Canadian Venture Capital Association at www.cvca.ca.

● **Labor-sponsored funds.** One source of venture capital financing that is unique to Canada is the labor-sponsored venture capital fund. These were created specifically to provide a new source of capital to fledgling businesses. Units in these funds are sold to the general public and offer a federal government tax credit of 15% on investments of up to $5,000 per year. Many provinces offer similar tax credits.

The managers of these fund are constantly on the lookout for new opportunities. However, they are highly disciplined in their screening process, so only companies with good prospects and a sound business plan are seriously considered.

Some of these funds specialize in specific industries, such as the Canadian Medical Discoveries Fund. This fund concentrates on new developments in medical research. Others limit their activities to a single province, such as the Crocus Investment Fund in Manitoba. So before you approach the management of one of these funds, do some research and be sure your business fits their profile.

● **Limited partnerships.** Many entrepreneurs aren't aware that limited partnerships can be used as a source of financing. They can be a useful way to raise capital, but you will need to find investors who are prepared to put money into fledgling ventures and they will probably demand above-average returns for the risk they are taking. You'll have cede control over your business to the partnership (even though you may be the operating or "general" partner) and you'll be expected to provide cash flow guarantees to your investors. They may also want a guarantee that their principal will be repaid at some point.

Successful Financing

Here are three important rules of seeking financing, regardless of its form or source:

1. Keep your proposal presentation clear, concise yet informative and easy to absorb. A potential funding source should be able to quickly understand your business, your reason for requesting funding and the benefits of providing that funding—without having to ask too many questions.

2. Don't sign away too much in your effort to obtain financing. In equity financing, it is very important to be cautious about the amount of control you relinquish. When taking on debt backed by personal guarantees, try to exempt certain assets, such as your home.

3. If you're turned down, find out why—in writing, if possible. Then, if feasible, rework your financing proposal to meet the objections and either resubmit it or try a new source.

Source: Jacob Weichholz, tax partner in the entrepreneurial services group of Ernst & Young, 787 Seventh Ave., New York, NY 10019, specializing in the tax and organization needs of small and medium-sized businesses. Additional input from Gordon Pape.

Useful Sources of Information

There are a number of valuable sources of information for Canadians looking for business start-up capital, seeking tax information, or looking for guidance on operating a small business. Here are the best of them.

Your Guide to Government of Canada Services and Support for Small Business. The document can be downloaded at http://strategis.ic.gc.ca/sc_mangb/smeguide/index.html.

Sources of Financing. This section of the Industry Canada website contains a wide range of information on financing possibilities, including a useful lease or buy calculator. (http://strategis.ic.gc.ca/sc_mangb/sources/engdoc/homepage.html)

Royal Bank's Online Guide to Small Business Financing. A section of the Royal Bank's informative website, it offers background information on various programs offered by the Business Development Bank as well as other financing options. (http://www.royalbank.com/sme/guides/financing/gvtsources_q3.html)

CIBC Small Business Services. Another big bank website with some helpful information. (http://www2.cibc.com/english/business_services/small_business/index.html)

Library of Links for Entrepreneurs. This useful website is privately run. It contains a wide range of information and links of use to Canadians who run their own business or want to start one. (http://www.gdsourcing.com/gds6.htm)

Toronto Public Library. This comprehensive website offers a lot of information and many links about every topic relating to setting up, operating and selling a small business. (http://smallbizxpress.tpl.toronto.on.ca)

Canadian Customs & Revenue Agency. Very important tax information for your small business. (www.ccra-adrc.gc.ca/tax/business/smallbusiness/index-e.html; http://www.ccra-adrc.gc.ca/tax/menu-e.html)

Strategis Canada. Tax resources for entrepreneurs and small business owners. (http://strategis.ic.gc.ca/SSG/mi06741e.html)

CanadaOne. Bills itself as "Canada's Small Business Hub." Toolkit section contains some useful forms, calculators and general guidance. (http://www.canadaone.com/)

Small Business Info Centre. A useful e-business source in Atlantic Canada. (http://www.smallbizinfocenter.com/info.asp?Category=15)

Microsoft bCentral.ca. Small Business Solutions. Information on marketing, technology, finance, etc., for small businesses. (http://www.bcentral.ca/articles.asp)

Your Own Business. All kinds of tips for starting on your own. (http://www.life.ca/hb/)

Home Business Report. Tips on home businesses sponsored by Telus. (http://www.homebusinessreport.com/)

HomeBasedWork.com. Articles dealing with home business problems and solutions. (http://www.homebasedwork.com/index.html)

Unconventional Ways of Raising Capital

When companies need cash to grow, the vast majority turn to proven sources: family and friends, commercial banks and venture capital funds. The choice depends on the amount of money needed, the stage in the corporate life cycle, and how fast the plan is to expand. But other capital avenues are open to the shrewd entrepreneur that may suit the company's needs better than the traditional ones. These include corporate ventures, joint ventures, R&D limited partnerships and marketing partnerships. It may even be possible to combine two or more of these sources in a total funding package.

Corporate ventures: The corporate venture, a direct equity investment by a large corporation in a smaller entrepreneurial company, is becoming a popular alternative to traditional venture capital investing. Corporate ventures are generally not entered into for the sake of profit alone. The investing business also may have an interest in identifying windows into new technology, screening potential acquisitions, leveraging available skills or enhancing a staid corporate image.

By the same token, the entrepreneurial company generally receives more than just cash: Its corporate

HOW TO FIND A VENTURE CAPITALIST

Are you looking for venture capital? Don't reach for the Yellow Pages. The goal is not just to find a venture capital firm, but to identify the right one for you. After a successful funding, your company will be married to the firm—in spirit as well as in equity. Finding the perfect match takes research, contacts and patience.

Anxious about the prospect of raising capital, entrepreneurs are often tempted to use the "shotgun" approach: printing up hundreds of copies of the company's business plan and distributing them to anyone wearing a suit. Unfortunately, this method wastes time and money and can damage the reputation of the company.

A targeted approach can improve your chances. The majority of venture capital firms specialize in particular types of deals. Some look only at high tech, others won't touch it. Some prefer leveraged buyouts, others work strictly with start-ups. High- versus low-tech preferences are important to determine, as well as discriminations on the basis of geographic area, industry, company growth stage or amount of money sought. Like other professionals, venture capitalists tend to stick with what they know best.

After you've figured out what kind of firm specializes in your kind of deal, the next step is to locate them.

It's a good idea to read articles in business or trade magazines for news of venture firms—take special note of deals in your industry or area.

Before you contact any venture firm, you should have developed a sound business plan and financial projections with your accountant, lawyer and banker. Stay in constant contact with them and remind them that you're interested in meeting venture capitalists. People whose businesses are already venture-backed can be particularly helpful. They've been through the process and may know venture capitalists looking for a deal like yours. *One steadfast rule:* A personal referral is infinitely preferable to a blind letter—it will get you and your venture more attention.

Is there a venture capital club in your area? Over 50 clubs have been established across the country, with more added every year. They offer entrepreneurs and investors a place to meet and exchange ideas. For beginners, this is a good way to learn the rules of the game and the buzzwords. In the best situation, you can meet people who are willing to support your company—either with money or experience—or to tell you honestly that it isn't likely to take off.

Venture capital clubs can be difficult to find, because they want to attract only serious entrepreneurs and investors, not hucksters. Again, it's always best to get involved with an organization like this through a friend or business associate.

While the "whom do you know" side of the process may be frustrating to an eager entrepreneur, don't despair. The creative and managerial synergy produced by a well-matched venture capital firm and an entrepreneurial company is well worth the trouble it takes to find a mate.

Source: Michael A. Reagan, partner, Deloitte & Touche, 695 Town Center Dr., Suite 1200, Costa Mesa, CA 92626. He is a member of the firm's emerging business services practice. He specializes in the high-tech industry, working with companies seeking growth financing.

partner may provide additional value in the form of credibility, a built-in customer-supplier relationship, or expertise in planning, marketing, R&D or distribution. Further, entrepreneurs entering into these strategic alliances generally don't need to give up as much equity as they would to a venture capitalist. Finally, corporate partners can offer deep pockets for later-stage financing.

Businesses likely to receive this type of investment are often smaller, technology-driven companies that have a logical "fit" with the sponsoring companies. However, unless you have a corporate partner experienced in this type of investment, you run a much higher risk of clashing corporate and entrepreneurial cultures.

Joint ventures: Joint ventures pair companies with complementary strengths on specific projects. For instance, a company that has designed a salable product may lack the cash to manufacture it. If the company can identify a partner with the right manufacturing capabilities, the two then can form a joint venture, divide the profits and eliminate the need for cash exchange.

Joint venture financing holds promise for the future in terms of providing emerging companies with a way of achieving the financial weight necessary to compete with larger corporate entities. There is plenty of room for imagination in setting up business arrangements of this type. One company was able to develop a software program for farmers and is now successfully marketing it through booths in feed stores.

Limited partnerships: A limited partnership can offer tax advantages that may be attractive to investors and thereby encourage them to put up money even though the returns won't be guaranteed. This is possible because losses incurred by a partnership can be passed through to investors and deducted from personal income. For example, suppose your business plan indicates it will take two or three years to achieve break-even (very common in start-up companies). These losses could be attractive to limited partners, because they can claim the write-offs on their own returns. The effect is to reduce the net amount of capital they have at risk in your business.

Limited partnerships don't have to involve large amounts of money and may involve only a small number of participants. This keeps set-up costs

down, because a prospectus doesn't have to be filed. They can be set up by lawyers or small brokerage firms that specialize in this type of venture and who have clients seeking such opportunities.

Source: David T. Thompson, partner, Deloitte & Touche, Crocker Center, 333 S. Grand Ave., Los Angeles, CA 90071, an international accounting and consulting firm. Additional input: Tom Slee, CFA, CGA, a financial consultant and tax specialist.

How to Appeal to Investors

To be a successful entrepreneur, you need more than a good idea. Among other things, you need money. One option is to raise the funds from family, friends and other personal sources (second mortgages, insurance policies, etc.). But if such funds are either unavailable or inadequate, you'll have to know where to find other avenues of financial backing.

Investment Sources

● **Informal investors.** These wealthy groups or individuals generally put up $10,000–$25,000 (but sometimes as much as $100,000) per investment. These investors can be found through the "in" accounting or law firms. As well, some well-connected brokerage firms may have a list of clients who are looking for attractive private deals.

● **Labor-sponsored venture capital funds.** These may invest several hundred thousand dollars (even more in some cases) if the project is attractive enough. They look for young companies that have products ready for market and demand a substantial chunk of the company's ownership.

● **Traditional venture capitalists.** These include private firms supported by insurance companies, pension funds or wealthy families and corporate venture-capital firms.

● **Investment bankers.** This group includes small local firms and the giants—CIBC Capital Partners, TD Capital, etc. They aid young companies that can't get venture capital by helping them go public. Some firms have both a venture-capital and an investment-banking arm.

Your Next Move

Entrepreneurs see all the possibilities for making money and usually downplay the risks. Investors, on the other hand, focus more on risk than on opportunity. They know there are more losers than winners among new businesses. Therefore, before approaching investors, it is critical to draft a detailed business plan. The plan should be 20–40 pages long, complete with a table of contents and summary (which includes the highlights of the plan). Without such a written plan, submitted in advance, few investment groups will grant an interview. *The plan should include:*

● **A clear description** of your business product or service.

● **Hard evidence of the marketability** of the product or service and the benefits to users.

● **Financial justification** of the chosen means of selling or distributing the product or service.

● **An explanation of product development** and the manufacturing process and their associated costs.

● **The qualifications of each member** of the management team.

● **Believable financial projections** that are not out of line with industry norms.

● **A statement of what the founders expect** to have accomplished three to seven years into the future.

The aspiring entrepreneur must also be prepared to give a concise and thorough oral presentation and to answer potential investors' questions.

What Turns Investors Off

● **Too much product orientation.** Entrepreneurs are often so obsessed with their product or technology that they talk too much about that instead of about who will be the user and what the user wants.

● **Insufficient attention to budgeting and finance.** There must be someone who is watching every penny and who is knowledgeable about matters such as what to do when the company needs a loan and whether it should go public.

● **Too much custom engineering.** When investors see that a company's product must be specially designed or altered for each customer, a red flag goes up. *Standard problems:* high costs and low profits. Investors also shy away from products that don't promise enough volume.

● **A one-man band.** Venture capitalists like to see a well-rounded management team of at least three players—encompassing marketing, finance, production and

research. You should have the team players outlined on paper, even if the slots have not yet been filled.

The least risky venture, from an investor's point of view, is a going concern with an established market. At the other end of the spectrum is a start-up venture whose single founder has an idea and whose market is assumed but not yet proved. Investors are especially leery of putting in money that will be used for unproductive research and development. And the greater the risk the investor perceives, the greater the ownership interest he or she will insist on.

Source: *Stanley R. Rich, founder of MIT Enterprises Forum and coauthor of* Business Plans That Win $$$, *HarperCollins. He is also an entrepreneur who has started nine ventures.*

When to Incorporate and When Not To

Enormous confusion surrounds the question of the best way to organize a business—as a proprietorship, partnership or corporation. Yet it is possible to make some sense out of the issues by examining the potential advantage and disadvantages of incorporating in light of specific tax and business considerations. Here are some basic rules.

When to Incorporate

● **If you, as owner, wish to enjoy tax-free fringe benefits.** A proprietor or partner is not an employee of a company and therefore can't participate in tax-free or tax-advantaged fringe benefit programs such as the pension plans that employees enjoy.

● **If you are trying to build working capital in the business.** This may be the single best reason for a profitable company in the growth stage to incorporate. You can conserve cash by saving tax dollars, since part of your total income will be taxed at corporate rates (with a special reduced rate for small businesses) rather than personal rates.

● **If you want to divert income to dependent family members.** You can hire members of your family as long as they do real work and are paid a reasonable wage.

● **Limited liability.** An incorporated business is an independent entity. Unless you have given personal guarantees, your own assets are not at risk if the corporation runs into financial difficulties.

● **Tax-advantaged compensation.** As the owner-manager of an incorporated company, you can decide on how you want to receive income. A mixture of salary and dividends will result in a lower personal tax rate because of the application of the dividend tax credit. However, dividends are not tax-deductible to the company and do not count toward CPP and RRSP eligibility, or in calculating a pension contribution. You may wish to discuss the matter with a tax adviser.

● **The capital gains exemption.** Owners of qualifying small businesses are eligible for a capital gains exemption of up to $500,000 when they sell.

When Not to Incorporate

● **If you expect losses in early years that you can offset with other personal income.** When you operate a new business on an unincorporated basis, start-up losses can be deducted from other taxable income.

● **If you want to avoid hefty start-up costs.** There are expenses involved in setting up a company. These include legal fees, government incorporation fees, etc.

● **If you want to keep on-going costs down.** As a private company, you will have to file annual corporate tax returns. You must maintain your books in good order in the event of an audit. You will also incur legal expenses to maintain company minute books.

● **If you hate paperwork.** You'll become a tax collector. Your company will need to register for the GST and, if applicable, for provincial sales tax. You'll be required to collect the appropriate amounts and remit them to government on a regular basis, along with the necessary forms.

● **Overall, management and administrative considerations favor use of a corporation.** The bigger the business, the greater the administrative advantages.

SIX WAYS TO TAKE MONEY OUT OF A CLOSELY HELD BUSINESS

If you are the president and sole or part owner of an incorporated business and you want to take money out of the business, you really have only four options. The one you choose may be largely determined by the varying tax implications. Here are the possibilities:

1. Sell the business. The first and most obvious method is to sell all or part of the business to a third party. Under Canadian tax law, your incorporated small business may qualify for a capital gains exemption of up to $500,000, provided certain conditions are met. If your business is eligible, you may be able to walk away without paying a cent in tax to the government.

Before you take any action, review the situation with a tax professional who has specialized expertise in this area.

2. Take a large salary or bonus. A simpler route—assuming you don't want to sell and the business generates the necessary cash—is to pay yourself a generous salary or bonus. This money is deductible from the corporation's earnings and taxed as ordinary income to you. This is not the most tax-effective alternative, but it is a direct way to get cash with no strings attached.

3. Take advantage of perquisites, benefits and amenities. Another alternative is to let the company pay for business-related expenses not considered taxable benefits, such as a club membership.

However, the CCRA may take an interest if you reward yourself too generously or overspend on expense account meals.

• **Personal legal considerations** also favor incorporation, because of the financial protection offered by limited liability.

Source: Vernon K. Jacobs, CPA, CLU, tax and financial adviser, 4500 W. 72 Terrace, Prairie Village, KS 66208. He is the author of Tax Factors in Choosing a Form of Business and has written more than 300 articles about legal methods of tax avoidance. Additional input from Gordon Pape.

The Top Home Businesses

Millions of North Americans commute to work these days by staying home. Some want to stay close to growing kids. Some find that technological advances make it easier—and often cheaper—to work from home.

Here are the best home businesses to start now. We've chosen them based on income potential, ease of entry, growth rate, stress level, ability to resist a recession and low start-up costs.

Important: Some businesses do require specialized skills. But often they're the computer skills you've learned and used at the office. And some of our favorite home businesses don't require special skills—only the willingness to learn and work hard.

• **Multimedia production.** This is a play on the business world's increasing appetite for multimedia presentations, which today almost always include computer-generated art and animation. Large and small businesses are accustomed to farming out such work. This does require computer skills. And if you have them, there's enormous potential here.

Requirements: An $8,000 to $25,000 up-front investment in hardware and software. You'll need a very large hard drive, CD-ROM drive that runs at triple speed, sound board, color scanner, laser printer, graphic design software and probably an authoring system that ties it all together.

Income potential: You can make up to $100

Generally, the CCRA holds that executives cannot receive company-provided amenities tax-free, especially when the perks are not available to all employees. But under CCRA guidelines, a company can pay for such job-related expenses as entertaining clients or traveling to a convention, within reason. These costs are deductible, at least in part, by the company and tax-free to the executive if they are deemed to primarily benefit the employer and not the employee.

4. Pay dividends. Another way to get money from a closely held business is to declare and pay substantial dividends to the shareholder(s)—in this case, you. Dividends receive a tax advantage, through the application of the dividend tax credit which alleviates, but does not eliminate, the effect of double taxation. You must pay dividends after corporate income taxes have been paid and declare them as

personal income. You claim the dividend tax credit when you file your personal tax return.

5. Employ family members. You can hire your spouse and/or your children to work for your company and pay them a salary. This results in income-splitting, which is often advantageous in terms of reducing total tax payable. The children do not have to be adults. However, it is important that family members perform legitimate work and that their pay be appropriate in the circumstances. If you use the going rate for a comparable job in the private sector, you should be fine.

6. Set up a pension plan. Although Individual Pension Plans (IPPs) aren't right for all circumstances, they can be useful in moving money from the company into your hands (albeit indirectly) without attracting tax. In fact, pension contributions are tax-deductible to the

corporation. Consult with an accounting firm that specializes in such plans before proceeding.

Clearly, there is no perfect way of taking money out of a business, but if you decide to do it, keep three basic rules in mind:

• Sell any portion(s) of the business that will not cause you to relinquish control of the company.

• Take "reasonable" salary an bonuses, for yourself and family members.

• Take advantage of all CCRA-allowed benefits and perks.

Source: Brian D. Dunn, principal with Towers, Perrin, Forster & Crosby, 245 Park Ave., New York, NY 10167, specializing in incentive compensation and organizational design. He has been published and widely quoted in professional journals and newspapers, and has spoken before the Human Resources Planning Society, the American Society of Personnel Administrators and the New York Chamber of Commerce. With additional input from Gordon Pape.

an hour—or as much as $5,000 for producing a three-minute video.

● **Video production.** There are two growing markets here. On the business side, the proliferation of TV channels is creating a huge appetite for programming. (*Consider:* 500 channels require 12,000 hours of programming per day.) As the number of channels grows, each channel attracts fewer viewers. That cuts the cost of advertising, making TV increasingly affordable for smaller advertisers.

Strategy: Watch cable TV to find businesses with poorly executed commercials. Convince them you can do a better job.

The second market is the consumer. More and more people will pay for professional, edited videos of weddings, parties and family histories.

Requirements: Video camera, computer with Intel 486 chip and editing/production software can all be acquired for as little as $6,000.

Income potential: $25 to $100 per hour.

● **Repair services.** Consumers don't really want to junk expensive purchases after warranties have expired. With even advanced-amateur skills—or aptitude and a willingness to learn—you can make money as either a jack-of-all-trades handyman or a specialist.

If you have the technical training, consider the fastest-growing area—high-tech products (computers, printers, copiers, fax machines and scanners).

Strategy: If you go into high-tech repair, consider concentrating on the home and home-business markets. They now account for 51% of all PC sales.

Requirements: Up-front equipment costs vary by field, as does training.

Income potential: $15 to $100 per hour.

● **Cleaning services.** You can do the cleaning yourself or hire employees. Both the business and the consumer markets are targets (consumers are increasingly willing to pay for convenience services). Niche markets include services to clean carpets, floors, ceilings, draperies and upholstery, venetian blinds, air ducts, swimming pools and much more.

Requirements: A little up-front investment in cleaning supplies and perhaps some training. The downside is that the work isn't easy or absorbing.

Income potential: $25,000 to $100,000 per year.

● **Mailing list service.** With a computer, this is one of the easiest businesses to start from home—and it

can really take off. You can create and maintain mailing lists for customers, produce your own list and then sell names to clients, sell monthly updated lists or market, support and educate users in mailing-list software.

Requirements: Start-up costs will range from $2,500 to $6,000. You'll need a computer with a large hard drive, printer, database or special mailing-list software, business cards, letterhead, envelopes and a price list.

Income potential: $10,000 to $75,000 is typical annual gross.

● **Rubber stamps.** A surprisingly hot business. People love rubber stamps and buy them at craft shows, in specialty stores and via mail order. You can use metallic and glow-in-the-dark inks to boost sales.

Requirements: It's not difficult to make rubber stamps and you can use free public domain clip art for designs. Or you can create your own designs. You can now produce rubber stamps with a computer, laser printer and photopolymer system (*Cost:* $2,800).

Income potential: People have been known to sell $2,000 to $5,000 worth per day at arts and crafts shows.

Source: Paul and Sarah Edwards, authors of The Best Home Businesses for the '90s, Working From Home *and* Making Money with Your Computer at Home, *Jeremy P. Tarcher/Putnam.*

How to Profit From a Merger or Acquisition

The thousands of mergers and acquisitions announced each year are only the tip of an enormous economic iceberg: For every deal we read about, several others take place more quietly. Mergers and acquisitions are almost considered routine, yet the rewards are not always worth the risks. Participants on both sides of the deal need to keep their strategies sharp.

The Buyer's Strategy

Most acquisitions don't work out because buyers outnumber sellers, giving sellers the edge, and because it's almost impossible to predict all of the problems involved in combining two companies. Also, diversification per se is not a sufficient reason to acquire. Most companies can't handle a totally new business.

To improve the odds of making an acquisition successful, make sure you first have a clear understanding of your own company first:

- **What do you do well—or badly?**
- **Do you undermarket your products or services?**
- **Do you challenge your managers sufficiently?**
- **Has technological development begun to pass you by?**
- **Will selling new products and services help your sales force?**
- **How much of your own capital can** you really spare for acquisition?
- **How do your shareholders feel about risk?**

Self-analysis helps you decide when to acquire—you may decide that now is not the time. An acquisition will quickly put you into new products, services or markets, but is speed worth the risk and disruption? Acquisition makes the most sense when you have the resources to succeed, the opportunity to add something you're lacking and the chance that you'll suffer if you move too slowly.

Self-analysis also helps you develop general acquisition criteria: Industry, company size, location, growth history and prospects, profitability, debt leverage, management objectives and purchase price. More specific criteria can include union status, customer profile, competitive posture, technology levels and image. Combining your criteria with a weighting system saves time and further reduces the risk of a poor acquisition.

Identifying Candidates

How you apply your acquisition criteria depends on how you identify candidates. The two search strategies are the passive approach and the active approach. The former involves networking in the business community, especially among investment bankers, business brokers, lenders, accountants, and the like, with the goal of uncovering owners who have decided to sell or at least to think about it. The active approach involves identifying, screening and contacting companies whose owners don't yet plan to sell. The search can be conducted by your own staff, consultants or intermediaries. Which method you use to identify candidates depends on your management depth. If your management team is "thin," the active approach usually won't work unless you hire outsiders.

If the companies on your list aren't for sale yet, it's especially important that actual contacts be made discreetly, possibly by a third party. *Before you make the contacts, answer these key questions:* Who controls the stock? What are the current "hot buttons" ("clean up your estate"; "preserve company's existence"; "add to your marketing clout"; etc.)? Who should make each approach? How? How much are you willing to say about your own company? What must you learn? And, what should the next step be?

The passive approach to identifying candidates costs less, but can involve spending a great deal of time fielding calls without seeing the best targets—the ones on the market may not be right for you. The active method, on the other hand, focuses on the best corporate fits, but the principals in the companies have to be convinced to sell. This can be an emotional process.

The Seller's Strategy

Sellers obviously have a very different view of the acquisition process. As the owner of a company, you may be under no pressure to sell, and the years you've spent building up the business can keep you from pricing it rationally. If you want to sell and you've minimized taxes, rather than maximized earnings, your company may not even be an attractive target.

In at least one way, selling a business does resemble buying one: Both require preliminary self-analysis. Do your shareholders need liquidity? Is selling to outsiders the only way to get it? Does the company need more growth capital than your current owners can provide? Are there other gaps, in production, marketing or management, that can't be closed except by selling? Is the future rosy enough to attract a buyer at the right price?

> " **As the owner of a company, you may be under no pressure to sell, and the years you've spent building up the business can keep you from pricing it rationally.** "

Eight Ways to Evaluate a Business Before You Buy It

Emotional and other less-than-pragmatic considerations often play major roles in deciding how much a business is worth. For buyers who want to rely on more logical techniques, there are eight basic methods for evaluating a closely held business with no publicly traded stock and owners who are near retirement:

1. **Capitalized earnings.** The value is judged according to the previous year's earnings, income over the last few years, or projected earnings.

2. **Corporate and shareholder earnings.** Both of these are capitalized. This amount is paid out over a period that is usually two to four times the capitalization period. *Example:* If earnings were capitalized for the previous two years payment could be over the next four to eight years.

3. **Percentages of future profits.** The definition of profit can include any items that management determines. Payments can be spread over a number of years and arranged in diminishing stages.

4. **Book value.** The sum of assets as they appear on the books (excluding goodwill) less liabilities.

5. **Adjusted book value.** Current values are applied to the balance sheet. *Example:* Fixed assets are valued at either their replacement or their knockdown value rather than as they appear on the books.

6. **Book value plus pensions.** Consideration is given to retirement plans in effect at similar companies and an equitable compensation program for the retiring sellers.

7. **Start-up cost.** A buyer who wants to enter an industry will often pay more than a business is actually worth. *Reason:* The price may still be less than the cost of entering the field from scratch.

8. **Industry custom.** Some types of businesses are valued on the basis of historic formulas. *Examples:* Dental practices may sell for the previous year's gross income. Insurance brokerages can sell for a price equal to the first year's retained renewals.

Source: Edward Mendlowitz, partner, Mendlowitz Weitsen, CPAs, 2 Penn Plaza, New York, NY 10121.

One way to attract buyers is to prepare a well-organized corporate profile containing: an executive summary, a financial history, adjustments to show true asset values and earning power, an industry survey, the position of your company in the industry, your products or services, marketing methods, management résumés, your labor environment, brochures, etc. Such a profile can deflect casual buyers. Once they've read it, you can insist that their next step be a bid. (This also will reduce onsite "tire kicking" and employee rumors.)

Another way to identify potential acquirers is to consider your current customers, competitors, and suppliers. You may find you already know good contacts. Intermediaries may be useful, too.

Intermediaries and Confidentiality

Whether you are a buyer or a seller, intermediaries can be used as a buffer and to maintain secrecy. Most intermediaries charge nonrefundable retainer fees, along with commissions or "success fees," with total charges computed as a percentage of the purchase price—often 1% to 5% for smaller businesses. Check on the intermediary's charges, terms and credentials before making a commitment. Intermediaries can be paid by either party, or at closing. Most intermediaries prefer to be paid by the seller, since that symbolizes the seller's commitment to sell. Above all, keep in mind that most intermediaries are transaction-oriented and will push hard to close a deal quickly, even if you haven't made up your mind.

There are several ways an intermediary can help a seller maintain secrecy. He can provide you with background information on each potential buyer, use an anonymous fact sheet for each first approach, limit the number of potential buyers approached simultaneously, have each prospect sign and return a confidentiality letter before you send your profile, and provide you with a weekly status report. However, these steps can delay the selling process, so you may need to balance your desires for secrecy and speed.

Valuing the Target

How does each side arrive at a price? This is particularly difficult if the target is privately held or part of a larger company, but three valuation methods are generally used:

1. Asset appraisal, which assumes that a business derives more value from assets than from earnings or cash flow.

2. Discounted cash flow, which assumes that a business's value is attributable to its cash flow.

3. Comparable-company multiples, which assumes the best way to decide a company's worth is to study what investors have paid for similar companies.

The seller and buyer independently use these valuation methods to arrive at their assessments. Negotiations typically proceed from that point.

The seller's minimum price depends on the seller's alternatives. For example, if the company has shareholders' equity of $6 million and net earnings of $1 million, a buyer might bid $8 million–$10 million. But if the current owners collectively take out $1 million or more each year—while retaining control—this offer might not give the owners as much as they already have.

The buyer's maximum price depends on synergies that could improve the target's earning potential. This requires the buyer to make two calculations: How much is the target worth, on a stand-alone basis? And, how much more can the buyer offer, if necessary, to reflect the company's potential value?

The result of the negotiations will depend more on the people involved than even these calculations of maximum and minimum price. (This is why the initial contact between companies is always a challenge.) The negotiating process underscores how important people are to the acquisition process as a whole. Many times, one party will walk away from a perfectly reasonable offer because he or she simply doesn't want to deal with the other party. At times like these, or when such a problem seems likely to arise, intermediaries can be helpful in buffering the parties from one another. However, whether you are the buyer or seller, remember that any merger or acquisition involves people—no price can make up entirely for ill will.

Source: *Stephen Bennett Blum, CPA, co-director of the merger and acquisition department, KPMG Peat Marwick, 345 Park Ave., New York 10145.*

Something for Nothing—How a Leveraged Buyout Works

Any investor who has participated in a successful leveraged buyout (LBO) may have reason to question the age-old axiom You can't get something for nothing.

In a typical LBO, the amount of cash the investors put into the venture in the form of equity is a small percentage of the total acquisition cost. Most of the purchase price is financed through debt, secured by the company's assets and cash flow. The cash flow of the business is used to pay interest and debt amortization. Also, less profitable segments of the business are sold to pay down the debt. At the conclusion of the transaction, the investors have something—ownership of an operating company, for next to nothing—their initial investment.

Since operating management usually obtains an equity position in the ongoing venture, increased productivity and profits often result from the entrepreneurial spirit of the new owners. If everything goes well, it may be possible to return the investors' original investment in the form of fees or proceeds from the sale of new stock (often a public offering). When this happens, the investors can find themselves with an ongoing business that has cost them nothing.

Minimizing the Risks

Obviously, not every company can provide investors with a windfall. To minimize the risks, look for the following general indicators of a good LBO candidate:

● **Strong, predictable operating cash flow** that is neither cyclical nor affected by interest rates.

● **Opportunities to reduce costs** by eliminating unnecessary overheads.

● **Assets with fair market values** in excess of net book values.

● **Management with a strong entrepreneurial spirit.**

Once you've chosen an LBO venture, there are still risks involved in making it pay for itself. Since the LBO is heavily dependent on debt financing, interest rate movements can have a significant impact on the company's ability to service its debt. One way to reduce this risk is to negotiate an interest rate cap with the financing sources. Another is to arrange to have interest charges in excess of a certain percentage deferred for a period of time.

To ward against the chance that profits don't increase as quickly as originally planned, investors can keep a cash reserve available for future investment in the company. A small additional investment may be all that is required to put the company over the top.

Although LBOs involving millions of dollars of investment get most of the attention from the business press, smaller LBOs continue to be a strong investment opportunity. You may need to take some high short-term risks, but prudent analysis of cash flow and proper attention to management can help you get something for nothing.

Source: *Kevin M. Smith, partner and director of entrepreneurial services for the New York metropolitan office of Ernst & Young, New York. He is responsible for providing financial accounting and consulting services to middle-market companies.*

Selling an Unprofitable Business

There are four kinds of potential buyers for money-losing assets.

● **Large public companies** with a specific need for products or assets.

● **Risk-playing entrepreneurs** with expertise in the industry.

● **Foreign companies** looking for a toehold in Canada or for access to the North American market.

● **The business's own management,** backed by venture capital.

To find a buyer: Figure out which one of these groups will most logically profit from acquiring the business. Then quietly send out feelers to candidates within that group to see if they express interest in acquiring.

If word gets out that the business is for sale, capitalize on the publicity. Use it to flush out as many potential buyers as possible, then pit them against each other.

Caution: Publicly putting a business on the block hurts employee morale. If a business is labor-intensive, it's generally best not to publicize the intended sale. Labor-intensive companies on the block get raided. The loss of their top talent depresses the business's value. *Sales strategy:* Know the strengths and weaknesses of the business. Address both of them openly when negotiating.

Important: Don't be tempted to spread false turnaround tales. When an owner tells a prospective buyer that the business is about to turn around, the buyer will only wonder why the owner wants to sell it. This casts doubt on the owner's credibility. *Pricing strategy:*

● **Price the business** at least 30% higher than the final acceptable figure.

Warning: Don't overbluff.

● **Keep marginal prospects** in the picture to foster competition with serious potential buyers.

Choices if the sale is not made:

● **Liquidate.**

● **Remove the business from the market** for the time it takes to revive it and increase its salability.

Source: The Profit Line. *Durkee/Sharlit Associates.*

What You May Not Know About Franchises

If you're considering the purchase of a franchise, you should understand first that franchises are not typically the bargains they once were. The costs and risks of running a franchise have increased, and the payback periods are longer than they were in the past.

You also should be aware of the trap that lies in the common business cycle of heavily franchised industries. In the initial phase of the cycle—launching the new product or service, or entering the new geographic area—competition and pricing pressure are generally quite low. Franchise fees may not seem like a burden to the operation experiencing rapid sales growth and strong cash flow.

As business lines mature and new competition enters the field, bringing increased pressures on profit margins, the franchise operation may find itself at a disadvantage compared with the independent competitor. With equal sales and gross profit margins, the independent business should make more money—franchise fees limit a franchisee's ability to meet price competition and still make a profit, unless the franchise provides some unique competitive advantage.

> "Publicly putting a business on the block hurts employee morale.... Labor-intensive companies on the block get raided. The loss of their top talent depresses the business's value."

Very important here are the franchisor's experience and attitude. Some franchisors not only are conscientious about helping franchisees who are in trouble, but also have the experience to anticipate and avoid problems of this sort. Unscrupulous franchisors, on the other hand, may simply let individual franchises fail and then resell them.

Aside from larger economic questions, specific difficulties and pitfalls can arise in franchise schemes. *Here's what you should know about:*

● **Hidden costs.** Not all franchise agreements clearly spell out the full fees the operator will be called on to pay. To avoid unpleasant surprises when the franchisor assesses fees for national advertising, administration, group accounting and the like, be sure to find out about all costs ahead of time. Total fees paid to the franchisor could be as much as the net earnings of the franchisee.

● **Product exclusivity.** If you are paying for the right to sell a unique product or service, ask yourself: how long will it remain unique? Early in the game, buying a franchise may be the only way to obtain the right to sell a particular product. But in our free market system, it doesn't usually remain this way very long. Typical complaints from franchisees in this situation are that not enough is spent on advertising the franchise name; that anyone can get the product; that the franchisees pay a higher price because they are locked into buying from the franchisor; and that they cannot get the latest or enough merchandise.

● **Location.** Selection and provision of a business location are often the purview of the franchisor. Can you count on the franchisor to provide a good location? Are the best locations reserved for company ownership rather than franchise operations? Will the franchisor refrain from selling other franchises close enough to compete with yours? These are important questions to have answered.

● **Standards.** Are standards of quality, appearance of premises, levels of service, etc. detailed in the franchise agreement? Are they enforced? A poorly run franchise in your area may reflect badly on your operation and the rest of the system. A franchisor needs to be able to identify these problems and take corrective action before other franchise locations are adversely affected.

● **Business and management assistance.** Theoretically, this is part of the package with almost all franchise operations, but in practice the assistance may have little value. Good franchisors hold regular training sessions and have experienced and knowledgeable corporate personnel to assist individual franchisees. Some bring in successful franchisees to help. However, in other instances, assistance may be limited to printed manuals or forms backed up by little or no hands-on help. For a first-time business owner, this may be inadequate.

● **Stability of the franchisor.** It may not matter how successful an individual franchisee is if the franchisor fails. For example, a clothing store franchisor had a policy to restrict franchisees from carrying and selling other brands of merchandise. The franchisor failed. Most of the successful franchises failed, in turn, since they had no existing relations with other vendors.

Lawsuit Guidelines

There are many exceptions, but as a rule:

● **Don't sue for less than $25,000.** A lawsuit will cost so much that even if you win, you can only break even.

● **Keep in mind that the legal bills** may cripple or kill your company.

● **Remember that if your company is sued** by a determined one that's much bigger than yours, your company doesn't stand much of a chance. The legal help your company receives depends on the size of its bankroll—the facts of the case are only incidental.

● **Don't be the first to suggest a settlement.** The unreasonable party usually wins.

Source: David W. Swanson, president, Daavlin Co., Box 626, Bryan, OH 43506.

● **Power of the lease.** Who holds the lease to the franchise location? If the franchisor owns the lease, a franchisee who gets in trouble and misses a payment may be evicted instead of getting expected help and support from the organization.

All in all, it is an excellent idea to investigate and evaluate the experience and reputation of the franchisor when considering buying a franchise system. Talk to other franchise owners and review the applicable laws in your province. Ontario, for example, passed new legislation in early 2001 designed to protect franchise purchasers.

You can find details on the website of the Canadian Franchise Association (CFA), at http://www.cfa.ca. The CFA also provides a list of established and reputable franchise companies and offers advice on how to evaluate an opportunity.

If you do not have access to the Internet, you can write to the CFA at 2585 Skymark Avenue, Suite 300, Mississauga, Ont. L4W 4L5.

Source: Donald Murray, partner and director of the enterprise and retail group Deloitte & Touche, 1000 Wilshire Blvd., Los Angeles, CA 90010. He has published several articles on retailing and frequently lectures at universities and to business groups.

The Many Benefits of Franchising

Franchising can help you avoid much of the risk of going into business on your own. For an establishment fee and continuing royalties, a franchise offers benefits that are otherwise unobtainable.

● **A franchise is your own business**—preplanned, prestructured, preestablished and pretested.

HOW TO MAKE THE MOST OF RETIREMENT PLANNING

As we live longer and pension investments become more important, it is crucial that people take a more active role in their retirement planning. Thus, it is very important to become more knowledgeable about investing and, especially, about asset allocation—how to divide your money between stocks, bonds, cash and other investments to get the best and safest return.

Those who already have a stockbroker or who keep up with the financial press know that all the big brokerage houses issue asset allocation recommendations periodically, suggesting that institutions keep their money in stocks, bonds, and cash in various percentages. *Here are some points to be aware of:*

● **The brokerage houses's fore-**casts relate to large institutional accounts. Individual planning does not need to be adjusted as often.

● **Blanket advice won't fit everybody.** The younger you are, the more risk you can take (that is to say, the more aggressive stocks you can own). As you grow into middle age, you will need to be more conservative and choose more bonds and balanced (between stocks and bonds) mutual funds.

● **Reallocating assets over the short term is disruptive to long-term planning** because it is essential for individuals to consider five-, 10-, or even 15-year time horizons to give investments a chance to turn a healthy profit.

See the Big Picture

View all your assets together, then plan your investment strategies. A reminder: try not to achieve only short-term results.

Some people invest too heavily in cash and term deposits (TDs) for one-year maturities and money-market funds, which all have low, low returns. And they are too afraid of the risk associated with stocks, which historically offer the best long-term rewards.

What's Your Current Allocation?

Make a comprehensive list of your current assets, noting the current yield for each. Mark all taxable items.

● **Savings accounts.**
● **Term deposits (TDs) and guaranteed investment certificates (GICs).**
● **Stocks.** List the number of shares of each stock and the current value of your holdings.
● **Bonds.**
● **Mutual funds.**
● **Real estate.**
● **Corporate savings plans.**
● **Deferred annuities and life insurance.**
● **Pension plans usually are paid out as an annuity in fixed monthly payments.** List the estimated annual

- **A franchise is based on more than "a good idea"**—it involves the previous establishment of pilot operations that have proved successful.

- **You are in business for yourself,** but not by yourself, since the franchise organization is behind you. The franchisor has extensive experience in implementing the business and can effectively guide you along the right path.

- **In-depth training is available to you at the outset,** with refresher training at subsequent periods. Workshops on management, communications and personal finances also may be offered.

- **The program is thoroughly documented**—manuals cover all aspects of the operation.

- **Selection of an effective site for your business** is based on standardized marketing procedures.

- **Economies are achieved from group advertising and purchases,** accelerating as the franchise system grows.

- **Each individual benefits from the whole.** As the network expands, the value of the individual franchise grows too.

- **The franchisor provides services that you often cannot afford,** because they require either too much time or too much money. These services include researching and developing new products, ideas and promotions, and the tools to help implement them. The franchisor's staff also can assist in problem solving.

Source: David D. Seltz, president, Seltz Franchising Developments, Inc., 30 Ridge Rd., New Rochelle, NY 10804, an authority on the franchising and marketing fields. He has served as chairman of the International Franchise Congress, has conducted seminars and is a prolific writer.

income for both employer pension plans and the Canada Pension Plan (CPP), as well as for Old Age Security (OAS).

- **An RRSP,** which includes investments of all types.

- **Liabilities.** List all your liabilities, such as a mortgage, car loan, student loan, etc.

Investment Strategies

The first step is to determine what income you need and what assets you already have (your house, valuable antiques, etc.) and then make some crucial personal decisions. How important is safety? Do you need safety of principal or safety of buying power?

If inflation persists at its recent historical rate of 3% a year, your money will lose one-third of its buying power in 10 years. That's why, even if you are 65 years old and have a net worth of $300,000, we would advise you to keep 25% to 35% of your assets in growth investments, such as stock or real estate.

How important is your need for liquidity and what is your comfort zone? Most retirees don't need more than three months' living expenses in quickly available funds, but some older people don't feel comfortable without $100,000 in a savings account.

By keeping only $10,000 in the bank and investing $90,000 in a low-risk bond or dividend fund, you could earn an extra couple of thousand dollars each year. If the income is received as dividends from a taxable Canadian company outside a registered plan, it will be eligible for the dividend tax credit.

The need for some reallocation of assets is usually revealed after you've looked at your overall financial picture.

We also advise clients to make their portfolios safer by weeding out any stocks that don't currently rate "1" or "2" for timeliness and safety by Value Line Reports (available in many brokers' offices and libraries) and any mutual funds that are not given four or five stars by Morningstar, Inc.

Source: William W. Parrott, president, Creative Retirement Planning, Inc., One Hollow Lane, Suite 306B, Lake Success, NY 11042. He and his son John L. Parrott are coauthors of You Can Afford to Retire: The No-Nonsense Guide to Pre-Retirement Financial Planning, Simon & Schuster's New York Institute of Finance.

Dealing With Banks, Credit & Debt

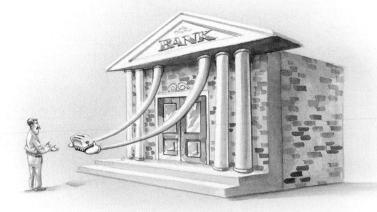

5

How Safe Is Your Bank?

Banks don't have to fail in order to hurt the customers with whom they do business. Even as financial problems are just beginning to develop, the bank's operations may begin to deteriorate, and ultimately the bank may need to rein in its growth.

When banks run into financial problems, they behave like any other troubled company. They sometimes try to hide problems and limp along the best they can. For the customer, services can quickly deteriorate. Growing companies can be especially hurt because most rely on their banks to expand credit lines. Unfortunately, a troubled bank too often will call in its loans because the bank needs the money—not because the customer is at any growth risk.

As a result, thousands of customers are hurt. Many could have avoided problems by watching for early warning signals of bank weakness. These signals can show up as early as two years before a failure.

Banks in Canada rarely fail, but it has happened. Chances are good that your bank is among the vast majority of healthy ones in the country. But ignoring the signs of problems may add to your future risks.

Bank problems often stem from decisions to grow aggressively. Some American banks that have failed funded an ambitious growth strategy with "purchased" funds (such as large GICs), as opposed to deposits from their customers. That strategy puts them on shaky ground.

Customers who have dealt for some time with banks in this situation usually sense something is wrong:

- **There's high turnover** among the officers.
- **Paperwork and record keeping** become sloppy.
- **The bank encourages customers to extend credit** when officers know it really isn't necessary.

But even when customers suspect that a bank is going through some sort of change, they rarely take the trouble to find out if it's merely because of routine personnel problems or because of more serious financial trouble.

Essential steps: If a friendly bank officer has recently quit, invite him or her to lunch and ask tough questions about his or her former employer. If you think there's a problem, get a copy of the bank's most recent financial data (annual reports, quarterly reports). These documents will tell you a great deal about the financial conditions of a bank. (In fact, regardless of whether a customer senses trouble, he or she should routinely get financial data for banks with which the customer does business.)

Most Canadian banks are public companies, so their financial reports are public documents. You can obtain them online at the bank's website or through the bank's investor-relations department. If you encounter any problems, the data is also available from the Office of the Superintendent of Financial Institutions website at http://www.osfi-bsif.gc.ca/eng/institutions/banks/financial/index.asp.

What to look for: By comparing financial figures over time, a customer can read the warning signals. According to Cates Consulting Analysts, Inc., the signals include:

- **Rapid expansion** as reflected in a big increase in loan yield relative to other similarly sized banks.
- **Loan recovery rate of less than 20%.** This is the percentage of written-off bad loans that a bank is ultimately able to recover. It should be well over 20% and is an excellent indication of how riskily the bank is willing to operate.
- **Low return on assets for a bank its size** (can range from 0.6% for large banks to well over 1.0% for a small bank).
- **High overhead ratio.** Failed U.S. banks had overhead expenses that amounted to nearly 80% of their income base, compared with a nationwide average of 56%. Bank failures in the United States have decreased in recent years, and we haven't seen one in Canada since the Bank of British Columbia suffered that fate in 1986. But that's no reason not to be diligent—it's your money. If your money is with a trust company, you should be even more cautious—Canada has seen several trust companies go under in the past 25 years.

> "With the careful management of your accounts, it's possible for you to go far beyond the $60,000 insurance limit offered by the CDIC."

How to Protect Yourself Against Bank Failure

Banks can have financial problems, but no companies or individuals should lose money if they understand how the banking system works. In order to protect against the possibility of bank failure, depositors must know how to:

● **Judge the different types** of insurance that banks can have.

● **Spread deposits legally** to maximize insurance coverage.

● **Evaluate a bank's financial data** for early warning signs of trouble.

Insurance Quality

In view of possible bank difficulties, the Canada Deposit Insurance Corporation (CDIC) was created to insure deposits at all Canadian banks, trust companies and loan companies. Credit unions, life insurance companies and brokerage firms are not eligible to be CDIC member institutions.

The CDIC protects up to $60,000 of your deposits. Be very cautious about doing business with independent financial companies that issue investment certificates through a trust company or credit union. The CDIC won't insure deposits you make as investment contracts with nonmember organizations.

Other problems: Even though RRSP and RRIF accounts are protected by the CDIC, you stand to lose a lot of money if you have a large retirement account that exceeds the $60,000 limit. Also keep in mind that certain types of securities, such as mutual funds, are not protected. And remember, the CDIC only protects your Canadian currency deposits. U.S. dollar deposits are not covered.

Beyond the Limit

Surprise: With the careful management of your accounts, it's possible for you to go far beyond the $60,000 insurance limit offered by the CDIC.

● **Each depositor is insured up to $60,000** at each institution, including its branches. All savings and chequing accounts owned by the same person, with the exception of RRSPs and RRIFs, are lumped together to reach the $60,000 limit.

● **Sole proprietorship business accounts** are insured separately from individual accounts.

● **All valid joint accounts** are insured separately from individual accounts.

These rules still leave a lot of leeway. Deposits owned jointly under such conditions as joint tenancy or community property are insured separately from deposit accounts individually owned by the co-owners. *Example:* A couple can insure up to $300,000 by opening five $60,000 accounts—one in each spouse's name, one in a joint name and two retirement accounts.

Opportunity: Another way to expand insurance coverage at the same bank is to open revocable testamentary or trust accounts that name beneficiaries in case of death. *Benefit:* There's a $60,000 insurance maximum on the accounts for each beneficiary.

For a complete explanation of CDIC insurance, ask for the *Protecting Your Deposits* brochure from your bank. You can also visit the CDIC website at http://www.cdic.ca/ for more information.

Pension Strategy

Similarly, a company's pension and profit-sharing deposits are considered to be trust funds. If they meet certain conditions and record-keeping requirements, these pension and profit-sharing accounts are separately insured for up to $60,000 per participant at each depository bank. Check with bank officers to make sure the company meets CDIC regulations governing such accounts.

The most common insurance traps:

● **Believing that securities held by a bank** in RRSPs and other accounts come under insurance plans. They don't.

● **Creating a corporation or other type of organization** with the sole purpose of using it to get more deposit insurance. Federal rules say that an organization must be engaged in "independent activity" in order for it to qualify for deposit insurance.

● **Using a variation of your name to open another account** in the hope of getting more insurance. Varying names or Social Insurance numbers on joint accounts usually isn't illegal. But it won't get you more deposit insurance.

Safety Checks

Just as a business would check the financial health of a supplier or customer, it's a sound practice to keep a running check on the viability of the company's banks.

Check on the following points:

● **Liquidity.** Look at the bank's cash and securities that are readily convertible into cash as a percent of total deposits. A one-to-four or one-to-five ratio is pretty good. A lower ratio could be a signal of some serious trouble.

● **Capital requirements.** Total primary equity at commercial banks should be 5½%–6% of total assets.

● **Loan losses.** These shouldn't exceed 1% of a bank's total loan portfolio on an annual basis.

● **Net interest margin.** This is simply the difference between what the bank pays for funds and what it must pay out in interest.

● **Bond portfolio.** Compare current market value with the book value of bonds carried on the bank's financial statements. With many of these bonds, the actual liquidation value could be substantially less than book value.

Source: Herbert F. Mueller, president, North Valley Bancorp, 1377 South St., Redding, CA 96001. He has been a member of the American Bankers Association's advisory panel that explains banking practices to bank customers.

How to Question Your Banker

If you are concerned about the safety of the bank, there are things you should look for:

● **Any bank should be able to give you its financial statement.** Most banks publish them quarterly and annually.

● **Read the statement,** looking at the net worth, the number of "workouts" (situations in which bank officers are helping troubled companies get back on their feet), and the amount of real estate owned.

What you're trying to determine is the quality of the bank's investments. This is easier if the bank is a publicly traded company, as most are in Canada. The exceptions are some foreign banks with operations in this country. These companies must file with the Office of the Superintendent of Financial Institutions.

● **Look at the bank's track record over time.** If the bank has gone through extraordinary growth, it means that the institution has put out a lot of money, and it may have taken more risk.

● **If you are depositing over $60,000** (the limit for CDIC coverage), you should be able to discuss the kind of investments the institution has made.

● **You should also look at the accountant's report (included in most shareholder's reports).** Each institution has one. Be sure to read the "exceptions" to the accountant's statement.

● **Ask about the bank's "at risk" loans or "scheduled items"** (loans that have been in default for 60–120 days).

And, of course, be sure that your bank is insured by the CDIC. (*Editor's note:* For a complete explanation of CDIC insurance, ask your bank for its free brochure on coverage of accounts.)

Sources: Gordon Pape and Kendrew Pape; and Franklin H. Ornstein, chairman, Central Federal Savings Bank of Long Beach, Long Beach, NY. He is the author of Savings Banking: An Industry in Change, Prentice-Hall.

Protection for Your Insurance Company Savings

Insurance companies do not come under the protection of the CDIC. For a century, insurance company failures in Canada were rare so no one worried too much. But some high-profile collapses in the 1990s, including the flame-out of giant Confederation Life,

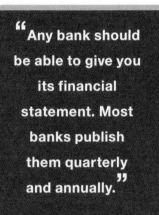

" Any bank should be able to give you its financial statement. Most banks publish them quarterly and annually. "

heightened concerns. Fortunately, you are protected, up to a point.

Both federal and provincial governments supervise the insurance business in Canada. The federal Office of the Superintendent of Financial Institutions oversees the solvency and stability of Canada's insurance companies. Additionally, agencies such as A.M. Best Ltd. assess companies' financial strength by reviewing their assets, liabilities, funds available to pay unexpected expenses, and its reserves. These agencies also review the companies' business plans, underlying assets (bonds, mortgages, real estate investments) and profits, and arrive at ratings that range from A (highest) to F (lowest). In addition to familiarizing yourself with the ratings issued by these firms, you should try to stay abreast of current business events. Read the business sections of Canada's major daily newspapers and scan media websites. Stay informed.

But if things go wrong, there is protection. The Canadian Life and Health Insurance Compensation Corporation (CompCorp) is a federally incorporated, nonprofit company established by the Canadian Life and Health Insurance Association (CLHIA) to protect policyholders, within limits, from the loss of benefits in the event of the failure of an insurance company. It is funded by CompCorp's member companies, about 200 strong. Protection is automatically extended to eligible policies issued by member insurance companies. There is no need to apply.

Coverage highlights per person are as follows:
● $200,000 of life insurance death benefits.
● $60,000 for non-registered policies, including money accumulation products and cash values in life insurance policies. Separate limits for individual and group contracts.
● $60,000 for registered policies, including RRSPs, RRIFs and registered pension plans (RPPs). Separate limits for individual and group contracts.
● $2,000 of monthly income under annuities or disability income policies.
● $60,000 of health insurance, other than disability income policies.

To be eligible for CompCorp protection, a policy must:
a) Be in Canadian currency.
b) Provide either life insurance, health insurance, money accumulation (RRSP, pension plan), annuity income (life income, term certain, RRIF) or disability income.
c) Be written by a member company in Canada, or shown on the books of a Canadian branch of a member company.

> "It's amazing how people go out of their way to get an extra eighth of one percent on an investment certificate—and then pay their banks much more than that in fees they have been told are unavoidable."

d) Not be covered under any other similar plan. (Note: There are no other similar plans at present in Canada.)

CompCorp provides no protection where policy benefits are backed by assets that are segregated from the insurance company's general assets (if there is a guaranteed minimum benefit set out in the policy, then that guarantee is eligible for protection under CompCorp).

If you want additional information, you can call the consumer assistance center toll-free at 1-800-268-8099. In Toronto, the number is 416-777-2344.

CompCorp also has a Montreal office. You can contact this office at 1-800-361-8070 if you wish to receive service in French.

Source: *Gordon Pape, based on information provided by CompCorp.*

Former Bank President Tells How Not to Be Outsmarted by Your Bank

It's amazing how people go out of their way to get an extra eighth of one percent on an investment certificate—and then pay their banks much more than that in fees they have been told are unavoidable. *Reality:* Banks don't want you to know their fees and interest rates *are* negotiable. Often all you have to do is ask. *Example:* Most banks will give senior citizens, the disabled and students free chequing accounts. But you have to ask. *Strategy:* Learn the chain of command at your bank. If you encounter a bank employee who won't negotiate fees, then ask to speak with his or her boss. Most senior personnel would prefer you to be happy with the bank, especially if you are a good customer.

Here is how to minimize most of your bank charges, such as fees for using the automated teller machine (ATM), overdraft charges and the penalties for falling below minimum balance requirements:
● **Use a small bank.** Your bank should be one of the smallest in your area. A big bank often won't go

the extra mile for you because it doesn't feel it needs your business. A small bank will be flexible because it needs satisfied customers in order to attract new customers and to grow.

● **Don't use ATMs**—except in emergencies. Not only can they be costly, they prevent you from establishing important personal relationships with bank officers. Those cordial relationships can help you get better rates and terms on bank loans and services.

● **Avoid overdraft charges.** Ask your bank to electronically monitor and "red flag" your chequing account and telephone you if it is over-drawn. See if you can strike an arrangement with your bank to give you until 3 P.M. the same day to come in with a deposit before they bounce a cheque—saving you a $15 to $25 overdraft charge and the embarrassment of a returned cheque. However, that kind of arrangement has become increasingly difficult to find in this era of computerization and centralization.

● **Ask for minimum balance requirements to be waived.** Many banks will waive these requirements if you insist. If your bank won't, then perhaps you should consider a credit union, which usually is cheaper and offers better service. For more information, visit Credit Union Central of Canada on the Internet at www.cucentral.ca.

● **Plan before you borrow.** Go into the bank and update your personal financial statement every six months or so—even if you don't need a loan. Strike up conversations with the people who help you. *Reason:* You want at least one teller, one loan officer and one bookkeeper to know your face. Anyone can borrow if they have good collateral. But if you need a loan based only on collateral, you're much more likely to get it if you and your credit history are familiar to the bank's employees.

● **Refuse unnecessary products.** Banks are intimidating to average consumers, who are afraid to question what is put in front of them. *Example:* Most people are so happy to get a car loan, they're afraid

F ree Help From the CDIC

● **CDIC insurance is carried by all commercial banks in Canada.** However, surprisingly few depositors know just what it does—and doesn't do—on their behalf. *Information:* Canada Deposit Insurance Corporation, 50 O'Connor Street, 17th Floor, P.O. Box 2340, Station D, Ottawa, Ont., K1P 5W5. Ask for a free copy of *Protecting Your Deposits.*

● **Trouble with your bank?** The Canadian Deposit Insurance Corporation will answer questions and take complaints. It deals only with banks supervised by the CDIC. Call toll-free, 1-800-461-2342. You can also reach the CDIC by e-mail.

Source: Kendrew Pape, personal finance commentator for CBC Radio.

to refuse the overpriced credit life and disability insurance the bank often adds to the loan. Even worse, they don't realize that because the insurance cost has been added to the loan, the premium is subject to a finance charge.

Source: Edward F. Mrkvicka, Jr., is the author of Your Bank Is Ripping You Off, *St. Martin's Press.*

Negotiate to Reduce Your Bank Costs

Nearly every fee charged by your bank is negotiable. It's also easy to request better terms.

Key steps:

● **Consider opening an additional savings account or investing in a GIC in the future.** Some banks will negotiate only with customers who already have established different types of accounts with the institution. The promise of more business may per-suade the representative to give you a better deal. Point out that a better rate will encourage you to do more business with the bank.

● **Ask about direct payment options.** Many lenders will lower car loan rates by as much as one percentage point if you agree to have payments auto-matically removed each month from one of your accounts. Other banks give better savings rates if you have your paycheque directly deposited.

● **Ask to have loan fees waived.** Whether the transaction is a mortgage or a home equity loan, the bank is going to make a lot of money from your business. As a result, it can afford to let several hundred dollars' worth of fees slide if it thinks you'll go elsewhere for the mortgage.

● **Repeat your request if you're turned down.** In some cases, the person with whom you're speaking may deny your request because he or she does not appreciate your value to the bank. Just go over the person's head. Don't be embarrassed about being persistent. It's your money, and you're lending it to the bank. You're entitled to a good deal.

Source: *Edgar Dworsky, director of consumer education at the Massachusetts Executive Office of Consumer Affairs and Business Regulation, One Ashburton Place, Boston, MA 02108.*

How to Beat the Banks Before They Beat You

Banks vary widely in their services and in the costs of those services. In order to turn the best profit, banks depend on the fact that customers don't know what to ask for. *How you can get the most for your banking dollar:*

● **Using telephone,** PC or Internet banking can save time and transportation costs and often service fees.

● **Ask about chequing accounts.**

● **What is the minimum-balance requirement?** How does the bank calculate it? Watch out for a minimum-balance calculation that uses the lowest balance for the month. A figure based on the average daily balance is best.

● **Does the balance on other accounts** count toward the chequing-account minimum balance?

● **What is the overdraft charge?** Many banks charge $25.

● **Don't buy loan insurance from a bank.** Credit life or disability insurance is often routinely included on loan forms and added to the cost of your loan. Don't sign any such policy when you take out a loan.

Caution: This insurance benefits the bank—not you. It covers the bank for the balance of your loan should you die or become disabled. You can get more coverage from an insurance agent for half (or even less) of what the bank charges.

> **"The average family overpays its bank more than $100,000 over the course of a 40-year relationship . . ."**

● **Avoid installment loans.** *These loans are front-end loaded:* Even though your balance is declining, you're still paying interest on the original balance throughout the term of the loan. Ask for a single-payment note with simple interest and monthly payments, or an installment loan calculated on a simple interest basis.

If you do have an installment loan, don't pay it off early—this actually adds to its real cost.

● **Avoid ATMs.** The farther bankers can keep you from their tellers and loan officers, the more money they'll make and the less responsive they'll be to your needs. Bankers like ATMs because people can't argue with them, and they're extremely profitable.

● **If you have to use an ATM,** use one from your own bank to avoid paying Interac fees. Always use full-service ATMs. Cash counters will often charge separate transaction fees.

● **Negotiate interest rates.** This sounds simple, but it means combating banks' tendencies to lump loans in categories—commercial, mortgage, retail, etc. For example, many banks offer a longtime depositor the same interest rate on a car loan as they do a complete newcomer. But often all it takes to get a better rate is to say, "I think my car loan should be 2% lower. I've been banking here for 15 years, and I have $10,000 in my savings account."

● **Forget CDIC security.** Given the option of a higher interest rate investment with a secure major corporation that probably has more reserves than the CDIC, many people will still automatically opt for the bank investment because of CDIC insurance.

● **Ignore the banks' amortization schedule for mortgages.** When you make your monthly payment, especially in the early part of your mortgage, very little goes toward the principal. However, if you choose to pay a small amount extra every month, this will go toward the principal and save you an enormous amount of money.

● **Don't put all your money in one investment certificate.** Split your deposits to get the same interest rate and more liquidity. If you put your money into a $10,000 or $20,000 GIC and then find you need to take out $1,000 or $2,000, you will have to pay a horrendous penalty. Your best strategy is to buy 10 or 20 $1,000 GICs.

Source: Edward F. Mrkvicka, Jr., *is the author of* Your Bank Is Ripping You Off, *St. Martin's Press.*

Picking the Right Bank for You

● **Banks are suppliers and should be evaluated as such.** Judge a bank's performance as you would that of a vital supplier—in terms of tangible factors (pricing, satisfactory performance, etc.) and intangible ones (loyalty, dependability and a willingness to be flexible).

Source: Cash Management *by business journalist John M. Kelly.*

● **Shop for a bank before deciding where to keep your personal savings.** *Check to see:* **(1)** How rush-hour traffic is handled. **(2)** If there are express lines. **(3)** If there are branches near your home and your work. **(4)** If bank officers are accessible. **(5)** If all types of services are offered.

Source: How to Invest $50–$5,000 *by financial analyst Nancy Dunnan, Harper & Row.*

How to Choose a Bank Account

Banks offer a bewildering array of accounts and rates to choose from. In order to compare, ask:

● **Is the account tiered?** Are there different rates for higher balances?

● **What are the fees and charges if the account balance drops below a minimum?**

● **What are the monthly maintenance fees?**

● **What are the transaction fees?** How many cheques can be written at no charge? What is the cost per cheque beyond a certain number a month? Is there a charge for using the automated teller machine?

● **Is there a penalty for closing the account early?** (At some banks you can be hit with a charge if you close a new account within the first 90 days.)

● **How is the account insured?** (CDIC insurance provides $60,000 per person, including principal and interest.)

● **Eight banks in Canada have agreements with the federal government** to make a standard low-fee account available to all customers. Does your bank offer a low-fee account?

Source: Investor's Daily, *New York. Additional Canadian content by Kendrew Pape.*

How to Protect Yourself From Your Banker

The average family overpays its bank more than $100,000 over the course of a 40-year relationship—borrowing money for mortgages, home improvements and auto purchases, and using chequing and savings accounts. But any knowledgeable customer—large or small—can easily and effectively beat the banking system.

What the banks don't want you to know:

● **When you make a deposit,** your bank can put a hold on your deposited cheque, even if it's government issued. There is no federal legislation that requires banks to clear your cheques quickly, even though a cheque will take no more than three days to clear when it is posted from one Canadian financial institution and deposited in an account at another Canadian financial institution. But some banks provide accounts that won't put holds on deposited cheques. *Helpful:* Ask your bank for its policy on clearing cheques, and compare it with that of some others. If you run a lot of money through your account, it may pay to switch to a bank with the swiftest cheque-clearing policies and accounts.

● **Most loans,** whether for mortgages, property insurance or car purchases, are negotiable, and it does not matter how much or how little you've deposited with the loaning bank. You will have to push for a better deal. No bank will simply volunteer one.

● **Bank safe-deposit boxes aren't as safe as you've been led to believe.** Although you'll be told that the boxes are fully insured, it's difficult to collect on losses unless you can prove to the insurance company which contents you lost. If the bank is robbed or burns down, proving your loss is almost impossible.

Not Like the Good Old Days

People used to view their bank as a partner in financial dealings. It was said that if you bundled all your business at one bank, you'd have a friend for life. The loyalty of a personal relationship would be there to help when the need arose. But, unfortunately, this is no longer the case.

Today's bankers are concerned with only one thing: the bottom line. The so-called Five-C's by which banks used to determine credit-worthiness—collateral, capital, condition, character and capacity—are now referred to as the "Three C's." They no longer care about character and capacity. Even if you once starved so that you could pay off a note, your past performance will mean nothing when you apply for a new loan.

Chequing and Savings Accounts

The best chequing account is what the banks call a "combination account" because it pays interest on outstanding balances while allowing chequing privileges as well. However, the interest rate paid is likely to be very low in most cases.

Important: How interest is computed, when it accrues and at what point you can write cheques against deposits.

Best: Interest should be figured on a day-of-deposit-to-day-of-withdrawal basis, compounded and paid daily. It's almost impossible to reach a decision by comparing the offerings of all banks in your area. **Helpful:** Ask officers at several banks, "If I put $1,000 in my account at the beginning of a quarter and write ten cheques totaling $750, how much would I have—after adding interest and subtracting bank fees (charges, per-cheque fees, charges for deposits)—at the end?"

Overdraft: If you write a cheque that can't be covered by your account, the bank will usually return the cheque unpaid and charge you for the trouble. Some banks charge as much as $25 for an overdraft. **Real out-of-pocket cost for the bank:** About $1. To beat the overdraft system, negotiate with the bank for your own personal overdraft policy. You can often convince a bank officer to cover the cheque with funds from, for example, your savings account and reduce the overdraft charge to a nominal fee.

Negotiating a Loan

Research the total cost of a loan at a minimum of three banks. Let each bank know that you're investigating others. Compare every aspect of each bank's deal—interest rates, legal fees, points, etc. Then, visit the manager of the one offering the best deal. Explain that in addition to opening an account, you'll also be interested in borrowing some money. Ask for an introduction to the loan officer. **Benefit:** When you're ready to take out the loan, you'll have access to the one person who can adjust the rules to your advantage.

Keep in mind that no matter how hard-nosed the bank seems, it's more profitable for it to knock a half a percentage point or more off the loan than to have you walk out the door, especially if it believes you'll take your other accounts with you.

● **Mortgage loans.** The bank calculates a fixed monthly figure to cover your repayment over the term of the loan. Early payments usually cover only the interest. As the loan matures, payments begin to reduce the amount of principal you owe.

Surefire way to cut your costs:

Deliberately overpay each month, even by just a few dollars. **Benefit:** Extra payments are automatically used to repay part of the principal—and the less principal outstanding, the less you'll pay in interest on it. **Example:** Paying off a $100,000, 25-year loan at 7.5% by increasing the monthly payment from $731.56 to $800 will reduce the total interest charges over the life of the mortgage by more than $28,000.

It would be unusual, but the bank might refuse to accept the extra payments. Discuss it with the manager. If you get nowhere, take it up with the bank ombudsman first, then the Canadian Banking Ombudsman 1-888-451-4519/416-287-2877. You're sure to get your way.

● **Installment loans.** You pay interest on the full amount of the standard installment loan even though you pay it off bit by bit and therefore don't have full use of the money during the life of the loan. That's costly compared with a loan you pay off all at once at the end of the term (a "single-payment note").

Not all banks are willing to provide single-payment notes—installments are much more profitable. But shopping around can save you hundreds of dollars on a typical auto loan.

Safe-Deposit Boxes

Plenty of safe-deposit boxes have been robbed, burned or otherwise compromised. Banks assure customers that with the bank's millions in insurance, the customer's valuables will be covered.

Trap: If you can't prove your loss—and most people can't—you won't collect a penny.

Self-defense: You'll have to forgo secrecy about the contents of the box. Appraise valuables and take the appraisal to the bank. A bank officer will then verify that the appraised items are in the box. Next, request from the bank a "safekeeping receipt" and list all the valuables—jewels, bearer bonds, cash, etc. Each time you open the box, take a bank officer with you to note on the receipt the removal or addition of any items. The receipt will guarantee reimbursement in the even of a loss.

It's also a good idea to insure items in your safe-deposit box through an "off-premise" rider on your homeowners policy.

Sources: *Gordon Pape and Kendrew Pape; and Edward F. Mrkvicka, Jr. He is the author of* Your Bank Is Ripping You Off, *published by St. Martin's Press.*

What Banks Don't Tell You

● **Some banks may put a "hold" on cheques** deposited to your account to allow them to clear. The length of time of the hold will vary, although it shouldn't exceed two or three days. Ask about your bank's policy on this. During the hold period, you do not have access to the funds, which can be a problem if your cash flow is tight.

Protection: Establishing a stable relationship with a bank branch is the best way to minimize holds. Be sure you know the manager or at least one assistant manager personally.

> "The best loan deal . . . (for a given interest rate) is a single-payment, simple interest installment note, with a provision for monthly payments."

● **Cheques dated more than six months ago are usually not cashable through normal channels** no matter how much money the issuer has in the bank.

● **If the amount written on the cheque in words is different** from the amount written in numbers, the bank will pay the sum shown in words.

● **Be careful when endorsing cheques.** To prevent loss of money, when sending cheques by mail for deposit, write "For Deposit Only" above your signature on the back. That limits the endorsement. An endorsed cheque with nothing but a signature is the same as cash and may be used by anybody if it's lost or stolen.

Sources: *Gordon Pape; and Lana J. Chandler, author of* Putting Your Money to Work, *published by Betterway Publications.*

Interest Rates Aren't Always What They Seem

One of the banker's lucrative stocks in trade is the average customer's innocent belief that 10% is always 10%. Like so many aspects of the financial business, it's not that simple.

Banking laws allow financial institutions to use varying methods of computing interest—both interest charged and interest paid. Interest can be calculated with daily, weekly, monthly or annual compounding.

This means that in shopping for the best deal, either on a loan or on a savings account or other deposit vehicle, the customer must be aware of the method of interest computation in order to make a valid comparison and choose the best.

Savings Accounts

Don't believe the posted interest rate on bank savings accounts. Even with the high-interest accounts at places like ING Direct, you need to figure out what you're really earning after inflation and taxes. It's not the total interest rate (the one you're receiving) that is most important—it's the real rate that matters. When you earn high interest rates while inflation is high, you could be worse off than when interest rates and inflation are low. If interest rates were 12% and inflation was 10%, you are only earning 2% (before taxes). But if interest rates are 6% and inflation is 1%, you are earning 5% (before taxes).

But be aware: In today's low-interest-rate environment, after figuring in taxes and inflation, you'll at best break even when you deposit your savings in a bank.

Loans

What about loan rates? They're even more complicated, since loan officers tend deliberately to perpetuate the mystique of borrowing. The best loan deal you can get (for a given interest rate) is a

SAFEGUARDS FOR SAFE-DEPOSIT BOXES

Valuables stored in bank safe-deposit boxes are not automatically protected against loss through burglary, flood or fire. To be compensated for missing valuables, depositors may have to initiate a lawsuit against the bank. The chances of winning are very, very slim.

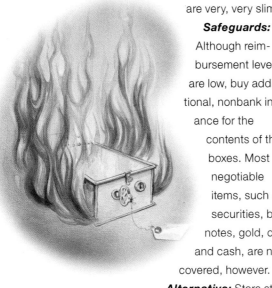

Safeguards: Although reimbursement levels are low, buy additional, nonbank insurance for the contents of the boxes. Most negotiable items, such as securities, bank notes, gold, coins and cash, are not covered, however.

Alternative: Store stocks and bonds at the brokerage house where they were purchased. These firms have a legal and financial responsibility to guard securities stored with them.

single-payment, simple interest installment note, with a provision for monthly payments.

Suppose you're shopping for a new car loan of $7,000. One bank offers it to you at 10.25% annual percentage rate (APR) for 48 months on the above terms, and another bank offers you a standard installment loan at the same APR. On the second note, with exactly the same principal, the same term, and the same collateral, you would end up paying a total of $140 more in interest over the term of the loan.

CDIC Insurance

Many banks claim that their Canada Deposit Insurance Corporation (CDIC) coverage provides security for depositors at no retail cost. Customers—particularly the elderly—often will deposit only in insured accounts, reasoning that the security provided in a bank as opposed to the market justifies a lower interest rate. However, since bank depositors normally receive interest rates 2% to 3% below those available on other deposit vehicles, it's fair to say that customers do pay for CDIC insurance.

From an investment standpoint, it would be better to ignore the CDIC insurance and opt for higher market rates as long as you investigate the investment carefully. It is important to substantiate corporate reserves that would be used to repay depositors/investors in the case of default. (For example, many deposit vehicles are backed by government-issue bonds.) Corporate investment opportunities frequently have better reserves than the CDIC.

Sources: *Kendrew Pape; and Edward F. Mrkvicka, Jr. He is the author of* **Your Bank Is Ripping You Off,** *St. Martin's Press.*

More on Safe-Deposit Boxes

Can you locate all your important papers and documents quickly? Guarantee it with a safe-deposit box. Important papers will be at your fingertips and protected from fire, theft or other casualty. Of course, you can use the box to protect your jewelry and other valuable things, too.

The fee for renting a bank safe-deposit box is surprisingly low. Only two keys are made to fit the box, and you keep both of them. The box cannot be opened without your permission until you die or you don't pay your rental fee for a year.

In a nonpayment situation you will receive a registered letter to give you one last chance to pay the fee. If you don't, the contents of the box will be removed in the presence of a bank official, inventoried, verified, and then stored in a safe place until you eventually claim them.

Documents to keep in your safe-deposit box:
- **Birth, marriage and death certificates.**
- **Divorce or separation agreements.**
- **Title papers to real estate, car, etc.**
- **Mortgage papers.**
- **Contracts and legal agreements.**
- **Stock certificates.**
- **Military discharge papers.**

In addition, many people keep credit cards and photographs of the inside and outside of their home in the safe-deposit box to support insurance claims.

Smart idea: Make copies of these records before you put them into the box for easy reference.

This is also important should your bank branch burn down—the vault may be the last thing to burn, but it will burn.

Final check: Make sure someone knows where the safe-deposit box is and where the key is, too.

Important: Safe-deposit boxes taken out in a corporate name don't get sealed upon the death of one of the principals. This might be very useful for closely held firms.

Some items should not be kept in a safe-deposit box:
- **Keep your will at your attorney's office,** with only a copy in the safe-deposit box. *Reason:* Your safe-deposit boxes may be sealed at death until the CCRA sees what's inside. This could prevent relatives from getting into the box right away to see if a will even exists.
- **Don't hide money in a safe-deposit box to prevent taxation on it.** This is illegal, and your heirs might be taxed on the money at your death anyway.

Source: *Rudra Nath, vault custodian, Safe Deposit Department, Marine Midland Bank, NA, 140 Broadway, New York, NY 10015.*

> "Don't hide money in a safe-deposit box to prevent taxation on it. This is illegal, and your heirs might be taxed on the money at your death . . ."

Hidden Costs of Automated Teller Machines

Hidden fees for using automated teller machines (ATMs): Canadians are the largest group of ATM users in the world. Most banks charge for withdrawals and for deposits at ATMs not owned by the bank. *Fees:* 10¢–$2.50. For the bank's own ATMs, you can open no-fee and low-fee accounts if you make regular use of ATMs. Read the fine print on the ATM agreement with your bank. If you're paying fees, shop around for a bank whose ATM use is free. Beware the white-label cash-dispensing machines now showing up in malls and convenience stores. They charge exorbitant fees.

Sources: *Kendrew Pape; and Study by Sheshunoff Information Services, Inc., a leading provider of banking-industry data, analysis and management tools.*

ATM Fees Are Rising

Almost all banks charge customers who use machines owned by other banks. Now many of those other banks are charging customers access fees as well. *Result:* The average cost of withdrawing money from an ATM anywhere other than your own bank has risen to about $3.

Self-defense: Use a bank teller...or use your own bank's machine. If you must regularly take out funds elsewhere, withdraw larger amounts less often. The average ATM user withdraws only $55. At an ATM with a $2 fee, the withdrawal cost is a very high 3.63%.

Source: *Edward F. Mrkvicka, Jr., is the author of* Your Bank Is Ripping You Off, *St. Martin's Press.*

Overseas ATM Use Alert

Notify your bank if you will be using your ATM card to make cash withdrawals overseas, especially if you are not a frequent traveler. A series of withdrawals from unexpected places might lead your bank to block your account.

Cardholders should check with their banks to be

sure a primary account has been designated (chequing or savings). Many banks outside Canada do not allow you to choose the account from which you make the transaction. If your primary account is not designated by the Canadian bank, the overseas bank will make the decision as to which account the transaction will affect or, in some cases, deny the request.

Important: If your ATM card is lost or stolen, notify the bank within four business days in order to limit your liability to no more than $50. Many delay reporting it missing, in the hope that they will find it.

Sources: Gordon Pape; and David Keenan, vice president for operations of the MasterCard/Cirrus ATM network, Westchester, IL.

Beware the Black-Market Foreign Exchange

Classic setup: You're in France and the official exchange rate is 0.70 euro to the dollar. On the street a well-dressed gentleman offers to change your money for 0.80 euro to the dollar.

Sting: He hands you a bankroll to count—it's correct. You hand it back to get out your money. He does a quick switch, substituting a sham bankroll for the real one, hands you the roll, and disappears.

Self-defense: Exchange money only at banks and official currency-exchange locations.

Use only approved exchange locations to get currency-exchange receipts. These are often needed when you change the currency back into dollars. (Receipts are proof that currency was obtained legitimately.)

Cashing a Letter

If you have an account with chequing privileges, you can write cheques to others as a way of paying for goods and services. A cheque is simply a written order to the financial institution to pay a specific amount of money from your account to the party named on the cheque. Letters or telegrams may serve as cheques. *Requirements:* The letter must be addressed to a bank. And it must state that a specific amount is to be paid on demand, from a specific account, either to the bearer of the letter or to the order of a named person, signed by the holder of the

account listed. *Point:* If any one of these requirements is not met, the letter will not be valid as a cheque. Of course, the bank will make its usual effort to verify that the "cheque" is valid.

Cheques Marked "Payment in Full"

If there's no dispute as to the amount, a cheque tendered for less than the amount due and marked "payment in full" (or the like) may be cashed without prejudicing the right to recover the balance.

If there's a bona fide dispute as to the amount owing, the creditor must be wary.

Alternatives: Reject the cheque and demand full payment. *Or:* Accept the cheque but risk that payment will be deemed to have settled the disputed claim for the lesser amount. It's easy for a debtor who wants to pay less than the amount he or she was billed to create a dispute on the basis of quantitative or qualitative deficiencies in the goods or services supplied.

How to Spot a Forged Cheque

● **See if the cheque has perforations on one side.** (A false cheque often has four smooth sides, since the forger cuts them with a paper cutter after printing.)

● **The code numbers printed on a legitimate cheque reflect no light.** They are printed in magnetic ink, which is dull.

● **About 90% of all hot cheques are drawn on accounts less than one year old.** The numbers in the upper-right-hand corner of the cheque indicate the age of the account. Be suspicious of those that are numbered 101–150 or 1001–1050 (the starting numbers).

Source: Frank W. Abagnale, once a master forger and now a consultant to banks and retailers, writing in Real Estate Today.

Bank Fees Self-Defense

Bank fees are on the rise. *Here are ways to reduce or avoid them altogether:*

● **Automated teller machines (ATMs).** The average cost for making a withdrawal at your own bank is now up to $1. But this fee can rise to as much as $3 when you take out cash from an ATM that is not owned by your bank.

Self-defense: Stick to your bank's ATM and find a bank that charges for ATM use only if your account balance falls below a specific amount.

You can also cut down on ATM fees by using the machines less frequently. Plan a weekly budget, and use the ATM only once each week to withdraw enough cash.

● **Minimum-balance fees.** An increasing number of banks now charge a fee if your balance dips below the minimum requirement for even a single day. Other banks still base the fee on your average daily balance over the course of a month.

In both cases, such fees can be avoided.

Self-defense: Look elsewhere for a better deal. Small banks, credit unions and trust companies tend to have much lower balance requirements and substantially lower fees. Before giving up on your current bank, however, ask if it has a different type of account—one with fewer "bells and whistles"—that would be more cost-efficient for you.

● **Nuisance fees.** Believe it or not, some banks now charge customers $3 just for calling to find out their balances.

Self-defense: If you already have an account at such a bank, threaten to take your business elsewhere unless those charges are rescinded.

Call the bank manager and begin by saying politely that you have been a good customer for a long time. If you don't get any satisfaction from the manager, speak to the bank's ombudsman.

Warning: This approach probably won't succeed if your account is at a large bank. Generally, the smaller the bank, the more flexible it will be. If you must switch, don't sign up for a new account without reviewing the institution's full fee schedule.

● **Safe-deposit boxes.** When banks send out renewal forms for safe-deposit boxes, some ask you to

Use It or Lose It Credit Card Alert

Credit cards are being revoked from customers with good credit standing but who do not use the cards to the issuer's satisfaction. One U.S. bank canceled 100,000 no-fee credit cards it considered unprofitable because holders did not use them often enough. Another American bank threatened to close some accounts that paid no interest. It said people who want to keep the cards would have to charge $2,500 within six months...transfer a $1,000 balance and pay interest...or have their accounts closed. There are no similar situations in Canada...yet.

Source: Ruth Susswein, executive director, Bankcard Holders of America, 524 Branch Dr., Salem, VA 24153.

pay for insurance on the box's contents. This insurance coverage is optional, and, in most cases, it is best to decline it.

Reason 1: Such insurance shouldn't be required to protect your valuables. The bank's vault is supposed to do that.

Reason 2: The insurance may be useless. If the boxes are robbed, the claims adjuster may not believe that the items you say you stored were actually in the box. *Better:* Insure the contents of the box through an off-premise rider to your homeowners policy.

● **Inactivity/activity fees.** Some banks now have penalties for depositors with idle accounts. Conversely, some tack on extra fees for customers who make "too many" withdrawals and/or deposits. *Strategy:* Ask your bank about its activity-fee policy. If it doesn't make sense, write a letter to the president or bank manager politely threatening to withdraw your money.

Source: Edward F. Mrkvicka, Jr., is the author of Your Bank Is Ripping You Off, *St. Martin's Press.*

All You Need to Know About Debit Cards

Pros: Using a debit card is safer than carrying cash and handier than writing cheques. Fees are comparable to using a bank automated teller machine (ATM) card. If you make many purchases, you can get a card from an issuer that charges only a flat annual fee—rarely more than $24.

Cons: Some merchants might charge you a fee for using a debit card, but since they get their money instantly, this is an extraordinary charge. Be sure to ask if they intend to impose this charge before using your card.

If you already have a bank ATM card that works like a debit card in stores, you won't need a VISA or MasterCard debit card unless you travel.

Editor's note: As debit card purchases are instantaneously deducted from your account, you lose the grace period you likely would have with a credit card purchase.

Source: *Gerri Detweiler, consumer credit consultant in Dale City, VA, and author of* The Ultimate Credit Handbook, *Good Advice Press.*

If You Lose Your Debit Card

Every so often, you'll read a horror story in the paper about someone who lost a debit card and had hundreds or thousands of dollars in unauthorized

WHAT TO DO IF YOUR CHEQUE BOUNCES

If you have been unlucky enough to bounce a cheque recently, you may well have been shocked at the size of the charge ($10, $15, $25 or more) assessed to your account for this misdemeanor. Does it seem strange that with the advent of all that cost-cutting automation in the banking industry, the expense of processing an overdraft should have risen so sharply? It should. The fact is that many banks have decided to transform the return of customers' cheques into a profitable industry by assigning purely punitive charges, totally unrelated to the real cost of processing the transaction. (The procedure involves no monetary outlay on the bank's part—unless the bank pays your cheque, which is unlikely—and the in-house paperwork cost averages about $1.25 per cheque.)

What You Can Do

The basic precept to keep in mind is, don't allow your bank to invade your personal finances any more than you would a thief. Most people are surprisingly passive about this trespass—they feel helpless, bound by the rules. But never forget, it's your money, not theirs, and they have enough ways of making your money work for them that you needn't put up with high-handed penalties for non-services.

If the overdraft was the result of a bank error (losing track of a deposit, charging other customers' cheques to your account, etc.), you should demand not only to have any and all charges removed, you should also see that a letter goes out from the bank to each party to whom a cheque of yours has been returned, explaining that the bank was at fault.

Here are some tactics that will help you prevail:

● **Be firm.** Be persistent. Don't hesitate to go over people's heads. It is usually easier for a bank employee or officer to give in to your demands than have the matter come to the attention of his or her superior.

● **Don't forget that you have access to small claims court,** and don't be shy about making sure the bank is aware that you know this. Small claims court is a great leveler—it makes you the equal of the bank and all its lawyers and accountants. And, again, it may cost a bank considerably more to make an appearance in court than to give in to your point of view.

● **If the threat of small claims court doesn't work,** you might mention the possibility of legal action on a grander scale. One customer of a major Chicago bank brought a class-action suit against that institution for $10 million in punitive and actual damages equal to the bank's earnings from its cheque-clearing policy over a 10-year period.

Of course, if your overdraft is purely a result of your own negligence or poor arithmetic, you may well have to bear the consequences as cheerfully as you can. Meanwhile, look for a new bank, one that will not charge you for this sort of "service"—or at least keeps such charges within reason.

Source: *Edward F. Mrkvicka, Jr., is the author of* Your Bank Is Ripping You Off, *St. Martin's Press.*

purchases charged against it. Just how great is your risk if your card is lost or stolen?

Actually, it's zero, providing you take prompt action to notify your financial institution. The Canadian Code of Practice for Consumer Debit Card Services says that debit card holders are not liable for losses "resulting from circumstances beyond their control." That includes use of a lost or stolen card or PIN number.

However, you could have problems if the debit card is misused before you discover it's gone or if you delay in notifying the financial institution. That's the kind of situation that most often leads to disputes and those scary newspaper stories.

If your card is misused because you've been a victim of coercion of any kind (in other words, an unwilling accomplice), you're also absolved from any loss as long as you report the incident promptly and cooperate in the subsequent investigation.

Source: *Gordon Pape, based on information from the Canadian Bankers Association website: http://www.cba.ca/cba/eng/publications/debitcode/debitcode.htm.*

Borrow From Several Banks

Many business advisers believe it's best to bank in one place to get more influence there. But in a tight money market, that one bank can squeeze you—by recalling your loan or putting pressure on you to pay it off in a way you didn't anticipate. *Better:* Spread loans among a few banks. That way, if any one of them creates trouble for you, there's somewhere else to go immediately. This is similar to the principle of investment diversification—never put all your eggs in one basket.

Source: Take a Chance to Be First *by Warren Avis, the founder of Avis Rent-a-Car, Macmillan.*

financial institution could still release any funds deposited in less than the 6 to 10 days (or even higher, in some banks surveyed) that many financial institutions currently hold deposited amounts. Hold periods of any kind on government cheques are also completely unjustified, given that the government indemnifies banks against fraud.

Sources: *Canadian Payments Association and Canadian Community Reinvestment Coalition (CCRC) at http://www.cancrc.org/english/accesssurvey.html.*

When the Bank Can't Bounce a Cheque

The bank may have to honor a cheque if it takes too long to bounce it. They should take some action by midnight of the business day after they receive the cheque.

But the bank gets more time if there's an emergency beyond its control, for example, computer breakdown.

If there is a dispute and the amount of money involved is substantial, don't take the bank's word for what the law says. Protect yourself; see a lawyer.

How Fast Should Your Cheques Clear?

No legislation exists to ensure the speedy processing of your cheques. Even government cheques can be held for processing by your bank. However, Canadian Payments Association (CPA) standards make it highly unlikely that a cheque will take more than three days (and should only take two) to clear when it is posted from one Canadian financial institution and deposited in an account at another Canadian financial institution. As a result, even in the case of an individual with a bad credit rating, a

Postdated Cheques

Although cheques pass though one or more clearing houses before being processed, mistakes can happen and postdated cheques can sometimes be cashed early. To avoid people cashing your postdated cheques early, draw attention to the date with a highlighter or circle it with a different color of ink.

Source: *Kendrew Pape.*

If Your Statement Is Wrong and the Bank Won't Help

When you receive a chequing account statement that appears to be incorrect, your first move should be to balance the account. This means making sure that all the additions and subtractions to the opening balance do in fact produce the final balance. If you have difficulty doing this, your bank should be willing to help. Ask if your branch has a bookkeeper who specializes in balancing accounts. (If this takes longer than a few minutes, the bank will charge a fee, but it's worth it.)

This process of reconciling your records and arithmetic with those of the bank should reveal the discrepancy. Most of the possible explanations will be simple to deal with. It's either your error or the bank's—a cheque or routine charge not recorded by you, a deposit not credited to your account, that sort of thing.

If the problem is one of those mysterious "adjustments" or "miscellaneous debits," the bank is, of course, obligated to identify and justify what the situation is to you. If the bank cannot do so within a period of two or three days, insist that the disputed amount be credited to your account pending clarification.

> "If the problem is one of those mysterious 'adjustments' or 'miscellaneous 'debits,' the bank is, of course, obligated to identify and justify what the situation is to you."

Once you know what the bank has charged you for, you will have to pursue getting the charge dropped if you think it's unfair. For this, you will need to talk to the manager (who may be hard to locate, due to the size and organization of large banks). Discuss the dispute with him or her face to face. If you don't get satisfaction, go straight to the top—the head office of the financial institution.

A contact name and telephone number may be obtained from the Office of the Superintendent of Financial Institutions, at http://www.osfi-bsif.gc.ca/eng/consumers/contact/index.asp.

If you don't get satisfaction on this level (don't be surprised if some other bank officer—possibly a customer relations professional—intervenes at this point), you should then contact the bank's internal ombudsman.

Your final option is to e-mail the Canadian Banking Ombudsman (mail@bankingombudsman.co), toll-free telephone 1-888-451-4519 or toll-free fax 1-888-422-2865.

Then change banks.

Sources: Gordon Pape; and Margaret "Marty" O. Tunnell, vice president and region manager, San Francisco Regional Corporate Center, 405 Montgomery St., San Francisco, CA 94104.

Getting a Bank Loan After You're Refused

It's unfortunate but true that banks are not only decidedly conservative in choosing whom to entrust with their money, they are also often intimidating. Banks know that a customer who is on the defensive either will be afraid to question a refusal or will be so happy to receive an approval that he or she won't try to negotiate a better loan rate. But it doesn't have to be this way.

Preparation

The person who goes to the loan officer armed only with some vague figures entrusted to a faulty memory is not likely to be successful (unless he or she is the bank president's golf partner, in which case it won't much matter). By the same token, any potential loan customer who comprehends all the ramifications of a loan request, is on top of all the facts and figures, and has it all down on paper stands a very good chance of getting what he or she asks for. That kind of preparation impresses loan officers—it commands their respect.

If you are applying for a personal loan, bring an updated financial (net worth) statement. If the request is for a business loan, besides the financial statement, thorough documentation should include back tax returns for two to three years (if available), profit and loss projections for two or three years into the future, and a pro forma sheet describing clearly why you need to borrow, how you intend to use the money and how you intend to generate enough income to pay the tariff. A competent presentation accompanied by neat, clear documentation may make all the difference in your request, and will help lower the interest rate offered.

Persistence

If your banker turns you down, you can, of course, go elsewhere with your request, but the chances are that pursuing the matter with your original bank will eventually pay the desired dividend. Most customers, in fact, don't follow up a loan denial, possibly because they're convinced that once the bank has spoken, the answer is written in stone. This is simply not the case—these decisions are often reversed "on appeal."

Your first move after receiving a turndown is to approach the loan officer and request an in-depth explanation. Having gotten the true word, ask the loan officer what it would take to elicit a positive response. Believe it or not, this simple gambit will often be enough to turn the trick! *Explanation:* Sad but true, loan officers often turn down perfectly legitimate applications because, on some level, they can't be bothered. Yet when a customer requests that officer's assistance, this bit of flattery often has the effect of motivating him or her to take the time that should have been taken in the first instance.

Assertiveness

If the gambit does not work and the loan officer will not help, go to his or her supervisor—or at least make it clear that you intend to do so. Bankers don't like people going over their heads and will go to great lengths to avoid that eventuality, including granting loan requests. The same principle operates with bank officers on all levels.

If you are not getting satisfaction and are convinced you are being discriminated against, you should enter a formal complaint under the bank's dispute resolution process. All the banks have one, with an ombudsman to review the problem. If that doesn't work, you can try sending letters of complaint to the Canadian Banking Association, the federal Superintendent of Financial Institutions, your

> **"Most customers... don't follow up a loan denial, possibly because they're convinced that once the bank has spoken, the answer is written in stone. This is simply not the case..."**

provincial ministry of finance and the Canada Deposit Insurance Corporation, with copies to the offending bank. Your point is not so much to bring these forces into play as to cause the bank to take notice. Any of these alternatives will likely get the bank's attention, and once it realizes you are serious about what you're doing, you may find your loan denial is turned into an approval. Your last resort is the legal system, but you'll need to have a strong case and a lot of patience before going that route.

Source: *Edward F. Mrkvicka, Jr., is the author of* Your Bank Is Ripping You Off, *St. Martin's Press.*

Finding the Right Loan Officer

● **Shop for loan officers if you are seeking funding for your business.**

Key factor: Loan application approach. Before putting in your application, talk with the officer about your plans. Ask what the chances are of your loan's being granted. If the answer is something like "The committee will make that decision," try a different loan officer or another bank.

Best reply: "I've been in this business 15 years and have had only three loans turned down. I don't take an application unless I expect it to be accepted."

● **Bad credit need not prevent you from getting a bank loan.**

Key: Find a banker with clout. Junior loan officers in most banks are sternly warned never to lend to people with bad credit, no matter what explanation the applicant may offer. But a more seasoned loan officer, at the vice-president level or higher, often has the experience and authority to bend the rules.

Source: *Take a Chance to Be First by Warren Avis, the founder of Avis Rent-a-Car, Macmillan.*

Tricks Banks Play With Interest Rates

Banks teach their loan officers a number of strategies to get extra percentage points from borrowers.

Recognize some of their tricks:

- **Doing the negotiating at the bank,** which is familiar territory to the banker, intimidating to the borrower.

- **Not mentioning the rate at all,** but simply filling it in on the note.

- **"Since you need the money today, let's write it up at X%.** Then we can talk later about changing it." The banker hopes you'll never bring it up again. He or she certainly won't.

- **Flat statement:** "The rate for this type of loan is X%." (Never true except for small consumer loans. There is always room to negotiate.)

- **Postponing the rate discussion as long as possible,** hoping the borrower will weaken under deadline pressure.

- **Ego building.** The bank president or manager stops by during negotiations.

The banker looks at the customer's account as a package, including loans, average balances maintained and fees for service. *Borrower options:* Trade off higher average balances for a lower interest rate on borrowings, or vice versa.

The borrower is at a disadvantage because he or she negotiates a loan only once a year or less, while the banker is negotiating with customers full time. So prepare carefully for negotiations. *Good tactics for the borrower:*

- **Ask the interest rate question early**—in your office, not the bank. Don't volunteer suggestions.

- **Negotiate everything as a package**—rate, repayment schedule, collateral, compensating balances. The banker's strategy will be to try to nail down everything else and then negotiate the interest rate when the borrower has no more leverage and no room to maneuver.

- **React with surprise and shock** when the banker mentions the interest rate, no matter what the figure is.

Source: *Lawrence T. Jilk, Jr., executive vice president, National Bank of Boyertown, PA, in* The Journal of Commercial Bank Lending.

A Standard Bank Loan Rip-Off

Many loan customers are not even aware that they're paying credit life and disability insurance as part of their loan costs, but it is the standard policy of many banks to include this coverage in all personal loans.

A credit (or mortgage) life and disability policy is one that guarantees repayment to the bank of any unpaid portion of the debt concerned in the event of the customer's death or disability. The policy offers no benefits (other than possible peace of mind) to the customer or the customer's family. It is understandable that a bank would wish to minimize the problems that might conceivably arise in the event of such an unhappy occurrence, but asking the customer to bear the cost of this self-protection is unconscionable.

Even assuming that a loan customer is so compulsively financial-security minded as to want to cover all such eventualities, there are many more cost-effective ways to do this while securing some benefits for his or her family. A whole life policy is one such vehicle. And the chances are that such a policy, covering at least the initial debt balance, could be bought more cheaply through the family insurance agent. What makes it even more outrageous is that the coverage is often treated as part of the loan obligation, and, as such, the bank charges you hidden interest!

To top things off, the bank will also be receiving a direct cash kickback of up to 40% of the premium, just for writing the policy. Practically the only way a financially responsible adult could let such a state of affairs come about in the first place is through ignorance. Your banker will often gloss over this facet of the deal he or she is offering you.

The standard practice is to write the provision into the loan papers with nary a mention from the banker. Under these circumstances, it's easy for a customer, assuming he or she notices the provision at all, to assume it is a necessary condition (which it almost always is not) and therefore fail to question it.

All in all, it's one of the best money-grabbing scams the commercial banking system has going for it. An informed loan customer should be alert to the policy and prepared to negotiate it out of any loan agreement he makes.

Source: *Edward F. Mrkvicka, Jr., is the author of* Your Bank Is Ripping You Off, *St. Martin's Press.*

How the Banking Ombudsman Can Help You

If you have a problem with your bank, bring your complaint to the Canadian Banking Ombudsman. This is a little-known, independent organization based in Toronto that acts as a watchdog for individuals and small businesses. All of the major banks and several smaller financial institutions are participants.

The findings of this organization are not binding on either you or the bank, but if the bank doesn't act on the decision it will be made public. To date, the office reports that all recommendations it has made have been accepted.

However, there are several important issues the organization won't deal with, including pricing, credit card charges, credit granting policies, interest rates and service charges. That means that if a bank refuses to grant you a loan, this line of recourse won't work for you.

It is recommended that you first try to resolve your dispute with the bank through its internal complaint resolution process. All the banks now have their own ombudsman to handle such problems. Only if that fails should you go to the Canadian Banking Ombudsman—in fact, you cannot get their attention unless you have completed the first stage and are not satisfied.

You will not forfeit your rights to legal recourse should you not get satisfaction from the Banking Ombudsman.

You can contact the Canadian Banking Ombudsman by calling their toll-free number at 1-888-451-4519, although all you may get is an automated response system that offers no opportunity to be connected to a human being unless you have a name or extension number.

A better choice is to e-mail this organization at mail@bankingombudsman.com. You can also write to this organization at The Canadian Banking Ombudsman, 4950 Yonge Street, Suite 1602, North York, Ont. M2N 6K1. The website is http://www.bankingombudsman.com/ombud/english/pages/home/ehome.html.

Source: Gordon Pape, based on information from the Canadian Banking Ombudsman website.

Foreign Bank Account Loopholes

Canadian individuals, corporations and trusts are required to declare all foreign investment property if the total value exceeds $100,000 at any time during the year, as well as all foreign income. This includes cash held in foreign bank accounts, shares in foreign companies, rental properties, holdings in offshore trusts or mutual funds, etc.

Loopholes: Even if you do have foreign assets, you can avoid declaring them. They consist of personal-use property. According to the Canada Customs and Revenue Agency, this may include "a vehicle, vacation property, jewelry, artwork, or any other such property," as long as it is intended primarily for your own enjoyment and use.

Source: Gordon Pape, based on information from the CCRA website.

Offshore Scam

Beware of offshore business trusts (contractual companies) that promise to give you financial privacy and protect your assets from the CCRA.

Problems: Potential for CCRA litigation, high cost, extreme complexity and high profile (which defeats the purpose of a foreign trust).

Source: Jerry Schomp of INVESTigate.

Negotiating a Policy Exception Loan

Financial institutions determine their own policies and guidelines regarding operating, business and credit decisions. You may wish to consult further with the financial institution to discuss your options. *Here are the primary policy reasons for credit refusal:*

- **Bad credit history.**
- **Excessive debt-to-income ratio.**
- **Inadequate collateral.**

Normally, to get a loan once you've been turned down on a matter of policy, you will have to try to negotiate a "policy exception loan"; this is best done face-to-face with someone you know who has the authority to make such a policy exception. If the reason was bad credit history, however, you should check this out before proceeding further.

EARNING MONEY ABROAD

Earning income from investments or employment overseas can be profitable. What most people don't realize, however, is that nearly all of this income is subject to Canadian taxes, or will be soon.

By law, Canadians are required to pay tax on their worldwide income. However, in the 1990s a booming industry developed in offshore tax shelters, which were supposedly designed to shelter money from the long arm of the Canada Customs and Revenue Agency (CCRA).

Some of these actually worked. There were some loopholes in the law that enabled wealthy Canadians to earn offshore profits without having to pay tax on them as long as certain conditions were met, including not withdrawing compounding assets.

In recent years, however, the federal government has been cracking down on the tax-haven business. The first step was the implementation of a rule that requires all Canadians who own more than $100,000 worth of foreign

assets to make such a declaration on their annual tax return. It's important to note the distinction between assets and income here. You may have zero foreign income, but still come under the $100,000 asset rule.

The CCRA requires that any individual, corporation, partnership or trust that owns more than $100,000 worth of foreign assets at any time during the year must file an annual T1135 return.

Foreign assets are defined as including virtually any type of investment, but does not include personal-use property. That appears to exclude a home in a state in the U.S. sunbelt if it is not rented or used to generate income.

Foreign assets include shares in non-Canadian companies. However, they do not include mutual funds that are registered in this country, even if they are made up of 100% foreign content.

Be aware that penalty for failing to comply can be stiff. If you don't file a report for two years and the government believes that you deliberately tried to conceal information or made false statements about your foreign assets, they can sock you for 5% of the total value of your foreign holdings.

But form T1135 was just a start. In the 1999 budget, the federal government announced that it would introduce sweeping measures to put a stop to tax losses resulting from offshore investments.

The Department of Finance justified this by saying that aggressive tax planners had developed techniques for offshore investing that created "unfair income tax advantages using foreign-based investment entities in comparison with Canadian-based entities."

In doing so, the department acknowledged that existing rules were "ineffective" in stopping the bleeding.

The new rules are very complicated, but the main thrust is to extract taxes from Canadians who participate in what are called "foreign investment entities" (FIEs). These entities can include any offshore trust, corporation, limited partnership, association, joint venture, etc.

The main thrust of the FIE rules is to trigger imputed income from such former tax shelters. In other words, you have to pay tax on any profits, whether you actually received any payment or not.

This is the equivalent to taxing unrealized capital gains. Think of it this way. Suppose you owned a vacation property in Whistler that went up in value each year. If similar rules were applied to it, you would have to pay tax on each year's capital gain, even though you won't receive any money until you actually sell it.

The proposals caused much controversy and implementation has been postponed several times. At the time of writing, the Department of Finance planned to implement the new rules starting in 2003, but further postponements or changes are possible.

Source: *Gordon Pape, author of* 6 Steps to $1 Million, *published by Viking Canada.*

Dealing With Banks, Credit & Debt

197

Dealing With the Reporting Agency

The bank will give you the name and address of the credit-reporting agency on whose records their negative decision is based. The agency is then required to give you one free copy of your file per year, on signed request.

In order to obtain your credit rating, you'll need to make your request in writing. Your request needs to include your present address, previous address, social insurance number, your full name, phone number, birthdate and two pieces of government-issued ID. If the information in the file is incorrect, write to the agency and say why.

Ask the reporting agency to contact the lender who has turned you down. Also contact the company that reported you to the credit reporting agency in the first place—send them a letter and appropriate documentation, requesting an answer. It is important to follow it up in 30 days if you don't hear from them. There are three national credit rating agencies: Trans-Union Canada (fax: 905-527-0401), Northern Credit Bureaus (fax: 800-646-5876) and Equifax Canada (fax: 514-355-8502).

Returning to the Lender

To find the person who can grant your "exceptional" loan request, start with whomever you originally dealt with and patiently work your way up the chain of command until you get to the person who answers "yes" to the question, "Do you have the authority to make exceptions to company policy?" This is the person you must convince with all your powers of persuasion. Arrange a meeting and prepare to bring documents supporting your case.

If the turndown was for bad credit history, you will have to explain how the report was inaccurate (if it was), or make a strong case for why it will never happen again. You might also offer a cosigner with a clean payment record.

● **If it was a large debt-to-income ratio,** be prepared to point out additional income the lender didn't count or expenses it overcounted. Are there obligations you could pay off or credit lines you could close to reduce your potential monthly outlay? (For example, the bank may consider your fully paid up $3,000 VISA credit line as $3,000 you *owe*.)

● **If the problem was inadequate collateral,** explore flexible alternatives. Find out how big a loan your collateral will support. If it seems appropriate to you, suggest that the difference be made up in an unsecured loan of shorter term (more profitable to them, to cover the higher risk).

If after fighting the good fight they turn you down again (less likely than you may think), you can always seek a lending institution with less conservative lending policies.

Source: Margaret "Marty" O. Tunnell, vice president and region manager, San Francisco Regional Corporate Center, 405 Montgomery St., San Francisco, CA 94104.

> " Traditionally, credit unions have offered the lowest rates on loans for consumer purchases . . . and for student loans. Even credit life or credit disability insurance may be offered at a much lower cost than . . . elsewhere. "

How to Deal With Credit Unions

You can't get rich overnight by keeping your money with a credit union. But you can find a combination of old-fashioned personal attention, modern financial services and the lowest-cost personal financial services available. The advantages are substantial. Credit unions commonly pay higher returns on bankbook savings, certificates and money-market accounts than do other financial institutions.

Traditionally, credit unions have offered the lowest rates on loans for consumer purchases, such as cars, boats and home improvements, and for student loans. Even credit life or credit disability insurance may be offered at a much lower cost than is available elsewhere. Some credit unions make loans for business purposes, generally in the form of a personal loan.

When you work for a company that has a credit union associated with it, you often can arrange to have your pay cheque deposited into your transaction account for immediate access, to have loan payments automatically deducted and to direct part of your pay into a savings or money-market account.

Chequing/savings accounts—the credit union's version of the banks' combination accounts—generally have very low minimum balances and service fees and may offer higher interest rates. Check with the credit union you're planning to join for details of the various account options they offer their customers. No-fee accounts are usually available for seniors. At some credit unions, you may find that accounts of this kind are also available to customers by special request.

Credit cards from credit unions are also cheaper than cards from conventional financial institutions. Most do not charge an annual fee, and many charge substantially lower rates than other card issuers. The one drawback is that some credit unions charge interest from the date of purchase.

Your funds are safer in a credit union than in a traditional bank. Credit union deposits are guaranteed by provincial guarantee corporations, although the amount may vary from province to province. In many cases, these guarantees are higher than those available through regular banks under the Canada Deposit Insurance Corporation (CDIC). *Here are examples from different provinces:*

In Alberta, Manitoba and Saskatchewan, deposits are 100% guaranteed, with no limit.

In Nova Scotia, the limit is $250,000 per account, with insurance provided by the Credit Union Deposit Insurance Corporation of Halifax.

Ontario deposits are guaranteed up to $100,000 through the Deposit Corporation of Ontario. RRSPs, RRIFs, joint accounts, etc., are eligible for separate coverage.

Privacy and Credit Reports

Credit reports and credit-reporting agencies are closely regulated and monitored to assure the privacy of the information in your credit file. Who has access? No individual or company may have access to the information contained in your credit report unless there is a "permissible purpose," or a bona fide business reason for inquiring into your credit history. Any creditor who inquires into a credit bureau's database must certify a legitimate business need for the information and be a customer of the credit-reporting agency. An agency may not release information to any individual or company regarding your credit history unless the information is required by that individual or company to make a decision concerning the extension of credit to you.

Source: *Thomas G. Collins, Jr., director of planning for one of the five major credit-reporting companies in the United States, The Credit Bureau, Inc., 1600 Peachtree St. NW, Atlanta, GA 30309. His responsibilities are business, marketing and strategic planning for the firm.*

British Columbia residents also receive $100,000 coverage, through the Financial Institutions Commission, based in Vancouver. Their website is located at www.fic.gov.bc.ca.

In New Brunswick, Prince Edward Island and Newfoundland, credit union deposits are only protected up to $60,000.

Source: *Credit Union Central of Canada; and Jim R. Williams, president and CEO of Credit Union National Association, Inc., and CUNA Service Group, Inc., P.O. Box 431, Madison, WI 53701. He is also president of U.S. Central Credit Union. CUNA is a trade association serving over 90% of U.S. credit unions, while CUNA Service Group provides financial, operational and telecommunications services to the industry.*

Who Can Join a Credit Union

Membership in some credit unions is limited to people who have so-called common bonds—working for the same employer, living in the same neighborhood, etc. But anyone can use one of the larger credit unions, like VanCity in Vancouver, as their financial institution.

Check with the Credit Union Central of Canada for a list of credit unions in your area. Their website is located at www.cucentral.ca.

Establishing Consumer Credit

Canadian businesses and consumers have come a long way from the days when credit was available only to the wealthy. Recent changes in the area of consumer credit have made it possible for almost anyone with a steady job or steady income to expect some form of credit and to keep it.

What hasn't changed are the basic criteria for getting credit. You still must have the financial capacity to pay your bills when they come due. And to build a strong credit history, you must also have a consistent record of on-time payments over an extended period.

Credit for Young People

Many credit grantors will make credit available, on a limited basis, to young people just entering the labor force. The only requirement is a steady job that assures the income necessary to meet payments. As income increases and a reliable credit history develops, credit limits will usually be increased. Also, less lenient creditors that might have rejected a young person's credit application the first time around will probably make credit available.

Advice for young people: Start small and build big. Certain credit grantors, such as oil companies, large department store chains and major credit card companies, employ relatively lenient evaluation policies. Most of these organizations solicit young people while they are still in college. If there are no service charges, accept the offer. If a credit application is at first denied, don't be discouraged. Changing economic times can cause credit grantors to change their evaluation policies from month to month.

Which Bills to Pay First

In a cash crunch, it's important to know which bills you can't put off paying without damaging your credit rating—and which you can "defer." *To pay immediately:* Bills from credit cards issued by department stores (Sears, Zeller's, etc.) and banks (VISA, MasterCard, etc.). *Reason:* They submit "full-file" reports (reaching back 12–24 months) on all customers every month to credit-reporting agencies. *Less likely to file regular reports:* Oil companies and utilities. Professionals and organizations that don't have contracts with credit-rating bureaus (most dentists and hospitals) don't file at all.

Credit for Women

Federal and provincial laws and regulations make it illegal for credit to be denied on the basis of race, creed, color or sex. The Canadian Charter of Rights and Freedoms and various acts passed by provincial legislatures assures that women will not be discriminated against when they apply for credit because of their sex or because they have been widowed or divorced or because they plan to have children.

Advice for married women: Establish credit jointly with your husband but report to credit bureaus in your name as well as your husband's name. That way you can build up your own credit history independent of your husband's.

It is a misconception that a married woman who doesn't earn a separate income cannot obtain credit in her own name. If you would like credit entirely in your own right, simply apply in your name. Credit grantors recognize that a woman has a legal claim to half of the family's assets and income and will base their credit evaluation on that assumption.

Source: *Walter R. Kurth, president and chief executive of Associated Credit Bureaus, Inc., 16211 Park 10 Place, Houston, TX 77084, the international trade association of the credit reporting and collection services industry. He is also vice chairman of the American Society of Association Executives and a member of the board of the U.S. Chamber of Commerce.*

What Information Is Contained in a Credit File?

The information contained in a credit file consists of computerized records on your payment history, how much you owe and to whom, indications as to whether payments have been received promptly or late, and information regarding legal action that may have been taken as a result of your inability or unwillingness to pay bills satisfactorily. There is also a brief section on your identification, which is used to assure that the applicable information is delivered to the inquiring creditor. This section includes your name, address, Social Insurance Number, date of birth and other similar pieces of information regarding your identity.

Source: *Thomas G. Collins, Jr., director of planning for one of the five major credit-reporting companies in the United States, The Credit Bureau, Inc., 1600 Peachtree St. NW, Atlanta, GA 30309. His responsibilities are business, marketing and strategic planning for the firm.*

What You Need to Know About Your Credit Report

Under consumer legislation governed by each province, you are entitled to a copy of all the information a credit agency has on you. There are three national credit agencies that can tell you the contents of your credit report. If you were denied credit, insurance, employment or a mortgage based on information in a credit report, you can contact the reporting credit bureau for more information.

To obtain your credit report, send a request to a Canadian credit reporting agency or call them directly. The two largest are Equifax Canada Inc. (1-800-465-7166) and Trans Union of Canada (1-800-663-9980). Equifax has a request form available on their website (http://www.equifax.ca). You will be sent a copy by regular mail within five working days. There is no charge.

If you don't want to wait for your credit report to be mailed to you, there is a faster method. Equifax offers personal credit files online. You can purchase a basic report ($14.50) or a more sophisticated detailed report ($21.95). Once you've paid, your report is available instantaneously over the Internet. You can continue to view it free of charge for 30 days.

A range of security measures prevent your credit report from falling into the wrong hands. This service is available in all Canadian provinces except Nova Scotia.

You have the right to dispute any item in your credit file. But remember that credit bureaus only store information supplied to them by others regarding your payment history. The rating you receive when applying for credit is assigned by the credit grantor, based on your payment history.

Sources: *Kendrew Pape; and Thomas G. Collins, Jr., director of planning for one of the five major credit-reporting companies in the United States, The Credit Bureau, Inc., 1600 Peachtree St. NW, Atlanta, GA 30309. His responsibilities are business, marketing and strategic planning for the firm.*

Your Credit Rights

A useful source for information on your rights relating to obtaining credit is the "Money Savvy" series on the Industry Canada website. Here are some key points to note.

Some tips on reviewing and correcting your credit report:

● **You have a legal right to see your credit bureau reports.**

● **Credit reporting is regulated provincially** by the ministries responsible for consumer protection.

● **Check your credit report for errors,** and positives that are missing, such as a successful repayment, or an asset like a car that could be used for security.

● **If you find an error, ask the credit agency to correct it.** Send them a certified letter, with documented proof, such as a photocopy of payment. Or, you could also ask a creditor to make the correction for you. For example, if your credit report states that you have been delinquent with your VISA payments and you know that you have not, ask VISA to contact the credit bureau and make the correction.

● **If your report contains someone else's information,** contact the credit bureau and ask them to investigate.

● **If the credit bureau won't correct your file,** ask them to mark the file "in dispute." You may also exercise your right to have up to 100 words inserted into your credit report to explain your side of the story to potential creditors.

● **Beware of credit repair scams,** or companies claiming to fix your bad credit report—for a fee. There is no way to fix a bad credit report, only a history of good credit practices over time.

Source: *Industry Canada. http://mmprodnt.ic.gc.ca/mmpub consumer affairs/english/ca01629e.html#credit_ratings.*

Credit Card Secrets

The next time you want to switch credit cards in an attempt to get the lowest possible interest rate—*watch out*. A growing number of card issuers have been quietly adding penalties and restrictions to their applications in an effort to make up for lost revenues.

Self-defense: Forget what appears on the outside of a promotional envelope or in an advertisement. Instead, read the disclosure box that, by law, must appear on the back of all credit card applications. Unfortunately, fewer than 10% of all consumers read these boxes. Those who don't read the fine print can end up paying unexpected fees if they violate their agreements.

Disclosure-Box Red Flags

Beware: **No mention of a grace period.** More than 90% of credit card issuers offer a grace period of about 25 days—which means you have 25 days to pay for your purchase without being charged interest.

Self-defense: Stay away from any card whose application doesn't mention a grace period. You will pay interest on all charges—even if you pay the card's bill in full each month. That's because interest starts the day you make a purchase.

Beware: **A high annual fee.** It's easy today to find a no-fee credit card with a decent interest rate or a low-fee card with a very good interest rate.

Key question: If the issuer charges a high annual fee, are there enough benefits you can use to justify the rate?

Beware: **A low interest rate that is too good to be true.** If the interest rate is lower than 10%, chances are it's an introductory rate—one that's offered for only a short time.

Important: The card issuer must disclose how long the rate lasts and what the new rate will be. A 7% rate that jumps to 18.9% after six months is a bad deal—unless you're sure that you'll have all charges paid off before the introductory rate expires. *Formula:* If the difference between a card's introductory rate and its long-term rate is greater than six percentage points, look for a better deal.

Beware: **Any type of penalty interest rate.** Some disclosure boxes may tell you that a higher interest rate goes into effect if you fail to meet the requirements of your account. Those requirements are not always spelled out clearly.

Violation of these standards usually includes making a late payment or exceeding your credit limit.

Limits are most often exceeded when staying at hotels, which charge you after you leave.

In some cases, there are more obscure provisions. Your interest rate can be raised if the bank decides you've become a poor credit risk. Some banks monitor credit files semi-annually.

Important: Issuers do not have to spell out in the disclosure boxes when the higher rates go into effect. Furthermore, they don't have to tell you when you will be late or over your limit. You may not even learn that your rate has increased until you get a bill that includes the new rate.

Self-defense: Call the issuer to ask about penalties before signing up.

Beware: **A "two-cycle average daily balance" method.** If this phrase appears in the disclosure box, throw away the application. The two-cycle method is the sum of the average daily balances for two billing cycles. *Better:* More than 85% of the industry uses a method that calculates the balance by adding all new purchases to the outstanding debt and then dividing by the number of days in the billing cycle. This is the preferred method.

> "Forget what appears on the outside of a promotional envelope or in an advertisement [for a credit card]. Instead, read the disclosure box that, by law, must appear on the back of all credit card applications. Unfortunately, fewer than 10% of all consumers read these boxes. Those who don't . . . can end up paying unexpected fees if they violate their agreements."

Dealing With Banks, Credit & Debt

202

PLAYING THE BILLING-DATE GAME

If you play by the rules of the game, you can keep more of your funds earning interest while you spend someone else's money (at least temporarily). Credit cards provide opportunities to maximize your earnings at the expense of creditors.

Creditors' Policies

Credit card issuers differ in the interest rates and annual fees they charge (if any). They also differ in their payment terms and finance charge calculations. *Reason:* Most issuers, such as VISA, do not set national billing procedures—the bank issuing the card sets its own policies. So, billing policies vary from bank to bank.

When do banks start charging interest? Banks use one of three options in charging interest on credit cards. The first is to begin charging on the transaction date (that is, the date the customer makes the purchase). The second is to charge from the posting date (the date your bank receives notification of your purchase). The third is for a bank to begin charging interest on the billing date (the date the bank makes up your bill and sends it out). There can be a lapse of several days or even weeks between each of these successive dates. *Helpful:* Find a bank that charges interest from the billing date; then you can save interest charges that might accrue from the transaction date to the billing date—in some cases well over 30 days. Avoid banks that charge interest beginning on the transaction date. You will start

paying interest charges immediately, no matter how long the merchant takes to deliver your sales draft to his bank; or the merchant's bank takes to transmit the sales data to your bank; or your bank takes to post the transaction to your account and bill you. In effect, you foot the open-ended bill for the system's inefficiencies.

Don't Pay Bills—Plan Disbursements

When paying credit card issuers, take advantage of interest-free grace periods and payment due dates. If you pay off your credit card bills in full every month, most creditors provide an interest-free grace period of 30 days. But some creditors provide less —25 days, 15 days or even no grace period. Because they vary, know what your creditors' rules are in advance.

When your creditor stops charging interest (or credits your payment) can make a difference too. Although creditors are required to credit payments on the date of receipt, there are some notable exceptions. A few creditors credit payment receipts as of the payment postmark date, which means you can mail your payment several days later than usual and still receive timely payment credit.

Be careful of late-payment charges for "nonconforming" payments. For example, bank card issuers usually

specify that payment be sent to a post office box. If that payment is received anywhere else, it is considered a nonconforming payment. Further, if you pay your VISA bill at the local branch of the bank that issued your card, your bank can defer crediting payment for up to five days after you hand over your cheque. Should this occur, you could incur finance charges or late-payment penalties on the entire balance in addition to losing use of your funds for those five days, even though you made payment to your card-issuer bank's branch on time.

Tip: Some banks permit online transfers from your chequing account to pay your credit card bill. These can be entered in advance, to take effect on the due date. Be sure to print a copy of the transfer confirmation in the event the payment doesn't go through so that you'll have evidence to show that the fault was not yours.

Managing your credit card funds means shopping for payment terms that best suit you. If you pay off your credit card bills in full each month, you should be indifferent to creditors' interest rates and to the timing of initiation of finance charges, but highly sensitive to annual fees and card payment terms. If, on the other hand, you incur finance charges, then interest rates and the timing of finance charge initiation would be the dominant concerns. In either case, the object of playing the billing-date game is the same—to maximize your use of your creditors' money and/or minimize your payment of finance charges.

Source: *Patricia L. McFeely, author of* Plastic Card Float and the Profitability of Cash Management Services.

Dealing With Banks, Credit & Debt

203

Beware: **Balance-transfer restrictions.** Some cards limit the amount you can transfer from another card, while others cap the number of transfers you can make in a particular period.

Other card issuers treat balance transfers as cash advances, hitting you with a ridiculously high interest rate and charging you interest immediately rather than waiting until after your first bill arrives.

The information provided in the disclosure box is often vague. Sometimes an issuer will say that balance transfers are just like cash advances, but they won't mention the cash-advance rate.

Beware: **Bad cash-advance terms.** Issuers must tell you what they charge if you use your card to borrow cash. The fee is usually 2% of the total borrowed.

Trap: They don't have to disclose the interest rate for borrowing the cash. It is often much higher than the interest rate on your card's balance. For example, it's not unusual for a credit card company with a 15% interest rate to raise that rate to 21.9% for a cash advance transaction. *Solution:* Call the issuer's 800 number and ask about its cash-advance terms *before* you borrow money.

Source: *Robert McKinley, president of RAM Research, a supplier of credit card data to consumers and businesses, Box 1700, Frederick, MD 21702.*

Cards With Favorable Terms

Here are some of my favorite credit cards. These have the lowest rates and none of the problems cited above:

● **Royal Bank VISA Classic—Low-Rate Option.** This card has an annual fee of $25 and co-applicant cards are free. The annual percentage rate (APR) is 10.5% and the grace period is 21 days. (Minimum credit limit is $1,000.)

● **Wal-Mart TD VISA card.** This card has no annual fee and comes with an interest rate of 15.48%, with a 6.88% rate on initial balance transfers.

● **Bank of Nova Scotia Value VISA card.** Interest grace period is 26 days. Interest rate is 11.9%/no annual fee, 9.9%/$26 annual fee.

● **Caisse Desjardins offers a Classique VISA card** with 8.9% interest rate and a 21-day grace period for an annual fee of $25.

Source: *Kendrew Pape, personal finance commentator for CBC Radio.*

What MasterCard and VISA Don't Tell You

One MasterCard or VISA card could be very different from another MasterCard or VISA card. What counts is the bank issuing it.

The MasterCard and VISA organizations do not issue credit cards themselves. They provide a clearing system for charges and payments on the cards and license banks to use the VISA or MasterCard name. It is the issuing bank that determines the interest rates and fees.

Choosing which card to take is becoming more difficult. Individuals must be especially careful about accepting any offer that might come in the mail.

Aside from the actual rates and fees, individuals must carefully check the fine print of their contracts. Most banks, for example, do not charge interest on balances stemming from purchases until the customer is billed for such purposes. If the bill on which the charges first appear is paid in full by the stated due date, there is no interest charge to the holder. But some banks begin charging interest as soon as they receive the charge slip and make payment to the merchant. Thus, interest begins accumulating even before the cardholder receives the bill. These interest charges continue until the

No-Fee Cards for Seniors

Senior citizens may be able to get permanent no-fee cards by signing up for special package deals just for seniors. *How it works:* They open savings, money-market and chequing accounts with an institution, and it provides a no-fee card. These packages may not be publicly advertised, so make a point of asking. Best: Shop around.

Source: *Consumer banking expert Robert Heady, publisher,* 100 Highest Yields *and* Bank Rate Monitor.

CREDIT CARD SELF-DEFENSE

Credit card fraud hurts everybody, not just the people whose cards are stolen or used illegally. It results in higher annual fees and finance charges, fewer free services from card issuers and higher retail prices. And rather than improving, the problem's getting worse.

Common Scams and Self-Defense

● **Telemarketing rip-offs.** These ploys succeed by preying on victims' gullibility and greed and succeed surprisingly often. *Scenario:* A phone caller informs you that you've been selected from a market survey as one of several winners of a free luxury trip, big appliance, etc. (Callers often pick numbers from the phone book at random, counting on the chance that the victim has a credit card. Or, dishonest employees at card-issuing companies sell names of new cardholders to crooks.)

All you need to do to claim your prize is verify your identity by providing the number from a major credit card. *What you've really won:* A major hassle. You won't hear from these people again until your next credit card bill, which is sure to be loaded with charges for merchandise you never ordered and cash advances from banks with whom you never did business.

Defenses: Obviously, never give your number over the phone. Inform the card issuer immediately of any potential fraud. *Liability:* Up to $50 if you don't inform the card issuer before charges are made to your account.

● **Credit card receipts.** An easy way to fall prey and you won't know anything happened until you get the bill. *Scenario:* You pay for gas by swiping your credit card through the payment slot, but you forget your receipt. The attendant throws it away. Thieves remove it from the trash and use your card number to buy items by phone.

Defense: Remember to take your receipt, and always tear up credit card receipts before you throw them away.

● **Stolen cards.** Whenever possible, keep credit cards separate from personal identification cards like your driver's license. A thief who has all your ID can easily misrepresent himself or herself as you and run up a staggering amount of charges in a single afternoon. Check your cards daily. Thieves often steal only one card, betting that you won't miss it for a few days. Always inspect monthly statements for unfamiliar charges. The sooner you inform the card issuer, the less you'll have to pay.

Source: Jack Taylor, U.S. Secret Service Special Agent.

bank receives payment from the customer.

Source: Robert A. Bennett, banking correspondent, The New York Times.

Premium Card Traps

Don't be lulled into getting "premium" credit cards, such as Gold MasterCard or Premier VISA. The only significant "premium" is the $20–$25 extra that you pay in higher annual fees. Besides the fancy finish on the plastic, you get marginally useful benefits, such as travel insurance and protection on lost or stolen credit cards. Since by law you are liable for only up to $50 if your regular card is stolen or lost, the zero liability offered by these premium cards is not worth the extra money.

Potential huge trap: Credit cards tied to home-equity lines of credit. Banks are pushing them hard. *Attraction:* Interest paid may qualify for a full tax deduction if you use the money for investment purposes, but there are more efficient ways to borrow money for investment, the banks' risk is minimal with the credit line secured by the equity in your home.

Home-equity card rates are typically one to three percentage points above prime, and credit lines start at $10,000 and go as high as $100,000.

Cardholder risk: If you can't make the payments, you may lose your house.

Source: Consumer banking expert Robert Heady, publisher, 100 Highest Yields and Bank Rate Monitor.

Traveling With Credit Cards

We all use our credit cards when we travel, but do you have any idea what that convenience costs you? Most people are unaware that credit card companies and the financial institutions that issue the cards tack on an administration fee every time you make a purchase in foreign currency—this is over and above the profit the banks make on their normal conversion rates. The total charge will vary from one bank to another and will be set out in the card holder's agreement. In the case of Royal Bank VISA and the popular CIBC Aerogold VISA, for example, the fee works out to 1.8%.

MasterCard says it does not charge an administration fee in Canada although individual members may do so. In fact, the MasterCard issued by Bank of Montreal hits you for a hefty 2.5% on all foreign purchases. So be sure to check with the issuer of the card you're considering regarding the policy in this regard, especially if you'll be spending a lot of time outside Canada.

Even if you do pay a conversion fee, the credit card companies claim that you get a better rate by using your card than you would by withdrawing U.S. cash from an ATM or exchanging traveler's cheques in a foreign bank because their huge volume enables them to benefit from wholesale rates.

You can avoid conversion charges altogether if you have U.S. dollar assets. In that case, get a credit card denominated in U.S. currency and use it whenever you travel to the United States. Your invoice will be in U.S. dollars and you can pay the bill directly from your U.S. account. Several banks offer them, including CIBC.

Source: *Gordon Pape writing in* FiftyPlus *magazine, the official publication of CARP, Canada's Association for the 50-Plus.*

Shopping for Exchange Rates

There is little point spending a lot of time shopping around for the best exchange rate unless you have a lot of money to convert. Why make a lot of phone calls or run from bank to bank if you are exchanging a relatively small amount of cash? But if the amount is significant, say several thousand dollars, you may want to do some shopping.

The rates at the major banks are unlikely to vary much, so the best approach is to contact the financial institution where you normally do business and ask what their rate is. Then immediately call a couple of foreign exchange specialists—you'll find them listed in the yellow pages—and ask for their rates. Look for companies that offer consumer services; some of these organizations cater only to large businesses that have hundreds of thousands of dollars to change.

Remember that rates fluctuate constantly, so for an apples-and-apples comparison you have to obtain them at the same time. Also, there is no guarantee the same rate will apply when you show up. However, you can get a pretty good idea of which companies consistently offer the best rates from this type of comparison shopping.

You can also search for currency exchange rates

Special Charge Card Trap

There are superhigh interest rates on charge accounts at a growing number of stores that offer their own cards. The biggest offenders are electronics retail chains that can charge from 21.6% to 24% on outstanding balances. There's also a minimum of $100–$500 that must be charged the first time the card is used. ***Alternatives:*** Bank credit lines and traditional retail charge cards.

on the Internet but it's a frustrating experience and I have not found any site that offers up-to-the-minute comparisons of retail rates.

One other point, you aren't allowed to take more than US$10,000 in cash or marketable notes into the United States for money laundering reasons. If you need more than that, set up an account at a U.S. bank and arrange for a transfer.

Source: *Gordon Pape writing in* FiftyPlus *magazine, the official publication of CARP, Canada's Association for the 50-Plus.*

How You Can Beat the System

Credit cards have become a way of life for most Canadians. However, very few people realize the unnecessary costs they incur by not utilizing their cards to their advantage or by not choosing the least expensive card to begin with.

Credit cards can be used as a bargaining chip to receive a discount from a merchant. Merchants typically pay a fee of 2%–7% of your charge when you use your credit card.

With an American Express or Diners Club card, merchants may have to wait a while to get paid. It may be to the advantage of the merchant to go along with your suggestion of a 5% discount if you pay cash.

Another way to beat the system: Some credit cards, like the Bank of Montreal Low-Rate Gold card, offer a lower interest rate on cash advances than on merchant purchases. Take a cash advance on your credit card and pay directly for goods and services, rather than charging them if bank-interest charges are less for cash advances. If you already are being charged interest for merchandise purchases, take a cash advance and switch the balance due to the lower rate.

If no interest charge has yet been levied, then time the cash advance to a day or two before the bill would be past due and pay off the merchandise portion of the bill. *Reason for the timing maneuver:* Cash advances are charged interest from the day that they are taken. Multiple credit cards are handy if you want to go to the limit of allowable cash advances on each without having to use your card to buy merchandise at high rates.

If you have gotten in over your head, it may be best to take out a consolidation loan to pay off a number of credit card bills. Although the consolidation loan rate may not be much cheaper than the credit card cash-advance rate, it can be significantly cheaper than the card's basic interest rate on merchandise purchases. In addition, since bank credit card payments are based on a 24-month term, one big advantage to consolidating such debt with a 36-month loan is lower monthly payments.

Source: *Edward Mendlowitz, a partner with Mendlowitz Weitsen, CPAs, 2 Pennsylvania Plaza, New York, NY 10121.*

BIG, BAD NEW CREDIT CARD TRAPS

Beware of complicated interest-calculation methods that can wipe out the benefits of a credit card's grace period. With the two-cycle billing method, you'll need at least two back-to-back, no-balance months to avoid interest charges. *Also:* Grace periods themselves are being shortened—some banks give only 20 days, down from 25 to 30.

Self-defense: When switching cards, avoid both traps.

Source: *Gerri Detweiler, author of* The Ultimate Credit Handbook.

A Loan Trap to Watch Out For

A consolidation loan will do nothing but get you deeper in debt if, after paying off your credit card debt, you start charging things again.

Best: Pay off your credit card debt with a consolidation loan and then use your credit cards only for emergencies.

Source: *Edward F. Mrkvicka, Jr., is the author of* Your Bank Is Ripping You Off, *St. Martin's Press.*

How to Sidestep Late-Payment Penalties

Late-payment penalties on credit card accounts are becoming more common. Some credit cards issued by Canada's gas companies are guilty of highway robbery, charging 24% interest as well as stiff late-payment penalties—even if payments miss the deadline by only a day or two. Some cards will waive the penalties, but the cardholder has to ask for the correction. A good payment track record and a reasonable excuse are usually sufficient grounds for having the charge lifted.

Source: U.S. News & World Report.

Advantages of Credit Card Purchases

● **Overseas purchases on a credit or charge card can be less expensive than expected.** It all depends on exchange rate fluctuations and how long it takes for the card company to process the paperwork. *Rule of thumb:* When the value of the dollar is increasing, the longer it takes to post and clear a charge, the cheaper the purchase becomes. When the dollar is falling, however, you'll want to have the paperwork cleared as quickly as possible. *Clearing times:* American Express—0 to 7 days; Diners Club—2 to 5 days; MasterCard—0 to 3 days; and VISA—3 to 6 days. Larger retailers in big cities tend to process paperwork daily—or even immediately—electronically. On the other hand, purchases made from smaller merchants and those in remote villages can take up to a week to clear.

Source: Condé Nast Traveler.

● **Pay for mail-order purchases with a credit card, rather than with a personal cheque.** *Reason:* If you don't receive the merchandise or it's not what you expected, you can refuse to pay until the matter is resolved. But if you've paid by cheque and the mail-order company cashes it, you may have trouble getting a refund.

Source: Good Housekeeping.

Signs That Mean You're in Trouble

Warning signs of excessive debt: You pay more than 20% of your discretionary income (after mortgage, taxes and utilities) on debt, you fail to pay all your creditors each month, you use a cash advance from one credit card to pay the bills from another, you feel nervous about how much money you're spending.

Source: National Foundation for Consumer Credit, 8701 Georgia Ave., Silver Spring, MD 20910.

● **Simple credit-card expense recording.** With every purchase you make with your credit card, it is advisable to write down for whom and why on the slip when you sign it. This will enable you to keep track of your business tax deductions and expenses in a single step.

Good Reason to Use Your Credit Card

Credit cards can protect you if a purchase turns out to be a lemon. Refuse to pay and demand that the amount be charged to the merchant. *What to do:* First, make an effort to settle the dispute. Then notify the credit card company, in writing, about the transaction, the amount of money involved, the name of the merchant and the attempts that you have made to settle the matter. Act quickly. Once you've paid for the merchandise, your only recourse is to sue the merchant.

Source: Jean Noonan, credit-practice attorney, Federal Trade Commission, quoted in U.S. News & World Report.

When Tax Status Depends on Which Credit Card You Use

The general rule is that you only get a tax deduction in the year you actually pay for a deductible expense. But there's an important exception when you pay with a credit card. For tax purposes, payment is considered made on the date of the transaction, not on the date you pay the credit card company. You can sign now and deduct this year but pay next year.

Many charities accept credit card donations. You can claim a charitable contribution deduction in the year the contribution is charged. The same rule applies to payment of medical or dental expenses with a credit card.

American Express Card Advantage

People with duplicate credit cards from a joint American Express account don't have to worry about a stop being put on both cards if one card is lost or stolen—each card has a special identifier code. This goes for the Optima Credit Card, too. *Latest information:* Neither VISA nor MasterCard plans to institute such a coding system.

Beware of Low Credit-Card Rates

Bank cards with the lowest rates—11% to 14%—can often cost more than cards with traditional 18% to 21% charges. *Reason:* A growing number of banks begin tacking on interest charges the minute a transaction is posted to their books. This charge accrues until the charge amount and the interest are paid in full. The TD Emerald VISA offers a 10.9% interest rate, but no grace period.

Even if you pay off your charges as soon as you get your monthly bill, you'll still pay an interest charge.

Solution: If you pay in full whenever you use a credit card, choose a bank that charges interest only on balances that are still outstanding following the payment due date on the bill.

Source: Money *magazine.*

Prevent Credit-Card Rip-Offs

Here's a simple trick: Pick a number and, if possible, make sure that all your credit card charges end in that number. *Example:* Say you choose the number 8 and your dinner bill comes to $20.00. Instead of adding a $3.00 tip, add $3.08. When your bill comes, check to see if all the charges have 8 as the last digit. If they don't, compare them against your receipts and report discrepancies to the card issuer.

Credit Card Protection

● **Photocopy the cards themselves** to keep track of which ones you have. It's much more convenient to have all accounts on a single sheet of paper than to rely on keeping all the original agreements together. Keep one photocopy at home where it can be used to notify card issuers if a card is lost or stolen. Put another in a safe-deposit box or other safe place.

Source: Leon Gold, Phillips Gold & Co., CPAs, 1140 Avenue of the Americas, New York, NY 10036.

● **Avoid being charged for goods or services you didn't buy by** scribbling over the shaded sections labeled "delayed charges" and "revised total" when you sign credit card slips. Often, unscrupulous merchants will add charges there, hoping the customer won't notice the discrepancy on his or her bill. By scribbling over these areas on each slip, you deter such acts of theft.

Credit Card Errors

Come January, many people find themselves in disputes over credit card charges that were mistakenly billed to them during holidays. Here are the most common problems and how to straighten them out:

● **There's a problem with the merchandise purchased with the card.**

Solution: You can withhold payment on a credit card charge if the merchandise you purchased was different from what you ordered—or it was delivered on the wrong day—or it was delivered in the wrong quantity.

You can also refuse to pay a credit card charge for merchandise you did not accept. *Example:* A new refrigerator was delivered to your home, but it was the wrong color, so you refused to accept delivery and the delivery people left with the refrigerator.

How to dispute the charge: Once you notice the charge on your statement, write a letter to your credit card issuer at the address listed on your statement for billing errors and inquiries.

Don't include the letter with your payment for other items on your bill. And don't procrastinate. In your letter include your name, address, account number, the charge you're disputing and why.

> "With every purchase you make with your credit card . . . write down for whom and why on the slip when you sign it."

Send your letter by registered mail, return receipt requested. *Your dispute will in all likelihood be rejected if:*

● **You have changed your mind about a purchase.**

● **The merchant has a clearly posted "no refunds" policy.**

● **You are disputing the "quality" of merchandise or services you bought.** *Helpful:* If you're buying something valuable, such as gems, artwork or antiques, always get the seller to write on the sales slip all promises about quality and authenticity.

● **You want to dispute a charge because of the poor quality of goods or services.**

● **There's a charge on your bill you don't recognize.**

Solution: You have the right to ask your credit card company to provide documentary proof of the charge.

If the issuer produces proof, such as a sales slip, but you did not make the charge or authorize someone else to make the charge, the most you can be responsible for is the first $50 of the unauthorized charge—and that's only if your card was actually used in the transaction. *Example:* If someone stole your credit card number and used it without the plastic card, you are not responsible for any of the unauthorized charges.

If the issuer balks at taking the unauthorized charge off your account, tell the issuer you want to sign a "fraud affidavit" certifying you didn't make the charge. That should indicate you are serious about not paying.

Credit background: Keep all records relating to any type of credit problem—or credit report problem—for a period of seven years. That's the length of time negative information can be reported on your account.

If your account is transferred to another financial institution, for example, you could find the same problem popping up again. Keep your records to quickly clear up misunderstandings about past accounts.

Source: Gerri Detweiler, consumer credit consultant in Woodbridge, VA, and head of public policy for the National Council of Individual Investors. She is the author of The Ultimate Credit Handbook, *Plume.*

Easy Way to Get Over Credit Card Addiction

> **Once you know how much you've earned over your lifetime—net—and compare it with your current net worth now, the difference will likely convince you to make radical changes in your lifestyle and spending habits.**

People who are in debt over their heads often blame their credit cards. *Reality:* Most of those problems are related to poor money management.

Even people who are not in trouble may want to reconsider their use of credit cards, unless they always pay the entire bill each month. *Reason:* Credit card interest is not deductible.

It might be tempting to just cut up your cards and go cold turkey. But it's important to learn self-discipline and good spending habits to take advantage of the convenience of credit cards. *What to do:*

● **Limit yourself to two or three credit cards.** A bank card covers almost all purchases. Add to it a gas credit card and, perhaps, a card from your favorite department store. (Shop around for low-fee or no-fee bank cards. Don't get hooked into expensive "status cards.")

● **Record your charges in a memo book.** Because there's no written running balance, as in a cheque book, it's easy to lose track of how much you're spending.

● **Put a ceiling on your spending.** Don't let the credit card companies set a ceiling for you. They're only too happy to increase your limit each year because you're such a "good customer." You'll be tempted to spend that much more.

Warning: Sometimes mortgage applicants may have difficulty obtaining the mortgage if they have a high credit card ceiling—even if they don't use it. (They could, in theory, get into that much debt overnight.)

● **Spend no more than 20% of your monthly take-home income on consumer debt.** (This is a general guideline. Low incomes should allow a lower percentage.) This includes car loans, credit cards, etc. If your monthly payments for debt exceed that amount, you're headed for trouble.

Solution: Stop incurring debts until all your credit cards are paid off. Then follow a budget faithfully.

If you are heavily in debt from credit cards or any kind of unsecured debt, find a nonprofit consumer credit counselor who can set up a repayment program and appeal to card companies to lower your monthly payments until the debts are paid off.

It is best to pay as much as possible as soon as possible, since interest usually continues to accrue on unpaid debt.

● **Use savings as an alternative to credit cards.** Too many people are forced to use credit in an emergency because they have no savings on which to fall back. *Change your approach:* Save to establish an emergency fund with *at least* three months' income. Use the money only in an emergency, and pay back that money as you would a bill.

● **Know your goals and budget accordingly.** Don't incur too much debt by trying to keep up with the Joneses. Know what you want out of life. *Suggestion:* Write down your goals, a time plan for achieving them and the approximate costs. Then determine which goals are important and focus your budget on the high-priority items.

Source: Cathy Pietruszewski, executive director and vice president, Consumer Credit Counselors of San Francisco and the Peninsula, 31 Geary St., San Francisco, CA 94108.

Credit and Divorce

If a loan to one spouse is secured by property that the court awards to the other spouse in a divorce settlement, the collateral can't be claimed by the creditor to settle the debt—it must take action against the original debtor in order to recover the loan.

Even a registered lien isn't valid if it's dated after the divorce petition was filed. *Example:* A husband buys a car in his name after he and his wife petition for divorce. The wife is awarded the car as part of the settlement. The car financing company can't repossess the car if the husband stops making payments. In this case, the company's only option is to sue the husband.

Editor's note: Although this is based on a U.S. court ruling, the same principles apply in Canada. However, family law comes under provincial jurisdiction, so the rules may vary somewhat.

Source: Hoyt *vs.* Amer. Traders, *SC Oregon, 9/3/86.*

Credit Card Debt Can Be Dangerous to Your Wealth

If you take a hard look at your credit card statements, you will probably notice that most charges are for goods and services that you really don't need. The temptation to spend money is great, but excessive spending is financially dangerous and can lead to debt.

To effectively cut back on your spending—and avoid putting off long-term dreams—you must do more than merely hide your credit cards. You must change the way you think about money. Whether you earn $10,000 or $200,000 a year, here are the steps you can use to avoid debt and save more income:

Step 1: **Look at what you already own.** Throw open your closets and drawers, and make a list of everything you see. By cataloging your possessions, either on paper or in your mind, you will be able to size up the true quality of your current life. You'll also likely discover you already own plenty of everything.

By recognizing that you have enough to be comfortable, you will be more likely to stop yourself the next time you think you must have something you

Stretching Due Dates on Bills

Due dates on bills can be stretched—but not far—without risk. *Typical grace periods:* Telephone companies, eight days. Gas and electric utilities, 10 days. Banks and finance companies, 10 days. Even after a late charge is imposed on an unpaid bill, your credit rating should be safe for 30 days.

can't afford. *Example:* A woman I know opened her closet and counted 30 pairs of shoes. And she realized that she rarely wore most of them.

A quick and easy way to have such a revelation is to ask yourself the following penetrating questions:

- **What do I have?**
- **What does it mean?**
- **Do I still want this in my life?**
- **Do I need it in my life now?**
- **Can I give any of this stuff away?**

Step 2: **Compare your lifetime earnings with your current net worth.** This step is important, and calculating the data isn't hard. Once you know how much you've earned over your lifetime—net—and compare it with your current net worth now, the difference will likely convince you to make radical changes in your lifestyle and spending habits. *Strategy:* Estimate your total earnings over the years. Use tax returns to determine your past income. Estimate any gifts or capital gains from investments. Set the total aside.

To calculate your net worth, simply add up all of your assets and subtract from that number your total debt. Look at the two figures. You'll probably be shocked at the difference. *Example:* A friend of mine, a TV producer, found that she had made $3 million in her lifetime but had less than $100,000 in assets to show for it. She asked herself, *Where did it all go?* She realized a lot of it had been wasted on nonessential luxuries she couldn't even remember enjoying. The assessment convinced her to change her spending behavior.

Step 3: **Calculate your real wages.** When you spend money, you have to spend energy to earn it back. *Example:* If you earn $40 an hour, you must figure in all the extra expenses—such as child care, commuting and clothes. You also need to include the extra hours you spend commuting and unwinding from your job at the end of the day.

After you do those calculations, you may realize that you don't earn $40 an hour—you actually only earn $20 or $25.

> "Many people deny that they have debt problems. They refuse to admit that the problems exist or believe that their debts will just go away by themselves."

The objective is to find out how much you actually get paid for your energy and to force yourself to confront the fact that you may be spending way over your head.

Step 4: **Track your daily spending pattern.** Many people ignore the fact that they are spending far too much money. They simply withdraw cash from their bank account or use their credit cards and ignore the consequences.

Solution: Devise a system to track your daily expenses. Keep a little notepad with you, and write down every purchase you make. Then calculate how much time you must work to meet the expenses you pile up in each spending category. *Example:* Say you spent $200 last month on dining out—and your real hourly wage is $20 an hour. That translates into roughly 10 hours of energy spent. Ask yourself if you received 10 hours of fulfillment from those restaurant meals.

Lots of people keep track of every penny, but they don't evaluate whether their expenses are worthwhile.

To assess the quality of your purchases, place an up or down arrow next to each expense to indicate whether or not it was fulfilling. *Some questions that you might ask yourself:*

- **Did I get fulfillment from the purchases that I made?**
- **Was I happy to work that much time for each expense?**
- **Do my buying habits really reflect values that I consider important?**

Chances are the answers will be all the encouragement you need to give up many unnecessary expenses.

Step 5: **Consciously lower your expenses.** Your expenses will decrease by 20% to 25% after you follow the previous steps. You'll become aware of the ways you spend your life energy. *Example:* One man recently sold the red Jaguar for which he was paying $390 a month in car payments and $140 a month in insurance. He laughed when he realized that he had gotten the car to impress people. He sold the car, paid cash for a used car and cut his high monthly car payments and insurance costs by 50%.

Source: *Vicki Robin, president of New Road Map Foundation, an organization that helps people gain greater control over their money and their lives, Box 15981, Seattle, WA 98115. The foundation offers a money-management audiocassette course. Ms. Robin is coauthor, with the late Joe Dominguez, of* Your Money or Your Life, *Viking Penguin.*

How You Can Get Out of Debt and Stay Out of Debt

Many Canadians are trying to reduce their credit card debt. Faced with increasing financial responsibilities, many are looking for ways to eliminate the bills and free up some of their income.

Fortunately, most debt is manageable—if it is addressed early enough. Here's what I tell people who are overburdened with debt:

● **Acknowledge the problem.** Many people deny that they have debt problems. They refuse to admit that the problems exist or believe that their debts will just go away by themselves. The fact is that if you owe money on your credit cards and cannot pay the entire amount when the bill arrives, you have debt. If your debt grows too large, you run the risk of being unable to meet your monthly payments and seriously damaging your credit rating.

The biggest drawback to debt is that it uses up income that could have been invested or spent elsewhere. You are also paying more for something over time than if you had paid for it in full right away. Even if your debt is only temporary, immediate action must be taken to minimize interest payments.

● **Put everything in writing.** To determine how much debt you are carrying monthly, calculate how much you owe. Then determine your monthly income and expenses. If your debt is higher than your monthly income, you should take steps to reduce it. *Strategy:* Make two lists—one for expenses that are essential and the other for those that are optional. Some expenses that seem essential may have to be reclassified as optional. Hold a family meeting to plan cutbacks. While debt may be a difficult subject to discuss with your family, it is essential that all family members make sacrifices.

● **Don't slash expenses too dramatically.** Just as total-deprivation diets do not help you lose weight permanently, budgets that completely eliminate anything that hints of fun do not permanently eliminate debt. Cutting back is better than cutting out. *Example:* Maybe you can no longer dine out twice a week. But you could go out once a month for special events. Your new budget should accommodate these occasional excursions.

● **Work hard to stay on course.** Paying off debt is an incremental process. Try not to take on new debt or go on a spending binge as a reward for being frugal.

If you're having trouble making payments, don't ignore the bills. That only gets you into deeper trouble. Instead, contact all of your creditors to work out less onerous repayment plans or to assure them that you will keep making regular payments. That is what your creditors really want to hear, since regular lower payments are better than no payments at all.

Source: *Alexandra Armstrong, chairman of Armstrong, Welch & MacIntyre, Inc., a Washington, DC-based financial advisory firm. She is coauthor of* On Your Own: A Widow's Passage to Emotional and Financial Well-Being, *Dearborn Financial Publishing.*

Anyone Can Get Out of Debt

When I was young and single, I spent all of my money. When I was married with two incomes, no children and a monthly rent payment of only $95—my husband and I spent all of our money.

No matter how much money there was, there was never enough.

By the early 1980s we had two kids. I quit work, and my husband was earning $20,000 a year as a teacher. We also were $7,000 in debt.

Our First Mistake

In the beginning, we tried the conventional approach to paying off our debts. Every month, I'd pay as much as I could toward our seven different outstanding credit card bills.

But this approach was a total failure. It didn't leave us enough money to live on. We were four people living on one modest income. We could have used a good chunk of that credit card payment for food and household expenses.

As a result, a few weeks into every month, we had to use credit cards to buy things like toothpaste, soap and gas for the car. By the start of the next month, instead of our credit card bill going down, it was *higher* than the month before.

Our Solution

Finally, I found a plan that worked for us. It freed us emotionally, so we were no longer held hostage to the ridiculous concept that joy and fulfillment are only possible if you have no bills. I recognized that unpaid bills are like dirty dishes—no one likes them, everybody has them and there will always be dirty dishes if you eat. But dirty dishes and bills don't have to rule your life. *Here's how we got out of debt:*

● **Don't worry if you can't pay large sums toward your balances.** The conventional wisdom is

HOW TO LIVE FEE-FREE

It's easy to save $1,000 or more by reducing or eliminating annual financial fees:

● **Banking.** Many banks charge monthly cheque-writing and/or ATM fees that add up to as much as $150 to $300 a year on chequing accounts, and $150 to $200 on ATM fees.

Don't make the mistake of passing up a no-fee chequing account just because it requires a minimum balance. It often makes sense to take money out of some investments and deposit it in the bank to meet the no-fee minimum.

● **Brokers.** If you're an active investor and you make your own investment decisions, consider a discount broker. It can drastically reduce your commissions.

But discounters aren't all the same. Traditional discounters such as Bank of Montreal InvestorLine (1-800-387-7800) and Royal Bank Action Direct (1-800-769-2583) offer some services such as free investment research. They will also save you as much as 40% on commissions. Deep-discount online brokers such as Solium (1-877-380-7793) and eNorthern (1-888-829-7929) take a more bare-bones approach but offer even bigger commission cuts.

Potential annual savings: It depends on how many trades you make each year. The greater the number, the greater the savings.

● **Credit cards.** If you run a balance of $1,000 a year, a low-rate card could cut your interest costs in half. If you pay off your balance every month, it is best to choose a card without an annual fee.

Potential annual savings: $35 to $100 for a no-fee card, or $72 in interest charges if you run a balance of $1,200 and switch from a 19% card to a 13% card.

● **Mutual funds.** Many mutual funds sold by brokers carry sales charges—or "loads"—of 2% to 5%, which are used to compensate the people who sell them to investors. *Better:* Choose no-load funds, such as those sold by the banks, Altamira or Phillips, Hager & North. On a $1,000 investment, you'll save as much as $50. *Alternative:* Ask your broker to sell you front-end load funds on a zero commission basis. Some brokers will do so just to earn the annual "trailer fees" the funds pay.

Also avoid high annual fees that some funds charge. *Ideal:* Choose stock funds with annual fees of less than 2.50% and bond funds with annual fees of less than 1.75%.

Potential savings: As much as $150 on an investment of $10,000 annually.

Sources: Gordon Pape and Kendrew Pape; and Jonathan Pond, president of Financial Planning Information, Inc., was the host of the PBS television special "Finding Financial Freedom With Jonathan Pond."

that you should pay more than the minimum required, so you can eventually extinguish your credit debt.

I began by paying only the minimum. That's because it was the only way I could start to reduce our debts and still have enough money to live on. After years of paying more than the minimum, running out of money mid-month and winding up deeper in debt the following month, I'd decided there had to be a better way. *Example:* Instead of pulling a whopping $100 out of our small chequing account and sending it to our card issuer, I'd pay the suggested $22 minimum. That left us with $78 to spend on things like car repairs, laundry soap and groceries. I reveled in the freedom and the feeling of control that came with having some cash.

Important: Make sure that the bank that has issued your credit card requires a minimum payment that is large enough so that it pays off some of the principal, as well as the accrued interest, on your balance. Otherwise, you'll never, ever succeed at getting out of debt.

Also, make sure that the interest rate you're paying on your outstanding balance is not too high. In today's low-interest-rate environment, you should consider switching banks if you're paying much more than 6.9%.

● **Stop using your credit cards.** The only way to wipe the slate clean if you're paying the minimum due on your credit card bills is not to run up a higher balance. But not using credit cards is more easily said than done. If you have become dependent on your credit cards, it may take a few months of minimum payments and socking away cash before you can make it through the month without charging. *Strategy:* My new approach worked because my goal was to enjoy life with the money we already had, not to be prisoners of our bills. By making the choice to put less

The Truth About Credit Card Security Plans

Credit card security plans that protect against unauthorized charges won't save you more than $50 per card, and thus are rarely worthwhile. *Reason:* Your liability for unauthorized charges is limited to $50 per card. Your liability will be zero if you report your credit card as lost or stolen before any improper charges are made on it.

Self-defense: When a card is lost, notify the card issuer immediately by phone and in writing through a letter sent by registered mail. Your receipt is proof of the date on which you sent notice to the issuer. This can be valuable if a question arises over whether disputed charges were incurred before or after the card was lost.

Source: *Gerri Detweiler, consumer credit consultant and author of* The Ultimate Credit Handbook, *Good Advice Press.*

toward the bills and more for our independence, I felt in control. Feelings of empowerment replaced the helpless feeling of relying on our credit card to get us through the month.

● **When you completely pay off a credit card's balance,** reward yourself by setting up a special savings fund. I'll never forget how excited I was when I paid off my first credit card balance under this new system. It was a $300 department store bill that had required a fairly steep minimum payment of $60 a month.

When it was paid off, it was like getting a $60 raise. There were all sorts of things I could do with that newfound money. I decided to put $10 a month into a family-camping account, $20 a month into an account for future car repairs and to leave $30 a month in my chequing account for other purchases.

If you follow this approach, you are emotionally and financially free to make real choices about what to do with your money. It's no longer just work and bills, and bills and work.

Source: *Carol Keeffe, who leads workshops on money, time and family management, Box 1965, Lynnwood, WA 98046. She is the author of* How to Get What You Want in Life With the Money You Already Have. *Little, Brown & Co.*

Holding the Line on Medical Costs

6

How to Get the Best From Your Doctor

With medical care getting more complicated, and with the growing number of specialties and even subspecialties, the field of doctoring is becoming a more impersonal industry. To the person with no medical problems, that's usually an academic point. But for the ill and the elderly, the new situation is creating additional heavy burdens.What used to be a simple doctor-patient relationship is now very complicated. For example, how do you...

● **Maintain continuity** of your medical records when you move from one specialist to another?

● **Identify the right doctor** to diagnose and treat various illnesses?

● **Evaluate the medical advice you're given**—and find the many alternative treatments that may be better for you than the conventional ones?

Taking an Active Role

Increasingly, patients are discovering they can no longer be passive in the doctor-patient relationship. They have to take an active interest to be sure they get not only the best care but, in some instances, just adequate care, as the soaring number of medical malpractice suits seems to indicate.

Here is a valuable checklist of potential problems and advice for dealing with today's doctors:

● **Checkups.** The usual procedure is that a doctor performs a checkup and lab work-ups (if needed) during the examination. Then, a few days later, the doctor's nurse calls and relates an oversimplified assessment of the lab results. *Instead:* Arrange for a preliminary visit so that lab work can be done before the physical exam. That way, the doctor can go over the results of the tests in detail, answering any questions during the regular exam. If there is need for further lab work, it can be done later.

● **Medical records.** In most cases, your medical records are kept by the doctor. So if you move, decide to change doctors or subsequently see a specialist, you have to go through a long procedure to get your records. *Instead:* Ask the doctor for copies of all records and keep them in your own permanent file. *Especially useful:* Electrocardiograms, blood tests and X rays. The doctor might charge you a nominal fee to make copies.

> " If you or the doctor feels that the drug you're taking may not be fully effective—but is the best currently available—consider doing some of your own research.... Check medical journals that specialize in the condition you have. "

● **Selecting professionals.** It's generally very hard to find out whether a doctor treats your particular problem or uses the procedure you need until you visit the office—a waste of your time, since you'll probably have to wait for the appointment. *Instead:* Try to get as much, if not all, information over the telephone.

● **Doctor-patient relations.** Doctors usually prefer to be called "Doctor." Yet they often call patients by their first names. That small difference helps to perpetuate the role of doctor as parent and patient as child—where the patient isn't expected to question the doctor's orders. This leaves the patient in a position of not sharing responsibility for his own health. *Instead:* As a symbolic gesture, settle whether the two of you are on a first- or last-name basis.

More Ways to Win

● **If the doctor always keeps you waiting,** call before you leave for your appointment. *Even better:* Ask someone else to call and explain that your professional duties make your schedule very tight.

● **If the doctor diagnoses an illness and prescribes drugs,** take notes on the name of the condition and the drugs being prescribed.

● **If you're overcome by the news of the illness** (which isn't unusual), call the doctor after you've had some time to calm down and frame any questions about the prognosis and the method of treatment. Also, arrange to bring a relative or friend with you to emotionally charged doctor visits. That'll give you the emotional space to "collapse" or to go temporarily "deaf" to bad news, while your companion is able to listen, ask questions and interpret what the doctor says. The period right after serious illness is disclosed is hard to handle, so make arrangements to compensate for it.

Drugs

Since even the "safest" drugs usually have some side effects, it's prudent to insist that you be included in any decisions about prescriptions. Frequently, the decision isn't only which drug to take, but whether one should be taken at all. In some cases, there are alternatives to drugs—changes in diet, lifestyle or exercise. Many doctors believe, perhaps correctly, that most patients don't feel that an office visit for an illness is complete unless a pill is prescribed. Make it clear that you don't feel that way.

● **Insist that the pharmacist include the manufacturer's fact sheet** with any prescription you're given. It's technical, but with the aid of a medical dictionary you may discover things about the drug you'll want to discuss with the doctor. It's hard, if not impossible, for doctors to know current information on all drugs. You may discover that the dose is excessive or that the drug is no longer effective for your condition.

● **If you do take a drug that has side effects** (i.e., dizziness, stomach distress), start taking it during a weekend or when you're home, so you'll be in a safer place when the side effects hit.

● **If you or the doctor feels that the drug you're taking may not be fully effective**—but is the best currently available—consider doing some of your own research. *Sources:* Check medical journals that specialize in the condition you have. Also, some brokerage firms run stock analyses of leading drug companies and include comprehensive reports on new drugs. The problem then is to find a doctor running clinical studies with the new drug. Only that doctor can legally use it if it doesn't have Health Canada

approval. Be aware, too, that you're running a risk in using the drug. However, some new drugs have already been given full approval in other countries.

Source: Susan G. Cole, editor of The Practical Guide to Cancer Care, Health Improvement Research Corp.

Cost-Cutting Secret

Get free drugs simply by asking for them. Doctors are constantly visited by salespeople from drug companies who leave samples, and the samples usually sit forgotten in a desk or filing cabinet. At today's prices, they're worth asking about.

Medical Test Rip-Off

Six out of 10 medical tests are unnecessary. Doctors order them because of insecurity, pressure, curiosity or habit. *To avoid wasting your time:* Ask your doctor whether each test is really needed.

Source: Study at the University of California, reported in the Journal of the American Medical Association.

How to Avoid Becoming a Victim

Studies show that one quarter of the surgical procedures performed in the United States each year are of very limited benefit, or entirely useless. *Part of the problem:* In the past 10 years, the number of surgeons has increased, while the demand for operations has remained constant. As the opportunities per surgeon dwindle there, the pressure mounts to perform surgery that is only "marginally" indicated. Although this is not the situation in Canada, where many communities face the opposite problem of doctor shortages and limited availability of surgeons, unnecessary procedures are sometimes performed.

Relatively few victims of unnecessary surgery come to harm, but all are burdened with needless

Generic vs. Brand-Name Drugs

Generic drugs aren't always cheaper than brand-name equivalents. Although pharmacies pay less for generics, many mark them up more than they mark up brand-name drugs. *Helpful:* Comparison shop for each drug instead of assuming that you'll always save by picking the generic.

Source: Journal of the American Medical Association (JAMA).

worry, inconvenience (hospital stays can be lengthy) and usually some expense. Operations also entail some risk if they require general anesthesia. Before you agree to surgery of any kind, make sure you are comfortable with the diagnosis.

Self-Defense

Unless you're a physician, you can't diagnose your own illnesses and decide whether or not you really need an operation. But you can and should seek a second—and third—opinion if you're considering any operative procedure.

Important: Get at least one opinion from a doctor who is not a surgeon. Call a teaching hospital in your area and ask to see a specialist.

Unwarranted operations are sometimes inspired by some patients who complain so frequently that their physicians finally recommend surgery as a way to relieve the patients' subjective complaints, if not treat their disorders. Because pain is subjective, it's hard for doctors to determine through medical tests alone whether the conditions are serious enough to warrant surgery. Physicians must rely on a patients reports of pain.

Warning: The more you complain of pain, the more likely that your doctor will recommend surgery. *It's valuable to become familiar with the types of procedures that may be performed unnecessarily, including the following:*

● **Arthroscopy.** A surgical technique to diagnose and repair cartilage injury in the knee. The operation is performed mostly on injured athletes. A good number of orthopedists recommend it. But for many injuries, a few months of rest and rehabilitation may be just as effective a cure. Arthroscopy doesn't necessarily prevent future knee problems or pain.

● **Biopsy of the skin.** One of the most common surgical procedures in North America. Several million are performed each year to remove moles and lesions—many of which may be nothing to worry about. *Potentially dangerous lesions:* Moles that change color, darken, bleed or grow rapidly may be potentially malignant. The procedure is simple and not high-risk. Nevertheless, you should definitely seek a second opinion.

● **Breast biopsies.** Because of the malpractice liability crisis, doctors have become fanatical about not missing any lump and women also are scared that any lump means cancer. *Result:* Numerous unnecessary breast biopsies. These operations may require one to two days in the hospital and involve pain and the normal surgical risks of doctors' errors, infection, death under anesthesia, etc.

Women under 40 may be the victims of unnecessary breast biopsies. In some cases, if the doctor and patient just wait two or three months, the lump may disappear. But waiting more than four months can be risky. *Better:* If two reputable doctors tell you that you need a breast biopsy, get one. If the surgeon asks you to sign a paper allowing him or her to perform a lumpectomy (removal of the malignant lump) in the lymph nodes of the axilla (armpit), give your consent and have it all done at one time to avoid a second anesthesia. Breast biopsies are almost never wrong, and if cancer is found, the doctor should take care of it surgically.

Caution: If the surgeon wants to perform a mastectomy (removal of the entire breast), withhold your consent until you can get second and third opinions. The need for mastectomies in some patients is controversial.

● **Carotid endarterectomy.** An operation to unclog neck arteries.

Problems: The operation offers little relief for nearly 30% of patients, and the risk of complications may be great when performed on older people. *Helpful:* Consult a neurologist and a vascular surgeon. Neurologists may suggest more conservative forms of treatment.

● **Coronary bypass.** Very much in vogue, but about one-third of the 225,000 bypass operations performed each year in the United States are only marginally indicated. (In Canada, about 22,500 bypass surgeries are performed annually.) The major benefit—a longer life—doesn't occur in at least half of all cases. Quality of life usually improves after the operation, but there's no guarantee.

Danger: This is a major operation. And the weaker the patient is from his or her heart condition, the more perilous it may be.

Possible attractive alternatives: Angioplasty (cleaning out of arteries via a catheter) or control by medication.

● **Endoscopy.** Over a million endoscopies are performed yearly in North America, but only 60%–65% are beneficial. The operation involves inserting a tube through the patient's mouth or anus to check for internal bleeding or tumors. It costs $550–$650 and, for some patients, it may be uncomfortable.

Risks: Possible perforation of the intestines. *Helpful:* Since there is a tendency for some endoscopists to overoperate, when you go for a second opinion, consult a doctor of internal medicine who isn't an endoscopist.

● **Hysterectomy.** Be wary. Some physicians believe the mere presence of a uterus in a woman age 40 or older with gynecologic complaints indicates the need for a hysterectomy.

● **Lumbar laminectomy.** The removal of a disk that is pushing against the spinal cord and causing neurological impairment.

Problem: Only 20% of back-pain sufferers have a disk problem, and of these, remarkably only two-thirds benefit from this painful operation. The decision to operate sometimes depends upon the patient's report of pain.

Alternative: Live a healthier lifestyle. One that will help you lose some weight. A large number of chronic back problems are caused just by excess weight and lack of exercise.

● **Tonsillectomy.** Many unnecessary tonsillectomies are performed at parents' insistence—they just can't stand their kids being sick all the time.

Problem: If recurring sore throats are caused by a virus, they may continue even after a tonsillectomy. The operation is most commonly indicated only if a child gets more than five strep throats per year. These bacterial infections travel through the blood and can cause problems in the heart and kidneys. If this is not the case, there may be little reason for an operation. Consult a reputable pediatrician.

Surgery You Don't Really Need

● **Most back-pain sufferers don't need surgery.** *Also:* Three out of 10 of the most common back operations (laminectomy and spinal fusion) are failures—and 10% make patients worse.

Source: Dr. C. Norman Shealy, founder of the Pain Rehabilitation Center, Springfield, MO.

● **Gallbladder trouble doesn't always necessitate surgery**. *Breakthrough:* Gallstones can now be dissolved by flushing the gallbladder with a form of ether known as MTBE. Recovery is faster, and there is minimal nausea and vomiting.

Source: Dr. Johnson Thistle, Mayo Clinic.

Same-Day Surgeries

You can often safely skip the inconvenience and discomfort of an overnight hospital stay after: hernia repair, tonsillectomy and adenoidectomy, cataract extraction, some plastic surgery, removal of a tissue lesion or cyst, dilation and curettage (D&C), tubal ligation and drainage procedures for glaucoma.

Source: Whole Life Times.

Don't Be Surprised If You Get a Bill

The government health plans cover the basics that most of us would need. They pay for most doctors' appointments and services, hospital care, bandages, medications administered while you are in hospital, nursing care, X rays, ultrasounds, blood tests and other diagnostic work.

But some kinds of treatments and services that might appear to be in the same category are not covered. As lauded as the Canadian system is, it doesn't cover everything. For instance, cosmetic surgery is generally not covered, unless it is performed as the result of an accident or is deemed "necessary" by the surgeon, and some fertility treatments are not covered. Some provincial plans limit the number of eye examinations you may have at public expense in a certain period of time. It's entirely possible that your grandmother's flu shot may be covered because she is elderly, but yours may not.

The most commonly used services that are not included in government plans are dental care and drugs. There have been many debates about whether there should be socialized dental and drug programs, and some provinces do provide assistance to their most needy residents. Most of us, however, turn to private plans purchased by our employers or increasingly, to individual private health care plans.

Source: The Insurance Book, by Sally Prasky and Helena Moncrieff, published by Prentice Hall Canada. Sally Prasky is editor of the Insurance Canada website, located at www.insurance-canada.ca.

Opting for Extended Health Care Insurance

This type of insurance is meant to pick up where your government plan ends. In some provinces, a ride in an ambulance will cost you money whether you ordered it yourself or were picked up unconscious following an accident. Extended health care insurance would cover such an expense. Prosthetic appliances, and medical supplies and equipment also fall under privately paid extended health care. In addition, it covers services you might need for a longer period of time than your government plan will support. For instance, depending on the plan, it might cover physiotherapy, home care and nursing, visits to a psychologist or speech therapist or a registered massage therapist or chiropractor.

Just remember, private plans have limits that might not necessarily match the cost of what you pay. Even if you have planned in advance and purchased insurance, always be prepared to be out of pocket if you have a problem. Nothing covers everything. If such a product did exist, the price would likely be so high that no one would buy it.

Source: The Insurance Book, by Sally Prasky and Helena Moncrieff, published by Prentice Hall Canada. Sally Prasky is editor of the Insurance Canada website, located at www.insurance-canada.ca.

The National Numbers

Many Canadians opt for supplementary health insurance. According to statistics published by the Canadian Life and Health Insurance Association, 109,200 group contracts covered about 6.2 million Canadian workers and their 8.9 million dependents for extended health care benefits at the end of 2000.

In addition to this, 3,400 group contracts provided 1.1 million workers and their dependents with

Questions to Ask a Surgeon

To protect against unnecessary surgery, ask the physician hard questions beforehand:

- What are the risks?
- What is the mortality rate for this operation?
- How long will it take to recover?
- What is the likelihood of complications? What sort?
- Are there alternative ways to treat this condition?
- How many people have you seen with similar symptoms who have chosen not to have surgery?
- How many of these operations have you done in the past year?

Once you receive answers, then get a second opinion.

supplementary hospital expense insurance only, while 7,500 group contracts supplied 848,700 workers and their dependents with prescription drug expense insurance only.

As far as individually purchased contracts, 367,400 people were covered for extended health care and an additional 293,000 for supplementary hospital care benefits. That's a lot of insurance!

Take a Tip Before Buying Your Health Insurance

No one looks forward to buying or renewing their insurance, but here are some tips that will make the process a little easier.

- **Ask your insurance provider what the policy doesn't cover.** The perils that are not covered are called "exclusions," and every policy has them. Find out what they are now, rather than at claims time.

They are listed on your insurance policy. Therefore, ask your insurance provider to explain the exclusions before you buy the policy. That's what he or she is paid to do.

● **Generally, you get what you pay for.** If you're shopping around, make sure you're always comparing apples with apples—not all insurance policies are alike. And, while minor price variation among companies offering similar kinds of coverage is likely, if one insurer is charging substantially less, beware. It may not be the ideal company to deal with at claims time.

● **Review your insurance needs on a yearly basis.** Your circumstances may have changed during the year, and some of these changes should be reflected in your insurance coverage. Don't wait for your insurance provider to ask—most don't.

Source: The Insurance Book, *by Sally Prasky and Helena Moncrieff, published by Prentice Hall Canada. Sally Prasky is editor of the Insurance Canada website, located at www.insurance-canada.ca.*

Pricing Your Policy

How do insurers decide what to charge for insurance? It's all based on something called "risk factors." The more risk involved in insuring you, the more you will pay for your insurance. That's where underwriters come in. They decide on what terms to accept a risk, and then price it accordingly.

Keep in mind that there are certain risks that no insurer will agree to cover, because the odds are too great that a loss will occur. You may not be able to buy certain types of travel medical or health insurance if you have what is called a "pre-existing condition"—an existing or previous illness that the insurer believes is likely to worsen or recur.

Source: The Insurance Book, *by Sally Prasky and Helena Moncrieff, published by Prentice Hall Canada.*

Health Insurance Problems to Avoid

Insurance companies are in the business of selling security and peace of mind. But when it comes to settling claims, most insurance companies are in the business of saving money. While millions of policyholders have their claims settled with a minimum of fuss, there are many areas in which abuses by insurers are widespread. *Rule of thumb:* The higher the cost of your claim, the more likely you are to have trouble with your insurer. The most common ways insurers shortchange policyholders:

● **Unwarranted rescissions.** Attempts by an insurer to rescind—or cancel—a policy *after* a claim has been filed are common in some kinds of insurance claims. Wrongful rescissions make up 25% of the cases I handle. *How it works:* Many insurers don't investigate your insurance application until you've filed a claim. This procedure is called *post-claims underwriting.* An adjuster audits your records, not for the purpose of paying your claim—that's a separate department—but to see if you forgot to include something on your application.

Self-defense: Case law on this subject is abundantly clear. If you had no knowledge of a medical problem at the time of your policy application, if you failed to appreciate the significance of an omission or if the omission is immaterial or trivial to the underwriting of your policy, your coverage cannot be rescinded.

When applying for insurance: Answer all questions honestly, *yourself.* Insurance agents often paraphrase answers.

● **Failing to fully investigate claims.** According to consumer-protection laws, it is the insurer's duty to investigate policyholders' claims *in good faith.* But insurers are sometimes adversarial when it comes to paying claims (although in Canada there has always been a fairly good track record for health insurance claims). *Result:* Insurers may deny claims without consulting the appropriate experts—doctors, appraisers, contractors—or do so only to find a reason *not* to pay.

Self-defense: If your claim is unfairly denied, enlist the help of your insurance agent and submit statements from experts who can support your claim. If your claim is for property damage, visual documentation—photographs, videotapes—can help as well. If the insurer refuses to consider your evidence, contact a trial attorney.

● **Overturning medical opinions.** Insurers must often review medical questions—*Was this treatment really necessary? Is this person really disabled?* For this purpose, most insurers use in-house medical examiners or hire "independent" medical examiners who may not be unbiased since they have ongoing

WORST TIMES FOR HOSPITAL CHECK-IN

Avoid weekend admissions for tests or elective surgery. Chances are that you will lie in bed for two days with little or no medical care. Because most patients are discharged by the weekend, hospitals trying to fill beds will encourage weekend admissions. As a general rule, insist that you be admitted right before a test or procedure is scheduled.

Also avoid admissions during major holiday seasons, such as Thanksgiving or Christmas. Staffing at most hospitals is particularly low during those periods, so you may end up sitting around waiting for things to be done.

Warning: If you are really sick, staff shortages may mean lower-quality care. The worst time to be admitted to a hospital is in the month of July. Why? July is the month when residents and medical students are rotated. A major portion of day-to-day care in teaching-affiliated hospitals is performed by newly graduated resident doctors. Young residents who have just arrived or those who have just taken on greater responsibilities will not have the same level of skill as more experienced physicians.

Source: Arthur A. Levin, MPH, director, Center for Medical Consumers, 237 Thompson St., New York, NY 10012, publishers of **Health-Facts,** *a monthly newsletter that critiques medical practices.*

business arrangements with the insurers. *Result:* Thousands of claims are unjustly denied every year when insurers' "medical experts" override the opinions of policyholders' doctors.

Self-defense: Most major medical policies pay for a second opinion—be sure to get one whenever possible. Shop around. You may have to find doctors who are willing to go to bat for you if their opinions are contradicted.

● **Narrowly defining disability.** Most employers define disability as the inability to perform steadily in a job to which you are reasonably suited by education, training, experience, opportunity and physical and mental capacities.

But most disability insurance policies ignore this and define disability as the inability to perform any job. By this definition, an executive who suffers a debilitating stroke would not be considered disabled if he or she could still wash dishes, and could be denied the benefits he or she expects based on his or her salary.

Self-defense: Look for a disability policy that covers you for your "own occupation." CPP disability, for example, has the "any occupation" definition, so it rarely pays. When filing a disability claim, describe the nature of your work to your doctor and precisely how your injuries affect your ability to work. Make sure this information is included in your doctor's report to the insurance company.

Source: William M. Shernoff, attorney, who specializes in consumer claims against insurance companies, Claremont, CA. Mr. Shernoff is the author of How to Make Insurance Companies Pay Your Claims, *Hastings House.*

Travel Health Insurance

Nobody likes to think about getting sick or injured while away on vacation—but it can happen, and when it does you should be prepared. No matter how cautious we are, accidents and illnesses do happen. One round of food poisoning could quickly see you rack up a bill of thousands of dollars a day for hospital care. If you'd rather spend those thousands on your next vacation, you may want to consider spending the tens of dollars travel health insurance would cost instead.

Consider this: If you have a health problem when you are away, your government plan will pay only what the Canadian costs would be, not the real costs in the country you are visiting. For instance, provincial plans would cover from between $75 and $800 a day for a hospital stay. But the charge in a U.S. hospital could be several thousands of dollars a day, as high as $10,000 a day for intensive care! Physicians' fees tend to be higher in the United States as well, something we don't usually have to consider at home. Our provincial plans will cover from about $50 to $100 for each visit to a physician. American fees are well beyond that. So although your government plan would cover some of your expenses, it wouldn't cover everything.

Don't count on advice from your cousins in the next province, by the way. Each provincial plan is different; an allowable expense under British Columbia's plan, for instance, may not be covered under Newfoundland's plan. Recognizing their own limits, the provincial health ministries themselves recommend you purchase extra insurance when you leave the country.

Depending on the package you purchase, travel health insurance might offer benefits for emergency hospital or other medical services, prescription drugs, X rays and lab fees, ambulance services, private nursing or wheelchairs. Caught a ball at spring training? Your travel health insurance would probably pay for emergency dental work too.

If you have to get back to Canada for immediate medical treatment, your insurance plan might pay for a plane ticket on a regular flight with a medical attendant accompanying you. If you can't travel on a regular flight, an emergency air ambulance flight might be included with a doctor and nurse on board. Your coverage may also get a relative to your bedside, or get your vehicle back home.

Source: The Insurance Book, by Sally Prasky and Helena Moncrieff, published by Prentice Hall Canada. Sally Prasky is editor of the Insurance Canada website, located at www.insurance-canada.ca.

Things to Know Before You Go Abroad

If you are traveling out of country, here are the top 10 questions to ask your insurance provider before you purchase your travel health insurance.

1. What is not covered in the plan (including certain sports or other activities)?

2. Are there any other limitations (time period permitted for travel, age restriction, etc.)?

3. Is there a deductible? If so, how much?

4. How is a "pre-existing condition" defined? How do I determine if I have such a condition?

5. If I do have a pre-existing condition, can I still be covered for other, unrelated illnesses or injuries?

When you have a claim…

6. How do I make a claim?

7. Do I have to ask the insurance company before I receive treatments?

8. Will the claim be paid directly, or do I have to pay up front?

9. Will the plan pay for an air ambulance to transport me home in the case of a serious emergency?

10. Will the plan pay for someone to fly to my bedside if I am seriously ill or injured?

Source: The Insurance Book, by Sally Prasky and Helena Moncrieff, published by Prentice Hall Canada. Sally Prasky is editor of the Insurance Canada website, located at www.insurance-canada.ca.

A Good Person to Talk To

If the need should arise during the course of your treatment, many hospitals today are staffed with a designated patient representative. This person answers your questions, acts on your concerns and intervenes between you and your doctor or you and the nursing staff if needed. In fact, a patient representative is your interface on any type of problem that might occur during your hospital stay.

Source: Ruth Ravich, director, patient representative department, Mount Sinai Medical Center, New York.

Hospital Stays Can Be Hazardous to Your Health

Shorter hospital stays can keep you healthier. *Fact:* The longer you stay in a hospital, the greater the risk you will end up with a problem you didn't have when you first arrived.

Medication errors and hospital-borne infections are only two of the dangers. A research study of more than 800 consecutive hospital admissions revealed that almost 40% of the individuals checked into the hospital ended up with new doctor- or hospital-caused problems.

Source: Arthur A. Levin, MPH, director, Center for Medical Consumers, 237 Thompson St., New York, NY 10012, publishers of **HealthFacts**.

Claiming Medical Expenses on Your Tax Return

If you have extra medical expenses that you have paid for out-of-pocket, they can add up to a non-refundable tax credit which reduces the amount of federal income tax you pay.

How much? *The General Income Tax and Benefit Guide for 2001* suggests that, in order to be beneficial, your total expenses have to be more than $1,678, or 3% of your net income, whichever amount is less.

Here's how it works:

You can claim medical and dental expenses paid for yourself, your spouse or common-law partner and your dependents for any 12-month period ending in the year for which you submit your return (as long as you haven't already claimed them in the previous year). You can only claim the portion of the medical or dental expenses for which you were not and cannot be reimbursed.

The following are some examples of medical expenses you can claim:

1. Payments to a medical doctor or certain other medical professionals, dentist or nurse, or to a public or licensed private hospital.

2. Payments for artificial limbs, wheelchairs, crutches, hearing aids, prescription eyeglasses, contact lenses, dentures, pacemakers and prescription drugs.

3. Payments for certain prescription medical devices.

4. Some expenses for modifying a home or vehicle can be claimed if your mobility is limited or you are physically impaired. The expenses will be allowed if the modifications make you more mobile and functional. They will also be allowed in cases where you can make such claims for another person.

5. Expenses incurred for guide dogs and hearing ear dogs.

6. Premiums paid under the Quebec Prescription Drug Insurance Plan, and premiums paid to private health service plans, other than those paid by an employer.

In addition:

If you had to travel at least 40 kilometers to obtain medical services that were not available locally, you can claim transportation costs for yourself, your spouse or common-law partner, or a dependent, for trips to and from medical facilities, including the hospital, clinic or doctor's office.

Furthermore, if you had to travel at least 80 kilometers to get medical attention, you can claim reasonable travel expenses, such as meals and accommodations, in addition to the transportation costs.

A simplified method of calculating transportation costs allows you to multiply the kilometers you drove for your trips relating to medical expenses by the cents per kilometer rate for the province or territory where your travel began. (Note that the rate per kilometer varies depending on your province or territory of residence from 38.5 cents per kilometer to 48.5 cents per kilometer.)

For meals, a simplified method allows you to claim a flat rate of $11 per meal, to a maximum of $33 per day per person, without receipts.

As you can see, it is certainly worth your while to keep track of any and all costs related to medical expenses that you've been required to pay out of your own pocket.

> "Some expenses for modifying a home or vehicle can be claimed if your mobility is limited or you are physically impaired. The expenses will be allowed if the modifications make you more mobile and functional."

Source: Claiming Medical Expenses, *Canada Customs and Revenue Agency.*

Negotiating an Informal Contract With Your Therapist

If you're in need of any kind of psychological help, try to negotiate an informal contract with your

YOU CAN SHORTEN THE LENGTH OF THERAPY

Depending on the type of psychotherapy you require, you may or may not have to pay for it yourself. Here in Canada, almost all psychiatric services are covered by our government health care system—but psychological services are not. If the type of psychotherapy you need requires you to consult a psychologist, be prepared to get a bill. It is possible, however, to facilitate the progress of psychotherapy, shorten its duration and save money. Here's how.

1. Outside your therapy sessions, establish an internal dialogue patterned on the one you have with your therapist. Continue the process of self-exploration, introspection and honest self-confrontation.

2. Make notes on your dreams and fantasies and bring them to the sessions. They are shortcuts to the unconscious.

3. Attempt to recognize any resistance you may have to the therapy. Resistance to change is part of the process of psychotherapy and is largely unconscious—patients often spend many sessions overcoming it. Recognizing resistance and developing a therapeutic alliance with your therapist will shorten this defensive stage.

4. At regular intervals, ask your therapist to join you in an evaluation of the progress of your treatment. Lengthy impasses may require a consultation with another therapist.

Source: *T. Byram Karasu, M.D., professor of psychiatry, Albert Einstein College of Medicine/ Montefiore Medical Center, 2 E. 88 St., New York, NY 10128. He is also chairman of the APA Commission on Psychiatric Therapies and of the APA Task Force on Treatment of Psychiatric Disorders.*

treatment. Many psychological problems are caused by narrowly definable conflicts that create corresponding defense mechanisms in the patient. These conflicts frequently lend themselves to short-term psychotherapies. Only lifelong characterologic problems and personality disorders may require long-term psychotherapy or analysis.

Try to have your symptoms treated independently of your life and interpersonal problems. Although such problems are usually inextricable, it is quite possible to treat manifest symptoms with medication and to achieve behavior modifications quickly. At the same time, you and your therapist can work on your life problems at a slower pace.

Source: *T. Byram Karasu, M.D., professor of psychiatry, Albert Einstein College of Medicine/Montefiore Medical Center, 2 E. 88 St., New York, NY 10128. He is also chairman of the APA Commission on Psychiatric Therapies and of the APA Task Force on Treatment of Psychiatric Disorders.*

The Dollars and Sense of Being Fitted With Contact Lenses

Acquiring a pair of contact lenses is quite different from buying any other consumer product. Lenses have a critical job to do and must do it without causing irritation or injury to the wearer's eyes. Of course the physical lenses themselves are a "product," but what the contact lens wearer is actually buying is a service—an effective solution to a health problem.

Choosing a Practitioner
Cutting corners when choosing a practitioner would obviously be foolish. Fees for a contact lens fitting

therapist before you begin treatment. Your discussion should include the fee and optimum required frequency of visits.

What makes therapy expensive is its open-endedness and its lack of focus—or its having too many different factors on which to focus. This makes it worthwhile to negotiate the goal of the therapy, its focus and the process.

Also ask your therapist to estimate the length of

GETTING THE MOST EFFECTIVE PSYCHIATRIC HELP

In Canada, psychiatric services are covered by our government health care system. However, even though it's being paid for, your time is still a valuable commodity and you should ensure that you're getting the best treatment possible. Psychiatric conditions that require professional help range from existential questions about oneself to disease entities such as schizophrenia, bulimia and a large variety of symptoms and syndromes such as impotence, marital conflicts, alcohol abuse and psychosomatic disorders. Many means are available for treating problems like these, but the effectiveness of a particular treatment program depends almost entirely on the condition being treated.

The Correct Diagnosis

The primary rule of effectiveness is to get the correct diagnosis. If you get an incorrect diagnosis in the beginning, you may become involved with a long and drawn-out treatment regimen that does not adequately correct your condition.

Once you start a particular program, it is usually difficult to end it. Patients have a tendency to stay with a familiar therapist even though, by all objective criteria, the therapy is not successful.

An incorrect diagnosis may be made if you select the "wrong" clinician—one competent in only a narrowly defined area, or whose treatment philosophy is not the one best suited to dealing with your particular problem. The correct diagnosis usually requires finding an eclectic psychiatrist with the training and capacity to synthesize multiple points of view.

Referrals by friends and family are always a good place to start looking for a well-qualified psychiatrist. Most good internists are also able to make recommendations. Check therapists' academic credentials—affiliations with academic institutions are a good sign. After you've narrowed the field, arrange to meet prospective therapists face-to-face. *Caution:* Beware of psychiatrists who talk too much, ask the same question over and over, lecture or drop names of patients.

Even if you don't intend to be treated by a psychiatrist, consult with one before deciding on a specific treatment and therapist. Psychiatrists can determine whether a psychological disorder has a physiological basis—a possibility you should at least rule out before beginning therapy.

After the Diagnosis

Depending on the diagnosis, a variety of practitioners are available to provide treatment. Psychiatrists in private practice are the best option for people with major psychiatric disorders such as depression, anxiety and thought disorders. Since they are also M.D.s, psychiatrists are capable of comprehensive medical evaluations and can also write prescriptions when pharmacological treatment is needed.

If you have no medical or organic problems (symptoms that require medical intervention), a psychologist or other mental health worker can be considered.

For interpersonal problems, group therapy can be very effective. Although it is less confidential and less time is available for individual issues, it is possible to get around these problems by complementing group sessions with individual sessions. Couples therapy, especially when conducted in a group, can be an effective way for spouses to resolve marital problems. *Advantages:* You and your spouse become part of a support group where you can examine your relationship, be comforted that you are not alone in your struggle, learn different styles of communication and identify with the survivors of interpersonal conflicts.

Clinics, especially those associated with medical schools, deliver good-quality, comprehensive care, even though they are largely staffed with trainees. Institutes (psychoanalytical, behavioral, etc.), also primarily staffed by trainees, specialize in more narrowly defined therapeutic approaches. By choosing carefully, you can find the type of practitioner who will provide the most effective treatment for you.

Source: T. Byram Karasu, M.D., professor of psychiatry, Albert Einstein College of Medicine/Montefiore Medical Center, 2 E. 88 St., New York, NY 10128. He is also chairman of the APA Commission on Psychiatric Therapies and of the APA Task Force on Treatment of Psychiatric Disorders.

Holding the Line on Medical Costs

can vary greatly, depending on the lens type and the complexity of your case, as well as the quality of the service rendered. But knowing up front what the charges and refund policy will be (within reasonable limits) will help you evaluate the cost-effectiveness of the care. In addition to investigating cost, then, here are several points to consider when choosing a practitioner:

● **Reputation.** Ask friends and acquaintances who wear contact lenses for their recommendations.

● **Competency.** Inquire about the doctors' credentials and areas of expertise. Focus on practitioners who specialize in contact lenses and be sure they employ *at least* three or four various lens types from different contact lens manufacturers.

● **Compatibility.** A pleasant, comfortable relationship with the practitioner and staff will help ensure that your needs are met. It is advantageous to work with the same doctor each time you return. This will lead to a more consistent approach in satisfying your contact lens needs.

● **Personal comfort.** Pleasant surroundings are a valid consideration when selecting a practitioner, since correct fitting requires substantial amounts of time.

The Fitting Process

A proper contact lens fitting consists of four phases. Understanding the purpose of each phase will put you in a better position to make evaluations and choices along the way.

1. In the initial consultation, you and your practitioner will mainly exchange information. If you are going specifically for the purpose of discussing contact lenses, this visit will probably not be covered by your provincial or territorial health plan (so be sure to find out about the cost beforehand). You will be questioned about your health history and your requirements, goals and expectations concerning wearing contact lenses.

> "Patients with complex cases and those who plan to wear their lenses for extended periods and/or sleep while wearing their lenses should plan on more frequent initial fitting appointments. Every daily-wear contact lens wearer should return once or twice a year thereafter for regular checkups..."

This visit is also your opportunity to question your practitioner on his or her experience, credentials and affiliations, as well as details about the further course and cost of the fitting.

It is important that you use this opportunity to eliminate many potential surprises down the line. At the conclusion of this consultation, it is a very good idea to request a comprehensive and detailed fee schedule.

If, for any reason, you do not feel comfortable with the practitioner—or anything else about the situation—this is the time to terminate the relationship and look for another practitioner. You will, of course, have to pay for the consultation.

2. Assuming all went well at the initial consultation, you will return for a diagnostic evaluation. Your vision-correction needs will be determined through careful examination of your eyes and eyelids. Based on the information collected and the goals agreed upon in the consultation and the findings of this exam, a limited selection of indicated lens types will be tried out and evaluated.

Normally, this will lead to a final selection of one or more applicable lens types. If no available solution fulfills your goals, either you and your practitioner must agree on new goals or the fitting process should be terminated at this point.

3. Following a successful diagnostic, you will return for the dispensing appointment, at which the selected lenses are tried on and evaluated. Again, assuming all is well, you will be instructed in their proper use and maintenance. It is imperative that instructions pertaining to wearing and disinfection and cleaning procedures be followed scrupulously. Failure to do so is fast becoming one of the leading causes of serious eye complications.

4. The final phase of lens fitting—every bit as important as any of the preceding one—is follow-up care. Proper follow-up to a typical

ARE VITAMINS WORTH THE COST?

According to a 2001 Gallup Survey conducted by Roche Vitamins Canada Inc., a full 44% of Canadians take vitamin/mineral supplements. To date, however, the importance of these extra doses of vitamins to our health and nutrition is largely unknown.

The controversy rages on two fronts: How helpful are moderate supplements of vitamins in maintaining maximal health—and how helpful are large (mega) doses of vitamins in either preventing or curing certain diseases and conditions?

Regarding the second question, little evidence has been gathered to show conclusively that megadoses of vitamins cure or prevent serious medical conditions. The first question has proved easier to answer.

Are Moderate Supplements Necessary?

For some, definitely yes—for others, probably. For individuals who have clinically proven vitamin deficiencies, vitamins are clearly worth the cost. These people need extra vitamins because either their behavior results in a deficiency or their medical problem or treatment results in a deficiency. *Examples:* Heavy smokers are thought to be very deficient in vitamin C; women on birth control pills, defi-

cient in thiamin, some B vitamins and vitamin C; those taking diuretics for high blood pressure often become deficient in B_6.

Although the proof is less conclusive, most health practitioners would agree that moderate amounts of vitamin and mineral supplements are needed even by those of us who eat three square meals a day and don't have the clinical deficiencies described above. Exercise, stress, alcoholic beverages, dieting and pollution are all believed to deplete the body's reserve of vitamins and minerals.

Source: *Arthur A. Levin, MPH, director, Center for Medical Consumers, 237 Thompson St., New York, NY 10012, publishers of* HealthFacts, *a monthly newsletter that critiques medical practices.*

dispensing of contact lenses without complication involves approximately four visits during the initial fitting period.

Patients with complex cases and those who plan to wear their lenses for extended periods and/or sleep while wearing their lenses should plan on more frequent initial fitting appointments. Every daily-wear contact lens wearer should return once or twice a year thereafter for regular checkups, and, in the case of overnight lens wearers, as often as four times a year.

Source: *Barry Farkas, O.D., FAAO, doctor of optometry, 30 E. 60 St., New York, NY 10022. He is a diplomate of the contact lens section of the American Academy of Optometry.*

Health Foods: Do You Get What You Pay For?

Since the 1960s, North Americans have had a love affair with health foods. Food products labeled "healthy," "natural," "additive-free," "no preservatives" and "nothing artificial" have become not only highly marketable, but also highly expensive.

While health foods are usually more expensive than other food products, they are sometimes no better or safer. Many "natural" foods have added ingredients with little nutritional value.

For example, a typical granola bar is no more nutritious than a Snickers bar and does not contain fewer calories.

Furthermore, because there are many "natural" toxins in foods, the term does not even guarantee safety. It always pays to read labels carefully and be a little skeptical about the claims made for any product.

A Better Value

Being healthy does not require spending extra money to eat only "health food." It is much more important to select foods that have high nutritional value and avoid those that have little or none at all.

As a general rule, avoid processed food products and opt for fresh or fresh-frozen ingredients instead. This will help you minimize your intake of salt, fats, chemicals and empty calories.

The best advice is to maximize your intake of fresh vegetables and fruits, whole grains and sources of protein low in saturated fat. Many supermarkets are carrying some of the grains, juices and additive- or preservative-free products formerly found only at "health food" stores—and the supermarkets are doing this at lower prices.

Source: Arthur A. Levin, MPH, director, Center for Medical Consumers, 237 Thompson St., New York, NY 10012, publishers of HealthFacts, *a monthly newsletter that critiques medical practices.*

How to Get the Most Nutrient Value Out of the Food You Buy

● **Buy whole-grain products,** or at least enriched refined ones.

● **Buy fresh or frozen fruits and vegetables, not canned.** The best choice is freshly picked, ripe produce. Frozen produce is often more healthful than fresh, however, because it is frozen when the nutrients are largely intact.

● **Low-fat dairy products** should be fortified with vitamins A and D, which are fat-soluble.

● **Don't soak fresh produce** for long periods of time. Also, don't wash rice. This will preserve water-soluble vitamins.

● **Avoid cutting and/or cooking vegetables** until right before use.

● **Avoid boiling vegetables.** Pressure cooking and steaming preserve more nutrients.

Source: Arthur A. Levin, MPH, director, Center for Medical Consumers, 237 Thompson St., New York, NY 10012, publishers of HealthFacts, *a monthly newsletter that critiques medical practices.*

Looking for Health and Medical Information on the Internet

With so much health and medical information available on the Internet today, more and more people are educating themselves about everything from nutrition and fitness to the latest treatments for heart disease and cancer. But with this wealth of information comes an abundance of fraudulent claims and scams.

Remember: Anyone with the right equipment can create a webpage, and some of these websites can look extremely professional and legitimate. You could lose time and money and, even worse, your health if you are duped by inaccurate or erroneous information.

Protect yourself from fraudulent and potentially dangerous health or medical advice by checking out your source of information very carefully. *Ask these questions:*

● **Whose site is it?** The most dependable sources are medical schools and universities (.ca), government agencies (.gc.ca) and some not-for-profit health agencies (.org). Always bear in mind that some practitioners and commercial organizations may have hidden agendas.

● **Are the names and credentials** of the people who prepared the site listed? How available are they? Can they be contacted?

● **When was the site last updated?** Frequent updates mean timely information.

● **Does the site link to other health and medical websites?** Be careful, though; anyone can link on to a legitimate source to make his or her website appear credible.

An extra caution: Be suspicious of websites that promote treatments that use words such as "miracle," "revolutionary," "secret," or "breakthrough," or that are pushing you to purchase a remedy or product.

Bottom line: Any information that you gather from the Internet should be double-checked with your health practitioner.

Source: Food and Drug Administration Consumer Health Information Online.

Friends, Family & Your Money

7

- Financial Strategies for Working Couples

- Prenuptial Agreements versus Marriage Contracts

- The Canada Child Tax Benefit

- How to Protect Your Savings Against Catastrophic Illness

- Lending Money to Family and Friends

- Choosing a Retirement Home or Supportive Residence

- Transform Your Relationship With Money

Financial Strategies for Working Couples

Few two-income couples take full advantage of their financial power. And they don't concentrate on making their money work for them.

Attitudes About Money

There are two types of people—savers and spenders. For better or worse, they tend to marry each other. The result is often conflicting views of money and how it should be spent and invested.

Solution: Sit down with your partner and confront your money attitudes. Then discuss how best to handle your finances. Take a close look at your overall financial picture. Ask yourselves:

● **How much of your respective incomes do you want to save?**

● **What are your savings goals** (vacation, new car, down payment on a house, university for the kids, retirement, etc.)?

● **Should you be accountable** to each other for all of your spending or should each of you have a private account?

● **How many credit cards will you use?** Or will you cut up all but one of your cards and take a weekly cash allowance?

Another way to limit the amount of damage is to set up separate accounts for a portion of your earnings. Pay your household expenses out of one joint account. *Remember:* Depending on your province of residence, you may be responsible for your spouse's debts, and your spouse's bill-paying habits could affect your credit report.

Reconcile Tax Strategies

Spouses often have different views about how to handle their income taxes and organize their records, especially if they prepare their own tax returns.

Important: You should both file a tax return, even if one spouse has no taxable income. Your family may be eligible for various government tax credits, such as the GST and the Child Tax Benefit. Eligibility is based on your combined income, evidence of which will be provided in the two returns. *Warning:* When you sign the return, you are liable for any mistakes, disallowances (when the CCRA disallows a deduc-

tion) or penalties. *Strategy:* Seek professional tax-filing help. Find a tax preparer with whom you are comfortable. It may be worth the extra expense to give you peace of mind about your taxes.

An Investment Strategy for Two-Income Families

Once you've worked out a savings program with which you're comfortable, your strategy should be to implement it in such a way that the lower-income spouse receives any investment income. That's because he or she will be taxed on that money at a lower rate, leaving more money for future investing.

You achieve this by having the lower-income spouse provide all the investment capital. For example, suppose the husband is earning $80,000 a year as an office manager while the wife earns $25,000 a year as a freelance writer.

We'll assume the husband's marginal tax rate is 42% and the wife's rate 25%. So for every $100 in interest income received by the husband, about $42 will go to the Canada Customs and Revenue Agency (CCRA). If that interest is received by the wife, only $25 of every $100 will be taxed.

Clearly, if this couple decided that, between them, they could put aside $500 a month for wealth building, they'd be much better off if the wife made the investments from her personal earnings. That's because the CCRA would regard any income earned on that money as hers alone—and assess tax at a lower rate.

How much of a difference can this make? Let's say this couple put aside $6,000 a year in a non-tax sheltered interest-bearing investment (like a GIC) for 10 years, with the money compounding at 5.5% annually. At the end of that time, they'd have about $77,000. That would be generating interest at a rate of about $4,200 a year (assuming the same rate, which in real life is unlikely). If the GIC were in the husband's name, the tax bill would be about $1,800 annually (assuming his tax bracket hadn't changed). In the wife's name, the tax bill comes to just over $1,000. It's clearly worth the planning involved.

Source: Building Wealth in the '90s, *by Gordon Pape, published by Prentice Hall Canada. Gordon Pape's other books include* Retiring Wealthy in the 21st Century, *published by Prentice Hall Canada;* 6 Steps to $1 Million, *published by Prentice Hall PTR; and* Making Money in Mutual Funds, *published by Prentice Hall Canada.*

Life Insurance Needs

If both of you are working, you might need additional life insurance to replace some of the income that would be lost if one spouse died.

That means you must figure out how much supplemental income you would need, especially to cover long-term expenses such as mortgage payments. *Helpful:* Comparison shop for the least expensive term life insurance from a highly rated company. *Alternative:* If you don't have a policy, consider buying a first-to-die whole-life policy. It will insure the life of the person who dies first and might be as much as 40% cheaper than buying separate policies.

Important: Make sure that the policy can be converted to cover a surviving spouse without a new physical exam.

Health Insurance

Be careful about tampering with your health insurance. Since both of you have jobs, you may be able

MONEY SIDE OF A COMMUTER MARRIAGE

The term "jet-setter" no longer applies exclusively to the wealthy hopping from one resort to another. Today it may more aptly describe a new generation of working couples who must travel from one home to another to maintain their two careers as well as their marriage.

Commuter marriages have increased in the past several years from approximately 700,000 to over a million. If you are faced with the possibility of entering into a commuter marriage, do not make a decision until you have given the issue careful thought and research.

A major consideration in commuting is the financial expense—it can be large, and the less obvious financial details can become very significant. Contact an accountant, who will acquaint you with the present tax laws and give you information regarding commuter marriages.

When a corporation is involved, take the time to understand the corporation's tax and legal responsibilities. You will also need to know the company's relocation procedures and schedules if you must negotiate for financial assistance.

If a home is involved, know whether your company will take responsibility if your home remains unsold: Will it absorb the cost of the sale? Will the company give rental assistance? Will it absorb the cost of your transportation from one location to another? You may need to move household goods twice in the same year—will the company pick up the tab in both cases?

A variety of options is available when it comes to arranging housing. Some couples buy homes at both ends, some rent and buy, some choose to sell their present home and buy or rent two new ones. Mobile homes and houseboats can be options as well.

If you decide to maintain two residences, be sure to budget realistically. Make up an initial budget for a two-residence arrangement, and for safety add 10%–15% to that figure. The major surprise to many couples is the cost of duplicating household items.

Items such as another set of dishes, tools, etc., can add up quickly, and many of the purchases can't be deferred. Consider renting furniture rather than buying it. In some places you can rent linens, dishes and small appliances as a package.

There are some less obvious expenses that you must also add in when budgeting for two homes:

- **Transportation costs** to and from airports, train stations or bus depots.
- **The possible need** for two or more cars.
- **Additional insurance** on rented household items.
- **Additional costs for certain services,** such as telephone and cable television.
- **Time off from work** to set up the new household and maintain your relationship.

Establishing a commuter marriage is a big step, but if it's well planned, the arrangement can be rewarding.

Source: Elaine Kay, president, Settlers Inc., 1713 Waterford Ave., Fort Collins, CO 80525, a nationwide relocation consulting firm advising corporations and real estate firms on how to better understand and assist the transferee.

Friends, Family & Your Money

235

to save some money on your coverage. For example, you might opt out of one partner's plan and let the other plan cover you both.

Warning: Such a move could leave you vulnerable if the covered spouse loses his or her job.

Compare the two plans, and figure out how much you could save by dropping one of them. If the savings are considerable, find out if you can temporarily drop one and then get back into it later—without being subject to restrictions for preexisting conditions. If not, it might be best to keep both plans, despite the extra cost. It is much better to be secure with two policies than run the risk of having no health insurance.

One Income

Just because both of you are working now doesn't mean your family will always have two incomes.

Bottom line: Being a two-income family gives you power, leverage and maneuverability right now. Change your attitudes about spending and saving. Think of spending less now not as a penalty, but as a form of deferred consumption with a real bonus—the interest or gains you can earn on the money you save. *Remember:* If you don't see the money, you won't spend it. Start automatic monthly deductions from your paycheque or chequing account into a stock or money market mutual fund. Let your money work as hard for you as you work for it.

> **"Being a two-income family gives you power, leverage and maneuverability right now. Change your attitudes about spending and saving. Think of spending less now not as a penalty, but as a form of deferred consumption with a real bonus— the interest or gains you can earn on the money you save."**

Source: *Gordon Pape; and Terry Savage, the well-known personal financial expert and registered investment adviser. She is the author of* **Terry Savage's New Money Strategies for the '90s,** *Harper Business.*

Drawing Up a Marriage Contract

Marriage contracts have only been made available by Canadian law for a relatively short period of time. Most provinces gave couples the ability to sign marriage contracts only as recently as the late 1970s and early 1980s.

There are lots of reasons to have a contract. Perhaps the bride's parents are giving the couple a substantial sum of money, say $100,000, toward their first home. The couple may be perfectly confident about the marriage, but the in-laws are not. So the couple makes a contract to please the parents.

Perhaps one of them has a significant piece of property, an heirloom and inheritance, or other special asset that they want to protect for their children. For example, in the case of a second marriage, the bride may want the children from a first marriage to receive specific pieces of property. Her new husband can accommodate that wish through a marriage contract.

Other couples wish to make it clear what will happen with their property when they die. In a strange sort of way, they combine their will and a marriage contract.

In some families, the children's education and religious upbringing are very important. So their parents put it in a contract that their children will be raised as Catholics, as Jews or whatever.

The best reason to have a marriage contract is predictability and certainty. If you have special needs around children, property or finances, then a marriage contract may offer you a way of strengthening the relationship.

Prenuptial Agreements versus Marriage Contracts

The expression "prenuptial" or "prenup" is used in the United States more than in Canada. Every prenup is a marriage contract, but not every marriage contract is a prenup.

Prenuptials are marriage contracts signed *before* the wedding takes place. They are contracts made in anticipation of the marriage. Once the ceremony is over and the marriage is consummated and therefore legally complete, the terms of the contract come into force. All the same rules apply to the prenuptial as to the marriage contract.

Marriage contracts can be signed after the marriage has taken place. For example, the husband in a five-year-old marriage may be a member of a law firm and learn one day that he is going to be made a partner. His other partners may ask him to have his wife sign a marriage contract in which she agrees that in the event of a separation and divorce, she will not sue for a share of his partnership. In other words, she agrees to give up an interest in property that he has acquired. Why should she do that? Usually the husband will substitute another piece of property for the business interest. He could say, for example, that she will keep the entire value of the matrimonial home in the event that they separate. In a way, they orchestrate a prearranged trade off so his partners can relax and not worry about lawsuits if one of them gets divorced.

Adding Up the Legal Costs

Most experienced family law lawyers charge between $150 and $250 an hour. Some can be as high as $400 an hour. The key is to find reasonably priced experience. I suggest that you not spend more than $200 to $250 an hour for this kind of advice.

The size of the bill reflects the number of hours the lawyer works on the contract. So, you can see that if you do a lot of work yourself in advance, your fees will be lower. In addition, there is no substitute for being an informed consumer of legal services and having control of your own marriage contract.

Barring some unusual problems, the cost of the contract for each of you should be about $800 for a total cost of about $1,600—a lot less than you probably spent on the flowers and the photographer for the wedding! A bargain considering the financial and emotional toll you may encounter down the road.

A Checklist for Discussion

1. If possible, plan to discuss the idea of the marriage contract or the cohabitation agreement well in advance of the wedding or moving in together. Leave yourself lots of breathing room.

2. Look upon the discussion as an opportunity to have a positive dialogue on several options, including will, power of attorney, business partnerships, household and life insurance and other things that can help the relationship.

3. Make a plan for the discussion that includes the specifics of why there might be a need for a contract. Be prepared to discuss what would or could happen without a contract and how one could help the relationship and create certainty. In the plan, focus on the children, financial planning and property that either of you already own.

4. Identify two or three experienced family law lawyers who have done marriage contracts or cohabitation agreements before. Don't forget that you will each need one! Find lawyers who respect your opinion, who have an hourly rate of no more than $250, and who will not take an adversarial approach to the negotiation of the contract. If it could be a tricky or complex discussion, consider getting the help of a mediator or financial advisers.

5. Once you have an idea of what you both need, go to the lawyers. Don't try to draft it on your own. There is too much potential for error and/or misunderstanding. The use of independent legal advice will make it more likely that the agreement will be enforceable later.

6. Keep it simple. Trying to anticipate everything that might happen will take time and money for the lawyer's fees. Avoid trying to dictate who does what in the marriage. These provisions are tough to enforce anyway. Stick to the children, finances and property.

7. Be fair with each other, be open and be realistic. Listen to each other. Remember, the vast majority of marriages work out just fine. The likelihood that you will need to refer to the agreement is small.

8. Consider putting in clauses that have the agreement expire on a certain date in the future. If you are going into a second marriage and are worried that it might not last, then why not put in a clause that says the contract expires on your 15th wedding anniversary (unless there are third parties, such as business partners, relying on the existence of the agreement).

9. Be fair. Show respect. This is your life partner, after all.

Source: For Better or For Worse: The Canadian Guide to Marriage Contracts and Cohabitation Agreements, *by Michael G. Cochrane, LL.B., © 1999 by Michael G. Cochrane. Reprinted with permission from John Wiley & Sons Canada, Ltd.*

Marriage Breakup and the CPP

When a relationship ends, there's a division of family assets. But what happens to future entitlements, such as Canada or Quebec Pension Plan benefits, particularly in cases in which one spouse may have contributed to the plan while the other didn't?

In fact, both the CPP and QPP make provision for what is known as "credit splitting," although the rules are somewhat different in each case. We'll focus on the CPP here; Quebec residents should call their local office of La Régie des rentes du Québec for details.

Credit splitting can be used by married couples who file for separation or divorce or by common-law couples (including same-sex couples) who are breaking up after having lived together in a conjugal relationship for a year or more.

The principle behind this is that both contributed to the financial accumulation of assets and therefore both are entitled to share in the benefits.

Basically, the procedure involves transferring CPP credits from one spouse (or partner) to the other. The greater the difference in the salary level between the two and the longer they've been together, the more credits will be transferred to the lower-income person. However, if both had the same "pensionable earnings" record while they were together, there would be no credits to transfer.

The end result is to equalize the CPP credits earned during the period the couple was together. Credits earned prior to marriage are not affected.

A spouse who never worked will benefit most under the formula since he or she will receive half the credits earned by the working partner during the time they were together.

Many people are unaware of the credit splitting process and there have been cases of retroactive application. However, the date the relationship ended is a factor on whether a couple qualifies. Any divorce that took place before 1978 is not eligible. From 1978 to 1986, only marriages that ended in divorce or annulment qualify. In 1987, the rules were broadened and same-sex breakups became eligible after July 31, 2000.

If the split took place before 1987, you'll need to file a formal application with the CPP to start the process. Otherwise, simply notify Human Resources Development Canada (HRDC) that there has been a divorce or separation and provide the needed documentation, such as the length of time the couple was together.

For more details, go to http://www.hrdc-drhc.gc.ca/isp/cpp/credit_e.shtml or contact the CPP.

Source: Gordon Pape, *author of* Retiring Wealthy in the 21st Century, *published by Prentice Hall Canada.*

Obstetric Alternative

Midwives offer parents more control over how their babies are born and their services are typically partially or completely covered under provincial health care. Licensing and safety issues are covered by separate provincial guidelines. Visit www.canadianmidwives.org for more information. ***Drawback:*** Midwives are not as well equipped as doctors to handle high-risk deliveries.

More Than Baby-Sitters

Trained nannies provide child care, deal with medical emergencies and other household duties. *Training:* Child growth and development, health and safety and interpersonal skills. In the United States, 200 hours of classroom instruction and 50 hours of supervised child care are required of nannies trained at schools accredited by the American Council of Nanny Schools.

Other countries apply their own standards, so be sure to inquire about the credentials of anyone you are considering hiring. British-trained nannies have long been considered to be the best in Canada, but they are hard to find and tend to be expensive in comparison to nannies from other countries.

Important distinction: A nanny is someone who has completed a rigorous training program and who may be a Canadian citizen. An au pair is a foreign visitor who is here only temporarily and who may have little formal training in child care. An au pair will certainly cost less, but her stay will be limited by immigration rules.

There are several agencies in Canada that can be used to locate and hire a competent nanny. Check the yellow pages or go online. A search under Nannies Canada should bring up several suggestions.

How to Find the Best Day-Care Services

Day-care centers often are a must for couples who both have to work to make ends meet. Yet locating high-quality care that serves a child's individual needs can be a difficult task, particularly when it comes down to making a final selection.

First thing to do: Find out the services available in your community or contact your province's child-care licensing agency (the name will vary from one province to another; look for the word "Family" in the ministry name. *Examples:* In Ontario, responsibility is under the Ministry of Community, Family and Children's Services; in Manitoba, the Department of Family Services and Housing is the governing body). *Other sources:* provincial or national child-care advocacy groups; your employers; or ask other parents.

This is one field where the Internet is invaluable. You can easily conduct online searches for day-care schools and centers. *Two useful sources:* The Internet Preschool and Daycare Database (Canadian entries at http://www.starcreations.com/ipdd), Relocate Canada (day-care and child-care section at http://relocatecanada.com/daycare.html).

There are also day-care associations that serve various regions of the country and which can be very helpful in addressing your concerns: identifying reputable day-care centers, understanding the rules and regulations in your province, contacting other parents, etc. *Some examples:*

Toronto & District Parent Co-operative Preschool Corporation. Website: http://www.web.net/~pcpc/index.html. Telephone: 416-410-2667.

Southern Vancouver Island Family Care Association. Website: http://geocities.com/svifcca.

Western Canada Family Child Care Association of B.C. Website: http://www.cfc-efc.ca/wcfcca. Telephone: 604-592-1008; or toll free: 1-800-686-6685.

Other possibilities: the local YM/YWCA, religious groups, local colleges, vocational schools or any of the sources listed above for information on child-care providers. In addition, local chapters of the Red Cross, the public library, and groups such as the Junior League are good sources of information regarding programs in your community. Don't overlook newspapers and bulletin boards. A useful source of online information on all aspects of child care is the Child Care Canada website at http://www.childcarecanada.org/.

What to Expect

The most important criteria for choosing a day-care center are quality and appropriateness of care to your child's needs. The next most important are cost, location and hours of operation.

There is a broad variety of child-care centers from which to choose. Settings range from private homes to large day-care centers or facilities located within a sponsoring institution or business. To begin the screening process, look first at licensed child-care centers. Any place that takes care of a group of three to four or more unrelated children is required to be licensed by most provinces.

Warning: Since licensing and registration requirements vary considerably from province to province, the fact that a child-care center is licensed does not necessarily mean high quality. It doesn't hurt to contact your province's child-care licensing agency to find out exactly what the licensing requirements are.

Many family day-care providers are unaware of licensing regulations and would be willing to become licensed. Parents who rule out all unlicensed care may deprive themselves of an excellent alternative. However, be cautioned that such a caregiver should be willing to become licensed.

Unannounced Visits

Before reaching a final decision, be sure to visit the prospective child-care program. You should feel free to drop in unannounced. A good child-care center expects this. What do you look for in a visit?

● **Staffing.** Find out the extent of the caregivers' training and experience. A good program has enough qualified adults to ensure that children receive individual attention. A good rule of thumb is one teacher and one assistant for the following groups of children:

- ● **Infants**—4 to 6 children.
- ● **One- to two-year-olds**—6 to 8 children.
- ● **Two- to three-year-olds**—8 to 14 children.
- ● **Four- to five-year-olds**—11 to 20 children.

Group sizes should reflect these ratios, since children generally do better in small groups.

● **Adult/child interaction.** Check to see that children are busy, happy and absorbed in their activities. Observe the adults. Are they interested, loving and actively involved with the children?

● **Cleanliness.** This is a high priority for young children. Cleanliness can control the spread of infectious diseases. Check to see that teachers and other adults wash their hands frequently. Do children wash before eating and after going to the toilet? Are the rooms, toys and equipment cleaned regularly?

● **Safety and emergency.** Emergency plans should be clearly posted near the telephone and include telephone numbers for a doctor, ambulance, etc. Smoke detectors should be installed and fire extinguishers readily available.

● **Play equipment.** Check to see that there is a variety of interesting play materials. Many organizations involved with child care publish guidebooks. You might want to read one before you begin your visits, but good parental judgment and monitoring are the only ways to ensure high-quality care.

Source: Carolyn Strand, 603 First St., Hoboken, NJ 07030. She is the former deputy director, Child Care Action Campaign, New York, which is currently the only national agency concerned with all aspects of child day care. She has been a day-care teacher and instructor of vocational child-care classes.

The Canada Child Tax Benefit

There is no federal tax credit for children, but you may be eligible to receive the Canada Child Tax Benefit (CCTB). This is a monthly payment that is made to families with children under the age of 18. As a bonus, it's tax-free—one of the few tax-free payments you'll get from Ottawa.

The CCTB is the federal government's contribution to the National Child Benefit. Each province has its own plan that is combined with Ottawa's to create the total package.

The basic benefit for all provinces except Alberta was $95.91 in 2002 for each of the first two children, plus $6.66 a month for additional youngsters. There's a $19 a month supplement for children under age seven, but that's reduced if you claim child-care expenses.

You receive the full amount if your family net income is below a specified level. This was $32,960 in 2002 and is indexed for inflation, as are the payments. For higher-income families, the payment is reduced according to a complex scale. However, even if your income is substantially more, you may be eligible to receive some money, especially if you have several children.

The CCRA provides an online calculator to help you determine if you are eligible for the benefit and, if so, how much you can expect to receive. You can access it by going to http://www.ccra-adrc.gc.ca/benefits/calculator/cctb-disclaimer-2001-e.html.

A Little-Known Tax Break

The CCTB is considered to be a payment to the child. Therefore, it is the child's money for tax purposes. This provides an excellent opportunity for income-splitting.

Open a separate account in the child's name and deposit the money cheque into it. Make sure no other money goes into it, especially gifts from mom and dad or close relatives.

Use the money in the child's account for investing. You can start with something easy like Canada Savings Bonds. When a large enough pool has been accumulated, move into assets with more growth potential, like mutual funds.

Since the money is the child's, income attribution rules do not apply. Any interest, dividends or capital gains earned by the investments will belong to your son or daughter. File an annual tax return on their behalf, and be sure to declare the investment income, to avoid problems later. There will be no tax payable as long as they do not have substantial income from other sources.

Source: Gordon Pape, author of 6 Steps to $1 Million, published by Viking Canada.

ABOUT THE POWER OF ATTORNEY

Most of us are familiar with the process of planning for death by writing a will. But how would your personal and financial affairs be handled if you were disabled by illness or accident?

The power of attorney is a written document that allows you (called the principal or the donor) to appoint another person (variously called the attorney, agent or donee) to make your financial decisions for you if you become disabled. The document is simple to create (forms are available at most stationery stores). However, it usually costs very little to have a lawyer prepare it if the work is done at the same time as you are writing or reworking your will. Once it is created, you are in no way bound by a power of attorney—the procedure is voluntary and can be revoked at any time.

The amount of control a power of attorney hands over to an agent can be either broad (your agent has the power to do anything you could have done) or limited (your agent has only the power to sell your car). The duration of the document is equally flexible. It can remain in effect even if you lose mental capacity (called the enduring power of attorney). The only limitation is that its powers end automatically upon the death of either party.

Know the Risks

The greatest risk involved with creating a power of attorney is choosing the right agent. Once a power of attorney is enacted, there is very little accountability of your agent, and he

or she could misuse the power. For this reason, it is important that you choose an agent in whom you place the greatest trust. The best choice is usually a close family member with a good head for finance and knowledge of your personal needs. For further protection, don't give the power of attorney to the agent. Rather, tell him or her where it is. Without the document itself, the agent can do nothing.

There is also a risk that the power of attorney might not be accepted. Most banks will question an agent to determine if the power was revoked or if the principal has died. Some banks insist that their own power of attorney form be used—some insurance companies will not honor a power of attorney if it is more than six months old.

Using the Power Of Attorney

Legislation being passed in a growing number of provinces would enable you to appoint an agent to make medical decisions for you when you are physically unable to do so. This is known as a power of attorney for personal care. This arrangement would be most appropriate for situations in which you might have to undergo a serious medical procedure that would leave you unable to decide the next medical step to take. *Example:* Before undergoing serious exploratory

surgery, a patient appoints a close relative to make necessary medical decisions. While the patient is under anesthesia, the doctor who is carrying out the surgical procedure can consult with the agent about what has been discovered and the possible options.

Your risk? The agent might not make a sound decision. Pick an agent who is likely to know what decision you would make, and put your conclusions in writing so he or she will have guidance. Two agents can be appointed and both required to approve any decision. What is the risk of not appointing an agent? In medical situations in which there are a number of options—each with a chance of failure—lengthy, expensive legal proceedings might be necessary before the doctor or hospital is willing to act.

Special application: A great deal of public attention has been paid to situations in which medical patients who are not able to make decisions for themselves are kept alive by extraordinary means. However, doctors and hospitals cannot remove life-support equipment unless they have consent from someone legally appointed by the patient. For those patients who are older and do not have any immediate family members, it would be wise to create a power of attorney for this purpose.

POWER of ATTORNEY

DURABLE   LIMITED

Teaching Children About Money

I am often asked how to teach children about money. It's not easy. You don't want to put so much emphasis on the subject that your children become obsessed with it—something that is very easy to do. On the other hand, you want your children to develop a sensitivity to the value of money and a basic understanding of the purposes it can serve beyond being just a medium of exchange. It's a fine line, but one that's worthwhile trying to draw. Wealth building is a long-term process, one that should involve all members of the family unit. If your children learn the right techniques and attitudes at home, they'll benefit when it comes time for them to establish their own families.

But be careful. Avoid trying to do too much too soon. That's a mistake I made in the case of my own family. My lack of early financial training undoubtedly contributed to it: I didn't want my children to waste the most efficient wealth-building period of their lives because of a failure on my part to give them the grounding they needed.

But like everything else in life, timing is critical in imparting this kind of information. Preteens simply aren't ready for it. In fact, most of them can't handle anything more complicated than allowances, a bank account and some simple explanations of the relationship between value and money.

It's around the time children hit their mid-teens that they become more sensitive to the subtleties of money management. This often coincides with a first job or a highly prized but expensive objective they want to achieve, such as paying the additional insurance costs so they can drive the family car. That's the point at which you can start going beyond the basics in laying the groundwork for a more sophisticated approach to money and wealth.

You're going to have to commit some of your time and imagination to the process, though. You can't just hand them a copy of this book and tell them to read it. The time will come when they'll seek out more information on their own and absorb it avidly. But not at the outset.

Source: Building Wealth in the '90s, *by Gordon Pape, published by Prentice Hall Canada. Gordon Pape is also the author of* Retiring Wealthy in the 21st Century, *published by Prentice Hall Canada.*

Summer Jobs for Kids

Friends and relatives are the best source of help in finding summer jobs. Ask them for contacts or ideas. *Two great options are:*

● **Summer camps hire students.** Usual requirements: Camp experience, age 19 or older and at least one year of college.

● **Parks Canada** provides over 1,000 summer jobs each year. Applicants must be full-time students at a secondary school, CEGEP, college, technical institute or university, and planning to return to class in the fall. Preference is given to Canadian citizens. You must be of legal working age in the province where the job is located. Another option is Young Canada Works. It provides 350 summer jobs for 16- to 18-year-olds at selected national parks and national historic sites across Canada. *For information:* http://www.parcscanada.gc.ca/Employment/jobs/english/students_e.htm.

Another good option: Advertise your services on local store and community-center bulletin boards. Two brothers kept busy painting houses (a very profitable enterprise) after putting up a notice in a supermarket advertising their availability.

Note: Many countries let foreign students work in temporary, seasonal jobs. The pay is usually low, but jobs can be interesting.

Hire Your Own Kids

If you have a family business, consider hiring your kids. They have to perform a legitimate function and be paid a fair wage. As long as you're careful about that, you should have no problem. But what can my kids do, you may ask? Lots of things—use your imagination. I once hired one of my daughters to handle all my filing when she was in her early teens. It saved me a lot of time, and the small amount I paid her was more than worth it. Another daughter worked for me in the summer, doing much of my research and handling correspondence. My son helped with computer work. There's a lot your family can contribute, if you give it some thought.

The advantages are substantial. The children learn the discipline of working for their money from an early age. Because the company pays them, their income is tax-deductible to your business. And, who knows—they may find the work interesting enough to want to join the company full time when they complete their education.

Source: Building Wealth in the '90s, *by Gordon Pape, published by Prentice Hall Canada.*

Work-Ethic Myth

Myth: Part-time jobs make teenagers more ambitious about education and careers. *Reality:* Typical dead-end jobs foster bad grades in school, more money for drugs and alcohol and a jaded attitude toward work in general.

Source: Laurence Steinberg, professor of child and family studies, University of Wisconsin.

Parent's Guide to Corporate Training Programs

What can you do to help your child land the right job?

A corporate training program may be the answer, because it permits recent graduates to earn while they learn. Such programs give in-depth training in a specific industry while also offering a practical view of the corporate world. This hands-on training is useful in whatever field the student finally picks. Best of all, most corporate training programs pay well. Starting annual salaries for trainees may range from $20,000 to $30,000, depending upon the field of expertise.

Competition for corporate training programs is fierce. The applicant usually has to face a number of rejections before he or she is offered a job.

How to prepare: Encourage your graduate first to learn about the industry that interests him or her. Then, once he or she understands the industry and the key players, he or she can zero in on particular companies. He or she should study their annual reports and recruitment materials, and articles written about them. (Articles can be obtained by telephoning a company's public relations department to request a press kit.)

Information interviews in advance of a job interview can also be helpful. Alumni from your son's or daughter's alma mater who are already working for that company or in that industry are often willing to take a few minutes—either over the phone or in person—to offer insights into what it's like to work there. Your own business contacts and friends may also be able to serve as informal career advisers.

Questions the job hunter should ask: What are the most satisfying aspects of your job? What are your priorities in an average workweek? What do you wish you had known about this career field before you entered it? What about this employer?

Source: Marian Salzman, author, with Deirdre Sullivan, of Inside Management Training: The Career Guide to Training Programs for College Graduates.

How to Protect Your Savings Against Catastrophic Illness

Nursing-home care, now more often referred to as long-term care, is not covered under Canada's national Medicare plan. However, all provinces do contribute toward these expenses. The Ontario Ministry of Health and Long-Term Care, for example, pays for expenses relating to nursing and medical care. Residents of these facilities are expected to contribute toward their own room and board. This can cost from $16,000 to $20,000 annually depending on the type of accommodation, according to the Ontario Long Term Care Association. In Alberta, the annual cost to the individual is between $11,000 and $12,000 annually. Even with government support, however, the life savings of a middle-class family can be wiped out in a very short time. That being said, planning can prevent this and ensure proper care.

The first step is to review your employer or private extended health care coverage. See if it offers any long-term protection. If it does, it's probably limited either in terms of the length of time allowed or the annual cost. Home care for any long-term debilitating illness will likely be treated in a similar way, if it is part of the package at all.

Families that must pay for such care have two alternatives—pay cash, or rely on special long-term care insurance.

Paying in cash is an option only for the very rich. Although long-term care policies tend to be more expensive if you wait until your 70s to purchase them, the cost can be reduced by co-insuring the risk—using what you can afford of your assets and income to pay some of your long-term care costs.

More companies are offering long-term care policies and the cost and benefits can vary significantly according to the plan selected. A typical policy covers two types of long-term care.

● **Facility care.** This coverage picks up your share of the cost if you enter a long-term care institution on the advice of a doctor. Protection is usually for the rest of your life.

● **Home care.** This covers expenses arising from prolonged home confinement, such as 24-hour nursing care. The time period is often limited, typically to a maximum of two years. You may find that the coverage only kicks in after the first 60 days.

Important: If you're considering this coverage, take a close look at the benefit levels. Compare them to the actual costs you would be facing, after the province pays its share. If you don't need the maximum allowable benefit, ask to have it reduced. That will lower the premium.

Long-term care insurance can be very expensive. A couple aged 65 and 66 was recently quoted a combined premium of $5,645 a year by a major insurance firm. If your province provides a high level of financial support, such coverage may not be worth the expense. Weigh the options carefully and get all the facts before making a decision.

Housing Alternatives for Aging Parents

There are several housing and care options available to Canada's seniors. Each option provides different levels of accommodation, care and support. The one that is right for your parents will depend upon an assessment of their needs and preferences. While housing and care services may vary somewhat from province to province, here are the seven basic categories:

● **Adult lifestyle retirement communities.** They provide independent housing options which may include detached bungalows, town homes, semi-detached homes or apartments. Tenure may be on a freehold, land-lease, life-lease, condominium or rental basis. In most cases, the residential campus includes a club house or central recreation center offering a variety of amenities such as a party room, games room or indoor swimming pool, as well as social and recreational activities. This option is geared primarily to those seniors who are able to live fully independently

and who want to enjoy the company of their peers in a vibrant, active community.

● **In-home health.** The objective of this, also referred to as in-home care, home care or community support services, is to allow people to live in their own homes and communities and to function as independently as possible through the provision of a variety of care and supportive services. Many different programs and services are available which are provided by government agencies, municipalities, homes for the aged, charitable, not-for-profit groups and for-profit, private organizations. These are some of the services typically offered:

1. Personal nursing care
2. Physiotherapy
3. Occupational therapy
4. Speech therapy
5. Day programs
6. Counseling
7. Friendly visiting
8. Transportation
9. Homemaking
10. Home maintenance
11. Meals on Wheels
12. Respite care
13. Emergency response

The best place to go to access these services is through your local community care access center. A person's needs will be thoroughly assessed there, and the most appropriate services will be recommended. Depending upon the individuals' needs, some of the services may be covered by government funding, regardless of their financial situation.

● **Independent/supportive living.** This option provides both the advantages of living independently in an apartment and the availability of supportive services and amenities typically provided in full-service retirement residences. These options offer accommodation in spacious studio, one-bedroom and two-bedroom apartment suites, most with full kitchens or kitchenettes—usually in multistory apartment complexes. Tenure is usually on a life-lease, condominium or rental basis. Many such facilities are operated by not-for-profit organizations and may be partially funded through the government. In these cases, a number of units are made available on a rent-geared-to-income basis. In some of these buildings, the purchase of a minimum supportive services package is mandatory, which may include services such as concierge, 24-hour emergency response, social/recreational programs and one or two daily meals.

● **Retirement homes.** These residences meet the needs of those individuals who need greater security or who are no longer able to manage all the activities of daily living by themselves. These facilities aim to allow residents to continue to live with dignity and as independently as possible, while providing the security, care and supportive services necessary. Retirement residences vary widely in terms of care and supportive services provided (limited services to assistance with daily living and personal nursing), amenities offered (dining/living room to extensive common areas), types of accommodation (shared rooms to spacious apartments) and physical structure (small converted house to high-rise buildings). Accordingly, prices also vary widely. Since most retirement residences are privately owned and operated, and do not receive any government funding, the resident has to pay the full cost. Tenure is typically rental and rates are subject to rent control. Most retirement residences provide accommodation, meals, social/recreational programs, 24-hour supervision, laundry and housekeeping services.

● **Assisted living.** Refers to retirement homes that cater to persons who are very frail and require constant supervision, hands-on personal nursing care services and frequent assistance with activities of daily living such as bathing and dressing. Care is usually provided in a designated section of the residence.

● **Long-term care.** The purpose of long-term care homes is to meet the physical, emotional, social, spiritual and personal needs of persons whose functional capabilities are chronically impaired or at risk of impairment and who, because of age or disability, can no longer be cared for in the community. The objective is to increase or maintain the health and well-being of individuals to their maximum potential. Long-term care homes include nursing homes and homes for the aged. Some nursing homes operate on a profit basis, others on a not-for-profit basis. Homes for the aged, both charitable and municipal, operate on a not-for-profit basis. Accommodation in long-term care homes is usually simple but comfortable. Rooms are private, semi-private or ward. In order to be placed in a long-term care home, seniors must first go through their local community care access center where their care needs will be assessed. If they qualify, they will be certified as a potential long-term care home resident and placed on a waiting list until a bed comes available. Depending upon the facility, waits vary from two to three months up to one to two years.

● **Palliative/hospice care.** This option provides services at home or in a homelike setting to persons with life-threatening and terminal illnesses and their families. The aim is to help people live as comfortably and as fully as possible. Care is usually provided by an interdisciplinary team of professionals and volunteers including doctors, nurses, therapists, clergy, homemakers and other counselors and caregivers. The goal of the team is to ensure the emotional, spiritual, physical and practical needs of both the client and their family. Typically, people do not enter hospice care until the final few months of life. Most palliative and hospice-care providers are charitable, not-profit groups that provide the services at no cost.

Source: TheCareGuide.com—Canada's guide to seniors' housing and care services including retirement homes, nursing homes, home health care, adult lifestyle retirement communities, supportive housing and palliative hospice care. Visit their website at http://www.thecareguide.com.

Lending Money to Family and Friends

Loans to friends or family members can sometimes become a sticky business.

Number one rule: Use the same care—or more—when lending money to a friend or relative as you would when lending money to an institution.

When a friend or family member approaches you about a loan, inform him or her that this is a business deal and will be evaluated as such. By taking this approach, you help remove some of the emotional strain involved for both of you. In the long run, you will also reduce the risk of losing your money. *Analyze the situation as a banker would:* How good is your friend's credit? How will your friend use the money? How and when will your friend repay the loan?

Examine Alternatives

Always check to see that your friend or relative has examined the alternative sources for a loan.

The most obvious include:

- **Banks.**
- **Second mortgage on house.**
- **Loan on whole life insurance policy.**
- **Company pension,** profit-sharing or savings plan.
- **Brokerage account.**
- **Business Development Bank of Canada,** if the loan is for a new or existing small business.

The advantage of this exercise is that it casts you in the role of financial adviser, not just friend or relative. More important, you may help the other person pinpoint a source of funds he or she overlooked.

Put It in Writing

Whether a loan is to a friend or a member of your family, any agreement should be in writing. Forms of promissory notes (also known as IOUs), which are often available in stationery stores, can be used for this purpose. What should be included in the agreement? At a minimum, it should specify the amount of the loan, its terms and the interest rate, if any.

You may want the interest on the loan to compensate you for the income forgone as a result of making the loan. For example, on a one-year loan, consider charging the going rate on one-year guaranteed investment certificates.

Try to eliminate possibilities for future misunderstandings. *If you can, address the following questions in your agreement:* Will the loan be amortized? Will payment of principal and interest be made monthly or quarterly, or will only interest be payable at fixed intervals, with a balloon payment specified at the end? Will the loan have a fixed term,

CHOOSING A RETIREMENT HOME OR SUPPORTIVE RESIDENCE

As we grow older, our lifestyle undergoes changes. For example, we may no longer need or want a large house, particularly when our offspring have finally left the nest to start lives of their own. At this stage, we may decide we prefer accommodations of a more manageable size. Our house may no longer be suitable because the demands for maintenance increase or because we experience physical difficulties such as managing to climb the stairs, mowing the lawn, raking leaves or shovelling snow from the driveway. For many seniors, children or grandchildren who could help with physical chores live in another city or province. For some seniors, the demands of daily living may make it difficult to achieve the lifestyle they desire. They may find that it is difficult or tedious to shop for groceries and prepare nutritious meals. Some individuals might be living alone and feeling a little isolated. They may want the company of others who share their interests or concerns. And, if housebound seniors have health concerns, they may seek a more supportive environment with health care facilities close at hand.

To find out if a residence suits your needs and preferences, you will need to personally visit it, if possible, on more than one occasion. Call ahead to the residences that interest you when you plan to schedule a tour. If you visited a residence during the day, consider going back a second time in the evening. Try to observe "a day in the life" at the home, talk to residents and don't be afraid to ask plenty of questions. Ask if you can just wander around on your own to get a better feel for the place, after all, it could be your new home. Attend some of the activities or stay for a meal. Like neighborhoods, each retirement residence has a unique atmosphere. It's important to consider if the "feel" of the home is right for you. Many homes offer short-term trial stays ranging from a few days and nights to a few weeks, which is the best way to truly know if a home is right for you.

When making the decision to choose a retirement residence, it's important to remember that parents as well as other key family members should be involved in the process. Making life choices can be emotionally stressful and may strain relationships. To avoid this, assign one family member to assist with all the necessary decisions and arrangements.

Source: TheCareGuide.com—Canada's guide to seniors' housing and care services including retirement homes, nursing homes, home health care, adult lifestyle retirement communities, supportive housing and palliative hospice care. Visit their website at http://www.thecareguide.com.

or be payable to you "on demand"? What are the consequences of nonpayment?

The following is an example of a simple promissory note that covers these questions:

$5,000   Dated:_____

Promissory Note

FOR VALUE RECEIVED, I_____

("Borrower") promise to pay to the order of

_____ the sum of *Five Thousand* dollars

($5,000.00), payable commencing on_____

_____ , 20____ , and each succeeding month

thereafter for _____ months in equal monthly

installments of principal and _____ % interest in

the amount of_____dollars

($_____).

_____(Borrower)

The signature of the borrower is essential to making the promissory note legally enforceable. The main purpose of a written agreement is not to frighten your friend or relative into thinking you'll haul him or her off to court, but to emphasize that borrowing money is a serious business.

Source: Karen F. Stein, Ph.D., associate professor of consumer economics at the University of Delaware, Newark, DE 19716. Author of numerous publications on consumer affairs, she is the former executive director of the American Council on Consumer Interests.

How to Talk to Your Parents About Their Money

Adult children may be genuinely concerned about how their parents are managing their finances. But some parents may resent that concern as an unwanted intrusion.

Guidelines for Discussion

● **Examine your motives.** Are you more interested in making sure your parents are protected against possible financial disaster—or in preserving the size of the estate you hope to inherit?

● **List the subjects to discuss.**

● **Location of financial records.**

● **Insurance**—health (company and personal), life, long-term care (for nursing-home expenses), mortgage and homeowners.

● **Investments**—safety of principal, rate of return, goals and whether savings are sufficient to last through retirement.

● **Be diplomatic.** Don't criticize, patronize or act as though you have all the answers. *Ineffective:* "I'm worried about the way you're handling your money." *More effective:* "What financial information do you think I need in case something should happen to you? For my own peace of mind, I'd like to learn something about your financial situation. Maybe each of us has information that can be useful to the other." *Very helpful:* Financial-planning forms as a neutral way to introduce the subject. These forms are available from some company pension programs and in many popular financial-planning guides at your library and bookstore.

● **Prepare.** If you want to get involved, be prepared to spend a lot of time, even months, on research into insurance and investment options.

● **Respect your parents' rights.** It's their money to do with what they choose. Once you've expressed your desire to learn more about their finances, it's up to them to agree to your involvement, or refuse it. Accept their decision. When we were growing up, we expected our parents to let us live our own lives and make our own mistakes. Parents deserve the same freedom from us.

Source: Robert Atchley, Ph.D., director of the Scripps Gerontology Center at Miami University, Oxford, OH.

Transform Your Relationship With Money

I changed my views on money years ago, and today live comfortably on an annual income of $9,000. And I save as much as $3,000 a year. By understanding the basics of money, you will be able to get rid of debt, save and live happily within your means.

The Myth of More

People identify money with all sorts of wonderful things—security, pleasure, power, prestige, quality, etc. And all too often we get locked into a lifelong struggle to obtain the "more" that money is supposed to bring.

SOME TAX BREAKS IF YOU'RE SUPPORTING A PARENT

The cost of supporting an aged parent or parents can run into thousands of dollars a year. Fortunately, the government does provide some tax relief to help you out. The main items to look at are:

● **Amount for an eligible dependent.** This tax credit is available if you support a parent and do not have a spouse. So you must be single to claim it (people who are divorced, separated or widowed are considered as "single" for this purpose). The tax credit is claimed most often by single parents on behalf of a child, but can also be used in a case of parent support if your father or mother is living in your home. (Grandparents are also eligible.) Note that you cannot make this claim if the parent has net income in excess of a specified amount. Consult the current *CCRA Income Tax Guide* for more details (line 305).

● **Amount for infirm dependents 18 or older.** If your parent is mentally or physically infirm (examples: Alzheimer's, crippling arthritis, blind-

ness), you can make use of this tax credit. You enter the appropriate amount at line 306. You'll need a signed statement from a doctor that confirms the nature and severity of the disability. Note that you can claim both this credit and the amount for eligible dependent for the same person. But if anyone else claims the eligible dependent amount, you cannot make this claim. Here again, there are limits on how much income the dependent can have. Get a copy of the special tax guide called *Information Concerning People with Disabilities* for more details.

● **Caregiver amount.** This tax credit can be claimed at line 315 of the return if the parent is living with you, dependent on you for support and is age 65 or more. Note that you cannot claim both this credit and the infirm dependent credit. Use the worksheets that you will find in the Forms book that accompanies the tax guide to calculate which is more beneficial for you.

● **Transfer of disability amount.** Disabled people receive a special tax credit, which is normally claimed at line 316. However, if you have a disabled parent who can't make use of this credit because his or her income is too low, you may be able to transfer it to your return. To be eligible, you must have been able to claim at least one of the other tax credits on behalf of the parent. Make the claim at line 318 of the return.

● **Medical expenses.** The costs of prescription drugs, glasses, dental work, etc., that are incurred by a dependent parent living with you can be included in your family medical expenses at line 330 of the return. However, if the parent had net income in excess of a certain limit (which is adjusted annually for inflation), you have to reduce the amount of the claim at line 331. See the tax guide for details.

Source: Gordon Pape, author of 6 Steps to $1 Million, *published by Viking Canada.*

More is never enough.

If you've just bought a bigger house, there's yet a bigger house to yearn for. Happiness is always just around the corner. Turn around that old maxim "Time is money" and look at it this way: "We pay for money with our time." *Example:* Your old stereo system gives you hours of pleasure each week. Would you buy a new stereo if you were aware that you net $20 an hour after taxes and work-related expenses

(clothes, transportation, etc.), and that it will cost nearly three weeks of your working life to buy the new system?

Enough—and Then Some
The constant question: "When I buy something, what am I actually getting for the hours of labor I put into earning the necessary money?" "Will I get happiness?" "Does this purchase conflict with my values?"

As you ask the questions, the answers will lead you to become a natural saver. You will, in short, have transformed your relationship with money.

Financial independence has nothing to do with being rich. It is knowing when you have enough. Enough for you may be different from enough for your neighbor—but it will be a figure that is real for you and within your financial means.

Where Does It All Go?

The only way to learn about your spending behavior is to keep track of every cent that comes in and goes out of your life.

Only after writing this down will you become conscious of how you actually handle money, as opposed to how you think you do.

After a month you will have a wealth of specific information on how you now handle the money in your life.

Use this daily money log to set up spending categories that reflect your actual behavior. Don't over-simplify the categories in your budget log.

Instead of a broad category of food, for example, you may see there are actually several different types of foods to track—food you eat at home, in restaurants, in snacking, lunches at work, etc.

This exercise isn't just accounting. It's a process of self-discovery. And the next time you ask yourself, "Where does it all go?" you'll know the answer.

Making Money Real

Knowing these answers isn't enough. You must translate the dollars you spend into the hours of your life to reveal the trade-offs you now make for your lifestyle.

I'm not talking about being cheap, making do—or being a skinflint. I'm talking about *creative* frugality.

Ten Sure Ways to Save Money

● **Pay off your credit cards.** You pay anywhere from 8.5% to 20% interest on credit card debt. That's

like working a five-day week and getting paid for four. On average, every $100 of debt costs $18.66 a year in interest. If you are in the 28% tax bracket, you have to earn $25.98 before taxes to pay for the privilege of having spent that $100.

● **Don't go shopping.** Although 70% of all adults visit a regional mall weekly, only a quarter of them are actually looking for a specific item.

● **Wait until you have the money before you buy something.** He who hesitates saves.

● **Take care of what you have.** Regular oil changes extend the life of a car. If you ignore a funny noise in your car's engine, you could burn out a water pump or otherwise incur major (and costly) damage.

● **Wear it out.** Think about how much money you would save if you decided to use things 20% longer.

● **Do it yourself.** Whenever you're about to hire an expert, ask yourself, "Can I do this myself? What would it take to learn how?"

● **Anticipate your needs.** Forethought is a huge cost saver. Blank cassettes bought at the supermarket cost less than half as much as the local convenience store charges.

● **Bargain.** Buy through mail-order discounters and discount chain stores. Ask for discounts at local stores. Haggling has become a way of life in North America.

● **Comparison-shop by phone.** *Example:* I was able to shave $4,000 (33%) off the highest price on a car years ago by calling every dealership within a 100-mile radius and buying a deluxe demonstrator model with 3,600 miles on it.

● **Buy it used.** Clothing, furniture, kitchenware, drapes—often of high quality—can all be found in thrift stores.

Source: Vicki Robin, coauthor, with the late Joe Dominguez, of Your Money or Your Life, Viking Penguin. Ms. Robin heads the nonprofit New Road Map Foundation, an organization that helps people assume greater control over their money and their lives (Box 15981, Dept. BL, Seattle, WA 98115).

Financing
an Education

8

- Adding Up the Costs

- The Scholarship Game

- Costliest Mistakes in the Scholarship Game

- Millennium Excellence Awards

- Financial Planning Steps for Your Education

- Top Government Student Loan Mistakes

- Ten Surprise Expenses for College and University Students

Adding Up the Costs

The price of a university education goes up every year. In an effort to keep track of the increases and provide up-to-date information on the costs, the USC Education Savings Plans organization surveys universities across Canada annually and publishes the results in a special brochure. They have been doing this for more than 20 years. Not all universities participate, but enough take part (30 in the most recent survey) to offer a clear picture of current costs and future projections. For instance, the UCS's *2001-2002 Guide to University Costs in Canada* reported that the average cost for a year at an Ontario university (including tuition and fees, room and board, books and supplies, but not including incidental expenses) is $11,259. In Quebec, that figure is slightly lower at $10,377, while British Columbia is even lower still at $8,058. The study predicts, however, that by 2010 the national average for the first year of university (including residence) will be $19,095. This figure is projected to skyrocket to $28,870 by the year 2019. When you figure that your child will most likely be enrolled in a four-year program, it's easy to see just how expensive a post-secondary education can be and why it's important to plan ahead as far as possible.

Source: Updated from Head Start, *written by Gordon Pape and Frank Jones, published by Stoddart Publishing Co. Limited. Based on figures compiled by University Scholarships of Canada.*

Using Registered Education Savings Plans to Save

Registered education savings plans (RESPs) have been around for many years. However, they didn't attract much interest from Canadian parents until the mid-1990s when university tuition fees began to soar and articles appeared in the newspapers about the heavy student-loan-debt loads many graduates had incurred by the time they received a degree.

An RESP is a government-approved tax shelter specifically designed for education savings. However, despite the similarity in name, it operates quite differently from its cousin, the registered retirement savings plan (RRSP). For example, contributions to an RESP are not tax-deductible. Any money that goes into the plan is contributed on an after-tax

basis. Once in the RESP, however, any future investment income that is earned remains tax-sheltered until it is withdrawn.

An RESP may be set up for a child at any time. The maximum annual contribution is $4,000 per child. You can contribute for up to 21 years, but the total cumulative amount of the contributions cannot exceed $42,000 per beneficiary. Unlike an RRSP, unused contribution room cannot be carried forward. Plans mature 25 years after they are set up (too soon, in our opinion). If the money has not been used for education purposes at that time, special rules come into play.

● **Few restrictions.** Interestingly, although the Income Tax Act says the proceeds from an RESP must be used for education, there are no hard and fast rules as to what this actually covers. You can't get a pamphlet from the federal government telling you what the money can or cannot be spent on, since no regulations have ever been put into place. Generally speaking, education payments include tuition fees, books, equipment, lab fees, student fees, sports fees, accommodation and transportation. However, if the student is in full-time attendance at an approved postsecondary institution, the government doesn't require any receipts or other evidence of how the money is spent. So a lot is open to personal interpretation. For example, there is no reason why a full-time student living at home could not direct some of his RESP money to his parents for room and board. That could be worth several thousand dollars a year and is an excellent strategy for getting money out of a plan, while still keeping it in the family. If they wished, and could afford it, the parents could put the money aside and gift it back to their child as a graduation present.

● **Check the rules.** You must be careful about which institutions qualify for payments under an RESP. The government's definition is quite broad and includes Canadian universities, community colleges, Quebec CEGEPs, junior colleges and technical schools. Universities outside Canada also qualify, as do some correspondence courses and certain other postsecondary institutions. However, you must check with the sponsor of the specific RESP you are considering to see if they allow this broad latitude. Some of the older programs offered by the pooled plans are quite restrictive in this regard. Even within the same RESP sponsor, some plan options may carry different rules relating to the eligibility of an educational institution. So be very careful. Most parents want the maximum possible flexibility. There are no governmental restrictions on the level of degree an RESP may be used to obtain (although here again individual plans may vary). Your child could, in theory at least, go all the way through medical school on RESP funding. However, this is an example of how the 25-year limit on the life of an RESP can be a problem.

● **Healthy bonus.** The 1998 federal budget introduced a new program that is intended to make RESP saving even more attractive for parents and grandparents. It's called the Canada Education Savings Grant (CESG) and it amounts to a government subsidy to your own savings. It works like this: The federal government will add an extra 20% to your annual RESP contribution each year, up to a maximum of $400 annually. So you need to put at least $2,000 into the plan each year to qualify for the maximum payment. The maximum lifetime grant per child is $7,200. That's $400 a year for 18 years. The grant will be paid directly into the RESP, not to you or the child personally. Children are eligible for it up to age 17. However, in the case of teenagers aged 16 and 17, a grant will only be paid if there have been contributions to the plan of at least $300 a year for a minimum of four years before the child turned 16, or if total previous contributions had reached $4,000 before that time. The idea here appears to be to discourage people from setting up a last-minute RESP just to get a grant.

Since the grant limit is $400 a year, you won't get credit for a contribution in any given year that is in excess of $2,000, even though you're allowed to put up to $4,000 into the plan. However, you can carry forward unused grant room. This is a wonderful program—that is, if the child or an alternate beneficiary

> "[RESPs] have been around for many years. However, they didn't attract much interest from Canadian parents until the mid-1990s when university tuition fees began to skyrocket and articles appeared in the newspapers about the heavy student-loan-debt loads."

chooses to make use of it. If not, the trustees of your RESP have a responsibility to ensure Ottawa gets its money back. That's correct; if the child does not go on to college or university, the government will take back CESG repayment equal to 20% of any amount withdrawn from the plan.

● **Still a risk.** There is a financial danger in using an RESP for education saving—a very real one that does exist and you must take it into account before setting up a plan. The problem arises if the child does not go on to postsecondary studies and there is no one else that can be substituted as a beneficiary. In this situation, all the accumulated income is at risk. The original capital can be withdrawn, because it was paid with after-tax dollars. But the earnings are another matter. You risk having part or all of that money taken from you. The Income Tax Act stipulates that the earnings inside an RESP must be used for education purposes. Although, as we have seen, that can be defined very broadly, the fact is that the plan beneficiary must take some postsecondary studies to make use of the money. Before setting up a plan, make sure you understand exactly what will happen to the accumulated interest if your child doesn't turn out to be college material.

● **Improving the odds.** One way to reduce the risk, which many RESP promoters have introduced, is to set up a family plan if you have more than one child. It will cover all the children in your family, so if one decides not to go on to college, the others can benefit from the extra money. This at least provides a measure of protection against having the government snatch most of it back 20 years or so down the road. However, the 25-year maturity rule can pose a real problem for younger children, who may not have adequate time to complete their university studies before the RESP must be wound up.

● **The fine print.** There are a number of other rules governing RESPs of which you should be aware if you're considering a plan. These are government requirements; individual RESPs may impose additional restrictions.

● **Short-term studies.** Some RESP promoters have made much of the fact that if a child chooses not to go on to university, a parent can designate himself or herself as the plan beneficiary and use the money to take short-term courses. This is allowed, but the 1998 budget limited the amount that could be withdrawn from an RESP for courses of less than three months to the cost of tuition plus $300 a week. Application can be made to Human Resources Canada to have the $300 limit increased, but you'd need to supply a good reason. This restriction appears designed to clamp down on the idea of using RESP money to take three-week art courses in Bali or on the Riviera.

● **Time limit on contributions.** Although an RESP does not have to be terminated until December 31 of the year the plan reaches its 25th anniversary, contributions are only permitted for the first 21 years.

● **Repayment of CESG.** There are other circumstances under which the Canada Education Savings Grant would have to be repaid to the government besides a child not going on to postsecondary studies. They include:

1. When an RESP is terminated or revoked.

2. When income is taken from an RESP for non-educational purposes.

3. When a plan beneficiary is replaced, unless the new beneficiary is under 21 and is either a brother or sister, or both beneficiaries are related to the subscriber by blood or adoption.

4. When there is a transfer to another RESP that involves either a change in beneficiary or a partial transfer of funds.

● **Taxation.** Payments from an RESP to a student are called education assistance payments (EAP). They are taxable in the student's hands as "other income." Students should receive a T4A supplementary slip from the company that administers the RESP reporting such payments.

● **Overcontributions.** If you put too much money into an RESP (remember the maximum is $4,000 a year to a lifetime limit of $42,000 per beneficiary), you'll be hit with a penalty tax on the excess. It amounts to 1% a month on the extra

money and is payable until the overcontribution is withdrawn. However, the overcontribution penalty does not apply when a child under 21 replaces another one who is also under 21 as a beneficiary and both beneficiaries are related to the subscriber. There is also no penalty if the new beneficiary is under 21, and a brother or sister of the former beneficiary.

● **Time limit.** RESP contributions must be made by December 31 of any year. Note this is a different deadline than that which applies to RRSPs.

Source: Head Start, *written by Gordon Pape and Frank Jones, published by Stoddart Publishing Co. Limited.*

Finding the Funds: Navigating the Financial Aid Maze

Financial aid plays a big role in financing many students' education. That financial aid will basically fall into one of two categories: nonrepayable and repayable. The more of the former and the less of the latter that students access, the less financially scathed they are likely to be upon graduation.

What's equally important to know is that within the nonrepayable sources, access is largely based on either need or merit, or in some cases, a combination of the two. Generally scholarships are awarded based on merit, while bursaries and grants are given based on need.

Loans and grants are generally made available to supplement what a student is able to contribute to their postsecondary education along with, in the case of dependent students, what their parents are able to contribute. Thus in applications for government assistance based on need, there is the assumption that a parent(s) will be contributing to the cause. How much both parents and students will be contributing will be assessed based on a variety of factors such as income, resources, assets, number of siblings being supported through school, along with, of course, how much it is determined that the student will need to attend.

Expected need is basically assessed by what the cost will be minus what you as a family are able to contribute (i.e., from savings and resources). Thus of course, a student that will be attending school while living at home is generally assessed a lower need than one attending half way across the country. At the same time, a parent who is assisting three of his or her children with their education simultaneously will be expected to contribute a lower amount for any one child.

The Scholarship Game

One of the most lucrative ways for a student to haul in the scholarship cash is to excel in the classroom. In fact, as colleges and universities compete for students with outstanding high-school grades, the size of scholarships has increased plenty. That means it may be more worthwhile for a student to aim for the highest grades rather than toil away flipping burgers.

Why are scholarships such a great thing? Simply put: they are free money. No employment insurance deductions, pension deductions, union dues—it all goes to the students' education. The only drawback is that the total combined yearly amount a student receives from scholarships, grants and awards over $3,000 is taxable—however, with the great variety of tax breaks available to students, this is maybe a nonissue.

Scholarships are, for the most part, based on the marks a student pulls off in their last years of high school or their grades in college or university. Occasionally, colleges and universities also consider such factors as community involvement, extracurricular activities, athletics and leadership skills.

When factors other than marks are considered, the handouts are generally called "awards." Some may be specific to a particular faculty or program. They may range in value anywhere from $100 to more than $10,000 per year. You don't have to be an accounting major to realize that's not a bad haul! Not only that, some of these awards are renewable for up to four years.

Scholarship awards are paid out in different ways. Some deliver the cash, others cover tuition, some pay for residence room and board, and still others give you a certificate to redeem at a campus book or computer store. Some company-sponsored awards even include an offer of summer employment, perhaps offering a solution to a student's summer job quandary as well. All in all, they spell out a significant financial bonus.

● **Main entrance scholarships.** Often called National or Presidents' Scholarships, these are like the Oscars of the scholarship Academy Awards. Prizes, including cash and non-monetary gifts, can run as high as $10,000 a year in total value. Some are one-shot deals, although many are renewed each year, as long as a student continues to pull off the high grades. The funds for these scholarships often come from the college or university itself, or from a particular faculty, or out of the deep pockets of some very well endowed individuals.

Simply by applying for admission to a particular school, you may automatically be considered for many scholarships and awards. However, you will need to apply separately for others. Some scholarships even require you to write a short essay or pass an interview.

If you are a top high school student, your guidance counselor should alert you to these scholarships— but don't count on it. Sometimes they're asleep behind their copy of *High School Counselor Quarterly*, and miss their cue. So don't let thousands of dollars slip away due to a missed application deadline. Enquire at the college or university awards office directly. Keep in mind that deadlines for these scholarships are early at many schools, so enquire well ahead of time—even a year or more before you plan to attend.

● **Other admission scholarships.** If you don't walk away with the big trophies, not to worry. Unlike the Academy Awards, you can lose the Oscar and still bring home some valuable prizes. There are many other admission scholarships, often funded by distinguished donors (and undistinguished donors with lots of money), as well as by corporations,

255

agencies and institutions. Many are sizeable and therefore worth pursuing, and some also continue each year, provided you maintain a high average.

Source: Murray Baker's best-seller: The Debt-Free Graduate: How to Survive College or University Without Going Broke, *published by HarperCollins. Murray Baker is a writer and popular speaker on saving and managing money for postsecondary studies. He can be reached at mbaker@debtfreegrad.com or through his website www.debtfreegrad. com.*

Digging for Gold: It May Be in Your Own Backyard!

Automatic consideration for scholarships when you apply to a college or university, or if you are already in attendance, based on your performance in the program, also has its drawbacks: It also means every other student is automatically being considered. Competition can be tough! However, because many other scholarships for which you must apply separately are sparsely advertised and hence attract less competition, some digging on your part may pay off. The trick is to explore all connections and affiliations that you or your family has.

So, Who Has the Treasure Chests?

Start by looking at all personal affiliations that you or your parent (or guardian) may possibly have. *These may include:*

● **Employers.** Better than a pen set or employee-of-the-month plaque, some employers dig deep for scholarships for their employees and their families. See if you or your parent's employer offers scholarships to family members, or if they belong to a particular industry organization that offers scholarship funding.

● **Unions.** Whether you lean to the left or lean to the right, you may stumble into some respectable

> "Assuming that scholarships only go to the highest grade students. While there is no doubt that high marks are an asset in the scholarship game, there are plenty of awards out there that look at more than excelling in the classroom. Many awards look at other factors such as community service, leadership ability, innovation and even motives for pursuing a particular area of study."

awards offered by various employee unions to members and their families.

● **Location.** You may be eligible for an award based solely on where you live: province, county, city or town. If you are from a small town where you are the only person furthering your studies, you may be a shoo-in.

● **Cultural clubs.** They may offer scholarships simply for being of a certain heritage . . . along of course with some good marks.

● **Religious affiliations.** Your prayers may be answered when it comes to funding. Not all, but some denominations offer awards to parishioners and their families.

● **Service clubs.** Dad's club with the funny little hats and the secret handshakes may just mean cash in your pocket. Service clubs such as Kiwanis, Optimist or 4H, for example, offer scholarships to their members and their families.

● **Veterans groups.** If your parents were involved in wartime service, you may be eligible for one of their scholarships. Head down to the legion hall and check to see what they are offering.

● **Permanent disabilities.** If you have a disability such as a physical or learning disability, you may be eligible for special scholarships. Check with your university disabilities office for details.

● **Athletic organizations.** While sports scholarships are not officially offered by institutions in Canada, some sports organizations do offer scholarships to their members or to students in general. Run, skate, ski or swim to the particular sporting organizations to which you belong.

● **Special skills, interests, knowledge.** A variety of skills, such as a foreign language, musical ability or dance, might lead to funding. Consider any skills at which you excel and check to see whether related organizations offer anything in the way of prizes.

● **Special situations.** A number of special situations may bring a windfall your way. Single parents, females, minority members and other distinct groups may be eligible for specific scholarships.

Where to Dig?

● **Interrogate the admission office** at the postsecondary school you will or are attending. Find out all possible scholarships based on year of study, marks and program of enrollment, etc. Start your search a year in advance or more, since the deadlines can vary considerably.

● **Check with the department or faculty in which you are enrolled** as well as bulletin boards and counseling offices on campus. These often list not only scholarships for your institution, but also funding for programs for study abroad. Also find out what criterion is required for different scholarships so you can maintain your eligibility (i.e., will dropping that Interpretive Slam Dancing 101 course disqualify me from consideration?).

● **Look at private-sector contests.** In this age of tight funding and some record corporate profits, various corporations are dusting out their wallets and offering open scholarship contests to students. Some of these scholarships offer various serious coin, while others offer both money and a guaranteed summer job!

● **Keep your eyes open for any possible link to some free cash giveaways.** Some relatively obscure scholarship and award gems you may just uncover by accident—just when you thought you'd explored everywhere!

Regardless of which scholarship you apply for, read in detail the criterion for qualifying for the award and, in the case of continuing scholarships, what you have to do to maintain your prize. Better to avoid disqualifying yourself and having to forgo what could pay for a big chunk of your education.

Source: Murray Baker's best-seller: The Debt-Free Graduate: How to Survive College or University Without Going Broke, *published by HarperCollins. Murray Baker is a writer and popular speaker on saving and managing money for postsecondary studies. He can be reached at mbaker@debtfreegrad.com or through his website www.debtfreegrad.com.*

Costliest Mistakes in the Scholarship Game

● **Assuming that scholarships only go to the highest-grade students.** While there is no doubt that high marks are an asset in the scholarship game, there are plenty of awards out there that look at more than excelling in the classroom. Many awards look at other factors such as community service, leadership ability, innovation and even motives for pursuing a particular area of study. A great example of this is the Millennium Excellence Awards, which seek to reward students of a well-rounded nature rather than those whose strengths lie strictly in their classroom performance. Created in 1999, the award can range from $4,000 to $4,800 with some of these renewable for up to four years.

● **Ignoring the large number of public and private scholarships that are available to students.** Institutions and government do award large sums of cash to students for higher education; however, there is plenty that is awarded by corporations and various nongovernment agencies. These often require the most work to find out about; however, they can be well worth the effort.

● **Failing to prepare yourself as the ideal recipient of a scholarship.** Just as any of us would try and make themselves an ideal candidate for a job through making sure we had the sought-after skills and experience, so too should we view trying to land a sought-after scholarship as requiring appropriate preparation. Because many awards look at other skills and experiences such as community involvement, leadership roles and other abilities in addition to grades, it's important to ensure that these are developed early on. For example, perusing scholarships and their selection criteria early on in high school will give a student an idea of what particular scholarships are looking for in an ideal candidate. Thus you'll have ample time to try and meet the criteria they have set out.

● **Assuming that competition for all scholarships is equal.** Every so often one hears of a scholarship that goes unclaimed. And while these are likely in the minority, they do occur. However, what is more common is that certain awards have very few applicants, meaning competition can be much less than for some of the more high profile awards. And while these may not always be the mother lode of awards, they can still be significant. For example, some organizations may have money for the creation of certain scholarships and awards, but not the huge budgets to publicize their existence. Thus extra effort to track down these lesser-known awards could be a big boost to the school-funding account.

● **Assuming that you have to pay a fee to track down scholarship matches.** There are services that offer to help students track down all the scholarship money that is potentially available to them. The only catch is the cost: this service will usually set you back $150–$200, with no guarantee it will come up with anything. These services are not worth it. Fortunately there are now plenty of web-based search engines and resources that won't cost you a cent. So save yourself the cash. With a little digging, you'll be able to unearth this precious metal yourself.

Source: Murray Baker's best-seller: The Debt-Free Graduate: How to Survive College or University Without Going Broke, *published by HarperCollins. Murray Baker is a writer and popular speaker on saving and managing money for postsecondary studies. He can be reached at mbaker@debtfreegrad.com or through his website www.debtfreegrad. com.*

Bursaries

If a student hasn't, er .... shall we say, excelled in the academic area, there's always another route to the loot: good old-fashioned need. A gift of money given to a student who demonstrates a genuine need is called a bursary.

But before a student heads out the door to spend this money in advance, remember a couple of things. You may not have to be the brightest bulb in your class, but you do have to demonstrate some sort of academic competency—like passing, and even maintaining, say, a B or C average. Primarily, though, bursaries are based on a demonstrated financial need.

Unlike some scholarships, you need to apply for bursaries. Colleges and universities tend to chase down high-grade students more aggressively than they do students who are broke. What do you need to qualify for these gifts? The following factors are generally considered:

● **How good you look . . .** on paper, that is. Some schools will take into account your resources, such as income and savings, along with those of your parents (if you are classified as a dependent student). They will also look to see that you've worked out a reasonable budget of modest spending to arrive at that need.

● **Bursaries, like scholarships,** are sometimes partially based on qualifying factors such as ethnic background, single-parent status, gender in certain areas of study or disability. Contact Human Resources Development Canada (HRDC) for further details on programs such as the Canada Study Grants, which provides these need-based awards. (HRDC's website is www.hrdc-drhc.gc.ca/common/home.shtml.)

● **Bursaries sometimes look at outside activities** that you've been involved in; community work, athletics, leadership roles and volunteer work are often considered. Since marks aren't the prime consideration in awarding bursaries, these other factors may be given closer attention.

● **Check into bursaries that are offered to part-time students.** Some students are part-time for the very reason that they are financially strapped.

TAX IMPLICATIONS FOR SCHOLARSHIP WINNERS

Only the first $3,000 in scholarship money is tax-free. This also covers fellowships, bursaries, study grants and artists' project grants. If the total amount you receive from such sources is less than $3,000, it needn't be reported. If it is more than $3,000, subtract that amount and only report the balance on your tax return. For example, if you receive $4,500 in scholarship money, you need only report $1,500.

Source: Head Start, *written by Gordon Pape and Frank Jones, published by Stoddart Publishing Co. Limited.*

There are bursaries offered specifically for such students. Check with the department or faculty of part-time studies or mature student organization at your school to see what is offered.

● **Many bursaries are specific to certain faculties or areas of study.** It could be that some alumnus was cash-strapped as a student, then graduated and actually paid off his loan, and left some money to help other financially struggling students.

● **As with scholarships, if your parents have affiliations** with service clubs, organizations or a generous employer, especially a college or university, you may be eligible for certain bursaries or awards.

● **Another potential bursary source is athletic teams or clubs.** They may offer bursaries to members in need.

Other Points to Remember in the Bursary Bonanza Game

Bursaries, like scholarships, have the disadvantage of being taxable on amounts over $3,000. So if you do receive one, keep this in mind when planning your tax strategies.

● **Like scholarships, some bursaries are open only to Canadian citizens.** However, special private-donor bursaries for international students may be available at your school. Check with your campus international student or financial aid office.

● **Because some bursaries are given out continuously as qualified students** apply (until the money runs out) each year, you may find it pays big to apply at the earliest date possible (first come, first served!). There are more and more students dipping into a limited pool of funds. Ask for this information from your school well in advance (when you apply for admission).

Source: *Murray Baker's best-seller:* The Debt-Free Graduate: How to Survive College or University Without Going Broke, *published by HarperCollins. Murray Baker is a writer and popular speaker on saving and managing money for postsecondary studies. He can be reached at mbaker@debtfreegrad.com or through his website www.debtfreegrad.com.*

Millennium Excellence Awards

The Millennium Excellence Awards are given out by the Canadian Millennium Scholarship Foundation to students entering their first year of full-time undergraduate studies. There are 100 national awards of $4,800 and 200 provincial awards of $4,000, both of which are renewable for up to four years. In addition, there are 600 local awards of $4,000, which are not renewable. These awards represent approximately 5% of the money given out by the federally mandated foundation, with the other 95% going to need-based bursaries through the provincial student aid programs.

The Excellence Awards look beyond the measurable and quantifiable. Fundamental to their selection criteria is a student's demonstration of community service, academic achievement, leadership and innovation. The application seeks to derive:

● Your motivations for what you've done.

● Your future direction.

● How your life experiences translated into positive action.

● The type of goals and passions you have.

Students can pick up an application at a high school guidance office or online at: http://www.forums.millenniumscholarships.ca/en/excellencea/howapply/.

Source: *Murray Baker's* The MoneyRunner, *a free web magazine of personal finance for students (available at www.debtfreegrad.com). He is the author of the best-seller:* The Debt-Free Graduate: How to Survive College or University Without Going Broke, *published by HarperCollins. Murray Baker is a writer and popular speaker on saving and managing money for postsecondary studies. He can be reached at mbaker@debtfreegrad.com or through his website www.debtfreegrad.com.*

Tax Breaks for Students

Tax breaks for students and their families are nowhere near as generous as some Canadians feel they should be, especially given the rapidly escalating costs of higher education. Instead of easing the financial pressure on all parents through tax advantages, governments at different levels have instead opted for programs such as the Millennium Fund that will benefit only a relatively small percentage of Canadian students and their families. Perhaps that will change in the future. But in the meantime, it's important to understand the tax advantages that are available so that you can benefit from them if you're eligible. *There are many, but here's a rundown of the most important ones.*

Tuition tax credit. Tuition fees have always been eligible for this tax credit. However, you are now also allowed to claim other college/university fees such as athletic and health service assessments. But some charges, such as student association fees, are not eligible. The fees must relate to courses you took during the year for which the credit is being claimed, and must total more than $100. If you are attending a university outside the country, the tuition costs may also be claimed provided you were enrolled full-time in a degree course for a period of at least 13 consecutive weeks. In all cases, special forms must be completed to make the claim; consult the *General Income Tax Guide* for full details.

Books, residence fees, etc. No tax relief is available for the cost of books (other than those that are included in the total fees for a correspondence course), equipment, residence or other such expenses. More often than not these make up the bulk of the costs for many students.

Education tax credit. You are allowed a tax credit for every month or part-month you were enrolled in a qualifying postsecondary program during the year. Until recently, this credit was only available to full-time students, unless you were disabled, but that has changed. The basic amount allowed for a full-time student has now been increased to $400 per month. If you were attending a regular university program, you would be eligible for a claim covering eight months.

Moving expenses. Students who move more than 40 kilometers to attend college are technically eligible to claim moving costs. These may include travel expenses to the destination, the cost of shipping personal effects and the like. But here's the catch: The expenses are only deductible from income earned at the new place of residence. For a student, this means he or she will have to receive scholarship money or perhaps a research grant of some type. But even if the child does get an academic grant, it may not be enough to put him or her into a taxable situation. So the deduction won't be of any use. Unfortunately, the parents, who are the ones who will probably actually pick up the tab in most cases, cannot claim these costs against their own income. This is just one more example of how the tax system places a burden on parents trying to help pay for their children's education. There is one angle that may apply down the road. If the student returns home (or goes to another city) to work at a summer job, moving costs are deductible against income from that source.

Student loan interest tax credit. Mounting student debt and the social and financial problems it creates has forced the government to take steps to provide more relief in this area. The 1998 budget contained measures that will allow students to claim a federal tax credit on the interest charges they pay for federal or provincial student loans. This could work out to be an important tax break, since the average student debt load is now about $25,000.

Part-time students. In recent years, the government has been moving to provide more tax assistance to part-time students. Part-timers are now able to claim an education tax credit in the amount of $120 per month. To be eligible, they had to be enrolled in a course that lasted at least three weeks and that included a minimum of 12 hours of course work per month. Part-time students are also eligible for the tuition tax credit, providing the rules are met regarding length of course, etc.

GST/HST credit. Although this is not a student tax credit as such, many students miss out on it because they do not file a tax return. The GST/HST credit is available to anyone age 19 or older who qualifies from an income perspective. This is a refundable credit, which means that if you don't owe enough tax against which to write it off, Ottawa will send you a cheque. Most university students qualify for it. But many don't receive it, because they don't file a tax return to make the claim.

Source: Head Start, *written by Gordon Pape and Frank Jones, published by Stoddart Publishing Co. Limited.*

Financial Planning Steps for Your Education

Getting the Money to Go

Nowhere, perhaps aside from saving for retirement, is starting early more important than in saving for college or university. The earlier both parents and students start planning and saving for an education, the more options they will likely find open to them and the less likely these options will cost in the long run.

Starting the process early and approaching it as a shared effort will go a long way toward lessening the financial impact that funding an education can have on both students and parents. Here's my guide for prospective college students on how to proceed.

Early High School or Before

Assess your situation carefully. Talk to anyone who may be helping finance your education: parents, other relatives, significant others, etc. For many students, the biggest source of financial support will be parents, guardians or other family members. It's something you may have to bring up yourself, and the discussion may seem awkward, but it will start things off in the right direction. *Here are some tips on what to talk about:*

● **Discuss early in high school the education goals** and objectives for postsecondary study. Keep in mind this may change several times; however, by keeping the channels of communication open it will mean you'll be able to better plan how to make these objectives a viable option. Better to assume your parents want you to do an undergraduate degree at the local campus, before you think about getting degrees at distant universities.

There's another big reason to discuss these issues early: It tends to lead to action and along with less reliance on debt. The ACUMEN Research Annual University Applicant Survey has found, for example, that students and parents who discuss these issues early are more likely to start planning their saving for education early and are looking to student loans to fund a much smaller portion of their education.

● **Talk about how much everyone involved can contribute each year.** Get some clear commitment or figures to cover specific costs—i.e., how much parents will contribute, how much from the student. For example: "We'll pay your residence and transportation costs" or "We'll pay for books and tuition," not "We'll

> "The 1998 budget contained measures that will allow students to claim a federal tax credit on the interest charges they pay for federal or provincial student loans. This could work out to be an important tax break, since the average student debt load is now about $25,000."

do what we can" or "We'll see how the year goes"—only the government can get away with such vague promises. Be conservative in your estimates of how much can be contributed from savings, investments, summer and part-time jobs, along with other earnings.

● **Find out what your parents expect.** Do parents expect you to work part-time? Do they expect straight "A"s? Or do they expect both, along with you being VP of the student council and captain of the basketball team? Their expectations can greatly affect how much you need to have them assist with funding.

● **Decide on a plan of action.** Will an investment account be set up? Will an RESP be set up and/or an existing one added to? Perhaps a student will commit to having 20% of their summer earnings go into some sort of investment plan. Or it could be that parents will match this amount dollar for dollar in the plan? By taking a shared interest in the process, both students and parents (or guardians) have a shared stake in the postsecondary education objective.

● **Implement a game plan.** This may involve setting up one or more investment vehicles. It may also involve doing some joint research on the specific options (i.e., you may have decided to put some of the money into mutual funds). It now may involve the process of deciding which ones are best to attain your funding objectives. Books such as Gordon Pape's annual *Buyer's Guide to Mutual Funds* can be a great resource for comparing the specific options.

● **Do a periodic follow-up on your investments.** This could be done quarterly and would allow you to see how your investments are doing and make any adjustments that will better assist you in meeting your objectives. For example, you may have a large portion of your money in stock mutual funds early on and want to gradually shift this to less volatile and more predictable funds as you approach the start of your postsecondary studies.

As the Start of College or University Approaches

● **Laying the cards on the table.** That little chat about plastic—exposure to credit cards is unavoidable. In fact, card companies want students to have them, and they'll do their best, through incentives and high-pressure pitches, to convince them that they're about as essential to a student's existence as a knapsack.

Have a chat about the plastic—including the caveats that come with the cards—before school starts. Perhaps no singular item is more problematic for many students than incurring large debts due to misuse of credit cards. In fact, the situation has become so severe that some schools have moved to restrict or even prohibit the marketing of credit cards on their campuses, while in the United States, some states are pursuing legislation that would limit and restrict their presence on campus.

● **Discuss the emergency options.** Plan ahead on what to do if there is a shortfall. Emergencies do arise and it is best to know what options are available to avoid those forced errors of personal finance. For example, that computer that you had hoped would make it through the first couple of years of university may have taken its final crash, leaving the expense of a replacement. Best to know that emergency options are available (i.e., backup savings or, if need be, a reasonably priced line of credit), rather than having to resort to one of the costliest of traps that many students fall into—ringing up balances on credit cards.

TOP GOVERNMENT STUDENT LOAN MISTAKES

If you qualify for a student loan, don't do anything that may jeopardize your financing. Here are four traps to avoid.

● **Dropping from full-time to part-time status, without considering the financial impact.** In Canada, student loans are available to both full- and part-time students. However, the government's generosity in making your interest payments for you while you are a student tends to only extend to those taking a full-time course load. Thus a student dropping a couple of courses could trigger a most unwelcome situation: Having to start making interest payments on your government loans while still a student. Always check the implications of dropping courses with the loans center, as well as with your academic counselor and scholarship provider—since dropping courses could also affect your eligibility for some ongoing scholarships.

● **Failing to notify the loans center that you are continuing on as a student.** Once the school year ends, it is up to a student to notify the student loans center (and provide the supporting documentation) that you are returning to school. You have six months after the end of your school year to do this; otherwise you may be required to start making payments on your loans.

● **Failing to keep in touch with the student loans center after you graduate.** Once you graduate, you may be all too eager to flee the life of a student. But whether you are moving home, to a new job, or embarking upon some travel, you are required to keep in touch with the loans center and arrange for loan repayment to begin after the six-month grace period. A significant amount of students fail to follow this process. The result can be putting your loan in default and even negatively affecting your credit rating—which could affect your future ability to borrow money at a reasonable interest rate.

● **Consolidating your government student loans with other loans.** Consolidation of your loans and debts is great if it can reduce your interest payments and make repayment more manageable. However, there can be a costly problem when you mix your government loans with, say, your debt from bank loans and credit card debt. The reason is that you can claim a deduction for the interest that you pay on your student loans on your income tax, but you can't for the interest you pay on debt from most other sources, such as bank loans and credit cards. Thus you may have a problem if you mix the two—something that may jeopardize this tax break in the eyes of the Canada Customs and Revenue Agency.

Source: Murray Baker, author of the bestseller: The Debt-Free Graduate: How to Survive College or University Without Going Broke, *published by HarperCollins, and* The MoneyRunner, *a free personal finance web magazine for students. A writer and popular speaker on saving and managing money for postsecondary studies, Baker can be reached at mbaker@debtfreegrad.com or through his website www.debtfreegrad.com.*

● **The when and where of your student cash.**
Plan ahead with regard to the expenses of the school year as well as when and where the money will come from when you will need it. For example, set up any term investments so that they mature just prior to the times when they will be needed. You'll ensure that there is not the last-minute scramble, not to mention stress, of having to find the cash to pay bills (or the costly expense of having to redeem investments prior to their maturity).

To help plan the year's budget, try the interactive budget calculator located at www.debtfreegrad.com/new_mr/mr_achive/mr_jan_2001/features/charts_jan_2001/f1bgt_chart_tstspt_may.htm.

Source: Murray Baker's Debtfreegrad.com, a free personal web portal for students and parents on managing money for college or university. He is a popular speaker and author of the bestselling student financial survival guide: **The Debt-Free Graduate,** *published by HarperCollins and can be reached at mbaker@debtfreegrad.com.*

Costly Mistakes of Financial Aid

Many students need financial help when they are paying for a college or university educations. Unfortunately, many parents and students are not at all familiar with the best ways to apply for and receive financial aid.

Here are the most common mistakes people make when applying for financial assistance from a college or university:

Mistake: **Assuming that you are not eligible for financial aid.** Of course there's only one real way to ensure not getting financial aid, and that is to not apply! However, it's far better to at least apply even if you have doubts that you'll qualify.

If you don't qualify now, situations can change. You and/or a parent or spouse may lose a job, a divorce may occur, etc., changing your financial situation. You may find that your application may be looked at much differently under such changed circumstances.

Even if you are loan averse, there's another reason to apply: Millennium Foundation bursaries, which are nonrepayable. The trick here is that you have to apply for provincial financial assistance to be considered for these bursaries, which can range from $1,000 to $4,500. Students who have

successfully completed 60% of their first year of postsecondary studies and are deemed to have need under the provincial financial assistance criteria may be eligible.

Mistake: **Applying late for financial aid.** Too often there is a last-minute realization that financial aid may be needed. By taking stock of your financial picture early on, you'll avoid missing deadlines and/or delays in having the money available when it is needed. Keep in mind that late applications may still allow you to access loans but may mean a missed deadline for consideration of such nonrepayable sources as the Millennium bursaries.

I'd also suggest looking at the application forms a couple of years ahead of time, which will give you a chance to plan out your application. For example, in a separated family the supporting parent is considered to be the one for whom the son or daughter is a dependent. Thus, in a case where one parent is making $25,000 annually and the other $90,000, it is clear that if the supporting parent is the one hauling in the $90,000 salary, there'll likely be a much lower chance of qualifying for financial aid than if the supporting parent situation were reversed.

Mistake: **Not paying attention to the details of the financial aid applications.** A simple error in documentation could delay, reduce, or even preclude a student's financial aid assessment. Check figures carefully, particularly figures related to income and assets, as a missed decimal could mean missed dollars. Yes, there is recourse if you notice an error; however, the delays of this correction process can be significant.

Mistake: **Accepting a "no" as final.** While you may have your application for financial aid declined, "no" doesn't always mean no. There are a number of reasons a student could be turned down, including an error in assessment or an error in the application form. There could also be circumstances that have changed and/or did not come across in the application process. What is important to know is that you do have the right to appeal if you feel you should have received some type of financial aid.

Mistake: **Not being aware of alternative loan options . . . and the strengths and weaknesses of each.** If qualification for government loans is not an option, there are other alternatives. What's most important to know is that some options are far better than others—not only in the interest rate they charge but also in the repayment terms. For example, many banks offer student lines of credit; however, the interest they charge both during studies and after can vary significantly. Many institutions offer interest terms in the prime plus 1% range when in school. However, the interest rate paid following graduation can vary significantly along with the flexibility of repayment terms. For example, the grace period for repayment of principal following graduation can vary from as little as six months to as much as one year.

It's also important to know that if a student is receiving Canada Student Loans it may affect their ability to access a financial institution's student lines of credit.

***Mistake:* Not maintaining a good credit rating.** Not only can being in default on a loan affect your ability to borrow money when you have graduated, it may also affect your ability to receive further funds for your education now. Having loans in default may make you ineligible for some provinces' financial assistance, which in turn may prevent you from qualifying for other aid such as the Millennium Foundation bursaries. There's another pitfall. Being in default may preclude you from some relief measures on your government student loans.

Source: *Murray Baker, author of the best-seller:* The Debt-Free Graduate: How to Survive College or University Without Going Broke, *published by HarperCollins. A writer and speaker on saving and managing money for postsecondary studies, he can be reached at mbaker @debtfreegrad.com or through his website www.debtfreegrad.com.*

The Good, the Bad and the Ugly of Student Loans

With rising costs of an education and a decrease in the availability of some grants, there has been an increase in the reliance of loans to pay for college or university. Of course, this means that the debt level

> "Colleges generally have lower tuition fees while many universities allow you to transfer credits in some of their programs. You should always check on the transferability of your credits with the school you would be transferring to before you choose this option."

that students graduate with has also been rising. Early planning and saving by both parents and students can certainly reduce the need to access borrowed money; however, for some this will still be a necessary option. What is important to know is that of the various types of loans available to students, some are much better options than others.

Government Loans: Your First Option in the Loan Pool

Government loans have changed, so that the federal government has become the direct lender of Canada Student Loans. Instead of various banks administering the loans, EDULINX Canada Corporation now handles all federal loans for public institutions (with BDP Canada administering them for private institutions). In addition, provinces such as Saskatchewan and Ontario have harmonized their loan programs as part of the move toward one student, one loan—a much easier and cheaper situation for a student to manage once they begin to pay off these loans.

Although nonrepayable sources like scholarships and bursaries are preferable for funding and education, if you do have to borrow, then Canada Student Loans should be looked at first. They have a number of advantages:

1. The loans are interest-free while you are in school full time—a potentially huge benefit.

2. You don't have to start paying back the loan or the interest until six months after you graduate. This could mean sizeable savings for you. Federal and provincial governments have agreed to pay the interest for you until you graduate.

3. The interest rate you pay on these loans is limited by the government. The two possible rates are:
● A maximum floating rate of prime plus 2½%.
● A maximum fixed rate of prime plus 5%.

4. Depending on your situation when you graduate, you may be eligible for interest relief.

5. If after a period of time whereby you are unable to pay in full and have exhausted the interest relief measures, you may be eligible for forgiveness of some of your loan.

6. The interest that you pay on your loan is, of course, tax-deductible.

Four Tips to Cut Your Cost of Higher Education

● **Consider attending a local institution and living at home for your first few years of study.** If you are taking a general program, this may make particular sense. You can then always transfer into a more specialized program out of town, if necessary, during your senior years of study. While this may not be an option if you are living in Smallsville, Canada, if you live in a larger metropolitan area, this is a great way to cut costs during your first couple of years. Keep in mind that many students are undecided about, or end up changing, their major, during their first year or two of studies, which perhaps makes this a good option for some. If the field you want to study is not offered locally, raising finances is more important.

● **Consider all the costs of various schools.** Tuition costs vary from province to province. Quebec and British Columbia have the lowest average tuition fees, while Nova Scotia and Ontario have the highest. Housing, food, books and transportation all drive up the cost. Also, trips home for the holidays, storage of furniture during the summer or work term, along with moving costs should all be considered. To help you get a picture of what it costs to study at a particular institution in Canada (along with the cost of living for those provinces) now and in the future, you can use an excellent interactive tool at http://www.canlearn.ca/financing/planner/cost_calculatorI.shtml?lang canlearn=EN.

● **Consider attending a college for a couple of years and later transferring to a university.** Colleges generally have lower tuition fees while many universities allow you to transfer credits in some of their programs. You should always check on the transferability of your credits with the school you would be transferring to before you choose this option. Some provincial education systems are set up so that this is more easily done than in others.

● **Consider the employment rates as well as the default** rates of students at various institutions. Some provinces, such as Ontario, require institutions to publish these figures. These can be a good resource to aid you in your choice of institution—particularly for the often more expensive private institutions. An institution with a very high default rate and a very low employment rate for its graduates may be a red flag.

Source: Murray Baker's: The MoneyRunner, *a free personal finance web magazine for students (available at www.debtfreegrad.com). Murray Baker is also the author of the best-seller:* The Debt-Free Graduate: How to Survive College or University Without Going Broke, *published by HarperCollins. A writer and popular speaker on saving and managing money for postsecondary studies, Baker can be reached at mbaker @debtfreegrad.com or through his website www.debtfreegrad.com.*

Fire the Boss, Hire Yourself

If you've had it with ruthless, demeaning and unappreciative bosses, or if you just can't find a job, there may be a position for someone you really know and trust: You! Each year, thousands of students decide to take the path of self-employment rather than work for someone else. And while it may be more of a risk and you may actually toil harder than you would for someone else, the rewards can be not only financially rewarding, but also excellent business experience.

Students come up with some amazing ideas, everything from clothing lines to website development to in-line skate schools. Some student businesses even end up as big-time operations. College Pro Painters went from a Canadian summer enterprise to a business doing $40 million a year in sales. One provincial program reported summer businesses started on venture capital (loans or grants given to start a new business) had sales averaging $15,000, with some upward of $80,000—not bad for a summer's work!

However, what usually carries a creative student idea to an actual successful business is how well thought-out it is. One of the most critical factors in the success of a small business is the plan. Laborious to do, the business plan acts almost like a road map that outlines details such as financing, strategy, expected expenses and revenue, direction, etc. As with any business there is no guarantee of success, but there's plenty you can do to increase your financial odds.

TEN SURPRISE EXPENSES FOR COLLEGE AND UNIVERSITY STUDENTS

● **Books.** They can take an unexpected bite out of a student budget—sometimes topping the $800 to $1,000 range. Buying used can save you a big chunk of this. Check free textbook trading sites such as www.textbooktrader.ca or your campus used bookstore to save on this major expense. Also, while you can't get away with not buying the core texts, you can save by pooling with classmates for the purchase of supplementary readings. One caveat: Always check the edition to make sure that it matches the textbook your professor is using.

● **Full-year leases.** If you live off campus, you may be required or asked to sign a one-year lease—still figuring you can sublet out your accommodation for the summer. Keep in mind that those looking to rent out their place for the summer usually outnumber those looking for summer accommodation by about two or three to one, meaning you'll only recover about one- to two-thirds of the rent thay you are paying. If you can stick to an eight-month lease, you may be able to save yourself several hundred dollars.

● **Supplemental health insurance.** Some schools negotiate a supplemental health plan covering items such as dental, prescriptions, etc., and build the cost into your student fees. While this is often a good thing for students lacking such health coverage, it's an unnecessary expense for those who already have this protection. However, if you are covered under a parent's or spouse's plan, you are usually able to recoup this fee by supplying documentation by a set deadline proving you are already protected and thus "opting out." Make sure that you provide this documentation by the required date or you may be paying for coverage twice.

● **Contents insurance.** Heading outside your hometown to school means you'll be carting off at least part of your worldly possessions. Often these may be covered under a parent's insurance policy—but not always. Check to ensure that they are protected (for replacement value) and inquire as to whether there are any limitations. In some provinces, policies may not cover items such as bikes, or certain policies may limit coverage on items such as cash or jewelry, meaning you may have to pay additional premiums for sufficient coverage. Shop around. It is worth it because students are particularly fair game for thieves, as the security of a house full of roommates tends to give way to more of an open-door policy.

Tips for the Process

● **Write a thorough business plan.** There are plenty of resources to help guide you through the often agonizing process of writing a business plan. You can access a free online guide or use an interactive planner to assist you. Regional small business centers as well as campus and local libraries are also useful.

● **Use local community small business centers.** You may have the most amazing idea and have labored over a business plan, but having someone review your plan can help enormously. It varies from province to province, but many local small business centers will provide initial consultation to students for free, while others may charge a nominal fee. These centers also have some great books and publications that you can access, usually without charge.

● **Consider balancing a summer business with a part-time job.** Starting your business on a part-time scale may give you a glimpse of whether it is likely to fly and whether or not "running your own show" is for you—before you wager your whole summer earnings on it.

● **Additional school fees.** Tuition can be costly, but you'll likely need to shell over for at least some additional fees such as athletic, activity, council and perhaps residence fees, to name a few. These can add up. In addition, don't forget the other little extras such as student card fees, charges for transcripts and lab fees. Most are required, but occasionally you may be able to opt out. Don't forget to keep track of these required fees, as some may be eligible for tax credits.

● **Trip home costs.** This is often forgotten in calculating costs. A trip home at Christmas or Hanukkah, and perhaps Easter or Thanksgiving, can add up—especially for the long-distance student. If your trips home involve flying, keep an eye out for seat sales and book well ahead when possible. And don't forget those other little gems the airlines and government have tacked on, such as fuel charges, security fees and airport improvement fees which can add up to more than the flight cost itself if you've found a deep-discount ticket! Waiting until the last minute for these peak holiday travel times could also leave you paying top dollar. If you are traveling shorter distances, check ride boards on campus to take advantage of car pooling.

● **Application fees, prep course expenses.** If you are applying to grad or professional schools, you may have the added expenses of entrance exams, such as GMAT, LSAT, MCAT, GREs, etc. These can be costly, with fees ranging from $100 to $200—and in U.S. dollars, no less! If you take a course to prep for these exams, you may be looking at several hundred more dollars on top of that, and perhaps more for practice tests, etc. Check registration deadlines carefully as most of these exams charge an additional US$50 for late registration.

● **Transportation expenses.** If you have a car (which is a major drain on any student trying to pay for school), you'll also have some extra expenses. You may have parking fees in residence or in your building along with parking pass fees on campus. Of course, you can always forgo the campus pass and take a chance on parking—which can lead to something more expensive: a pile of parking tickets from an overzealous campus parking patrol!

● **Damage deposits.** Whether you live in residence or off campus, you may have to put up an additional damage deposit. If your place stays in good shape, you'll get some or all of this back —the likelihood of which is usually directly related to the frequency and size of your hosted parties.

● **Internet connection fees.** If you are wired as most students need to be, you'll usually pay some sort of monthly or term internet access fee. If you are off campus and have roommates, you can usually split this (along with other cable and utility fees) to cut your costs. A cheaply purchased hub and a moderately techie friend can also help you network your place to cut costs. Competition between cable and ADSL providers is strong, so you can usually negotiate a bit to get the installation fee waived or a free trial. Check for beginning of school specials among the internet service providers.

Source: Murray Baker, author of the bestseller: The Debt-Free Graduate: How to Survive College or University Without Going Broke, *published by HarperCollins. A writer and popular speaker on saving and managing money for postsecondary studies, Baker can be reached at mbaker@debtfreegrad.com or through his website www.debtfreegrad.com.*

● **Talk, and more importantly listen, to other entrepreneurs in similar type businesses.** The best sources are those successful entrepreneurs that are not only willing to share their success stories, but also their mistakes as well. Check first with family or friends who have gone the entrepreneurial route.

● **Look thoroughly into sources of funding.** Funding for your summer job can sometimes be very time-consuming. Fortunately there are programs set up specifically for students, which offer interest-free or low-interest loans and occasionally grants.

● **Enhancing your worth.** Your summer small business may lead to a life of entrepreneurship—or perhaps solidly convince you that you'd rather work for someone else. Even if that turns out to be the case, the experience that you gained along with a demonstration of motivation, initiative and risk-taking could go a long way toward improving your marketability for those better summer and even full-time jobs in the future.

Source: Murray Baker's: The MoneyRunner, *a free personal finance web magazine for students (available at www.debtfreegrad.com).*

Retirement Planning

9

Formulas to Use in Retirement Planning

A big problem in North America today is most people lack an adequate retirement plan. In the United States, out of every 100 people who retire, 3 are financially independent, 27 must continue to work to maintain their standard of living, and 70 remain dependent on family and social welfare to survive. In addition, the U.S. Social Security system reports that 85% of all Americans reaching age 65 do not have as much as $250 in personal savings.

In Canada, research shows that the average older family (head of household age 65 or older) tries to make do with less than half the income of younger, working families. Statistics Canada found that in 1999 the older families had average household income of just $25,937, compared to $56,998 for younger family units.

The main reason for this problem is simple—lack of planning. People often forget that their prime earning years, between 30 and 60, should be spent earning enough income to support themselves and their families, but also accumulating enough funds to live from age 60 to 90.

My first and most important piece of advice: Don't wait until you're 65 to start thinking about what you will realistically need for retirement.

The first planning step is to determine the three major factors for your future retirement—present resources, income needs at retirement, and income resources from investment assets and other sources when you have retired. The goal of any retirement plan is to accumulate as large a fund of investment dollars as possible, with the ultimate goal of reallocating those funds into a mix of assets that will provide you with a steady income and some growth potential. In all scenarios, inflation will be your worst enemy. (At 2% inflation, the purchasing power of a pension drops by 50% after 20 years.) To protect yourself against inflation, invest a portion of your retirement funds in growth assets. The majority of your funds, however, should be

ARITHMETIC TO DO BEFORE YOU RETIRE

How to size up your financial situation:

1. List your assets. Include income-producing assets (stocks, bonds, annuity-generating insurance policies, real estate, company profit-sharing plans), plus nonincome-producing assets (paid-up life insurance, furniture and household goods), and assets that require expenditures for maintenance (houses, cars, etc.). Estimate total dollar value, factoring in appreciation.

2. Figure out postretirement income. Add up income from assets, pensions and programs like Canada Pension Plan and Old Age Security.

3. Calculate postretirement expenses, then deduct costs stemming from work (commuting, clothes). Next add on the cost of benefits (e.g., health insurance) that will no longer be covered by an employer. Estimate an annual dollar figure. Factor in the inflation rate.

4. If postretirement expenses outstrip postretirement income, develop a plan for liquidating assets. *Rule of thumb:* The percentage of total capital that a retired person may spend annually begins at 5% at age 65 and increases by 1% every five years. At age 80, it is 10%.

invested in secure income assets to provide a reliable income base. Expect your retirement needs to be approximately 85% of your present working gross income, although officially the federal government sets a lower target of 70%.

Retirement Worksheet

The following formulas and examples illustrate how to determine what you should set aside each year to maintain a satisfactory lifestyle during retirement.

Note: You will need access to a business calculator, a personal computer or present value of annuity tables in order to complete this worksheet.

Assumptions: You will retire 10 years from now. You will require $100,000 per year for 22 of retirement. You now earn $200,000 gross pretax income.

Step 1

Gather all financial data. Establish balance sheet, cash-flow needs and rough tax analysis (use the current year).

Step 2

Determine assets available:

a)	Cash/cash equivalents	$ 50,000
	Invested assets at fair market value:	
	Guaranteed investment certificates	$ 60,000
	Treasury bills	$ 20,000
	Stocks	$ 70,000
	Real estate	$ 300,000
	Total (a)	$ 500,000
b)	Investment debt	$ 0
	Bequests	$ 200,000
	Other	$ 0
	Total (b)	$ 200,000
c)	**Total available assets (2a – 2b)**	$ 300,000

Step 3

Determine the future value of available assets:

a) Total from Step 2(c) $ 300,000

b) Future value (FV) calculation

Number (n) of periods (years) until retirement 10

Rate of return (i) after tax 6%

Future value factor $(1 + i\%/100)^n$

$(1 + 0.06)^{10} = 1.791$

c) Multiply 3(a) by future value factor to determine value of available assets at retirement.

Future value of assets at retirement—

FV: $(300,000 \times 1.791) =$ $ 537,300

Step 4

Estimate retirement income fund:

a) Annual income needs during retirement $ 100,000

b) Expected Canadian Pension Plan and other retirement benefits and income from other resources $ 60,000

c) Net income needs during retirement— subtract 4(b) from 4(a) $ 40,000

d) Income adjustment for inflation

Number (n) of periods (years) until retirement 10

Rate of return (i) after tax 5%

Future value factor $(1 + r\%/100)^n$

$(1.05)^{10} = 1.629$

Multiply 4(c) by future value factor to determine annual income needs during retirement adjusted for inflation.

$(40,000 \times 1.629) =$ $ 65,160

e) Retirement fund needed:

Number (n) of periods (years) of retirement assumed 22

Rate of return (i) after tax 6%

Rate of inflation (r) 5%

Annual income after retirement— Payment (PMT) $ 65,160

Calculate the lump sum needed at retirement to provide PMT over (n) years.

Adjusted interest factor— $\dfrac{(1 + i\%/100)}{\left[(1 + r\%/100) - 1\right]}$

$\left[\dfrac{1.06}{1.05} - 1\right]$ $f =$ 0.00952

Lump sum $= \textbf{PMT} \times (1 + f) \times \left[\dfrac{-(1+f)^{-n}}{f}\right]$

Lump sum =
$65{,}160 \times (1.00952) \times \left[\dfrac{1 - (1.00952)^{-22}}{0.00952}\right] =$

$1,300,100

Step 5

Amount needed for emergency fund at retirement:

a) Emergency fund needed in today's dollars $ 20,000

b) Future value calculation

Number (n) of periods (years) until retirement   10

Rate of inflation (r)   5%

Future value factor $(1 + r\%/100)^n$

$(1.05)^{10} = 1.629$

Multiply 5(a) by future value factor to determine future value of emergency fund needed at date of retirement.

Future value of emergency fund—

FV: $(20,000 \times 1.629) =$ $ 32,580

Step 6

Determine additional savings at retirement:

a) Resources needed

From Step 4(e) $ 1,300,100

From Step 5(b) $ 32,580

Total resources needed $ 1,332,680

b) Resources available

From Step 3(c) $ 537,300

c) Subtract 6(b) from 6(a) total

Additional savings needed at retirement: $ 795,380

d) Deflation calculations

Number (n) of periods (years) until retirement   10

Rate of inflation (r)   5%

Present value factor— $\dfrac{1}{\left(\dfrac{1 + r\%}{100}\right)}$

$\dfrac{1}{1.05^{10}} = 0.614$

Multiply additional savings needed at retirement by present value factor to determine the savings needed at retirement in today's dollars. Present value of additional savings needed at retirement.

$(795,380 \times 0.614) =$ $ 488,360

Step 7

Determine the amount of money (after tax) that needs to be saved annually:

a) Savings (S) needed at retirement from Step 6(d) $ 488,360

b) Serial savings calculations

Number (n) of periods (years) until retirement   10

Rate of return (i) after tax   6%

Rate of inflation (r)   5%

Calculate the first serial payment to be invested at the end of the current year.

Adjusted interest factor— $\dfrac{(1 + i\%/100)}{[(1 + r\%/100) - 1]}$

$\left[\dfrac{1.06}{1.05} - 1\right]$ $f = 0.00952$

First serial payment— $PMT = \dfrac{S}{\left[\dfrac{(1 + f)^n - 1}{f}\right]}$

$\dfrac{488,360}{\dfrac{(1 + 0.00952)^{10} - 1}{0.00952}}$ $ 46,780

c) Inflation adjustment

Annual savings required from Step 7(b) $ 46,780

Rate of inflation (r)   5%

Multiply annual savings by inflation rate (written as $1 + r\%/100$).

Adjusted serial payment

$(46,780 \times 1.05) =$ $ 49,120

d) Percent of income needed to be saved

Annual adjusted savings $ 49,120

Gross income (pretax) $ 200,000

Divide annual adjusted savings by gross income to determine percent of income to be saved.

$(49,120 \div 200,000) =$ 24.6%

Source: *Paul E. Ferraresi, president of Founders Group, 11 Greenway Plaza, Suite 3030, Houston, TX 77046. Mr. Ferraresi advises individuals and corporations on investment, tax and estate planning. He is also an instructor and lecturer, as well as the publisher of a newsletter,* Personal Money Management.

A Threat to Retirement

Baby boomers have to secure their retirement future now, or they'll be forced to continue working "forever." Companies are offering decreasingly generous pension plans; many people no longer stay at one job long enough to accumulate significant pension benefits; Old Age Security—burdened by the growing elderly population—is now subject to an income-related tax clawback, some provinces are trimming health-care benefits for older people.

Self-defense: Establish a savings and investment plan now to meet current and future needs.

Source: *Anna Rappaport of William M. Mercer-Meidinger Hansen, Inc., financial consultants, Chicago, IL.*

More Income

Becoming a partner in her husband's business and drawing a salary could boost a woman's ultimate retirement benefits. By doing this, the woman will have earned income, eligible for Canada Pension Plan and RRSP contributions. When she reaches retirement, her benefits will be based on that income. This could add significantly to her retirement benefits. If she had no earnings on which to compute her CPP entitlement, she would get nothing from that source.

Source: *Dr. Robert S. Holzman, professor emeritus of taxation at New York University and author of* The Encyclopedia of Estate Planning, *Boardroom Books.*

Spotting Trouble in Your Pension Plan

Many people take their company's pension plan for granted. Although most pension funds are sound, there are some that bear watching, and it is in your interest to know if yours is one of them.

First, you need to understand the kind of plan or plans your company offers. There are two basic types: Defined benefit plans and defined contribution plans. Your company may have one or the other or, possibly, both.

Checking Up on the CPP

The Canada Pension Plan (CPP) payments you receive monthly upon retirement will depend on both the age at which you retire and the dollar amount of earnings credited to your account by Human Resources Development Canada (HRDC), which administers the program.

Problem: The HRDC's records may reflect less than your earnings. CPP records should be checked every two years to ensure that the right amounts have been credited. If you find any errors, locate supporting documents—such as tax returns and T4 slips—for the periods in question, and take them to your local HRDC office.

How to do it. Ask for a personal Statement of Contributions by completing an Application for a Statement of Contributions and mailing it to: Contributor Information Management, Canada Pension Plan, P.O. Box 9750, Postal Station T, Ottawa, Ont. K1G 4A6.

You can download an application form at the HRDC website (www.hrdc-drhc.gc.ca), or call 1-877-454-4051 to have one mailed. If you contribute to the Quebec Pension Plan, you can request a Statement of Participation by contacting: Régie des rentes du Québec, Service des cotisants, P.O. Box 5200, Quebec, Que. G1K 7S9. The service is free. Don't be taken in by companies that offer to obtain your savings records for a fee.

Source: *Human Resources Development Canada*

Defined Benefit Plans

Defined benefits are the more traditional type of plans. Under such plans, at retirement you receive a set yearly income—your defined benefit—from the pension fund. The payments continue for the rest of your life. How much you are paid annually is based on a number of factors, including the number of years you worked for the company and your salary level.

Contributions to the pension fund under a defined benefit plan are made annually, usually by the company alone. The fund is invested by its trustees, who are appointed by the company and often include company officers. If the pension fund makes higher earnings than expected, the company can contribute less in future years. Conversely, if the pension fund underperforms, the company will be obliged to contribute more.

If you believe that your company's defined benefit plan is underfunded, there isn't much you can do about it.

Defined Contribution Plans

Defined contribution plans don't have a predictable payout. Your benefit depends on how much money is contributed to your account in the fund and how well it is invested. When you retire, you will receive only the amount that has accumulated in your name, usually in a lump sum.

Profit-sharing and money-purchase plans are examples of defined contribution plans in which the company usually makes all the contributions.

Group RRSPs are funded primarily by employees, although companies often match some part of the employee's contribution.

The size of your pension from such plans is dependent on the investment judgment of the trustees.

Checking the Financial Statements

The law requires that pension plans submit annual reports to governing bodies (provincial or federal, depending on the jurisdiction). Large funds are required to prepare audited statements and these are available to all plan members. They tell you how much money is in the plan, how much money the plan made (or lost) in investments and what the administrative costs were for that year. For larger funds, you are likely to also receive a detailed list of all the investments held by the fund, the amounts paid to people providing services to the fund, and a report by a certified accountant that the figures are reliably reported.

If you don't receive an annual report detailing the finances of your plan, request one from your employer or the plan's administrator.

PENSION BENEFITS TRAPS

The bottom line in retirement planning today: Don't count on anticipated pension benefits being available when you need them. With general restructuring and cost-cutting efforts, many firms have been finding ways to terminate or reduce their pension obligations. *Changes to watch out for:*

Terminating a Pension Plan

It has become very popular for companies to terminate their pension plan and recapture any excess funds to help pay off the debt in a leveraged buyout. The law says that employers must distribute the assets of the plan to employees, but with the money often moved into locked-in RRSPs, you still come out behind because you lose any pension guarantees and any further employer contributions.

Deducting CPP Benefits

Companies often take workers' Canada Pension Plan payments into account when figuring pension benefits. They reason that since they paid half of those premiums, they're entitled to reduce their share of your defined benefits by half of whatever you'll be receiving from CPP.

Problem: Most think pension benefits are separate from CPP.

Protection: Ask your employer annually for a benefits statement

Learn to read your plan's annual report. Heavy investment losses and high administrative costs are signals that you should look further into the performance of the fund.

Blowing the Whistle

If you discover any questionable information in the report, such as excessive fees paid to fund managers or transactions made with company or union officials, their relatives or those with close connections to the plan, you may wish to contact the office of the regulator responsible for overseeing your plan. This authority is divided in Canada. Approximately 1,100 federal-registered pension plans are supervised by the Office of the Superintendent of Financial Institutions (OSFI) in Ottawa. The mailing address is 255 Albert Street, Ottawa, Ont. K1A 0H2. They also have a toll-free number you can call: 1-800-385-8647.

If a federally regulated fund is involved in illegal practices, the Office of the Superintendent of Financial Institutions can take action.

OSFI offers a booklet titled *Pension Guide for*

Members of Federally Regulated Private Pension Plans which contains useful information about pension plans in Canada, including frequently asked questions, a glossary of terms and information on the Old Age Security Program and the Canada Pension Plan. You can download a copy at: www.osfi-bsif.gc.ca/eng/pensions/index.asp.

For matters relating to provincially regulated pension plans, contact your provincial government to find the appropriate supervisory body.

Source: Office of the Superintendent of Financial Institutions (OSFI) 255 Albert Street, Ottawa, Ont. K1A 0H2, and Karen W. Ferguson, the director of the Pension Rights Center, a nonprofit advocacy group at 918 16th St. NW, Washington, DC.

Can Your Employer Change the Plan?

Yes, but what you've earned so far is protected.

● **Your employer is allowed to change your pension plan with two provisos.** First, the plan text must allow for amendments—and they generally do. Second, the amendment must not reduce any

showing how much you would receive at retirement if you left the company now or at various points in the future. Ask for the figures with and without salary increases, since those are not guaranteed. Never assume that person benefit projections will hold up 100%.

Goal: To replace at least 50%–70% of your final salary. That's considered a minimum for living in relative comfort during retirement.

Changing Vesting Requirements

Companies must vest their employees after two years of participation in a pension plan.

Implications: Before making a job change, take into account these vesting requirements and the relative pension benefits. Even if a new job looks attractive, you may lose earned pension benefits by moving now.

Self-Protection

Nowadays the responsibility (as well as the risk) for retirement planning is being shifted away from companies and onto the shoulders of individual employees.

Our advice: If possible, contribute the maximum to your RRSP, even if this means taking money out of the bank. If the combined contributions earn, say, 8% a year, each $100 you contribute will be worth $216 after 10 years. Plus you will have received a tax deduction for your contributions. That is a very good deal.

Employees who belong to a pension plan must deduct the value of their "pension adjustment" to determine how much RRSP room they have available. However, if you are self-employed or are not covered under a company pension plan, the law allows you to contribute considerably more to an RRSP, so no pension adjustment is applied. Your annual deduction limit is 18% of the previous year's earned income, up to the current government ceiling.

Source: Gordon Pape, author of Retiring Wealthy in the 21st Century, published by Prentice Hall Canada; and Kenneth P. Shapiro, president, Hay/Huggins Co., Inc., the benefits and actuarial consulting subsidiary of Hay-Group, Wanamaker Bldg., 100 Penn Square East, Philadelphia, PA 19107-3388.

benefits you've already earned. (There is an exception to this rule for multiemployer plans.)

● **While benefits earned so far are safe, an amendment can reduce those earned in the future.** For example, a flat benefit plan that provides a pension of $40 a month for each year of service might be reduced to $30 a month for those years after the amendment takes effect. Or the accrual rate for a final average plan might be reduced from 2% to 1%— but only for those credits earned after the change is made; retroactive reductions are not allowed.

● **Every amendment must be registered with the plan's regulator.** The plan can implement that change once the registration application is made, but would then have to undo everything if the regulator rejects the request. Regulators won't register an "adverse amendment" unless plan members are notified and given 45 days to comment. An adverse amendment is one that reduces future benefits or affects the rights and obligations of plan members. If the amendment is accepted, the plan must notify its members, the affected former members and any relevant unions.

Conversions

In recent years, employers have shown considerable interest in converting defined benefit (DB) plans to defined contribution (DC) structures. The impetus may come from younger employees who do not feel the DB structure meets their needs, or from employers who make their pension costs more predictable by shifting the investment risk to their employees.

There are basically two ways to structure a conversion. A "prospective" conversion would freeze the benefits already earned under the DB plan and switch to DC credits for service going forward. A "retrospective" conversion would give you the option of going DC all the way. Your DB credits earned so far would be converted to an amount that becomes the opening balance for your DC account.

There are strict rules on how this balance is to be calculated, and you must be given detailed information on your rights and options at the time of the conversion. You can't be forced to accept a retrospective conversion. If you don't, your DB credits would be kept intact.

Winding Up

Sometimes a defined benefit plan is shut down and its assets distributed. That's called a "wind-up." The employer might instigate the wind-up or it might be ordered by the pension regulator if the employer goes bankrupt or fails to make the contributions required by law. Some jurisdictions have the concept of a "partial wind-up," usually triggered by a plant closing or other large-scale terminations. Under a partial wind-up, the plan is effectively divided into two parts. The part covering the terminated employees is wound up. The part covering ongoing employees remains unchanged.

● **When a plan is wound up, the assets must be distributed.** Usually the money is transferred to some form of locked-in RRSP, such as a locked-in retirement account (LIRA), or used to buy an annuity. The plan's surplus, if any, must also be disposed.

● **Each member must be given notice of the wind-up** and a statement detailing his or her entitlements and options. The members are also entitled to see the special actuarial report that details the plan's financial position and the proposed method of dealing with any surplus or deficit.

● **At wind-up, you have the right to full vesting** of the benefits you've earned so far—even if you haven't reached the normal vesting date. You also have the right to transfer the value of your benefits no matter what the normal plan rules say. But—aside from benefits for current pensioners—no money can leave the plan until the regulator approves the wind-up.

● **What if there's not enough to go around?** Current retirees get first claim. Next come those employees now eligible for pensions. Remaining money is then divided among the rest. Yes, there is a risk that you might not get the benefits you were promised. Therefore, keep an eye on your plan's health through your annual statement and ask questions if there has been a substantial deterioration. The Ontario government maintains a fund, financed by pension sponsors, that's earmarked to cover shortfalls on wind-ups.

● **Ontario and Nova Scotia have special benefit** provisions that kick in on plan wind-up. These are known as "grow-in" rights. A member whose combination of age and years of employment adds up to 55 or more is entitled to these rights, which can be very valuable if the plan has early-retirement subsidies.

● **Basically, the grow-in rule assumes the employee would have stayed** on long enough to qualify for an unreduced pension. Take Peter, who is now 50 and has 10 years of service. Due to a wind-up, Peter is leaving the plan whether he wants to or not. Normally, a 50-year-old who leaves his plan early has the right to a pension starting at 65, but one who stays until 60 can then retire on a full pension without actuarial reduction. The grow-in rules assume Peter would have stayed on. So, at wind-up, his earned pension is enhanced to make it payable at age 60 instead of 65. In his case, this increases the value by about 30% and he has the right to transfer that amount out of the plan.

What if Your Employer Is Sold?

That depends on how the pension plan is structured. If the plan covers all employees, the new employer would have to set up a new pension plan and transfer in assets from the old plan. Does the new plan have to be as good as your current one? No, but as we noted at the start of this chapter, the benefits you've earned so far are safe. Any negative change would apply only to the benefits you earn in the future.

● **Some companies have a separate pension plan** for each facility or division. In that case, the new owner could simply assume responsibility for the plan and continue it as before, but with a new name.

● **The new owner must get regulatory permission to transfer assets** from your current plan to a new one. Based on complex rules, the regulator will see if the benefits of plan members are protected by examining a report that details what's going to happen to the fund's assets and liabilities.

Source: The Pension Puzzle: Your Complete Guide to Government Benefits, RRSPs, and Employer Plans, *by Bruce Cohen & Brian Fitzgerald, © 2002 Bruce Cohen and Brian Fitzgerald. Reprinted with permission from John Wiley & Sons Canada, Ltd.*

Deferred Profit Sharing Plans (DPSPs)

DPSPs are not too widely used. Those that exist are like a defined contribution registered pension plan (RPP) in some ways and a group RRSP in others.

● **The plan is subject to federal tax rules but not pension legislation.** This might change. Pension, insurance and securities regulators view DPSPs as "capital accumulation plans"—just like group RRSPs—and are working on defining the responsibilities that employers who sponsor them have.

● **The employer is the only one who can make contributions.** Before 1991, employees could make nondeductible contributions, but now employee money can go in only if transferred from another registered plan. Since funding is one-sided, the contribution limit is half that for a DC RPP. The money goes right into the DPSP. There is no salary bump-up as with a group RRSP, so the contributions are not subject to C/QPP or EI premiums.

● **Unlike an RPP, the employer does not have to contribute each year.** Indeed, one reason why an employer might have a DPSP is to keep the cost of its retirement plan funding in line with its profits.

● **As with other money purchase plans,** the employer's contribution is included in the employee's pension adjustment dollar for dollar.

● **The employer can reclaim its contributions** if the employee leaves within 24 months of joining the plan. After that, all contributions immediately become the employee's property.

● **Plan members cannot lend the employer money** through notes or bonds, but can invest in its common stock. Indeed, the employer's stock might be the only investment option—these plans lack the safeguard that prohibits a formal pension plan from putting more than 10% of its assets into any one stock. On leaving a DPSP you can take the stock with you and not face capital gains tax until you actually sell it.

● **A retiring employee can take his or her money as a lump sum;** it need not be structured to provide periodic income. That's a big difference between this type of plan and an RPP. Here are some other important differences:

● **DPSP proceeds must start to be paid out no later than 90 days** after you leave the company or die. The only deadline for an RPP is that the pension must start before age 70.

● **The DPSP payout can be made in installments over as many as 10 years.** Aside from death benefits, RPP payouts must generally be spread over the recipient's lifetime.

Source: The Pension Puzzle: Your Complete Guide to Government Benefits, RRSPs, and Employer Plans, *by Bruce Cohen & Brian Fitzgerald, © 2002 Bruce Cohen and Brian Fitzgerald. Reprinted with permission from John Wiley & Sons Canada, Ltd.*

Retirement-Related Links Across Canada

Here's how to contact pension regulators and securities regulators, plus some handy web sites as well.

Pension Regulators

● **National**
Canadian Association of Pension
  Supervisory Authorities
www.capsa-acor.org

● **Federal**
Federal Office of the Superintendent of
  Financial Institutions
www.osfi-bsif.gc.ca
1-800-385-8647

● **Alberta**
Alberta Finance
www.treas.gov.ab.ca/business/pensions
780-427-8322

● **British Columbia**
Pension Standards Branch
www.labour.gov.bc.ca/psb
604-775-1266

● **Manitoba**
Manitoba Pension Commission
www.gov.mb.ca/labour/pen
204-945-2740

● **New Brunswick**
Superintendent of Financial Institutions
www.gnb.ca
506-453-2055

● **Newfoundland**
Insurance & Pensions Division
www.gov.nf.ca/gsl/cca/ip/about.stm
709-729-2594

● **Nova Scotia**
Pension Regulation Division
www.gov.ns.ca/enla/pensions
902-424-8915

● **Ontario**
Financial Services Commission
www.fsco.gov.on.ca
1-800-668-0128

● **Prince Edward Island**
No regulator: Pension Benefits Act not yet
proclaimed into law.

● **Quebec**
Régie des rentes du Québec
www.rrq.gouv.qc.ca
1-800-463-5185

● **Saskatchewan**
Pension Benefits Branch
www.saskjustice.gov.sk.ca
306-787-7650

Securities Regulators

● **Continental**
North American Securities Administrators
  Association
www.nasaa.org

● **Alberta**
Securities Commission
www.albertasecurities.com
780-427-5201

● **British Columbia**
Securities Commission
www.bcsc.bc.ca
604-899-6500

● **Manitoba**
Securities Commission
www.msc.gov.mb.ca
204-945-2548

● **New Brunswick**
Justice Department
www.gov.nb.ca/justice
506-658-3060

● **Newfoundland**
Securities Commission
www.gov.nf.ca/gsl/cca/s/default.stm
709-729-3699

● **Nova Scotia**
Securities Commission
www.gov.ns.ca/nssc
902-424-7768

● **Ontario**
Securities Commission
www.osc.gov.on.ca
1-877-785-1555

● **Prince Edward Island**
Attorney General
www.gov.pe.ca
902-368-4550

Source: The Pension Puzzle: Your Complete Guide to Government Benefits, RRSPs, and Employer Plans, *by Bruce Cohen & Brian Fitzgerald, © 2002 Bruce Cohen and Brian Fitzgerald. Reprinted with permission from John Wiley & Sons Canada, Ltd.*

Correcting a Mistake

If you claim an RRSP contribution as a deduction on your tax return, then realize that you forgot to actually make the contribution to your RRSP, what should you do? Chances are the Canada Customs and Revenue Agency (CCRA) will disallow the claim because you will not have filed any supporting documentation and send you a notice of assessment requesting additional payment. In the unlikely event this doesn't happen, don't file an amended tax return. Instead, send a completed Form T1-ADJ, T1 Adjustment Request, to the CCRA. Alternatively, you can send a letter providing details of the error. They will issue a notice of reassessment which you should pay promptly to avoid additional interest charges on the overdue amount.

The Basic Rules of RRSPs

The registered retirement savings plan (RRSP) has to rank as one of the best tax shelters available to the ordinary person, not just in Canada but throughout the world. The government gives you a big tax write-off every time you contribute, plus you can shelter all the investment income earned inside the plan until the time comes to make use of it.

The result is a government contribution to a more comfortable retirement that could be worth tens, even hundreds of thousands of dollars over your lifetime.

An RRSP should be one of your two top financial priorities, home ownership being the other. If you don't have an employer pension plan, your RRSP should be your largest single source of retirement income. Even if you have a pension, it should still form a considerable portion of your total retirement income package. But that will only happen if you do two things:

1. Contribute the maximum possible amount to your plan each year.

2. Manage your RRSP assets so as to obtain the highest possible return, consistent with the degree of risk you're prepared to accept.

Here are some basic rules governing RRSPs.

If you already know all, you can skip ahead. But if you're just starting out, you'll need this information to get off on the right foot.

Eligibility. Everyone age 69 or under may contribute to an RRSP, as long as they have earned income. There is no minimum age for setting up an RRSP. Even a child can have a plan, as long as he or she has earned income.

Contribution limits. The basic rule is that you can contribute up to 18% of last year's earned income, to a maximum of $13,500 a year. (This is scheduled to rise to $14,500 in 2004 and $15,500 in 2005, after which it will be indexed to the average national wage.) Members of registered pension plans and deferred profit sharing plans must deduct their pension adjustment (PA) from the amount they're allowed to put in. Your employer will supply that number.

Deadline. The last day for contributions for previous tax year is 60 days from January 1 of the next year. That usually makes the deadline March 1, except in a leap year or when that date falls on a Sunday.

Carryforwards. If you don't make your full contribution, you can carry forward any unused portion to a future date. The Canada Customs and Revenue Agency (CCRA) will track this for you and update your current RRSP status each year when you receive your notice of assessment.

Eligible investments. You can invest your RRSP money in almost anything you can think of, including guaranteed investment certificates (GICs), term deposits, Treasury bills, Canada Savings Bonds, savings certificates, most types of bonds, Canadian stocks listed on recognized exchanges, shares of foreign companies listed on recognized exchanges (within limits), over-the-counter stocks traded on

NASDAQ and the Canadian Dealing Network (CDN), some limited partnership units, units in labor-sponsored venture capital funds, shares of small businesses, mutual funds, mortgages—including your own—call options, warrants and rights issued by companies listed on Canadian exchanges, bankers' acceptances and Canadian cash. Major exclusions from RRSPs include gold bullion, foreign currency, real property and collectibles.

Foreign property. The federal government wants you to keep most of your RRSP assets at home. As a result, foreign assets may not exceed 30% of the book value of each individual RRSP. However, there are many ways around this rule.

Number of plans. You can open as many separate RRSPs as you like, in any number of financial institutions. This allows maximum flexibility, but it can also create problems. Too many plans may be difficult to

THE BEST WAYS TO MAKE YOUR RRSP GROW

All growth inside your RRSP is tax-deferred. Choose investments that have the best solid long-term growth. Keep in mind that all withdrawals from an RRSP is taxed as ordinary income, even if the underlying investment produced capital gains or dividends for your account.

Decide how much risk you want to take. Choose investments that are very safe or at most have only modest risk. *Not recommended:* High-risk investments of any kind.

The Best Investment Choices

● **Mutual funds.** These are set up by financial managers who pool many investors' contributions and invest in 50–150 different stocks or bonds. You share proportionately in the income and gains or losses. *Advantages:* You greatly reduce the risk of taking a large loss that could result from putting your entire contribution into one stock or only a few different stocks. You can invest in a mutual fund that has a higher risk/higher growth potential or in one that invests in conservative common

stocks with significantly reduced risk potential.

Duration of investment: Plan on leaving your RRSP in a common-stock mutual fund for at least four years to get the advantage of the long-term growth trend and to reduce the effect of short-term market fluctuations.

What to expect: On the average, common-stock investments have grown at a rate 6% better than the rate of inflation when measured over a period of many years.

● **Self-directed RRSPs.** With a self-directed RRSP you manage your own investments rather than pooling with others and relying on a professional manager.

Caution: Self-directed RRSPs are appropriate only for very experienced and knowledgeable investors. Don't even consider a self-directed RRSP unless you know how to choose investments or know how to work with a broker—and you or your broker has

had a successful track record over a long period of time. But if you fit into this category and believe in risk taking, the growth potential may be worth it.

● **Bank money-market accounts and money-market funds.** These are the safest kinds of investments for an RRSP and are best for people who don't want to take risks because they are near retirement. You earn interest on the money, and your principal is completely protected.

Bank guaranteed investment certificates (GICs) of deposit are longer-term and usually give you a higher interest rate. However, if interest rates go higher than the rate you are earning, and you take the money out of the certificate before maturity, you will probably be penalized.

Source: Arnold Corrigan, economist and investment adviser.

keep track of. Also, they can be expensive, depending on what type of RRSPs you set up. It becomes more difficult to make full use of your foreign content when you're dealing with multiple plans. So even though there's no official limit on the number of RRSPs you can have, use some common sense.

Claiming deductions. You must file an official receipt with your tax return to claim an RRSP deduction. If you've lost it, ask the financial institution to issue a duplicate. Deductions do not have to be claimed for the year a contribution is made; if it is to your advantage you may carry them forward and claim them when you are in a higher tax bracket.

Spousal plans. You may set up an RRSP for your spouse and contribute to it as long as he or she is within the RRSP age limit. The total contributions you make to your own plan plus the spousal plan may not exceed your personal limit. Common-law and same-sex couples are also allowed to use spousal plans.

Transfers. You may transfer from one RRSP to another without penalty. Complete Form T2033, which can be obtained from the CCRA or the financial institution to which you're making the transfer.

Withdrawals. Any withdrawals from an RRSP are taxable at your marginal rate, unless they are made under the Home Buyers' Plan or the Lifelong Learning Program. You are allowed to withdraw part of the assets from a plan without having the whole plan deregistered.

Source: Retiring Wealthy in the 21st Century, *by Gordon Pape, published by Prentice Hall Canada.*

The Importance of an Early Start

The younger you are when you begin saving in an RRSP, the better. The more years your money can compound in the tax-sheltered environment of a registered plan, the more capital you will have accumulated when it comes time to retire.

The following table shows you what happens to people who contribute $1,000 a year to an RRSP, based on their age when they open the plan. In all cases, we'll assume retirement at age 65, an average annual compound rate of return of 6%, and contributions made at the start of the year.

THE ADVANTAGE OF AN EARLY START		
STARTING AGE	TOTAL CONTRIBUTIONS	FINAL VALUE
20	$45,000	$225,508
25	40,000	164,048
30	35,000	118,121
35	30,000	83,802
40	25,000	58,156
45	20,000	38,993
50	15,000	24,673
55	10,000	13,972
60	5,000	5,975

Take a look at the lines for the 20-year-old and the 40-year-old. The younger person contributes $45,000 to the RRSP over the years and ends up with a plan worth more than $225,000. The 40-year-old contributes $20,000 less. But her plan is worth only $58,000 at retirement, a difference of $167,000. That's the price she pays for the late start.

Source: Retiring Wealthy in the 21st Century, *by Gordon Pape, published by Prentice Hall Canada.*

Strategies for Late Starters

Unfortunately, not everyone can get an early start on their RRSPs. The money may not be available during the family formation years. Or they may simply procrastinate until retirement suddenly begins to loom on the horizon.

What to do? The reality is that the older you are when you begin to seriously address this issue, the more you need to save, save, save. There just isn't any way around it, short of winning the lottery. Here are five strategies that will help late starters to make up for at least some of the lost time.

Take more risk. Normally, younger people are told that it's all right to take more risk because they have lots of time to recover from any losses. Older people, on the other hand, are urged to be more cautious. But in this case, we have to stand things on their heads. The older you are when you begin your retirement planning process, the more risk you are going to have to take in your effort to make up lost ground.

The reason is that you must earn a higher return on your invested money if you are to build the pool of retirement capital you need. Essentially, this means that an older person cannot afford the safety of putting GICs or stripped bonds into a retirement plan, the way the person who starts young can do. Equities, usually in the form of mutual funds, will be the key to success for the 40 or 50-plus starter. If world stock markets do well over the next few years, you should end up all right. If they don't, be prepared to cut back on your lifestyle after you retire or make plans to work until age 70.

Consider a catch-up loan. One way to make up some of the lost time is to apply for a catch-up loan that will enable you to use all your unused RRSP carryforward credits immediately. Let's say you're age 40 and you now have 10 years of back credits available. If you can swing it, take out a loan for the full amount and put it in your RRSP immediately. Space out your deductions over several years to maximize the refund you receive from the CCRA.

Forget early retirement. This may come as a shock to baby boomers, but if you haven't begun to seriously save for retirement by the time you're 40, early retirement will never be anything more than a dream. It is impossible for you to accumulate enough capital to retire comfortably at 55 or 60. Unless your employer comes through with a golden handshake as an incentive for you to depart early, count on staying at your job, or one like it, until you reach at least the age of 65.

The financial reality of early retirement is that it gives you fewer years to save money and more years to spend it. Unless you plan extremely carefully, you run the risk of finding yourself in difficulty before you hit 70.

Sell your house. It's not as radical a step as it may sound. If the kids have left home, you may no longer need that large four-bedroom house in the "burbs." A two-bedroom condo might be better suited to your current lifestyle.

Many people in their 40s and 50s have a lot of

Borrowing From Your RRSP

You are allowed to borrow from an RRSP legally by making use of the Home Buyers' Plan to acquire a first home or the Lifelong Learning Plan to continue your education. No interest is charged on such loans, but they must be repaid according to the government's schedule. If you skip a repayment, that amount will be considered as taxable income for the missed year.

equity tied up in their homes. If you've owned the house for 20 years or more and you live in an area where prices have escalated (e.g., Vancouver, Calgary, Toronto), you may have a lot of money tied up that could be used to give a kick-start to your retirement savings program.

Remember that capital gains on the sale of a personal residence are not taxed in this country, so your home is actually a form of tax shelter. You can turn those paper profits into real money by selling your home and either renting or purchasing smaller accommodation at a lower price.

Cut costs. If you need to find more money to direct to your retirement plan, you may have to cut back on some of your living expenses. Savings should increase as the children leave home to start independent lives. *But further sacrifices may be needed:*

Cars. If you have two, think about whether you really need both. Also, plan to make your car last longer. Don't automatically trade it in every three or four years. Instead, the next time you need to replace your car, choose a model that has established a reputation for longevity and plan to keep it for the next five to seven years. A two-year-old top-rated car, like a Honda Accord or Toyota Camry, will be the best buy.

Vacation home. If you have a summer cottage and the kids are grown up, ask yourself how much use you'll continue to make of it. Cottages can be very expensive in terms of the capital they tie up and the maintenance costs.

Leisure expenses. Do you belong to an expensive club? If so, are you getting enough use out of it to justify the cost? Or could you better use the annual fees for your retirement savings plan? What about vacations? If you tend to overspend on them, look for ways to cut back. Do you really need as many cable outlets in your home? Are you dining out more than is necessary? Do you need a $20 bottle of wine when a $10 bottle will do just fine? In short, look at all the ways in which you spend your leisure money and resolve to cut back by at least 25% if you need to boost your savings.

Get a second job. If cutting spending seems too harsh to you, explore the possibility of getting a second part-time job or becoming a mini-entrepreneur from your own home. Many people are discovering that a small Internet marketing venture geared to a personal hobby or skill (anything from selling home-made quilts to offering consulting advice) can provide some welcome extra income. You can also get some valuable tax breaks, such as deducting the cost of a home office, in this way.

Exercise self-discipline. When it comes right down to it, the only way late starters can be successful is if they genuinely want to build a good retirement plan and are prepared to exercise the self-discipline and make whatever sacrifices are needed. It won't be easy, but if you have the determination it can be done.

Source: Retiring Wealthy in the 21st Century, *by Gordon Pape, published by Prentice Hall Canada.*

HOW INFLATION CAN RAVAGE AN RRSP

When looking for an investment vehicle for your retirement funds, always remember the disastrous effect inflation can have on those funds. Even low levels of inflation can easily negate the benefits of compounding.

For example, an average inflation rate of 5% over 35 years will reduce the purchasing power of $1,387,145 to the paltry sum of $344,634. The further away you are from retirement—or the longer your retirement—the greater the impact.

To avoid this consequence, keep an eye toward growth. Consider using mutual funds as the vehicle for your RRSP investment.

Helpful: Split your annual contribution into two parts, with one half invested in a high-quality bond fund and the other half invested in a growth mutual fund.

In alternate years, substitute one of your investments with an investment in a real-estate income program, such as a real estate investment trust (REIT). Your returns should still be relatively high, your risk minimal and your investment will be hedged against the possible onset of high inflation.

As you approach retirement, begin reducing the amount devoted to the growth portion of your funds—but don't do away with it altogether. Even retired people need protection from the danger of inflation.

Source: Geraldine Parrott, certified financial manager for Stifel, Nicolaus & Co., 615 E. Michigan Ave., Suite 400, Milwaukee, WI 53202.

What to Put in Your RRSP

The rules are very generous when it comes to qualified investments for an RRSP. However, there are some taboos, such as gold bullion and foreign cash. These are allowed in your plan:

● **Annuity contracts.** Your RRSP can hold a deferred annuity contract, as long as payments have not begun.

● **Bankers' acceptances.** These are short-term notes issued by financial institutions. Brokerage firms often use them instead of Treasury bills or money market funds because of their slightly higher returns.

● **Call options.** These options give you the right to purchase a security at a predetermined price for a certain period of time. They may be held in RRSPs provided they're listed on a recognized Canadian stock exchange.

● **Canada Premium Bonds.** These securities are designed specifically for RRSPs and backed by the federal government. The issues have 10-year terms, with

WHAT TO EXPECT FROM YOUR RRSP

Y ou should make every effort to contribute the maximum amount you're allowed to your RRSP each year. Last year's notice of assessment from the CCRA will tell you how much room you have available, including any unused credits from prior years. Use it as your guideline.

The following table shows how much an RRSP can grow over time assuming a modest and very achievable average annual compound rate of return of 6%.

ANNUAL CONTRIBUTION	VALUE AFTER			
	5 YRS.	10 YRS.	20 YRS.	30 YRS.
$1,000	$ 5,637	$ 13,181	$ 36,786	$ 79,058
2,000	11,274	26,362	73,571	158,116
5,000	28,186	65,904	183,928	395,291
10,000	56,371	131,808	367,856	790,582
13,500	76,101	177,941	496,606	1,067,286

As you can see, a higher contribution goes a long way. If you contribute $1,000 a year to your plan, it will grow to just over $79,000 after 30 years. But if you are able to increase the annual contribution to $2,000, you'll end up with almost $160,000 in retirement capital upon which to draw.

The $13,500 line represents the maximum annual amount anyone can contribute to an RRSP, up to 2004. Of course, only people with very healthy incomes will be able to take advantage of it.

Source: Retiring Wealthy in the 21st Century, *by Gordon Pape, published by Prentice Hall Canada.*

escalating interest rates for the first three years set at the time of issue.

● **Canada Savings Bonds (CSBs).** These are safe fixed-income investments and can be held in no-fee government-sponsored RRSPs, as can Premium Bonds. The latter are the better choice because of their higher interest rate.

● **Cash (Canadian).** As long as the money is legal tender in Canada, it's okay. Direct cash deposits in a foreign currency cannot be held in an RRSP.

● **Corporate bonds (Canadian).** All debt securities (bonds, debentures, etc.) issued by a Canadian company with shares listed on a recognized stock exchange are eligible.

● **Corporate bonds (foreign).** Bonds and debentures of firms whose stock trades on an eligible foreign exchange may be held in RRSPs as foreign content.

● **Covered call options.** This is a particular type of call option, sometimes used by RRSP holders to generate additional revenue. The procedure involves selling options on shares you own within the RRSP. The premiums received from selling the options add to the RRSP's cash flow and have the effect of reducing the net price paid for the stock. However, some financial institutions do not permit such transactions within their self-directed plans because of the administrative problems they present.

● **Credit union shares.** Shares or similar interests in a credit union may be held in an RRSP.

● **Exchange-traded funds (ETFs).** These are index-based products that track a specific underlying stock or bond index. There are many available, and some will be considered foreign content.

● **Government bonds (Canadian).** These include all debt obligations (bonds, debentures, notes, mortgages, etc.) issued by the Canadian government or one of its agencies. This brings in the federal government, provincial governments, municipalities, Crown corporations (defined as at least 90% government-owned), and educational institutions and hospitals if the security has a provincial guarantee.

● **Government bonds (foreign).** Only foreign government bonds that have an "investment grade" rating with a recognized bond rating service are allowed. The most common type of foreign government bonds offered to Canadian investors is State of Israel bonds. Most Israel bonds are denominated in U.S. dollars.

● **Guaranteed investment certificates (GICs).** These are among the most popular forms of RRSP investment, along with mutual funds. GICs are fully RRSP-eligible as long as they are issued by a Canadian financial institution.

● **International bonds.** Bonds, debentures and notes issued or guaranteed by a number of international banking organizations may be held in an RRSP without counting as foreign property. These include the International Bank for Reconstruction and Development (better known as the World Bank), the International Finance Corporation, the Inter-American Development Bank, the Asian Development Bank and the Caribbean Development Bank.

● **Investment contracts.** These must be government-approved and issued for RRSP investing.

● **Labor-sponsored venture capital funds.** These investment funds are designed to raise capital for fledgling businesses. Investments in these funds are usually eligible for tax concessions from the federal government and some provinces. In 1998, these funds became qualified as small businesses, a change that gives investors the opportunity to bump up the foreign content limit of registered plans. Ownership of small-business shares in an RRSP increases allowable foreign content by three times the value of those shares.

● **Limited partnership units.** These are RRSP-eligible, but some rules apply. Only units that trade on Canadian stock exchanges are allowed and this excludes most limited partnerships, since the bulk of this trading is done over-the-counter on the Canadian Dealing Network (CDN). The largest eligible partnership is the Mackenzie Master Partnership, which trades on the Toronto Stock Exchange. In the past, these units would have counted as foreign content, even though the company is 100% Canadian. In May 2000, new rules that allow Canadian-based limited partnerships to be counted as Canadian content were passed into law.

● **Manitoba Rural Economic Development Initiative (REDI) and Grow Bonds.** These bonds are issued by the Government of Manitoba to encour-age investment in rural areas of the province. Those purchased after July 1991 are eligible for inclusion in self-directed RRSPs.

● **Mortgages.** Mortgages on Canadian real estate are eligible RRSP investments. This includes your personal mortgage or mortgages on real estate owned by members of your family. There is nothing in the rules that requires the investment to be a first mortgage, so second and third mortgages could also be held in your plan. Mortgage mutual funds are also eligible, as are shares in a mortgage investment corporation that is listed on a stock exchange.

● **Mutual funds.** Mutual funds that invest primarily in qualified RRSP investments are eligible in their own right. Funds that invest mainly in foreign securities will be limited by the foreign property rules. Real estate mutual funds (both open-end and closed-end) are RRSP-eligible, even though you're not allowed to hold real estate directly (however some may be classed as foreign content). The same is true of precious metals funds—you can hold mutual funds that invest in gold, but not gold itself.

● **Provincial savings bonds.** Several provinces, including British Columbia, Ontario and Quebec, issue their own savings bonds. They may be held in self-directed RRSPs.

● **Rights.** Rights allow the holder to purchase a security at a set price within a specified time. As long as the rights relate to a security that in itself qualifies for an RRSP, they are eligible.

● **Royalty trust units.** Royalty trust units that trade on a recognized Canadian stock exchange and derive their value solely from Canadian resource properties are eligible RRSP investments.

● **Saskatchewan Community Bonds.** Like Manitoba Rural Development Bonds, Saskatchewan Community Bonds are eligible for RRSP investments. These bonds are designed to support economic development in the province where the principal is guaranteed by the Saskatchewan government.

● **Savings certificates.** These are term deposits issued by some Canadian financial institutions (mainly smaller trust companies) that are cashable at any time. They are also called cashable GICs and are fully RRSP-eligible.

● **Small-businesses shares.** Investments in small businesses are allowed as long as a number of conditions are met. These include shares and limited partnership interests in small businesses. Small-business investments used to be limited to 50% of the value of your RRSP, but this restriction has been lifted. If you're interested in investing in a small business, consult a tax expert.

● **Stocks (Canadian).** Common or preferred stocks listed on any Canadian exchange are fully eligible for RRSPs. If you're not sure whether a particular company qualifies, check with a taxation expert before acquiring its shares for your RRSP.

● **Stocks (foreign).** Shares in foreign companies traded on recognized stock exchanges may be included under the foreign property rule.

● **Strip bonds.** These bonds are eligible for RRSPs if the underlying debt security would normally qualify.

● **Term deposits.** The definition of a term deposit is muddy. Some financial institutions allow early redemption of term deposits, with a penalty, but do not allow GICs to be cashed in ahead of their maturity date. Others refer to certificates with a maturity date of less than a year as term deposits, while those maturing in one to five years are GICs. Others use the terms interchangeably. Regardless of the definition (which you should clarify before you make your investment), term deposits are fully RRSP-eligible if they are issued by a Canadian financial institution.

● **Warrants.** Like rights, warrants allow the holder to buy a security at a set price within a fixed time period. They are eligible for RRSPs as long as they meet the conditions outlined under Rights.

Source: Gordon Pape's Buyer's Guide to RRSPs, *by Gordon Pape and David Tafler, published by Viking Canada.*

> "Unless you . . . can't wait for the first nip of frost, a white Christmas and delicious, sweet sap running from the maples, you're probably dreaming that your magic retirement address will be somewhere in the Sunbelt."

Five Ways to Reduce Your RRSP Costs

Managing an RRSP doesn't have to be expensive. Some types of plans cost nothing at all; others charge only a small annual administration fee. But if you're not careful, you can run up some fairly hefty bills which will not be tax-deductible and will be paid from the proceeds of your plan. Here's what to watch for and how to beat those high expenses.

● **Mutual fund commissions.** Many mutual funds charge a front-end load when you buy. While you shouldn't pay more than 4% (and 2% is a better target to shoot for), this can still add up to a lot of money over time. *Solution:* Buy no load funds or ask your adviser to sell you front-end load funds at zero commission. Some will be more than likely to do this to get your business and earn the annual trailer fees paid by the fund companies.

● **Mutual fund redemption fees.** If you buy a back-end load (also called deferred sales charge) fund for your RRSP and then decide to cash in your units, you may be assessed a redemption charge depending on how long you've held it. *Solution:* Switch to another fund within the same family. Switching fees are no more than 2% and your dealer may do it without charge.

● **Broker's commissions.** Every time you trade a stock, you'll pay your broker a commission. You'll also pay when you buy Treasury bills, stripped bonds and regular bonds. These charges won't be as obvious because they're built into the price you pay for the security, but they're a drain on your RRSP money nevertheless. *Solution:* Use a discount brokerage service and/or trade on-line. Fees are less.

● **Transfer fees.** If you switch your RRSP elsewhere, you'll probably have to pay a fee to the transferring institution. *Solution:* Don't move your money around unless it is absolutely necessary.

● **Self-directed RRSP fees.** Annual administration fees typically run between $100 and $150. This can add up over the years. *Solution:* Some companies now offer low-fee or no-fee plans, although they may have some limitations on them. Shop around.

Source: Retiring Wealthy in the 21st Century, *by Gordon Pape, published by Prentice Hall Canada.*

Nine Winning RRSP Tips

● **Invest only in things you understand.** The list of possible RRSP investments is long and ranges from the relatively simple, like Canada Savings Bonds, to the ultra-sophisticated, such as covered call options. Stay with securities with which you are comfortable and you won't go far wrong.

● **Diversify your plan.** Don't put all your RRSP eggs into one basket. The best-performing RRSPs contain a mixture of securities. A diversified approach will improve your prospects for better returns while at the same time reducing your risks.

● **Invest for the long haul.** You and your RRSP are going to be together for a long time. Your investment strategy should reflect that. Virtually every decision you make should have at least a five-year horizon, with the exception of cash movements. That doesn't mean you should never sell a security you've held for less than five years, but you should have a good reason for doing so.

● **Keep your costs low.** Any money your RRSP spends on fees or commissions is lost to the plan forever. That's why you should keep such charges to a minimum. If you're purchasing mutual fund units, favor no-load or back-end load funds (in cases where you're not saddled with high management fees). If you buy a front-end load fund (which means sales commissions must be paid at the time of purchase), negotiate the lowest possible rate.

● **Keep your losses low.** Since you can't replace RRSP money lost as a result of bad investments, you should do everything in your power to keep any losses to a minimum. That means avoiding speculative investments and not selling high-quality securities if they go into a temporary slump because of corrections in the stock or bond markets.

● **Maximize the effect of compound growth.** The key to building a million-dollar RRSP is steady compounding over many years. Your plan should include securities that maximize the effect of this, such as high-yielding bonds, strip bonds, mortgages and Guaranteed Investment Certificates.

● **Pay attention.** Review your RRSP holdings at least once every three months to see how well they're performing and if any adjustments are required. You should also review every statement you receive from the company administering your RRSP. Errors creep into these reports occasionally; check to make sure that you've received credit for all interest and dividends and that the administrator's list of your assets corresponds with yours.

The Benefits of Early Retirement

Collecting Canada Pension Plan early if you're eligible can pay off. Even though benefits are reduced, they'll usually add up to more in the long run. *Example:* If full benefits are $800 per month for retiring at age 65, you can get reduced benefits of $560 a month by retiring at age 60. You'd have to collect full benefits for almost 12 years to make up the $33,600 you would receive during the five years of early payments.

Source: Changing Times, *Washington, DC.*

● **Contribute regularly.** RRSP contributions shouldn't be determined by whatever's left over in your bank account. A regular contribution program, preferably on a monthly basis, will ensure your plan continues to grow at a steady rate and will eliminate the last-minute scramble for cash at deadline time. Many RRSPs now offer an automatic deduction plan, which enables you to authorize a specific amount for transfer from a deposit account into your RRSP at regular intervals.

● **Don't ignore stocks.** There is a raging debate among financial experts as to whether stocks should be included in an RRSP. Under ideal circumstances, they should not because you lose the benefits of the dividend tax credit and the favorable capital gains tax rate when stocks are held inside a retirement plan. You're better off keeping the stocks outside the plan and holding more highly taxed interest-bearing securities in the RRSP. But that assumes you have adequate assets to run two investment portfolios. Most people don't. If your RRSP is your only investment portfolio, we recommend you hold at least some stocks in your plan, preferably in the form of high-quality equity mutual funds. The younger you are, the stronger this recommendation. That's because, over the long haul (which is, after all, what we're discussing here), common stocks have a better growth record than any other type of investment you can make.

Source: Gordon Pape's Buyer's Guide to RRSPs, *by Gordon Pape and David Tafler, published by Viking Canada.*

WORKING AFTER RETIREMENT

Many retirees would like to keep working after retirement, at least part-time. But those who want to work for financial reasons should be aware of these drawbacks:

● **You can work and still collect Canadian Pension Plan benefits,** but if you are 60–64 you cannot begin drawing CPP unless your earnings are below the maximum monthly CPP benefit at the time you stop work. If you qualify for an "early" pension (the normal age for collecting is 65), you will retain that entitlement even though your part-time earnings may rise above the minimum level in future. At age 65, you can collect full CPP no matter how much part-time income you earn.

● **Be careful that any part-time earnings** don't put you into a position where your Old Age Security benefits will be subject to the Clawback. This is a special tax that effectively reduces your OAS benefit by $1.50 for every $10 you earn beyond a certain threshold ($56,968 in 2002).

● **If you continue working part-time for the same company,** you may not be eligible to collect your pension. One way around this, if the company will go along, is to retire as an employee and return as a freelancer. Since you're now self-employed, your pension won't be affected.

If you work full-time or part-time, you may be able to make RRSP contributions until the end of the year in which you turn 69. The annual limit: 18% of the previous year's earned income.

Source: William W. Parrott, a chartered financial consultant, Creative Retirement Planning, 1 Hollow Lane, Suite 306-B, Lake Success, NY 11042, and Gordon Pape, author of Retiring Wealthy in the 21st Century, published by Prentice Hall Canada.

The 12 Most Common RRSP Mistakes

Mistake 1

Not having a plan. Many people who could afford to contribute to an RRSP don't bother, especially while they're relatively young. In reality, they are forgoing the prime years for RRSP growth, and the longer the delay, the more capital they lose by default.

Mistake 2

Choosing the wrong plan. Many people think one RRSP is the same as another. They don't appreciate there are several different types of plans, each with its own built-in strengths and weaknesses. Typically, this is the person who dashes into a bank on the day before the RRSP deadline, writes a cheque on his or her account, and gives instructions to put it into an RRSP. If he or she doesn't specify the type of plan, the money will almost certainly be directed to a guaranteed investment certificate, which provides a very limited return in a low interest rate environment.

Mistake 3

Ignoring the money once it's invested. Many people believe their RRSP task is finished once the money is in the plan. But you should never go to sleep on your money, especially if you've chosen a mutual fund plan or a self-directed RRSP. Conditions change, new opportunities arise, once-successful mutual funds fall by the wayside—there are dozens of factors that can sharply reduce the returns on your registered plan. Remember, all the profits earned within your RRSP are tax-sheltered until the money comes out. So do everything possible to manage the plan effectively and to maximize your return potential without incurring undue risk.

Mistake 4

Gambling with your RRSP. Some people tend to treat the assets in their RRSP as Monopoly money. They know they won't have access to it for many years, so they do silly things like chasing hot tips. This "go for the big score" rationale usually ends in large losses—money that cannot be replaced (the Canada Customs and Revenue Agency does not allow extra contribution room for investment incompetence). Your RRSP should be conservatively managed, with capital preservation high on the priority list. If you want to gamble, do it outside your plan where at least if you lose money, you can claim a capital loss for taxation purposes.

Mistake 5

Trading too frequently. It costs money to buy and sell securities if your RRSP includes load mutual funds, real estate investment trusts (REIT), royalty income trusts, stocks or any of a variety of other assets. These commissions must be paid from inside the plan. So if you do a lot of trading, a sizable por-

tion of your capital is going to vanish over time. If your trading profits are high enough, perhaps you won't care. But if you are going to have a lot of this kind of activity, make sure they are.

Mistake 6

Not using asset allocation. A well-crafted asset-mix strategy is one of the best disciplines you can use in building an RRSP portfolio, yet most people don't do it.

Mistake 7

Misusing the carryforward. There are times when using the carryforward may make sense for tax planning reasons. But usually, resorting to it is a bad idea, especially if the money is being used for a non-priority purpose. If you have carryforward credits from previous years, make use of them as soon as possible.

> "Most RRSP investors can make the best use of their retirement funds by putting them into stocks, particularly a family of no-load mutual funds."

Mistake 8

Not contributing the maximum each year. A lot of people make a partial RRSP contribution every year, and carry forward the balance of their entitlement. It's a sort of halfway house approach: "Well, at least I did something." Certainly, half a loaf is better than none, but the wise investor tries for the whole bundle. The easiest way to achieve this is to set up an automatic monthly contribution plan. Divide your RRSP contribution entitlement by 12, and have the required amount transferred directly from your chequing or savings account to your RRSP each month.

Mistake 9

Not considering borrowing. Every survey on this subject shows that the overwhelming majority of Canadians wouldn't even consider borrowing to make an RRSP contribution. Many of these same people probably carry credit-card debt, however. This suggests a fundamental misunderstanding of how to make the best use of other people's money. Properly done, an RRSP loan is an almost surefire way of making a profit.

Mistake 10

Waiting until the last minute. It has actually become a joke: we have five seasons in Canada, spring, summer, fall, winter, and RRSP. Every January and February, people pour millions of dollars into their retirement plans in a last-minute scramble to beat the tax deadline. The problem is that this frantic rush can have several negative effects. For starters, it reduces the returns within your plan. *Look at it this way:* If you'd made your contribution several months earlier, the money would already be earning tax-sheltered income. Over time, that extra money can add up to thousands of dollars. A second problem is that last-minute deposits often mean hasty investment decisions—and rushed decisions can be bad decisions. So this year, plan to get the money in sooner (or at least part of it), and take your time deciding where and how you want it invested. It will pay off in the long run.

Mistake 11

Not making use of foreign content. You're allowed 30% foreign content in your RRSP. Use it! *The reason is simple:* Better diversification. Canada represents a very small player on the world financial stage. History has shown that our stock market is highly vulnerable to boom/bust cycles because of its heavy weighting toward the resource sector, and that our currency is vulnerable to political shocks, like separatism. Until the government makes a change, we're required to keep the majority of our retirement capital in this small, uncertain market. But you can reduce the risk (and increase the return potential) by using the foreign-content allocation you're allowed.

Mistake 12

Not managing the Home Buyers' Plan properly. Almost a million Canadians have borrowed money from their RRSPs to help finance a home. In the overwhelming majority of cases, they'll pay for this privilege in the future because their RRSP will never make up for the lost years of compounding. But it doesn't have to be that way. There are techniques that can be used to manage the Home Buyers' Plan effectively so that you not only end up with your house, but with an enhanced retirement savings plan

as well. It's the ultimate in eating your cake and having it, too.

Source: Gordon Pape's Buyer's Guide to RRSPs, *by Gordon Pape and David Tafler, published by Viking Canada.*

The Deductibility Loophole

Say you are covered by a company deferred profit-sharing plan (DPSP), but the company won't make any contribution to the plan this year because it won't make a profit. Can you make a deductible RRSP contribution? Yes.

The RRSP contribution formula for DPSPs is 18% of your previous year's earned income to a maximum of $13,500 (this figure scheduled to rise in 2004), less your prior year pension adjustment. Your pension adjustment in this case cannot be more than 18% of your annual compensation or $7,250 in 2003 and $7,750 in 2004 (the maximum deductible DPSP contribution), whichever is less. If your employer makes no contribution to your plan in any year, you're entitled to make your full RRSP contribution, with no pension adjustment applied.

Source: Gordon Pape's Buyer's Guide to RRSPs, *by Gordon Pape and David Tafler, published by Viking Canada.*

Picking the Right Stocks for a Retirement Account

Most RRSP investors can make the best use of their retirement funds by putting them into stocks, particularly a family of no-load mutual funds. But the volatility of the stock market means that there are still times when an RRSP owner should get out of the market to reduce risk.

How do you determine those times? There is a technique for keeping your eye on only two simple indicators—both of which have to be positive to enter or remain in the stock market.

Follow the Prime Rate

The market's major direction depends in large part on the trend in interest rates and in Federal Reserve Board policy in the United States and the Bank of Canada's stance in this country.

The prime rate is especially convenient to use as an indicator because it generally doesn't change frequently. And changes in the prime are hard to miss because they always make headline news. *When to take action:* If the U.S. prime is below 8%, a sell signal occurs on the second of two increases in the prime or on an advance of a full percentage point in the rate.

Tracking the prime in the future:

● **If the prime has been climbing but hasn't yet reached 8%,** move into stocks at the first drop in the rate.

● **If the prime is climbing and is 8% or higher,** move into stocks only after two consecutive drops in the rate or a full percentage point drop.

● **If the prime is dropping but is still 8% or higher,** move out of stocks whenever the rate starts to rise again.

Pay Attention to Price Trends

Guidelines:

● **Keep a record** of each weekly close of the *Value Line Composite Index.* You'll usually find the figure in the weekend financial pages of most major newspapers and in *Barron's.*

● **Check to see if the index climbs 4%.** A 4% change, not simply a four percentage point change, on a weekly closing basis indicates a move to stocks.

● **Maintain that position as long as the weekly index doesn't drop 4% or more.**

The price trend indicator is right only about half the time, but stock profits made from the times that it's right are substantial. If you prefer to switch investments less often than this indicator might provoke, simply increase the "4% rule" to 5% or 6%.

These indicators can be used by the most conservative RRSP investors to minimize risk.

How to do it:

● **Wait until both the prime rate indicator and the price trend indicator** signal "buy," choosing stocks over money-market instruments.

This conservative system will occasionally miss an up market, but you'll be able to sleep at night, and you'll be playing the stock market only when the odds are greatly in your favor.

Source: *Martin Zweig, chairman of the Zweig Fund ($370 million under management) and author of* Martin Zweig's Winning With New IRAs, *Warner Books.*

Transferring Your RRSP

The time may come when you want to switch your RRSP from one company to another. The reasons for making a change are many and varied. It may simply be that you've moved to a new location and want to switch your RRSP to a financial institution that's more conveniently located. Or it may be something more serious—investments that are underperforming, escalating fees or a personality clash with your account representative. Whatever the reason, our advice is to think it through carefully before you act.

While the procedure for moving RRSP assets from one company to another is fairly straightforward, the actual execution of the move can sometimes be immensely frustrating. We constantly hear complaints from RRSP investors who have been forced to wait weeks and even months for a requested transfer of funds to take place. Some unhappy RRSP holders have actually brought suit in small claims court for lost revenue resulting from lengthy delays—and won.

Financial institutions have an annoying habit of burying the paperwork involved in these transfers. After all, if the account is being transferred to someone else, why break your back to service the customer? We'll get around to it—when everything else has been done.

All major financial institutions now charge fees to transfer your money among accounts or to other institutions. These are generally around $25 per transfer. So not only will they take their time moving your money, they'll penalize you as well.

It's not only frustrating for RRSP holders, it can cost them money on top of the fees. That's because the transferring company will "freeze" your account once it receives the transfer instructions. That means you won't be able to conduct any transactions until the switch is completed. A transfer of funds that is delayed for several months could mean missed investment opportunities and lost income.

Here's how to protect yourself from having that happen if you decide to move your registered plan:

● **Find out what guidelines** your financial institution has adopted for transfers to another organization. No standardized guidelines exist to cover the whole industry. Most industry associations have policies in place, but usually these are voluntary guidelines with no teeth.

● **Make sure the transfer is really necessary.** If it's not, leave the funds where they are. You can always open a new RRSP with the company to which you intended to transfer your money.

● **Keep close track of the maturity dates** of all GICs and term deposits in your plan. If you want to transfer assets from any of these sources, have the appropriate paperwork ready well in advance. This will ease the pressure on yourself and your financial institution.

● **For a faster procedure,** don't initiate the transfer during January or February—the peak RRSP season. Wait for a quieter time (say, mid-summer) when your request is less likely to be put on hold.

● **Review all paperwork for accuracy** before signing. If you've obtained a time-limited rate guarantee from another institution, make sure that you inform your broker, bank or trust company both verbally and in writing. Attach a copy of the written notification to your paperwork.

● **Keep checking on the status of the transfer.** If no action has been taken within a reasonable time, speak to the manager of the RRSP department of the transferring firm. If you do business with the company in other ways (deposit accounts, mortgages, etc.) and intend to keep doing so, mention the fact—presumably, they'd like to hold on to you.

Consider a self-directed RRSP within the same company as an alternative to transferring your assets to another organization. You'll find the staff much more accommodating and the whole operation should be done quickly.

If you have trouble, make a pest of yourself until the job gets done. We don't like having to give that kind of advice, but the workings of some financial institutions in this situation make it necessary.

Source: Gordon Pape's Buyer's Guide to RRSPs, *by Gordon Pape and David Tafler, published by Viking Canada.*

Withdrawing Money From Your RRSP

You can take money out of your personal RRSP at any time, as long as you're prepared to pay tax on it. RRSP withdrawals are treated as income in the year they're made; you don't get any special tax concessions, such as a lower rate for any capital gains in your RRSP. You'll pay tax on your RRSP withdrawals at your marginal rate—the rate that applies to the last dollar you earn in any given year. And, if you withdraw a large amount, you may find yourself in a higher bracket as a result.

The trustee of your RRSP is required by law to withhold tax at source on any withdrawals you make from a plan. The rate of withholding tax increases with the amount you take out, on the following basis:

	Federal	Quebec Residents
Up to $5,000	10%	23%
$5,001 – $15,000	20%	31.5%
Over $15,000	30%	36.5%

When you file your tax return, you may claim any tax withheld as a credit.

Special tip: To minimize the impact of withholding taxes, consider making a series of small withdrawals from your RRSP rather than one large one. Four withdrawals of $5,000 each will be subject to only $2,000 in withholding taxes everywhere but in Quebec. One withdrawal of $20,000 will have $6,000 withheld. Unfortunately, some financial institutions discourage this practice because of the paperwork involved. This is done by putting a limit on the number of annual withdrawals or by charging a fee for each one. Check the policy of the company that holds your RRSP before proceeding.

Source: Gordon Pape's Buyer's Guide to RRSPs, *by Gordon Pape and David Tafler, published by Viking Canada.*

All About Rollovers

A rollover is simply another way of describing the injection of additional money into your RRSP from a source other than another tax-sheltered retirement plan. There is only one way this can happen: if you leave your job and receive a retiring allowance.

A retiring allowance may refer to money you receive when you retire and can be a euphemism for severance pay—money you received because you were fired, whether or not as a result of legal action. However, retiring allowances do not include any pension benefits, death payments or benefits received for counseling services that are part of a dismissal arrangement.

Any eligible payments may be transferred directly to an RRSP (or to a registered pension plan, but not to a RRIF) without being taxed, within certain limits. The transfer can be done in one of two ways:

● **By arranging to have the money** transferred directly into your RRSP. In this type of arrangement, you avoid having income tax deducted at source. To do this, complete Form TD2, Tax Deduction Waiver in Respect of Funds to be Transferred, and give it to your company's payroll department.

● **By receiving the money yourself** and making a contribution to your RRSP within 60 days of year-end. In this case, tax will be withheld on the payments when you originally receive them, but you'll get part or all of the money back when you file your return, depending on how much goes into the RRSP. To make a claim, show the total amount of the retiring allowance you received on Line 130 of your return. You can then claim a deduction for the amount transferred to an RRSP at Line 208. Be sure to attach a receipt for this amount to your return.

The maximum amount of retiring allowances you can transfer directly to an RRSP is $2,000 times the number of years or part years you were with the employer, up to and including 1995. No credit will be granted for any year or part year from 1996 forward.

You may also claim an additional $1,500 for each year or part year prior to 1989 for which no money was vested for you in a pension plan or deferred profit-sharing plan.

The formula looks like this:

$2,000 × years of service before 1996
+ $1,500 × non-pension years before 1989
= eligible retiring allowance

For purposes of this calculation, any part of a calendar year is considered a full year. As an example, if you had been with an employer for 24 years starting in 1980 and ending in 2003 and had no pension plan, your maximum retirement allowance eligible for RRSP rollover would be:

($2,000 × 16) + ($1,500 × 8) = $32,000 + $12,000 = $44,000

If you were fully vested in the company pension plan for all those years, your maximum would be:

$2,000 × 16 = $32,000

Source: Gordon Pape's Buyer's Guide to RRSPs, *by Gordon Pape and David Tafler, published by Viking Canada.*

Creditors and Retirement Accounts

Unfortunately, your RRSP is not safe from creditors in Canada, with a few exceptions.

The tax people can get at retirement accounts through the use of section 160.2(1) of the federal Income Tax Act, which allows the government to seize unpaid taxes from a retirement savings plan upon the plan holder's death. In this case, the assets of the RRSP are considered income in the year of death, and taxed accordingly.

Thankfully, the Canada Customs and Revenue Agency (CCRA) has no strong claim against your plan while you're still alive, although not for lack of trying. The Trust Companies Association has advised regulators that its members will not surrender any funds from RRSPs unless they are served a court order to do so. This declaration comes after a member company was successfully sued by an RRSP holder when the institution complied with a CCRA request.

Locked-in RRSPs are not subject to seizure, even under court order. However, annuity payments can be garnisheed, that is, amounts owed can be deducted from this type of income by the CCRA, or any other creditor who makes a valid claim.

Also safe from creditors are employee-sponsored pension plans and life income funds (LIFs) that hold money from pension plans.

But most personal and group RRSPs aren't protected in any way. If your marriage breaks up, your spouse will usually have a claim on the assets of your plan. Even if your marriage is solid, your RRSPs could fall prey to zealous bill collectors, who have come up with a number of ingenious approaches to separate you from your money.

The main justification used by creditors seeking to grab your retirement money is that, since RRSP holders can dip into their plans whenever they want for consumer purchases, an RRSP is really just a deposit account. As such, it should not be shielded from creditors. This argument has been used by creditors seeking access to the holdings of financial institutions and insurance companies that have gone bankrupt. In some cases, the courts have gone along with them.

There is one type of RRSP that creditors have

difficulty seizing: the plans offered by life insurance companies that form part of an insurance contract. Retirement savings in this form are covered under provincial insurance legislation, which protects life insurance from the claims of creditors. That includes segregated funds, which are essentially mutual funds with an insurance component, and RRSPs issued by insurance companies. In most provinces these laws don't cover retirement plans from banks, trust companies or other financial institutions.

There have been some court rulings recently that seemed to undermine the creditor-proof status of insurance company RRSPs. These are usually related to the length of time a plan was opened before a bankruptcy was declared. As a result, there were concerns that perhaps these plans weren't as secure as they appeared; that their assets could be seized in certain circumstances. A ruling by the Supreme Court of Canada in February 1996 has put those fears to rest. The case involved a Saskatchewan doctor and was extremely complicated. The bottom line, however, is that the Court upheld the creditor-proof status of insurance company retirement plans. Moreover, the ruling even appears to have strengthened the position of these plans.

A more recent ruling by the British Columbia Court of Appeal in January 1998 further strengthened the creditor-proof status of segregated fund and deferred annuity RRSPs. In this case, the Court overturned three lower-court judgments that denied creditor-proofing protection to these contracts.

Naturally, the insurance industry was delighted by these rulings since they confirmed one of the unique selling points of their retirement programs.

But, overall, the whole creditor-proofing issue is still confusing. And it's made even more complex by the fact that authority in this field is under provincial control. So the vulnerability of RRSP assets will vary from one province to another, at times turning on a technical phrasing in the law.

This doesn't mean you should run out and switch your RRSPs to insurance companies because creditors are breathing down your neck. Bankruptcy laws include provisions that prevent people from shifting funds simply to avoid creditors. But it does mean that, in most cases, you'll get better protection from your insurance company than anywhere else.

Prince Edward Island offers the best creditor-proofing legislation, extending the protection that life insurance companies enjoy to all RRSP (and RRIF) holdings, regardless of the issuing institution.

British Columbia's laws aren't as generous, but they exclude RRSPs from the estate of the plan holder on death if an irrevocable beneficiary designation was made. This effectively shelters the funds from people with claims against the estate.

Quebec offers limited creditor protection to certain types of RRSPs where the money will be used to buy an annuity. This protection extends to fixed-term annuities issued by provincially chartered trust companies.

RRSP holders elsewhere in Canada whose plans are not with insurance companies are at risk.

In the face of all this uncertainty, there are some things you can do to at least reduce the chance of your RRSP becoming the target of creditors, governments, corporate failures and political unrest. Here are a few ideas:

● **Designate a beneficiary.** If your RRSP has a named beneficiary (e.g., your spouse), instead of simply passing to your estate, it may help shield the plan from creditors. Unfortunately, this protection isn't absolute. In 1989, the Canadian Imperial Bank of Commerce won a court ruling that allowed the bank access to funds in an RRSP upon a plan holder's death. Even though the man had named a beneficiary, the bank was granted the legal right to the funds in order to satisfy an outstanding loan.

● **Familiarize yourself with CompCorp.** RRSP assets are protected up to $60,000 under the Canadian Life and Health Insurance Compensation Corporation (CompCorp) program, in the event of an insurance company bankruptcy. For a free brochure explaining how the coverage works, call 1-800-268-8099 (in the Toronto area, phone 416-777-2344). You can also visit the web site at www.comp-corp.com.

● **Set up a spousal RRSP.** If you're worried that creditors may come after you at some point, create a spousal RRSP and make all your contributions to it. If your spouse is not a party to your debts, bill collectors will have a much harder time trying to get at that money. Don't try this after you've run into trouble, however, because the courts will probably rule it was just a sham to avoid your debtors.

● **Use an insurance plan.** Insurance company RRSPs have a higher degree of creditor protection than ordinary plans in most Canadian provinces. The Canadian Life and Health Insurance Association advises that if the plan has a designated beneficiary that is the parent, spouse, child or grandchild of the policy holder, it's protected against creditors. Quebec's rules are even more liberal, extending the protection to family members even further removed.

The growing concern over these issues is one of the reasons behind the move of many traditional mutual fund companies into segregated funds. You pay a higher annual management fee, but that buys you the benefit of creditor protection as well as guarantees against loss.

Source: Gordon Pape's Buyer's Guide to RRSPs, *by Gordon Pape and David Tafler, published by Viking Canada.*

Inheritances and Your Retirement Plans

In most circumstances, you can keep your retirement savings out of Revenue Canada's hands when you die by willing it to your spouse. The tax people will only come calling when your assets pass to the next generation.

● **This requires a little planning.** It's important, for example, that your spouse be designated as the beneficiary for your RRSP. For an RRIF or LIF, your spouse should be named as beneficiary or successor annuitant. If your retirement plans are left to your estate, they may be taxed. At the very least, they'll wind up in probate and it may be some time before your spouse can get access to the funds.

● **You have an opportunity at the time** you open an RRSP or RRIF or join a pension plan to designate a beneficiary. Some people fail to specify anyone, however, in which case your estate will get the proceeds of your plan.

● **If you don't know who your beneficiary is,** ask. If it's your estate, arrange to have the beneficiary switched to your spouse, unless you have some strong reason for not doing so. It could save your loved one many financial headaches if anything should happen to you.

● **Plan for the next generation.** Sooner or later, both you and your spouse will be gone and another generation will inherit your assets including, perhaps, some of your retirement savings or benefits. There is one important point about which you should be aware when preparing for that day. You can, in special circumstances, pass some of your retirement savings on to a child or grandchild who is financially dependent upon you, even if your spouse is still living. This can be done with the proceeds of an RRSP and RRIF.

The definition of a financially dependent person for these purposes is very tight, however. The income of the child or grandchild has to be less than the basic personal tax amount in the year before your death. If the dependent child or grandchild is physically or mentally disabled, the proceeds from your RRSP or RRIF can be transferred directly into an RRSP in the youngster's name. The money can also be used to buy an annuity.

In the case of children who are not disabled, the only way to avoid tax is to purchase an annuity that provides payments for a term not longer than 18 years minus the age of the child at the time of purchase. Thus, if a child were 13 years old when the annuity was bought, the term could not exceed 5 years. The annuity payments will be taxed as ordinary income in the child's hands.

The inherited money could also be included in a child's income, in which case it would be taxable—but perhaps at a lower rate than the estate would pay.

Source: Retiring Wealthy in the 21st Century, *by Gordon Pape, published by Prentice Canada.*

Retiring Abroad

If you remain a Canadian resident and simply spend a few months a year in warmer climes, you shouldn't encounter any major problems. However, if you spend a great deal of time in the United States, you need to be aware of the "closer connection" rule.

If you don't take appropriate steps, you may be classified as a "resident alien" by the U.S. Internal Revenue Service (IRS). To determine if you might be exposed to this possibility, take their "substantial presence test." It works like this:

● **For the current year,** count every day spent in the United States as one day.

● **For last year,** count every day as one-third of a day.

● **For the year before that,** count every day as one-sixth of a day.

● **If the total exceeds 182 days,** you meet the substantial presence test. If so, you have to file a U.S. tax return and report your world-wide income. For example, suppose you spent 125 days in the United States in each of the past three years. That's about four months a year. *Here's the calculation:*

This year = 125 x 1 = 125 days
Last year = 125 x 1/3 = 42 days
Prior year = 125 x 1/6 = 21 days
Total = 188 days

Even though in this case you never spent more than about four months in the United States in any one year, you qualify as a resident alien of that country.

You can get around this problem if you meet three conditions:

● You were in the United States less than 183 days in the current year.

● Your tax home is in Canada, meaning you are employed in this country or live here regularly.

● You have a "closer connection" to Canada than to the United States. This can be determined by a variety of things, from where you vote to the church to which you belong, etc.

In this case, you have to advise the IRS by filing Form 8840, *Closer Connection Exception Statement.* You'll find a copy in a useful pamphlet published by the CCRA titled *Canadian Residents Going Down South.* The pamphlet also outlines your obligations both as a resident alien or nonresident alien in the United States. If you plan to spend any significant amount of time in that country after you have retired, we strongly recommend that you get a copy of it.

If you do end up paying any U.S. income tax as a result of all this, you may be able to claim a foreign tax credit when you file your Canadian return.

Should you decide to live abroad permanently after retirement, there are several factors to consider. The precise rules will depend on which country you choose and the tax treaty that prevails between that nation and Canada. We'll use the United States for our illustrations since that's where most Canadians choose to go if retiring abroad.

● **RRSPs/RRIFs.** The value of an RRSP when you become a U.S. resident is considered capital, and is therefore not taxable. Any income earned within the plan after you become a U.S. resident may continue to compound tax-free. You only become liable for U.S. taxes once you start making withdrawals from the plan, and then only on those amounts which relate to income earned in your RRSP *after* you became a U.S. resident, plus any unrealized capital gains. This makes it a sound strategy to take any capital gains in your RRSP before you leave Canada, thereby reducing the U.S. tax for which you'll eventually be liable. If you've lost money in your RRSP to the extent that the plan's value is less than your total contributions, you'll face no U.S. tax at all.

You will have to pay a withholding tax of 25% in Canada when you make withdrawals from your RRSP after you become a nonresident by moving to the United States. Periodic payments from an RRIF or annuity are subject to a 15% withholding tax. If you become a non-resident, the CCRA will regard the withholdings as your full payment. This means you'll pay tax at a much lower rate than would have been the case had you stayed home. Some tax may be assessed in the United States, but such tax will only be payable on a portion of your withdrawals, as we've seen. Morever, you should be able to claim a credit for your Canadian withholdings against your U.S. taxes payable.

● **To get this tax break,** you have to make a declaration to the IRS that you intend to make use of this provision of the tax treaty. This requires a special election, which is made with the first U.S. return you file. You'll be required to supply detailed financial information about your RRSP at that time.

● **The same rules apply to registered retirement income funds** (RRIFs) as well. They're simply regarded as a substitute for an RRSP.

● **Currency protection.** Investing strategies need careful consideration if you decide to leave Canada for good. Don't risk leaving too many of your assets here and then seeing the Canadian dollar fall in relation to the currency of your new country of residence.

The best way to avoid this is to switch a large proportion of your investments into securities denominated in the currency of the country in which you'll be living. You can convert Canadian dollar securities into U.S. dollar denominated assets quite easily, even in registered plans such as RRSPs and RRIFs.

U.S. dollar-denominated bonds from Canadian issuers such as the federal and provincial governments are considered to be 100% Canadian content for RRSP/RRIF purposes. So are mutual funds which invest in these securities.

Some financial institutions issue U.S. dollar term deposits and GICs which are considered Canadian content for RRSPs. As well, some Canadian stocks are denominated in U.S. dollars and pay dividends in that currency. Ask your broker for a list.

In the case of your non-registered investments, there are no barriers of any kind in switching to a U.S.-dollar-based portfolio. It's simply a matter of selecting which securities you want. U.S. equities, as a group, tend to outperform Canadian stocks, so that could be a plus if you want to maintain a growth component in your portfolio.

● **Departure tax.** The Canadian departure tax can make leaving the country very costly. The government doesn't call it that, of course, but a departure tax is really what it comes down to—and it may make it financially difficult for you to take up residence in another country, depending on your situation.

It works like this. On the day you leave Canada, the CCRA takes the position that you sold all your stocks, bonds, mutual funds and other securities. This is called a deemed disposition. You must declare any capital gains (or losses) that result from this fictitious sale on your final Canadian tax return. If you have a lot of invested money, the tax liability could be huge.

There are a few exceptions to the deemed disposition rule. You don't have to declare any Canadian real estate you own, any Canadian business property (if the operation is run from a permanent Canadian address), pensions and other rights, stock options and certain property of short-term residents.

You can, if you so choose, defer paying the tax on property subject to this rule until it is actually sold. The catch is that you have to provide the CCRA with "acceptable security" to ensure they will eventually get paid.

You must also provide the tax people with a list of all your world-wide assets if their fair market value totals more than $100,000.

Source: Gordon Pape, *author of* Retiring Wealthy in the 21st Century, *Prentice Hall Canada.*

Forced Retirement: The Courts May Not Help

Many Canadians have attempted to obtain legal damages as a result of mandatory retirement, and some of the cases have gone all the way to the Supreme Court of Canada on the grounds that the person's Charter rights had been violated through age discrimination.

In most cases, the courts have upheld the principle of mandatory retirement. A landmark case was Dickason *v.* University of Alberta, in 1992. The Supreme Court dismissed a claim by Prof. Olive Dickason that she was unlawfully forced to retire at 65, holding that the university was within its rights.

Source: Dickason *v.* University of Alberta, *Supreme Court of Canada, File No. 22700.*

Retirement-Savings Mistake

Many employees over age 40 who leave their companies use any lump-sum severance benefits or Group RRSP assets to pay bills.

Problem: Any lump-sum payment or RRSP withdrawal will be taxed as income in the year you receive it at your marginal rate, which could be close to 50%. *Better:* Take advantage of the "Retiring Allowance" provisions to roll as much of any severance payment as possible into an RRSP. Leave money in your group RRSP account (which will be in your personal name) untouched. If you need money, take out a home-equity loan or explore taking monthly distributions from your RRSP, spread out over more than one tax year to reduce the government's bite.

Source: Gordon Pape, *author of* Retiring Wealthy in the 21st Century, *Prentice Hall Canada.*

Insurance Tactics
& Strategies

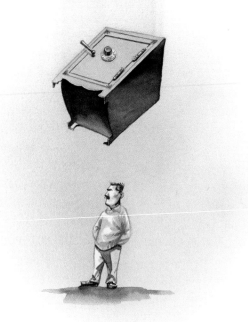

10

How to Pick an Insurance Company

Your number one consideration as you're selecting an insurance company should be its financial strength. Buying insurance (especially life and health insurance) is—we all hope—a long-term proposition. You want to be sure that the company you are buying from will be healthy for many years.

Nevertheless, most people fail to verify the strength and stability of the company they are choosing. It has taken the failure of several firms to drive home the point that not all insurance companies are created equal. But analyzing a company on your own is virtually impossible. Their statements are inscrutable, even to accountants without special training. Leave the analysis up to the professionals.

The Rating Firms

There are five rating firms that evaluate the strength of life-health insurance companies in the United States and publish ratings: A.M. Best (908-439-2200), Duff & Phelps (312-629-3833), Moody's (212-553-0300), Standard & Poor's (212-208-8000) and Weiss Ratings (800-289-9222). You can find information about all these ratings services at http://insurance.about.com/cs/companyratings/.

In Canada, A.M. Best has set up a subsidiary based in Toronto that reports on more than 230 property and casualty companies and virtually all of the life insurers licensed to do business in Canada. They can be reached at 133 Richmond St. W, Suite 600, Toronto, ON M5H 2L3, tel.: 416-363-8266, fax: 416-363-2673. Their website is www.ambest.ca.

Consumers should be aware that ratings can change (either up or down) in a short period of time, so it's best to get current updates by phone or on the Internet. There may be a charge for the information, depending on how much detail you want. For example, A.M. Best provides basic insurance company ratings to consumers without charge, as long as you registered on their website. But if you want a full, in-depth report on a company, there is a $35 charge.

> " You should...read the rating firms' reports about a company. [It] may... only [be] a few pages, but...it gives... insight into the company's strength. "

A rating is an expression of the firm's opinion about the strength of a company. The higher the rating, the greater the likelihood the company will fail.

The opinions of rating firms about a company's strength are often similar, but opinions sometimes differ. For that reason, you should check all the available ratings of a company that interests you. *Helpful:* You should also read the rating firms' reports about a company. A report may consist of only a few pages, but often it gives useful insight into the company's strength.

Helpful Guidance

To understand what a rating means, you need to know where it fits among a rating firm's categories. *Example:* A+ looks like a top rating, and it is Weiss' highest category. However, it is Best's second category, Duff & Phelp's fifth category and Standard & Poor's fifth category. Similarly, A1 looks like a top rating, but it is Moody's fifth category.

You can find information on the most recent financial statements from all Canadian insurance companies by going to the website of the Office of the Superintendent of Financial Institutions at www.osfi-bsif.gc.ca. Click on Financial Data.

Quality of Service

Financial stability is not necessarily an indicator of how fast or well a company pays claims. The best way to gauge the service of an insurance company is to find out how satisfied its current customers are. Unfortunately, there is no comprehensive nationwide ranking.

The best alternative: A few U.S. state insurance commissions publish "complaint ratios" for companies licensed to operate within their borders. These give consumers some indication of the kind of service a company will provide. Since many of the same companies operate in Canada, this information may provide some guidance when you're selecting an insurer. *Example:* Each year, the Illinois Department of Insurance issues pamphlets that compare the

PROTECTION FROM UNREALISTIC EXPECTATIONS AND SALES ILLUSTRATION GAMES

Cash-value life insurance remains one of the few investments whose earnings can build up tax-free and that can protect your family from the financial consequences of your untimely death.

But be wary. In the scramble to persuade you to buy their products, some life insurance companies and their agents are using misleading sales techniques and aggressive investment practices that have turned once boring (but usually safe) policies into high-risk gambles. *How to measure risks:* The first thing to understand is that sales illustrations are not projections or guarantees.

● **Using "unguaranteed" rates of return that are higher than current market rates.** The government bond market may be paying 7½%, but the insurance agent shows you an illustration using an unguaranteed rate of 10%–11%. Or the agent uses illustrations based on "past experience," for example, choosing interest rates from years ago, when rates were much higher, without showing what is currently being credited.

Protection: Find out if the company pays a guaranteed rate and what it is. Ask the salesperson to rework the illustration using current market rates.

● **Illustrating nonguaranteed results for unreasonable lengths of time.** Salespeople who guess at future interest rates may add to the deception by extending the illustration to periods as long as 40 years. *Result:* Expected earnings will be greatly exaggerated. The difference between 7% and 10% annual rates of return compounded over 40 years can be enormous.

Protection: Ask for demonstrations using realistic rates for shorter periods of time, e.g., 10 years and 15 years.

● **Offering high first-year interest rates.** Some companies entice buyers by inflating the first year's interest rate, then reducing the rate in following years. Because of high expenses in the first year, during that time there is usually little cash in the policy to earn the tantalizing interest.

Protection: Find out exactly how much of your first-year premium will be eaten up by expenses and commissions and how much will be left to earn interest. Ask how the company is crediting rates on older policies.

Dangerous Investment Strategies

Some companies are wooing buyers by offering high rates of return on their most conservative fixed-rate products.

Danger: They may have turned to increasingly risky investment practices to sustain these rates:

● **Investing in low-quality, high-yield bonds.** In the old days, insurance companies invested in conservative government and top-rated corporate securities. In the 1980s, some companies turned to higher-risk, higher-yield bonds. That trend has reversed, but conservative rates mean lower returns.

Protection: Request a copy of the company's investment portfolio to see what percentage is devoted to bonds rated BB or lower. There is reason for caution if junk bonds comprise over 10%–15% of the company's portfolio.

● **Investing in longer-term securities—such as 30-year bonds.** *Better:* less volatile short-term securities, such as 5- to 10-year bonds. Although long-term bonds pay higher rates than short-term bonds, the value of a long-term bond declines much more rapidly than the value of a short-term bond if interest rates increase, causing returns to diminish. If they fall significantly, dissatisfied policyholders might surrender their policies to take advantage of higher rates elsewhere. *Likely consequence:* The insurance company would be forced to raise cash quickly by selling its investments at depressed prices— which would further reduce its returns and threaten its financial security.

Protection: Find out the average maturity of the company's investment portfolio. Any term that is longer than 7 to 10 years is cause for concern.

Source: Charles Rohm, senior vice president, The Principal Financial Group, Des Moines, IA. The firm provides a wide range of financial services, including insurance for individuals and corporations, pensions, and residential mortgages.

number of complaints made against each insurance company with the dollar value of the premiums that the company has written in the state. Each figure is listed separately. The companies are ranked, from the best to the worst, in terms of complaint ratios.

The Illinois Department of Insurance offers four complaint-ratio pamphlets: Automobile, Home-owner's, Life and Accident & Health. They are available from the Illinois Department of Insurance, 320 W. Washington St., Springfield, IL 62767.

A company that offers poor service in one U.S. state is unlikely to do much better in another, or in Canada. Some states list all calls to their insurance departments as "complaints." Check to be certain lists are for complaints only.

Some provinces offer a consumer complaint service for insurance-related problems and will assist in reaching a settlement in certain situations. The Financial Services Commission of Ontario is one example. Their website is www.fsco.gov.on.ca.

Source: Joseph M. Belth, publisher of "The Insurance Forum," a newsletter for the insurance industry. He is professor emeritus of insurance at Indiana University and author of Life Insurance: A Consumer's Handbook, *Indiana University Press.*

Answers to Challenging Insurance Questions

Despite everything you have read about insurance, buying any type of policy need not be complicated or expensive. Shrewd consumers only have to remember two rules:

● **Seek protection against catastrophes**—not inconveniences.

● **The more completely your needs are covered**—instead of having partial coverage through various policies—the better the deal.

Answers to today's big insurance questions:

When does it make sense to drop a cash-value life insurance policy and buy term instead? Cash-value policies have two parts—a savings account and life insurance protection that can last until you're 100 years old. As a result, these policies—sometimes known as whole-life policies—cost a lot more than term insurance, which only provides insurance coverage for a set period of time. They are also more confusing.

What to do: If your cash-value policy doesn't pay dividends, you might want to drop it and buy a term policy. Call your insurer or agent to find out if it pays dividends on your policy.

If your cash-value policy pays dividends, the answer becomes complicated. If you've held the policy for two or three years, there may not be much cash value to withdraw from the policy. Typically, much of your premium in each of the first few years goes toward the agent's commission and other charges. There will also likely be a surrender fee, even if you change policies with the same insurer.

You have to assess how much you'll be losing and what you'll be saving to see if it's worth the switch. ***Rule of thumb:*** For a one-income family with two children, insurance would have to cover five to seven times annual earnings.

Do I really need disability protection if my company already provides me with coverage? It's quite likely that you need additional coverage. Very few employers provide enough long-term disability coverage.

Corporate disability policies often don't start until six months after you are disabled—and pay a percentage of your salary. While the amount is certainly better than nothing, it's too often not enough.

Drawback: Disability coverage can be expensive. A policy that provides replacement for $50,000 in annual income can cost $600 or $700 a year, or more. You can cut this in half by increasing the *elimination period*—the waiting time before benefits start—to six months rather than 30 or 60 days. This is the point at which you should tie in your starting date of coverage to what your employer offers.

Warning: Disability coverage is one of the areas in which insurance companies tend to sell you too little insurance.

Policies are to replace the income you have lost because of disability—not to make you rich. Insurers worry that some policyholders may not hurry back to work if they have excessive coverage.

Tip: If your employer pays the premiums for your long-term disability coverage at work, any benefits you draw are taxable. If you pay the premiums yourself, they are not. Suggest to your employer that you pick up the tab for those costs in exchange for the company paying for something else, perhaps dental

INSURANCE YOU SHOULDN'T WASTE YOUR MONEY ON

The best rule when purchasing insurance: Buy only comprehensive policies that will protect you against all catastrophic economic eventualities in a particular category.

Piecemeal policies leave gaps in coverage. After years of paying premiums, you get absolutely nothing if your accident or illness falls between the policies' provisions. In addition, piecemeal coverage is always more expensive than comprehensive coverage.

Policies to avoid:

● **Cancer insurance.** If you wind up in a hospital or bedridden at home, you'll want to collect for *any* disease.

● **Air-travel life insurance.** Fear of flying aside, this is a terrible deal statistically. If you have a dependent, you need good life insurance to cover any cause of death. Besides, your survivors can sue an airline.

● **Accident life insurance.** Will your survivors need more money if you die in an accident rather than from natural causes?

● **Automobile medical insurance.** Your comprehensive health plan will cover your medical expenses, while auto liability coverage will take care of your passengers.

● **Rental-car insurance.** When you had to assume only a $500 deductible, this was easy to ignore. Now that the deductible is commonly $3,000, it's a tougher call. But before you fork over an exorbitant $17 a day (to cover liability and physical damage to the car), call your agent. Your current auto policy may already cover cars you rent. Another possibility: If you pay with a premium credit card, you may qualify for coverage through it.

● **Credit insurance.** This policy pays off loans in the event of your death—for a usurious fee.

Example: A three-year policy on a $5,000 loan costs $144 in annual premiums, for average coverage of only $2,500. (Coverage decreases as the loan is repaid.) But a 40-year-old man can buy $250,000 in annual renewable term life insurance for $350 a year—100 times the coverage for less than triple the premium.

● **Mortgage insurance.** Again, annual renewable term is a superior deal. With mortgage policies, your coverage slides as your debt declines. With term life insurance, your coverage is constant—unless you choose to reduce it to cut your premiums.

Source: J. Robert Hunter, director of insurance, Consumer Federation of America, 1424 16 St. NW, Washington, DC 22207.

insurance. Don't claim a tax deduction for the cost of the premiums or you will lose the tax-free status of the benefits.

How do I know if I have enough homeowner's insurance? Most homeowner's insurance companies automatically increase your premium—and coverage—each year to keep pace with rising real estate values and construction costs. They say the increases protect policyholders against inflation should the need to rebuild arise.

Problem: Most policy increases reflect *average estimated costs* in a region. Real estate values and construction costs can vary between neighborhoods.

Solution: Every three years, determine the current repair value of your house (excluding land value), and compare it with your insurance coverage. If you're insuring for a high home value, ask your insurer not to raise the premium. If the cost to rebuild exceeds your current protection, raise your coverage.

Source: Robert Hunter, director of insurance, Consumer Federation of America, 1424 16 St. NW, Washington, DC 20036.

Life Insurance Savvy

If you find that you need more life insurance, don't replace your current policy with a bigger new one. Instead, keep your current policy and supplement it with a small second policy.

Trap: A bigger new policy actually benefits the agent, not you. The bigger the policy, the bigger the agent's commission. You will have to pay for that as well as new administrative costs before you get any return. In addition, the new policy may have higher premiums and exclude some causes of death covered in the old policy.

Source: Robert Hunter, director of insurance, Consumer Federation of America, 1424 16 St. NW, Washington, DC 20036.

Insurance You May Not Know You Own

● **A homeowner's policy usually covers** stolen purses and wallets, lost luggage, and property taken in a car break-in. It also may cover many offbeat accidents, such as damage to a power mower borrowed from a neighbor; trees, shrubs, fences or tombstones; damages by vandals or motor vehicles; and property lost or damaged while moving.

● **$25,000 in travel life insurance is sometimes provided** if a ticket is bought on a premium credit card. Check the details of the benefits provided if you have such a card.

● **Many clubs and fraternal organizations** have life and health benefits.

● **It's possible to collect twice on car accident** injuries, once through health insurance and through the medical payments provision of auto insurance.

● **Family health policies** usually cover children at university. Check before buying separate policies.

The Secrets of Avoiding— or Fighting—Bad Ratings

The discovery that an insurance company is charging you extra for an individual health, life or disability insurance policy can be infuriating—especially when you're not told why. Almost 10% of all health, life and disability insurance applicants are hit with extra charges (ratings, in insurance jargon) for medical or moral reasons.

What They Can Pin on You

● **Health problems,** such as high blood pressure or obesity—which you may have had years ago and since resolved.

● **Drug or alcohol abuse.** Occasional use is easily exaggerated by malicious colleagues or neighbors.

TROUBLE WITH A CLAIM?

Before a Claim

Before you have a claim, it is a good idea to read your insurance policy closely. Write a letter to the company informing it of what you think the policy covers. If you are right, it will tell you. If you are wrong, it should say so—you can then ask the company to change the situation, or choose to go to another company.

If there is ultimately a problem with a claim, the courts should hold any ambiguous language in the policy in your favor, since the insurance company wrote it and you were stuck with the language. Further, the courts look to the "reasonable expectation" of the insured when a claim occurs. State your expectations in writing up front when you first purchase coverage, and they will more than likely be binding later.

Also, know what you are insuring before a claim: Keep detailed records of what you own and their condition. For example, make records of the condition in which you keep your car. Then, if an accident occurs, you will be able to prove that the car was in excellent shape. Make an inventory of your home. It's surprising how many important items people are not able to recall after a fire. Document ownership with photos to give the claims adjuster sufficient evidence. All valuables should also be documented with sales slips or periodic appraisals. Be sure to keep these records in a safe-deposit box or at work—records are not much good if they're destroyed along with the contents of your home.

After a Claim

● **Do not sign any insurance company releases without careful consideration.** *Document everything that happens first:* When did the insured event occur? What were the circumstances? Who are the witnesses? When did you inform the agent or company? Whom did you talk to? What did that person tell you?

● **Keep a complete record of each contact with the insurance company.** Your ability to have a claim paid will be directly related to the

- **Psychiatric conditions.** Even light therapy may make extracautious underwriters nervous about your mental stability.
- **Criminal associations.** If a relative or close friend is a known member of organized crime, you're considered a greater risk.
- **Homosexuality.** Not just because of AIDS, but merely for moral reasons.

In-Depth Investigation

When you sign an insurance application, you give an insurance company permission to undertake a thorough investigation of your medical, social and financial history. When they delve into your past, insurance companies look for consistency—a straight story. They ask the same questions of several sources and ask each source the same question three or four times from different angles. The more inconsistency they find, the more they dig. *Sources:*

- **You.** When filling out applications or answering questions at medical examinations, keep it simple. Make yourself as small a target as possible.

Important: If you hide a condition that later forces you to make a claim within the so-called "contestability period"—usually one to two years—an insurance company will cancel your policy because you have misrepresented yourself. For example, if you hide a known heart condition and die of cardiac arrest six months later, your life insurance policy will be canceled and your family will collect only a half year of returned premiums.

- **Your doctor.** Ask your physician to examine your medical file to see if it conveys an accurate picture of your current physical condition. If an item could be misconstrued, ask for an explanatory note.
- **References.** Insurance companies usually ask for an accountant, a friend and a business associate. Pick carefully.
- **Your agent** must file a report on you but is unlikely to be a problem, since an agent is always interested in making the sale.
- **Information-gathering services** investigate you, looking for both medical and moral problems. (Most companies now use Equifax Canada. You can obtain a copy of your personal file by visiting their website at http://www.equifax.com/EFX_Canada/.)

quality of your record keeping. If the company tries to delay or reduce the size of the claim, you will be able to document what is happening and will have the evidence you need to appeal higher up in the company or to the appropriate federal or provincial regulatory body or, if need be, to court.

If you go to a lawyer, you will not only have a better chance in court with good evidence, but if the insurance company gives you an abusive

CLAIM FORM

I DON'T THINK SO

runaround, you may also be entitled to sue for punitive damages in some jurisdictions. Before you sue, though, which could take a long time and be costly, consider other help. If the problem relates to life or health insurance, call the Helpline Consumer Assistance Centre of the Canadian Life and Health Insurance Association (1-800-268-8099 in English or 1-800-361-8070 in French). It will refer you to sources of help, answer basic questions, help to locate lost policies, and

contact company consumer divisions on your behalf. Also worth noting is the new National Financial Services OmbudService (NFSO), which began operation in 2002.

Complaints should be directed first to the company (write to the president). Be reasonable, but don't believe everything the insurance company tells you. If that avenue of relief fails, appeal to the appropriate regulatory agency. Be brief and factual. Clearly state the relief you want. If you do not get a satisfactory response from the regulator and the money is significant, you may have to be prepared to go to an attorney.

Source: J. Robert Hunter, director of insurance, Consumer Federation of America, 1424 16 St. NW, Washington, DC 22207.

● **The Medical Information Bureau** (MIB) compiles information on previous insurance applications and claims in search of special health situations. They have an office in Toronto and you can apply to see your file by visiting their website at www.mib.com. Click on Canadian residents under "Request Your Record" for the correct forms.

Knowing You're Rated

All your careful efforts notwithstanding, you've been rated if:

● **You are rejected outright for coverage.**

● **The premium charged is higher**—or the benefits less—than your agent originally quoted. With disability insurance, terms may be less favorable.

● **Your policy arrives with the words** *rating* or *modified benefit* printed on the page where your name appears.

● **You are required to sign a rider or an amendment.**

Fighting Back

You must refute the existing underwriting records. An insurance company's information may be completely mistaken or, more likely, out of perspective —old, exaggerated or misinterpreted. Unfortunately, the nature of the negative information will not always be volunteered. The law requires, however, that an insurance company surrender the reason for a rating to you—or your doctor, if medically oriented—upon written request.

A good agent can make your case to the company. *Advantage:* If the agents are respected, their arguments will carry more weight.

● **Medical situations.** Generally, you or your agent will have to present a letter and test results from a

Mistakes in Filing Property Claims

● **Failure to accurately calculate losses.** It's hard to believe, but many people can't accurately determine their losses—whether by damage or theft. They fail to maintain effective accounting and record-retention procedures to document the losses. It's not uncommon to hear of a situation where a theft loss amounted to $250,000, but the claimant could only substantiate $100,000 of the loss. It's important to plan ahead with your accountant to determine the best procedures for demonstrating what you own, should you have to make a claim.

● **Overstating the loss.** This is a subtle problem. If a claimant purposely overstates the loss to the point where the insurance company could question his or her integrity, the company will take a hard line. Generally, if the claimant takes a fair position, the insurer will still bargain over the loss claim but will be more reasonable.

● **Underestimating the loss.** This sounds like a contradiction of the above, but it's not. Immediately after losses are claimed, an adjuster will ask the claimant for an estimate of the damage, not an accurate, justified number. The insurer requires such a rough estimate, but be wary of providing a number before taking time to get a reliable estimate. If the adjuster reports a number that's too low and then must go back later to the insurer and restate it much higher, his or her credibility and yours are hurt, making future loss negotiations tricky. Tell the adjuster about any problems in coming up with a number.

doctor to the company's medical director. Suppose you had high blood pressure when you first applied for insurance, but that was because of stress on your old job. If a physician can show that you no longer have this condition, the company may reconsider.

Trap: The insurance company may have received information from your physician with a request that it be kept from you. You won't get that information from the insurance company. You will be told, however, that the rating is based on confidential information from your doctor.

● **Moral ratings.** These can be hard to fight. Often, you will not be told the exact source of a bad reference. You will just get a very general statement. Such sources may be vindictive or mentally unbalanced.

While you won't have an opportunity to answer these charges directly, you can ask the insurance company and its sources to recheck their facts.

If the charge is proven wrong, the insurance company will probably correct its files. If the charges are based on opinion rather than fact, have your own response placed along with the allegations in your file. Ask the company to talk with other sources. Give the company personal references.

Battling an insurance company requires patience and dedication. However, if you make enough noise, and with good reason, your chances of erasing a costly insurance rating are very good.

Source: *Leonard B. Stern, president, Leonard B. Stern & Co., an insurance and consulting firm, 305 Madison Ave., New York, NY 10165.*

Finding a Lost Insurance Policy

Hundreds of life insurance policyholders die each year and their named beneficiaries either don't know they are beneficiaries or can't find the policies. If you suspect that you are the beneficiary of a lost policy, don't expect a life insurance company to volunteer the information. The search is up to you.

Check the obvious places first: the box with the tax records, the desk with the cubbyholes full of papers and the safe-deposit box. Talking to family lawyers and insurance agents helps, too. If you don't find what you're looking for, try these:

● **Cheque books.** Cheque stubs often tell the tale. Keep alert for cheques made out not only to insurance companies but also to trusts, trade associations, alumni organizations and individual agents.

● **Employers.** Company personnel offices can provide information on benefit plans, including voluntary programs, life insurance and severance benefits.

● **Supplemental life insurance agents.** They may have had contact with your loved one in or out of the workplace. They usually remember.

● **Money orders.** Try the company credit union, the local bank or Canada Post to find out if a money order was purchased to pay for an insurance policy.

● **Insurance agents.** Anyone in the insurance business—friends, acquaintances from religious organizations, relatives or neighbors of the deceased—can be a source of facts.

● **Old policy applications.** These are always a good place to look because they contain a list of previously owned insurance.

● **Veterans Affairs.** If the deceased was ever in the armed services, check to see if he or she had any veteran's coverage.

● **Relatives.** Older members of the family may recall a policy taken out as a present.

● **Loan documentation.** Frequently, this will reveal insurance policies used as collateral.

● **Possible former beneficiaries.** These can include a former spouse or lover or anyone else who may have been a beneficiary at one time.

● **The funeral register.** Former insurance agents, unknown associates and acquaintances may have the information you're looking for.

● **The Medical Information Bureau.** This clearinghouse for medical and lifestyle information has computerized facts about many who have applied for insurance, but does not readily provide information—you may have to hire a lawyer or go to court to find out anything. The Canadian address is MIB, Inc., 330 University Ave., Toronto, ON M5G 1R7, tel.: 416-597-0590.

If you uncover a company name through this search, the next step is to write to ask about policies that might have been in effect when your loved one died. Provide the company with the deceased's full name, any other names the person might have used, date and place of birth, and Social Insurance number. If you still find nothing, you can contact all insurance companies in provinces where the deceased lived. The names of these companies are available at provincial ministries responsible for insurance administration, although the lists won't include companies no longer in business or mail-order companies.

● **If all else fails,** there is the Canadian Life and Health Insurance Association. This trade organization will forward your inquiry to their member companies, who represent about 98% of the policies in force in Canada. Their website is http://www.clhia.ca. They have offices in Toronto, Montreal and Ottawa.

Source: *Benjamin Lipson, president, Benjamin Lipson Associates Insurance Agency, Inc., 7 Bulfinch Pl., Boston, MA 02114. Mr. Lipson is an independent insurance broker specializing in insurance for people with medical problems. He is also the author of* How to Collect More on Your Insurance Claims *and writes a weekly newspaper column.*

When a Lawful
Claim Is Refused

When you buy an insurance policy, you are purchasing protection for yourself, your family and your possessions. If your car is totaled or you're disabled by a fall or your home is burglarized, you submit a claim and wait a reasonable time for your cheque. It's a simple enough transaction in theory.

But now, in too many cases, the cheque never gets there. The insurance company balks and refuses your claim or it offers a sum far lower than your actual loss. What do you do then? In 9 of 10 cases, people do nothing. They figure there is no use in fighting this $200 billion industry. And that's a shame, because policyholders have strong legal rights under both statute law and case law. You can take on an insurance company and win.

The right tactics:

● **Never inflate your claim.** This will annoy the claims adjuster and make payment more difficult. At worst, it can make you vulnerable to a criminal charge of fraud. An honest claim lays the foundation for further action, should the company refuse to settle.

● **Request a written explanation of why your claim was denied.** If the explanation cites some technicality, such as failure to file on time, the company is probably out of line. Even if you are months late in filing, your claim is still valid unless the company can show that its investigation was harmed by the delay.

● **Keep in mind that the company's interpretation is not gospel.** Insurance firms are no friendlier than other corporations—the fewer claims they pay, the larger their profit. They can be very subjective, and even ridiculous, in interpreting a policy's language. *Example:* One company refused to pay a claim for a patient on a respirator in an intensive-care ward. The company insisted the patient had received "custodial" care, which was excluded in the policy. Even in an honest disagreement, courts have often ruled for the policyholder whenever a policy was deemed unclear.

Bottom line: If you think your interpretation is reasonable, stick to your guns.

● **Don't be bullied by the fine print.** If your claim was denied because of a fine-print "exclusion," take heart. Most courts have ruled that the company must prove that such exclusions were phrased clearly, plainly and conspicuously.

● **Ask your agent to go to bat for you.** Insurance agents want to see valid claims paid, if only to keep their customers happy. A nudge to the home office may help grease the wheels. But the most honest agent in the world may have little influence over a distant adjuster.

● **If you're still not satisfied, take your case to higher-echelon people in the insurance company**—make your first contact by telephone, then follow up by mail. The company may decide to pay your claim after hearing your side of the story. But if it fails to respond to two letters, write a third letter that says you intend to commence legal action within 30 days. Given the size of some recent court awards, this approach can often work wonders. While you wait for their anticipated move, be sure to keep a log and a copy of all communications.

> " **Never inflate your claim; an honest claim lays the foundation for further action, should the [insurance] company refuse to settle.** "

● **Contact your province's insurance regulatory body.** In some provinces, these departments are helpful consumer advocates. Ontario even has its own insurance ombudsman, operating under the aegis of the provincial Superintendent of Financial Services. You can read their instructions for disputing a claim at their webpage at www.fsco.gov.on.ca. Or you can contact them at the Office of the Insurance Ombudsman, 5160 Yonge St., 4th Floor, P.O. Box 85, North York, ON M2N 6L9.

In British Columbia, complaints about insurance companies can be addressed to the Insurance Council of British Columbia, 300–1040 West Georgia St., Vancouver, BC V6E 4H1, tel.: 604-688-0321.

In other provinces, the regulation of insurance companies can fall under a variety of ministries, from the Department of Finance to the Department of Justice. The best bet is to visit the provincial government website and search for insurance regulation or insurance complaints.

● **Take the company to small claims court.** You can represent yourself, and you will get quick results.

One major drawback: Most of these courts have a jurisdiction limit. In Ontario, it is $10,000. Check for the limit in your province before proceeding.

● **If all else fails, see a lawyer.** To find someone experienced in this particular area of the law, contact your provincial or local trial lawyer's association or consumer advocate group. Many attorneys will take insurance-claims cases on a contingency basis. If you win your case, the lawyer keeps a portion of the award, usually one-third. However, if you lose, you pay nothing.

About 95% of insurance suits are eventually settled out of court. But cases in which a policyholder's attorney can demonstrate "bad faith" by the insurance company can result in huge punitive awards.

Source: *Gordon Pape, author of* Retiring Wealthy in the 21st Century, *published by Prentice Hall Canada; and William M. Shernoff, partner, Shernoff, Bidart & Darras, a law firm that specializes in consumer claims against insurance companies, Claremont, CA. He is the author of* How to Make Insurance Companies Pay Your Claims, *Hastings House.*

The Most Common Mistakes in Buying Life Insurance

In addition to offering protection for your family, life insurance can be a good investment. But life insurance policies are complicated, and without facts and comparisons, it's easy to spend a lot of money for the wrong coverage. Here's a list of the most common mistakes to avoid and recommendations on what you should buy.

Mistake: **To buy life insurance when you have no dependents.** Agents tend to create needs where none really exist in order to sell policies. If you are single, you don't need life insurance.

Mistake: **To buy mail-order insurance.** It's a bad bargain for most people.

Mistake: **To buy life insurance for your children.** Unless there's some extraordinary reason, there are better ways to save money.

Mistake: **To put money into a cash-value life insurance policy,** unless you have fully funded any RRSP for yourself and your spouse. Cash-value policies are whole life, universal life, variable life, or any form of life insurance with a savings element.

Be cautious about variable life, which tends to have high built-in expenses and must, like any cash-value policy, be held until death to maximize tax

advantages. Traditional whole life policies bought from mutual life insurers generally offer better value than universal life or interest-sensitive whole life. Any policy bought from an agent must be held at least 20 years to amortize heavy up-front charges. Term insurance is safer.

Mistake: **To buy a cash-value policy from a high-pressure salesperson.** Keep in mind that agents make 5 to 10 times as much commission selling you a $100,000 cash-value policy as they would on a term policy for the same amount. So you should always be alert to the hard sell for such policies.

Mistake: **To buy life insurance and not disability insurance.** People may automatically buy life insurance without realizing that a long-term disability can be an even worse financial event for their families than dying. If you're disabled, you not only lose your income, but you are still around, incurring expenses.

A majority of workers lack the proper amount of disability insurance. Everyone is covered by Canada Pension Plan disability, but it's very restrictive. To qualify, your disability must be "severe and prolonged." The definition of "severe" in this case means your condition prevents you from working regularly at any job (not necessarily your current job or profession). "Prolonged" means your condition is long term or may result in your death.

Mistake: **To buy riders on your policy,** such as the accidental death benefit or the additional-purchase option. These should be treated like options on a car—high-profit items that are best avoided. *Example:* Double indemnity—contrary to popular belief, you're not worth more dead in an accident than dead by other causes.

Controversial rider: The waiver of premiums in case of disability. You don't need it if you're covered for disability. If you become disabled, you'll have enough money to keep up your life insurance premium.

Smart Buying

For young buyers, annual renewable term is probably the best choice in term life insurance. *Rule of thumb:* Buy five to seven times your annual gross income—choose the lower multiple if you have group life insurance at work. For those 45 and up, level premium term is a good choice. Pick the period of coverage that suits your needs. *Helpful:* Compare any cash value or term quotations you receive to rates quoted by doing some selective Internet searches. Some useful sites include:

www.insurance-canada.ca—for insurance information and quotes for all types of insurance, with direct links to many insurance companies.

www.insurance-auto-quotes.com/canada—quotes offered on life policies as well as auto and home insurance.

www.cheaplifeinsurance.ca—quotes available for universal and term life as well as critical illness, disability and long-term care insurance.

Caution: If you buy insurance on-line, find out about the reputation of the company, its viability and its claims procedures. Review a copy of the policy first before signing any agreement. Just because the rate may be cheaper than that quoted by an insurance agent or broker doesn't mean that it's the best choice.

Some policies are so complicated that it's impossible to figure out exactly what you're getting without a special computer program. *Example:* If a universal life policy says it pays 6.5%, that may be figured on whatever is left after a lot of expenses. You have to compare it with what you would have earned if you had bought term and invested the difference. Assuming you hold the policy 20 years, 6.5% may turn out to be more like 5.5%.

Reevaluate your older policies. If your old policy is a term policy, you should assume you can replace it with a lower-priced policy, at least if you're a non-smoker. If your old cash-value policy doesn't pay dividends, it probably should be replaced. If it does pay dividends, you'll be better off keeping it, especially if it has a low policy-loan interest rate that allows you to borrow on it and reinvest the money elsewhere.

Source: Gordon Pape, author of Retiring Wealthy in the 21st Century, *published by Prentice Hall Canada; and James H. Hunt, a life insurance actuary with the Consumer Federation of America.*

> " If you are requesting that dividends be paid directly to you in cash, one of the best bargains in insurance is what the industry calls *paid-up additions.* Policy dividends are used to buy tiny single-premium policies. "

More Life Insurance Mistakes That People Make

Mistake: **Buying life insurance without keeping other financial goals in mind.** Providing for loved ones is important, but so is buying disability insurance, and so is saving for your children's university educations and your own retirement.

Every dollar you spend on life insurance is one dollar less for retirement—and most people are not likely to die before they retire.

Important: Buy life insurance—and every other financial product—as part of a well-conceived plan, not as a reaction to a sales pitch.

Mistake: **Failing to take advantage of level-premium term products.** In today's marketplace, healthy people can get terrific term policies with low premiums that are guaranteed to remain at those levels for 15 to 20 years. *Example:* Recently I worked with a 46-year-old man who wanted insurance coverage of $1.5 million for 20 years. At that point in his life, he would be retired and his children would be out of school. One of the best term policies I found would cost $4,275 a year for 20 years—guaranteed—and the company was financially sound.

I compared this policy with a competitive annual renewable term policy offered by another sound company. In present dollars, that policy cost $2,565 for the first year—increasing annually to $4,560 by the eighth year and to $21,690 by the 20th year.

The first policy was far better. The present value of premiums calculated at a 4% discount rate would be $60,400 over 20 years, while the other policy would cost $102,100.

Important: The equation changes if you think that your insurance needs will change. *Example:* If you bought the first policy and dropped it in the 12th year—when you would have spent a total of $41,700 in present dollars on premiums—you would have been better off with the increasing-premium policy, for which you would have spent a total of $40,700.

In addition, if the level-premium policy expires after 20 years and you find that you still need insurance, you will have a problem getting life insurance if you're in poor health.

Mistake: **Failing to shop around for insurance.** Premiums vary widely. By making a few phone calls, you can get a good sense of what the product you want might cost.

● **For instant term life quotes,** I contact Quotesmith at 1-800-556-9393 or on their websites www.quotesmith.com and www.quotesmith.ca. They will scan the rates and coverages of many companies and mail a price-comparison report in one day for free.

Mistake: **Replacing existing cash-value policies.** In most cases, it is a mistake to replace a policy after you have paid the heavy up-front costs. Even if the policy is a poor one and merits replacement, evaluate what you stand to lose. *Example:* A woman with a poor-quality, $400,000 universal life policy was unable to keep up with the premiums. She wanted to drop the policy but would have been charged $3,000 to do so. I suggested that she obtain less-expensive coverage elsewhere and leave just enough money in the old policy to keep a reduced policy in force for a few years until the surrender charge disappeared. The effective rate of return on her small "investment" will exceed 20% a year, with almost no risk.

Mistake: **Failing to make optimal use of existing policies.** Cash-value policies that have flexible premiums, such as universal policies, allow you to pay less—or more—than the required annual premium, may be a good place to put additional tax-deferred savings. You can pay more, and the money will grow tax-deferred until you take it out. In many cases, no taxes are due when you withdraw.

If you are requesting that dividends be paid directly to you in cash, one of the best bargains in insurance is what the industry calls *paid-up additions.* Policy dividends are used to buy tiny single-premium policies. Then the death benefits and cash values of these tiny policies are combined with your major policy. You'll be getting more insurance without paying additional commissions.

Finally, ask your agent if your insurance company has any *update programs.* With these, you get a higher dividend rate in exchange for agreeing to pay a higher rate if you borrow money against the policy.

Mistake: **Dropping a policy when you no longer need life insurance.** This occurs when your children have grown up, eliminating the need to pay higher premiums for a cash-value policy that was purchased to protect them. But rather than drop a policy in which you've invested, ask to convert it to a *reduced paid-up policy.* This means that you use your accumulated cash value to buy a policy that charges a single premium.

In effect, it converts your whole life policy into a single-premium policy that still carries a death benefit that is lower than your original policy. It also will provide a relatively safe investment that is competitive with a short-term bond fund.

Mistake: **Paying premiums semiannually, quarterly or monthly rather than annually.** Opt to pay once a year. If you decide to pay more frequently, the policy will cost you more. The interest charge for "fractional" premiums is often quite high.

Mistake: **Not paying enough attention to early cash values.** The cash value of your policy is money that is available to you to withdraw or borrow against. A sizable cash value reduces the risk of losing money if you want to drop the policy for any reason.

Compare the first year's cash value with the annual premium. The higher the cash value, the better.

Source: *Glenn S. Daily, a fee-only insurance consultant, 234 E. 84 St., New York, NY 10028. He is the author of* The Individual Investor's Guide to Low-Load Insurance Products, *International Publishing Corp.*

How Much Life Insurance Do You Really Need?

The function of life insurance is to replace the economic value of a family member and to provide

> **"[When buying insurance] determine your family's income needs. Most people underestimate the amount of money it takes to live from month to month."**

liquidity to meet the surviving family's cash needs as the estate is settled. The amount of insurance you *need* is not necessarily the amount you can *afford*. Before you visit with a life insurance agent, take a few minutes to understand the logic involved in determining your life insurance needs.

● **Talk with your spouse or "significant other."** What would he or she do if you were not around? The answer dramatically affects the amount of life insurance you need. He or she could decide to stay at home and care for the family or return to work. Returning to work may require paying for some additional education. Alternatively, relocating the family may drastically reduce the amount of income needed to maintain a similar lifestyle.

● **Determine your family's income needs.** Most people underestimate the amount of money it takes to live from month to month without a change in lifestyle. Try working from a cash-flow page to estimate what costs would change if you were no longer in the picture. *Cash flows will differ as the family ages:* **(1)** while children live at home, **(2)** after the children leave home, **(3)** while your spouse is in retirement.

● **Determine what will generate the required amount of income.** Remember that funds can be invested in a number of ways, each of which will generate a different amount of income. Also keep in mind the effects of taxes and inflation on your family's income stream.

● **Evaluate your liabilities.** Some liabilities should be paid off immediately at your death. Others, like a 7% home mortgage, may not be difficult for your surviving spouse to meet.

● **Estimate a university education fund.** Determine the amount of money that you would have to invest today to meet the expense of university for your children when they turn 18.

● **Estimate readjustment-emergency funds.** Most people go through a period of grieving, when it may be impossible to earn income and start a new life simultaneously. Funds will be needed for ordinary and unanticipated expenses during this time.

● **Calculate last expenses.** In addition to funeral costs, there is the expense of getting your estate passed to your heirs. Assume that between 7% and 9% of the total value of your estate will be needed for administrative expenses.

● **List your assets.** Know what is already available to your survivors.

Once you've done some thinking, make the following calculations to determine your insurance needs. And don't forget to reevaluate these calculations at least once a year.

Add	
Lump sum necessary to provide income:	
While children are at home	
After children leave home	
For spouse in retirement	
Debts that should be paid off	
University education fund	
Readjustment/emergency funds	
Last expenses Amount of estate required	
Subtract	
Available assets	
Existing insurance payable to survivors	
Amount of insurance needed	

Source: *Karen P. Schaeffer, president, Schaeffer Financial, 7855 Walker Dr., Greenbelt, MD 20770, a financial-planning firm affiliated with Hibbard Brown & Co.*

A Quick Way to Estimate Coverage

The multiples-of-salary chart was developed to permit a breadwinner to estimate life insurance requirements in the event of premature death. There are many factors besides these multiples, but the chart will give you an idea of what to expect.

The calculation is based on your current income and on the assumption that your family will receive Canada Pension Plan survivor benefits in addition to insurance proceeds. It also accounts for your spouse's age. For example, if your gross income is $30,000, your spouse is 45 years old and your goal is 75% net income replacement, you will need a policy worth 8.5 times your gross income, or $255,000.

MULTIPLES-OF-SALARY CHART

YOUR PRESENT GROSS EARNING	25 YRS. 75%	25 YRS. 60%	35 YRS. 75%	35 YRS. 60%	45 YRS. 75%	45 YRS. 60%	50 YRS. 75%	50 YRS. 60%
$15,000	4.5	3.0	6.5	4.5	8.0	6.0	7.0	5.5
23,500	6.5	4.5	8.0	5.5	8.5	6.5	7.5	5.5
30,000	7.5	5.0	8.0	6.0	8.5	6.5	7.0	5.5
40,000	7.5	5.0	8.0	6.0	8.0	6.0	7.0	5.5
65,000	7.5	5.5	7.5	6.0	7.5	6.0	6.5	5.0

Source: Morton Tolchin, chartered life underwriter with HL Financial Services of New York, Inc., 780 Third Ave., New York, NY 10017, is a member of the American Society of Chartered Life Underwriters and the Association for Advanced Life Underwriting.

Inflation Calls for More Insurance

The classic solution to the problem of how to increase one's estate when income and the stock market aren't enough is to take out additional life insurance. A life insurance policy without the necessity of taking a physical examination is the best possibility. If it is group insurance, the costs are appreciably less than they would be if the employee took out his own individual policy.

The solution, then, is to locate an employer that has a liberal group term-life insurance program for its employees. The best possibility for an aging executive who wants to move is to sign up with an executive search agency, the sizable fees of which are tax-deductible in most instances. If, in your preliminary interview, you ascertain that this agency hasn't done its homework about analyzing compensation packages well enough to know of the group insurance plans available from various employers, seek help elsewhere.

Source: Encyclopedia of Estate Planning by Robert S. Holzman, Boardroom Books.

Where There's Smoke...

More and more insurance companies are using a test to detect smokers who say they don't smoke so they can get lower premiums on new life insurance policies. How the test works: When you visit your doctor for the required physical, insurance forms instruct the doctor to send your urine sample to the insurance company's lab for testing (the form usually doesn't say what kind of testing). The test looks for traces of nicotine and has never given a false-positive reading.

Although the test supposedly shows whether you've ingested nicotine within the 36 hours prior to giving the sample, it's really effective for only 24 hours. The test isn't sensitive enough to pick up nicotine traces in those who live or work with heavy smokers.

Alternatives to Whole Life Policies

If you're interested in permanent life insurance, what kind should you buy? Here's a primer on some alternatives to whole life policies illustrating their strong and weak points.

Enhanced Whole Life Policies

If you need more permanent protection than you can immediately afford with whole life, you may be interested in an "enhanced whole life" product. This is an option that combines whole life and term insurance, with dividends used over time to convert the term to permanent protection. The advantage of this approach is that you can buy permanent protection at a cost lower than that of ordinary whole life. The policy builds a cash value, and you can borrow from it at any time.

A limited number of life insurance companies now offer flexible life insurance that extends the limits of earlier programs of this type. The new approach is a flexible combination of the three basic life insurance types—whole life, term and paid-up insurance. Generally, the insurance is backed by a company's entire investment portfolio, which softens the impact of dramatically changing interest rates.

This type of policy allows you to custom-design your insurance at time of issue. You decide the premium you can afford and direct the proportion of your premium into permanent insurance, term insurance and paid-up additions. You can also use a lump sum—a single premium—at issue and buy a chunk of single-premium insurance to obtain tax advantages and to increase cash-value buildup.

ARE YOU SPECIAL?

People with chronic physical ailments or who enjoy risky hobbies must take special measures to obtain adequate life insurance coverage. Insurance companies make their money by selling insurance to the "right" people—people in good health who lead "low-risk" lives. Special-risk people—such as those who suffer from cancer, diabetes, nervous disorders, alcohol problems, or hypertension, those who have had bypass surgery, are older, or are scuba divers or pilots—are not the kind of clients insurance companies favor.

If you have any reason to believe that you are a person with special risks, don't be afraid to "sell" yourself to the insurance company. It's legal and moral, and you owe it to yourself and your family to be properly protected.

Passing the Physical

● **Go early.** People who have physicals early in the morning are most likely to pass. Your weight is lower in the morning, you are usually under less stress, and you haven't eaten, so you are prepared for a blood test.

● **Control your vices.** Don't eat, smoke or drink before your physical examination. Alcohol, salt and coffee can produce an undesirable effect on your blood pressure or blood analysis.

● **Try to provide a urine specimen before your blood pressure is taken.** Urination reduces blood pressure. If you jog or exercise heavily, be sure to tell the doctor. Oftentimes, heavy exercise will cause urine specimens to turn up "abnormal."

● **Don't withhold information about your smoking habits.** If you smoke, admit it. Chances are the physician will find out anyway, and you could be rejected for withholding information.

● **Consult your own doctor** *before* **the insurance physical.** The doctor should know precisely what your condition is—in order to help answer possible questions by the insurance company. Be sure to ask about stress and/or other special tests you might be given. Some of these may not be safe for you, and your own doctor can recommend suitable equivalents.

● **Don't change your medical routine just before the insurance examination.** Your system may react badly or unusually. Always provide a record of any medication you're currently taking.

● **Preparation counts.** Try to find out what questions you'll be asked. Plan your answers and obtain records to back up your statements. Try not to forget anything—if the insurance company thinks you're withholding information, you may be rejected.

● **If you've just gotten over a cold or are feeling tired,** you won't test well, so it's smart to reschedule the exam. Once you've been turned down for a medical reason, an insurance company will rarely reconsider.

Beyond the Physical

Apart from passing the insurance physical, there are other things you can do to get coverage. Undergo regular physicals and keep records of the results. Underwriters can be swayed by evidence that you've controlled a chronic condition such as hypertension or diabetes.

Shop around. High-risk insurance candidates are renowned for frequently failing to shop enough.

If you've already been rated and assigned to an expensive, high-risk premium category, don't give up. Ratings can be reversed. For example, three years after a cancer operation, you could legitimately receive a removal of a rating that imposes a surcharge of $15 per $1,000 of coverage. New information, actuarial studies and correcting simple errors may make it possible to reduce your premiums over time.

Remember, if you face special risks, don't apply for insurance in the usual manner. Know what your options are, keep records, be patient and never take no for an answer.

Source: Benjamin Lipson, president of Benjamin Lipson Associates Insurance Agency, Inc., 7 Bulfinch Pl., Boston, MA 02114. Mr. Lipson is an independent insurance broker specializing in insurance for people with medical problems. He is also the author of How to Collect More on Your Insurance Claims and writes a weekly newspaper column.

The "Econolife" plan from London Life is one of the better-known programs of this kind in Canada. Under this plan, dividends are used to buy an additional death benefit that is a combination of permanent and term insurance. Other companies offer similar programs under their own trademark.

Universal Life

In the late 1970s, in response to high interest rates, some insurance companies began offering universal life insurance—a flexible premium insurance plan that combines term insurance with a separate investment fund often tied to short-term interest rates but which may offer a range of other investment options, including mutual funds, GICs and index-related securities. A prime feature of universal policies is that premium payments are optional. Like whole life policies, earnings on the cash reserve portion of a policy are tax-deferred and the proceeds of the investment portion are paid out tax-free at death. However, there are limits on how much you can shelter from tax in this way, in the same way as the government limits RRSP contributions.

Although policy owners may find the flexibility of universal life insurance convenient, there can be problems. The ability to reduce or even stop premiums may be too tempting and may override your commitment to your insurance program's future. Another potential problem is that the short-term investments that back many universal life products make them vulnerable to major investment or interest rate changes.

How do you compare whole life, economatic and universal life products? The flexibility available with an economatic policy may make it more attractive than whole life insurance. Because of its emphasis on long-term investments, the economatic policy also may be a better choice than universal life. However, for careful policy owners, universal life may be preferable because it permits skipping a premium or paying a lower premium than originally planned.

Variable Life

For policy owners who want to control how their cash values are invested, some companies now offer variable life insurance. It has a fixed annual premium, and you can borrow against a policy.

The unique feature of variable life is that part of your premium is invested in an investment pool of your choice. The pool can be a money-market fund, a stock fund, a bond fund or a managed combination of the three. These are known in Canada as segregated funds. Some companies will let you invest part of your premium in each, and switch among funds.

If your investment pool fares well, the cash value and pure insurance value of your policy will increase. If your investments don't fare well, neither will your cash value, although your insurance benefit will never drop below its initial value.

Source: Mark J. Lucius, advertising and corporate information officer for Northwestern Mutual Life Insurance Company, 720 E. Wisconsin Ave., Milwaukee, WI 53202.

Understanding Term Insurance

Term insurance is usually the least expensive form of insurance to get for a maximum of five years. *The choices:*

● **Yearly renewable term.** The rates start low and rise annually as your age (which increases the risk) goes up. Choose this policy if you're in a short-term venture (for example, a construction project or a short-term contract).

● **Five- and 10-year term insurance.** Appropriate for a person starting a high-risk or highly leveraged business, when the bank may insist that the entrepreneur's life be covered by a large policy for a specified period of time. The premium is averaged out on an annual basis over the life of the policy.

● **Yearly renewable term policy with a reversion to lower premiums on evidence of insurability.** This is a recent development. At a specified time (usually after four or five years), if you pass a medical exam, the premiums can be reduced by perhaps 35% of what they might have been. *Example:* If your insurance premium starts at $1,000 a year and climbs $200 annually, you must pass an exam during the fifth year to get the premium lowered to $1,200.

Potential problem: Bad health at examination will negate the possibility of lowering the premium.

● **Avoid term insurance even for the short haul if you are almost 70 years old.** Since the risk at that age is so high, the point at which the term and straight-premium rates would cross would be attained within five years. At that point, a permanent (or straight) life policy is best.

● **If you need life insurance for more than five years, permanent insurance is usually best.** The reason for this is that the total acquisition price usually evens out over a period of 10 years. If you are relatively young, say in your thirties, the cash value of the policy may increase at a greater rate than the premium after the third year. The straight-life policyholder may borrow on the cash value at a low rate of interest.

Alternative: Some creative insurance agents combine the two types of coverage, thus lowering premium costs and ensuring cash value.

Source: *Leon Sicular, president, Leon H. Sicular Associates, New York, NY.*

News About Life Insurance Replacement

People who hold old cash-value life insurance policies are being urged to replace them with new policies with higher returns. Although such substitutions make financial sense in some situations, in other cases the client stands to lose.

Best-case scenario: The client who changes saves up to 25% on premium costs.

Drawback: Since the client's buying a new policy, he or she has to pay the acquisition cost—which often amounts to as much as one year's premium.

People buy cash-value life insurance for two reasons, one of which usually takes precedence:

● **Permanent insurance protection.** If this is your primary reason for owning a policy, you may

BORROWING FROM YOUR LIFE INSURANCE POLICY

Is your life insurance policy a good source of readily available funds? When should you consider borrowing from it?

The rate at which you can borrow from your life insurance policy depends primarily on when you bought it. If your policy dates back to the 1970s or earlier, you may be able to borrow at 5% or 6%. Newer policies generally have 8% loan provisions. If you've purchased a policy in the early 1980s, your policy may have either an 8% loan provision or a "variable loan rate." The latter means that the rate at which you can borrow varies and is pegged to an index such as Moody's Corporate Bond Index. Newer policies may not specify a fixed loan rate so check with your agent.

One certainty is that, regardless of the rate at which you can borrow, policy loans are somewhat more expensive than they used to be.

Despite this, borrowing from a life insurance policy is still less complicated than most other borrowing. You can borrow from your policy without delay— and without the approval of a bank officer.

However, because the cash accumulation inside a life insurance policy is tax-deferred, and depending on your tax bracket, you may find that you are better off borrowing from a bank than borrowing from your policy. This is particularly true when interest rates are low. Borrowing from a life insur-

ance policy at 8% is convenient, but may prove more costly in the long run. Why? You may find that borrowing from your policy affects the dividends you receive from your life insurance company. If you have a "participating" life insurance policy— one that pays dividends—talk to your agent or life insurance company before borrowing. If dividends are calculated by a technique called "direct recognition," you may get higher dividends and greater tax-deferred cash accumulation if you don't borrow from your policy.

Source: *Mark J. Lucius, advertising and corporate information officer for Northwestern Mutual Life Insurance Company, 720 E. Wisconsin Ave., Milwaukee, WI 53202.*

come out ahead by switching. Even though you're buying insurance at an older age (which carries a higher premium base), new actuarial tables could lower your actual premium layout.

● **Accumulation of capital.** If this is your primary reason for owning coverage, you may lose in a replacement. Usually you do better by negotiating a conversion of your existing policy to a higher rate of return than by paying a second set of acquisition costs. *Example:* Most insurers will raise your interest to the current T-bill rate if you agree to pay them the market rate for loans.

Important: Your math must be correct, and so must your reason for buying the insurance.

What to Do

Without a detailed financial and actuarial analysis, it's impossible to predict whether a replacement is prudent. There's no rule of thumb, since companies have reacted to the rash of replacements with incentives (such as higher dividends on old policies, premium discounts on new insurance and even free insurance for up to 10 years) for customers who keep their original policies and agree to pay the market rate on loans.

Insurance brokers should not make a replacement without first conducting a full analysis, submitting substantiating evidence to the insurance company and having the client sign a statement verifying that he or she saw all the data before making the decision.

If, without making an analysis, your broker categorically tells you a replacement is good for you, he or she is acting in his or her best interest, not yours. On the other hand, if your broker suggests doing the analysis to find out whether you can gain, he or she is acting on your behalf.

Source: Arthur Schechner, chairman, Schechner Lifson Corp., insurance agents and brokers, Millburn, NJ.

Understanding Deferred Annuities

Annuities have been offered by insurance companies for many years, but many people don't understand how they work or how to use them effectively. This is especially true of deferred annuities. These are simply the life insurance industry's equivalent of a guaranteed investment certificate (GIC). The primary difference from an ordinary GIC that you'd buy from a bank or trust company is that with a deferred annuity, the proceeds from the plan must be used to purchase an annuity (or be redeemed) by a specific date. This may be a specific number of years, or may relate to the investor's age.

There are also some other differences from an ordinary GIC of which you should be aware.

● **Beneficiary.** You can designate a beneficiary for a deferred annuity, who will continue to receive payments if you die. This is not so with regular GICs.

● **Pension tax credit.** Income from a deferred annuity is eligible for the pension tax credit. Ordinary GIC interest is not.

● **Creditor protection.** If the beneficiary of the deferred annuity is your spouse, a child or a parent, creditors cannot make a claim against the invested principal. They can go after payments made to you.

● **Liquidity.** Most deferred annuities can be redeemed prior to maturity. Ask the company with which you're dealing about its policy in this regard. In most, but not all, cases, bank and trust company GICs cannot be cashed before maturity.

● **Security.** GICs from banks and trust companies are protected by deposit insurance up to $60,000, as long as the term does not exceed five years. Life insurance companies are not members of the Canada Deposit Insurance Corporation. However, they have their own insurance fund, CompCorp, which protects deferred annuities to the same dollar limit as deposit insurance. There is no maximum term.

A deferred annuity enables you to lock in your interest rate when rates are high, but to delay receiving payments until you need them. So you can go shopping for an annuity several years before you actually expect to draw the money. This is an important advantage which allows you to set up the maximum possible income flow from your annuity.

The level of interest rates is an extremely important factor in buying an annuity. If you lock in for a long term when rates are low, you'll end up sacrificing thousands of dollars in retirement income.

So time your annuity purchases for maximum return. If interest rates are low when you're shopping, postpone the decision.

Source: Retiring Wealthy in the 21st Century, *by Gordon Pape, published by Prentice Hall Canada.*

Profit From Life Insurance

It's possible to get a tax break by donating a paid-up life insurance policy to charity.

Key: Your contribution will be valued at the policy's cash value at the time of the donation, and you will receive a charitable receipt for that amount that can be claimed on your next tax return. If the policy has been in existence for a long time, the cash value may be significant, resulting in a large tax deduction.

Trap: There are limits to the amount of charitable donations you can claim in a given year, based on your income. Make sure that your claim is within those limits.

Source: *Gordon Pape, author of* 6 Steps to $1 Million, *published by Prentice Hall Canada.*

How to Collect Claims From Insurance Companies

In many situations, you can negotiate successfully with an insurance company without retaining a lawyer. It is important to know when to negotiate yourself and how to negotiate effectively.

Where to start:

● **Your insurance agent,** if he or she is not an employee of the insurer, should be the first line of inquiry. An independent agent is better able to assist in obtaining the full amount to which you are entitled. A good relationship with clients keeps an agent in business.

He or she will often present your claim, negotiate it and obtain a satisfactory settlement for you without charge. An agent is especially valuable on smaller claims. Also, if you negotiate yourself, he or she can be a major source of information and advice.

Should you hire a lawyer?

● **The major deciding factor is economics.** On small claims, a lawyer's fee might be prohibitive, but on larger claims you could lose money by negotiating with an insurance company yourself.

In some cases, you might simply pay a flat fee for the attorney's review of your claim. Initial consultation will usually provide you with helpful information and assist the attorney in deciding whether or not it will pay for him or her to take your case.

Other considerations:

● **Subjective factors.** If you don't feel comfortable retaining a lawyer, go it alone.

● **No-fault versus at-fault jurisdictions.** Negotiating your own claim makes a lot more sense in a no-fault jurisdiction, where the insurance company is bound by law to reimburse you for your losses. But even in a no-fault province, or if you don't apply in time for all of the benefits to which you were entitled, your claim may not be honored if the forms are presented incorrectly.

● **Language.** Understanding the convoluted terminology used in insurance policies and law is a major stumbling block for the layperson. To negotiate successfully, you must be comfortable with the language.

● **Reputation.** Some insurance companies deal fairly and quickly. Others are notoriously difficult and slow. Ask your insurance agent or a negligence attorney about the company you are dealing with. You may need legal help to negotiate a favorable settlement with a difficult company.

● **Pain and suffering.** When multiples of out-of-pocket expenses are involved due to pain and suffering, it is best to hire a lawyer. Lawyers can point out losses you have not even thought of. Also, the insurance company will take into account what you are saving by not hiring a lawyer and offer you less.

If you go it alone:

● **Read the policy very carefully.** Pay special attention to exclusions and coverages. Before presenting your claim, take a close look at the policy. Make sure you're presenting it in a way that makes it evident that your claim is covered. (If you can't find your policy, the insurer is obligated to give you a copy.)

● **Document everything completely.** It is the most important part of an insurance claim. Support every aspect of your claim, including medical bills, receipts for medicines, transportation for medical reasons and a letter from your employer stating lost wages. Think of everything. Witnessing an injury to a loved one may cause compensable emotional trauma. A husband or wife may recover for the lost services and companionship of his or her injured spouse.

> " Claims for bodily injury can be the most complicated and negotiable, especially when based upon pain and suffering. "

● **Find out what your claim is worth.** Consult with your insurance agent or a negligence lawyer to determine what a reasonable offer would be in your circumstances.

● **Be prepared to take a discount.** There has to be a motivation for the insurer to settle a claim. One advantage of negotiating without a lawyer is that a quick settlement may be offered to avoid legal expenses. So decide what amount you are willing to settle for. The settlement offer will depend on various factors, including clarity, proof of coverage, damages, documentation, how likely you are to prevail at trial and the caseload of the court in which you would have to sue. (Some insurers offer nothing until the trial date.)

Bodily injury:

Claims for bodily injury can be the most complicated and negotiable, especially when based upon pain and suffering.

● **In a no-fault jurisdiction,** which applies in most of Canada, there are limits on your ability to see damages through the courts. However, lawsuits are permitted everywhere except Manitoba and Quebec, according to the Insurance Bureau of Canada (IBC). In Saskatchewan, you may recover only with respect to gross income losses that exceed a specified amount. In Ontario, your ability to sue for loss of income is subject to conditions: you can sue for medical, rehabilitation and related costs only when injury is very serious (catastrophic, as defined by law).

You can sue for pain and suffering, except in Saskatchewan, Manitoba and Quebec, where such lawsuits are not permitted. Ontario allows suits only if the injured person "dies, or sustains permanent serious disfigurement and/or impairment of important physical, mental or psychological function" (the court assesses damages and a deductible applies). For more details, visit the IBC website at www.ibc.ca.

● **Don't miss damages.** Start at the top of your head and go down to your toes, to include every part that's been hurt.

● **Photograph your injury.** In addition to medical reports, photos are a good documentation of suffering.

● **Consider every aspect of your life affected by your injury.** Include your career, sports, hobbies, future interests and family relationships.

● **Ask what a lawyer would ask**—at least twice the actual expenses when there has been no permanent disability. Where liability is clear, the insurance company will be likely to give you what you ask, if they believe that you really had difficulties and were out of work for a few weeks. However, where there has been permanent disability, multiples of expenses do not apply. *Example:* Your medical bills for a lost eye might have been only $3,000, but a jury might award you 50 times that amount.

If you cannot reach a settlement: An insurance company has a fiduciary duty (a relationship based on trust, like that with your lawyer or stockbroker) to deal fairly and in good faith with its insured.

What to do if you are not treated well:

● **If you feel that the company** is either unreasonably delaying your claim or acting in bad faith, make a complaint to your provincial insurance regulatory agency. In many cases, the agency will write a letter to the company.

● **If your time is being wasted** by the insurance company's bureaucracy, the small claims court may be appropriate. Such action will pressure the company to settle with you more quickly on your terms.

Many provinces have laws penalizing an insurer for bad faith. If you feel the company has been acting in bad faith, you can initiate a lawsuit and possibly collect a multiple of your claim in punitive damages.

Source: *Dan Brecher, a New York attorney.*

What Insurance Companies Don't Tell You

Consider two houses, side by side, both destroyed in a disaster. One homeowner gets an $18,000 cheque from his insurance company to rent temporary housing. The other gets just $500 a month—and must haggle each month to get it.

Sound unlikely? As a supervisor, I saw this happen after the 1989 San Francisco earthquake. People who trusted their insurers to look out for them often received fewer and smaller benefits.

What you don't know about your homeowner's policy could permanently reduce your standard of living after a calamity. It could even cost you your home.

Rules for Insurance Self-Protection

● **Don't rely on fluffy language.** Regardless of how a policy is advertised, read the fine print of a homeowner's policy before you buy. Don't depend solely on your insurance agent. To wrap up the sale quickly, he or she has an incentive to sell you something basic and cheap.

● **Read your policy now.** If you aren't sure what your policy covers, if something isn't absolutely clear, have your insurer or agent explain it and confirm the conversation in writing.

● **Don't expect the insurer to put you first if disaster strikes.** If the company had known you were going to have a loss, it would never have written a policy on you.

How to Buy the Protection You Need

● **Buy coverage to restore your home** exactly as it was before the disaster. This is the "face value" of the policy. Coverage for other possessions, such as furnishings and landscaping, are usually expressed as a percentage of the replacement cost.

The cost of restoration has nothing to do with the price you paid for the home.

Key question: What would it cost to exactly reproduce this dwelling on this property?

Answer: Only an expert contractor can tell you. Invest $150 or so to get an estimate.

● **Tailor the insurance to your own home.** Insurance companies like to base their payments on the cost of modern, tract-house-style construction. Your home—especially if it is older—could have more costly features, like lathe-and-plaster instead of sheetrock walls. *Strategy:* Buy a policy that provides "Guaranteed Replacement Cost" (GRC) coverage. This will pay the cost to replace your dwelling regardless of the "face value." *Helpful:* Some policies that claim to be GRC have a limit usually expressed as a percentage of the face value. Even if the policy has GRC on the dwelling, the other coverages that are expressed as a percentage are usually a percentage of the face amount, not the actual replacement cost.

● **Don't neglect "code and ordinance or law" coverage.** After Hurricane Andrew, many Florida homes had to be elevated 13 feet—or they couldn't be rebuilt. After the San Francisco quake, new homes in the area had to have much stronger foundations.

Homeowners without this additional protection had to pay those extra costs themselves. The cost of code protection is about 10% of the annual premium.

● **Know what replacement cost means.** While your coverage may say "full replacement cost," you must complete the replacement to collect.

If you can't—because you can't afford to elevate the home or build that new foundation—you might collect only the "actual cash value" of the lost home, which might be one-third less.

● **Your possessions.** Make sure your furnishings and possessions are covered for replacement cost, not current value. A used sofa is worth half its replacement cost, at best—but you won't replace it with used merchandise.

Most policies cover the contents of a home only up to 50% or so of the face amount. If your possessions are worth more than that, pay around $1.50 per each $1,000 of coverage per year.

● **Your valuables.** If you have artwork, collections, antiques or other valuable personal property, study the "limits of coverage" section of your policy to see how much of the value of lost or destroyed valuables the insurer will pay.

Consider a "floater" to provide supplemental coverage. It will cost about $0.25 to $2.50 for each $100 of coverage.

● **Know about "other structures."** Structures separated from your dwelling are covered separately in your homeowner's policy—usually for 10% of the "face value" amount. But what about attached decks and patios? Are they considered other structures, or are they included in the face amount?

Any kind of structure that is "attached" to the dwelling should be included in the face value, but be sure to clear this up at the time of purchase.

● **Take inflation into account.** Construction costs rise every year. So do the costs of replacing your furniture, snowblower, kitchen appliances, etc. Unless you have replacement value coverage, make sure the policies covering contents—as well as the dwelling itself—are protected with a rider that raises coverage periodically to reflect rising costs.

● **Buy all the liability coverage you need.** Standard policies provide some protection in the event your neighbor trips over your sprinkler and breaks his leg. But consider "umbrella" coverage, which unifies liability under all your policies—house, car and boat.

Umbrella policies often cover hazards that homeowner's insurance does not, such as a claim of slander when your neighbor doesn't like what you said about him or her. You would pay about $100 a year for $1 million of umbrella coverage.

● **Protect yourself in case of disaster.** Make sure the policy will pay all expenses necessary to maintain your standard of living for as long as necessary, while your home is being restored.

Important: Avoid coverage of "actual incurred costs." That will skimp on paying for temporary quarters and force you to argue with your insurer over every receipt.

● **Don't be penny-wise/pound-foolish.** The best coverage doesn't necessarily cost more. In fact, insurance companies price their best policies very competitively because "better" customers are good prospects for the companies' other products.

INSURANCE TRAPS: BUYERS, BEWARE

Don't buy life insurance from television or mail-order advertisements. No matter how much you trust their paid shills, it is a rip-off.

Serious drawbacks: These companies accept anyone who applies—no matter how high the risk—and charge a monthly fee about twice what other insurers charge per $1,000 of life insurance coverage.

Major trap: You don't receive any coverage until you've made at least two years of monthly payments. If you die before that, your estate receives only the premiums you've paid—without interest. *Much ado about very little:* One of the policies we reviewed paid out only $1,900 after two years. After age 55, the payout dropped annually. *Example:* If the insured dies between the ages of 75 and 80, the estate receives only $200. *Exception:* Some university alumni insurance programs are less expensive and are legitimate.

Source: Robert Hunter, head, Consumer Federation of America, 1424 16 St. NW, Washington, DC 22207.

● **Don't just buy a policy and forget it.** Every few years review your coverage to make sure it still meets your needs. And then shop around to make sure you're still getting the best price. *Helpful:* Start with your current agent. He or she may be willing to improve your coverage—and trim the price—if he or she fears losing the annual commission.

Source: Ina De Long, executive director of United Policyholders, a nonprofit group devoted to consumer education on insurance. Box 2071, Merced, CA 95344.

Your Life Insurance Is Protected From the CCRA

Good news. In the United States, the cash surrender value of a life insurance policy is subject to a lien by the Internal Revenue Service for unpaid taxes. But that's not the case in Canada. Insurance contracts of any type are creditor-proof in this country, and that protection extends to the CCRA. The tax people will have to look elsewhere to satisfy any claims.

What to Do When Your Insurance Company Says No

North Americans spend billions of dollars on health and life insurance every year to protect against financial ruin in case of a serious illness in the family or the death of a family breadwinner.

But when we file insurance claims at times of crisis, it can feel like a betrayal of life-threatening proportions when an insurer is slow to respond, refuses to pay a claim or digs in its heels when challenged. Here are the best ways to ensure your claims are paid the first time through—and what to do if your claim is denied.

Before You Make a Claim

● **Tell the truth on all insurance applications.** Many health-insurance policies have a contestability clause, which allows the company to rescind the policy at any time if it discovers a "material misstatement" on the application. *Examples:* Omitting an existing medical condition, understating the severity of a condition.

The insurer may not review your application until after you file a claim, even if you have been paying premiums for years. If a misstatement is discovered, you could lose benefits at the very time you need them the most.

Self-defense: Don't leave out information you consider unimportant or fear will result in your application being turned down. *Example:* High blood pressure. Your position is far stronger if the insurer sees evidence of your truthfulness.

● **Ask which percentile your health insurance company uses** to determine "reasonable and customary charges." Most extended-care health insurance policies agree to pay a percentage of the "reasonable and customary" fees for medical services. Insurers calculate what is reasonable and customary in each area of the country, sometimes even by postal code, by various fees, then limiting their coverage to the 70th, 80th or 90th percentile. *Result:* The same procedure or service may be covered for a different amount, depending on your carrier. But the fees the insurer has decided are reasonable and customary may not be representative of *your* own experience.

● **Have expensive procedures and fees preapproved.** This can be especially important for things like pricey dental services, such as bridges and braces. Whenever possible, ask your practitioner for an advance estimate, have the procedure preapproved by the insurer—and ask how much it will pay.

● **Negotiate with your practitioner.** Often, they will agree to perform services for the amount your insurer will cover, if it's not already covered by your provincial health care program. It is also not unusual to "negotiate" with dentists and other practitioners on fees. Here your agent could be very helpful.

If Your Claim Is Refused

● **Don't panic—your first round with an insurance company need not be final.** Here are the major reasons an insurer may deny a claim and what you can do about it. *If the insurer says:*

"This procedure/condition isn't covered."

● **Read your policy and/or descriptive booklet carefully.** Enlist the help of the agent who sold you the policy or your company-benefits manager.

● **Get a letter from your dentist or other health care professional** explaining what he or she did and why it should be covered. If the practitioner feels the procedure is covered based on your policy booklet, often a letter is sufficient.

"This procedure/condition isn't covered because it is considered experimental."

● **More and more insurers are willing to negotiate on this point,** with the result that many procedures once considered experimental are now fully or partially covered. *Examples:* Bone-marrow transplants, liver transplants, some fertilization procedures.

● **If your problem is chronic,** let the insurer know of the future claims for medication and treatment for which it will be liable for the rest of your life if it doesn't pay for the procedure. Clearly demonstrate to the insurer it is in its long-term interest to try something new, even if it is a long shot.

"We'll only pay a portion of your fees."

● **Ask your health care professional to clarify which procedure was done.** It is possible the code for the procedure that was performed does not accurately describe your case. *Example:* A dental procedure that should have taken 20 minutes took several hours because complications set in.

● **Ask your health care professional to write the insurer as to why the fee is reasonable and customary.**

● **Have your health care professional submit the appropriate reports to the governing body of his or her profession for peer review.** If he or she refuses, you know that the fee is out of line.

Virtually every insurer will accept the verdict of a peer review committee. Often, the finding is that the practitioner has overcharged. In the unlikely event a committee says the insurer should pay less than it agreed to, insurers will generally stick to the amount originally promised.

If Your Claim Is Contested

Most life insurance claims are paid automatically. But insurance companies occasionally investigate some claims. Reasons:

● **Suicide.** In the event there is a question, insurers will generally rely on police reports.

● **Misrepresentation of age.** If the deceased has claimed to be younger in order to qualify for lower insurance rates, insurers will prorate the claim.

● **Misrepresentation of smoking.** The insurer must have evidence to suspect a policyholder was a smoker at the time of application. If you are a smoker, you should tell the insurance company at the time of the application. If you don't provide this information, the insurance company can generally rescind the policy at any time—even after death.

● **Accidental death.** If the policyholder was insured for an accidental death benefit, or double indemnity, the insurer may investigate an ambiguous cause of death. *Example:* Did the deceased have a heart attack, then drive into a tree—in which case the heart attack was the cause of death and the insurer is not liable for the double benefit—or did the crash cause the heart attack, in which case the insurer must pay up? In this case, the family will have to rely on medical reports to support their claim.

Source: Sam E. Beller, CLU, ChFC, president of Diversified Programs, Inc., an insurance sales organization based in New York City. He is the author of The Great Insurance Secret, *William Morrow & Co.*

What You Need to Know About Viatical Settlements

We should begin our discussion of viaticals with a warning: Viatical settlements are currently illegal under provincial insurance legislation in many Canadian provinces. If the concept is of interest to you, check with your agent or insurance company to see if it is an option where you live.

The term "viatical" is derived from the Christian doctrine of viatica, the administering of the Eucharist to a person near death. The practice became prevalent in the United States with the increase of deaths due to AIDS, but has moved beyond that to now include any person nearing death who wants cash from a life policy.

Viatical settlements offer a potentially important financial option to individuals facing a life-threatening illness. Where they are legal, viatical settlements are business transactions whereby the beneficiary's interest in a life insurance policy is transferred to a third-party investor, called the viatical settlement provider. In exchange, the seller of the policy (called a viator) will receive a discounted cash settlement.

In the United States, individuals who have a life insurance policy can sell all or part of the policy for

> " [When applying for insurance,] don't leave out information you consider unimportant or fear will result in your application being turned down. *Example:* High blood pressure. "

immediate cash, with no restrictions on how they use the money. Most insurance policies qualify. The money to purchase the policy comes from investors (corporate or individual) who expect a rate of return based upon many factors, most significantly the insured's remaining life expectancy. Not only are viatical settlements an excellent opportunity for financial growth for the investor, they can also provide the insured with the freedom to live the remainder of their lives with more dignity and fewer financial concerns.

Let's look at a simple example. John Doe owns a life insurance policy of $100,000 from BigLife Corp. Upon becoming terminally ill, John agrees to sell the policy to Mrs. Mary Smith for 75% of the policy's face amount. Mrs. Mary Smith pays Mr. Doe $75,000, becoming the owner of the policy, and takes over premium payments on the policy. Upon Mr. Doe's death, BigLife Corp. pays Mrs. Smith the $100,000 face value of the policy.

Under a viatical settlement, the purchaser pays the premiums on the purchased insurance policy and the viatical settlement provider, or its agent, maintains contact with the viator to monitor their medical condition. Upon the death of the viator, the insurance company will pay the insurance proceeds directly to the new beneficiary.

While this whole issue strikes some as morbid, it is important to recognize the financial and emotional benefits that will accrue to the insured having funds to see them through their illness.

Source: G. Pierce Newman, coauthor of Fiscal Fitness, *published by Prentice Hall Canada. This article originally appeared on 50Plus.com, the official site of Canada's Association for the Fifty-Plus (CARP). The website is www.50plus.com.*

The Best Buys in Health Insurance

Finding the absolutely best deal in supplementary health insurance would probably require a company-by-company and policy-by-policy search. To avoid spending most of your free time for the next several months doing that kind of research, try following a few general rules to help keep costs down without sacrificing coverage.

The first rule: If buying private health insurance individually, get only the coverage you need. For example, there is no point in paying high premiums for eye care if no one in your family wears glasses.

● **The second way to contain costs is through group insurance.** Most employers offer some form of group insurance at a cost that may be 20%–40% less than individual coverage. You usually don't have to take a physical, and coverage stays in force until you leave the company.

The number of employees in the group will determine the most inexpensive type of coverage. If more than 100 employees are involved, self-insuring may provide substantial savings. The one problem with this type of approach is the risk of a large claim during the first few years of the plan, before a sufficient reserve has accumulated. However, the company may be willing to assume this risk or to obtain regular group coverage during the accumulation period.

● **Group underwriting offers another way of cost cutting through shared funding.** The employer, employee and insurance company share in the losses up to a predetermined limit, say $10,000 per individual. After the limit is reached, the insurance company assumes full responsibility up to the limits of the policy. The split among the three parties is determined on an actuarial basis. Under either a self-insurance plan or a shared-funding plan, you must calculate in advance whether there are true cash-flow gains or whether the payments have simply been deferred to the end of the contract year.

● **Another cost-containment strategy for group health plans is precertification.** Under a precertification contract, employees must obtain authorization for prospective expensive treatments in order to be reimbursed. Prior to any procedure, the employee submits a detailed plan from the health care professional to the company outlining the procedures to be undertaken and the estimated costs. Any expenses incurred without approval, except emergency procedures, are not covered by the policy.

Editor's note: Yet another cost-containment strategy for group health plans of small employers and self-employed individuals is using high deductible plans.

● **Some insurance companies seek to reduce costs and lower premiums** by requiring second opinions before any major treatment. Although the second professional's appointment may increase the up-front costs, the reduction in unnecessary procedures more than offsets it. These savings may be in the form of reduced premiums for individual as well as group plans.

● **A final trend toward lower costs in group health insurance** is restricted access for employee dependents. Many companies are offering insurance only to their employees, requiring substantial if not total contribution for any benefits to the employees' families. The result is a reduction in premiums for the company, but the plan may not be the best one for you, depending upon your family's needs.

Source: Karen P. Schaeffer, president, Schaeffer Financial, 7855 Walker Dr., Greenbelt, MD 20770, a financial-planning firm affiliated with Hibbard Brown & Co.

Collecting More on Your Company Health Policy

Health insurance policies are not etched in stone. There are contractual provisions in the insurance policy that are negotiable. Most companies give health insurance to engender goodwill among employees. Many problems in collecting the maximum due you are a result of incompetence or of negligence on the part of the administrators in your company who handle insurance benefits. They may be too busy or unaware of how to get more for you. *Three ways to improve your ability to collect:*

● **Know the insurance contract and all its provisions.** Be aware that everything is negotiable. *Example:* Home health care by someone other than a registered nurse or practical nurse is not covered in the policy. Contractually nothing needs to be said, but administratively an alternate source of home health care could be covered. It is a question of negotiation.

● **Have the company's insurance broker help negotiate with the insurer.** The broker is the one who is making the money from selling your company the policy. He or she also has more leverage than you do with the insurance company. If he or she is unwilling to help, encourage your company to switch to a more cooperative broker.

● **Set up a liaison.** The individual in your company in charge of claims should have a good working relationship with the insurance company. If a settlement is too low or doesn't fully cover your needs, the claims person at your firm can make a better settlement. After all, the insurance company is selling policies.

If your claims person is uncertain whether you can get more compensation for a treatment, ask to contact the broker. The broker should know the terms of your contract and be familiar with the people at the insurance company. He or she should have an idea of how to get the claim paid.

Unallowable Treatments

Trying to make specifically unallowable treatments allowable: This is between the health care professional and you. *Example:* If you want to claim an experimental procedure not covered by provincial health care but that could prolong your life or improve its quality, convince your doctor to help you. If he or she won't help, you are not going to get anywhere with the insurance broker, the personnel at your office or the insurance company.

If you're stuck with a flawed company policy and have huge deductibles and other uncovered expenses, take out a personal policy that coordinates with the company's.

Source: *Leonard Stern, president, Leonard B. Stern & Co., an insurance consulting and brokerage firm, New York, NY.*

Buy the Right Protection

If you are among the millions of North Americans who do not receive health coverage at work, it is still possible to find a great health insurance policy. There are even options for people who are dissatisfied with the coverage they receive from their employers. *Here are the most important questions people are asking me now:*

When Employees Need More Insurance

Even if you have an extended health care plan at work, you may need additional coverage.

Here are some of the most common questions asked by employees when considering adding a personal plan to their employer benefit.

● **I have a plan through my job. Shouldn't that be enough?** If it's a good one, yes it should. But check it out and know what is included. The plan's efficacy depends on the agreement your employer has struck with the insurer and how many benefits are included in the package. A small employer, or a cheap plan, might not offer as many benefits as you would want.

The downside to plans from work is that they are dependent on your employment and are not portable. A private plan is yours if you pay the premiums.

● **Where do I start looking for private insurance?** To get an idea of the full range of companies out there, look in the Yellow Pages under "Insurance—Life and Health." If you want detailed information to get you started, watch for pamphlets at pharmacies. Some companies arrange to have them displayed in drugstores, and have probably paid a fee to do so. Don't take the display to be an endorsement by your pharmacist. If you have access, look on the Internet. Some quick comparisons can be made of larger companies with websites. Some insurers will even allow you to apply for insurance by e-mail. If you have an insurance broker or agent, ask if he or she carries health insurance, remembering that brokers and agents do not necessarily cover every company's products.

You may also buy health coverage through a professional organization or other group to which you belong, and take advantage of a group rate.

● **How do I decide what I need?** Weigh the options and consider your needs, both today and in the future. Do you wear glasses? Does anyone in your family? Does your family history indicate that you likely will? If so, you might want to consider a plan that includes coverage for eyewear. Do you plan on having children? That almost guarantees a hospital stay. Would you want a semiprivate room? Do you have children who might need regular dental work? Could you afford to pay for it yourself? Do you have a condition that requires regular or expensive medication? Can you afford the cost of that? Will your health insurance company cover drugs for a preexisting condition? For example, if you are diabetic and require insulin, your condition would be taken into account in the underwriting process. Will the company cover your medication and any further complications? You will also have to decide how much you can afford in premiums.

● **Are there bells and whistles?** Yes, to a degree. Some companies offer newsletters with tips on how to maintain good health. The same type of information is available for free in some pharmacies. Other companies provide access to a telephone helpline staffed by nurses offering medical information. Again, some pharmacies offer similar services. You could also purchase insurance that would give you cash should you be hospitalized. This covers personal expenses that are tough to avoid while you are in hospital—the forgotten toothbrush, your favorite soap, television or telephone rentals.

● **Can I buy health insurance like I would buy a pair of shoes, or must I apply for it?** Despite what some advertisements and brochures say, you must apply for health insurance. A lot of promotional material will have you think that after filling out a brief form and sending in a cheque, you're covered. Not so. The fine print will tell you that what you have filled out is not a contract, and that a policy will be issued after your application is approved.

● **Will I have to undergo a medical examination?** Generally, no. Unlike life and disability insurance, health insurance tends to have fairly strict limits on what is covered and for how much money. You either have a prescription for medication or you don't. The drug is either covered or it's not. You are either in a semiprivate hospital room or a ward. There are fewer gray areas. Completing a medical questionnaire is usually all that's required of you and, for some policies, you may not have to fill out a medical form at all.

● **Is there any way to cut the cost?** Check out any associations in which you have a membership. Sometimes university alumni associations, unions or professional clubs arrange to have group insurance available for members. The price might be lower, although the plan might not be what you were after.

● **Take care of yourself.** The fewer ailments you have, the better the risk you are and the lower the price you will be charged for coverage.

Something to Tide You Over

Temporary health insurance is available for periods when you're between jobs, starting a new business, etc. Policies are sold for specific periods of 30 to 180 days and are generally renewable only once. Most don't cover pregnancy or preexisting disabilities. Rates are low.

● **Check out companies that offer choices in plans.** You may be able to pick the services you want without having to pay for those you are less likely to use to the max. You may need help with dental care but not need drug benefits, for instance.

Source: The Insurance Book, *by Sally Prasky and Helena Moncrieff, published by Prentice Hall Canada. Sally Prasky is editor of the Insurance Canada website, located at www.insurance-canada.ca.*

Health Plans for the Self-Employed

Extended health care plans are available for the self-employed, but be prepared to pay a price for the coverage. Like many products, when you buy in bulk, you save money; when you purchase single units, it costs more. So you won't be able to buy as much as a large employer does at the same cost. Rates range from about $25 to $100 a month, depending on your age and the plan you purchase. Generally, the older the applicant, the higher the prices. Basic drug plans are available at the lower end of the scale, with plans combining drugs, dental, vision, extended health care, travel coverage, and accidental death and dismemberment at the higher end of the price range. For some categories, monthly premiums charged to seniors are higher, but so are some of the benefits.

In addition, some insurers offer à-la-carte service for other coverage you may wish to add on or buy separately. For instance, you may not need ongoing benefits like drug, dental, and vision care, but you would like an extended health care package to cover you in the event of a health catastrophe.

The key phrase in most of these packages is "some conditions apply." The conditions may not allow you to get what you need, and at a price you can afford. On the other hand, it might be better than no coverage at all. You must weigh the risks of developing a health problem with your ability to pay for care.

Source: The Insurance Book: What Canadians Really Need to Know Before Buying Insurance, *by Sally Praskey and Helena Moncrieff, published by Prentice Hall Canada.*

Provincial Health Care: What It Doesn't Cover

Don't think that all your medical needs will be taken care of by your government health care program. These program are riddled with coverage gaps, which will vary from province to province.

Major problems with government plans:

The following exclusions relate to the Ontario Health Insurance Plan (OHIP). Other programs may differ in some details, so consult the provincial ministry (usually the Department of Health) for details in your area.

● **Certain physicians' services.** Not everything your doctor does is paid for by the government. Physicians may bill you for such services as transferring files to another doctor, telephone consultations, certificates of fitness to work, physical examinations for schools or camps and missed-appointment fees.

● **Cosmetic surgery.** Normally not covered unless required as the result of an accident.

● **Fertilization treatments.** These can be very expensive and are not covered by OHIP.

● **Experimental procedures.** Some are covered by provincial health care, but many are not.

● **Podiatrists, chiropractors and osteopaths.** Services provided by these health care providers are only partially covered. You must pay for the rest.

● **Dental care.** Most dental services are not covered. OHIP only pays for some dental surgery, including fractures or medically necessary jaw reconstruction, when done in hospital. *Exception:* The Children in Need of Treatment program (CINOT).

● **Eye care.** OHIP insures optometry services every two years for persons 20 to 64 and once a year for those under 20 and age 65 and over. More frequent checkups are at your expense, unless you have a condition that requires treatment. Glasses are not covered by provincial health care.

● **Prescription drugs.** Not covered, unless you are over 65, in which case many (but not all) are supplied free or at reduced cost.

● **Immunization for children.** Surprisingly, not all shots are covered. Sometimes the bureaucracy is slow in approving coverage for new vaccines. Check with your doctor.

● **Some diagnostic procedures.** Certain tests aren't covered by provincial plans.

● **Audiology services.** In a controversial decision, audiology tests were dropped from OHIP coverage in 2001, except under certain conditions.

● **Hospital accommodation in private or semiprivate rooms.**

● **Special equipment and services.** Things like wheelchairs and artificial limbs are not paid for by your public plan.

● **Long-term care services.** OHIP does not cover the cost of long-term care, either at home or in a facility, although it will pay for medical treatment received under such conditions within limits.

● **Costs incurred outside Canada.** Only a fraction of the actual expense may be covered. Be sure you have travel health insurance before leaving.

For more information on health care coverage, visit the website of your provincial plan. In Ontario, you'll find it at www.gov.on.ca/health/english/program/ohip/ohip_mn.html. For other provinces, go to the Ministry of Health site.

The Payment Process

For most services that are covered by provincial health care plans, payment is made directly to the health care provider. However, if you have to pay a charge that you believe is covered, such as an expense incurred outside Canada, you'll have to fill out an appropriate form and submit an itemized bill to your nearest provincial health care plan office. This should be done within six months of receiving treatment. With your bill, send:

● **Details of your treatment.**

● **Your original receipt for payment.**

● **Your name and current address.**

● **Your provincial health care plan number.**

If you expect to make an additional claim to a private supplementary health plan, include a letter asking for the return of the original receipts.

EXPLANATION of YOUR HEALTH PLAN

What to Consider Before Choosing a Nursing Home

Cost of nursing homes in your locale; whether the policy requires hospitalization before entering a home; the amount of the deductible; coverage for custodial care as well as for skilled care; the duration of coverage; inflation coverage; whether mental illnesses are included or excluded. A policy that excludes mental illness only if there is no organic cause still protects you in the event of Alzheimer's disease. The younger the insured, the lower the premiums.

Source: Norma Severns, former nurse practitioner and fee-based financial planner with Armstrong, Welch, and MacIntyre, 155 Connecticut Ave. NW, Washington, DC 20036.

Disability Insurance

Most people shy away from buying disability insurance because they think they'll never become disabled. Statistics show, however, that at age 37, you're three and a half times more likely to become disabled than to die, and that disability remains more likely than death until you're age 68. Many people suffer injury or illness severe enough to make them unable to work, but insufficiently serious to kill them.

Disability policies are among the most confusing to decipher. *Look for:*

● **Noncancelable by the company**—only by you.

● **Guaranteed continuable** until age 65–70 (75 is even better).

● **Restrictive riders** shouldn't be added by the company when the policy is issued. Look for the broadest coverage you can find.

● **Premium cost should be guaranteed not to rise before you reach 65.** *Trade-off:* Your coverage will remain flat, regardless of inflation. You can pay extra for a cost-of-living adjustment rider to pick up the slack.

● **Prompt processing of claims**—within 10 business days, unless the claim is complicated. (One otherwise good company processes claims through its zone managers. If a manager has a bad quarter with a lot of claims, there is a chance your claim might be held back and not processed until the following quarter.)

How Disability Is Defined

A useful definition of disability is "your inability to perform the material and substantial duties of your occupation." Under this definition, for example, an anesthesiologist who contracted hepatitis and could no longer practice had to change his profession to hospital administrator, and he was covered. He received $4,000 a month from the insurance company in addition to his regular salary.

Bad definition: One that deals with your inability to work—period. A policy like this won't protect you at all. (The definition used by Canada Pension Plan is the inability to perform any occupation.)

Injury versus sickness. Insurance companies handle injury claims differently from claims due to illness. Illness-related claims almost always pay fewer benefits than accident claims. Sometimes the company will simply change the classification to its own advantage. *Example:* In a policy, the wording "After a stated period of time after your accident, we'll pay you as though you were sick" will reduce both the amount of money you'll receive and the length of time that you'll receive it—sometimes from a lifetime (the longest possible length of payments for an accident claim) down to as little as five years. *Much better:* That payments for injuries due to an accident remain in the injury-claim classification, regardless of how much time elapses.

● **Disability insurers also use tricky language to define exactly when you get sick.** Since getting a claim approved hinges on when you became ill, using the wording "when the illness first manifests itself" permits the company to deny the claim on the grounds that the illness predated the policy but wasn't diagnosed until after the policy was signed.

Typical: An insurer denies a claim for cancer because the policyholder had the disease for years before the problem became apparent.

● **Occupational classes.** Disability benefits are dependent on your occupation at the time of the accident or illness. How long you'll receive benefits depends on the complexity of your training for your current job and the ease with which you might be trained for a new one. *Examples:* Surgeons are covered for life; managers, 10 years; salespeople, 5 years; etc. Good insurance agents help find companies and individuals with the most favorable length.

DISABILITY INSURANCE: WHAT YOU NEED, WHAT TO LOOK FOR

Too many people overestimate their ability to withstand the financial impact of a disability lasting more than 90 days. *Their most common misconceptions:*

● **Their employers "will take care of them,"** either through a formal income-replacement program or by simply keeping them on the payroll.

● **Their family's standard of living can be lowered** to accommodate the loss of income.

● **A spouse who has not worked outside of the home for a number of years** can attain a relatively high-paying job in a short period of time.

● **A growing net worth,** which may be invested in illiquid assets or assets that could only be sold at a substantial discount, can cover their loss of income. Don't underestimate your needs for adequate disability protection. If you aren't in a position to self-insure against the risk of a disabling accident or illness, you need some insurance to help fill the gap.

Maximizing Value

Whether you are seeking employer-provided or individually purchased coverage, the objectives and criteria for selection are essentially the same. The key in both cases is to maximize the value of the premium dollar by budgeting for smaller losses and insuring against the catastrophic occurrences that could ruin your personal financial plan.

A major point to consider when choosing a plan is the need to keep your "waiting or elimination period" (the period during a disability when the insurer is not responsible for paying you benefits) between three and six months. These are usually financially acceptable waiting periods. Purchasing the traditional 30-day elimination period can be as much as 40% more expensive and often provides unnecessary coverage.

The "benefit period"—the length of time you can expect to receive disability income—should extend to at least age 65 for each separate incident of disability. For extra safety and where the family unit is relatively young, pay a higher premium in exchange for a lifetime benefit period.

As you get older, you can reduce your coverage and save money by increasing your policy's elimination period and/or reducing the benefit amount. In most cases, a family's financial burdens decline over the years and its ability to meet those burdens improves. As children move out and investment assets are accumulated, the necessity for maintaining disability insurance declines, although it may not be eliminated. However, you should generally avoid cutting costs by reducing your benefit period. If you were struck by a catastrophic disability, you would want benefits for as long a period as possible.

Another major concern is the manner in which the condition of disability is defined in an insurance contract. Some policies use the "pure residual" approach, with the reduction in the level of earnings as the sole criterion. Since this approach is relatively objective, such contracts are frequently less expensive than those using the alternative approach: evaluating your ability to perform the duties of an occupation or profession. This approach has many variations, ranging from "ability to perform any duties of any occupation or profession" to "ability to perform the material duties of your profession until age 65." Since the approach is more subjective, premium rates are generally higher.

Normally, the policy with the broadest definition of disability is best, unless you can claim true "specialist" status and justify the added cost. Therefore, the residual approach is suitable for occupations offering the flexibility of reduced hours and duties, while the "ability to perform" approach is best for professions that lack that flexibility—for example, the medical profession. Some policies do feature characteristics of both approaches.

Source: Andrew E. Gross, treasurer and shareholder of Dennis M. Gurtz and Associates, Inc., 4910 Massachusetts Ave. NW, Suite 112, Washington, DC 20016, a financial-planning and consulting firm. The author has an extensive academic and professional background in accounting, risk management and other financial-planning matters.

● **Specialties within a profession.** Some insurance companies don't recognize specialties, and, for example, lump together all their insured lawyers. Avoid these companies. Look for an insurer that differentiates between a litigator and a patent attorney and differentiates in payments for, say, a broken leg, which obviously incapacitates the litigator much more than the patent attorney.

● **Residual (partial) disability.** This desirable rider—available at extra cost—will pay you if, after an illness, you can work only one or two days a week. Usually, if you lose 20% or more of your earned income, you are considered to be residually disabled.

Exclusionary Period

You can choose from exclusionary periods (also known as elimination or deductible periods) of 7, 14, 30, 60, 90 and 180 days—the number of days after the onset of illness or injury it will take for payments to begin. The longer the period, the lower the cost of the policy. Your choice should depend on what other insurance benefits you have.

Recommended: 60–90 days.

● **Amount of coverage.** Most companies won't insure you for more than 50%–60% of your earned income. Payments are tax-free if you—not your employer—have paid for the policy. You often can end up with as much as 85% of your after-tax income.

● **Best package.** If your funds to buy insurance are limited and you're a professional or an executive, buy lifetime accident coverage, sickness to 65 (lifetime, if you can afford it) and residual disability, with a 60- or 90-day exclusionary period. Cost-of-living adjustment riders can be added or dropped each year.

Traps

Here are some serious drawbacks to group disability plans that can leave you high and dry in the event of an accident or illness:

● **The issuer can cancel the policy.**

● **Premiums aren't guaranteed**—the issuer can raise them dramatically.

● **Coverage and claims practices favor the company, not the insured.**

Source: Leonard B. Stern, president, Leonard B. Stern & Co., a financial services and consulting firm, 305 Madison Ave., New York, NY 10165.

How Much Disability Insurance Is Enough?

Before buying disability insurance, it is important to assess what resources you already have that would enable you and your family to manage in the event of an accident or illness. Compare these resources with your expenditures. Then, make up any gap with disability insurance.

Key questions:

● **Would you get partial pay from your employer?** How much? For how long?

● **Do you have a benevolent family member** you could count on to keep you going or at least to help?

● **What assets do you have that could be converted quickly?**

● **Are you already covered by disability insurance policies?** (Don't forget to check what's provided by credit cards and association memberships.)

● **What could you expect from Canada Pension Plan (CPP) disability coverage?** You should always reassess your disability coverage whenever:

● **Income changes.** Almost everyone increases lifestyle and financial needs when income increases.

● **Financial responsibilities increase.** *Examples:* A new child, a new mortgage, or building a new house.

There is a CPP trap to watch out for in planning your insurance needs. To get disability payments from CPP, you must have contributed to the Canada Pension Plan in four of the last six years. (This rule applies to anyone who became disabled after Dec. 31, 1997. During that period, you must have earned at least 10% of each year's maximum pensionable earnings (YMPE). The YMPE changes each year. Check with CPP administration if you're unsure about your eligibility.

Warning: There may be errors in the CPP records, and you may find out too late that records are wrong and you're not covered.

Safeguard: Get a statement of contributions from CPP and check it over to ensure it is accurate. If there's a mistake, immediately notify the CPP office. It does not matter how long ago the mistake was made.

If you do not automatically receive your statement of contributions in the mail, you can request one. Fill out an application for a statement of contributions, which you can download from the CPP website (www.hrdc-drhc.gc.ca/). Or you can ask that a form be sent to you by calling 1-877-454-4051. Mail the completed form to: Contributor Information Management, Canada Pension Plan, Human Resources Development Canada, P.O. Box 9750, Postal Station T, Ottawa, ON K1G 4A6.

What Happens If an Insurance Company Fails?

Most insurance companies are financially sound, but bankruptcies are not unknown in Canada. The biggest failure was the collapse of Confederation Life in 1994.

The good news is that if things go terribly wrong with your insurer, you do have protection. It is provided by the Canadian Life and Health Insurance Compensation Corporation (known for short as CompCorp), which is a federally incorporated, non-profit company established by the Canadian Life and Health Insurance Association (CLHIA) to protect policyholders, within limits, from the loss of benefits in the event of the failure of an insurance company. It is funded by CompCorp's member companies, currently almost 200 strong. Protection is automatically extended to eligible policies issued by member insurance companies. There is no need to apply.

Coverage highlights per person are as follows:

● **$200,000 of life insurance death benefits.**

● **$60,000 for non-registered policies,** including money accumulation products and cash values in life insurance policies. Separate limits for individual and group contracts.

● **$60,000 for registered policies,** including RRSPs, RRIFs and registered pension plans (RPPs). Separate limits for individual and group contracts.

● **$2,000 of monthly income under annuities** or disability income policies.

● **$60,000 of health insurance,** other than disability income policies.

To be eligible for CompCorp protection, a policy must:

a) Be in Canadian currency.

b) Provide either life insurance, health insurance, money accumulation (RRSP, pension plan), annuity income (life income, term certain, RRIF) or disability income.

c) Be written by a member company in Canada, or shown on the books of a Canadian branch of a member company.

d) Not be covered under any other similar plan. (*Note:* There are no other similar plans at present in Canada.)

CompCorp provides no protection where policy benefits are backed by assets that are segregated from the insurance company's general assets (if there is a guaranteed minimum benefit set out in the policy, then that guarantee is eligible for protection under CompCorp).

If you want additional information, you can call the Consumer Assistance Centre toll-free at 1-800-268-8099. In Toronto, the number is 416-777-2344. There is a Montreal office at 1-800-361-8070 if you wish service in French.

Source: *G. Pierce Newman, coauthor of* Fiscal Fitness, *published by Prentice Hall Canada. This article originally appeared on 50Plus.com, the official site of Canada's Association for the Fifty-Plus (CARP). The address is www.50plus.com.*

Homeowner's or Renter's Insurance

Homeowner's insurance provides protection for risks such as fire, lightning, wind, hail and theft. It does not cover some catastrophic events such as flood, earthquake and nuclear accident. Policies also include liability coverage in case someone sues you for an accident other than an auto claim, such as a dog bite or a fall on your property.

Renter's insurance, which is usually inexpensive, covers your own personal property (furniture, etc.) and most liabilities you may incur when renting a property. Similar coverage is available for owners of condominiums, cooperatives or mobile homes.

Buying Suggestions

To decide how much homeowner's coverage you need, get an appraisal of the cost to rebuild your home if a disaster happens. *Don't* insure to market value. An appraisal calculates the cost per square foot by builders in your area. You don't want to insure the land or basement. Your insurance agent usually appraises homes free. Or you can get a professional appraisal for around $200 and up.

For example, if it would cost $50,000 to replace your home, only insure to $50,000, not more. But don't insure for *less* than 80% of its value, because you'll forfeit the right to collect full replacement, at today's costs, of your home and possessions. Instead, you'll only get its *actual cash value.* That's what it costs, less depreciation.

When shopping for a homeowner's policy, keep in mind that you can usually save money by buying from a direct-writing insurer (one that doesn't use so-called "independent agents").

Source: J. Robert Hunter, head of the insurance group, at Consumer Federation of America, 1424 16 St. NW, Washington, DC 22207.

How to Avoid Homeowner's Insurance Pitfalls

Most people buy their homeowner's insurance from the company that gives them the best price. And for many buyers, that's the smart way to go. But if the insured's property—home and belongings—is valued at more than $200,000 or if they also have a vacation house and some jewelry, silver and fine art, they may be inadequately covered or may be wasting money on overlapping coverage.

Insurance companies usually aim for one segment of the marketplace. Most go after the big middle market—homes valued at under $200,000 and owners who have few or no valuables such as fine art, jewelry, furs or silver. And for those people, the homeowner's policies issued by these firms are indeed adequate. In fact, the cost of that type of coverage is usually quite competitive because so many firms are fighting for a share of that large pie.

But when the value of property starts to climb, the owner should look at insurance in a fundamentally different way. Are the changing values of possessions being tracked? Prices for fine art and jewelry don't remain static. They may rise or fall, depending on market conditions. Some fine art posts dramatic swings, especially the moderns.

With mass-market insurance policies, upper dollar limits are usually built into the coverage. These limits vary for different parts of the country.

Of course, you can consider buying additional coverage for items that exceed the upper dollar limit. This extra coverage is called a personal articles floater (known as a PAF in the trade). However, in order to get higher-value PAF coverage, you will have to prove the value of those items, either by providing a bill of sale or by getting an appraisal from an expert in the field.

Insurance firms that aim for the middle market may discourage such special coverage for valuable items because they don't really have a ready-made policy to offer. Their prices for special items are usually not competitive. Before offering coverage, they may require an appraisal (inconvenient and not that inexpensive) on an item valued as low as $1,000.

Some people who started out adequately covered by the midrange homeowner's policy when they were young find after several years that they are starting to grow beyond the protection of their coverage. Many people buy "inflation guard," coverage that increases protection automatically, about 1% every four months. This increases the premium, but not significantly.

What to Do

Just as some insurance firms specialize in the middle market and thus offer the best prices for that one, other insurance firms specialize in the narrower, higher-bracket markets. Once the value of your home and belongings exceeds $200,000, you should investigate what coverage is available from these firms. They may offer not only a better price, but also policies that are tailored to your special needs. If your current agent represents only middle-market firms, ask him or her to recommend an agent or broker that can service you. Other routes: Contact your local insurance association, or call the Insurance Bureau of Canada.

Second Home

If you own a vacation house in addition to your main residence, be aware of the gap trap or the overlap trap. Often a vacation-home owner buys coverage from a broker or agent in the vicinity of the dwelling on the theory that if anything should happen, the representative is here. That is logical—up to a point.

Problems:

● **The agent at the vacation spot** may assume that, for example, a small boat is covered by the insured's main policy. As a result, he or she omits it from the vacation-home policy. Or the insured may have the boat covered under both policies. With two uncoordinated policies, the insured may be paying for too much coverage.

● **There is no discount for coverage on two houses,** as there is for coverage on two or more cars.

Other Considerations

Important basic: Many midrange policies guarantee to pay the actual cash value (ACV). That certainly sounds good—until you discover (perhaps belatedly) that the insurance company subtracts from the actual cash value the damaged article's depreciation.

To see how ACV works, let's use as an example a damaged sofa that cost $5,000 new and has a useful life of 10 years. It has depreciated by $500 a year. If the sofa is eight years old when damaged, the owner will wind up with a settlement cheque of $1,000 (minus, probably, a $250 deductible).

Some policies have a four-times-ACV clause for settlement, which means the owner of the sofa will get a cheque for $4,000 (minus the deductible). And still other policies call for payment of full replacement cost of the damaged item. Considering inflation, that could put the settlement cheque at something like $7,500.

A conscientious agent will point out these and other differences.

Source: Robert Fergusson, assistant vice president and personal client services marketing manager, Marsh & McLennan Companies, Inc., New York, NY.

BETTER HOME INSURANCE BUYING

Many people spend far too much money for home insurance and then end up with the wrong coverage.

Key: Don't waste money protecting yourself against small losses. *What you should look for:*

● **Home replacement coverage:** Protect yourself against the total destruction of your house. Urban and suburban home-owners may need to buy coverage for only 80% of the replacement value of a home because local fire services in the city are quicker to respond than those in rural areas. If your insurance is for a dollar amount, check annually to see if it will still pay for a replacement home.

● **High deductibles:** A $1,000 deductible can cut insurance premiums by 15%. The savings will more than make up for the cost of repairing minor damage such as a broken window.

● **Extra coverage of high-value items:** Most policies limit payment for certain valuable items. *Typical:* Jewelry losses can't exceed $1,000–$2,000 (depending on the company you use), silverware, $1,000. To insure these for their true value, get a personal articles floater that spells out what the company will pay in the event of a loss.

Adequate liability protection: Some policies provide only $200,000 for personal liability. That's the most common minimum limit in Canada, although most policies now provide for coverage of $1–$2 million. But even that may not be enough coverage if you have above-average income and assets. *Better:* An umbrella policy that picks up where your home-owner's and automobile insurance policies leave off (a particularly good idea for pool owners, for example).

Source: Rodale's Practical Homeowner, Emmaus, PA.

You're Covered— or Are You?

An "all-risk" homeowner's policy isn't necessarily what its name implies. Some policies may not give you protection against heavy damage caused by a flood, hurricane or other natural disaster.

For adequate protection, insure your house for at least 80% of replacement value—the cost of rebuilding it with the same materials, at today's labor rates. Also, pay the added premium for a "replacement cost endorsement" on your home's contents. Otherwise, the insurer will pay you only a depreciated amount on those items that suffer wear and tear.

Source: *Benjamin Lipson, Benjamin Lipson Associates Insurance Agency, author of* How to Collect More on Your Insurance Claims, *Simon & Schuster.*

While You Were Gone...

Homeowner's insurance trap: Letting friends use your home when you're not in residence may invalidate your insurance. Insurance companies assume that the owner will take better precautions to protect the property than a renter will. If you rent out your vacation home, for example, purchase either "all-risk" or "special multiperil" insurance. These policies cost more, but they'll cover both theft and liability losses.

> "Homeowner's insurance trap: Letting friends use your home when you're not in residence may invalidate your insurance."

Source: Profit Building Strategies for Business Owners, *Scarsdale, NY.*

Protection for Renters

Only one renter in five has property or liability insurance.

Problem: The landlord's policy covers only the building, not tenants' possessions. *Here are some guidelines for renters:*

● **For adequate property protection,** buy a policy with full replacement coverage. This will cost 15%–40% more than the same policy at actual-cash-value coverage (replacement less depreciation), but is well worth it.

● **The standard policy sets a liability limit of $25,000,** inadequate for most people. For $10 or so extra, you can raise the limit to $100,000.

● **Expensive jewelry, watches and furs are best protected by a personal articles floater,** a policy amendment that insures each item individually.

● **You can save 10% by raising your deductible** from $100 to $250, and another 10% by increasing it to $500.

Source: Money, *New York, NY.*

How to Save on Auto Insurance

There are four major areas of coverage in a typical auto insurance policy:

● **Bodily injury liability,** in case you injure someone.

● **Property damage liability,** in case you damage someone else's property.

● **Collision,** in case you damage your own car.

● **Comprehensive,** in case your car is stolen, vandalized or otherwise damaged.

Each of these areas is subject to cost cutting.

● **Don't buy unnecessary auto coverage.** As a rule, every $1 of auto insurance premiums returns approximately 60¢ in claims—the rest is overhead. By self-insuring for the small risks you can afford, you can save up to 40%.

● **Avoid collision insurance on older cars.** This is generally expensive relative to other types of coverage and is not economical if your car is not very valuable. Comprehensive insurance is a less expensive alternative and, given the chance of total loss due to theft, should probably be purchased anyway.

● **Increase your deductibles.** Increasing your deductible $200–$500 could reduce your collision cost by 15%–30%. The trade-off is that you are required to pay for more small claims. Over time the savings in premiums should, however, more than pay for your claims if you are an average or better driver. And because small claims increase your premiums, filing fewer claims will reduce the chance that your premiums will rise in the future.

● **Avoid incidental coverages.** Buy good medical insurance and skip auto medical payments. (In no-fault jurisdictions, use medical insurance in lieu of personal injury protection, if you are able to legally.) Avoid coverage for substitute transportation, which pays for rental cars when your car is being repaired, for towing coverage and for memberships in insurance-company auto clubs, which are not good values.

● **Shop around.** Some companies charge two or three times what others charge for identical coverage.

Trouble Finding Coverage?

If you can't find coverage, call insurers that specialize in "nonstandard" risks, those for drivers with higher than average risk. Most agents can recommend one or two. In some provinces, government-sponsored automobile insurance programs are mandatory for basic coverage ("extras" can be sold by private firms). You can also try calling the office of your provincial superintendent of insurance for guidance. You'll have to pay more for the coverage. In many provinces, however, claims or other items such as where you live, or how you live, or even the whim of the insurance company, may cause inexpensive insurers to reject your application. As a result, you may be forced to seek insurance from high-rate companies that specialize in selling insurance to people who have difficulty finding coverage. In some cases, you may be better off going to a government-guaranteed assigned-risk plan if one is available rather than paying the rates of some of these high-risk insurers. These government programs must sell auto insurance to licensed drivers who have the money to pay their premiums. The Facility Association is the prime example. It is an insurance pool that all automobile insurance companies belong to and acts as an insurer of last resort for people who can't obtain coverage elsewhere.

Source: *J. Robert Hunter, head of the insurance group at Consumer Federation of America, 1424 16 St. NW, Washington, DC 22207.*

Children's Car Insurance Costs

You can cut car insurance costs when children who still live with you start driving.

● **List them as occasional drivers,** not principal drivers. That alone will cut the premium by up to one-third for boys and by one-fourth for girls.

● **Allow your child to drive only one of your cars** (if you have more than one), preferably the least expensive one. If more than one child has a driver's license, cover girls for driving the more expensive car.

● **Make sure the youngsters take driver's education.** Insurance discounts of 10% are available for those who pass.

● **Look into "good student" discounts.** For the minimum discount, your child must maintain at least a B average; maintaining a higher average increases the size of the discount. Good-student discounts commonly cut the premium by one-fourth.

● **If your child is at university more than 160 kilometers** from home and does not have a car on campus, try to get a university-student discount.

● **If your child has a car,** have it put on your policy. Multicar discounts can be anywhere from 10% to 25% depending on the insurance company.

Guarding Against the Uninsured

An accident with an uninsured or underinsured motorist can be financially ruinous. As part of your own policy, underinsured (in some jurisdictions) and uninsured motorists coverage is obtainable to deal with such accidents.

Uninsured Coverage

Most provinces have statutory requirements that automobile liability insurance policies include uninsured motorist's coverage.

● **Financial responsibility limits.** The law requires that uninsured motorist's coverage be provided in an amount mandated by the province. These financial responsibility limits vary.

● **Getting more coverage.** Usually you can buy coverage up to your liability limits. *Example:* If you carry $200,000 in liability, you can get the same amount in uninsured coverage.

● **Proof of fault.** Under uninsured coverage, your company has to pay only what the other party is legally liable for. The other party must be proved at fault.

● **Comparative negligence provisions.** In some no-fault jurisdictions, if the other driver is proved somewhat or entirely responsible, you can recover a proportional amount of your deductible from your own insurance company. So if, for example, you were rear-ended and it was determined that the other driver was 100% responsible for the accident, then you would not have to pay any of your normal deductible.

● **Making a claim.** You are placed in an adversarial position with your own insurance company. You must prove the extent of the injury, establish its value, and negotiate with your own carrier to settle. If you can't reach a settlement, most claims will go to arbitration.

Underinsured Coverage

This type of coverage is becoming more and more popular in the United States, although it is not widely available in Canada. Some jurisdictions require that underinsured coverage be offered. In others, it is optional. With underinsured coverage:

● **You must first recover the maximum amount** from the other party's liability policy before you can collect on your own policy.

● **As with uninsured coverage, you are in an adversarial position with your carrier** and must prove that the value of your injury has exceeded the liability limits of the other party's policy.

Important: Uninsured motorist's coverage will not pay you if the other driver has any insurance at all, no matter how inadequate. However, keep in mind that most Canadian provinces require a minimum amount of liability coverage and won't let you obtain a vehicle registration without it. In Ontario, for example, you must carry at least $200,000 worth of third-party liability coverage.

Source: *Richard P. Oatman, assistant claim counsel for Aetna Life & Casualty, Hartford, CT.*

No Fault Does Not Mean "Without Fault"

The term "no fault" has led to confusion and misunderstanding on the part of consumers. All it really means is that, if you are injured or your car is damaged in an accident, you will deal with your own insurer regardless of who was at fault for the accident. If party A was at fault for an accident, you, party B, don't have to go after party A's insurance company for compensation. You will deal with your own insurer, who will pay you for the loss or damage.

However, the term has had the regrettable effect of actually causing some consumers to believe that the notion of "fault" in an accident has been done away with. Nothing could be further from the truth.

Let's take this issue to the next stage. You have been injured in an accident in which you were the driver. Who pays your accident benefits? Does it matter who was at fault? You will receive accident benefits from your own insurer regardless of whether you were at fault or not. Your auto insurer will pay benefits to you as the driver, as well as to anyone else who was injured while in your vehicle regardless of whether they have their own automobile policy.

But someone must still be judged to be at fault, either completely or partially. The law requires it. There are "fault determination" rules incorporated in the provincial insurance acts. These rules are intended to help insurance companies deal with accident claims expeditiously. The extent of your "fault" according to these regulations will determine the amount of the deductible you will have to pay. So, if you're 50% at fault, you'll pay 50% of the deductible on whichever policy pays for the damages. And your fault, even if it is only a mere fraction, say 20%, will almost certainly result in an increase in your premiums.

The CLEAR System

CLEAR is the Canadian Loss Experience Automobile Rating system, a mechanism for rating vehicles for insurance purposes. Most Canadian insurers are now using this system, and Canadian consumers should be very happy that the system is in place.

Insurers take into account the claims experience of a particular vehicle (make and model) when they calculate your premium. This differs from the previous practice of using the manufacturer's suggested list price (MSLP) as the basis of your premium. What does this mean to you? It means that you can control your premium expense! Look at it from the point of view of the insurance company. Models that have fewer safety features, are stolen more often, or cost more to repair will cost more to insure.

Consider safety features such as air bags, antilock braking systems (ABS), and theft-deterrent devices. While they can add substantially to the initial price of a vehicle, they may nonetheless translate into lower premiums for car owners, since these devices can help to reduce insurers' claims costs.

For argument sake, let's say that you and your neighbor both own cars that cost $35,000. Under the old system, both cars would be rated the same for insurance purposes. Easy enough to follow, yes. But not fair. If one of the cars is stolen more frequently, is less roadworthy and thus involved in more collisions, and costs more to repair, is it fair to charge

HOW TO BUY AN UMBRELLA INSURANCE POLICY

The standard homeowner's policy in Canada usually provides for at least $1 million in liability coverage. That's significantly higher than in the United States, which is why umbrella insurance is not as popular in this country as it is south of the border. The coverage is available from some companies, if you want to add extra protection.

An umbrella policy protects your family's assets in the unlikely—but possible—event of your being sued for damages in a lawsuit. It also covers you against suits filed as a result of accidents beyond those that are covered by your basic homeowner's policy, as well as legal fees to defend against such a suit. One such case in Canada dealt with a well-known celebrity who was sued for more than the homeowner policy limits, in the belief that there would be additional assets (expensive home, etc.) or an umbrella policy to recover more than the "typical" amount. Since the wordings of umbrella policies vary, it is crucial that the insured understand what is covered and what is not. Some policies extend into professional liability (e.g., a doctor that is sued as a business and personally).

It's important to distinguish between an umbrella policy and an excess liability policy. The latter is an add-on—it cuts in only when your primary coverage has been exceeded. An umbrella policy stands alone—it is not a "follow form." It also provides protection against risks that may not be covered in a standard home-owners policy, such as libel and slander, although most people will never be at risk for damages for those reasons.

What a Policy Costs

Most umbrella policies are inexpensive. For $200 to $400 a year, you can buy up to $5 million in coverage. *Strategy:* If you don't want to increase your total insurance costs by adding umbrella coverage, increase the deductibles on your auto and homeowner's policies. *Shopping strategies:* When shopping for a policy, ask your insurer for a comprehensive breakdown of what is—and what is not—covered.

Important: Make sure there are no risky gaps between your umbrella policy and your auto and home-owner's policies.

Self-defense: Check your existing policies, and eliminate any gaps. If necessary, raise your auto or homeowner deductibles to balance out the cost of higher liability protection.

Shopping for a Policy

Start by contacting the insurers that have sold your family its policies. If their rates are reasonable and their coverage levels comprehensive, you'll reduce complications by keeping your coverage under the same roof. Ask your insurer if you can qualify for a discount by adding an umbrella policy to your coverage.

Special Needs

● **Operating a home-based business.** You may need a separate, commercially oriented umbrella policy to protect you against related liability risks. A total of $1 million worth of protection may not be sufficient. Ask your insurance agent for recommendations.

● **Owning more than one home.** If you own primary and vacation residences, a good policy should cover both. But it pays to investigate, particularly if one or more properties provide significant rental income.

● **Serving on a nonprofit board.** Some umbrella policies include directors and officers (D&O) liability protection, but others do not. This won't protect you against wrongful acts in the discharge of your duties, but it does cover you for liability relating to bodily injury, personal injury or property damage. If you are asked to serve on a board, ask if the board is covered by the nonprofit's insurance.

If it is not, check your own coverage before joining the board of your child's nursery school, your co-op building or any other nonprofit group. *Note:* As a rule, for-profit companies buy D&O coverage for their boards.

Source: Robert Hunter, head of the insurance group at the Consumer Federation of America (CFA), a consumer advocate organization, 1424 16 St. NW, Suite 604, Washington, DC 20036. He is the author of Buyer's Guide to Insurance, *available from the CFA. Additional input from Dave Way, National Property Portfolio Manager for Zurich North America Canada.*

each owner the same amount for their insurance? Obviously not, especially from the perspective of the owner of the safer car. Under CLEAR, motorists who drive safer vehicles, that are less expensive to insure, do not subsidize those driving vehicles with a higher loss experience.

Before you sign on the dotted line for that racy little number you've been eyeing, ask your insurer what the CLEAR system rating is for your dream car. It just may turn out that the insurance cost will be nightmarish.

Source: G. Pierce Newman, coauthor of **Fiscal Fitness**, published by Prentice Hall Canada. This article originally appeared on 50Plus.com, the official site of Canada's Association for the Fifty-Plus (CARP). The website is www.50plus.com

Title Insurance—An Often-Overlooked Protection

The use of title insurance in Canada by lawyers has grown by leaps and bounds in recent years. Yet, despite the fact that it has become a mainstream product, its benefits are relatively unknown to consumers. Canadians are very aware of the benefits of other forms of insurance—we insure our lives, our cars and the building we live in. But what about the quality of our title? How can we be sure we have acquired the bundle of rights to the property that we think we have? Are there unknown problems lurking within? What about protection against risks that threaten our right to enjoy the title to our homes? After all, we spend more on our homes than on any other single item we own.

What Is Title Insurance?

Title insurance is a policy for which there is a one-time premium that is issued at the time of closing, and which lasts as long as you own the property. It provides protection to the buyer or lender, or both, against a variety of perils that relate to the quality of title acquired by the buyer and the security against the property that the lender has. Simply put, it is an assurance of the bundle of rights acquired by the buyer, lender or both on closing.

When buying a home, title insurance can only be obtained through your lawyer. What makes title insurance so essential is not only the hitherto unavailable level of protection, but also the efficiencies lawyers are able to enjoy when they complete your purchase using a title insurance policy. It used to be that the lawyer, in closing a purchase, had to do two types of searches: title and off title. In a title search, the lawyer looks back in time to verify that the seller acquired title correctly and has the ability in law to deliver to you what is known as clear title. Off-title searches are mostly municipal and provincial government searches that address issues such as whether the property complies with all the appropriate zoning bylaws and more.

Further, the lawyer checks that there are no arrears of expenses or obligations that can impact on the clarity of title—such as property tax arrears. That kind of debt runs with the property, and one of the lawyer's responsibilities is to verify if there are arrears, and, if so, to adjust what is owing up to the day of closing. At the end of the day, the lawyer provided something called an "opinion" on title. The opinion was just that—a collection of the lawyer's thoughts on the quality of title based on the results of the searches performed.

In a closing where the lawyer is using title insurance, the deal closes not based on what the lawyer's opinion is as to the quality of title you are acquiring, but on the strength of the policy of insurance that the lawyer arranges for you and the lender. The policy provides assurance to the buyer and the lender as to the bundle of rights each acquires to the title of the property.

The assurance offered by a title insurer is backed by deep-pocket American insurance companies. There are several title insurance companies operating in Canada, and they all involve U.S. firms. That's a good thing for Canadian consumers, who benefit not only from the century of experience the U.S. insurers have in assuring title, but also from the financial strength these large firms bring to the real estate marketplace. This financial strength is typically greater than any of the lawyer's malpractice insurers. Quite simply, a title-insured closing provides greater protection for the consumer and the lender than an uninsured closing. But the benefits are far more than that. They include a smoother process and a greater likelihood that your deal will close on time and uneventfully.

It's a Direct Insured No-Fault Claims Process

When your lawyer places title insurance on your property, you and your lender become the direct insured. A title-insurance claim is a no-fault claim, and you are directly insured. The process of collecting on a claim often starts with a phone call. That process is superior to the old process of going after the lawyer first. There is no need to prove negligence against anyone to recover under the policy.

Consider this. Just about every bank in Canada has a program with one or more of the title insurers whereby they process their non-purchase transactions (such as refinance or secured lines of credit) in conjunction with a title insurance policy. You have to wonder whether banks know something ordinary consumers don't. The answer is they do. For years, they made loans in part on the lawyer's opinion on title. When a problem arose, they had to bear it or pursue the lawyer in the case of negligence. Title insurance changes and makes the lender the direct insured and they have a no-fault claims process.

Title Insurance Saves You Money

In recent years, municipal and provincial governments used title and off-title searches as revenue generators, steadily increasing charges to lawyers for the search results. The response time to search requests has often been extended—slowing down many closings. Worse, these searches often reveal little information and are usually marked "E & OE": errors and omissions excepted!

In a title insured transaction, the insurance company acts as a risk taker, assuming reasonable risk in exchange for a premium. When the lawyer uses title insurance, the need for certain searches becomes unnecessary as the results of those searches are covered by the policy. The savings vary within Canada. Generally, they are greatest in Ontario and the Maritimes, but less in the Prairie provinces and British Columbia. Moreover, you avoid the whole "E & OE" nonsense because you obtain direct coverage.

Title Insurance Eliminates the Lender's Requirement for a Survey

Across Canada, just about every lender requires a buyer to produce an up-to-date survey in order to obtain the mortgage funds. The lender needs the survey to be sure that the house has not been built in such a way so as to obstruct things like easements or conflict with municipal setback requirements (how far away the house or deck should be from the lot line). This is a simple requirement. But what often happens is that the survey is sold and does not show things such as alterations or additions or decks. Sometimes, a very old existing survey has simply been photocopied too many times and is hence not clear. When that happens, a new survey has to be obtained. The cost of a new survey ranges in Canada from about $150 in the western part of the country to about $800 in Ontario. Moreover, problems with existing surveys often appear at the very last minute, since that's when lenders tend to look at them—just before a scheduled closing. The closing then has to be delayed to obtain the new survey.

Just about all lenders in Canada will accept a policy of title insurance in lieu of a survey. Since the cost of the survey is greater than the cost of the title insurance policy most of the time, that translates into savings for consumers. That savings becomes even greater when compounded with the effect of avoiding the cost of unnecessary searches.

Title Insurance Gives Broader Protection Than the Lawyer's Opinion on Title

Without sounding too alarmist, there are risks out there that could imperil the quality of your investment in your house. Title insurance can protect you against these risks. The most obvious of those risks are fraud and forgeries relating to your title, such as someone else claiming to own an interest in your title or claiming to have a lien against your house. These types of problems tend to be catastrophic in nature and the best way to avoid these nightmare scenarios is to have title insurance. Other covered matters include documents in the chain of title not being validly registered; liens on the property (such as for nonpayment of taxes); certain work orders; and forced removal of structures (except for boundary walls and fences) because they violate zoning bylaws or they extend onto adjoining properties.

Source: Houserich, *by Howard Turk, published by Prentice Hall Canada. Copyright © Howard Turk 2002.*

Insurance Tactics & Strategies

Estate Planning

11

What Gets Taxed and How the Tax Is Calculated

To achieve your estate-planning goals, the first step you should take is to understand the size of your estate and the manner in which it will be taxed. The following guidelines should enable you to make estimates for tax purposes.

There Is No Estate Tax in Canada, But...

Unlike the United States, Canada does not have any estate tax as such (and it's being phased out in the United States as well). However, that does not mean that your assets will pass to your heirs without the government taking its share. There are two ways that taxes are extracted from estates.

● **Taxation of capital gains.** At death, all your assets are deemed to have been sold and the profits (if any) realized. These are then subject to tax at the capital gains rate. You may think that you don't have much, but consider more than just your investments—look at everything you own. For example, is there a lakeside cottage that has been in the family for many years? It may have appreciated in value significantly. That gain will be taxable when you, the owner, die. The tax bill could be substantial—so much so that the estate may have to sell the property to satisfy the Canada Customs and Revenue Agency (CCRA).

● **De-registration of RRSPs, RRIFs, etc.** When you die, any registered plans you have are deemed to have been cashed in and the assets are added to your income in the year of death. When your final income tax return is prepared, that money will be taxed at your full marginal rate—there are no tax breaks of any kind. If you have a lot of money in such plans, the CCRA will end up taking almost 50% of the total (the exact rate will depend on your province of residence).

A Reprieve for Spouses

The good news is that your spouse is protected from the big tax hit. In Canada, all assets may pass to your spouse when you die without attracting any of the taxes aforementioned. This ensures that a spouse won't be left impoverished as a result of your death.

When certain property is left to your spouse, or to a spousal trust, then the transferred assets attract no tax on your death.

In the case of stocks, real estate, etc., you are deemed to have disposed of your assets at a certain adjusted cost base, and your spouse assumes that cost base. Therefore, no capital gain will be triggered. The tax is postponed until your spouse sells the asset or dies.

Assets that are covered by this exemption:
● The family home.
● Joint accounts.
● Proceeds from an RRSP or RRIF.
● Stocks, mutual funds, or other assets which have appreciated in value.
● Registered plans (e.g., RRIFs, RRSPs).

Two criteria must be met in order for this exemption to apply:

1. You must have been resident in Canada immediately prior to your death.

2. Your property must have been transferred on or after your death to one or the other (or both) of your spouse (who was also resident in Canada immediately prior to your death) or a qualifying spousal trust. This is defined as a trust created by your will whereby your spouse is entitled to receive all the income of the trust that arises during their lifetime, *and* no other person may receive any of the income or capital from the trust. The trust must be held in Canada immediately after the property is settled in it.

Source: G. Pierce Newman, coauthor of Fiscal Fitness published by Prentice Hall Canada. This material originally appeared in the Money section of 50plus.com, the official website of CARP, Canada's Association for the Fifty-Plus.

The Effect of the Change in the Capital Gains Calculation

In October 2000, Finance Minister Paul Martin brought down a mini-budget that had significant long-term estate planning implications. The main effect was to reduce the tax impact of capital gains that are realized at death. Under the law, when you die any assets you own are deemed to have been sold for tax purposes. This means that all capital gains on stocks, mutual funds, real estate, etc., become taxable in the year of death, unless the estate is passing to your spouse or common-law partner.

In the mini-budget, Mr. Martin reduced the capital gains inclusion rate to 50%. The effect was to reduce the amount of tax payable on realized capital gains. This can be especially significant in situations such as that of a family cottage being passed from one generation to the next.

Source: Gordon Pape, author of 6 Steps to $1 Million, published by Prentice Hall Canada.

A Tax Trap to Watch For

If the beneficiary under your RRSPs or RRIFs is not your spouse and receives the proceeds of these plans directly, taxes will be payable. You will have been deemed to have cashed in the registered plans in the year of your death, taking the capital into income. The tax owing will be payable from the residue of your estate. Unless you plan for this situation, you could inadvertently leave one or more of your children (or another relative) in financial difficulty.

Source: Gordon Pape, author of 6 Steps to $1 Million, published by Prentice Hall Canada.

U.S. Estate Taxes and Canadians

Canadians thinking about buying a property in the Sunbelt to escape from our long, cold winters have for years faced a complicated and potentially expensive problem—U.S. estate taxes. However, there have been some recent changes that make estate planning much easier for Canadian snowbirds, at least for the time being.

The problem is that the changes the U.S. Congress recently introduced to the estate tax laws expire after 2010.

Here's some background. The United States adds up the value of everything you own and applies the appropriate tax rates to determine the value of an estate. There is no blanket exemption for spouses, although they do receive a partial tax break. Nor can you escape by giving your property away because the United States imposes a gift tax at the same rate as the estate tax. (Be aware that there is no gift tax in Canada.)

Until the mid-1990s, Canadians residing in the United States were entitled to an exemption of only US$60,000 on the value of their estate when they died. Anything beyond that was subject to American taxes at onerous rates that could run as high as 92% (federal and state), according to the Canadian chartered accounting firm of BDO Dunwoody.

It was not just U.S.-based property that was at risk. A Canadian estate could end up being taxed on anything with a U.S. connection, including bank accounts, stocks, bonds and other types of securities. It was a potential nightmare.

As a result of changes to the Canada-U.S. Tax Treaty in the mid-1990s, the exemption for Canadians was raised to US$600,000—the amount allowed for U.S. citizens and residents. But that wasn't an absolute amount. The exemption had to be prorated by the total value of a Canadian's estate, which meant that it might in fact end up being worth much less once your home in Canada, your RRSP or RRIF, your Canadian investment portfolio, your cottage on the lake and anything else you own was taken into account. So, many Canadian snowbirds with winter homes in Florida, Arizona, California, Hawaii or other states were still potentially on the hook.

In 1998, the U.S. Congress approved a measure to gradually increase the exemption for calculating estate taxes, and the higher limits also extended to Canadians under the tax treaty provisions. The limits have been rising gradually, and were fixed at US$700,000 in 2002–03. After that, they are to escalate sharply, reaching US$1 million in 2006.

When George W. Bush was elected to serve as president of the United States in 2000, one of his priorities was to eliminate the U.S. estate tax entirely, as part of his massive tax-cutting program. Legislation which appeared to fulfill that goal was passed by

Congress in May 2001. But the accounting firm of Ernst & Young commented after analyzing the measure in detail, that reports of death of the estate tax have been greatly exaggerated.

*Source: Gordon Pape, writing in **FiftyPlus**, the official publication of CARP, Canada's Association for the Fifty-Plus.*

No Gift Tax in Canada...But

There is no such thing as a gift tax in Canada. However, that does not mean that you can give anything to anybody tax-free as a strategy to reduce the tax burden on the estate at death. As usual, the CCRA is one step ahead of you.

To be a valid gift, several elements are required:
- The person presenting the gift must have had the intent to do so.
- The recipient must have accepted the gift.
- The gift must be irrevocable.

There are several types of gifts, including outright transfer of property, transfers to an irrevocable trust and creation of joint ownership.

A gift will avoid probate fees, but may well create other problems. If the recipient is a spouse or a related minor, any income from the property will be attributed back to you, and will be taxed in your hands. If, however, the recipient is anyone other than your spouse, you are deemed to have disposed of the property, and to have received the proceeds from the sale, at the fair market value of the property. This will trigger either a capital gain or a capital loss.

*Source: G. Pierce Newman, coauthor of **Fiscal Fitness**, published by Prentice Hall Canada. This material originally appeared in the Money section of 50plus.com, the official website of CARP, Canada's Association for the Fifty-Plus.*

Why Estate Planning Is Important

A major incentive behind estate planning is to minimize the taxes and fees your estate must pay on the death of the last surviving spouse. Your estate is a legal entity that is created upon your death. It holds all of your personal assets and assumes all of your personal liabilities. In Quebec, it is referred to as your *patrimony.*

Effective tax minimization is just as important for an estate as it is for an individual. Probate fees, which are essentially just another tax on your estate, can and should be minimized. However, a well-developed estate plan will do much more than just reduce taxes and fees.

What you want to avoid is the state deciding how your assets will be distributed. If you have broad or complex expectations about how your assets will be handled, a sound estate plan has to cover a wide range of issues. Sometimes these issues will conflict with one another. Carefully consider all the courses of action open to you, and weigh the advantages and disadvantages of each.

A comprehensive estate plan will prevent costly errors, no matter how well intentioned. You don't want to make a change in asset ownership to reduce probate fees, only to find out that this action has triggered greater capital gains taxes.

Proper estate planning will be a source of great comfort to your survivors. You will have relieved them of many painful decisions. Take a few moments, close your eyes, and imagine what the consequences would be for your family if you died without a comprehensive estate plan in place. This should motivate you to take action. Too many Canadians fail to act in a timely fashion here, and they place their families at risk. Dying without a will can expose your estate to needless taxation, delays in settlement, and potential legal challenges. It can produce emotional stress and financial hardship for family members while the estate is being settled, and possibly even beyond.

Three Key Steps to Building Your Estate Plan

As with any planning process, you should build your estate plan in stages. There are three key steps involved.

Step 1. Determine exactly what you own. Start by making a list of your assets, to estimate your estate's worth. This is also known as your "gross estate." Your list of assets might include:
- **Real estate.** Your home, perhaps a cottage or a rental property.

- **Personal property.** Cars, a boat, jewelry, art or antiques.
- **Canadian and foreign securities.** CSBs, GICs, bonds, mutual funds, stocks, etc.
- **Registered investments.** RRSPs, RRIFs, LIFs, pensions and annuities.
- **Insurance policies.**
- **Business interests** (proprietorships, partnership, etc.).

Remember to list not only what you own, but also how you own it. The latter will definitely influence your estate planning. For example, is your spouse the designated beneficiary on your RRSPs and insurance policies, or is it your estate? What about employer pension benefits? Clearly note which assets you own jointly (whether with your spouse, or some other person), and what you own singly. Your ownership of assets will decide whether they will pass to the beneficiaries *through* the will, or *outside* the will, and thus not form part of your estate for probate.

Then make a list of your liabilities—what you owe. This may include mortgages, bank loans and credit-card debt. It may also include business loans and accounts payable. Deduct these from your gross estate to arrive at your "net estate." Remember, after your death there will be other liabilities such as probate fees, income taxes, legal fees and executor's compensation which will be payable from your estate. An important part of your estate plan will be

SPRINKLING TRUSTS

With trusts often lasting 10 years or more, it's difficult for a settlor to predict what long-term tax and management benefits his or her beneficiaries will need. Many trusts in which income is uniformly distributed are too inflexible to adapt to beneficiaries' changing circumstances.

Classic problem: Income from a trust is equally distributed among beneficiaries in different tax brackets. The result is that income is eaten up by the taxes of the wealthy beneficiary, while too little income is directed to the beneficiary in a more favorable tax situation.

The flexibility to solve this problem can be built into a trust with an income "sprinkling" (or "spray") clause. This arrangement gives the trustee discretionary power to disburse or accumulate income and principal during the life of the trust. In Canada, these are known as "discretionary trusts," as opposed to "non-discretionary trusts," in which no flexibility is built in.

Income-sprinkling trusts can create two types of tax benefits. First, by favoring lower-tax-bracket beneficiaries, a sprinkling feature can produce family income tax savings. Second, a sprinkling trust can yield tax savings on the death of a surviving spouse by restricting the disposition of unnecessary income to him or her if it is not needed, thus avoiding buildup of the estate.

Here are factors to consider when establishing a sprinkling trust.

1. You must provide detailed and comprehensive guidelines for the trustee regarding the purpose and priorities of the trust.

2. Try to create a trust in which sprinkling is established between a beneficiary and his or her descendants, rather than among beneficiaries. By doing this you may eliminate potential conflicts over unequal distribution of trust income.

3. If the beneficiary is to be your surviving spouse, he or she should be provided with a set minimum amount of income that is excluded from the discretionary powers of the sprinkling clause.

4. If you retain benefits from or control over a sprinkling trust that is set up while you are still alive (an "inter vivos trust"), you will be taxed on the trust's income.

5. Careful consideration must be given to the trustee of a sprinkling trust. It is best not to have a beneficiary serve in this capacity.

Sources: *Israel A. Press, CPA, tax partner and Tom Spiesman, J.D., tax associate with Grant Thornton, 7 Hanover Square, New York, NY 10004. Mr. Press is the author of numerous tax articles.*

addressing how to pay the tax bill that is likely upon your death, or that of your spouse.

Step 2. Know what you want to accomplish with your estate plan. Your objectives here may be very broad or very simple. Many Canadians have common goals. But everyone has goals that are unique to themselves.

Your goals will be influenced by such factors as your age, marital status, the ages and needs of children, whether you are a business owner or an employee, etc. These factors can change over time. This is why estate plans need to be reviewed regularly. The estate plan of a 38-year-old parent with a mortgage, a spouse and dependent children will be different than that of a 60-year-old with substantial net assets and no dependents.

Here is a list of some common objectives to consider:

● Ensure that your estate has sufficient cash to pay taxes and other liabilities after your death.

● Provide financially for your loved ones.

● Select an executor who will manage your estate to your satisfaction.

● Ensure you leave as large an estate as possible to your heirs.

● Make sure your dependent children will have a suitable guardian.

● Distribute assets according to your wishes.

● Make gifts to your church, your college, or your favorite charities.

● Ensure that your children have sufficient funds to acquire a post-secondary education.

There are also some common problems that you should try to avoid:

● Leaving any financial burden on your family.

● Loss of assets due to excessive taxes and fees which could have been avoided.

● Delays in having your estate settled, causing increased costs and greater distress for survivors.

● Leaving assets to those who are incapable of managing them properly.

Here are some other complex issues to consider at this stage:

● **Who should benefit under your will?**
Take the example of a parent with a spouse and school-age children. Each spouse might want everything to go to the surviving spouse. It is common for spouses to designate each other as sole beneficiaries, but is that necessarily the best course of action? Can the surviving spouse manage the estate alone? Might it be better for the surviving spouse to receive only the income from the estate during his or her lifetime, without any rights to access the capital? If the surviving spouse has access to capital, does the spouse designing the will have any specific purposes in mind for which capital may be used, or are the surviving spouse's requests for capital to be at the discretion of the executor/trustee? What if the surviving spouse remarries? Will he or she (and the future spouse) continue to receive the benefit, or is the estate to be distributed to the children?

● **When should benefits be paid?**
Once it has been decided who will benefit, the next decision is what each beneficiary will receive, and when they will receive it. Should legacies (cash gifts) be paid to family members, your alma mater, a favorite charity or your church? If so, in what amounts? If the legacy is to be paid to an individual, at what age is it to be paid? And what happens if the person does not survive to that age?

● **What about your personal assets?**
There may be specific items such as antiques and artwork, a coin collection or a summer cottage which are left to certain named beneficiaries. It is wise to specify exactly who will receive which items in the will. This will go a long way toward eliminating the possibility of arguments and hurt feelings amongst survivors. Alternatively, a side letter, which has been signed on or before the date of the will, and is referred to specifically in the will, accomplishes the desired end.

Step 3. Put in place a plan to achieve your objectives. The final step is to involve the appropriate professionals to assist you in drawing together all these elements. At a minimum, you will probably be looking at completing a will and powers of attorney. Beyond that, your estate plan will be as individual as you are. Your estate plan may require the establishment of a trust, creative uses for life insurance or an estate freeze.

It is strongly recommended that you seek out the assistance of the appropriate professionals to guide you in the achievement of this important work.

The consequences of not doing so are potentially serious indeed.

Source: G. Pierce Newman, coauthor of Fiscal Fitness, *published by Prentice Hall Canada. This material originally appeared in the Money section of 50plus.com, the official website of CARP, Canada's Association for the Fifty-Plus.*

Types of Property

Since we're discussing assets, it's worthwhile to expand on the term "property." We often think of property as land, but actually the definition is much broader. There are, in fact, three main types of assets.

● **Tangible personal property** includes your car, boat, household furnishings, etc. These are physical items, therefore they're tangible.

● **Intangible personal property** includes such things as cash, GICs, share certificates, bonds, receivables, business interests, etc.

● **Real property.** This category is probably responsible for the general misconception regarding the term "property." Real property is real estate, which itself is the land and things permanently affixed to it: the buildings on the land and the rights of ownership that attach to them.

What You Need to Know About Probate

Probate is one of the least understood areas of the estate-planning process. But failure to plan carefully can tie up your assets for a long period of time and substantially increase costs.

The Latin word for proof is *probo,* from which we derive probate. It is the process of establishing (proving) the validity of the deceased's will.

There are several issues that need to be addressed in the probate process. Is the will valid? Does it satisfy legal requirements as set out by provincial legislation? Is this the deceased's true signature? Is this, in fact, the last, most recent, will of the deceased? The provincial courts will decide the validity of the will; that is, they will grant probate.

The document that the courts issue is called the grant of probate (or more commonly letters pro-bate), or, in Ontario, the certificate of appointment of estate trustee with a will.

Probate fees (really disguised taxes) are payable in all provinces except Quebec. They vary significantly from one province to another.

Probate fees are levied at the time the executor(s) applies to the courts for confirmation of appointment under the will and are based on the gross value of the deceased's assets on death. In some provinces, probate fees apply only to the value of assets situated in the deceased's province, while in others the fee is based on all of the deceased's assets, regardless of location. Debts may not be deducted from the gross value of the estate, but mortgages outstanding against real estate assets can be.

One of the problems with the probate process is that it can sometimes be extremely lengthy. This means the assets of the estate may be tied up for months or, in some cases, years, which could mean hardship for the heirs.

There are ways around this, however. Proceeds from an insurance policy are not subject to probate if they go directly to a named beneficiary. Assets that are held jointly are also excluded. These might include joint bank accounts, the family home, vacation property, etc. RRSP and RRIF portfolios avoid the probate process if a specific person, usually the spouse, is named as the beneficiary in the event of the death of the annuitant.

Using some of these techniques can ensure the quick transfer of assets after death, and to reduce the amount of the estate subject to probate fees—an important consideration since the fees usually rise with the value of the estate.

Source: G. Pierce Newman, coauthor of Fiscal Fitness, *published by Prentice Hall Canada. This material originally appeared in the Money section of 50plus.com, the official website of CARP, Canada's Association for the Fifty-Plus.*

Understanding Trusts

Once the domain only of Canada's wealthy, trusts are becoming key tools in the area of estate planning for many Canadians. Their use allows persons to transfer assets to family members, or others, while retaining some control over those assets. But don't look at trusts as simply a way to reduce taxes. Given the changes in laws, the establishment of trusts has more to do with the management of assets than it does with tax savings.

There is no statutory definition of a trust. Generally speaking, a trust is a relationship between two parties: the person(s) who hold the property (the trustees) and another person(s) for whose benefit the property is held. The relationship is said to be "fiduciary" (the Latin word for trust is *fiducia*). This means that the trustee owes a duty of "utmost good faith" to the beneficiaries.

The person who puts (settles) property into the trust, referred to as the settlor, creates the trust. The settlor must transfer property to the trustee with the clear intention of creating a trust relationship, as opposed to a gift of property, for example. It can be made clear that a trust relationship is intended using a formal trust agreement, a will, or a beneficiary designation.

It is important to note that the settlor and the trustee do not need to be different people—they can be one and the same person. A spouse, a third party or a trust company (or several of these acting together) could be designated as the trustee. The trustee holds legal title to the settled property. The beneficiary is considered to be the "beneficial owner" of the settled property. The trust assets can include real property (real estate), and tangible or intangible personal property.

A trust can be established for about $2,000. One of the reasons they are relatively inexpensive is that trustees are partially compensated from the trust's annual income.

There are three ways to create a trust:

1. By means of a distinct trust agreement.

2. A clause within a will establishing the trust.

3. A simple beneficiary designation within an insurance policy.

Testamentary Trusts

A testamentary trust is established in your will. It comes into effect when you die, and your will is probated. The assets that are the object of the trust are conveyed to the trustee just as though the trustee were a beneficiary under your will. The trust will endure for as long as you (the settlor) wish, subject to legal limitations.

One of the most common uses for a testamentary trust is to provide for the lifetime financial needs of the surviving spouse. He or she would likely be entitled to encroach on the trust's assets, and would also be entitled to receive income from it. The lion's share of the assets, however, would be preserved for eventual inheritance by the deceased's surviving children.

Other common uses for testamentary trusts are:

● Providing for specific uses, such as a child's education.

● Ensuring that monies left to minors be put into trust until they reach the age of majority, or some other specified age, at which time it can be distributed to them.

● Ensuring that funds left to a person who is incapable of managing his or her own affairs will last for their lifetime, and also be creditor-proof.

Inter Vivos Trusts

A testamentary trust takes effect after your death. An inter vivos trust, or "living trust," is set up while you are still alive. It can be used for a variety of purposes, including income splitting with other family members, reducing probate fees and estate freezes. But great care must be taken in creating them, or the income they generate could be taxed in the hands of the settlor.

Avoid Tax on Debts

Suppose your son owes you $10,000. Your will provides for cancellation of that debt upon your death. *Tax result:* Even though your estate does not collect it, the value of that debt is considered an asset of the estate. **Better way:** When the debt is first established, spell out that the payment obligation will cease at your death. **Result:** After your death, there is no repayment right for your estate and there is no asset to be included and subjected to probate.

Spousal Trusts

This is a special type of trust that is set up for your husband or wife. The two key requirements are that all the income from the trust must be paid to the spouse during his or her lifetime, and there may be no distributions of trust assets to anyone other than the spouse during the person's lifetime.

One important feature of the spousal trust is that the transfer of property to the trust takes place at the settlor's (donor's) cost—there is no triggering of accrued capital gains up to the moment of the transfer. In fact, the property is only taxed when it is disposed of, or when the spouse dies.

Insurance Trusts

An insurance trust is a specialized tool that gives a policy owner control over the timing of receipt, and the use, of insurance proceeds. While it is usually used for minor beneficiaries, it can be used in many other situations as well. Insurance proceeds directed to such a trust do not form part of the deceased's estate, and as such may reduce probate fees and may be protected from creditors.

An insurance trust can be useful in special situations. One example is in the case of a beneficiary who has yet to attain the age of majority. As a result, the insurer has three options regarding the disbursement of the death benefit. They must either:

● Pay the funds to a named trustee (the most common option).

● Pay the funds into court.

● Pay the funds to a public trustee.

The first option is the most commonly used for the following reasons:

1. It assures the policy owner that the funds are received for the benefit of the minor child.

2. It provides flexibility as to how the child will benefit from the proceeds, and the conditions under which the child may eventually receive the proceeds of the policy.

3. It prevents misuse of the funds by an irresponsible beneficiary.

A valid insurance trust will be created simply as a result of the beneficiary designation in the policy, where the proceeds are paid to the named trustee, with the additional words "in trust for (a named beneficiary)."

In this situation, the absence of any other trust documentation is likely to cause some minor problems, as the trust will be limited to the terms set out in applicable provincial legislation, and jurisprudence. These limitations may hinder the best efforts of a trustee, and may not be in keeping with the wishes of the insured. The potential problems of relying on the beneficiary designation alone include:

● The trustee will be unable to encroach on the capital of the trust regardless of the minor's needs.

● The minor child is entitled to receive the insurance funds when they reach the age of majority.

● The trustee may not have the discretion to ensure that the smallest amount of tax is paid on the earnings of the trust.

● The trustee will be limited by applicable legislation in the types of investments they can make. This may limit the returns that can be obtained while the funds are in the trust.

In creating an insurance trust, you must ensure that all legal documentation supports the same end. Thus the will, the beneficiary designation in the insurance policy, and other trust documentation (if there is any) must all support the same result. Here is a simple but damaging example of why.

Assume that an insurance trust has been set up in your will, or in separate trust documentation. You accidentally make a different beneficiary designation using the beneficiary designation in the policy. In such a case, which one will prevail?

Under provincial legislation, a later beneficiary designation will automatically revoke all prior designations. If a policyholder had made an earlier beneficiary declaration under his will, then the declaration within the will would no longer have effect and the intended insurance trust would not be created.

At one time it was possible to flow income out to a beneficiary without the income being payable to them. This was effected by what was known as the preferred beneficiary election. This is now not generally available, being restricted to cases where the beneficiary is mentally or physically disabled (defined as being able to claim the disability tax credit).

Source: *G. Pierce Newman, coauthor of* Fiscal Fitness, *published by Prentice Hall Canada. This material originally appeared in the Money section of 50plus.com, the official website of CARP, Canada's Association for the Fifty-Plus.*

The Role of a Trustee

If you are asked to be a trustee for any type of trust, think about it carefully before you agree. It's not an honorary role, like being a godparent. There is a lot of work involved.

Being a trustee involves great responsibility, with many legal implications. The trustee's actions are governed by provincial legislation, the principles of the trust relationship as established in common law, and the authority originally granted in the will (assuming it is a testamentary trust). If you fail to act appropriately, you could be held personally liable by the trust's beneficiaries. So in taking on the role, you are exposing yourself to some potential risk.

A trustee is responsible for the annual reporting requirements for trusts, as mandated by the Income Tax Act and must ensure the payment of any taxes owing by the trust. The basic duties and responsibilities of a trustee are established in law, and include:

The duty of care: A trustee has the responsibility to act in a reasonable and prudent manner.

The duty to act in the beneficiary's best interests and to avoid all conflicts of interest: Trustees may not profit from administration of the trust, and must treat beneficiaries without favoritism.

The duty to act personally: While a trustee may employ others to provide professional advice or administrative services to the trust, the trustee's responsibility for the trust cannot be delegated.

Trust and competence are the key qualities required of a trustee. Possible trustees would include family members, friends, trust companies,

---

GIFTS TO MINORS

For adult children, an outright gift of property is usually the most efficient and practical way for you to distribute assets to your beneficiaries—the title is simply transferred from you to the beneficiary. Since we have no gift tax in Canada, the only thing you need to watch out for is the "deemed disposition" rule. The Canada Customs and Revenue Agency (CCRA) takes the position that a gift is equivalent to a sale for tax purposes. If the deemed disposition triggers a taxable capital gain, you'll be on the hook to pay the CCRA.

Tip: You can avoid the deemed disposition trap by giving a cash gift. Also, giving the family home to an adult child will not trigger taxes because as a principal residence it is tax-exempt.

Giving financial gifts to young children is a different matter.

Here you risk running afoul of the "income attribution" rules. This means

that any interest or dividends earned by the money you give your children will be considered as taxable income in your hands, not theirs. The idea is

to prevent income-splitting within a family, whereby a high-bracket tax-payer transfers income into the hands of a related person who pays little or no tax.

However, the attribution rules do not apply to capital gains. If your financial gift is invested in such a way

as to grow in value through capital gains, those profits are considered to belong to the child, not to you, and are taxed accordingly.

So it is possible to put some of your assets in the hands of minor children and not suffer any tax consequences. The key is to have an investment program that will minimize or eliminate any interest or dividend income, at least until such time as the child reaches the age of maturity.

Another option is to set up an inter vivos education trust for the child. This can be done on an informal basis, but you need to ensure that you follow the proper steps if income attribution rules are to be avoided. You can also consider putting some money into a registered education savings plan (RESP). The income earned within these plans is tax-sheltered. When the accumulated income is withdrawn by the child to pay for college, it's taxable in his or her hands, not yours. The principal is returned to you, tax-free.

lawyers and accountants. (But a trustee should generally not be one of the beneficiaries of the trust.)

Often, joint trustees are named, with one being a family member or friend and the other being a professional who will look after all the details.

In theory, you don't have to appoint a professional to be a trustee. But unless it is a small family trust, you should seriously consider doing so. Trusts are complicated structures and they must file special tax returns each year. There are also investment decisions to be made and other administrative matters to be attended to.

Unless the person you are considering as trustee has the knowledge and time to deal with these matters, it would be better to use the services of a trust company, a lawyer, or some other competent professional to look after all this. Otherwise, your trust may end up in a tangled mess, which will cost more to sort out in the end.

Source: G. Pierce Newman, coauthor of Fiscal Fitness, published by Prentice Hall Canada. This material originally appeared in the Money section of 50plus.com, the official website of CARP, Canada's Association for the Fifty-Plus.

Tax Considerations for Gift Giving

Although there is no gift tax in Canada, that does not mean that you can give your assets away without any tax consequences. When you give an asset to someone else (say, for example, shares in a company), the Canada Customs and Revenue Agency (CCRA) takes the position that you sold it at fair market value. This "deemed disposition" triggers a taxable event. If the shares have risen in value, you will have to pay tax at the capital gains rate on the difference. The same rules apply if the assets are moved into a trust.

However, assets gifted to your spouse are exempt from this rule. They are deemed to pass to the

Head Off Trouble

If you own a tax shelter, or any investment that might involve you in a dispute with the CCRA, think twice before leaving it to your spouse or children unless they share your financial sophistication—and your willingness to battle the government.

Alternative: Leave it to someone with a lot of financial savvy, or put it in trust and appoint a smart trustee.

spouse at the current market value (which becomes the "adjusted cost base") and no tax is payable by you at the time of the transfer. Of course, that isn't of much help if your goal is to save taxes at death, because assets will pass tax-free to your spouse.

Giving assets to your spouse, and minor children, can give rise to a different kind of problem: the income attribution rules. These are designed to prevent income-splitting in families by making it difficult for a higher-income spouse to transfer income-generating assets to a spouse or children who are taxed at a lower rate. The law states that if you make this type of gift, you must continue to declare the income earned from the asset on your own tax return. However, future capital gains will be taxed in the hands of the recipient. Also, if the earnings from the asset are reinvested, income from the reinvested money will be the tax responsibility of the spouse or child. You're only on the hook for the original amount.

The attribution rules don't apply to adult children, however. You can transfer as much of your wealth to them with no tax implications beyond the initial capital gains potential.

Tax benefits: All income tax on gift property that is transferred outright or in a trust (with the income being distributed to the beneficiaries) is based on the donee's tax bracket, not on your income tax bracket, provided the donee (recipient), is not your spouse or, if a child, is an adult. Otherwise, if a minor child receives the income, it is taxed at the parent's top bracket. *Even trickier:* For property that is transferred through a trust but where the income is not currently distributable to the beneficiary, the trust itself is subject to income tax at the top marginal rate that is applicable in the province.

For gifts to be a legitimate transfer, you must relinquish all control over the transferred property.

Source: Gordon Pape, coauthor with Eric Kirzner of Secrets of Successful Investing, published by Prentice Hall Canada.

Why You Need a Common Disaster Clause in Your Will

Include a "common disaster clause" in your will to cover the possibility that you and your spouse (or other beneficiary) may die together in an accident. Otherwise, your provincial "simultaneous death statute" will govern all questions of inheritance, taxation, the marital deduction, the disposition of jointly held property, who receives insurance proceeds and all other questions of who claims your property.

The provisions of the law may not be to your liking. To be sure your wishes are carried out, put a provision in your will.

Source: *Alexandra Armstrong, a certified financial planner.*

Do-It-Yourself Will Kits

Will kits have become popular with many people who want to avoid legal costs. Without faulting their usefulness, in general anything more than a very basic estate would benefit from the knowledge of a lawyer. Certainly, a kit would be preferable to not having a will at all. But remember that lawyers are paid for their years of experience, not the cost to prepare a few documents. Just one mistake with a do-it-yourself will could cost your loved ones dearly.

Source: *G. Pierce Newman, coauthor of* Fiscal Fitness, *published by Prentice Hall Canada. This material originally appeared in the Money section of 50plus.com, the official website of CARP, Canada's Association for the Fifty-Plus.*

Keeping Peace Among Your Beneficiaries

A man's will provided that his daughter could choose "any three items in my estate," with the remainder distributed to others. His estate included 19 thoroughbred horses, and the daughter selected all 19 as a single item. The other beneficiaries sued—one horse, one item, they claimed. The judge disagreed—all 19 counted as one.

Although extreme, this example demonstrates the family discord that can arise over vaguely worded instructions regarding the disposition of property. The market value—not to mention the high emotional value—of furniture, jewelry and other tangible property makes it imperative to avoid carelessly planned dispositions that ultimately may have to be handled in court.

The Problem of Equal Shares

Suppose you own securities, tangibles of moderate value and a magnificent $300,000 desk. Everything is

Protecting a Valuable Collection

If breaking up your collection would greatly reduce its value, consider forming a corporation to inherit the collection under your will. It can then be sold as an entirety and the proceeds distributed to your heirs and beneficiaries (to whom you would specify numbers of shares in the corporation). If the collection is willed to various individuals, it may make the sale more difficult and less lucrative.

to go to your children in equal shares. With the desk indivisible, how can your children apportion all the tangibles and still maintain equality? *Solution:* Add a codicil to your will that allows for the disproportionate allocation of your securities to adjust for inequality in the tangibles.

Avoid catchall phrases in your will. References such as "the contents of my safe-deposit box" simply invite conflict. Allow for moderate inequality by permitting the tangibles to be divided in *substantially* equal shares. Making gifts during your lifetime also helps reduce friction after your death.

You don't have to amend your will every time the plans for your tangibles are changed—the will can refer to a nonbinding memorandum to be rewritten by you from time to time. However, if the executor of the will is empowered to make allocations, make sure he or she is not one of the beneficiaries.

Be wary of the impact of capital gains taxes levied on the estate. If an estate contains shares of stock, for example, a number of them may be sold to provide tax money. The same cannot be done with a valuable chair—chipping off a leg to raise taxes is impossible. Conflict is guaranteed if one beneficiary receives the chair and another pays the taxes derived from it.

Source: *Archie M. Richards, Jr., CFP, president, Archie Richards Associates, Inc., Ten Mall Rd. Burlington, MA 01803.*

Who Is the Spendthrift?

A testator (the person writing a will) may not be concerned so much that his or her son or daughter has spendthrift tendencies, but that this person's spouse is the one who is likely to be wildly extravagant or gullible. The testator may provide that anything he or she gives or leaves to a son or daughter is to be in the form of a life income from a trust, so that the principal cannot get into the hands of the spouse. The assets of the trust may subsequently be distributed as the testator sees fit—often the grandchildren are named, rather than the prodigal spouse.

Who Gets Your Money If You Don't Leave a Valid Will

Many Canadians don't have a will. And they probably have no clear idea what will happen to their property when they die.

Provincial laws vary, but the provisions of most are similar when someone dies without leaving a will.

● **Surviving spouse.** A surviving spouse is always entitled to a substantial part of the estate, sometimes all of it. If there are also surviving children, the spouse's share is usually one-half or one-third, or sometimes a specified amount plus a fraction of the balance. The exact amount allocated to each depends on provincial law (which is subject to change) and on

WRITING A WILL THAT WORKS

● **Include a simultaneous-death clause** that dictates how property will be disposed of in the event both you and your spouse die simultaneously in a common disaster. This prevents acrimony among the beneficiaries as well as potential litigation.

● **Consider a no-contest clause** to prevent a disappointed beneficiary from suing to have your will overturned. Such a clause says that any beneficiary who challenges the will must forfeit his or her share under the will.

● **Tailor bequests to the beneficiary.** Leave property to each beneficiary in the form that he or she can best handle. This may mean outright transfers. But depending on the beneficiary's age, experience, financial sophistication and personal inclinations, a trust or a custodianship or some other form of management, may be more appropriate.

● **Avoid giving complicated or risky investments,** such as tax shelters, to financially unsophisticated beneficiaries who may not have your desire to fight the Canada Customs and Revenue Agency.

● **Don't leave property in joint ownership** when one of the co-owners is likely to be dominated by the other.

● **Don't give undivided fractional interests in property** to beneficiaries who have very different and/or uneducated ideas about the management or selling price of the property. Instead, transfer the property to a corporation and give the beneficiaries voting shares.

● **Consider percentage bequests to favored beneficiaries,** rather than absolute dollar amounts. In inflationary times, an estate can turn out to be worth far more than anticipated. A bequest of a dollar amount, no matter how generous it seemed at the time you made it, may be embarrassingly small in relation to the size of the inflated estate.

Source: *Dr. Robert S. Holzman, professor emeritus of taxation at New York University and author of* Estate Planning: The New Golden Opportunities, *Boardroom Books.*

the number of children. In Manitoba, for instance, the law states that if surviving children are also the children of the surviving spouse, all goes to the spouse.

In all provinces but Quebec, if there are no children or grandchildren, the spouse takes the entire estate. Quebec, however, gives a share to parents or brothers and sisters. For example, if relatives are living, 33% of the estate goes to the spouse, 33% to the parents, and 33% to siblings. If the parents are deceased then 50% goes to the spouse and 50% to relatives. If there are no relatives, 50% goes to the spouse and 50% to parents.

It doesn't matter if the parties have been separated. Only a legal dissolution of the marriage (by divorce or annulment) will cut off the spouse's right to inherit.

● **Descendants.** Subject to the rights of the spouse, descendants usually have first claim on the estate. Each child takes an equal share, and the children of deceased children take the share their parent would have received. If all children are deceased, the grandchildren inherit. If great grandchildren enter the picture, the same rules apply.

The rules on adopted children may vary, although the trend is to treat them exactly the same as non-adopted children. Illegitimate children inherit from their mother. But the laws on inheriting from the father vary widely.

● **Ancestors.** In practice, this means parents. In rare cases, a grandparent may survive even though both parents are dead. If the deceased left any descendants, parents take nothing. If a spouse survives, but no descendants, parents only take a share in the province of Quebec. If there are no surviving descendants or spouse, the surviving parents or parent usually takes the entire estate. Some provinces divide it among parents, brothers and sisters.

● **Collateral relatives.** If there is no surviving spouse or relative, the estate goes to those with the closest degree of blood relationship to the deceased. Some provinces bar remote relatives by limiting inheritance to a specified degree of relationship.

If there is no relative who can inherit and no will, the property goes to the province.

One misconception: Lack of a will won't keep your estate out of the courts. Even holding property jointly won't necessarily do that. Most assets, such as stocks, bonds and savings accounts above a certain amount cannot be transferred without court administration.

● **Administration.** The court will appoint an administrator, usually one of the heirs. The administrator normally has to post bond, with the cost paid by the estate. If there's more than one heir, any unreasonable disputes among them (including who is to be administrator) must be settled by the court. Such family quarrels can be highly destructive, especially if the estate includes an ongoing business or any other assets that require management.

Once appointed, the duties of an administrator are the same as those of an executor: to collect and manage all the assets and distribute them to the proper persons.

● **Minor children.** If any of the heirs are minors, the court must appoint a guardian or trustee of the property. The trustee's job is to conserve the inheritance until the minor grows up. Income from the property can be used for the child's benefit or saved, but the principal can't be touched without a court order. This can mean a great deal of trouble and expense if money is needed to cover items such as educational costs or medical bills for the minor.

Here's how to avoid problems: The cost of a simple will (without trusts) drawn up by a competent attorney should be modest. A will can avoid many of the possible costs and problems of administration as well as making sure that your estate goes to persons you really want to have it.

Source: G. Pierce Newman, coauthor of Fiscal Fitness, *published by Prentice Hall Canada. This material originally appeared in the Money section of 50plus.com, the official website of CARP, Canada's Association for the Fifty-Plus; and Edward D. Moldover, senior partner, Moldover, Hertz, Presnick & Gidaly, New York.*

The Role of an Executor

An executor is one of those people we will never need in your lifetime, but who will be extremely important to the family after death.

This is a person, or an institution, appointed in your will, whose duty is to administer and distribute the estate's assets after a death. The executor is responsible for carrying out the deceased's wishes. The selection of an executor is one of the first and most important considerations in the process of will preparation. Often Canadians select a family member, a trusted friend or relative or a business associate, to act as executor.

It is recommended that more than one executor be appointed. An alternate executor should be named, since, upon death, the named executor might choose not to take on this responsibility, or he or she may have predeceased. It is also important to obtain the consent of the individual or individuals appointed before naming them in a will.

At the simplest level, the executor's duties are the same for all estates. However, given the complexity of a particular estate, they may appear very different. The tasks may be few, and simple to execute. Or they may be many and complex, and take years to complete. Irrespective of the size of the estate, the executor takes on great responsibility.

Here is a run-down of some of the responsibilities that are involved, and skills required. Let's look at them from the perspective of someone who has just assumed an executor's responsibility.

● **Locate and review the will.** Your first priority as executor is to obtain the most recent original copy of the deceased's will. Ideally, you will have been informed where it is, or you may already have a copy. If it cannot be located among the deceased's papers at home, check the safety-deposit box. This will necessitate calling the bank and making an appointment to come in to open the box. Bring the key, a copy of the death certificate (a burial certificate issued by the funeral home may suffice), and your identification. If the will is there, confirm that you are indeed named as executor. If so, you should be allowed to take the will with you. A bank employee will make a list of the contents of the box and will give you a copy of that list. Ironically, a safety-deposit box is a poor place to keep a will, for just this reason.

● **Organize a meeting.** Organize a meeting of the deceased's family, to review funeral arrangements, and allow you to confirm the whereabouts of insurance policies, investment statements, safety-deposit boxes, share certificates, etc.

● **Arranging the funeral.** Assuming the funeral has not been preplanned, it is one of your direct responsibilities as executor. You will, no doubt, want to consider the deceased's wishes as expressed in the will or elsewhere, and the wishes of the immediate family.

After the funeral, the funeral bills can be presented to the deceased's bank. The bank will give you an official cheque drawn on the deceased's account to pay the funeral home. Financial institutions will generally permit cheques to be drawn from the deceased's account, with minimal documentation, as long as these payments are for the funeral, and medical bills incurred immediately prior to the death. But if you try to go much beyond these costs, the financial institution will demand that all their documentary requirements be met before releasing further funds.

● **Routine financial matters.** Cancel all the deceased's credit cards, subscriptions, etc. Utility services may need to be terminated. If the deceased is entitled to CPP and OAS, make application for whatever benefits there may be. Communicate with the deceased's employer, if applicable, regarding any benefits that may have been available. Commence claims on any private life insurance policies that the deceased held. If you believe it to be appropriate, place an advertisement in a local newspaper asking creditors to come forward so that you can ensure that all of the deceased's legitimate debts can be paid.

● **Beginning to manage the estate.** Prepare an inventory of all of the deceased's assets. Remember that any assets that were owned in joint tenancy with another person, or where a beneficiary designation had been made—such as with life insurance policies, RRSPs and RRIFs—do not form part of the estate. Ensure that tangible assets are secure and that proper insurance is in force. In particular, ensure that homeowner's insurance does not lapse because the home may be vacant.

● **Distributions from the estate.** Payments on behalf of the dependants of the deceased may be permitted. But you should not make any distributions from the estate during the first six months without the surviving spouse's written consent, or an authorization from the court. In fact, you should wait six months before distributing any assets to the beneficiaries because the deceased's dependents have six months during which they may contest the will. Lastly, you may not make a final distribution of estate assets until you have a "clearance certificate" from the CCRA or Revenu Quebec, certifying that the estate has no income taxes owing.

For assets such as marketable securities and real estate, letters probate or letters of administration are almost always necessary for transfer of title. Financial institutions will generally require "notarial copies" of letters probate/letters of administration before they will amend the registration of a financial asset, or disburse funds to the executor/administrator. This protects the financial institutions from liability arising from claims by other parties.

● **Keep detailed records.** Ensure you keep full and accurate records of all transactions either in to, or out of, the estate account. If you are asked to do so, you must be able to provide a full accounting. Keep track as well of all your disbursements made in the course of your duties as executor. Lastly, when you do finally distribute the estate, obtain releases from the beneficiaries absolving you from any further claims.

Tip: Don't put yourself on the hook

Being the executor of an estate should not cost you anything personally, other than your time. But there are situations in which you could be held financially liable if a problem arises. Settling all the deceased's debts is one of these.

It's your job to make sure all creditors are identified and paid. It's a good idea to advertise for creditors, usually in local newspapers. Arrange for the payment of any debts, and funeral and testamentary expenses, including probate costs. If you do not do so, and a creditor turns up after all the money in the estate has been paid out, you as executor will be responsible for settling the debt.

Source: G. Pierce Newman, coauthor of Fiscal Fitness, published by Prentice Hall Canada. This material originally appeared in the Money section of 50plus.com, the official website of CARP, Canada's Association for the Fifty-Plus.

How to Choose a Guardian for Your Children

Whom do you want to take care of your children in the event you and your spouse die in the same unfortunate accident?

This important estate-planning question exasperates most parents. But if you don't appoint a guardian, a probate judge will. And you are likely to make a better choice than the judge. *To do the job right, follow these guidelines:*

● **Prepare a list of possible guardians.** Rate each individual or couple according to their degree of responsibility, accessibility, lifestyle, moral tenets, opinions on child raising, and personal compatibility with your children. *Other factors:* The candidates' ages, whether they have children and their ages.

● **Have meetings with the candidates.** From these meetings you should learn each individual's willingness to become your children's guardian, the individual's short- and long-range plans and his or her viewpoints on issues that are crucial to you as parents.

● **Select only individuals who satisfy all your criteria.** And remember to provide for a succession of guardians. Choose alternates in case your first choices become unable or unwilling to carry out their duties of caring for your children.

● **Keep in touch with the guardians you have appointed.** Meet with them from time to time to fill them in on the current needs and plans for your children. These meetings will also give the guardians a chance to voice changes in their own lifestyles that might have a dramatic impact on your children. You may decide to change guardians because of impressions you pick up. Use these sessions to let your children and their guardians get to know each other.

● **Prepare a memorandum of instructions for the guardians, and keep it up-to-date.** Include a list of things important to your children's well-being, such as their allergies, medical requirements, family medical history, personality traits and behavior responses. State your personal opinions about allowances, dating, schooling, driving, drinking and other areas of parental discretion.

● **Provide direction about spending funds to achieve short-range and long-range goals.** Indicate which goals have priority. For instance, are short-range goals such as a car or a vacation in Europe more important than long-range goals such as college or a nest egg for going into business?

● **Set a minimum monthly allowance** to be paid to the guardians for the children's day-to-day spending needs. This monthly amount should be reviewed from time to time for reasonableness. Give your trustee the power to increase the allowance to meet your specified spending goals or to adjust for inflation.

● **Project your estate's future cash flow.** How much will be available after taxes are paid on the income earned? You need this figure to set a realistic monthly allowance.

Powers of Attorney

A power of attorney is a written agreement between you and someone that you trust. It empowers that person to do certain things on your behalf while you are alive, and while you are unable to do so yourself. The person granting the power is the donor. The person to whom power is granted is the donee. It is a legal document, and it is signed before two witnesses.

Powers of attorney are an important part of a comprehensive estate plan. Remember that, like wills, this area of the law is a provincial legislative

WHAT YOUR EXECUTOR NEEDS TO KNOW

You choose your executor with great care and expect him or her to do a good job. But he or she can't be effective unless you provide some essential information. *Questions:*

● **How can an executor collect all of the estate's assets** if he or she doesn't know precisely what or where they are or the extent of your interest in them?

● **How can he or she prevent co-owners of bank or brokerage accounts** from drawing out funds if he or she doesn't know that the accounts exist? How can he or she put a stop payment on the accounts? How can he or she prevent safe-deposit boxes from being invaded by co-owners and those in possession of keys or combination numbers? *Solution:* Write your executor a letter listing all the facts he or she must have in order to effectively administer your estate. *Include:*

● **A complete list of what you own and where it is,** plus any identifying serial numbers (such as those on stock certificates, bank accounts and insurance policies). If there are co-owners or persons holding power of attorney over any of your property, supply the details.

● **The location of all documents the executor will need immediately**—your most recent will, cemetery-plot deed or number, marriage license, divorce decree.

● **A description of the rights you have, or may have,** under the retirement plans of all employers you have ever worked for. You may have vested rights under the plan of a company you worked for many years ago. If you were in the armed forces or with a government agency, identify which one and give your serial number. Are you a member of a fraternal organization or lodge that may provide death benefits or survivor rights?

● **The name of the person who prepared your federal income tax returns,** at least for the past three years. Who has the work papers? Who understands them?

● **The names of your insurance broker and stockbrokers.** Where are brokers' confirmation slips of all purchases you have made at any time?

● **A list of all money, jewelry or other property you've lent.** Are you the co-owner of any property that may not be in your possession? Does anyone, including the Canada Customs and Revenue Agency (CCRA), owe you money?

● **A list of all your debts,** including insurance policy loans and tax assessments.

● **A list of all documents that could establish the value of property** you own or the price that your executor could get for it. *Include:* Financial statements of closely held corporations in which you own stock, partnership agreements, buy-sell agreements between a corporation and its shareholders or between the shareholders themselves, real estate or jewelry appraisals, markets where estate assets such as collectibles might be sold at a good price.

Put the letter in a well-sealed envelope with your executor's name on it. Attach the envelope to your will or put it in your safe-deposit box.

Source: Dr. Robert S. Holzman, professor emeritus of taxation at New York University and author of Estate Planning: The New Golden Opportunities, *Boardroom Books.*

jurisdiction, thus there will be differences from province to province. Consult a lawyer on your government's specific provisions.

There are several different terms everyone should be familiar with before making a decision to execute a power of attorney.

General power of attorney. This grants very broad latitudes (and responsibilities) to the donee. It allows the person to manage your affairs completely. This could include making investment decisions, making withdrawals from your bank or investment accounts, or disposing of tangible property. It is also generally a continuing or enduring power of attorney, in that it remains in force during any subsequent incapacity of the donor.

Limited power of attorney. This allows the donee to act only in certain specific matters. If you spend your winters in Arizona, for example, you may want them to deposit your dividend cheques and pay your bills while you're gone. This is the scope of a limited power of attorney. You can revoke a limited power of attorney at any time while you remain mentally competent.

Power of attorney for property. This is the document most people probably think of when they hear "power of attorney." It covers the general management of a person's affairs, personal and business. Clearly, it should only be granted to someone in whom you place great trust. It usually provides for a broad range of powers. A power of attorney for property can be drawn for a specified period of time ("while I am out of Canada") or for a certain purpose ("to sell 100 shares of XYZ Corp."). But it is more common for it to be general in nature, and "continuing"; that is, it continues to be valid during any subsequent incapacity of the donor. To be "continuing," it must specifically address the issue of the donor's subsequent incapacity. Even a general power of attorney can have restrictions written into it. For example, you might give the donee authority over your financial affairs, but direct that your home could not be sold. The donee could not prepare or change your will, nor could he or she give away any property that was bequeathed to someone else in your will.

Power of attorney for personal care. This takes effect when the donee believes that you are

How to Avoid the Naming of an Administrator

To ensure that an executor of your selection will serve, this is what you should do:

✔ Sound out your designated executor to see whether he or she will actually serve if named in your will. Do this periodically. Is his or her health still satisfactory? Has he or she taken on full-time responsibilities elsewhere? Is he or she still interested in you and your beneficiaries? If not, replace him or her.

✔ Seek to ensure your designated executor's agreement to serve by recommending to him or her knowledgeable and able attorneys, accountants, and (where appropriate) appraisers and brokers who can help your executor to carry out his or her responsibilities without excessive detailed work with which he or she isn't familiar.

✔ Name one or more successor or contingent executors so that if the person of your choice doesn't serve, at least it will be your second or third choice, rather than an administrator whom you would never have engaged.

✔ Name a trust company as coexecutor. This virtually assures the permanence and continuity of an executor you have seen fit to name.

✔ Make certain that your will is valid so that the executor chosen by you will qualify. Have an attorney familiar with provincial law check such requirements as the minimum number of witnesses required. Laws vary as to the technicalities to be met.

✔ Be sure that your will can be found when the time comes to have it probated. A perfectly executed and technically correct will is useless if nobody knows where it is. Have your will in your attorney's office, or with your federal income tax work papers.

Source: Encyclopedia of Estate Planning, *Boardroom Books.*

incapable. You can set out in the power of attorney how you want that issue to be decided. You can also give the donee specific instructions on what you want to do in certain circumstances. He or she will have the authority to make decisions about your health care, shelter and clothing, nutrition, hygiene and safety if you are incapable. You can sign a power of attorney, or write a new one, if you are well enough to understand its meaning and purpose, even though you may already be getting help with your personal-care needs.

It is important not to confuse this document with a living will, which is neither a will nor a power of attorney for personal care, and will probably not have the legal force necessary to achieve your goals. The power of attorney for personal care, however, will give your donee the necessary legal authority to make health care choices on your behalf.

As with any element of an effective financial or estate plan, things should be done well before there is an actual need. This is particularly so as it relates to powers of attorney. You may execute a power of attorney only while you are of sound mind, and can understand what you are doing. Once you have become mentally incapacitated, it is too late to execute a power of attorney. And that is precisely the time when one will be needed, to ensure that your affairs continue to run smoothly, especially for the benefit of those who depend upon you. Don't delay.

Source: G. Pierce Newman, coauthor of Fiscal Fitness, *published by Prentice Hall Canada. This material originally appeared in the Money section of 50plus.com, the official website of CARP, Canada's Association for the Fifty-Plus.*

Prepaid Funeral Plans

Trap: Consumers who buy them may lose out if the company selling the plan misappropriates the money or if the funeral home goes out of business. Before investing in a prepaid plan, call your provincial attorney general's office and/or the Better Business Bureau to see if there are any problems with the company. Then, check out its track record, and review the contract with an attorney.

Safer alternatives: Set up your own trust fund or savings account, or add to your insurance policy to cover funeral expenses.

Pay-before-you-go funeral programs allow you to make all arrangements in advance, sparing your family difficult decisions. Payment can be made in installments through an insurance plan that covers all costs even if you die before all the premiums are paid.

Source: Joseph I. Swietlik, CA-7, No. 85-1887.

Estate-Planning Glossary

Administrator. The person, appointed by the court, who will administer the estate under the following circumstances: there is no will, an executor was not named in the will, all named executors have or all named executors are unwilling or unable to act. Also referred to as a personal representative.

Agent for the executor. This is a person or trust company, retained by the executor, to provide them with administrative services and advice.

Alternate appointment. This is another executor, appointed in the will, in the event the first named executor is unwilling or unable to act.

Asset. Anything that you own, or is owed to you, that has a value in economic terms. Obvious examples would include a car, a house, RRSPs, an investment portfolio, business interests, etc.

Attribution rules. These are rules under Canada's Income Tax Act, the aim of which is to discourage certain income-splitting arrangements. These rules may cause income and losses, or capital gains or capital losses, to be taxed in the hands of the transferor, not the person holding the property. This will depend on the circumstances of the individual case. These rules are very complex. Even if you believe you have found a way to circumvent these rules, the government can rely upon the General Anti-Avoidance Regulation to reverse actions you've taken. It is essential to seek professional advice before implementing any income-splitting strategies.

Beneficiary. The person receiving a benefit or gift under a will. Also, the person for whose benefit a trust is created. Can also be the recipient of benefits under a life insurance policy, an RRSP or a pension plan.

Bequest. A gift of personal property made pursuant to a will.

Capital gain. A capital gain is realized when an asset is sold and the proceeds of disposition, less selling expenses, is greater than the asset's adjusted cost base. Such a gain will often result in tax consequences. One-half of a capital gain is taxable. Examples include the sale of stocks, bonds and real estate.

Capital loss. A capital loss is realized when the capital gain calculation results in a negative number. In other words, the adjusted cost base is greater than the proceeds of disposition less selling expenses. One-half of a capital loss is an allowable capital loss, and can be used to offset taxable capital gains.

Capital property. Property which, if sold, leads to a capital gain or a capital loss.

Cash flow. Net income for a stated period, plus any noncash deductions (depreciation and amortization).

Certificate of appointment. *See* Grant of probate.

Codicil. A properly witnessed, written amendment to a will. The amendment could be a change or an addition. It is executed with all the formalities of the will it amends.

Custodian. A person legally responsible for overseeing the care and affairs of a minor or an incompetent person, should both parents be dead. Custodianships are appointed by the court. Also referred to as a guardian.

Donee. The person or party receiving a gift (from a donor). In the context of a power of attorney, the party to whom authority has been granted.

Donor. The person or party making a gift (to the donee). In the context of a power of attorney, the party who granted the authority.

Estate. The right, title or interest a person has in any property. This would include such items as monies, personal property, business interests, real property, receivables, etc.

Estate planning. The process of arranging for the orderly conveyance, to your chosen beneficiaries, of all of your assets at the time of your death.

Estate trustee. The individual or firm named, by the deceased in a will, to carry out the provisions of such will.

Estate trustee with a will. *See* Executor/Executrix.

Estate trustee without a will. *See* Administrator.

Executor/Executrix. The person (or persons) or institution appointed to administer an estate in accordance with the terms of a will.

Fair market value. The value of an asset sold by a willing vendor to a knowledgeable purchaser, neither party being under duress.

Fiduciary. An individual or institution having a lawful duty to act for the benefit of another party.

Grant of probate. A document, issued to an executor by the court, that confirms the executor's authority to administer a particular estate. Also referred to as letters probate. In Ontario, now referred to as certificate of appointment as estate trustee with a will.

Guardian. *See* Custodian.

Heir. A person legally entitled to receive property from a deceased through inheritance.

Holographic will. A will written completely in the testator's (the person writing the will) hand, signed and dated, but not witnessed. May not be a valid will in some jurisdictions.

Income splitting. A technique whereby taxable income from an individual in a high tax bracket is diverted to an individual in a low tax bracket, with the net result that total taxes for the two individuals are reduced.

Intangible personal property. Personal property that does not have a physical existence, such as cash in the bank, ownership of shares of a company, copyright and patent. The property, and its value, may be represented by a document, but the document itself, is not the property.

Inter vivos trust. A trust created during the lifetime of the settlor (the person creating the trust). Assets can be passed to the trust for the benefit of beneficiaries and in order to minimize probate expenses. Also referred to as a living trust. *See* Trust.

Intestate. A person who dies without a will is said to "die intestate."

Irrevocable trust. A trust which cannot be cancelled by the person who created it (the settlor). *See* Trust.

Issue. All those who are descended from a common ancestor. The term "children" is limited to the first generation.

Joint and last survivor. A feature of an annuity. Benefits are paid until the death of the second, surviving spouse, at which time they cease.

Joint tenancy. A form of joint ownership of tangible and intangible assets where the death of one of the joint owners results in the immediate transfer of ownership of the asset to the surviving joint owner(s). Also referred to as joint tenancy with right of survivorship, and abbreviated JTRS, or JTWRS.

Joint tenant. One of the tenants in a joint tenancy.

Legatees. Used in the province of Quebec, this is a person legally entitled to receive property from a deceased through inheritance.

Letters probate. *See* Grant of probate.

Liability. Debts or obligations of a person or company. Usually distinguished between current and long-term liabilities.

Liquidator. In the province of Quebec, the person who administers the succession of the deceased's patrimony. It is analogous to the executor in common-law provinces.

Living trust. *See* Inter-vivos trust. *See also* Trust.

Mandatary. The person or persons to whom authority is granted under a mandate. Peculiar to the province of Quebec. Equates to the donee in common-law provinces.

Mandate. The form of power of attorney peculiar to the province of Quebec.

Mandator. The person who grants authority to the mandatary. Peculiar to the province of Quebec. Equates to the donor in common-law provinces.

Patrimony. This term is used exclusively in Quebec. It is the total of the economic rights and obligations of a person. A person's patrimony begins when they are born, and lasts for their life. A person has only one patrimony.

Personal net worth (PNW). A person's total assets, less total liabilities. This is their equity.

Personal property. *See* Tangible personal property; and Intangible personal property.

Personal representative. *See* Administrator.

Power of attorney. A legal document that gives one person (the donee) authority to act on behalf of the person granting the power of attorney (the donor). Referred to as a *mandate* in Quebec.

Power of attorney for personal care. Also referred to as a health care power of attorney. The donee has authority to make decisions regarding the donor's health and personal care. This power of attorney does not extend to decisions regarding property.

Power of attorney for property. This power of attorney applies to personal, financial and business transactions (signing cheques, undertaking contracts).

If "enduring," the donee may continue to exercise authority during the incapacity of the donor.

Probate of will. The court process that certifies a will to be the valid, last will of the deceased. It also confirms the executor(s) named therein.

Settlor. The individual who establishes a trust.

Succession. A person's succession begins with their death, at the location where they were last domiciled. It is the process of conveying their patrimony (property) to their heirs and legatees. The term is peculiar to the province of Quebec.

Tangible personal property. This refers to physical personal property. This includes your home and household goods, car, clothes, boat, artwork, etc.

Taxable capital gain. That portion of a capital gain that is subject to taxation. Currently it is 50%.

Tenant in common. A form of joint ownership in which two or more persons have an interest in the same property. Upon the death of a tenant-in-common, ownership of the deceased's interest transfers to that person's estate, not to the other owner(s).

Testamentary trust. A trust established by a will, and that only takes effect after death. The will would normally specify what assets the trust will hold and for whose benefit the trust will function. The trustee, the person responsible for the administration of the trust, would also be identified in the will. *See* Trust.

Testate. Refers to a person who has died leaving a valid will.

Testator/Testatrix. One who makes a will.

Trust. A legal instrument established to hold property, such property to be managed by the trustee for the benefit of a third party or parties. One person (the settlor) transfers legal title for certain property to the trustee to manage for the benefit of a person or institution (the beneficiaries).

Trustee. A person or a trust company responsible for taking legal title to the settled property, and who has the fiduciary duty to follow the terms of the trust. Settlors may name joint or cotrustees, who exercise equal authority.

Will. A legal document signed by the person making it (the testator), and witnessed by two individuals, that takes effect on the testator's death, and directs survivors regarding the disposition.

Source. G. Pierce Newman, coauthor of Fiscal Fitness, *published by Prentice Hall Canada.*

Investing to Win

12

Setting Your Investment Objectives

In setting investment objectives, few investors effectively unify their understanding of their personal financial circumstances, risk preference and knowledge of the financial markets. Instead, a close inspection of most investors' objectives indicates a foundation of wishful thinking.

This lack of perspective and realism is exemplified in the financial press all of the time: Returns of 9%–10% are put down in favor of highly risky "opportunities" for 20+% returns. It may be true that 20+% returns would multiply an investment almost a hundredfold in 25 years—but how many people have enjoyed that kind of success?

Remember, too, that 10% is close to the long-term average return to common-stock investors, who have accepted considerable risk to achieve it. Identifying resources, including future earnings, carefully calibrating future needs, understanding personal risk tolerance and allowing low-risk investment returns to compound have worked magic for many investors.

Failure to diversify is another product of many investors' wishful thinking. Putting all of your eggs into one high-flying basket can be exciting and, if you are right, ultimately can lead to the greatest potential returns.

But if you have a lot to lose (such as your life savings), then disaster may be waiting just around the corner if you don't diversify. On the other side of the coin, hedging every potential development is probably only appropriate for the extremely wealthy. If you fall somewhere in the middle, always employ reasonable diversification, both in terms of types of investments and within the selected types. This will temper the risk and opportunity reflected in your investment objectives.

Source: M. David Testa, vice chairman and director, T. Rowe Price Associates, Inc., 100 East Pratt St., Baltimore, MD 21202. As chief investment officer, he oversees $140 billion in mutual funds and separate accounts.

Investment Strategies for High-Net-Worth Individuals

While only an in-depth analysis of an individual's risk tolerance and financial condition will produce an intelligent investment strategy, general strategies can be devised for the high-net-worth individual based on assumptions of changes in risk tolerance and in earning power that reflect the investor's age. *Four such strategies:*

EARNING POWER	AGE	INVESTMENTS
High	30–40	30% high-quality growth stocks
		30% aggressive growth stocks
		40% real estate (investments, not personal residences)
High	40–50	25% high-quality growth stocks
		25% high-quality bonds
		25% income stocks
		25% real estate
High	50–60	50% high-quality bonds
		25% income stocks
		25% high-quality growth stocks
None	Retirement	75% high-quality bonds
		25% income stocks

Source: Jeffrey J. Miller, CFA, executive vice president, Provident Investment Counsel, 225 South Lake Ave., Pasadena, CA 91101. Mr. Miller's responsibilities include portfolio management of over $400 million in assets, research and marketing. He serves on the board of directors of the Association of Investment Management Sales Executives and the board of governors of the Investment Counsel Association of America.

The Real Impact of High-Risk Investments

Some investors go for the quick kill. They select investments, not for reliable growth, but to attain riches they don't feel they can acquire through their own earnings. Some do this by investing in speculative stocks on margin; some purchase futures or puts and calls.

Success with high-leverage, high-risk investments requires tremendous attention and skill. It usually requires buying when most others are selling and selling when others are buying. Investing against the grain is no easy task.

The danger of high-flying investment strategies is that when you lose, you usually lose big. And, when you suffer an investment loss, your funds must work extra hard to make up for the loss.

For example, if you invest $100 in the stock market, suffer a 10% loss in the first year and realize a 10% increase the next year, your investment is worth $99, not $100. Even worse, if your $100 investment declines by 50% in the first year and increases by 50% in the second, it is worth only $75—far short of the original amount, despite a spectacular turnaround.

When an investment incurs a loss in the initial stages, it must work much harder thereafter to attain the initial objectives.

Let's say you expect an investment to appreciate at 10% a year for five years. But in the first year, its value drops by 10% instead. Your investment must now compound at a rate of 15.7% annually to catch up with your initial five-year expectations—such a high rate is usually attained only by buying common stocks at the depth of a recession and holding for a market recovery.

Source: *Archie M. Richards, Jr., CFP, president, Archie Richards Associates, Inc., Ten Mall Road, Burlington, MA 01803. Mr. Richards is a member of the Institute of Certified Financial Planners and has been admitted to the Registry of Financial Planning Practitioners. He is also a weekly newspaper columnist.*

An Investment Strategy for All Seasons

There is no investment for all seasons, but there is a season for each investment. The primary factor determining that season is inflation. During periods of decelerating or stable inflation, financial assets—stocks and bonds—are the superstars. During periods of accelerating inflation, real assets—real estate, precious metals and commodities—are winners.

The problem for investors is trying to determine whether inflation is going to remain stable, accelerate or decelerate. Inflation is primarily caused by government monetary and fiscal policy, so the most important economic indicator for investors to keep track of is what government policy makers are actually doing (not what they *say* they are doing).

The following guidelines should help you determine when inflation is beginning to speed up and

Portfolio Strategies

● **Conservative:** Invest 27% in domestic and 8% in international growth funds and 65% in cash equivalents.

● **Venturesome:** Invest 45% in domestic and 15% in international growth funds, 5% in international bond funds and 35% in cash equivalents.

Source: *William E. Donoghue, publisher of Donoghue On-line, an electronic mutual-fund performance service, Seattle, WA.*

when the best time is to change the character of your portfolio to take advantage of changes in the inflation rate.

Changes in Money Supply

The main ingredient for accelerating inflation is excessive growth in the country's money supply. If the percentage change in the money supply, measured on a year-to-year basis, begins to rise sharply, you can reasonably expect an increase in the inflation rate.

The lag between an acceleration in the money supply and an acceleration in the inflation rate is approximately two years. That gives the astute investor ample time to restructure his or her investment portfolio accordingly. On the other side of the coin, when the monetary growth rate begins to decline as measured by the year-to-year percentage change in the money supply, it is probable that inflation will also decline in approximately two years.

Acceleration

When the monetary growth rate accelerates for more than six months and rises by more than three percentage points from its low, it's time to prepare for an acceleration in the inflation rate. Since the trend may change slowly, it's best to first liquidate only half of your long-term financial assets.

Sell the remainder of your assets when bond and stock prices fall below their respective 39-week moving averages. *Helpful:* Initially invest the funds generated by the sales in short-term financial instruments such as term deposits and/or Treasury bills or money-market funds.

Investments in inflation hedges should be made only after the monetary growth rate has accelerated for more than six months and the year-to-year monetary growth rate is more than three percentage points from its recent low. Additionally, the economy should be expanding and an index of inflation-sensitive commodity prices should be above its 20-week moving average. The best equity investments in an inflationary environment can typically be made in mutual funds containing stocks of gold-and-silver-mining companies. Holding a portfolio of short-term money-market instruments is a conservative way to keep pace with inflation, since short-term interest rates rise sharply once inflation takes hold. Also, when inflation is accelerating in Canada, the dollar usually declines in value. To take advantage of a weakening in the dollar, invest in foreign stocks or mutual funds with portfolios of foreign stocks.

Deceleration

Use a similar process to anticipate decelerating inflation. Wait for the monetary growth rate to decline for at least six months and to fall at least three percentage points from its recent high. The economy should show signs of weakness, and an index of inflation-sensitive commodity prices should decline below its 20-week moving average. At that point, liquidate inflation-hedge investments and invest the proceeds in money-market instruments or money-market mutual funds.

Source: Dr. Roger Klein, president, The Interest Rate Futures Research Corporation, Princeton Junction, NJ, and money manager and consultant to financial institutions. Dr. Klein is editor of The Klein-Wolman Investment Letter and coauthor, with William Wolman, of **The Beat Inflation Strategy.**

Securities and Commodities Fraud

To reduce the chances of becoming a victim of an investment swindler, send for the free booklet "Investment Swindles: How They Work and How to Avoid Them," National Futures Association, 200 W. Madison St., Chicago, IL 60606. You can also find useful information on the website of the Ontario Securities Commission. Go to the Investor Resources page at http://www.osc.gov.on.ca/en/investor.html.

All About Hiring an Investment Counselor

The trick in hiring an investment counselor is to demystify the position. Put it in a realistic context—you are hiring an employee who works outside of your home or office. The longer he or she has been doing the job effectively, the more likely it is that he or she will continue to do so.

Until the early 1970s, the services of investment counselors were available only to the very, very rich. Computers have made it easier and more profitable for counselors to take on smaller accounts. Today, individuals with $200,000 to invest can find counselors willing to manage their accounts. (Until you have accumulated that kind of capital, your best bet is mutual funds.) *Three groups to avoid:*

● **One-man firms.** These are limited to the ideas of the founder, and the accounts can't be supervised when he or she is out of the office.

● **Bank trust departments.** They are generally disadvantaged by low salary levels and too many committees. Talented money managers cannot afford to stay at most banks.

● **Brokerage firms.** Their money managers are often limited to using research generated inside the firm. They also channel most of their clients' investments through their own firm.

Myths Debunked

Several misconceptions surround the investments-management business:

● **You will have a custom-designed portfolio.** *Reality:* At almost all firms, all accounts are managed essentially the same way.

● **You will receive personal attention.** *Reality:* Good portfolio managers do not have time to speak with their clients often. Most will talk to you once a quarter and meet you face-to-face annually.

● **Your existing portfolio will be scrutinized closely.** *Reality:* When you turn your portfolio over to the firm, the manager will scan the list to see if he or she actively follows any of the stocks. If not, the manager will sell them. If you do not want the stock to be sold, you should not have the issue managed.

What to Look For

Ask to see the performance record for the entire time the firm has been in business. Beware of 20-year-old companies that show you only 5-year results…what happened in the previous 15 years? Are they hiding anything?

Compare performance for each quarter of the last eight years with the S&P/TSX Composite Index (formerly known as the TSE 300), the Standard & Poor's 500 Index and any other major indexes that are relevant. The company should have outperformed the appropriate index, especially in down markets.

Look for a firm that is registered with your provincial securities commission. And ask the firm whether the people responsible for whatever success the firm has had still work there.

Meet the portfolio manager who will handle your account. Find out how the firm is organized, so you know who will make your investment decisions.

Get client references that take into account past periods of stock market adversity, such as 1973–74, 1977, 1981–82, 1987, and the downturn that has occurred since 2000.

What It Costs

Annual fees usually range from 0.5% to 3% of the amount of the account. Accounts over $1 million are able to negotiate fees at a number of good firms.

It is, of course, important to monitor your investment counselor. A reasonable rate of return on your money over several years is 1.2 times the 90-day Treasury bill rate. A 12%–15% compounded rate or a rate that beats inflation is a very good performance. If after a full market cycle (usually three to five years) the account has a gross return of less than 25%, you should look for a new counselor.

Source: Michael Stolper, president, Stolper & Co., a consulting and per-formance-measurement firm, 525 B St., San Diego, CA 92101.

How to Evaluate a Money Manager

Selecting a money manager takes more than just looking at recent performance numbers and picking the firm that ranks at the top. If it were that simple, you could pick a money manager using a computer. The four basic criteria to be considered before you place your money in someone else's hands are: (1) philosophy, (2) process, (3) personnel and (4) performance.

Philosophy

A prospective money manager's philosophy is his or her beliefs about how to successfully make money in the market and do better than the major stock averages. Does the manager focus on growth stocks or high-yield stocks? Or is he or she a contrarian, always investing in out-of-favor stocks? Investment philosophy can also include a manager's belief about his or her market-timing ability; that is, being 100% invested in equities in an anticipated bull market and then moving to cash-equivalent securities when the market is expected to be bearish.

Your main objective in determining a manager's investment philosophy or style is to see if the manager has been consistent over time, and whether his or her style goes along with your basic investment instincts. If a prospective manager's style has been continually changing, be cautious—a successful style should be able to stand the test of time. Also, knowing a manager's style helps you to evaluate performance. For example, a high-yield manager should do well when interest rates are falling, but might not be at the top of the pack when interest rates are rising.

Process

Be familiar with the way a manager chooses specific securities for his or her portfolios. One typical process is the "top-down" approach, whereby the investor begins with projections for the economy followed by a determination of the industries that should do well in the forecasted economic environment. Within the favored industries, specific stocks are selected that should benefit most from the industries' growth. Another process is the "bottom-up" approach, in which stocks are picked on their own individual merits and only secondarily on the basis of their industry and its relationship to the economy. Make it your objective to find a manager whose process makes sense to you.

Personnel

What is the manager's experience in the business and what kind of backup support does he or she have? How long has the individual been in the business? Has he or she been through the good and bad times? Is the manager a chartered financial analyst? Who manages the portfolios while he or she is out of the office? Are there other individuals who will be familiar enough with your account to handle it when the manager is on vacation?

Performance

The last consideration should be performance. What kind of long-term track record does the manager have? These figures may be difficult to get from the manager, but it's worth pushing a little to find out. When reviewing a prospective manager's track record, be sure to compare performance to the market (S&P/TSX Composite, Standard & Poor's 500) or to a universe of professional money managers (this information is available from various consulting services). The minimum time period to consider is one market cycle, which will show how a manager performed in both up and down markets. If he or she hasn't done better than the market or the average manager, it's probably a good idea to consider someone else.

Source: David C. O'Donovan, vice president, SEI Corporation, Funds Evaluation Services, 2 N. Riverside Plaza, Chicago, IL 60606.

Finding the Right Stockbroker

The risky and expensive way to find the right stockbroker is by experimentation—switching from one account to another. Instead, minimize the cost of your search for the right broker by considering the following points.

● **A broker's livelihood depends solely on commissions generated by transactions.** The pressures of the securities industry can cause some brokers to unnecessarily buy and sell securities in an account for the sake of generating commissions ("churning"). To resolve this issue, ask a prospective broker what his or her philosophy is regarding holding periods for stocks. If the broker is a short-term trader—one who usually holds stocks for a year or less—look elsewhere unless this matches your investment strategy. You may be in for heavy commissions.

● **How well do you communicate with the broker?** Will he or she be readily available? Does the broker answer your questions directly, or evade issues? The question of communication is most important for accounts in which you do not plan to give the broker discretionary power over buying and selling. Does the broker try to find out about your investment objectives and risk tolerance? How will the broker communicate with you on a regular basis—by newsletter, research reports, monthly calls, quarterly meetings? What will your responsibilities be as a client? Will you be expected to monitor your own account, or wait for the broker to make recommendations? It is essential that you clarify each person's responsibilities at the outset.

● **What is the average rate of return you should expect as a client?** Is the response you receive to this question realistic? Does the broker promise guaranteed returns? Beware if he or she claims to have a surefire way to beat the market.

● **Does the broker invest his or her own money in the market?** If the broker does not, why is he or she recommending that you do so? Ask to see the broker's own account record for the past several years. This will tell you what his or her past results were and the types of securities the broker buys and sells. Remember, however, that brokers sometimes buy riskier stocks for their own accounts.

● **Find out about the broker's clients, to determine if they are similar to you.** What is the average client like? Older? Younger? High-income? Are they high-risk investors? Are they more interested in investment vehicles such as limited partnerships, load mutual funds, and insurance products? Be sure to ask the broker for references—and call them. Since you will only be referred to the broker's most satisfied clients, always ask the clients how long they have been with the broker. This will be a strong indicator of whether or not they have gone through several market cycles with the broker.

● **What is the broker's experience?** How long has he or she been in the industry? Be wary of new brokers—in general, they rely on others to tell them what to recommend. This can be a problem if the firm is pushing its brokers to sell certain stocks, such as new issues. New brokers also have not had the invaluable chance to learn from their mistakes.

● **How does the broker pick stocks?** Does he or she have a system? If so, does it make sense? What does the broker read and whom does he or she listen to for advice? Does the broker talk directly to corporate officers and analysts?

● **What is the broker's firm like?** Are the rates charged in line with the services provided? Has there been a major change in the account executives recently? If so, are there problems at the branch office?

● Once you've signed on with a broker, review the broker's performance regularly. Is he or she really making money for you after you deduct commissions? Set regular periods for review of your account results with your broker. If the broker consistently reduces the value of your account in both up and down markets, it's time to apply these search ideas to the next candidate.

Source: Laura Waller, president, Laura Waller Advisors, Inc., 201 East Kennedy Boulevard, Suite 1109, Tampa, FL 33602. She is a certified financial planner, a registered principal of NASD, a registered representative of Investment Management & Research, Inc., and a licensed insurance agent. Southern regional director on the national board of the Institute of Certified Financial Planners, Ms. Waller is a frequent speaker and has been quoted in many financial publications.

What to Expect of a Full-Service Broker

If you like to map out your own investment strategy, do your own research and closely monitor all of your stock transactions, then you probably won't want a full-service broker. Why pay full commission when you won't utilize a broker's advice and services? However, if you're like many people and don't have the time to devote to watching over your stock portfolio, then a full-service broker can be well worth the extra money you will pay in heftier commissions.

What You Pay For

The process of choosing a full-service broker should be handled with care, since the quality of his or her advice will largely determine how well you do with your investments. The following will tell you what you should expect from a good full-service broker.

● **Advice.** A full-service broker is full of investment ideas. If he or she is good, those ideas will be tailored to fit your financial requirements and investing style. If the broker is very good, he or she will help develop your financial plans in the same way an accountant might handle your taxes or a lawyer might draw up your estate. *But remember:* A stockbroker only makes money when you make a trade. You must ask yourself if that type of incentive system bothers you.

> " Once you've signed on with a broker, review the broker's performance regularly. Is he or she really making money for you after you deduct commissions? "

● **Monitor your stocks.** A good broker can watch over your stocks and help you trade more effectively. An experienced broker will know trading techniques that might not be familiar to the average investor. You can decide the extent to which a broker monitors your portfolio—whether the broker calls you before each transaction or takes full control.

● **Research products.** Large brokerage houses spend millions of dollars each year on providing research products. Reports published by these firms can be of great value to the investor who wants to stay up-to-date on industries, specific companies, the overall stock market and new investment areas. Check to see that your broker's firm offers a high-quality research product. It should be meaningful, comprehensive and timely. (Each year, *Institutional Investor* ranks Wall Street's research departments according to their ability to provide the best investment advice.)

● **Other investment products.** A full-service broker will also provide you with a wide range of alternative investment vehicles, including income trusts, strip bonds, tax shelters, mutual funds, real estate investments and insurance. Other extras include free chequing, money-market accounts and borrowing facilities. Alternative investment products can become increasingly important during changing economic times, when you have entered a new stage in life, or when you have changed your investment strategy.

Choosing a Broker

Referrals from friends may not always be the best way to make your selection. A broker may have performed exceptionally well for your neighbor, for instance, but because of a different style or different financial profile, he or she may not be appropriate for you and your needs.

Before choosing a broker, always try to accurately establish your investment goals. There are many: Are you looking for safety, or are you primarily a speculator? Do you have need of immediate income, or will you need income in the future? How much risk are you willing to assume? What rate of return would adequately compensate you for assuming that amount of risk?

When you've decided what your investment goals are, take the time to meet and interview all prospective registered "reps." The primary trait to look for in a broker is compatibility. You want your broker's investment style and trading technique to be suited to your investment goals. For example, if you are looking for long-term capital gains, then stay away from brokers who are more interested in making short-term gains in the options market.

Always test a broker for personal professionalism, and examine his or her firm, noting the level of seriousness you find there. Is it a noisy office, with loud talk about sports, movies, etc.? A lack of adequate secretarial help is also a dangerous sign. (A firm building a relationship with the public relies on clerical help.) Are the employees doing their work? Remember, the level of seriousness of any investment company may be measured in direct proportion to the level of "horsing around" prevalent in its branch offices.

If a broker meets the compatibility test and the professionalism test, then it's time to ask for at least two references. Make sure that you ask for references from people whose goals are similar to your own. If their recommendations are strong, open an account and watch it carefully to check on the quality of your decision.

Source: The late Louis Ehrenkrantz of Ehrenkrantz King Nussbaum, investment advisers, New York, NY.

How to Make a Deal With Your Broker

Many companies charge a range of prices for the same goods and services. This means some people are paying less than you for the identical item—a hotel room, car rental—anything that can't be warehoused and sold later. That's why, although they'll never brag about it, most sellers actually need to negotiate.

So-called "standard rates" are almost always negotiable. Suppose you like your stockbroker but want to pay lower commissions and interest rates. Check the ads in the business pages or call a couple of discount brokers for their rate structures. Once you

have the facts, visit your broker and explain that other brokers charge much less than he or she does, and you'd like to discuss a new, fairer arrangement.

Show your proof (ads or notes you took while calling discounters). Expect the usual responses about excellent service, discounts that depend on volume, your account is too small, etc. *Your response:* "My account doesn't require much servicing, I don't use your research or other expensive facilities and I'm not asking for the moon. I just don't think it's fair that I have to pay the top rate."

If the broker says that he or she can't help you, find out who can. *Inside information:* The broker probably has more discretion than he or she is willing to disclose. He or she should be able to arrange a 20%–30% discount off the top rate. *That accomplished, ask for one last favor:* You're paying the firm's highest interest rate on your debit balance, and you'd like a one-percentage-point discount. Since brokers usually charge one-half to two percentage points above prime, a one-point reduction off the high end of this gravy isn't unreasonable—even for a small account. If you're told that rates are based on the size of the debit balance, explain that you know rates are negotiable, that others pay less and that you'd like the same treatment as those paying less. *Later:* Negotiate for your share of free stock guides and charts, access to the broker's financial library and/or the research section of their website and occasional shares of "hot" issues.

You have a right to these, but they won't be handed to you on a silver platter. You have to ask for them.

Source: Ralph Charell, former CEO of his own Wall Street securities firm, 242 E. 72 St., New York, NY 10021.

When Not to Listen to Your Broker

The few words the average investor finds hardest to say to his or her broker are, "Thanks for calling. I appreciate it, but no thanks." There are times when it is in your own best interest to be able to reject the broker's blandishments.

● **When the broker's hot tip** (or your barber's or tennis partner's) is that a certain stock is supposed to go up because of impending good news. *Ask yourself:* If the "news" is so superspecial, how come you (and/or your broker) have been able to learn about it in the nick of time?

Chances are by the time you hear the story, plenty of other people have, too. Often you can spot this because the stock has already been moving. That means that insiders have been buying long before you got the hot tip. After you buy, when the news does become "public," who'll be left to buy?

● **When the market is sliding.** When your broker asks, "How much lower can it go?" the temptation can be very great to try to snag a bargain. *But before you do, consider:* If the stock, at that price, is such a bargain, wouldn't some big mutual funds or pension funds be trying to buy up all they could? If that's the case, how come the stock has been going down?

It's wildly speculative to buy a stock because it looks as if it has fallen "far enough." The last thing you want to do is try to guess the bottom. After all, the market is actually saying that the stock is weak. That is the fact, the knowable item.

HOW TO CHOOSE A FULL-SERVICE BROKER

In today's increasingly complex financial world, it is almost mandatory for the busy individual to have a full-service broker at his or her disposal. And that doesn't just mean a stock picker. In fact, the term *broker* itself is no longer appropriate. The title *financial consultant* much more accurately describes the position. A full-service broker must belong to a firm that can provide superior investment advice, tax planning, estate planning and a menu of investment vehicles such as money-market funds, chequing and borrowing capabilities, stripped bonds, guaranteed investment certificates, bonds, commodities and options.

Referrals from friends are a good way to start. But remember, your investment style might not be the same. Find a broker who meets your needs, not someone else's.

If you have to start the search cold, it's a good idea to pick several large brokerage houses in your area that you think will be in business in the future. Be sure that the brokerage firms are members of all major stock exchanges

and that you are able to select from a wide variety of investment vehicles in addition to stocks and straight debt securities. Find out if the brokerage firms are properly insured. Also determine whether they have the necessary communications and computer equipment to execute transactions quickly and effectively.

When you've narrowed down your prospects to one brokerage house, go to the firm's largest office in your area. Speak to the senior manager of the office. (The trick is to start at the top and work your way down.) Carefully review with the senior manager your investment objectives as well as the kind of investments that appeal to you. Discuss the type of broker you are looking for. Finally, arrange a face-to-face interview with several prospective brokers recommended by the manager.

Questions to ask:

● **How long have you been a broker?**

● **How long have you been in the securities industry?**

● **How long have you been associated with this firm?**

● **What type of clients do you have?** Are they income, speculative, or tax-shelter oriented?

● **Do you specialize in any one area?**

● **What is your attitude toward risk?**

● **Do you advise any of the senior officers of this firm?**

● **Do you have any clients whom I could speak to regarding your performance?**

The last question is the most important. Referrals are the best test of a broker's quality. Equally important as a broker's performance record is his or her ability to communicate. Good rapport with your broker is critical.

Source: Stanley P. Heilbronn, first vice president, Merrill Lynch. Mr. Heilbronn advises clients—including individuals in the fields of entertainment and medicine—on their investments. In addition, he is a contributor to Medical Economics magazine.

● **Don't fall for the notion that a stock is "averaging down."** It's a mistake for the broker (or investor) to calculate that if he or she buys more "way down there," he or she can get out even. The flaws are obvious. The person who averages down is busy thinking of buying more just when he or she should be selling. And if a rally does come, the broker waits for the target price "to get out even"—so if the rally fades, the broker is stuck with the mathematical target.

Stock market professionals average up, not down. They buy stocks that are proving themselves strong, not ones that are clearly weak.

If Your Broker Goes Broke

Your money may be tied up for months if your brokerage house fails. Although brokerage accounts are insured for up to $1 million by the Canadian Investors Protection Fund, assets are frozen during the bankruptcy period. You will receive any gains, but market losses are not covered.

Alternative: Keep your stock and bond certificates in your safe-deposit box.

Source: Sylvia Porter's Personal Finance.

What to Watch Besides the Dow

Too many investors rely exclusively on the Dow Jones Industrial Average for a quick view of what the U.S. market is doing. But the Dow reflects only stock price changes of 30 large, mature companies. Their performance does not necessarily reflect the market as a whole.

If you invest in American securities and want insight into how that market is performing, the Dow should be supplemented with these indexes:

● **The Over-the-Counter Composite Index** gauges the cumulative performance of over-the-counter issues. It points to a bull market when it outpaces the Dow Jones Industrial Average and to a bear market when it is weaker.

● **TRIN, an acronym for the trading index,** measures the relative volume of rising and declining issues. The market is bullish when the TRIN falls from a reading of above 1.20 to below 0.70 during one day of trading. It is bearish when the TRIN goes from

below 0.70 to 1.20. A reading of 1.00 shows an even relationship between advancing and declining stocks.

● **The Quotron change,** named for the company that developed it, measures the daily percentage change for all issues on the New York Stock Exchange (the QCHA index) and the American Stock Exchange (QACH). It gives an excellent picture of what the market is doing in broad terms. Mutual funds track more closely with the Quotron change than the Dow Jones Industrial Average.

● **The Dow Jones Transportation Average** is a reliable lead indicator of intermediate trends. The Dow Jones Utilities Average reflects income- and interest-sensitive stocks. It's a good long-term lead indicator.

● **In a bull market,** the total number of shares traded expands on days when advances outpace declines. The opposite occurs in a bear market. A sign of market reversal is a high-volume day when the market moves in one direction all morning, then turns around.

Find Out Which Way the Market's Going

A quick, easy technique to determine the U.S. market's general direction: The outlook is bullish if the discount rate is greater than the three-month U.S. Treasury bill rate, the federal funds rate is lower than a year ago, the three-month U.S. T-bill rate is below 7% and lower than a year ago, and rates on seven-year U.S. Treasury notes and 30-year U.S. Treasury bonds are lower than a year ago but higher than rates on three- and six-month T-bills. The outlook is bearish if the opposite is true for all of the above. (All rates are listed in major business papers such as *The Globe and Mail Report on Business,* the *Financial Post* section of *The National Post* and *The Wall Street Journal.*)

Source: Elaine Garzarelli, chief quantitative analyst, Shearson Lehman Brothers.

How to Recognize a Stock Market Rally Before It Gets Going

Stock market rallies don't begin without some kind of warning. In most cases, market advances and rallies have been signaled long before their arrival. Most of the data required to track these indicators are available weekly in newspapers that provide extensive financial coverage. As Canadian stocks usually take their lead from what happens in New York, here are some especially accurate indicators that can help you predict when the U.S. market is likely to stage a major advance or rally.

● **Declining member short sales ratio.** Members of the New York Stock Exchange (NYSE) are usually very astute traders. When they cut back their short selling, it's likely that the stock market is ready for an advance.

● **Favorable Federal Reserve action.** The market loves to watch the U.S. Federal Reserve for indications of changes in monetary policy. Falling interest rates are usually very bullish for the stock market. A really strong signal is a drop in the discount rate (the rate the Fed charges for loans to banks) two times in succession without an intervening rise. This action implies a bull market that could last for months rather than weeks or days.

● **NYSE "new lows" reach a high level and then turn down.** Long market declines are usually concluded when the number of weekly new lows rises over 300 and then declines to under 150. Major bull markets often follow this signal.

● **The advance/decline line shows strength after an intermediate low point.** *Expect a sharp market advance if the following conditions are met:* (1) the NYSE Index falls to a four- to five-week low, then (2) the market stages a strong daily rally—850 more stocks advance than decline. Odds are good that the market advance will be strengthened if volume increases sharply.

● **Newspapers and magazines become overly bearish.** The public media always follow rather than lead the investment markets. You can tell a bear market has bottomed out when front-page articles

WHEN TO USE A DISCOUNT BROKER

If you are an independent thinker and like to make your own investment decisions, then a discount broker is probably for you.

Discount brokerage firms (independent or bank-affiliated) offer no advice, a limited number of products and services, salaried brokers to take your orders and much lower commissions. Generally, commission rates for discount brokers are 50%–70% lower than the published rates of full-service brokers. Of course, if you are a substantial investor, you can usually bargain for a discount from your full-service broker, but the commissions still won't be as low as a discounter's. (A substantial investor can always bargain with a discount broker as well.)

Discount brokers don't make sense when you invest infrequently and/or when your transactions are $2,000 or less. That's because most discounters charge minimum commissions of $20–$40. So, if you are only going to save $5 once in a while, you might as well use a full-service broker. At least then you'll get research reports and other services.

Discount brokers do offer some services. Some will give you copies of Standard & Poor's or *Value Line*

research reports, sell you mutual funds or income trusts and pay interest on your cash balance. Discounters affiliated with a bank will automatically switch your funds between your brokerage and bank accounts.

If you are nervous about relying solely on a discount broker, consider using both a discounter and a full-service broker. *Many substantial investors have two or more brokers:* a full-service broker for ideas research and for watching certain investments and a discount broker when the investor knows what he or she wants or when commissions cut too deeply into profit margins.

Source: *J. Bud Feuchtwanger, president, Feuchtwanger Group, 161 E. 91 St., New York, NY 10128. He is a consultant to commercial banks, savings and loans, insurance companies, and securities firms on marketing, product development and distribution.*

recall the crash of 1929 and unfavorable articles are written about major corporations such as IBM or General Motors. You can usually invest safely when such articles become commonplace.

● **Brokerage stocks start to show strength.** Brokerage stocks, such as Merrill Lynch, often lead the list in a bull market rally and can be very reliable in calling market turns.

Source: Gerald Appel, president, Signalert Corporation, 150 Great Neck Road, Great Neck, NY 11021.

Bullish Indicator

Stock mutual fund liquidity. Historically, mutual funds' holding a big portion of their assets in cash is a sign of an imminent stock market rally. *Reason:* Cash is buying power, and once it's poured back into the stock market, a new spurt in prices is fueled.

Source: Norman G. Fosback, editor, Income & Safety.

Downturn Warning

Investors must watch market signs closely and react quickly when indicators change.

A key indicator that the market is about to be bearish is a shortening of money-market fund maturities.

Traditional average: 30–45 days. Once these maturities drop down to 37–38 days, it's time to reassess your entire stock position—individual issues *and* mutual funds. When money-fund maturities shorten significantly, a stock market downturn will follow almost immediately.

Source: William E. Donoghue, publisher of Seattle-based Donoghue On-line (1-800-982-2455), an electronic mutual-fund performance service, updated daily.

When to Get Out of the Stock Market

Be ready to sell stocks as soon as a major market top starts to form. *Definition of a major top:* The begin-

GUIDE TO U.S. STOCK MARKET INDICATORS

● **Speculation index:** Divide the weekly trading volume on the American Stock Exchange (in thousands) by the number of issues traded. Calculate the same ratio for New York Stock Exchange trading. Divide the AMEX ratio by the NYSE ratio to calculate the speculation index.

To read the index: Strategists believe the market is bearish when the index is more than 0.38 (and especially so if it rises to 0.38 and then falls back). Less than 0.20 is bullish.

● **Member short selling:** Divide the number of shares NYSE members sell short each week by total NYSE short selling.

To read the index: It is bearish when readings of 0.87 are reached.

A reading below 0.75 is very bullish, particularly if it lasts several weeks.

● **New highs, new lows:** The market is usually approaching an intermediate bottom when the number of new lows reaches 600. The probable sign of an intermediate top is 600 new highs in one week, followed by a decline in number the next week.

● **NYSE short interest ratio:** The total number of outstanding shares sold short each month divided by the average daily trading volume for that month. A strong rally generally comes after the ratio reaches 1.75.

● **Ten-week moving NYSE average:** Compute the average NYSE index for the previous 10 weeks. Then mea-

sure the difference between last week's close and the average. *How to read it:* When the gap between the last weekly close and the 10-week average remains at 4.00 or below for two to three weeks, investors can expect an intermediate advance. Market tops are usually near when the last week's index is 4.00 or more above the previous 10-week average.

● **Reading the indicators together:** Only once or twice a year will as many as four of the five indicators signal an intermediate bottom, but when four do, it is highly reliable. The same is true for intermediate tops.

Source: All indicators are available weekly in Barron's. The Speculation Index was developed by Indicator Digest.

ning of a market decline that lasts from six months to several years. A typical long-term stock market cycle is about four years—from one major bottom to the next. To spot a top you must follow two different kinds of market barometers:

- **Fundamental indicators,** which warn when stocks are getting overpriced.
- **Technical indicators,** which provide early clues to market behavior.

When to Sell

- **Scenario 1.** The blue-chip stock averages keep hitting new highs, but the indexes of smaller, secondary stocks (the NASDAQ Composite and *Value Line*) stall. The rally won't have long to go.

Check the newspaper each week for the number of stocks making new 12-month highs on the New York Stock Exchange. If that number is falling while the Dow Jones Industrial Average (DJIA) is rising, a major market correction will probably hit within a few months—at the latest.

- **Scenario 2.** The DJIA stops rising, and market action begins to focus on the secondary stocks and stocks concentrated in a few select groups.

Trap: A speculative binge would be under way—and the smart money would have already begun to leave the table.

Whether the action starts to narrow in blue-chip stocks or in secondary issues, any sign that fewer investment sectors are participating in the rally should prompt defensive action.

Readying Your Defenses

- **Lighten holdings as soon as a major top starts forming.** You probably have two to eight months to act, so don't panic—but pay off any margin debts and accumulate cash.
- **Identify stocks you own that have stopped rising.** Either sell them or place protective stop orders with your broker. (A stop order is an order

given to a broker to sell a security at a specific price below the rent market price, if the security falls to that price.) If a market slide begins, those stocks will be sold automatically at the price you've specified.

- **Get out of any mutual fund whose net asset value suddenly drops 5% or more.** Be very cautious with aggressive growth funds.
- **Buy only cash equivalents** (money-market funds and Treasury bills) unless you're a very nimble seller. If you have a lot of cash and a recession comes along, you'll be in a position to buy up assets cheaply at the next market bottom.

Source: Gerald Appel, president, Signalert Corp., money managers, 150 Great Neck Road, Great Neck, NY 11021.

Bull Market Trap

When the market is in an up cycle, prices of many stocks with a weak earnings potential are pushed up by the market's overall momentum. Inevitably these issues will drop in value before the market as a whole declines.

Safeguard: If insider sellers greatly outnumber buyers, it's a clear signal to stay away.

Source: The Insiders.

How to Tell When Stocks Will Tumble

It is unfortunately the case that the investing public usually enters the stock market after prices have risen, rather than before. The obvious result is that the market soon reverses itself, and investors get caught in the downswing.

This doesn't have to be the case. The stock market tips its hand, so to speak, often far in advance of a general decline. Here are some standard guideposts to alert you to a coming downturn.

- **The U.S. Federal Reserve increases interest rates.** Stocks are extremely sensitive to actions taken by the U.S. Federal Reserve Board, especially with regard to interest rates. The market usually declines when it appears that the Fed is going to pursue a restrictive policy (i.e., increase interest rates). The time to be cautious is when the Fed has raised the discount rate (the rate charged by the Fed for loans to banks) three times in a row with no intervening reductions.
- **Heavy stock churning.** Market peaks are often marked by churning—volume is heavy, but prices go nowhere. The way to recognize churning is to check the number of issues advancing on the TSX or the

NYSE and the number declining. Expect a market downturn when advancing and declining issues remain in relative balance over a period of five weeks. A second method is to compare the number of the week's issues that reach 52-week highs versus the number that reach 52-week lows. The outlook is very bearish if 150 issues reach new highs *and* 150 or more reach new lows during the same week.

● **Excessively bullish sentiment.** When speculation is at its highest, the market is usually overpriced. That's the time to get ready for a correction. In other words, when everyone has fallen in love with the stock market, it's time to get out. Look for the following:

1. Frequent newspaper and magazine articles that feature discussions of a rising stock market.

2. A plethora of bullish investment advisory advertisements.

3. Sharp price rises in speculative stocks.

4. A flood of "hot" new issues.

5. A high level of secondary stock offerings.

6. Friends on the golf course boasting about profits they've made in the stock market.

7. Secondary markets fail to keep pace with the major market averages. Be cautious when gains in the stock market are limited to blue-chip issues. Check the percentage gain each week in the NASDAQ Composite Index. Be prepared to sell if, after several weeks, these gains do not match gains in the Dow Jones Industrial Average.

> "When speculation is at its highest, the market is usually overpriced. That's the time to get ready for a correction [and the] time to get out."

Source: *Gerald Appel, president, Signalert Corporation, 150 Great Neck Road, Great Neck, NY 11021.*

Sources of Information on Stocks

You don't have time to read every newspaper and financial publication or listen to all the investment advice available. Still, you should take your investment homework seriously. Informed investors—those who base investment decisions on careful analysis of a stock, the company's industry and general stock market conditions—are more likely to be successful investors.

A vast array of investment vehicles merit your attention: stocks, bonds, Treasury bills, money-market funds, mutual funds, commodities, etc. Similar resources provide important investment information regarding each of these vehicles.

● **Daily newspapers, financial publications.** Tracking stocks on a daily, weekly or even month-to-month basis can help you get a clear picture of what is happening to a company or an entire industry. *The Wall Street Journal* and the business sections of *The Globe and Mail* and *The National Post* provide extensive daily coverage of markets, industries and individual companies. You can expect that most pertinent business news will be printed in one or more of these publications.

● **Market guides and newsletters.** An exceedingly broad variety of publications provide detailed reports on individual stocks, industry trends, where pension and mutual-fund managers are investing and emerging growth companies. Many of these are based in the United States, but there are a number of Canadian publications as well. The list of subjects for market guides and newsletters is virtually endless. You can find publications devoted to one particular industry, a specific region of the world, leveraged buyouts, insider trading, specific investment vehicles, such as options or futures, or just plain old technical market analysis. The range in the quality of these publications is equally broad. Many have been very successful in forecasting trends in the economy or particular stocks, while others have not called a market turn in the history of their existence.

Although often worth the investment, subscription costs of market guides and newsletters can be high—$300 a year and more. Before you subscribe, visit a local library or call a stockbroker. Check the accuracy of the newsletter's past predictions. Make sure the newsletter bases its advice on substantial research. It helps if the publication employs a variety of market analysis techniques. Many investment firms will provide guides and newsletters to clients at little or no cost. In today's high-tech home environment, you can even gain access to research services on your home computer via database services.

Investing to Win

HOW BEAR MARKET RALLIES CAN FOOL YOU

Bear market rallies are often sharp. They're fueled, in part, by short sellers rushing to cover shares. However, advances in issues sold short often lack durability once short covering is completed.

Details:

● **Bear market rallies** tend to last for no more than five or six weeks.

● **Bear market advances often end rapidly**—with relatively little advance warning. If you are trading during a bear market, you must be ready to sell at the first sign of weakness.

● **The first strong advance** during a bear market frequently lulls many analysts into a false sense of security, leading them to conclude that a new bull market is under way. The majority of the bear markets don't end until pessimism is widespread and until the vast majority is convinced that prices are going to continue to decline indefinitely.

● **Although the stock market can remain "overbought"** for considerable periods of time during bull markets, bear market rallies generally end fairly rapidly, as the market enters into "overbought" conditions. An "overbought" condition occurs when prices advance for a short time at a rate that can't be sustained.

One way to predict a decline—using the advance-decline line as a guide: Each day, compute the net difference between the number of issues that rise on the Big Board of the New York Stock Exchange and the number that decline. A 10-day total of the daily nets is then maintained. During bear markets, be careful when the 10-day net differential rises to +2,500 or more, and be ready to sell immediately once this figure is reached and starts to decline. The decline will usually indicate that the advance is beginning to weaken.

able to potential investors either through stockbrokers or directly from the corporation. You can also find filings from all Canadian public companies and mutual funds by going to the Sedar website at www.sedar.com.

Note: No matter what a stockbroker or a friend may tell you about a "hot tip," always look at the company's financial statements before investing in it.

● **Personal knowledge.** Investors, and in particular novice investors, often overlook personal knowledge of a company or industry when making investment decisions. Some of the most successful investments may be sitting in your own backyard. If a local company has just concluded favorable labor negotiations, applied for a patent on a revolutionary new design, made a major sale to an international client or recently signed a long-term contract, take a closer look at the company. Think about the products you and your friends use. Try to avoid investing in companies and industries you know nothing about, have not carefully researched and whose business does not interest you.

Outside Help

You don't have to wade through this ocean of research by yourself. Your stockbroker can help, although you should make it your business to develop at least a general understanding of how to pick and follow an investment.

Large investment firms employ full-time staffs devoted to studying individual investments and market trends. In fact, the advice your stockbroker gives is largely based on the opinions of these experts— industry specialists, technical analysts who track and study market data, experts in particular types of

● **Corporate publications.** If you have been tracking a stock in the press and had your optimism reinforced by a market advisory report, the corporation is the next place to turn. Public corporations are required by securities regulators to publish documents describing almost every aspect of their current and historical operations. Annual and quarterly reports, proxy statements and certain financial filings are avail-

investments and economic research teams who follow the health of the overall economy and certain segments of it.

Any securities analyst's job is to use the available resources to determine which stocks are most valuable. He or she then makes buy, sell or hold recommendations accordingly. To analyze your own investments, do your homework—evaluate what you've learned and consider all the alternatives. Then, take advantage of your investment firm's research services. If its advice matches your own opinions, you can invest with added confidence. If there is a mismatch, find out why—you may want to rethink your choice to ensure that your final decision is one you feel comfortable with.

Source: Stanley P. Heilbronn, first vice president, Merrill Lynch, Pierce.

Economic Indicators for Profit and Safety

We hear these terms on the news all the time—*Gross Domestic Product, Consumer Price Index, Consumer Confidence Index,* etc.—yet most of us have no idea what these indicators are or how they affect the financial markets. Here are six of the most important economic indicators, when they are released and how to invest based on their results.

U.S. Federal Reserve Board Policy

The U.S. Federal Reserve Board directs monetary policy, which is largely influenced by the chairman, currently Alan Greenspan. He has the power to control the markets by tightening the money supply or pumping more into the system. This affects the value of money directly. *What to do:*

● **Whenever the chairman makes a public statement,** read the key sections and study the commentary of the professional Fed watchers. The chairman's viewpoint usually takes a while to work its way through the system—but eventually it has a considerable impact.

Interest Rates

Focus on long-term bond rates and the discount rate, which is the rate the Fed charges banks to borrow money, as well as the Bank of Canada overnight lending rate, which is the rate at which major partic-

ipants in the money market borrow and lend one-day funds to each other. Long-term rates change continually. The discount rate and overnight rates only change when the Fed or the Bank of Canada wants to make a shift in monetary policy. *What to do:*

● **Don't dive into the market—or bail out—at the first change in the bank rate.** That alone will not alter the overall direction of the market. You can lose money by reacting too early either way.

● **Two or three moves in the bank rate**—in either direction—constitute an unmistakable trend, and the markets will react dramatically. Know in advance how you'll respond if that second move occurs. If you're going to act at all, act fast.

● **If the interest rate trend is up,** rethink the asset allocation in your portfolio. Cash will likely outperform stocks and bonds. In this environment, choose a fixed-rate mortgage over an adjustable-rate mortgage, since you'll want to lock in at the low rate.

● **When the trend is down,** you should be buying stocks and bonds.

Gross Domestic Product (GDP)

The GDP is the dollar value of all goods and services produced in the country. It is announced at the end of March, June, September and December, and provides a snapshot of how fast the economy is expanding or contracting. The markets typically interpret GDP growth of between 0% and 3% as anemic…3% to 5% as robust and healthy…and more than 5% as frothy and probably unsustainable. When the GDP drops for two consecutive quarters, the economy is officially in a recession. A total of three consecutive quarters in which the GDP increases is considered a growth trend. *What to do:*

● **If the GDP is growing at a slow pace** following a steep decline, it's a good time to buy stock or real estate. The values of both will certainly rise as the economy strengthens.

● **If the GDP is growing at a fast pace,** quality growth stocks are good investments. Remember that with expansion comes contraction and the growth environment won't last forever.

Warning sign: If growth is 5% or more for two consecutive quarters, the Bank of Canada, which regulates the flow of money into the Canadian economy, will probably raise short-term interest rates to

INVESTING WITH THE INVESTMENT NEWSLETTERS

Investment advisory newsletters are there to help you choose individual stocks and bonds, put together investment portfolios and even time your moves in and out of the markets.

Some are highly focused, providing advice exclusively on small over-the-counter stocks, or on mutual funds or on more esoteric investments such as options and commodities. Others inform you of investment opportunities in a wide variety of markets.

Most investment newsletters originate in the United States, although there are a few that are written and published in Canada and which focus on our markets.

Think Twice About...

● **Newsletters that make near-impossible claims.** Virtually all investment newsletters are bought through the mail. To attract subscribers, many of them display outlandish quotes such as "I made 1,000% in one year with no risk." Be very cautious. Take the time to determine whether the claims are truly within the realm of possibility. *Preferable:* A newsletter that claims it made 20% a year during the last 10 years over one that claims 500% in just one year. Twenty percent annually over 10 years is a very respectable return. At least it doesn't insult your intelligence.

● **Newsletters that quote performance results out of context.** Since *Hulbert Financial Digest* is the only publication that ranks the performance of newsletters, many stretch the truth to advertise that they were listed among the best.

Problem: They may have been ranked in the top 10 for one month—but their overall performance may be horrible. Look for newsletters with consistent performance through good and bad markets over at least five years.

● **Unfamiliar newsletters that don't offer a trial subscription.** Most newsletters offer an inexpensive trial subscription for two weeks to three months. Such offers are an ideal way for you to study the newsletter's style, methodology and performance—and to see if it is truthful about its record.

Once You've Subscribed, Be Wary of...

● **Newsletters that quote selectively from previous issues.** Many newsletters provide both the bearish case and the bullish case. Then, two months later, they quote whichever case most closely corresponds to actual market events.

● **Newsletters whose recommended issues disappear** or fall through the cracks when their performance turns out to be poor. A bad newsletter makes lots of recommendations and then neglects to report on their later performance—especially when the performance turns out to be bad.

● **Newsletters that cover up or make excuses for their mistakes.** A newsletter that admits its mistakes and is objective about the future is preferable to one that spends most of its time making excuses and explaining why the market didn't do what it was supposed to do. A newsletter is supposed to predict the turn of events—not explain why the market didn't move in its favor.

● **Newsletters that do not make specific recommendations.** Some offer strict portfolio recommendations, telling you exactly what and when to buy and sell. Others are general and vague. If you're going to pay $150–$300 a year for a subscription, you should get concrete, worthwhile suggestions. You don't want to have to read between the lines, as you are forced to do with the more general newsletters. Remember, you don't have to follow advice just because it *is* specific.

● **Highly aggressive newsletters** (unless the potential returns are large enough to justify the risk). Many newsletters take incredible risks in an attempt to win a high-performance ranking to use in their advertising. But high-risk strategies don't always provide the best opportunity for high returns. *Irony:* In recent years the more conservative newsletters have actually performed better than the most aggressive newsletters on a risk-adjusted basis.

Source: Mark Hulbert, editor of **Hulbert Financial Digest**, *316 Commerce St., Alexandria, VA 22314.*

Investing to Win

slow borrowing and combat inflation. Consider selling some stocks and shifting the profits into long-term bonds.

● **If the GDP growth rate is declining,** review your stock portfolio. *My strategy:* Hold those blue-chip issues that are solid, long-term investments—and sell the rest.

Producer Price Index (PPI)

Released around the 15th of the month, the American PPI measures the rate of change in wholesale prices according to commodity, industry sector and production stage—or what it costs to manufacture goods. The PPI helps show the direction of inflation—I consider three consecutive months of movement up or down a trend. *What to do:*

● **When the PPI is rising slowly**—0.3% or less per month—inflation is under control. Combine that with a slowly rising GDP and investors have the best of all possible worlds. Be wary of a one-time jump in the PPI—either up or down. It won't move the markets significantly. Pay careful attention how the PPI is interpreted by the media and analysts—not just what the number is.

● **If the PPI advances sharply for two consecutive months** at the equivalent of a 6% annual rate (about 0.5% per month), it's costing companies a great deal to make goods. *My strategy:* Sell your stocks and bonds before the market overheats. Also, purchase big-ticket items before those wholesale prices are passed along to consumers.

● **If inflation is rising and the PPI rate of change starts to slow or declines,** buy stocks and bonds. Companies will be earning higher profits, as it costs them less to make goods, but they can still charge consumers higher prices.

Consumer Price Index (CPI)

Often referred to as the cost of living, the CPI measures the change in consumer prices for goods and services bought by households. It is released in the middle of every month—the U.S. version always appears one day after the Producer Price Index. *What to do:*

● **If the economy is expanding moderately** (a GDP of 4% or under) and the CPI is also rising at a modest rate (annual rate of about 3%), consider buying stocks or real estate—and avoid bonds because interest rates are likely to rise.

● **If the CPI moves up sharply for two months** and the cause of the rise is not easily explained by the economists, avoid bonds. *Attractive:* Stocks that will either profit from inflation or not get clobbered in the recession that may be looming.

● **If the CPI falls by 1% or more for two months,** I like stocks that pay dividends. To lock in yields before they fall, add quality corporate bonds and Treasury bonds to your portfolio.

● **If the CPI rises by 4% or more over four consecutive months,** expect interest rates to rise. It is best to buy short-term certificates of deposit (CDs).

Consumer Confidence Index (CCI)

The CCI reflects consumers' attitudes toward the economy, the job market, their own financial situations and the future. The U.S. government releases the CCI during the first 10 days of each month.

When assessing the CCI, remember that consumers account for two-thirds of all U.S. economic activity. So how Americans are feeling matters. *What to do:*

● **Don't react to the CCI's month-to-month ups and downs.** Rather, use it as a big-picture forecaster.

● **If inflation is high and consumer confidence falls below 80**—20% lower than the index's benchmark of 100—prepare for a recession.

● **If inflation is low and the CCI shows signs of reviving**—lower unemployment and rising auto or home sales, for example—bet on a stronger economy.

> "Until the 1980s, the pension obligations of North American industry were dramatically underfunded. Since then, pension assets have built up more rapidly than obligations. The result has been a vast net overfunding. Thus, what appears to be a liability—a pension obligation—is often a net asset."

Big-ticket durable goods, such as autos and appliances, may soon do very well.

Source: *Jay J. Pack, vice president of Burnham Securities, Inc., 1345 Avenue of the Americas, New York, NY 10105. He is coauthor, with Nancy Dunnan, of* Market Movers: A Complete Guide to Economic Statistics, Trends, Forces, and News Events—and What They Mean to Your Investments, *Warner Books. Canadian input, Gordon Pape.*

Hidden Balance Sheet Values

Most top Wall Street and Bay Street research analysts base their stock recommendations on a set of sophisticated earnings estimates. It's difficult for amateurs to develop comparable estimates because they lack professional investors' combination of experience, access to information source and ties to industry. *But there is a way for amateurs to beat the pros:* by looking for hidden value in a company's balance sheet.

The best tools for finding value are the annual report and the company's quarterly financial statements. This information can be acquired from the company itself or, in the case of Canadian public firms, found on the Sedar website at www.sedar.com.

Read the Fine Print

Begin your search with the footnotes. If taken seriously, a reading of the footnotes can reveal an abundance of information that many investors are simply too lazy to track down. The following list will point you on your way.

● **Company pension fund.** Until the 1980s, the pension obligations of North American industry were dramatically underfunded. Since then, pension assets have built up more rapidly than obligations. The result has been a vast net overfunding. Thus, what appears to be a liability—a pension obligation—is often a net asset that can be easily tapped by management as a source of ready cash. Exceptions to this overfunded situation are primarily companies in industries characterized by years of strong union domination.

● **Inventories.** A company that uses what is referred to as the LIFO (last-in, first-out) system of accounting for inventories may have a huge cushion of extra value hidden in its inventory account. That's because the LIFO method values inventory at historic costs rather than at the cost of the inventory if a company had to purchase it today.

To gauge hidden value, the investor must distinguish between raw materials and finished products. The closer inventory is to the raw materials stage, the more likely it is that the LIFO values in inventories can be ultimately realized.

● **Natural resources.** These assets may be well above their carrying value in the balance sheet. Thus the investor has to distinguish between raw materials that have declined in value and those that have risen. For example, even with the price of petroleum far below its peak levels, oil reserves are often carried at conservative valuations if their discovery cost was low. As a cross-check, use the calculation required by the U.S. Securities and Exchange Commission (SEC) of the present value of its oil reserves.

● **Business segments.** Probably the most important way to locate hidden value is through a careful analysis of a company's different business segments. The footnotes in an annual report provide fairly detailed information regarding a company's lines of business, separating them in terms of investment, capital spending, earnings and other important variables.

What investors should look for is a company's "crown jewel"—a highly profitable or potentially profitable segment—which may be masked by poor financial results in the company's other operations. The stock market's overall appraisal of the company may not reflect the potential of the profitable division. The payoff comes if you can find a diversified company with a top-performing division that may become the target for a potential acquisition. Acquirers of diversified businesses often look for one profitable segment, calculating that they will be able to dispose of the losers.

● **Company property.** The value of the company's property could be grossly understated. The annual report normally indicates how much square footage the company leases and owns. Most important is office and commercial space. Unless you are familiar with the particular real estate market in which the company's property is located, it may be difficult to estimate the property's value. However, by examining the company's plant account, with a close eye to location, you may find a clue to the value of company-owned real estate. Similarly, even though they are labeled as liabilities on the balance sheet, assignable leaseholds at below-market rates can be enormous assets.

● **Intangible assets.** Large hidden assets that have no place on the balance sheet may include the following intangibles: brand recognition, technology, distribution and marketing networks, franchises, etc. Intangibles such as these may have taken years to build up and could very well be a company's most important assets. They are usually of enormous value to potential acquirers.

Note: Beware of capitalized expenses for research and development costs. These expenses are treated as assets on the balance sheet. If the product to which the R&D is devoted does pay off, there may be an eventual write-off. Also beware of deferred marketing expenses.

Sources: Michael Metz; additional Canadian information by Gordon Pape.

Spotting the Traps in Earnings Figures

Figures on company earnings are usually deceptive. They are useful guides only to investors who interpret them correctly.

● **Retained earnings** for some North American companies can be overstated by significant amounts. *Example:* $1 in after-tax profit shrinks to just 60¢ after 40% is subtracted to adjust for the effect of inflation on depreciation and costs. Another 40% might then be deducted in order to pay out a dividend.

● **The real corporate tax rate is elusive.** *Reason:* Inflation boosts costs, resulting in inventory profits and underdepreciation of both plant and equipment.

Advice: Have more confidence in the earnings reports of companies that use last-in, first-out (LIFO) inventory accounting methods that make adjustments for inflation.

● **Return on equity is often one-fourth of the reported percentage.** *Reason:* Profits are nearly halved by inflation. But the book value is more than likely to be almost doubled when current prices are used to calculate.

> **"Assuming that a stock that's moving in a certain direction will continue to move in that direction forever. When a stock is heading for the moon, take profits—and when a stock is headed for zero, be a buyer.** Veteran's insight: Very few stocks get to zero, and none reach the moon."

In most cases, it is not worth trying to make a quick trade based on a quarterly report. *Reason:* There is almost always a correction that brings the stock price back to where it was before the report. *When to trade:* After the price settles back. *What to focus on:*

● **Deviation in the long-term trend** of a company's earnings.

● **Changes in net margin.** If sales move ahead but income is level, watch for a trend toward lower profits. And vice versa.

● **Underlying changes,** such as currency fluctuations, tax rate and number of shares outstanding. They all affect earnings per share. Translating the earnings figures into the price/earnings ratio (p/e ratio) is even trickier because the price of a stock is based on anticipated earnings, but the ratio is calculated on earnings in the previous 12 months.

Brokers are quite shameless about recommending one stock to a client as a good value (because the p/e ratio is low) and another as an excellent growth stock (because company prospects are so exciting that the p/e ratio is meaningless).

Rationale for buying low-multiple stocks: There is less downside risk in a declining market. And they have higher upgrade potential in an advancing market.

Rationale for buying high-multiple stocks: If the company really grows by 40% a year for the next 10 years, paying 40 times earnings is acceptable. Current earnings of $1 compounded for 10 years at a 40% rate amounts to nearly $30 of earnings 10 years from now. Even if the p/e ratio falls to 10 by then, the stock will have gone up more than seven times in value (from 40 to 290).

Bottom line: Keep a clear head when earnings, earnings forecasts and p/e ratios are being loosely presented as reasons to buy now.

Source: Peter De Haas, portfolio strategist, L.F. Rothschild, Unterberg, Towbin, New York, NY.

The Truth About Stock Buybacks

Offers by companies to buy back shares at premium prices usually are worth accepting. In fact, these buyback offers are often 10% or more above market levels. If you hold your shares, chances are they won't go up more than 2%–3% in the months following the buyback because the market will already have discounted the impact of the offer. In addition, buybacks divert large amounts of company cash from other productive investments, lowering the potential for future share price increases.

Source: Changing Times.

Wisdom From a Wise Source

Smart investors avoid the following big mistakes:

● **Assuming that a stock that's moving in a certain direction** will continue to move in that direction forever. When a stock is heading for the moon, take profits—and when a stock is headed for zero, be a buyer. *Veteran's insight:* Very few stocks get to zero, and none reach the moon.

● **Worrying about whether the stock market is too high.** The stock market isn't a single entity—it's a universe of individual stocks. *Smart investor's goal:* To buy value whenever it's reasonably priced. Even when the market as a whole is too high, there are always a few undervalued stocks around.

● **Believing every stock story you hear.** *Wise rules:* Never follow the crowd, avoid fads and investigate thoroughly every story that seems plausible.

● **Buying stocks for dividends.** This has become popular thanks to the dividend tax credit that effectively lowers the amount of tax you pay on dividends from Canadian companies.

Risk: Common stock dividends *aren't* guaranteed. If the going gets rough, as it can, many companies will cut their dividends.

Only source of guaranteed income: Top-quality bonds—but even these aren't risk-free. If interest rates rise, the market value of bonds falls. And if you have to sell the bonds before maturity, that can be a problem.

● **Paying too much attention to market gurus.** No one person has ever been able to predict consistently what's going to happen in the stock market.

MAKING PROFITS ON A STOCK SPLIT

When a stock splits, the average profit to an investor is 20%. But the greatest profits are generally made in the three to six months before the split is announced. The general pattern is that the price stays high for two days after the split announcement and then declines. *To spot a candidate for a split, look for:*

● **A company that needs to attract** more stockholders, diversify or attract additional financing.

● **A takeover candidate** (heavy in cash and liquid assets) whose management holds only a small percentage of the outstanding shares. (Companies with concentrated ownership rarely split stock unless there are problems with taxes, acquisitions or diversification.)

● **A stock priced above $75.** A split moves it into the more attractive $25–$50 range.

● **A stock that was split previously** and whose price has climbed steadily since then.

● **Earnings prospects so strong** that the company will be able to increase dividends after the split.

Likely prospects are small companies with current earnings of $2.5 million, at least $2 million annually in preceding years and less than 1 million shares outstanding (or under 2,000 shareholders). A stock split is necessary if management wants to list on a major exchange.

Source: C. Colburn Hardy, Your Money and Your Life: Planning Your Financial Future, *Books on Demand.*

Problem: Unpredictable events that affect the overall market, such as wars, assassinations, OPEC decisions, etc. *Safer:* Predicting that an individual stock will rise if the company's earnings are growing 20% a year and it's a leader in its industry. Whether or not somebody shoots the prime minister, its value will continue to go up.

● **Not being patient enough.** Patience is the key to making money in stocks. Unfortunately, 90% of investors—including institutions—lack it. Nowadays everybody thinks short term; what used to take six months to happen in the market now takes six days. *To beat the market:* Keep your eyes fixed on the long-term horizon. Do your homework, and then give your stock selections time to perform. Often it takes years for an investment scenario to play itself out.

● **Acting too quickly.** There's always time to buy a stock. If it's now at $22 a share and it's rising to $50, does it really matter if you pay $22 or $24.50?

Never take action until you understand why a stock is moving. *When to suspend judgment:* Triple Witching Hour—the third Friday in March, June, September and December—when stock index futures, stock index options and individual stock options all expire and the market often makes wild swings up or down. Wait at least a day to confirm the trend.

With the sophistication of computerized program trading, this extreme volatility has started to pop up on other days. Whatever happens, don't be panicked into making a move that you might regret later.

Source: *The late Louis Ehrenkrantz of Ehrenkrantz King Nussbaum, investment advisers, New York, NY.*

Those Great Old Investment Strategies

Ever since the stock market's inception, investors have been searching for strategies and rules of thumb to help them decide whether, how and when to invest in a particular stock. The strategies that have evolved range from the very complex (detailed calculations of risk, economics and financial analysis) to the very simple (tracking newspaper headlines or even gauging the strength of the tides). *Here is an analysis of today's most popular investment strategies:*

Strategies That Work

● **Small-firm strategy.** This is a tested, investment strategy. *How it works:* Small stocks (issued by companies with a market capitalization between $20 million and $100 million) have provided consistently higher returns over time than large stocks—even when adjusted for risk. *Probable reason:* The large institutions avoid many small yet high-quality stocks, leaving opportunities for individual investors. If the stock continues to do well, the institutions eventually jump in, bidding up the price of the stock significantly. *Results:* Since the Depression, small stocks have provided returns that, on average, are annually 2% higher than returns from large stocks. Over time that kind of spread can significantly boost the total return of a portfolio.

Risk: Small stocks are much more volatile than large stocks—when the market goes up, small stocks increase in value very rapidly, but when the market goes down, they fall fast, too. Large stocks move up and down at a much slower rate.

● **Contrarian-investing strategy.** Stocks that are out of favor (neglected by the big institutions, research analysts and the press) have provided higher returns than stocks considered "hot." *Best ways to identify out-of-favor stocks:*

● **Low price/earnings multiples** (low price to book-value ratios).

● **High dividend yield.**

● **Low institutional ownership.** If more than 10 to 12 institutions own a stock, it is probably too

Dividend Reinvestment

Dividend-reinvestment plans (DRIPS) permit shareholders to buy additional stock by automatically reinvesting dividends. There is a list of some Canadian plans at www.moneypaper.com. The subscribers to the *Canadian Moneysaver's* online service can find detailed information at www.canadianmoneysaver.ca/dripsandspps.htm.

popular. Monthly institutional ownership figures can be found in the *Standard & Poor's Stock Guide*.

Approach: When the market heats up, find the stocks investors are ignoring. Then research to determine whether there is a strong chance for future gains.

● **Calendar-effect strategy.** Although this one defies all logic, certain days do provide consistently higher returns than other days.

Best: Don't trade solely on the basis of calendar effects. *But keep these points in mind:*

● **The first half of the month** usually outperforms the second half. The difference between these two periods is significant—as much as 1% for the first half of the month. Over a year, that can really add up.

● **Preholiday trading days are very positive.** The day immediately preceding a major holiday tends to be bullish. The biggest preholiday day is December 31.

● **January is the best month of the year.** This is especially true for small stocks. This period includes the last trading days of December to the last days of January.

● **Dollar-cost-averaging strategy.** This is one of the most profitable ways to invest and to minimize risk. *How it works:* Invest a set amount of money in one particular stock at regular intervals over an extended period of time (usually one full market cycle)—regardless of whether the stock is up or down. *Rationale:* If you invest the same amount each time, you end up buying less of the stock when the price is high and more when it is down. Over time, the strategy irons out the wrinkles of a volatile market.

● **High-relative-price strategy.** A stock selling for a price that's high relative to its average historical price tends to do better than other stocks. You may not believe in technical analysis, but this simple stock-picker's rule has turned out to be a notable exception.

Strategies That Don't Work

● **Market-timing strategy.** Trying to move in and out of the market on the basis of short-term movements has never worked nearly as well as buying and holding a stock for an extended period of time. *Attraction:* Some investors can call market twists and turns for short periods. But no one can keep this up indefinitely.

Risk: If you lose, chances are you'll lose big. Also, the more trading oriented your investment strategy becomes, the greater your transaction costs.

● **Penny-stocks strategy.** "Small is beautiful" goes only so far. Although a high-quality small stock can do very well over time, an extremely cheap stock (issued by a company not listed on any major exchange) can be highly risky. Many investors think that a low-priced stock, such as a 50-cent stock, will offer a huge upside potential and little downside risk. Wrong. Studies have shown that portfolios of very low-priced stocks have performed far worse over the years.

● **Initial public offering strategy.** Buying stocks that are going public, particularly just after the initial offering, is a losing strategy. Plus, if you can get the stock at the offering price, you probably don't want it. All the really good IPOs are available only to the institutional investors.

● **Technical-analysis strategy.** Except for the high-relative-price strategy mentioned above, virtually all forms of technical analysis—stock-price runs, charting, moving average and so forth—have proved almost worthless as investment strategies.

Source: John Markese, Ph.D., president, American Association of Individual Investors, 625 N. Michigan Ave., Chicago, IL 60611.

How Stan Weinstein Beats the Stock Cycles

By tracking the price cycles of stocks, investors have a good chance of timing for maximum appreciation.

To plot the cycles, chart the 30-week moving average for stocks that you hold or may want to trade.

From the chart, you'll be able to recognize the four stages of each cycle:

● *Stage 1:* **The base.** The first sign of this stage is that daily prices start to nudge above the 30-week average. This typically occurs immediately following a major price decline. At first glance, it might appear that this is the time to buy—but don't buy stock at this stage. It's impossible to tell how long the price will remain flat, and you could have your money tied up for a long time with no movement.

● *Stage 2:* **The advance.** As this phase begins, prices surge ahead of the 30-week average. This is the ideal time to buy the stock—the major advance is first getting under way.

- **Stage 3: The top.** The surest sign of a top is that daily prices are no longer consistently above the 30-week average. Instead, they move within a narrow range above and below the average. Consider selling.
- **Stage 4: The decline.** Now the stock trades increasingly below its moving average. Stay away from the stock throughout this period.

Source: *Stan Weinstein, publisher,* The Professional Tape Reader.

Chart Patterns to Help You Time the Purchase and Sale of Stocks

Graphic representations of stock market trends are readily available to all investors. Each day, newspapers such as *The Globe and Mail, The National Post, The Wall Street Journal* and *The New York Times* print charts of the movement of the stock market for recent time intervals. Other financial

TRADING STOCKS BY THE CLOCK AND THE CALENDAR

Investors can increase their odds of successful stock trading by planning purchases and sales around certain times and dates. The following observations should be of help.

Best Times of the Day

- **Stocks usually reach low points each day** at around 10:45 A.M., 1:25 P.M. and again at around 2:50 P.M. If you plan to take a position in a rising market, try to purchase around these times.
- **Keep track of market action between 3 P.M. and 4 P.M. (closing);** pay special attention to activity during the final few minutes of the day. A strong final hour and/or a strong final five minutes usually means a strong opening the next day. If the market closes with a very powerful burst of trading, the odds are high that the next day's opening will be strong, but that stocks will sell off later that day.

- **High points during market rallies** tend to occur at 10:30 A.M., 2:30 P.M. and, if it is a strong day, at the close.

Best Days of the Week

- **Fridays tend to be weak days** for the stock market. If prices show little change for Friday, but edge up near the close, expect Monday, a stronger day of the week, to show a gain.
- **Mondays tend to be favorable days** for stocks. Most Mondays are good days for selling. You will notice that this is a reversal from the best selling days several years ago.

Best Days of the Month

- **The market is usually strongest** the final two to three trading days of one month and the first two to three trading days of the next month. This is a well-documented pattern—traders make extensive use of it. Price gains during these five-day periods often exceed gains shown in all the rest of the two months' trading days combined.

Best Months of the Year

- **Buy** in November and **sell** in April.

Holiday Buying

- **The stock market tends to be strong** one or two days before a holiday. A really good time is a preholiday period that coincides with turn-of-the-month strength.
- **Expect excellent performance** during the period prior to the U.S. July 4 holiday and between Christmas and New Year's.

The Political Cycle

- **Stocks tend to rise** during the two years prior to a U.S. presidential election, and have historically been weaker during the two years following an election.

A Special Coincidence

- **For no explainable reason,** years ending in "5" have proven to be extremely strong for the stock market.

Source: *Gerald Appel, president, Signalert Corporation, 150 Great Neck Road, Great Neck, NY 11021.*

newspapers and investment newsletters provide longer-term, sometimes weekly or monthly, charts of the same movements. Investors with home computers can even purchase moderately priced software that receives data and generates stock and stock market charts. Or you can access charts without cost at websites such as www.globeinvestor.com.

By themselves, charts cannot guarantee successful stock market trading. However, they can serve as useful tools for general market timing. The following tips should help you know when movements in the market are going to take place.

● **Congestion areas.** A congestion area is a price area in which a large amount of trading takes place without much price movement.

Prices tend to stall just under previously developed congestion areas (areas of resistance). The market is bullish if prices penetrate and rise above a previously formed congestion area. Conversely, price declines tend to stop just above previously formed congestion areas (areas of support). The market is bearish if prices penetrate downward through such an area.

● **Uptrends and downtrends.** Uptrends in price may be considered intact as long as prices continue to reach new high levels on each upswing and continue to find support at progressively higher levels. Downtrends may be considered intact as long as each decline carries the market lower and each rally fails to reach the highs of the previous rally. Remain in the market during uptrends—stay out during downtrends.

● **Double bottom formation.** A double bottom occurs when the stock market declines to a certain level, rises, declines back to the area of the first low, and then starts back up again. The entire formation looks like a "W" on a chart. When the "W" is complete, the market usually continues to advance. Patterns that take only a few trading sessions to develop indicate short-term rallies. Patterns developing over a period of several weeks suggest longer advances.

The reverse pattern appears as an "M" on a chart. It indicates a future market decline.

● **Volume patterns.** Most charts carry volume data in addition to price movement data. The following are bullish volume patterns.

● **Stock prices rise broadly off a low,** on sharply increasing volume. It is especially bullish if prices rise on strong volume at the same time a "W" formation is completed.

● **Prices pull back** after a few days of a strong advance on sharply reduced volume. Pullbacks during uptrends usually last for a week to 10 days. Expect prices to retrace about 40% of the gains recorded on the previous advance. This is a good time to accumulate positions if you missed the initial leg up.

● **It is usually bullish for the intermediate trend** (lasting for several weeks to a few months), if the Dow Transportation Average performs at least as well as the Dow Industrial Average. It is bullish for the major trend (lasting for months to years) if the Dow Utility Average performs at least as well as the Dow Industrial Average.

● **Time cycles and stock purchases.** Chart patterns often reveal time cycles that underlie stock price movements. Low points for stocks tend to occur at fairly regular intervals. Once you recognize those intervals, you can often anticipate when low points are likely to develop, sometimes weeks in advance. The following are regularly repeating cycles for the stock market.

● **Stocks tend to reach their bottom** in a minor price swing at 13- to 15-day intervals. Market lows tend to be spaced about three weeks apart.

● **A more important market cycle** is the six- to eight-week market cycle. Low points tend to occur at intervals of approximately seven weeks. Once the market turns up at the seven-week low point, expect the advances to last for about two to three weeks.

● **Important low points** tend to be spaced at approximate intervals of between 16 and 18 weeks. This very important cycle provides the most significant intermediate market movement.

● **It is very bullish** when a 16- to 18-week low point coincides with a seven-week low point. The nesting of these two cycles indicates a strong market advance for the future.

● **Very few market swings** last for longer than five to six weeks before a price reversal takes place. If the market has already risen for five to six weeks, wait to buy. If the market has been falling for five to six weeks without an intervening rally, then your gains are likely to be greater if you wait to sell.

Source: Gerald Appel, president, Signalert Corporation, 150 Great Neck Road, Great Neck, NY 11021.

Bear-Proofing Your Portfolio

If you're like most investors, you're probably nervous about where the stock market is headed over the next 12 months. The high-tech meltdown and the subsequent bear market left many people nervous about the future.

Here are strategies to consider for preserving the value of your portfolio—no matter what happens to the market during the coming months. By taking action now, you will be able to relax, no matter what occurs.

● **Sell half your position in stocks that have had big gains this year.** This is one way to have your cake *and* eat it. *Example:* Last year, you bought 1,000 shares of a company at $10 a share. Now the stock's price is $50. Even if you believe, for sound reasons, that the stock could go higher, you could protect your profits by selling 500 shares. That way, you would pocket $20,000 in gains and still profit from the company's future growth.

● **Set stop-loss orders to protect yourself** in case a stock fails to perform as you had hoped. Stop-loss orders authorize your stockbroker to automatically sell a stock once it reaches a price determined by you. This does not mean it will be sold at your price but at the available market price. *Example:* Let's say you buy 1,000 shares of a company at $10 a share on the expectation that its earnings will grow at 20% a year. But the company suddenly encounters supply problems and those expectations are dashed. Subsequently, the stock drops to $7 a share while you're away on a fishing trip. Had you placed a stop-loss order to sell your stake at $9 a share, your position might have been liquidated before the stock lost another two points.

A good rule of thumb is to sell automatically when a stock drops 20% below its highest price since you've owned it.

● **When buying stocks now,** only invest if there is little downside risk. Don't be dazzled by the prospect of big gains—without considering the possibility of big losses.

I hold on to a stock if it has the potential to increase its value by at least one-third over the next 12 months. But I won't buy a promising stock unless I also think its downside potential—its negative risk for investors—is *half that amount.* To put it another way, I look for a risk/reward ratio of at least two to one. *Example:* If we think a stock is likely to go up by 40% over the next year, it might be a potential purchase as long as we also think that it is unlikely to lose more than 20% of its value over the same period of time.

● **When in doubt, hold on to the stock.** The best approach to investing in stocks is to take a long-term view and to measure the success of your portfolio's performance over the next 5 to 10 years, not the next quarter.

This strategy allows you to filter out the temporary surges and dips in stock prices and focus instead on what hopefully will be the steady increase in their market value.

For this reason, there's something to be said for the advice of some successful older investors who say their secret was to buy stocks decades ago and stick them in a box. This strategy prevented the investors from selling when things got shaky or overheated. And because their stocks were generating dividends for them year after year, these investors got maximum mileage out of the enormous power of compounding—or the phenomenon of earnings producing more earnings.

● **Diversify by buying bonds.** Bonds generate a flow of income, which can be reinvested in stocks when a buying opportunity arises. There's no magic number for allocating a percentage of your portfolio to bonds or bond funds. Buy as much as you need to feel comfortable.

Source: *Douglas Raborn, chairman of Raborn & Co., an independent advisory investment firm for individuals and retirement plans located in Delray Beach, FL, 800-798-1124.*

If the Stock Market Makes You Nervous...

What should you do with your money now if you are nervous about the future? *Here are our strategies for stock investors who are uneasy:*

● **Don't change your strategy.** If you're a long-term investor with a time horizon of 10 years or more—and you're happy with the stocks and mutual funds you own—leave them alone. Presumably you have an investment strategy that is designed to work for you over the long haul, so stick with it.

Responding to every anticipated move in the stock market makes you a market timer. Even the great professionals have trouble timing the market consistently. *Better:* A long-term strategy that ignores temporary ups and downs in the stock market should give you a higher return over time. *Exception:* If you own stocks that have large profits and you're not comfortable with the market's future, sell some of your stocks. Remember the Wall Street adage that no one ever lost money taking profits. You'll pay capital gains taxes on only half of your profits—which effectively means that at least 75% of the gain will wind up in your pocket, even if you're in the highest tax bracket.

Important: If you're five years away from retirement—or will need the money soon to buy a home or pay tuition—you shouldn't be too heavily invested in the stock market. You're better off in more conservative investments.

● **Put the money you were going to invest in stocks into safer places instead.** If the stock market frightens you, shift cash to money-market accounts where it will be safe and readily available when the market quiets down. *Another alternative:* Treasury bills. They pay higher returns than bank accounts or money markets—and they have the absolute backing of the government, making them completely safe. You can buy them from a bank or broker, paying a commission to do so.

● **Rethink your asset allocation.** The key to successful investing is having the right mix of stocks, bonds and cash. The right mix depends on your own personal financial situation and current economic conditions. *Strategy:* Depending on your goals, you might want to examine your allocation annually—or at least every time there is a shift in the investment markets—to see if the mix still makes sense for you.

If the market makes you nervous, change the allocation by adding new money to bonds and cash.

Pay particular attention to your allocation after a long rally in the stock market. Maybe you started with 50% of your assets in stocks. Now, after a long market run-up, rising prices have pushed that stock allocation to 65% of assets. Take profits to restore your allocation to the way you want it to be.

● **Invest in foreign markets now.** Economies around the world move at different paces—and so do international stock markets. *Example:* The Japanese economy and the Japanese stock market stayed weak when the United States economy and the United States stock market were booming. *Strategy:* If you believe the United States and Canadian stock markets are turning sluggish, shift your money to foreign stock markets that are doing better. Most investors will be much better off buying shares in a foreign stock mutual fund.

Important: Pick *international* mutual funds, which only invest overseas. *Global* funds invest internationally *and* in the United States and Canada—the markets you want to avoid.

If you are a more sophisticated investor, you can invest directly in foreign stocks through American Depositary Receipts (ADRs). They represent shares of foreign companies but trade on U.S. stock exchanges. Any stockbroker can sell them to you.

● **Use investment money to pay off debts.** This offers a better return on your money than investing in a stagnant stock market. It is also better than putting the money in a low-return bank account. The higher the interest rate on the debt, the better the payoff to you.

● **Invest the money in your home.** Studies show that money spent on a new kitchen, master bathroom or extra room can add to the value of your house on a dollar-for-dollar basis.

● **Invest in yourself.** Use some of your money that might have gone into stocks to take courses that will improve your skills and learning potential. Adding to your education could help you find a new, better job. You could also use the money to launch a part-time or sideline business, which could grow into a full-time venture someday.

● **Give away the money.** Anyone can give money to anyone else each year and not incur taxes. Once the money is given away, it is out of your estate and your income taxes forever. *Caution:* Make sure the income attribution rules don't come into play. Gifts to your spouse and minor children are most at risk. Gifts of money to adult children are safe.

Strategy for minor children: Use the money to create RESP accounts for university-bound youngsters. The income on the investment will compound tax-free inside the plan. You will get your capital back when the RESP is cashed in. The only tax liability will fall on the young student and it will probably be very low as he or she is unlikely to have substantial income.

Warning: Never give away money you might need for your own security. Examine your finances—with the help of a financial adviser—before giving any money away, to make certain you can spare it.

Source: *Laurence I. Foster and Thomas J. Hakala, partners in the personal financial planning practice of KPMG Peat Marwick, LLP, the accounting and consulting firm, 345 Park Ave., New York, NY 10154.*

When You Invest Abroad

When you invest abroad, you invest not just in the foreign stocks or bonds you purchase—but you are also investing in the foreign currency. If the currency drops in value, so will the value of your investment.

When selling a currency that will keep its value, remember that over the long run, countries with high savings and productivity rates together with low interest rates have the strongest currencies. When selecting foreign investments, examine the fundamentals of the country you invest in as well as those of the business.

Source: *Getting Rich Outside the Dollar by Christopher Weber, investment consultant, Ormond by the Sea, FL, Warner Books.*

Quick Securities Analysis

You don't need an MBA to judge the financial health of a business in which you might invest. First get its latest financial statement. Then figure its *quick ratio*—cash and marketable securities divided by current liabilities. If this is more than 1.0, the company can pay its debts. If not, don't invest. Also figure its debt-to-capital ratio—total long-term debt divided by total capital, which consists of long-term debt plus the total value of all outstanding common stock. Long-term debt is part of the company's capital, so it is counted on both sides of the equation. Typical debt ratios vary by industry, but a ratio of more than 25% may be risky.

Source: *Barron's Guide to Making Investment Decisions, by John Prestbo, markets editor,* The Wall Street Journal, *Prentice Hall.*

Insider Buying Vs. Insider Selling

Insider selling is less meaningful than insider buying as an indicator of a company's prospects. Since sales may be made for a variety of reasons (diversification, shortage of cash, etc.), sales by two insiders in a company should be accorded roughly the same importance as one purchase by an insider.

Source: *Norman Fosback, editor,* Income & Safety.

Signal That a Large Block of Stock Is About to Be Dumped on the Market

Very frequently, knowledge that a large block of shares of a particular stock is up for sale can influence the decision of whether to buy or to sell those securities. For example, you might postpone or permanently avoid purchasing shares about to come under institutional liquidation. On the other hand, you might choose to sell before a competing large sell order becomes operative.

While mutual funds and other institutions don't "advertise" that they plan a liquidation prior to actual sale, such information not infrequently manages to "leak out," and this often puts a sizable dent in the stock's price. There usually are hints available to the alert investor that a liquidation of the block is imminent.

The major indication that a block is coming up for sale lies in a sudden shrinkage of the trading range of the issue in question. For example, a stock might usually demonstrate an average trading range of perhaps a full point or point and one-half between its daily high and low in a typical trading day. If, for two or three days, this trading range shrinks to, say, one-tenth to three-eighths of a point, you might anticipate a block is coming up for sale at near current market levels or below.

The shrinkage probably represents awareness on the part of knowledgeable floor and other traders that a large sell order exists and an unwillingness to bid up for the stock until the overhead supply, which is immediately forthcoming, is fully liquidated.

When to Sell a Stock

Buying stocks is easy. It's selling them that's hard. Many otherwise intelligent investors sabotage their stocks' performances by not recognizing the signs to bail out of positions. Greed and ego are the two major enemies. *But they can be controlled with these criteria:*

● **Sell when you reach your target price.** Planning an exit strategy in advance can help counteract your emotions. We always set a target sale price—based on a reasonable multiple of the company's expected future earnings. *Formula:* This target can be calculated by multiplying the company's expected growth rate by its earnings estimate for the next year. These numbers can be found in any broker's analyst report on the company.

● **Sell if the fundamentals worsen.** If a key executive departs, or if same-store sales worsen or if margins start eroding seriously, it's usually smart to sell a stock—even if the price doesn't yet suggest that you should.

● **Sell when the reason you bought the stock is no longer valid.** *Example:* You bought the stock because the company was the industry's dominant player, but now a competitor is doing better and is more efficient.

● **Sell when a stock is technically weak.** Watch out if your stock's price is declining while the volume—the number of shares traded—is large. A stock's volume is listed in the stock tables. For greater comparison, check with your broker.

● **Sell if a moving stop-loss is reached.** Think of a decline as an indication that something is probably wrong with the company. We *always* sell if a stock

drops 20% from its high during the time we own it. This not only limits losses but locks in profits. Using a 20% drop removes the emotion from a difficult decision. *Example:* If a stock that hit a high of 40 six months ago sags to 32, we unload it.

Source: *Douglas K. Raborn, J.D., chairman, Raborn & Co., an investment management firm, 777 E. Atlantic Ave., Delray Beach, FL 33483.*

The Biggest Stock-Picking Blunders

When the stock market begins to rise significantly, many people who have been sitting on the sidelines with cash will likely rush to invest. But as we have learned from the bear market that opened the 21st century, it's better to look—and then look again—before you part with your money. *Here are the biggest mistakes people make when investing in stocks:*

Blunder: **Not using critical stock-selection criteria.** Most investors are unaware of the fundamentals that make up a successful stock. Instead, they choose to buy fourth-rate stocks that are not market leaders.

A common method touted by experts is to choose stocks with low price/earnings ratios (p/e ratios). This strategy is a mistake. It's like saying you want to hire lousy players for your football team because they won't cost as much as great ones. *Reality:* The better stocks almost always have p/e ratios that are higher than the market average. As a result, these stocks look expensive.

I have studied the stocks that have done best during the past 40 years over all different types of market cycles. Because of their superior earnings records, most of them had p/e ratios that were higher than the market average at the time.

To differentiate between the great stocks with high p/e ratios and the lousy ones with high p/e ratios—read on.

Blunder: **Buying a stock whose price is declining.** We are a nation of bargain hunters. Individual investors are always looking for stock bargains and shopping for stocks that have reached new lows for the year. *Reality:* This is a good way to ensure miserable returns. A declining stock seems like a true bargain because it is cheaper than it was a few months ago. But the company may also be headed for an extended period of poor performance or even bankruptcy. Institutional investors occasionally buy these stocks because they have lots of money invested elsewhere to minimize the risk—and can make up any loss somewhere else. An individual with a handful of stocks in his or her portfolio cannot afford to bet that a stock has hit its absolute bottom.

Blunder: **Using the dollar-cost-averaging method** to buy shares of a stock whose price is declining. Dollar-cost-averaging involves investing the same sum of money at consistent intervals, regardless of the stock's price. The logic here is that you will be buying more shares as the stock price declines. *Reality:* Investors who follow a stock down can lose big. If you buy a stock at $50 and buy more at $40, your average price per share is $45. If it continues downward, you are throwing good money after bad. *Exception:* Using dollar-cost-averaging to buy shares of a growth mutual fund whose price is declining is a good strategy. *Reason:* A mutual fund's portfolio is diversified and will *almost always* come out of decline when the general market recovers.

Blunder: **Buying second-rate stocks because they pay high dividends.** Dividends are not as important as increasing earnings per share. In fact, the more the company pays in dividends, the weaker it may be. That's because the company may have to pay high interest rates to replenish the money that was paid out to shareholders. Realistically, you can lose the amount of a dividend in one or two days' fluctuation in the stock's price.

Blunder: **Continuing to hold on to declining stocks because the losses are small.** It's human nature to become emotionally involved with stocks and to keep hoping for a turnaround. *Reality:* In most cases, your loss will get much bigger.

The only way to prevent a huge loss is to take a small loss. The best way to do that is to set a loss limit. We sell when the stock has declined 8% from our purchase price. If you're indecisive, have your broker put in a stop-loss order at 8% below the purchase price. The stock will then be sold automatically. *Example:* If you buy a stock at $40 and it drops to $36¾, sell it.

This strategy is like taking out a little insurance policy. Otherwise, if you take a big loss, another

stock will have to produce an even bigger return to make up for it. Conversely, you should also avoid cashing in small, easy-to-take profits while holding on to losers. Many investors sell stocks with profits before they sell those with losses. The move helps them feel like winners rather than confirming that they've made a mistake. *Reality:* This is a bad strategy. If you're going to sell a stock, you should think of the process as if you were weeding a garden. You want to get rid of the poor performers.

Blunder: **Worrying too much about taxes and commissions.** Your key objective should be to make an overall net profit on your stock portfolio. Focusing on taxes often leads to . . .

● **Making unsound investments** in the hope of finding a tax shelter or a way to limit your overall tax burden.

● **Losing out on a good profit** because you don't want to be taxed on your capital gain.

If you hold a stock that can be sold at a gain to avoid taxes, the gain may disappear and you will miss an opportunity.

Commissions shouldn't be a key factor either. The cost of buying or selling stocks, especially through a discount broker, are minor compared with making the right decisions and taking action when needed.

Blunder: **Being influenced by events that are not really crucial to the stock's outlook.** Many investors focus on stock splits, dividend increases, news announcements and brokerage firm recommendations. None of these significantly contribute to a stock's advance. Instead, read the major daily and weekly business publications, take a look at the companies in which you have invested and develop selection criteria. There are always plenty of opportunities in the stock market. *Strategy:* Consider companies whose stocks showed large and improving percentage increases in their quarterly earnings per share.

Source: *William J. O'Neil, trader and stock analyst, founder and chairman of* Investor's Business Daily.

Stock-Churning Alert

Beware if your brokerage firm sends you a letter that thanks you for doing business with it, mentions your

HOW TO FIND TAKEOVER TARGETS

Short of consulting a crystal ball, the best way to tell if a company is a possible takeover target is by watching the buying patterns of investors with top track records. For U.S. stocks, you can do this by tracking SEC 13D filings.* They're required within 10 days of a purchase that brings an investor's holdings to 5% or more of a company's outstanding stock. For Canadian stocks, the limit is 10% and buyers are required to file insider trading reports with securities regulators, the largest being the Ontario Securities Commission. The OSC is working on a system called SEDI that will make this information available online; check their website at http://www.osc.gov.on.ca/index.html to see if it has been activated. Otherwise, you will have to phone the OSC for this information at 416-593-8314, toll free at 1-877-785-1555, or reach them through e-mail at: inquiries@osc.gov.on.ca.

That's not to say you should blindly follow what the insiders are doing. You must also analyze the company's balance sheet and market position.

When calculating a company's book value to compare it with its market value, research its adjusted book value—including assets that don't show up on the balance sheet (find them in annual report footnotes)—often, an overfunded pension plan or last-in, first-out (LIFO) inventory reserves. *Reasons:* Spectacular rises in the stock and bond markets boost the funds held in pension plans—and if a company uses LIFO accounting procedures, its inventory is usually worth more than stated on the books.

Insight can also be gained from looking at the company's securities portfolio, also listed in annual report footnotes. *Question:* Is the portfolio's market value higher than its stated book value? When the stock market indexes are as high, almost any company with a securities portfolio has these high off-balance-sheet assets.

Also take a look at the market value of a company's real estate holdings. *Where to find them:* the company's annual report, available from its investor relations department or for Canadian firms at www.sedar.com.

You'll have to research land values in the area—and will often find that the value of the property is higher than stated on the company's books. Find out from its annual report whether the company has a tax-loss carryforward that might benefit another party.

In addition to hidden balance-sheet assets, you need to know how the company is faring within its own industry. *How:* by comparing its price/earnings ratio with p/e's in the rest of the industry and with the general market. That gives an idea of whether it's fairly, over- or undervalued. ***Best:*** Undervalued.

Next area to investigate: The company's market share. Is it a major player or an also-ran? Always go for the major players.

*How to get 13Ds: *They're available from the SEC in Washington on the day they're filed (go to http://www.sec.gov) and in Chicago, Los Angeles and New York two days later. Other sources:* SEC Today *and* Street Smart Investing.

Sources: *Gordon Pape; and William Wood, senior vice president, Street Smart, Inc., publisher of* Street Smart Investing *and* 13D Opportunities Report.

account has been reviewed, expresses the hope that you are happy and asks if there is any way it can improve its service. This is not junk mail or a customer solicitation. It is a warning that an unusually high volume of trading has occurred in your account.

Trap: If you ignore the letter, then later discover improper trading and complain or sue, the firm can respond that it asked if you were happy with how your account was being managed and you did not request any changes.

Defense: Review statements immediately after receiving such a letter, and respond in writing if you have any complaints.

Source: *Dan Brecher, attorney of counsel, Fishbein, Badillo, Wagner, Itzler, 909 Third Ave., New York, NY 10022.*

About New Issues

Investors will always have a hard time solving the two big problems of initial public offerings (IPOs):

● **How to choose companies** that haven't been analyzed extensively by professional investors.

● **Where to find a broker** who will sell the newly issued stock, which is often grabbed up by a few of the underwriter's favorite clients.

> " **IPOs have risen in price an average 64% in the first year of being publicly traded. Some of them double in value after even minutes of being traded.** "

Profits and Safety

Conducting a shrewd analysis of companies that go public is the only way to minimize the enormous risk of investing in IPOs. As a group, IPOs have risen in price an average 64% in the first year of being publicly traded. Some of them double in value after even minutes of being traded. *The downside:* About 40% of all IPOs lose half their value in the first year, and a substantial number go bankrupt.

The document to ask your broker for is the final prospectus of the IPO. *What to look for:*

● **How money raised from the initial stock sale will be used.** Proceeds from the offering should be used to improve or expand what the company is currently doing. *Examples:* Increase production or pay for a major marketing plan. *Be wary when:* proceeds of an IPO go toward retiring debt or entering new fields.

● **What the IPO's past performance has been.** Even if the company has been operating for only a short time (less than three years), there's usually evidence in the prospectus of management's ability to find a market niche and make a profit. It there's no track record of this ability, avoid the stock.

● **How the original owners profit from the IPO.** When a company goes public, owners occasionally take out big cash profits for themselves. That's bad because big profits at an early IPO stage mean the owners are much more interested in making quick profits than in keeping an equity stake while they run the company.

Evidence of this should appear in the prospectus. If you can't find it, make inquiries. Look for a section titled *Principal and Selling Shareholders.* It's usual for an officer to take a small profit, but the prospectus also shows the percentage of each owner's shares that are being converted into cash. Be cautious about an IPO if all the officers as a group are selling more than 15% of their shares.

● **Who the underwriter is.** Brokerage houses have cycles of success and failure in taking companies public. For that reason it's usually safe to buy an IPO whose underwriter has had a good track record for the previous six months to a year. But don't expect an underwriter that had great success two years ago necessarily to maintain its pace today. (The success/failure record of underwriters is regularly reported in publications that specialize in new offerings and occasionally in the general financial journals.)

● **If warrants were issued to the underwriters.** Check the final prospectus to see whether the underwriter is receiving part of its fee in warrants that give it the right to buy the stock at a fixed price in the future. Willingness to accept warrants means the underwriter has more than average confidence in the IPO. Historically, these stocks have a better chance of appreciating in value than others.

● **Who the venture-capital investors are.** It's also a sign of confidence when prominent venture-capital firms are listed as shareholders, or if they put up capital earlier when the company started up. Participation of these firms is also assurance that new management talent can be brought in if the existing team falters. (Most brokers can tell you if a venture-capital firm has a good track record of backing start-up companies.)

Finding the Impossible

If demand for a new issue is high, it's usually impossible for any but the broker's favored clients to get shares at the initial price.

The first step is to get advance information on which IPOs are coming up.

Best sources: Securities commission filings (the Ontario Securities Commission, or OSC, handles most of the major IPOs in Canada) and publications that specialize in new issues.

Next, tell your broker as far in advance as possible which upcoming offering you're interested in. Because prices of new issues aren't decided until the last minute, give your broker a top limit on what you're willing to pay for the stock.

Caution: If your limit is $16 per share, for example, and the price is set at $18, you can cancel the deal. But don't expect your broker to put out an extra effort the next time around.

Even if the broker's own firm is participating in the underwriting, he or she may have trouble getting shares when demand is high. Only clients with large trading accounts can expect access to shares.

If your broker can't promise you the shares, it often pays to try a smaller, regional broker that is participating in the underwriting. If that fails, it pays to open an account with the brokerage firm that's managing the underwriting. The managing underwriter is usually allotted more shares than the others and may be willing to arrange a sale, especially for someone opening an account.

Don't take no for an answer, even if this ploy fails. As a last-ditch maneuver, call one of the directors of the new company directly. The director may be willing to ask the underwriters to reserve shares for you. This is especially likely if it's a local firm interested in signing up local investors.

If it's impossible to get shares in the initial offering, consider buying them in the first trading session after the initial offering. Usually the price won't have climbed too high, and some investors are quick to sell and take an immediate profit. Profits may be smaller by buying in this secondary market, but they can still be substantial. *Example:* During the roaring bull market of the late 1990s, Home Shopping Network shares sold in the initial offering for US$18. Within minutes after trading began, shares were going for US$38. Three months later, each of these shares was worth more than US$130. However, very few IPOs have experienced that kind of rapid price escalation in recent years.

In fact, if there's little demand for the IPO, it may make sense to wait to buy it until trading begins. *Reason:* There's sometimes a 10%–20% decline from the IPO's price in early sales. *Example:* When Shoppers Drug Mart went public in November 2001, the IPO price was $18. Once trading began on the Toronto Stock Exchange, the shares fell as low as $16.51. Investors who missed the IPO could actually have bought them more cheaply. By the spring of 2002, they were trading at more than $24. Those who bought while they were cheap made a profit of almost 50% in about six months.

Besides screening new issues carefully, the best protection is to diversify your IPO investments into different companies and industry groups. When the market as a whole is high, there won't be many long-term values in IPOs because their prices will be high too. These shares may be more attractive for short-term profits though, because prices may double or triple during the first few months.

If the market is generally weak and there's not much speculative excitement, it's time to look for long-term returns from IPOs. What to look for: As with other types of investments, look for young growth companies that can be bought for well below their value.

Sources: *Norman G. Fosback, editor,* Income & Safety; *Gordon Pape.*

How to Recognize Undervalued Industrial Stocks

A favorite investment approach is to look at unpopular stocks of good companies, particularly companies with small market capitalizations. Ignore the big names and the Wall Street "whiz stocks." They've already been touted and bid up way too far.

There are many small- to medium-sized companies that merit your attention because of their potential long-term appreciation. Sifting through them can seem like an overwhelming task, but there are two good techniques any investor can use for finding undervalued companies.

Price/Sales Ratio (PSR)

The PSR is computed by dividing the total market value of a company by the company's total sales. PSRs provide a useful valuation technique for comparing large numbers of potential investment candidates.

Oftentimes, good companies will have reduced earnings and temporary losses, but their sales will remain stable. Because of the decline in their earnings, Wall Street assigns a lower value to the stocks. However, since sales have remained the same, earnings will likely return to prior levels and the stock prices will rise along with earnings.

Debt Adjustment Factor (DAF)

Using the PSR you can sift out a large number of potentially strong, undervalued companies. The next step is to find the companies with strong balance sheets by using the DAF to determine whether a company has too much debt on its books.

To perform this calculation, divide the current assets by the current liabilities. This will give you the current ratio. Divide the current ratio by 4. Then divide shareholders' equity by total assets. Add the equity/assets and the current ratio/4. If the total is 1.00 or greater, the balance sheet is strong. If the total is less than 0.80, there is too much debt.

Using only PSRs and DAFs, you can consistently pick stocks that outperform market expectations. You can further improve your chances of picking an undervalued stock by utilizing other tools of fundamental analysis (evaluating the quality of management and competition, insider trading, etc.), but the key to winning with undervalued stocks is to buy unpopular stocks of good companies and to hold them long enough for their quality to be reflected in the stock prices.

Source: Kenneth L. Fisher, chief executive of the investment management firm, Fisher Investments, Woodside, CA 94062.

Contrarian Investment Strategies

A contrarian investment strategy involves buying financial instruments that are "out of favor," that are in industries that are shunned as boring or whose prices have fallen sharply. Contrarians invest "against the grain" of conventional thought. A contrarian assumes that the market frequently overreacts to both good and bad news, and invests counter to the consensus.

The history of the market is full of examples of low-expectation stocks whose results have exceeded those expectations. At the start of World War II, John Templeton instructed his broker to purchase 100 shares of every stock on the New York and American Exchanges with a price below $1.

Important: Templeton did not exclude those with the worst possible expected future—a third of the companies were in bankruptcy proceedings. Four years later his portfolio had quadrupled, significantly outperforming the market.

Conversely, there are also numerous examples of the demise of so-called "glamour stocks" whose future seemed particularly bright. Xerox, once dominant in duplicating office equipment, sold as high as $170/share in 1972 with earnings of only US$3.16. In 1985, earnings per share were only US$3.46, and the stock sold at about US$60. By 2001, the company was bleeding red ink and the share price had fallen to the US$6 range.

Techniques Used by Contrarians

Contrarians look at many signals of overly low or overly high market expectations. *These include:*

● **Low p/e investment strategies.** The classic contrarian investment strategy may be buying low p/e stocks. Given an earnings level, low p/e stocks tend to be stocks whose prices are depressed or at least are not lofty. Often, low p/e stocks have low expected earnings or are simply perceived as stodgy investments. *The key to the strategy is this:* If the low expectations pan out, there will be no negative surprises to cause selling of the stock. If, however, earnings exceed expectations, the surprise is positive and the stock will rise.

● **New highs, new lows.** Stocks that approach new highs are presumably more vulnerable to price drops on bad news. Stocks that reach new lows are more likely to have most or all of the bad news reflected in the low price.

● **Market newsletters/research reports.** A uniformly bearish consensus of market newsletters and brokerage house research reports is perceived as a bullish sign for the market. It is thought by some that investors who follow the advice of these newsletters would have sold all their stock in the face of bearish recommendations, making further selling pressure unlikely. As the opinions of the reports change to a bullish tone, these investors will more than likely buy back in, raising stock prices. *Conversely, a bullish consensus is considered a bearish sign for the market:* Market tops occur when all the bulls are fully invested, and market bottoms occur when all the bears have sold.

● *Institutional cash positions.* This is a popular and frequently used method to measure market sentiment. If institutions are fully invested—i.e., cash positions are low—new buying of stocks will be unlikely. On the other hand, high institutional cash positions (greater than 15%, for example) suggest untapped buying power.

BIG OPPORTUNITIES IN SMALL COMPANY STOCKS

Though investing in less-well-known businesses can lead to big payoffs, investors must be prepared to do more homework to find them than they'd do if they wanted to invest in better-known companies. Some data can be found in annual reports and filings with the Securities & Exchange Commission (U.S. stocks) or at www.sedar.com for Canadian companies. *Look for:*

● **A 15% annual revenue growth.** If a company's increase in sales is below that level, high dividends and stock appreciation are

unlikely. Also look for companies in industry segments that are growing.

● **Large market share.** This is especially important because small companies are very vulnerable to eco-

nomic slowdowns. Market share is about the only cushion that can carry them through rough times. The safest businesses for investors are those with at least a 20% share of their market.

Caution: Avoid investing in small companies that are competing against giants. They may do well in good times but be squeezed if the economy falters.

● **Good management.** This factor is the toughest to judge. Solid management is much more important to the success of a small company than to that of a big one, whose momentum can drive it for years. Look through the company's annual reports of several years—then look at its current filings to see whether performance has lived up to management expectations. In the case of a U.S. firm, a SEC 8K filing may reveal extraordinary changes in a company's situation, such as key management moves and litigation.

If possible, try to talk with the firm's executives, customers and suppliers. And, of course, get copies of research reports by the major brokerages.

● **Good value.** The lower the price/earnings ratio, the better.

Useful guideline: Invest in companies that have a price/earnings ratio well below the company's expected annual growth rate. A company with a price/earnings ratio of 12 and annual sales growth of 18%, for instance, is one that you would usually move into.

Also watch the relationship between the company's capitalization (total value of outstanding shares) and its sales. We look for companies whose market capitalization is attractive in relationship to their revenues. Avoid stocks of companies whose sales are very high in relation to their capitalization.

Avoiding the Pitfalls

Prices of secondary stocks are very volatile. And, there's danger that the company will issue new shares, which lowers the value of shares that are already in investors' hands. If there are rumors of a new issue, wait until all the new shares have been absorbed in the market. Then the price will almost certainly be depressed.

One of the biggest mistakes investors make is buying stock in industries with which they're not familiar.

Source: Richard F. Aster, president, Aster Investment Management Co., which manages the Meridian Fund, a no-load mutual fund specializing in secondary growth stocks, 60 E. Sir Francis Drake Blvd., Larkspur, CA 94939.

Investing to Win

● **Cash flow analysis.** Inasmuch as a primary tool for valuation is a p/e ratio, investors often focus on reported earnings. However, substantial depreciation and amortization (noncash) charges to reported earnings may mask a company's operating stability. For example, in 2001, Imperial Oil generated funds from operations of of almost $16 billion. However, net income was only $1,9 billion. Depreciation depletion and amortization charges (well in excess of capital expenditures) accounted for almost $700 million, but required no cash outlay. Accordingly, the cash flow (earnings plus noncash charges) measure of profitability reflects a much more stable and healthy operating picture.

While some allowance must be made for future capital expenditures and working capital needs, it is useful to look at cash flow. Often, companies with weak earnings figures may have relatively stable cash flows. Accordingly, a contrarian may see greater than perceived stability and value in a company with negative earnings but positive cash flow.

● **Asset values.** Companies that sell at a discount to asset value may be undervalued. A contrarian may buy companies with temporarily depressed earnings and stock prices if the assets of the company are perceived to be worth more than the current market price. Obviously, determining so-called "asset value" is an imprecise task. If these assets are worth more to another company, a takeover could yield significant profits to investors. Such would be the case of significant tax-loss carryforwards. Assets may also have a liquidation value in excess of current market prices (which may reflect only short-term earnings potential). While book value is not synonymous with asset value, companies with prices below book value are more likely to fall in this category.

Contrarian investment strategies often require patience because success requires a change in the market sentiment that initially created an overvalued or undervalued security. Moreover, contrarian investing is a more difficult investment strategy to follow because it involves investing against the tide of conventional wisdom. However, investors who bet against the prevailing short-term market sentiment may realize significant profits.

Source: Bruce H. Monrad, analyst, mergers/acquisitions & leveraged buyout department, Prudential-Bache Securities, Inc.

How to Find Values in the Market

We are value investors, which means we look for stocks whose prices are cheap compared with corporate assets. Instead of basing investment decisions on a company's earnings-growth potential, we look hard at companies that most investors ignore—searching for unrecognized value. *Here's how we pick value stocks:*

The Secret of Value Investing

We buy stocks that are selling at a deep discount to the company's value. To determine a stock's discount, we look at a company's current cash flows and earnings, the cash on its balance sheet and the values of comparable businesses. We try to determine what another company would pay for parts of the business.

By contrast, growth investors try to predict a company's future earnings in order to determine its current worth. We think the odds of getting this right are lower than using present valuations of a company.

Value investing may have less downside risk than growth investing. If a growth company stumbles and has one quarter of disappointing earnings, the damage to the stock's price can be severe, as investors try to get out while the price is high.

But if a company that is considered a value stock comes out with disappointing earnings, it may not matter as much. Because the stock is selling at a discount to what the company is worth, the investors may be less likely to sell.

We search for bargains in companies that are out of favor—and look carefully at those no one else wants to touch.

Value in Transition Companies

As value investors, we are always looking for good companies that are coming out of bankruptcy, being taken over, merging with other companies or selling off their assets. We especially like companies that are spinning off parts of their businesses—setting up divisions as separate, publicly traded companies. The big plus here is that the stock price of the parent company is often less than the sum of its parts.

Source: Franklin Mutual Series Advisers manages the assets of Franklin Mutual Series Fund.

Investing to Win

Time to Crisis-Proof Your Investments

The volatility of the stock and bond markets has left many investors yearning for an investment strategy that will let them sleep at night.

While dramatic rises in the markets result in speculation, profits and excitement, declines often follow, creating fear and anxiety. *Here are some easy steps that will help you invest free from daily worry:*

HOW TO RECOGNIZE AN OVERVALUED STOCK

How many times has your broker sent you a glowing report about a great company whose stock price is bound to skyrocket? How many times has he or she been right? Probably few or none. Investors need to take the upper hand and be able to identify quickly whether a company is overvalued in the stock market.

One of the best tools for determining whether a stock is overvalued is the price/sales ratio (PSR)—the price per share/sales per share. If the PSR is greater than 0.75, the stock is too expensive—investors are paying a premium for future growth, so the upside potential in the stock's price is dwarfed. *Example:* IBM reported revenues per share of $74.98 for its 1984 fiscal year. At the time, the price of the stock was $127.50. IBM's PSR was equal to $127.50 divided by $74.98, or 1.70. This was too high. While IBM is a great company, investors had already incorporated their expectations for growth in the current stock price. If you had bought the stock in 1983 at a price of $123.75, held it for a year and then sold it for $127.50, your total annual gain would have been only 3%. You would have been better off with an almost risk-free money-market fund.

It's important to know that initial public offerings (IPOs) are generally overvalued stocks. The purpose of a stock offering is to raise cash for a company, whether it's to open a new plant, pay off old debt or accomplish some other business purpose. Unless it is desperate, company management will wait to make the deal until it can receive the maximum amount of cash possible. As a result, the offering price of the stock will be at or near the highest price level to be expected—there is a very strong chance that the price of the stock will decline when it starts trading in the open market. How can you profit from this? Let the stock price drop after the offering, then buy the stock when the PSR is at a more reasonable level. (Of course, do not buy the stock from any offering without first checking the PSR.)

Insider selling is another good indicator of overvalued stocks. If management does not want to own its own company's stock, then why should you? Vicker's Stock Research of New Jersey publishes the *Weekly Insider Report,* which allows investors to see exactly who is selling how much of what stock. In Canada, the Ontario Securities Commission is developing an online service called SEDI (System for Electronic Disclosure by Insiders) that will make access to such information much easier for investors in this country. Often, insiders sell stock of firms with high PSRs.

High-PSR stocks are frequently high-price/book-value stocks as well. Book value is the company's assets minus *all* liabilities. In other words, it is the company's net worth on the books. You have a much better chance of making money with stocks selling at less than book value than those selling for more than book value. *Example:* 53 companies with high PSRs were featured in the *PSR Stockwatch* investment newsletter. During one year, 37 stock prices tumbled, compared to gains in only 16 companies. Many of the values were halved or worse, because the stocks had been too popular. If you don't beat everyone else to the investment, you can't hope to beat them to the profits.

Source: Gordon Pape; and Margaret Brill, a former stockbroker at L.F. Rothschild, Unterberg, Towbin, in San Francisco, and editor of a newsletter on undervalued stocks, PSR Prophet.

Determine the Right Mix of Stocks and Bonds

If you are going to reach long-term goals, invest at least some of your money in stocks.

But you should also hold some bonds so that you aren't totally at the mercy of stock market swings. As a rule, the younger you are, the greater the proportion you can commit to stocks because you can afford to ride out such fluctuations. *Strategies:* If you are a conservative investor, your age can represent the approximate percentage of long-term savings that you should invest in bonds. Invest the remainder in stocks.

If you want to take moderate risk, subtract your age from 110. The result is the minimum percentage of your long-term investment portfolio that should be allocated to stocks. Aggressive investors might use 120 as a factor. *Example:* At age 50, an investor who wants to take conservative risks should adopt a portfolio that includes a 50% stake in bonds and a 50% stake in stocks. If he or she wants to be aggressive, the investor could make at least 70% of the portfolio stock purchases and 30% bond purchases. It is best to rebalance with the RRSP portion of your portfolio, which is tax-deferred. To limit commissions on stock and bond sales, he or she should hire a discount broker.

Important: Short-term income investments—such as money-market funds or bank savings accounts—have no strategic place in long-term investment portfolios. They simply don't provide the returns you need to beat inflation over time.

Some people insist on holding large sums—as much as six months' or more worth of income—in such investments as an emergency reserve. But since most investments can be sold in a short period of time, even a matter of days, it doesn't make sense to keep money languishing for years on end in such low-paying investments.

Choose the Right Types of Stocks and Bonds

Studies have shown that long-term investment success is far more dependent upon allocating your money appropriately among the various investment categories than it is on trying to select the best-performing investments.

By far, the best strategy is to divide savings among a range of mutual funds. That way, some of your funds will be working for you even when others are not—and you won't feel left out when one sector is doing particularly well, since chances are you will own a piece of it.

Stocks: I advise my clients who are willing to take moderate risks to divide their holdings as follows:

- **Growth stocks** /20%.
- **Growth and income stocks** /40%.
- **Small-company stocks** /20%.
- **International stocks** /20%.

If you're an aggressive investor, split your stock holdings equally among those four categories.

Bonds: Divide your holdings equally between long- and either short- or intermediate-term funds that invest in corporate, municipal and federal government bonds.

Important: You will need approximately $25,000 to divide among the different stock and bond funds. If you have less, start by investing your stock money in growth and income funds and your bond money in government bond funds.

Beginning investors can easily start with one single balanced fund—one which divides its money between stock and bond investments.

Trap: Many investors start out by committing too much money to a *sector fund*, which invests in stocks of companies in a single industry or related industries. That is a risky approach. If you invest in sector funds at all, limit those investments to 5% to 10% of your long-term portfolio.

> "If you have to make a major change in your current investments right now to achieve an appropriate allocation of funds, do so gradually. Don't go from 0% in stocks to 50% overnight. You might wind up investing just before a major market decline that will cause you to suffer a heavy loss."

Periodically Rebalance Investment Allocation

This strategy is very important to the success of your long-term investments. Changes in the financial markets can have a big impact on your portfolio and possibly leave you with the wrong mix of investments. *Example:* A sharp run-up in stock prices might increase the value of your stock funds. The result is that they will account for a greater percentage of your overall portfolio than before. After a few years, you may be holding a much riskier portfolio than you realize or intended. *Strategy:* About every six months, return the investment allocation to the original percentages you established. *Example:* Let's say you set up a 60%/40% stock/bond split, but stock prices have climbed to the point that stock funds now account for 67% of your portfolio's total value.

Sell shares in your stock funds so that your stock allocation is 60%, and use the resulting money to add more to bond funds.

Important: If you have to make a major change in your current investments right now to achieve an appropriate allocation of funds, do so gradually. Don't go from 0% in stocks to 50% overnight. You might wind up investing just before a major market decline that will cause you to suffer a heavy loss. Instead, sell and reinvest gradually. *Example:* If you currently have 100% in cash investments and want to get to a 60%/40% stock/bond allocation—here is a sensible schedule:

● **For the first six months,** gradually build up to 20% stocks, 15% bonds and 65% money-market funds.

● **Then for the next 6 to 12 months,** go to 40% stocks, 25% bonds and 35% money market funds.

After two years, you can redistribute your investments to your desired 60%/40% split.

Source: Jonathan Pond, author of 4 Easy Steps to Successful Investing, *published by Avon.*

Spotting Low-Priced Stocks Ready to Bounce Back

The key to success in the stock market is knowing how to recognize value, and value has little to do with a good company versus a bad company. A top-quality large company selling at a high price/earnings multiple is less attractive than a lesser-quality company selling at a depressed price in terms of its past and future earning power, working capital, book value and historical prices.

Here is where analysts look for value:

● **Stocks that have just made a new low** for the last 12 months.

● **Companies that are likely to be liquidated.** In the process of liquidation, shareholders may get paid much more than the stock is selling for now.

● **Unsuccessful merger candidates.** If one buyer thinks a company's stock is a good value, it's possible that others may also come to the same conclusion.

● **Companies that have just reduced or eliminated their dividends.** If the stock is hit with a selling wave, it can create a good buying opportunity.

● **Financially troubled companies** in which another major company has a sizable ownership position. If the financial stake is large enough, you can be sure that the major company will do everything it can to turn the earnings around and get the stock price up so that its investment will work out.

● **Opportunities in stocks that are totally washed out**—that is, situations where all the bad news is out. The stock usually has nowhere to go but up. *How to be sure a stock is truly washed out:*

● **Trading volume slows to practically nothing.** If over-the-counter, few if any dealers making a market.

● **No research analysts** are following the company anymore.

● **No financial journalists,** stock market newsletters or advisory services discuss the company.

● **Selling of the stock** by the company's management and directors has stopped.

Signs of a turnabout:

● **The company plans** to get rid of a losing division or business. If so, be sure to learn whether the company will be able to report a big jump in earnings once the losing operation is sold.

● **The company is selling off** assets to improve its financial situation and/or reduce debt.

● **A new management comes on board** with a track record of success with turnaround situations.

● **Management begins buying the company's stock** in the open market.

Source: Robert Ravitz, director of research, David J. Greene & Co., an investment management firm, 30 Wall St., New York, NY 10005.

How to Make Big Money in Good Markets and Bad

Set strict rules about when to buy stocks and when to sell them, and never deviate from these rules.

The Ideal Company

● **Dominates its marketplace** as an "unregulated monopoly." *Example:* Paychecks Corp. is similar to Automatic Data Processing, which handles payrolls for firms with 100 or more employees. Paychecks' payroll companies have fewer than 100 employees. It now has an unregulated monopoly in that segment of the market and is thriving.

● **Grows more than 20%** per year in both earnings and sales.

● **Has a high return on equity.** Avoid off-the-wall companies and start-up companies. Buy companies with $300–$500 million in sales and a track record of at least five years.

> **"Look for companies with innovative managements that find a niche and fill it with a new product or service. Such managements usually have a dedication to quality rather than price and tend not to diversify. They also avoid building bureaucracies (no overstaffing or private planes)."**

Rules for Buying and Selling

In addition to the above criteria, buy only:

● **Stocks that are undervalued.** *How to measure:* A company that has grown 35% per year over the past five years and has a price/earnings multiple of less than half that rate (17) is attractive. Low p/e multiples are important. It's easier to expand the multiple from 10 to 18 than from 20 to 30.

● **Stocks that you think will meet a specific price objective.** For each stock you buy, set a goal based on its price over the past years. If it reaches your goal, take a hard look to determine whether you should stay with the company. Automatically unload stocks that report a decline in earnings. This decline is for a single quarter, compared with the same quarter the previous year. Never violate this rule. *Reason:* If you find enough good companies, you don't have to risk keeping one in decline. When something bad happens to a company, it takes time for it to turn around.

Source: Eugene G. Martin, executive vice president and portfolio manager, National Investment Service, 815 E. Mason St., Milwaukee, WI 53202.

Investing in Blue Chips

Conservative or blue-chip stocks often pay high dividends and can be owned with very little risk to the investor because their prices fluctuate relatively little. The advantage of conservative stocks is that when the economy goes into a recession and the market takes a turn for the worse, conservative stocks usually are the least affected. For this reason, blue chips can act as a cushion for the rest of your portfolio. The goal is to have about 30% or 40% of your portfolio invested in conservative stocks.

Selling the Successes and Failures

The best way to make money with blue chips is through constant turnover. Since you are not going to double or triple your investment with one stock, you have to be willing to sell your successes and reinvest in other blue chips immediately.

Say you have a portfolio of 100 blue chips. If one of your stocks rises by 20% or 30%, check the stock's fundamentals to see whether something really good is happening. If it is, you may want to add to that stock, but normally the best strategy is to sell it and add to a stock in your portfolio that has a chance of earning 30% for you. If you can make 30% returns six times in a year, you will quadruple your money. A problem is that investors in conservative stocks may make 30% on a stock, but instead of selling it immediately, hold on to it for three more years. The result is that a 30% gain turns into a 7% or 8% gain.

In addition to selling your successes, sell a blue chip whenever the fundamentals go wrong—for instance, when the industry or the product is about to deteriorate. Use the gains from all of your sales to invest in other companies with sound fundamentals whose stocks haven't appreciated.

Source: Peter Lynch, retired manager of Fidelity Investments' Magellan Fund, which soared in value during his tenure and beat the average equity fund every year he was at the helm.

Selecting Superstocks

Everyone dreams of finding another IBM or Microsoft or Hewlett Packard—a "superstock" that appreciates many times in value. The problem faced by all investors is that out of the thousands of stocks available for investment today only a small fraction of them will turn into the "superstocks" of tomorrow. In most markets, careful examination of the superstock successes has revealed each to have the following eight characteristics.

Small to Medium Size

Small- to mid-sized firms with annual sales of $25 million to $100 million usually are neglected on Wall Street and Bay Street, either because they are hard to analyze or, more important, because they do not represent enough liquidity (that is, they do not have enough tradable shares of stock) to interest institutions. Yet smaller firms usually represent outstanding value in terms of growth in earnings per share and assets.

Look for companies with innovative managements that find a niche and fill it with a new product or service. Such managements usually have a dedication to quality rather than price and tend not to diversify. They also avoid building bureaucracies (no overstaffing or private planes).

The most attractive prospects are smaller companies on the threshold of growth. Companies with $25 million–$500 million in sales usually combine management that is reasonably well-seasoned with a sales volume large enough to be generating a meaningful cash flow. The firm (or the market it serves) is generally not quite large enough to attract major competition and is eager to grow.

The bad news is that the smaller company is more vulnerable to industry downturns due to less diversification, is more in need of costly debt financing and has less staying power in a recession. These are the trade-offs investors must consider when attempting to reap the potentially higher rewards.

Rising Unit Sales Volume

Rising sales are essential to any growth company. How fast should sales be rising? As a general rule, growth should not be less than an annual rate of 12%–15% during a strong economic year. The

Rules for Picking Common Stocks

✔ **Try to buy the industry leader** or, at the very least, a company that has an important position in its industry.

✔ **Look for an industry** with a limited amount of competition.

✔ **Avoid an industry** that is an essential part of the Gross National Product or the Consumer Price Index, such as autos or steel. *Reason:* Highly visible companies are easy targets for government pressure.

✔ **Stick to stocks** that have price/earnings ratios lower than that of the Standard & Poor's 500 Index or the S&P/TSX Composite.

✔ **The stock should yield** at least $4\frac{1}{2}$% to 5%.

✔ **The company should have** a record of significant dividend increases.

✔ **The market price of the stock** should be close to book value per share.

✔ **Both the industry and the company** should have growth rates higher than the median of American or Canadian business, depending on which country it is located in.

One helpful rule of thumb: Sales and earnings ought to have doubled over the past decade. If they haven't, you probably won't be able to keep ahead of inflation in the years ahead.

✔ **Stay away from companies** that are too heavily in debt, especially in relation to industry-wide standards.

✔ **Look for companies** where managers are owners, too. Nepotism can be a danger in such situations. More often, though, owner-management is a big plus. Owner-managers have a real incentive to keep the company growing as well as to boost the stock's value.

Source: *Roy Papp, investment counselor, 5631 Echo Canyon Circle, Phoenix, AZ 85018.*

prospects of at least 15%–20% annual growth should not be out of reach.

It is important for investors to realize that a rising sales trend does not necessarily mean a company is enjoying greater prosperity. Sales may be going up, but the cost of producing products or services may be rising even faster. It's possible for a company to survive this squeeze temporarily by cutting expenses or producing more with the same or less labor and equipment, but without sales growth, a company is ultimately doomed as a viable investment prospect.

A good signal for investors is a three-year total sales increase (in percent) that is higher than the total increase in the Consumer Price Index over the same period. If sales growth is equal to or lower than that index, the company just isn't growing.

Rising Pretax Profit Margin

A company's profit margin can be defined as the relationship of income (profit) before or after taxes to net sales.

Best measure: The pretax margin reflects the efficiency of a company in extracting a profit from each dollar of sales. Also, more than any other ratio or percentage, the pretax margin indicates just how profitable and effective a company has been within its industry. Most experts favor pretax profit margins as an analytical tool, since the profitability of different companies can be compared without having to account for variations in tax rates.

Above-Average and Improving Return on Equity

The profit earned on the stockholders' investment is the indicator of management's efficiency in using the stockholders' funds remaining in the company. In other words, management's productivity of capital.

One Way to Spot a Good Investment

Big cash reserves usually mean companies are strong investment prospects. *Reason:* They can use cash to repurchase stock, fund expansion and invest in securities that bolster profitability. *Result:* The stock market favors firms with cash amounting to 15% or more of the market value of their shares, and so share prices perform comparatively well in market downturns.

Source: Merrill Lynch Market Letter, New York.

Return on stockholders' equity tells you how successful management has been with the stockholders' money. This profit, or the percentage return on stockholders' equity, is found by dividing net profit after taxes by stockholders' equity.

What constitutes an above-average return? There is no single answer, but in a superstock search, look for a company whose return is (1) better than the competition's, (2) above the aggregate rates of return of the companies in broad market averages such as the S&P/TSX Composite, Standard & Poor's and the Dow Industrial, and (3) above the prevailing level of interest rates. Any return on equity below 15% is unsatisfactory. Moreover, like pretax margins, the trend is important. As the company matures, its productivity improves and its assets are used to greater advantage.

Above-average returns are essential to growth. If a company earns 20% on stockholders' equity and pays out half in dividends, the remaining 50% will be plowed back into the business to produce a future growth rate of roughly 10% ($0.20 \times 0.50 = 0.10$); if the company pays out only 15% of earnings as dividends, the remaining 85% will sustain a growth rate of about 17% ($0.20 \times 0.85 = 0.17$).

Low but Rising Dividends

Dividend statistics are an important indicator of a company's value in the marketplace and its future growth. *Two dividend ratios can be used:* (1) The dividend yield is expressed as a percentage calculated by dividing the current annual dividend by the market price of the stock; (2) the dividend payout ratio is the percentage of the company's earnings paid out in dividends to the stockholders.

Dividends cut two ways. On one hand, the payment of at least a modest dividend helps stocks gain acceptance in the marketplace among institutional investors, setting the stage for eventual price appreciation. On the other hand, the higher the dividend payout, the less of a company's earnings remain for reinvestment in operations. Plowback of earnings increases the company's future earning power and, eventually, the price of the stock.

Low Debt Ratio

How much debt is too much? The answer depends on the industry and stability of earning power, the company's profitability and, of course, the level of interest rates. For utilities, where the markets are monopolistic (only one company in the area), a debt level of 50% to 60% of total capitalization is acceptable. For cyclical companies such as those in the steel, aluminum and copper industries, debt above 25% of total capitalization is dangerous. As a general rule, for growth companies, debt should not exceed 35% of total capitalization—when interest rates are high, debt should be even lower.

Institutional Holdings

Look for growth stocks that are relatively unknown, but not completely obscure. Since institutional research is intensive and thorough, buying stocks with some ownership by institutions vindicates your own research process and investment decision. The information on institutional ownership is available for most companies from services such as Moody's or Standard & Poor's.

Look for stocks with institutional ownership of less than 10%. When institutions own 20% or more of a stock, the growth company has been "discovered." The probable result is that your stock will become fully priced—no one will be left to bid up its price.

Increasing Price/Earnings Ratio

The price/earnings (p/e) ratio indicates investors' attitudes toward a company's earnings and growth potential. The ratio's significance stems from the fact that price appreciation in a growth stock is achieved by steadily increasing earnings per share, but also by the amount, or p/e multiple, the market is willing to pay for each dollar of the earnings.

To use the p/e ratios, first compare the ratios of companies within the same industry. Next, compare the ratio of your prospective growth company with the ratios of the overall market. (The S&P/TSX Composite, Dow Jones Industrial Average and Standard & Poor's are commonly used indexes.) Also examine trends in p/e ratios to discern how attitudes have changed over time.

Generally, investors pay higher p/e ratios in bull markets than in bear markets, and when interest rates are low. Speculative or "hot" stocks usually carry high ratios. Look at "undiscovered" growth stocks whose p/e's are rising rather than falling. If the earnings potential of two companies is the same, buy the company with the lower p/e (considering the other seven superstock characteristics, of course). The company with the lower p/e will be cheaper— the market might not know what it's missing.

Source: *Frank A. Cappiello, president of the investment counseling firm McCullough, Andrews & Cappiello, Inc., 502 Washington Ave., Suite 240, Baltimore, MD 21204. Mr. Cappiello is also chairman of The Carnegie-Cappiello Growth Fund, Carnegie-Cappiello Total Return Fund, and director of a number of publicly owned financial and industrial companies.*

Overcome Psychological Stumbling Blocks to Wise Investing

With more investors taking greater risks to achieve higher returns, many are finding that their anxiety levels are rising, too. Parting with money is hard enough, but investments that can erode in value can be nerve-racking.

Although the fear of losing one's money is perfectly healthy—and in many cases prudent—many investors are becoming overly fearful and paralyzed into inaction.

It is possible to overcome these fears. The first step is to recognize the characteristics of your investor type:

The Conflicted Investor

The conflicted investor is unsure of what he or she is doing and often embraces whatever financial opinion is being expressed at the time. He or she often feels relieved after losses and needlessly agonizes about trades. Successful trades even cause anxiety.

Action plan: Carefully analyze your mistakes and determine why they occurred. Were you investing in companies about which you knew little?

Then find a good investing role model by imagining your ideal self and finding a real-life character who best matches your image. This person will patiently explain to you how the markets work and how to find a good investment.

Use a notebook to keep a private record that charts your reasons and emotional reactions, wishes and thoughts. Put these comments alongside entries for your investments. This will help you come to grips with reality rather than allow you to wonder why you made certain investments.

Review this record often so you can see the patterns of conflict. Pay particular attention to the anxiety or agitation you feel. Open up to a friend or your spouse, who can help you develop confidence in your investment decisions.

The Consumed Investor

The consumed or revenging investor can't get enough of the investing scene. Investment talk is exciting. He or she may have suffered some serious losses and feels seduced, abandoned and betrayed by the market as a result. The consumed investor is determined to get even—to triumph over his or her adversary.

Revenging investors cannot bear rejection. They often feel anger at their losses or the financial gains of others and seek to get even by also making a financial killing.

Action plan: Shift your focus from past problems to new opportunities. One solution is an automatic investment plan that factors out your emotional input. Another is to find a mentor who can help you keep the right focus and develop a disciplined investment plan. Your mentor should be someone who shares common values, goals and ideals—someone whom you admire and aspire to be like.

The Masked Investor

The masked investor feels inadequate and takes on a bigger-than-life persona in an attempt to project a winning image. A favorite "mask" is that of the swashbuckling competitor. But such people wind up in competition with themselves. Often they are confused as they act against their natural impulses, and their confidence breaks down.

Action plan: Shed your mask. Identify your own strengths and talents—not the ones you wish you had—and be honest about your weaknesses as well. Then form an investment action plan that is consistent with your real personality.

Avoid uncomfortable strategies. An impulsive person, for example, will not be happy with a highly technical trading strategy, nor a cautious one with big risks.

The Fussy Investor

The fussy investor is orderly and tidy, checking and double-checking all the details of an order, and he or she often keeps detailed charts and records.

Action plan: Loosen up. Experiment by making a small trade based on gut feelings instead of mounds of research. Find friends, mentors or brokers who will push you to make quicker, smarter decisions. Find another outlet for your fussy feelings and talk it over with a friend.

The Paranoid Investor

The paranoid investor feels an intense need for a guru—often a broker or media personality.

But in reality, he or she trusts the judgment of no one and no system.

Paranoid investors look for scapegoats and assign blame when things go wrong, instead of doing a sound analysis of the trade that can lead to wise future decisions.

Overly cautious, they do not even trust themselves and feel embarrassed or disbelieving when complimented, but may risk everything on just one roll of the dice.

Action plan: Try to balance holdings among several low-risk investments. When things go wrong, find out the real reason, rather than blaming someone else.

The Depressed Investor

The depressed investor is unhappy, discontent and burned out. Everyone is depressed on occasion, particularly over events like a death in the family or the loss of a job. But if you are chronically resigned and apathetic, it's time to take action.

Action plan: Do not make important investment decisions when you feel depressed.

Successful investors are happy investors, so get together with family members or friends who can help you snap out of it. If there is a family history of depression, there may be a genetic basis, so get medical help.

Tools for a Sound Investor Psyche

Several psychological tools can help you become a happier, more disciplined investor, whatever your psychological type.

● **Keep a mind/money journal.** The journal may be set up separately or alongside your current market or financial charting system. The best size is 8½ inches by 11 inches, which is big enough to see and small enough to fit in a briefcase. It is for your eyes only.

Write five categories across the top of a piece of paper: Date, event, emotion, thought and fantasy/dream. *Example:* Under these headings might be: 8/30/03, new contract, hassled, too much work, vacation house; or 8/30/03, commission, cheated, not appreciated, second car.

Then write a succinct paragraph of what is on your mind, as well as trading moves. Jot it down quickly whenever you trade or make an important business move and review it at least weekly. Soon you will see a pattern of your emotions and how they are affecting your actions.

● **A personal money time line.** Make quick notes in five-year segments—zero to 5 years, 5 to 10 years, 10 to 15 years, etc., through your present age.

In each segment, write a paragraph of significant family events, particularly as they relate to money.

That snippet shows a background of family conflict over money that can lead to a conflicted investor. And several five-year snippets can help you discover more about attitudes you hadn't recognized.

Sources: *Ira Epstein, founder and president of Ira Epstein and Company, a Chicago-based discount brokerage house, and David Garfield, M.D., an associate professor of psychiatry at the Chicago Medical School. They are the authors of* The Psychology of Smart Investing, *John Wiley & Sons, Inc.*

Winning in Insurance Stocks

If you're looking for a sound investment, don't neglect the insurance industry—it's one of the longest-running growth shows in town. The insurance business is unique because it is populated both by 100-year-old companies that continue to grow and by fast-growing newcomers whose first-generation management is still in control. There are hundreds of publicly traded insurance companies in the United States. In Canada, our selection is much more limited. The demutualization of several insurance firms in recent years expanded the range of domestic choices for Canadian investors. Even with the increased choices for Canadians, if you want to build a broad insurance portfolio, you need to look on both sides of the border.

Diversity and Opportunity

Insurance companies differ in size, operating characteristics, profitability and stock market price action. This diversity can represent a potential headache for some but an opportunity for those who take their investment homework very seriously.

The three broad categories of insurance companies are life insurance, property/casualty and multi-line companies. Today, there are very few "pure" life or "pure" property/casualty companies. Most firms specialize in one or the other area, but have subsidiaries involved in a variety of other lines of the business.

Until the 1980s life insurance companies were considered relatively predictable investments. Any life insurer with good products, solid marketing and adequate expense control could be counted on to show healthy, stable returns over both the short and the long run. Property/casualty insurers were usually more cyclical than pure life insurers—their earnings were tied to competitive conditions and catastrophe experience—but over the long haul, property/casualty companies also produced healthy rates of return.

The life insurance industry went through a product revolution in response to high and volatile interest rates. The introduction of new interest-sensitive and investment-type policies caused problems for many traditional companies serving the upscale market, and created exciting opportunities for aggressive competitors. Some companies suffered substantial earnings declines for the first time in their operating histories while others have grown faster than most people believed life insurers could.

On the investment side of the insurance business, rising interest rates tend to boost investment income and operating earnings, but also tend to push down the market value of investments held. The reverse happens when interest rates decline. Reflecting this fact, neither high nor low interest rates can be proven to be best, but relative stability certainly helps management run its company most efficiently. The valuations (p/e ratios) of almost all stocks, including insurers, are benefited by a low inflation and low interest rate environment.

Guidelines for Investment

● **Look beyond the big names.** Size does not necessarily go hand in hand with growth, profitability or quality. The problem with the strategy of most investors, including a large number of professionals, is that they limit their participation in the insurance industry to the biggest, best-known insurers, usually because it's too much trouble to investigate and follow the lesser-known names. That's a mistake. The bigger the insurance company, the more efficiently priced its stock will be and the less chance you will have of making large price gains.

● **Emphasize the differences.** The insurance industry's diversity means that economic and other events can have equally diverse effects. In any typical year, apparently similar firms may experience opposite market price actions and valuations, particularly if they operate in limited geographical areas or specialized market niches. It pays to know the companies—how or why they are unlike their competitors—before you invest, in order to take advantage of low prices resulting from market inefficiencies.

● **Examine management.** The most important investment task is to recognize differences in managements and identify those best equipped for the partic-

ular demands of their business. While this is difficult to accomplish without personal contact, much can be learned from annual reports and the trade press. Is management motivated by the same goals as shareholders (i.e., long-term growth in earnings, dividends and market price)? Is management consistent—does it stick to areas that make sense in light of its resources and abilities? Is management willing to change when conditions point to potential problems? Beware, however, of companies that plan to move aggressively into a new or untested area of business. If the market is already filled with a large number of competitors, chances are that a new player will have little chance of making money.

● **Be an investor, not a trader.** A successful insurance operation takes time to develop—when you find a good one, stick with it. Overtrading, trying to catch popularity swings or profit cycles, can produce very poor results. By the same token, don't be afraid to change your mind if your ongoing research suggests a faulty initial premise or an adverse change in long-term conditions.

● **Diversify to reduce risk.** In an industry with hundreds of companies to choose from, it makes sense to invest in more than one or two issues unless you are certain that those are the best to own without any question. If your basic selection process is sound, diversification reduces the risk that an occasional loss will ruin your entire investment program.

● **Average your cost per share.** Since it's virtually impossible to predict the market's short-term direction, investing all of your available funds at one time is bad strategy. The safer alternative is to buy equal dollar amounts at intervals, buying more shares when prices are low, fewer shares when prices rise. The results are a lower average cost for your total holdings as well as an increased number of opportunities to reevaluate the soundness of your investment program.

Source: *William W. Dyer, trustee, Century Capital Management Inc., One Liberty Square, Boston, MA 02109, a mutual fund worth more than $200 million concentrated in insurance company stocks.*

Investors, Beware

Standard & Poor's created a risk rating for investments—an "r" rating indicating there is a significant risk that a security may lose market value.

Even a security with the highest AAA safety rating against risk of issuer default may incur the "r" rating. *How:* usually when it is a derivative whose value is tied to that of underlying assets, such as mortgage pools, currencies or commodities. The "r" rating was adopted because many investors mistakenly took the AAA rating—which applies only to risk of default—to indicate an investment is equally safe against price fluctuations.

Source: Leo O'Neill, president, S&P Ratings Services, New York.

Secrets of Playing It Very Safe

Not everyone wants to risk their money in stocks, bonds or mutual funds. Plenty of investors stay safe in Treasury bills and GICs. But even super-safe investments can be risky if you don't know the rules. *Here's how to use super-safe investments safely:*

● **Know your goals.** Start by deciding your time frame. Don't just park your money because you don't know what else to do with it.

Super-safe investments should not be long-term. If you need a lump sum in six months to a year, you can play it safe. If you are looking toward retirement, you are better off taking some risks.

● **Consider inflation.** The more conservative you are, the greater your inflation risk. A 3% return from an insured bank account is no return at all when inflation is near 3%.

● **Do it yourself.** You won't earn much by keeping your money safe. Therefore, you can't afford to give any of your return away. Bypass brokers and banks when possible. Their fees will eat into your return.

● **Beware of gimmicks.** Avoid anything touted as a "new" way to protect your investment and improve returns. Do yourself a favor—wait until there's a track record. Derivatives and portfolio insurance are both examples of strategies that promised higher returns, but turned sour. How do safe investments stack up today? Here is a list:

> "Beware, however, of companies that plan to move aggressively into a new or untested area of business.... Chances are that a new player will have little chance of making money."

● **Guaranteed Investment Certificates (GICs).** Yields have been low for several years, reflecting the general low interest-rate environment. If five-year rates return to levels above 6%, you may want to consider locking in.

Important: You may have to shop around for the best rate on a GIC because many banks aren't pushing them aggressively. They would rather push mutual funds, which, unlike GICs, don't require them to pay for deposit insurance. Start with the local newspapers, where you should find GIC rates published in the business section.

A brokerage house may get you a higher rate on a GIC because they can shop the market and have access to the latest quotes.

● **Money-market mutual funds.** They typically pay more than a short-term GIC—however, unlike GICs, where the rate is fixed, the return on a money fund will rise as interest rates rise. The shorter the average maturity of money fund investments, the quicker its return will rise in line with interest rates.

If you think or know interest rates will rise, look for a fund with more short-term paper. For this purpose, I like a 30-day average maturity.

● **Short-term Treasury issues.** Treasury bills (issued for one year or less) are guaranteed by the government of Canada.

If interest rates climb, your Treasury bills will lose value. You'd get less than the purchase price if you must sell early. The longer the maturity, the more the price is likely to fall.

● **Short-term bond funds.** You can buy short-term issues yourself. Or you can buy a mutual fund that invests in short-term securities. *You get the same advantages of any mutual fund:* Diversification and professional management.

Because bond funds actively trade their portfolios, the higher interest rates generally go, the more you'll earn on your fund. As with any bond or bond fund, the higher rates go, the lower prices will go.

Sources: Gordon Pape; and Scott Kahan, U.S. certified financial planner and president of a New York asset management firm.

How to Make Money in the Stock Market in Tough Times

Short selling is easier than you think—but it's risky. Short selling involves borrowing common stock from another investor and then selling it in the hope that the stock's price will fall and you'll be able to replace it at a lower price. But instead of going down, the stock's price could go up—and there's no limit to how high it could go—losses can be staggeringly large. *Classic example:* In 1901 Northern Pacific Railroad's stock shot up from under $150/share to $1,000 in just a few days—wiping out all short-sellers. Such a big move in a stock's price rarely occurs, but a swing of just 10–20 points can also be devastating to a short-seller.

Lesson: Never stay short when the market turns against you—buy the stock back quickly and get out.

Psychological Factors

Short selling is unpopular, and especially unpopular in bull markets, when people think that stocks will go up forever. Of course, no market goes up forever. *Signs of an overvalued market ripe for decline:*

- **Everyone talking about their market gains.**
- **Magazine covers emblazoned with a rampaging bull.**
- **No one urging caution.**

Even when investors think that the market may be headed for trouble, most either just refrain from buying stock or move to cash. These are solid protective steps. But they don't enable investors to make money in a downturn—as short selling does.

Underrecognized: Investors can actually make money much faster by selling stocks short than by buying them as investments. *Reason:* Stocks go down much more rapidly than they go up. Typically, if it takes a stock a year to go from $20/share to $30, it can fall back from $30 to $20 in as little as two or three days in a bear market.

There's a place for short selling in any kind of market. Investors who have a substantial portfolio ($50,000 or more) should hedge by putting 5%–10% of capital into short sales.

Selecting Shorts

Companies are always eager to talk about good news that they expect, but in order to find out about pos-sible earnings declines or dividend cuts, short-sellers must do their own homework. *Signs that a sector is overvalued:*

- **A sharp run-up in stock prices in that sector.**
- **Stock sector analysts** rationalizing the run-up and claiming that the stocks are still undervalued.
- **Extensive media coverage.**

Signs that a stock is overvalued:

- **A rapid price increase** on the promise of a concept that's caught people's imagination but hasn't yet been developed into a marketable product.
- **The company finally coming** out with a new product that was extensively promoted but doesn't measure up to its promise.
- **The stock hitting a new low** in volume after a long increase.

In general, when a sector weakens, it's best to short the companies that have been laggards. They will decline first and furthest.

Source: The late Louis Ehrenkrantzt of Ehrenkrantz King Nussbaum, investment advisers, New York, NY.

Selling Short in a Bull Market

Short-selling opportunities develop even during bull markets. Most such markets are interrupted at least once by a severe decline.

Suggestions for profitable short selling:

- **Sell only heavily capitalized issues** with a low outstanding short interest. They are much less likely to be subject to a short squeeze (sharp rallies caused by many short-sellers rushing to cover and too few shares available).
- **Cover short sales during moments of market weakness.** Take advantage of market declines that are stimulated by bad news to cover periods of weakness.

Warning: Do not wait for a rally to cover shorts. *What the pros do:* Cover short sales just before weekends in case favorable news triggers sharp Monday rallies.

- **As an alternative to selling short,** consider the purchase of puts (selling an option contract at a stated price on or before a fixed expiration date).
- **A stock that is sold short** can decline by only so much, but there's no limit on how much it can rise.

Result: Short selling bucks the odds because the ultimate risk is always greater than the potential reward. Place stop-loss orders to cover when the short sale goes against you by more than 10%–15%.

● **Sell short stocks** that show definite signs of overhead resistance (areas of heavy trading in that stock just above your short-selling level) on their charts. Such areas tend to impede upside progress.

● **Do not sell those short issues** that have just made new highs. Wait for definite signs of weakness before selling short.

Source: Personal Finance, *Kephart Communications, Alexandria, VA.*

When a Company You Have Invested in Goes Bankrupt

You basically have two choices when a company you've invested in goes bankrupt: Sell the stock and take a loss—or hold the stock and hope the company and its stock recover.

A bankrupt company will do one of two things. It may reorganize under the bankruptcy protection provisions available in Canadian law, in which case it is maintained as a viable public entity and given the chance to reverse its losses and pay back its creditors. Or, the company may be dissolved as a public entity, with its assets liquidated to pay back the creditors. Both outcomes are decided by a bankruptcy court on the basis of creditors' needs and the ability of the company to repay its debts.

The worst case for the owner of common stock occurs when the company is liquidated. After the firm's liquidation, taxes, wages and court costs receive top priority. Debt holders and preferred stockholders are next—common stockholders are last in line. Most often, liquidation barely raises enough cash for the company's debt holders.

HOW TO PICK LEISURE STOCKS

The great advantage of leisure companies—manufacturers of recreational products such as golf clubs, boats, running shoes, etc.—is that you don't need a Wall Street or Bay Street analyst or industry expert to tell you how a product works and/or how successful it might be. With most leisure stocks, your own judgment is good enough to pick out the potential winners from the losers.

For this reason, leisure stocks are perfect for the investor with an eye for changes in the public mood. Trends in sports or exercise or new developments in old products create opportunities for growth almost overnight. For example, a few years ago, there was a strong demand for a boat specifically designed for sports fishermen, one of the largest groups of boat buyers in the country. Several small, innovative companies recognized this need and produced what is now known as the "bass boat." The result was instant success for the companies involved and sizable stock price appreciation for the companies' stockholders.

The second advantage of leisure stocks is that they tend to be much less cyclical than industrial or high-tech stocks. It doesn't seem to matter whether the economy is good or bad, once Canadians take an activity to heart, money is no object in acquiring the equipment to pursue it.

Remember, however, that identifying emerging trends in the leisure market or potentially hot new products is only half the battle. You still have to make sure the company fulfills the rest of your investment criteria—strong growth rates; solid, innovative management; a strong balance sheet; etc.

Also, with any industry governed by popular taste, you have to be careful of investing in companies that rely on one particular trend for most of their earnings. If the trend is short-lived or brings with it a great number of competitors, as was the case with running shoes, you may see your company's profits squeezed from all sides.

Source: Scott Miles, president, Miles & West Insurance Agency, Inc., 12221 Merit Drive, Suite 940, Dallas, TX 75251. He is responsible for marketing and finance at the agency.

The best scenario for stockholders occurs when the company is allowed to reorganize, is made profitable in a relatively short period of time (a few years) and its creditors are paid back. Then the stock may recover a portion of its value or even return to its original price.

Sell or Hold?

There are several questions you must ask yourself, when deciding what to do with your stock. First and foremost, how likely is it that the company will be allowed to reorganize? If you think the firm will be liquidated, it's probably better to sell the stock when you can still get a fraction of its original value. However, if the company is allowed to reorganize, what are the chances of the stock recovering even part of what you paid for it? What are the opportunity costs of holding it—that is, what could you do with the money if you sold the stock? What value is the tax loss to you this year? Can you handle the emotional stress involved in holding a bankrupt company?

One of the decision-making problems you face is that you can't know how long bankruptcy proceedings will last: They may end in a couple of months or drag on for years without a satisfactory resolution. Another problem is that the company may come out of reorganization, not make a profit and fizzle back into bankruptcy later. Your biggest risk is that after the company goes into reorganization, it may run into hard times and be liquidated.

Risk Reduction Tactics

The best way to minimize your risk is to remain well informed at all times. Try determining what the bankruptcy court will decide before its decision is announced. Unfortunately, once a company goes into bankruptcy proceedings, information becomes scarce, but you can look for indications that the company can pay back even a portion of its debt.

The single most important indicator to look for is available cash flow. If the company has sufficient cash flow to pay down debts slowly at some modest discount from full value, it's likely the court will allow the company to exist. But beware of dilution. The company may try to issue new shares as a way of raising additional capital. While stock issues are a good sign that the investment community has faith in the company's future, they also mean that the value of your shares will decline.

Profitable divisions of the company can help your chances of recovering your equity. In many cases, bankruptcies are due to one or two unprofitable divisions of a diversified company. If a large part of the company is still profitable, there's a good chance the unprofitable divisions can be sold or shut down.

A strong equity holders' committee can help, too. These committees are established after a bankruptcy is announced and serve as the only means for stockholders to influence the outcome of the legal proceedings.

If you are a large stockholder in the company or just want to play an active role in the proceedings, you have a good shot at becoming a member of the equity holders' committee. This will give you access to a great deal of information. The only drawback is that you will be considered an insider by securities regulators and severely restricted in your buying and/or selling of the company's stock.

Source: *Kenneth L. Fisher, chief executive of Fisher Investments, Woodside, CA 94062, an investment management firm. Mr. Fisher is the author of a regular column in* **Forbes** *and of several books.*

Know All About Bonds

While most investors have a good understanding of how the stock market works, too few are even remotely familiar with bonds—or the bond market.

As a result, many individuals invest blindly and are unaware of the risks. That's unfortunate, because bonds deserve a place in every portfolio. Over time, they can produce higher returns than other fixed-income investments—if you understand what you are doing.

Bond basics:

● **The face value of a bond is fixed at the time it is purchased.** It is the amount a bondholder can count on getting in cash on the date the bond matures, which could be anywhere from one year to 100 years, depending on the particular bond.

● **The market value**—the price at which you can sell a bond any time before maturity—is profoundly affected by changes in interest rates. These rates are driven by expectations about the course of inflation. The longer the amount of time until a bond comes due, the more vulnerable it is to these expectations on a day-to-day basis.

● **When interest rates go up, the prices of bonds held by investors go down.**
Reason: Newer issues offer higher yields. For example, why would investors pay the $1,000 you paid for a 7% bond if they can get 8% on the $1,000 now. It is basic economic common sense.

● **A guess about the probable course of inflation** is built into a bond's interest rate—or "coupon"—at the time it is issued. For example, a bond paying 7% may assume a 4% inflation rate, for a real return of 3%.

But if inflation turns out to be much higher, you will take a beating if you have to sell a bond before it reaches maturity. You can, of course, hold a bond to maturity and collect its face value—but the dollars you will get back may have a lot less purchasing power than they did when you invested them.

How to play interest rates:

● **If you think interest rates will rise**—buy bonds with short or intermediate maturities, generally not more than 8 to 10 years. A spurt in interest rates after you buy the short or intermediate bond will not affect its price as much as it would a long-term bond because the substandard return lasts for a much shorter period. In other words, you will get back your principal sooner and be able to reinvest it at the new, higher interest rates.

● **If you think interest rates will fall further**—do yourself a favor and buy bonds with low coupons and long maturities (more than 10 years) that are selling below their face values.

● **If you have no idea** about which way interest rates are heading—"ladder" your investments. Buy bonds of different maturities—short, intermediate and long—to give you some protection against rate movements in either direction.

DRIPs

Investors in dividend reinvestment programs (DRIPs) should be aware of two tax-planning points: Extra shares bought with dividends through a DRIP are taxable income if the securities are in a non-registered portfolio, even though the DRIP does not pay out any cash with which to pay the tax. So you'll have to come up with cash from other sources to pay the tax bill. And if you invest automatically through a DRIP, you'll probably be buying small lots of shares at least quarterly, at different prices. You will have to maintain accurate cost records for each purchase in order to figure out your taxable capital gain (or loss) when you sell.

Important: If you sell just part of your holdings, pick the particular shares for sale that will produce the best tax results.

Source: *Charles B. Carlson, CFA, editor,* **Dow Theory Forecasts**, *7412 Calumet Ave., Hammond, IN 46324.*

Common problems and solutions:

● **Bonds can be difficult to buy at fair prices.** Bonds have always been a game for major players—commercial banks, insurance companies, pension funds and mutual funds—which buy and sell them in huge quantities and pay less for them than you could.

Self-defense:

1. Buy new issues. Initial offerings by governments, agencies and corporations usually sell for set prices. Commissions are generally paid by the seller, not you.

2. Shop around. Get quotes on comparable bonds from two or three brokers. Some discount brokers, such as E*Trade Canada, have programs that enable you to comparison shop online if you have an account with them.

● **Bonds can be hard to sell at fair prices.** Many issues rarely trade in the secondary market. Dealers don't like to handle small numbers of bonds and often cut prices to move them quickly. If you have to sell, the bid price may shock you.

Self-defense:

1. Hold bonds to redemption. This is almost always the best plan for individuals. Invest in bonds with the intention of holding them to maturity.

2. Buy bonds that are likely to have an active secondary market. If you feel the yield on long-term bonds is too good to pass up, choose those that are part of large offerings from well-known issuers. Find out if they are actively traded by asking your broker.

● **Bonds can be retired early**—or "called"—years before their scheduled maturity. Issuers can call bonds when interest rates fall if a call feature is part of the original issue. Just as homeowners rush to refinance mortgages, bond issuers reduce interest expenses by replacing old, high-interest bonds with new ones at much lower rates.

Even though the call price is usually slightly above a bond's face value, early redemption is almost always a blow to bondholders. They lose the high returns they've expected to earn for years and must then reinvest the principal at lower market rates. *Even worse:* An investor may have paid a premium for a high-yielding bond and so will lose income when it's called.

Self-defense:

● **Buy bonds that can't be called.** Read the prospectus on a new issue carefully to check for call provisions. If a bond is already trading in the secondary market, ask your broker whether it is callable before you commit. If you decide to buy a callable bond for the increased yield, you should understand the call provisions and how they may affect your investment.

● **Interest and principal may not be paid.** Corporations and municipalities sometimes do go belly-up. When they do, you may lose most of your investment.

Self-defense:

● **Look for quality.** Unless you have good reason to think a company that is facing hard times is due for a comeback, forget it. Invest in conservatively managed companies that are leaders in growing industries.

● **Insist on collateral.** Don't rely on an issuer's revenue stream to service a bond. If the assets pledged to secure the debt are valuable, chances are you'll get most or all of your money back if disaster strikes. Bondholders can force the sale of these assets to pay their claims.

● **Invest in government of Canada or U.S. Treasury securities**—the ultimate security, since governments aren't going out of business.

A case for bond funds:

● **Unless you have large amounts of money to invest in bonds,** beware of buying individual issues. You are bound to sacrifice diversification—either in terms of issuers or maturities—and it is easy to get lost in the intricacies of some of the markets.

Generally, individuals are probably better off investing in bond funds.

Drawback: Mutual funds don't "mature," so there is no guarantee that you will get back your investment on any specified date.

Be sure to match a fund with your own investment standards and invest in at least two of the following types of bond funds:

● **Longer term**—13 years or more—for the higher yield.

● **Intermediate term**—from 2 to 12 years to reduce risk.

It's important to know a fund's fee structure before you invest, so read the prospectus carefully. *Look for the following:*

● **Low expense ratios.** This is critical. An expense ratio of more than 1.5% is a big drag on your yield. *Example:* A bond fund with a gross return of 7.5% yields a net return of 7.0% if the annual expense ratio is 0.5% of assets, but yields only 6.0% if the ratio is 1.5%.

Tip: A few companies offer special Internet-traded bond funds with very low management expense ratios (MERs). TD Bank's "e" units are an example.

● **Loads.** Some funds charge a front-end load—or fee—when you invest. Others charge a back-end load when you sell. Back-end loads are generally reduced over time, for example, from 6% of net asset value on shares held less than a year to no fee at all on shares held five years or more. Clearly, it is more costly to sell before the fees phase out.

Sources: *Gordon Pape; and David L. Scott, Ph.D., professor of accounting and finance at Valdosta State University, GA. He is the author of* The Guide to Investing in Bonds, *Globe Pequot Press.*

Convertible Bonds

Convertible bonds are hybrid securities that carry a fixed interest rate like a bond, but may be exchanged for a specified amount of the issuing company's common stock. (Usually the issuer will spell out several limitations regarding when and how conversion can take place.) Convertibles' dual character produces dual advantages. The bonds provide you with interest income that is usually higher than what you would receive from a common stock dividend, but lower than the income from a straight debt security. At the same time, the bonds' convertibility feature gives you the chance to play the stock market.

Convertibles act as a compromise investment for times when you are uncertain about the future of the bond market and uncertain about the future of the stock market. When stock prices climb, convertibles rise. When they fall, convertibles don't fall quite as quickly, and still pay you reasonable current income. As a result, convertibles allow you to smooth out the effects of a volatile stock market.

What to Watch For

Keep an eye on the market for rare opportunities. There are situations in which the market for convertible bonds and the market for the bonds' underlying stocks are not well coordinated. The result can be inefficient pricing. In these situations, it is possible that (1) a bond's underlying common stock actually provides a higher yield than the convertible, and/or (2) the convertible bond is selling at or below its conversion value. Both situations would allow you to purchase the underlying common stock at a discount.

Convertibles are fairly complex instruments to understand. The pricing can get tricky, and most individual investors end up paying a fairly large premium for the opportunity to play both the bond and stock markets. By trying to have the best of both worlds, you can severely limit your potential gain from either one. If both the bond and the stock markets drop, the price of a convertible could decline.

Special notes on buying and selling:

● **Before buying a convertible bond,** check its "call" provisions—the right of the issuer to redeem your security. Call provisions can sometimes have a very substantial effect on the price of a bond over time.

● **When you decide to convert a bond into its common stock equivalent,** wait until after the next interest payout. Interest on convertibles is paid semiannually and normally does not accrue.

Source: *Jay Goldinger, president and chief investment strategist at Capital Insight, 190 N. Canon Drive, Suite 200, Beverly Hills, CA 90210, and author of* Keys to Investing in Government Securities, *Barron's.*

Stripped Bonds

Stripped bonds (so-called because the interest coupons have been stripped away) are often sold as a simple, predictable, risk-free investment. If that sounds almost too good to be true—believe me, it *is* too good to be true.

Stripped bonds are an appropriate investment only for people who are certain they will hold bonds until maturity—and who want to have a specific amount of money at a specific future date—to pay a college tuition, make a down payment on a house or pay off the mortgage at retirement.

For reasons I'll get to, a strip is very risky for anyone who might have to sell before maturity.

Important Differences

● **Traditional bonds** are sold at or near face value and pay periodic interest until maturity, when you get back your principal. You are paid interest every six months—so every six months you have new money to reinvest at whatever rate you can get at that moment.

● **Stripped bonds** are sold for a fraction of their face amount and pay all interest, along with principal, in a lump sum at maturity. Since no interest is paid until maturity, there's no need to keep reinvesting. *Advantage:* Strips are affordable because they're sold

GOOD WAY TO BUY FOREIGN STOCKS

Foreign stocks need not always be bought on exchanges abroad. *Easier:* Buying shares of a foreign company through American Depositary Receipts (ADRs). These instruments are available for some foreign stocks. They trade on U.S. exchanges and are treated just like U.S. securities. They generally are available in units that represent one to 10 shares of a foreign company's stock. They certify that the shares have been bought and are being held by a custodian outside the United States. *Advantages:* Lower brokerage commissions than on trades of actual foreign shares and dividends paid in U.S. dollars.

Source: Joseph Velli, ADR business manager at the Bank of New York in New York City.

at a deep discount. Say that today's rate is 7½% for long-term Canada bonds, you'd pay $1,142.21 for a 30-year stripped government bond that will be worth $10,000 at maturity.

Risk: Having an issuer solvent enough to pay off:

● **Government or Crown corporation strips** are sure to pay off.

● **Provincial strips** are also safe—if you buy good credit quality bonds and diversify by buying bonds issued by more than one province.

● **Corporate strips** are another story—and I recommend against them. *Reason:* A corporation generally issues stripped bonds because it has no money to pay current interest. What does that tell you about its quality?

Understanding the Risks

If you can't hold to maturity, strips are a wildly unpredictable investment—much more volatile than traditional bonds. *Here's why:*

● **When interest rates fall,** strips can be sold at premium prices because of the higher interest rate locked into the bond.

● **When interest rates rise,** the stripped bond's locked-in lower rate sharply reduces what it can be sold for. If the current long-term bond rate should rise from 7½% to 8½%, the strips you bought for $1,142.21 will be worth only $865.18.

Best prospects: Strips should be bought only by people who feel interest rates won't go much higher, know they won't need this money until the bonds mature and won't lose sleep over price fluctuations in the meantime. For the other 98% of investors, I'm not a big fan of strips.

Important: You're taxed every year on the interest you earn on a stripped bond, even though you don't receive it until the bond matures. Generally, you should buy stripped bonds only for a nontaxable account, like an RRSP.

Source: Lew Altfest, CPA, CFP, president of L.J. Altfest & Co., a financial planning firm, 116 John St., New York, NY 10038. He is the author of Lew Altfest Answers All Your Questions About Money, *McGraw-Hill.*

Create Your Own Bond Fund

You can do this by building a portfolio of laddered government of Canada bonds. *How:* Invest among bonds with varying maturities, such as one, three, five and seven years. You obtain the benefit of diversification—if rates go down, you earn capital gains from the longer-term bonds; if rates go up, you get more income when your short-term securities are reinvested. You also get the complete safety of government of Canada investments. For investors who don't require professional money-management services, this strategy will avoid bond-fund management fees that average about 1.8% annually—or 26% of a 7% bond yield.

Sources: Gordon Pape; and Bruce Ventimiglia of Quest for Value, retail investment advisory arm of Oppenheimer Capital, New York.

How to Guard Against Losses in the Options and Futures Markets

Most amateur investors lose money with high-leverage investments because they carelessly put most of their trading capital at risk in the hope of making large, quick profits—they invest on the basis of emotions rather than a disciplined trading strategy.

Contrary to popular belief, disciplined trading is the real way to make consistent profits over the long term in either the options or futures markets. The key to successful, disciplined trading is managing your capital, controlling your risks and watching the markets.

Managing Your Capital

Don't commit funds to leveraged investments that you can't afford to lose. Since you only make big profits in futures and options markets when you assume a correspondingly high level of risk, always limit the capital you commit to an amount you feel comfortable about losing completely. As a general rule, if you can't handle large losses over a short period of time, you probably shouldn't be trading in options or futures.

Once you've determined the amount of capital you can devote to trading, always keep a large portion of capital in reserve. Never risk all or most of it on a single trade, regardless of how successful you've been in the past or how attractive the next trade appears. *Remember:* There will always be losing trades. By compounding your capital after a few profitable trades, you can only expose yourself to potentially dangerous losses. This strategy will give you the staying power to ride out losses and, ultimately, to make a profit.

Controlling Your Risk

Diversify your positions. *The old rule still applies:* Never have all your investment eggs in one futures or options basket.

For futures trading, maintain a minimum of two positions in different futures complexes. (The major futures complexes consist of stock indexes, metals, financial instruments, meats and agricultural commodities.) A long position in gold and a long position in silver does not constitute diversification. Don't

just trade on the long side (buying with the hope that prices will rise). Since markets rise and fall, you must learn to trade on the short side as well (profiting from a decline in prices).

For options trading, maintain at least two positions in different underlying instruments. Also try to invest in puts as well as in calls.

Protect against major losses by using stop-loss orders. Diversification will help protect you against adverse moves in a particular market, but protective stop-loss orders will close out losing positions before they deteriorate into huge losses. Determine your stop-loss points in advance and stick to them; 50% maximum loss on your original investment is appropriate for most trades.

Watching the Markets

Many futures and options traders are short-term-oriented, and their approach tends to be technical in nature. This means that they analyze past trends in price and volume to predict future market direction. It is also possible to look at markets in terms of fundamentals, such as interest rates, inflation, production and demand. However, although these will ultimately dictate price movements, it is very difficult to translate them into profitable short-term trading programs.

Closely follow the markets that most interest you. It's the only way to gain a feeling for a market's underlying direction. Don't be afraid to utilize the advice and recommendations of outside advisory and information services. Most good traders rely on a number of excellent information sources beyond just the daily financial press to help determine market movements. Sources include investment advisory services, brokerage reports devoted to futures and options, chart services and computer databases.

Source: *Bernard G. Schaeffer, executive director, Investment Research Institute, Inc., 110 Boggs Lane, Suite 365, Cincinnati, OH 45246. He is coeditor of* The Option Advisor *and several other newsletters on short-term trading, as well as coauthor of* The Options Handbook *and* The Trader's Handbook.

How to Profit With Options: The Basics

The sad truth about options is that most people who invest in them end up losing money. That is primarily because few investors take the time to learn exactly how options work or, more important, how to use them to make money.

Good advice: Always learn the basics well, then proceed with caution. *For serious investors, options can serve three basic functions:*

- **High-risk speculation** on market direction.
- **Supplementing current dividend** and interest income from a portfolio.
- **Hedging** against portfolio risk.

But, again, options only provide these advantages to investors who know what they're doing.

The Basics of Options

An option is nothing more than a contract that gives you the right to buy or sell a security at a set price by a specified date in the future. *There are two types of options:* A *call*, the right to buy a security at a set price in the future; and a *put*, the right to sell a security at a set price in the future. *Example:* Company X's stock sells for $30 a share. You buy a call, which expires in three months, at $35 a share. This means that within three months, you have the right to buy the stock of Company X for $35 a share no matter how high the share price has risen.

The price of the option, or premium, is 50¢. This represents the time value of the option. It is based on the length of time before the option expires and the likelihood of the stock actually reaching the option's exercise price. If investors think there is only a small chance that Company X's stock will reach $35 in three months, then the premium will be

MORE ON STRIPPED BONDS

Stripped bonds are simply ordinary government or corporate bonds stripped of their coupon yields and sold at a deep discount from their face value. Like Treasury bills, they pay no current interest to the investor. Instead, the bonds increase in value until they mature, when they can be redeemed at full face value. Interest that normally would have been paid out to the investor over the life of the bond is used to increase the value of the bond.

For example, buy $10,000 worth of stripped bonds due in 10 years and appreciating at a compounded rate of 8.1%, and they will be worth almost $22,000 when they mature.

Return, Tax and Cost Advantages

Stripped bonds can offer some of the highest overall returns to be found among government-guaranteed securities. In addition, they provide a fixed rate of return for the reinvestment of your interest income. The problem with most bonds is that you have to reinvest your interest income. Stripped bonds eliminate the burden of reinvestment, because interest income is reinvested at the rate initially guaranteed to you when you bought the bond.

Stripped bonds are ideal fundings for tax-deferred investment vehicles. Their most popular uses are in qualified pension/profit-sharing retirement plans, RRSPs, or financing a university education. However, be careful how you fund the last. The best technique is to put them into a registered education savings plan (RESP), so that the compounding takes place in a tax-sheltered environment.

Think twice, also, about investing in stripped bonds if you're not using a tax-advantaged investment vehicle. Even though you don't receive interest payments on a stripped bond, the Canada Customs and Revenue Agency (CCRA) requires that you pay the annual income tax on interest you would have received.

Sources: Jay Goldinger, president and chief investment strategist at Capital Insight, Beverly Hills, CA 90210, and author of **Keys to Investing in Government Securities**, *Barron's. Canadian information, Gordon Pape.*

low. If, however, investors think there is a large chance that the stock will reach $35, then the price of the option will be higher. At 50¢, investors probably think there is relatively little chance of the stocks reaching $35.

A month later, the price of the stock jumps to $40. The value of the option is now $5, because you could exercise the option, buy the stock at $35 and then sell it for $40 in the open market. Your 50¢ investment is therefore worth 10 times its original value. If the stock did not reach the exercise price of $35 however, the option would expire worthless.

A put operates in the reverse fashion. If you think a stock will go down in price, you buy a put or the right to sell the stock at a set price in the future. *Example:* Company X is selling for $35 a share. This time, you think the price will go down, so you buy a put to sell the stock for $35. The premium you pay for the option is $1. One month later, the company experiences problems and the price of the stock drops to $30. You can now buy the stock for $30 in the open market and sell it for $35. Your profit is $4, or a 400% gain on your original investment.

Huge Returns—and Risks

With options, a very small investment can rack up huge returns in a very short period of time. To otherwise achieve the same results in the stock market would take massive amounts of capital and a great deal of patience.

The risk is that most options expire worthless. Unlike the stocks themselves, if an option's underlying stock or index does not perform according to your expectations, the options contract expires with no value at all—you lose your entire investment. Also, options are typically short-term investment vehicles—they usually involve a great deal of buying and selling. As a result, total commission costs can be very high.

Source: Carl A. Futia, investment consultant, 16 Colles Ave., Morristown, NJ 07960.

> "Unlike the stocks themselves, if an option's underlying stock or index does not perform according to your expectations, the options contract expires with no value at all—you lose your entire investment."

Options Investing Strategies

Professional investors have devised a large and impressive array of investing strategies utilizing the options market. Some of these strategies are exceedingly complex and, because of the large amounts of capital involved, are not recommended for use by individual investors. However, a number of basic options strategies can expand your investing capabilities significantly.

Selling Options on a Stock Portfolio

Selling options on a stock portfolio, better known as "writing covered calls," allows you to generate current income over and above the income received by dividends. Instead of buying call options, you actually "write" or sell them on your own portfolio. In return for selling the call option, you receive a premium from the investor who purchases the call. This strategy is used when you don't expect your stocks to move much either up or down. *Example:* You own 200 shares of Company X at $40 a share. Company X pays a regular quarterly dividend of $1 or an annual yield of 10%. This is a respectable dividend, but you want more current income. You believe that the stock of Company X is going to remain relatively stable, so you decide to write a covered call on your stock of Company X at an exercise price of $45. The investor who buys the call pays you a premium of $1.

As a result of this transaction, you have doubled your quarterly income in no time at all. The risk, though, is that your outlook for Company X is not correct and the stock's price will actually rise above $45. Then, your stock can be called away any time before the option expires. If this happens, you will not participate in the stock's gains beyond $45. And, if it is called away from you before a quarterly dividend date, you won't receive your dividend, either.

Sale of a Naked Call

This is a much riskier version of writing covered calls. The main difference between the two is that when you sell naked calls, you receive a premium without actually owning the underlying securities. Who should use this strategy? Investors who are willing to take on large and sometimes unlimited amounts of risk. Why are naked calls so risky? If you sell a naked call for $45 and the stock rises above that exercise price, you are responsible for purchasing the stock in the open market at the current market price. *Example:* If the naked call is exercisable at $45 a share and the price of Company X's stock rises to $50, you will have to buy the stock at $50 in the open market and sell it to the owner of the call for $45. Your loss will equal $5.

Straddles

Use a "straddle" when you think a stock will move dramatically up or down, but you're not sure which direction it will take. This situation might arise when a company's future earnings will be severely affected, positively or negatively, by a specific event—for instance, a court ruling on a series of new products, the movement of interest rates or a cutoff of supply of natural resources. *Example:* Company X's stock trades for $40 a share. A Health Canada ruling on a new product will dramatically affect Company X's potential for future earnings. You're not sure which way the stock will move, so you buy a $40 call and a $40 put. The cost of each option is $5—your investment is $10. Now, if Company X's stock goes above $50 or below $30 before the put and call expire, you will make a profit.

Hedging a Broad Stock Portfolio

Options on market indexes can be used to hedge against a portfolio's inherent market risk. Use this strategy when you own a broad portfolio of stocks and are uncertain about the future movement of the stock market as a whole and, hence, of your portfolio. If this is the case, buy a put option on the most comparable market index (S&P/TSX Composite, Standard & Poor's 500, Value Line, etc.). If the market and presumably your portfolio do in fact decline in value, you will make a profit on your put. If your prediction does not come true, then the rise in the value of your portfolio can offset the premium you paid for the option. Index options (unlike stock options) are settled with cash.

The advantages of hedging a portfolio, rather than liquidating it outright, are that you save a significant amount of money in brokerage commissions, and you are able to hold on to stocks you believe are fundamentally sound long-term investments. However, there are also risks. If your portfolio is not well correlated with a specific market index, you will not be fully protected. You can potentially lose money on your hedge and your portfolio. If the stock market goes up, you do not get the full benefit from the increase in the value of your portfolio.

Limiting Your Losses

Most first-time options investors lose. *So, be careful:* Don't let your losses amount to more than 50% of your initial investment. Options investors are notorious for waiting out a downturn in the market in the hope that their position will become profitable by expiration time. When your loss amounts to 50%, admit you were wrong and liquidate the position to ensure that the option won't turn into a 100% loss by expiration day.

Source: Carl A. Futia, investment consultant, 16 Colles Ave., Morristown, NJ 07960.

Investing in No-Load Funds

Beware of investment salesmen who try to convince you that load funds are better than no-load funds. To support their position, they will say that some load funds have outperformed no-load funds.

Then they will tell you not to worry about the load because you'll only have to pay that 3% or 5% or 8% fee *once.* After that, you'll be entitled to switch between funds in the same family, free of charge. *Reality:* Arguments are not convincing. No-load funds are still the only way to go—for individuals and institutions.

Since front-end load funds charge you money up front, they automatically have to work harder than no-load funds to produce real returns for investors. Back-end load funds don't charge any commissions in advance, but their MERs are sometimes more expensive and you may have to pay a deferred sales charge when you exit. Sure, some load funds outperform no-load funds, but there's no guarantee that they will.

Investing to Win

As for free switching—why is it beneficial to be limited to one fund family? No one fund family is going to have the strongest funds in every category.

The Power of No-Load Managers
What to look for in a no-load-fund manager:

● **Independent thinking.** Invest with someone willing to buck conventional wisdom, who has the courage of his or her convictions but can adjust a portfolio when the markets don't cooperate.

You can gauge this by looking at the manager's portfolio and reading the semiannual letters to shareholders.

● **Long-term track record.** The past is an imperfect guide to the future, but a record of excellence sure beats one of mediocrity.

● **Recent strength.** It's inevitable that top managers will sometimes underperform their peers.

TODAY'S CANADA SAVINGS BONDS

Canada Savings Bonds have changed a lot in recent years. In fact, if you haven't looked at them for some time, you may be surprised at the differences. They've come a long way from the days when your parents gave you a $50 CSB as a birthday gift when what you really wanted was a scooter.

There are now two classes of these popular investments: Canada Savings Bonds (CSBs) and Canada Premium Bonds (CPBs). Each is designed for specific investment purposes.

Canada Savings Bonds. For safety and liquidity, they're still hard to beat. CSBs are backed by the full financial weight of the Canadian government. Unless you think we're going into national bankruptcy any time soon, that makes them about as secure an investment as you will find anywhere.

The other big point in their favor is that they're as good as cash. You can walk into a bank any time with a CSB and they'll redeem it on the spot. But timing is important. Interest is only paid up to the end of the previous month. If you cash in your CSB on May 30, for example, you'll only get interest to the end of April. By waiting two more days, you earn an additional month.

CSB interest is now guaranteed for a three-year period and normally escalates on each anniversary date. You'll never receive less than the guaranteed amount and you could actually get more—if interest rates rise faster than expected, the government will adjust CSB yields upward to discourage people from cashing them in.

CSBs were once sold only for a couple of months each year. Now the sale period extends from November to April, with rates adjusted monthly.

Main drawback to CSBs—low returns, especially in the first year. When interest rates dropped to 40-year lows in 2001, first year CSB yields actually fell to below 2%.

Canada Premium Bonds. These are the new kids on the block. They're specifically designed for registered plans (RRSPs, RRIFs, etc.) and pay somewhat higher rates than CSBs— usually 0.5% to 1% more. The trade-off is that they're less liquid. Like CSBs, the rates are guaranteed for the first three years. Unlike CSBs, they can only be cashed once a year, on the anniversary date and in the 30 days immediately following.

Both types of bonds can be purchased through payroll savings programs.

The government has also created no-fee RRSPs and RRIFs, which are especially designed to hold CSBs and CPBs. For information, visit the CSB website at www.csb.gc.ca/eng/default.asp.

Source: *Gordon Pape, author of* 6 Steps to $1 Million, *published by Prentice Hall Canada.*

But if this happens for more than a nine-month stretch, I'm not happy, and we vote with our feet.

Important: Be sure you're comparing apples with apples. If *value investing* is out of favor, no *value manager* will beat the market. But if you insist on value investing, at least pick someone who is outperforming his or her value-stock peers.

● **Disciplined approach.** Invest with someone who has a clear view of how the world works and a willingness to stick with that approach.

● **Ownership stake in the fund family.** The fund family can tell you whether the manager owns shares in his or her own fund. That's obviously a positive sign. But there's another benefit to this as well. The more shares a manager owns, the more likely it is that he or she will stay put for a long time.

How to Check the Numbers

We use data from a variety of sources, including *Morningstar.* Other Canadian data sources include *Globefund, Financial Post* and www.sourcebook online.com, the website of the old *Southam Mutual Fund Sourcebook. Here's what to do with the data once you get it:*

● **Look behind the numbers.** Two similar funds may both have advanced 50% last year. That's tentatively appealing, but you have to see what the numbers mean. Did the manager profit from huge stakes in two or three highly speculative companies? Was the fund strong in the first half of the year but weak in the second half?

Key: Given a choice, we would always invest in the fund that came on strong in the second half of last year rather than in the first half. *Morningstar* has this information.

Investing Strategies

● **Don't just go for the famous fund-family names.** We believe that the most innovative and courageous fund managers are more likely to be found outside the large fund families.

● **Invest in the future.** Put some money where you think the market is *headed*, not where it has been. It's a wonderful way to enhance returns.

● **Consider applying a top-down approach.** This involves identifying those sectors of the economy you believe will outperform and overweighting your assets

to favor them. For example, if you think energy stocks are likely to outperform the broad market over the next two or three years, you will have a significant position in energy funds in your portfolio.

● **When a great fund closes to new investors, be careful.** When this happens, don't automatically put your money in a fund with a similar name.

Use careful analysis to try to find a fund with a similar investment philosophy and track record.

● **Paying too much attention to expense ratios can be penny-wise and pound-foolish.** An expense ratio—what a fund charges investors to cover its marketing costs—is crucial when it comes to bond funds but not as important for stock funds. That's because the ratio for bond funds tends to eat into total returns more so than stock funds.

More important: Check the results after expenses.

● **Diversify correctly.** Buying six different growth funds in an attempt to seek diversification is a mistake. Ideally, you want to own funds that will work in tandem. Our growth and real estate funds will often move in opposite directions.

You can only diversify intelligently if you know exactly what's in each of your fund's portfolios. The typical Canadian equity fund now probably has about 15% to 20% of its money in foreign stocks.

But some "domestic" funds have foreign holdings that push right up against the federal government's 30% limit for RRSP eligibility.

If you own such funds and also own several international funds, you may be overexposed to foreign markets. If that's a strategic decision, fine. If it's an oversight, adjust your portfolio.

Source: Robert Markman, president of Markman Capital Management, 6600 France Ave. S, Minneapolis, MN 55435.

How to Win the Mutual-Fund Race

Consistent—rather than spectacular—returns is the best way to build long-term wealth. *This approach eliminates several problems:*

Trap: **Altering your strategy when the market drops.** If your funds are highfliers, your portfolio's value will really sink if the market suffers a severe decline. It's hard for many investors to stay the course at such times.

Trap: **Underperforming by seeking maximum performance.** Losses really drag down a portfolio's return over time—as opposed to *gains* that are below the market indexes. It's very hard to make up for a bad year.

Trap: **Sustaining losses.** If you start with $10,000 and lose 50% the first year, you're left with $5,000. You need a 100% return the second year to be even. You would need a 142% gain to achieve a 10% annualized gain for those two years.

Strategy

Choose the tortoise, not the hare. When building a fund portfolio, pick consistent winners rather than top-10 performers.

But isn't it wise to buy a fund that has been red-hot lately? *Absolutely not.* Of the top 10 funds in any year, more than five will fall to the bottom half of all funds in performance within one or two years. When a home-run hitter doesn't hit home runs, he strikes out a lot. *Advantage:* Besides giving you relatively consistent returns over time, this approach offers peace of mind. When the market swoons—as it did in 1987 when the S&P 500 lost 30% of its value in six days, and in 2000–2001 when NASDAQ fell more than 60% from its highs—your portfolio will do much better. It won't look like the end of the world. *Added benefit:* At such times, this conservative approach will make it more likely that you'll be an opportunistic buyer rather than a rattled seller.

● **Investing shouldn't be exciting.** Most people would be better investors if they considered the process boring. They wouldn't be looking for instant gratification. They wouldn't be concerned about finding a hot fund that will give them bragging rights at their next party.

● **Don't expect too much.** The performance of your fund portfolios will not wow you during runaway bull markets.

● **Allocating your assets.** The average investor should employ a *fixed-mix* approach. Establish an asset-allocation mix at the outset and stick with it. It works. *Strategy:* Review the mix quarterly. If you started with 60% equities, 35% bonds and 5% money-market funds, make adjustments to get back to your original allocation. If the market has been soaring, you may need to lighten up on equities and put more into

bonds and money funds. If stocks fall, you'll add to equity holdings. *Advantage:* This imposes some buy low/sell high discipline that definitely can improve your overall returns.

● **Beware of sector funds and international fund risk.** Sector funds are simply too volatile and dangerous. Besides, the temptation is to pick a sector after it has soared, rather than before it begins a good move.

International funds, on the other hand, can add currency risk. Avoid funds that are not allowed to do currency hedging. Find out by reading the prospectus or asking the fund representatives. *Reason:* If the dollar rises, your international investments could be worth much less in dollars. *Better:* Buy global funds instead. They own international and North American stocks and often hedge their currency bets.

● **Objectives.** I think preretirement and retirement portfolios should be different, but not radically so.

A conservative preretirement portfolio might be 50% equities and 50% bonds. After retirement, the objective might shift slightly to the income (bond) side. *Result:* 60% bonds, 40% equities. In each case, you need significant equity holdings to withstand inflation.

● **Choosing specific funds.** I swear by the three P's: *performance, people and process.*

● **Any single year of grossly subpar performance should raise a red flag.** When analyzing a fund's past performance, ignore cumulative returns. Focus instead on year-by-year returns. You want a fund that is consistently profitable. This means you'll buy funds that almost never finish in the top 10 in an up-market year. In general, these tortoise funds tend to perform slightly better than the middle of the pack, year after year.

Studies show that over time, the best pension-fund managers do slightly above average for a long period of time. The same managers should have been running the fund for at least three years.

A fund should have a disciplined, well-defined style. If it calls itself a large-cap value fund, that's what it should be. How can you tell? Call the fund and request semiannual and annual reports for the past five years. See if it has lived up to its designation. If, in the past two years, the fund has been loading up on small-cap growth stocks, this isn't the right place for your money.

Source: *Michael D. Hirsch, chairman of the M.D. Hirsch division of Freedom Capital Management, a firm managing more than $250 million in mutual funds through private accounts and the Fund Manager Trust family of funds.*

A Simple Case for Mutual Funds

There are at least 100 variables that may influence the future values of any security. How can the amateur investor balance those variables and decide how each will affect an investment? By following a simplified step-by-step decision-making process that seldom requires dealing with more than two variables at a time.

● **Stocks or bonds?** Historically, the Standard & Poor's 500 Index has outperformed bonds almost three to one. If you are confident you can invest in stocks successfully, this decision is not difficult—go with stocks.

● **Do it yourself or delegate?** Although many investors think they can beat the system, it's smart to delegate stock-investment decisions to professionals. Historical results indicate that professionals have the advantage.

● **Stockbroker or portfolio manager?** It's best to delegate the decision-making process to fee-based portfolio managers. Stockbrokers graduate to fee-based management only if they are successful—when you choose a portfolio manager, you have a better chance of getting someone with a proven record.

● **Private or public portfolio managers?** Most successful portfolio managers have minimum account sizes of $100,000 to $5,000,000. If you are a smaller investor, you have the option of joining forces with other investors, retaining some of the best portfolio managers and investing in publicly owned mutual funds. These funds offer diversification to protect you from stock risk. Also, most funds are members of a family of funds, each with a different investment objective. Once you have invested in a family of funds, switching back and forth between funds usually can be accomplished without a commission or fee.

● **What kind of fund is right for you?** If you are young and have many years to retirement, you may be best served by a growth-oriented mutual fund. If you are nearing retirement, a more conservative growth and income fund may be appropriate. At retirement, many investors seek the extreme safety of bond or income funds.

● **Load or no-load funds?** No-load funds make the most sense for most people. Load funds charge up-front commissions or expensive liquidation fees. No-load funds have no commission at the time of purchase and can be liquidated without penalty. To date, no-load funds have performed as well as load funds, so there is no reason to accept the extra burden of a load fund.

● **Buy and hold or use market timing?** If you make the decision to buy and hold a mutual fund, you are relying on the abilities of a portfolio manager to diversify your investment among stocks that will generally go up in bull markets and not go down in bear markets. Yet diversification will not protect a portfolio from the 25%–50% declines suffered in a major bear market.

The goal of market timing is to be in equity funds during market advances and safely moving to money-market funds during market declines. Market timing of no-load funds can cut the risk of investing by approximately 50%. Most market timers are in equity funds about half of the time, during which they are exposed to whatever risk or volatility factor each fund carries. The other half of the time the funds are in near-zero-risk money-market funds.

● **Do it yourself or professional market timing?** This decision depends on whether you have the ability, time and desire to manage your investments on a daily basis. Although there can be no guarantees of profitability, hiring a professional market timer relieves you of this obligation and allows you to concentrate on evaluating only his or her performance.

> "Stockbrokers graduate to fee-based management only if they are successful—when you choose a portfolio manager, you have a better chance of getting someone with a proven record."

● **Newsletter or private management?** The key to market timing is the signal that instructs you either to be in equity funds or safely in money-market funds. Market-timing signals can be purchased from services that contact you through the mail or by telephone. Or, for those who do not want the responsibility of tracking a newsletter or contacting mutual funds, there are a handful of managers who will perform the switching function without client involvement. A few private management services provide timing for accounts as small as $2,000, but most have minimum account sizes of $25,000 to $100,000.

Source: Paul A. Merriman, registered investment adviser and president of Paul A. Merriman & Associates, 1200 Westlake Ave. N, Suite 507, Seattle, WA 98109. Mr. Merriman is publisher and editor of The Fund Exchange *and the author of* Market Timing With No-Load Mutual Funds.

Selecting the Right Mutual Funds for Your Portfolio

Selecting the mutual fund that's best for you hinges on five basic rules:

1. Diversify.
2. Analyze performance over a long period of time.
3. Seek funds with continuity of investment style.
4. Use your money fund wisely.
5. Recognize mistakes.

Diversify

Even with mutual funds, it pays to diversify your portfolio. Select at least three basic types of mutual funds as your foundation. Choose among the broad groups of "growth" and "growth and income" funds for your portfolio's anchor. To satisfy your opportunistic side, add a "sector" fund (which invests exclusively in a particular area, such as technology, health care, finance or energy) or a "small company growth" fund. Maintain a money-market fund as your reserve.

Consider a "fixed-income" fund if you are building your portfolio in a tax-sheltered retirement plan—the high yield will compound your tax-deferred income. You may be able to capitalize on volatility of interest rates or make this fund the longer-term reserve element of your portfolio. But, don't remain in long-term fixed-income investments if inflation begins to reemerge.

Analyze Performance

Evaluate a fund's performance over a long period of time in order to analyze how a fund performs under varying market conditions. Does it rise faster than the general market, but fall faster too? Does it climb steadily and hold its ground well? How do these characteristics mesh with your strategy?

Go to the rating services to evaluate a fund or group of funds. *Rating services generally can be grouped into two types:* Quantitative and qualitative. The quantitative services measure performance results, using total return as their indicator. The other services provide advice on market timing and reveal general attitudes toward funds, particular groups of funds and/or fund managements.

Seek Continuity of Style

Carefully read the fund's annual and interim reports, the proxy statement and statement of additional information. Call the president or the vice president of marketing of the fund for answers to these questions: Have there been important shifts in strategy? If so, when? How has this affected the fund's tactics? Did it help results? Have there been changes in personnel? Why? Who is the portfolio manager? For how long? If there have been any significant changes in style, strategy or personnel, it will be difficult to evaluate the past as a guide to future success.

Use Your Money Fund Wisely

Separate your cash-management money from your investment reserves. Emphasize convenience and service when selecting a money-market fund. The quality of the assets held in the portfolio is more important than the small difference in yield among money-market mutual funds. Also look for ability to exchange with other funds in a family of funds.

Recognize Mistakes

As with any other investment, cut your losses. Monitor your funds' strategies and their results. Most well-selected mutual funds will remain appropriate as investments for a long time. However, opportunistic funds are more vulnerable to changes in the economy—monitor these funds very closely.

Source: A. Michael Lipper, CFA, president, Lipper Analytical Securities, Inc., 74 Trinity Place, New York, NY 10006.

Mutual-Fund Selection Secrets

It's most important when picking mutual funds first to define your investment objective. Investors are interested mostly in preserving capital they already have (and invest for income) or they want primarily to increase their capital (growth). Few people shoot for 100% income or 100% growth, but you should choose a fund with investment objectives that are your own.

● **Identify several top-performing no-load funds that pursue your objective.** *Helpful: Mutual fund guides, websites such as Globefund and Morningstar, monthly fund reports in newspapers.*

● **Analyze performance in-depth.** Don't just glance at overall 5- or 10-year returns. For stock funds, look for 10 years of annual gains that have consistently beaten the S&P/TSX Composite or the Standard & Poor's 500 stock index in up and down years. If a stock fund did badly in 1973, 1974, 1977, 1981–1982, 1987, 1990, 1994 and 2000-2002, it may perform poorly when the next bear market hits. For bond funds, compare performance to an index that matches the maturity of your fund. Generally, it is best to stick with short-term and intermediate-term funds.

● **Opt for consistency.** If two funds have similar returns but one's share price swings widely while the other's is relatively stable, go for the least volatile. *Reason:* If you suddenly have to sell your shares, there's less risk they'll be significantly depressed.

● **Investigate the current portfolio manager.** Is the person managing the fund responsible for the fabulous gains of the past 10 years? Or has the star performer moved on to manage another fund? *Little known:* Many of the top-gun investment advisers who require a prohibitively large personal portfolio ($1 million or more) before they'll accept your business also manage mutual funds. You may be able to tap their brainpower with a tiny fraction of that amount.

● **Think small.** Mutual funds with more than $1 billion in assets have a harder time producing supe-rior results because they must invest in larger, more lethargic companies.

Dangerous pattern: A fund becomes a hot performer and suddenly receives a tidal wave of cash, the manager is forced from small stocks into big ones and the exciting returns evaporate.

● **Don't invest in new funds.** They don't have a track record.

● **Don't accept biased advice.** Brokers and financial planners who recommend funds often receive a commission when you buy in. Take their advice, but only if the funds they suggest meet the criteria outlined here.

● **Don't jump in and out of funds.** Professional investment advisers know that for growth, they must be in the market at all times—although the percentage of their portfolios kept in the market may vary depending on the outlook. For most people, market timing is a risky business and highly impractical.

Source: Kurt Brouwer, president of Brouwer & Janachowski, Inc., a San Francisco-based investment company managing over $500 million for corporate and private investors. He is the author of Kurt Brouwer's Guide to Mutual Funds, Wiley. He has written for Forbes, Barron's and the San Francisco Chronicle.

How to See Through Murky Advertising of Mutual Funds

Mutual-fund advertising often confuses investors—whether or not funds intend to do so. Mutual-fund advertising is actually more heavily regulated than advertising in banking, but most consumers are more familiar with personal banking than fund investing and are easily led astray.

Mutual funds and bank accounts are completely different animals. While a bank can promise you a federally insured account with a fixed yield, the stability of principal and rate of return in a mutual fund depend on market factors and can't be guaranteed. All numbers that appear in mutual-fund ads describe only past performance.

Potentially Misleading

● **Track records.** Every fund wants to tell the best story that it can within the strict regulations that govern on how performance numbers can be used in Canadian advertising. However, track records can be misleading. A fund may show a great 10-year record, but closer inspection may reveal that the big gains were recorded in the bull market of the late 1990s. The numbers since then may be very weak. *To make a significant comparison:* You have to compare funds' performance data for the same periods (available in the prospectuses or by phone from the funds).

Also, you must compare apples with apples. A value fund may have great three-year numbers compared to a growth fund that you're considering. But when compared to other value funds over the same time period, it may look second-rate.

● **"Current" yields.** The numbers in magazine ads are often two to five weeks old.

Trap: Using old yields to compare bond or money market funds.

● **Load (sales charge) status.** Unfortunately, funds aren't simply "load" (with a sales charge) or "no-load." Pure no-load funds and have no initial or deferred sales charge and no redemption fee—but if you buy them through a brokerage firm, you may discover that you do indeed have to pay a fee, either going in or coming out. Initial sales charges on front-end load funds are usually 4%–6%, however you may be able to negotiate a lower rate. The charge for buying or selling a no-load fund through a broker is usually a fixed dollar amount.

● **"100% insured" and "government guaranteed."** Many bond funds purchase issues whose principal and interest are guaranteed by a private insurer or federal, provincial or local governments, but bond funds themselves—unlike bank accounts—are *never insured or government-backed.*

Risk: If interest rates go up, the shares of all bond funds—even those that invest exclusively in government bonds—will fall in value.

● **Switching costs.** Some fund families allow brokers to charge up to 2% every time you move money from one fund to another. Others offer a limited number of free switches per year.

And if your money isn't in a tax-deferred account, remember that when you switch out of a fund in which you have made a capital gain, you must pay income tax on that gain unless the fund is in a registered plan.

Sources: Gordon Pape, author of Retiring Wealthy in the 21st Century, *published by Prentice Hall Canada; and William E. Donoghue, publisher of* Bill Donoghue's WealthLetter *(free sample issue on request), chairman of W. E. Donoghue & Co., Inc., registered investment advisers, and author of* Donoghue's Mutual Fund SuperStars, *Elliott & James, Box 360, 100 Medway Road, Suite 401, Milford, MA 01757, 1-800-982-2455.*

How to Buy a Money Fund

Money funds offer instant liquidity, full market rates of interest and a high degree of safety. Nevertheless, there are differences among money funds, and investors need to know those differences in advance of buying.

Yield

Money funds are mutual funds that invest their shareholders' assets in high-quality government and corporate securities, and in bank deposits. Their operating expenses are relatively low—all it takes to run a money fund is a portfolio manager, a computer, and a staff of telephone operators. As a result, money funds are usually able to pass through to shareholders upwards of 99% of their gross investment income.

Money funds can have the upper hand over banks. Banks have hefty overhead expenses, capital construction costs for buildings and stockholders who demand profits. Larger, efficient money funds therefore can afford superior managers, attract more shareholders and offer yields consistently superior to yields on consumer money-market accounts at banks and credit unions.

Most newspapers report money-fund yields on a weekly basis, but be careful when judging the results: They are based on historic returns. Returns going forward will directly reflect interest rate movements. So if rates are rising, expect higher yields in the months ahead. If rates are falling, yields will be lower than those you're looking at.

If you're a high-tax-bracket investor, remember that income from most money funds (there are a few exceptions) is taxed at your top marginal rate. So if the fund is generating a return of 4%, you may see only about 2% of that in your pocket after taxes.

Of course, money funds held in a registered plan are tax-sheltered.

Unlike money-market accounts in a major bank, money mutual funds are not entirely risk-free. Still, the money fund industry's record for safety has been relatively solid. To avoid any potential problems, pay close attention to the phases of the economic cycle and to the following three factors.

● **The quality of a fund's portfolio.** Some funds own exclusively government of Canada Treasury bills, the safest investment. Most other funds buy high-quality bank deposits and corporate securities. The highest-risk funds attempt to boost their yields by purchasing low-quality securities, such as low-grade or unrated commercial paper. Pay careful attention to the percentage of a fund's assets made up of these high-risk investments.

● **Average portfolio maturity.** The maturity of investments in a typical money fund is about 90 days. Watch out for funds that extend their portfolio maturity significantly beyond the industry average. These funds are probably trying to lock in higher yields from longer-maturing investments. If interest rates rise sharply, the value of longer-maturing securities can decline, resulting in losses. These are not reflected in a fund's net asset value (NAV), which it usually fixed at $10. But it may result in a suspension of interest payments for a period of time. This actually happened to a few Canadian money funds in the early 1990s when short-term interest rates jumped sharply.

● **Portfolio disclosure.** All mutual funds are required to publish details of their portfolios only twice a year. Since typical money market fund investments mature in just a couple of months, much can happen in a six-month period that goes unreported. Before buying any money fund, ask for a current or recent portfolio. Avoid funds that refuse to comply.

Service

Money funds offer a range of shareholder services. Be sure to check them thoroughly before investing. Minimum initial investments are usually quite low, typically about $500–$1,000. A few funds offer cheque-writing privileges, although this service is increasing hard to find in Canada, in contrast to U.S. money funds. Most funds can also establish special accounts for RRSPs and other retirement plans.

Liquidity is the greatest service. Investors can get their money back from a fund at any time without penalty. Interest is fully credited to accounts right up to the day of withdrawal. *Trap:* A few money funds impose a 90-day waiting period before allowing penalty-free withdrawals. Check the policy before investing.

It is actually easier to open a money-fund account than it is to open a bank account. Investors can call no-load money funds from their home or office on toll-free telephone numbers to obtain an account form, a prospectus and a current portfolio. Many money funds are also set up to handle wire transfers.

For investors who like to play the market, most money funds have relationships with other mutual funds that invest in stocks, bonds and other securities. A quick phone call can usually switch an investment from a money fund to another type of fund or vice versa.

Source: *Norman G. Fosback, editor,* Income & Safety.

Choosing Fixed-Income Funds

There's a tendency among younger people to think that fixed-income funds are for their parents. Dull funds for old folks, if you like. There's no action in bond funds, no excitement in mortgage funds, no drama in dividend funds. They may be okay some day, when retirement income is needed. But not now. Please!

Well, we have news for you. Yes, it's true that fixed-income funds are useful for generating retirement income. But there's a lot more to them than that. In fact, certain fixed-income funds offer significant capital gains potential—with all the risks that go with it.

Every mutual funds portfolio should contain some fixed-income funds. But which type of funds, and in what proportion, will depend on your investment goals and on general economic conditions.

Before we get into the strategies of fixed-income investing, let's run down the different types of funds that are available.

● **Regular Canadian bond funds.** These invest in a diversified portfolio of bonds and debentures mainly issued by Canadian governments and corporations. They may also contain mortgage-backed securities.

The portfolio is usually a mix of short-, medium- and long-term bonds, with the weighting adjusted by the manager depending on the prospects for interest rates and the bond market.

● **Short-term bond funds.** These funds started appearing in the mid-'90s, mainly in response to the crash of the bond market in early 1994. Think of them as a cross between a regular bond fund and a money market fund. The managers invest only in debt securities with a term to maturity of less than five years. This makes the fund less risky than regular bond funds, which are vulnerable to loss during periods when interest rates are rising. The price you pay for this increased safety is a lower return and almost no capital gains potential. These are defensive funds, for those who want to keep risk to a minimum, but obtain a better return than money market funds offer.

● **High-yield bond funds.** These funds specialize in high-yield bonds—you may be more familiar with their commonly used name, "junk bonds." They are issued by companies with a relatively low credit rating. As a result, the interest rate they have to pay to borrow is higher than would be charged to a blue-ribbon client like the federal government or a major bank. So you'll get a better return, but at a higher risk—companies with weak credit ratings are more vulnerable to defaulting, especially in a recession. If you're risk-averse, you should steer clear of these funds.

● **Foreign bond funds.** These invest in debt securities issued by foreign governments or companies, or in Canadian bonds denominated in foreign currencies. We have many foreign currency issues in our country. All levels of government frequently issue U.S. dollar bonds and you can also find issues in euros, sterling, Japanese yens and Swiss francs. Funds that specialize in Canadian foreign currency issues are fully eligible for registered plans (the currency isn't what counts, it's the issuer). Those that invest offshore are considered to be foreign content for RRSP and RRIF purposes. Foreign bond funds perform best when global interest rates and the value of the Canadian dollar are falling in tandem.

● **Mortgage funds.** For the most part, these funds invest in residential first mortgages and mortgage-backed securities, which are guaranteed for both principal and interest by Canada Mortgage and Housing Corporation (so, in essence, by the government of Canada). However, a few also hold commercial mortgages. After money market funds, mortgage funds are considered to be the lowest-risk type of mutual fund you can buy. Defaults by mortgage holders are rare in Canada, and the relatively short term of these funds makes them less vulnerable to price changes due to interest rate fluctuations. A few fund companies even go so far as to guarantee that any defaulting mortgages will be repurchased from the fund with no penalty to unitholders (Bank of Montreal does this for the BMO Mortgage Fund).

● **Dividend income funds.** We include these funds in this category because there's no other logical place for them, but we do so reluctantly since there is no consistency in the offerings from different fund groups. A pure dividend income fund invests almost exclusively in preferred shares and high-yielding common stocks, such as banks and utilities. The objective is to maximize dividend income, which is taxed at a lower rate than interest because of the application of the dividend tax credit. However, several so-called dividend funds have portfolios that don't truly reflect this philosophy. They may hold bonds, common stocks that pay little or no dividend, or even foreign securities that don't qualify for the dividend tax credit at all. If tax-advantaged income is your main objective, be very selective. *Useful: The Mutual Funds Update* newsletter publishes an annual survey in March of each year on the yield and tax effectiveness of dividend income and high-income balanced funds. This information is not available anywhere else. For subscription information and to read a sample issue: http://www.buildingwealth.ca/mfudemo.cfm.

● **High-income balanced funds.** Like dividend income funds, these do not fall perfectly into the fixed-income category, but there is no other logical place in which to slot them. These funds invest primarily in high-income securities like royalty income trusts and real estate investment trusts (REITs). The goal is to generate higher cash flow that you would receive from other types of fixed-income funds, often with some tax advantages. The trade-off is more risk. Like the securities in which they invest, these funds can be highly volatile.

● **Income funds.** These are something of a hybrid. The managers may invest in just about anything from the fixed-income securities list, from long-term bonds to mortgage-backed securities to royalty trusts. Before putting any money into one of these funds, it is best to find out where the portfolio emphasis lies and decide if that's consistent with what you're trying to achieve.

That's the rather lengthy list of fixed-income options. As you can see, there are many from which to choose, and not all the fund types will be right for everyone. The next step is to consider some of the most common fixed-income investing strategies and decide which of these funds best suits the specific goals you have in mind.

Before we get into that, however, there's a basic principle of investing that has to be taken into account whenever you're considering a fixed-income fund. It's this:

Interest rates and bond prices move in opposite directions.

Technically, this is called an inverse relationship. When interest rates decline, bond prices rise, and vice versa. It seems elementary, but many people aren't aware of it and don't understand how to use this principle to their advantage.

Although we've made reference to bond prices in stating the principle, the same principle applies to all fixed-income securities, including mortgages and fixed-rate preferred shares. However, it's important to note that the degree of impact on the price of any given security will be directly affected by its term to maturity. The longer the time remaining until maturity, the more the price will move when rates rise or fall.

FOR CONSERVATIVE INVESTORS

The best deals for conservative investors searching for high yields without significant principal risk are managed high-yield bond fund portfolios. First of all, these so-called "junk"-bond portfolios have greatly reduced the risks associated with the "Mike Milkin Bond" period (when more marginal issuers were encouraged to offer junk bonds for marginal purposes) of the early 1990s. Most of those earlier high-yield bonds are no longer considered investment quality. In fact, it can be argued that investing in a high-yield bond fund is much safer than investing in high-yield bonds because the fund can buy a better-quality bond, do better and more selective research among the thousands of offerings and invest larger amounts in the more liquid (at a fair price and narrower spread) issuances. Investing in a no-load

high-yield bond fund makes even more sense. *Advantages:* First, this type of fund can be better diversified among investment styles. Second, the fund managers can have an investment discipline that will tolerate only very limited amounts of volatility. Finally, such portfolios have long-term track records to demonstrate their success.

There are more than two dozen high-yield bond funds available in Canada. The largest by far is the Trimark Advantage Bond Fund, offered through the AIM Canada organization. While focusing on high-yield securities, it also maintains a core holding of government bonds to reduce risk and add stability. Other popular funds of this type include the Phillips, Hager & North High Yield

Bond Fund, the Mackenzie Yield Advantage Fund, the Renaissance Canadian High Yield Bond Fund and the Investors Canadian High Yield Income Fund.

Bottom line: Conservative investors should consider increasing after-tax returns and reducing investment risk and volatility by considering managed high-yield bond-fund portfolios. These are among the most imaginative and liquid conservative investment choices in recent years.

Sources: *Gordon Pape, author of* Retiring Wealthy in the 21st Century; *and William E. Donoghue, publisher of* Bill Donoghue's WealthLetter *(free sample issue on request), chairman of W. E. Donoghue & Co., Inc., registered investment advisers, and author of* Donoghue's Mutual Fund SuperStars, *Elliott & James, Box 360, 100 Medway Road, Suite 401, Milford, MA 01757, 1-800-982-2455.*

For example, suppose you have two bonds, each of which pays 7% annual interest. One matures next year; the other has 20 years to run. Interest rates drop and new issues are paying only 6%. That makes your bonds, with their higher coupon rate, more attractive to investors. But the bond with one year to maturity only pays the premium rate for a limited time. The other one continues to generate above-average income for two decades. It's not hard to figure out which one is worth more to other investors.

Keeping all this in mind, let's now look at some fixed-income fund strategies.

● **The compound interest approach.** This is the most common use for fixed-income funds. The idea is to use the steady returns provided by these funds over time to maximize the effect of compound interest in your portfolio. You can achieve the same result with GICs, of course, but a well-selected group of fixed-income funds will usually provide a better return over time. Mortgage funds and conservatively managed bond funds work most effectively. This strategy works best inside a registered plan, such as an RRSP, where tax sheltering will maximize the return.

● **The capital gains gambit.** Many new fund investors don't realize that bond funds are capable of producing some very healthy capital gains. This strategy seeks to take advantage of the interest rate/bond price relationship to generate this type of profit. The idea is to load up on bond funds during periods when interest rates are high and expected to fall. As rates move down, bond prices will react and fund unit values will rise. Holdings are reduced when rates appear to be bottoming out, so as to lock in the profits. Experienced investors wishing to use this strategy seek out bond funds where the managers have over-weighted their portfolios with long-term issues or such pure long-term bond funds as Altamira Bond. These are the ones that will do best in a falling interest rate environment. Obviously, this is a higher risk strategy—if you guess wrong and rates rise, you'll be looking at some heavy losses in your portfolio. If that happens, don't panic and sell. Rates will inevitably come back down. They always do.

● **The steady income plan.** One of the strengths of fixed-income funds is their ability to generate a regular income stream for investors. This makes them especially useful for people who have reached retirement age and are planning to live on their investment income. If this is how you want to use your fixed-income portfolio, find out how often the funds you're considering make distributions. Some investors prefer funds that offer monthly payments, to ensure a regular cash flow. Others are content with quarterly distributions. If a fixed-income fund's distributions are less frequent (only once or twice a year), it won't be suitable for this purpose.

● **The tax-advantaged income tactic.** Some of these funds can be used to generate tax-advantaged income. That means your payments will be taxed at a lower than normal rate. Dividend income funds are a good choice here because a portion of the money they distribute to unitholders qualifies for the dividend tax credit. High-income balanced funds provide a degree of tax sheltering, as some of their distributions are treated as "return of capital," which means no tax is payable in the year the money is received. To take advantage of these opportunities, make sure you keep your fund units outside a registered plan and choose funds that invest mainly in securities with tax breaks.

● **The capital protection strategy.** If safety is a prime concern for you, fixed-income funds can be used effectively to protect your capital from loss. In this case, you'll want to focus on the lowest-risk types of fixed-income funds. Mortgage funds and short-term bond funds would be most suitable for this type of portfolio.

● **The currency hedge.** Finally, fixed-income funds can be used to give your mutual funds portfolio some protection against possible future declines in the value of the Canadian dollar.

Unfortunately, our currency has a history of being highly volatile. In the past decade, the value of the loonie has declined by more than 30% against the U.S. dollar—far too much for the comfort of any conservative investor. By adding foreign bond funds to your portfolio, you can reduce this risk to some extent by introducing securities denominated in some of the world's strongest currencies into your mix.

But be careful. If the Canadian dollar rises sharply in value against other currencies, especially the U.S. dollar, it will have a negative effect on the value of these funds. Currency volatility cuts both ways. We suggest using these funds as a long-term hedge against continued devaluation in our currency, especially if you require significant amounts of U.S. dollars now or in the future.

Every mutual fund portfolio should hold some fixed-income funds as part of the total asset mix. As a general rule, not less than 25% of your holdings should be in these funds, with a maximum of 75% for older people who are looking mainly for steady income and safety.

We recommend that younger people who are just starting into fund investing begin with more conservative fixed-income funds. Psychology plays a big role in investing success; if you start with a high-risk fund and lose money, you could be put off fund investing for life. It's better to choose a low-risk fund at the outset. As the fund starts to show gains, your confidence level will increase and you can move on to other areas.

Source: Gordon Pape's Buyer's Guide to Mutual Funds, *by Gordon Pape and Eric Kirzner, published by Prentice Hall Canada.*

The Dividend Tax Credit

The dividend tax credit is intended to reduce the effect of double taxation by recognizing that corporate dividends are distributed to shareholders out of after-tax profits. This means a company has already paid tax once on the earnings. In theory, therefore, dividends should then be received tax-free, but governments aren't that generous. The dividend tax credit is a compromise measure. To calculate the credit to which you're entitled, you must first "gross up" the actual dividend you receive by multiplying the amount by 125%. You then multiply that number by 13.33%. The amount of the credit is deducted directly from your federal tax payable. Note that the dividend tax credit will only apply to dividends your fund receives from taxable Canadian corporations. Dividends received from foreign companies aren't eligible.

Safety First!

Here's how fixed-income funds rank on a safety scale, moving from least risk to highest risk. Note that these ratings are generalizations. The style of individual portfolio managers will play a major role in the risk level of any fund.

Mortgage funds	Low risk
Short-term bond funds	
Canadian bond funds	Medium risk
Foreign bond funds	
Dividend income funds	
High-yield bond funds	Higher risk
High-income balanced funds	

Source: Gordon Pape's Buyer's Guide to Mutual Funds, *by Gordon Pape and Eric Kirzner, published by Prentice Hall Canada.*

Investing in Mortgage-Backed Securities

Pass-through securities based on pools of mortgages are attracting investors interested in higher yields than those from comparable fixed-maturity securities. The size of the yields is the trade-off for variable cash flows and maturities and for the accounting problems associated with holding these securities.

Mortgage-backed securities reflect the underlying cash flows of their respective pools of mortgages. The mortgages produce monthly payments of principal and interest, but monthly prepayments can vary. This is a product of fluctuations in interest rates.

When interest rates are declining, mortgage holders generally speed up prepayments, effectively shortening the maturity of the pass-through security. For the investor, this means reinvesting the capital sooner—at the current lower rate. Conversely, as interest rates increase, prepayments decrease. The maturity of the security is lengthened just when the investor wants to shorten it to protect capital.

For this reason, "closed" MBS pools are available which do not allow for prepayments. Investors who want steady, predictable income with no surprises can use these.

The accounting problems attached to mortgage-backed securities stem from the need to keep track of monthly cash flows. For example, the investor must reduce his or her cost basis by the return of principal, and calculate whether there is a profit or loss. Also, the amount of the monthly interest—as opposed to principal—payment must be accurately recorded.

Government-Sponsored Securities

Any institution may pool mortgages and sell interests in those pools. The mortgages are all guaranteed by Canada Mortgage and Housing Corporation (CMHC) for both principal and interest. Effectively, that means they are backed by the government of Canada, making mortgage-backed securities a low-risk form of investment.

Buying Mortgage-Backed Securities

Brokerage firms are the best source of these securities, although some banks may offer them as well. They are traded like bonds and the price will fluctuate from day to day. Some business papers publish trading quotes on mortgage-backed securities.

Sources: Gordon Pape, author of Retiring Wealthy in the 21st Century, published by Prentice Hall Canada; and Jack H. Lemein, vice president and portfolio manager, Franklin Resources, Inc., Box 5994, San Mateo, CA 94402.

Investing in Equity Funds

Money market and fixed-income funds are valuable additions to any portfolio, but the real action is in equity funds. This is where you can score the biggest gains—or suffer the worst losses if you choose badly and the market moves against you. That's why you need to be extremely careful in your fund selection. Make sure you know exactly what you're buying, and the risks involved in the process.

There is a broad range of equity funds from which to choose. They fall into several categories, some of which may overlap. Here's a rundown of the key ones. As you go through it, keep in mind that a single fund may fit into more than one category; for example an international fund that specializes in small-cap stocks.

● **Single-country funds.** These invest primarily, although not necessarily entirely, in shares from a single country. Canadian equity funds, by far the most common type of stock fund offered in this country, fall into this group. U.S. equity funds also fit here. There are also about two dozen Japanese funds, a German fund and two Indian funds. As well, there are a few so-called "China" funds, but none are true single-country funds because most of the shares they hold are based in Hong Kong or in other Asian countries. No other single-country funds are offered directly here, although Canadian investors can buy a wide range of closed-end single country funds that trade on the New York Stock Exchange.

● **Regional funds.** These invest in shares of companies located within a geographic region. Included in this group are European funds, Far East funds, North American funds and Latin American funds. Usually, the manager of a regional fund has the freedom to acquire stocks from any country in the designated area for his portfolio. But sometimes there are restrictions. For example, several Far East funds specifically exclude Japanese stocks. The reason usually given is that Japan is a developed country, while the other Far East markets are not. This creates conflicts in the fund's investment approach. We believe the exclusion has more to do with marketing—many fund companies offer both a Far East fund and a Japan fund and want to maintain a clear distinction between the two.

● **International and global funds.** For the managers of these funds, the world (or most of it anyway) is their oyster. They have the freedom to invest wherever they want for the most part, and to stay completely away from countries they think are overpriced or are potential trouble spots. But there are some fine points you need to be aware of. For example, there is a technical distinction between the terms "international fund" and "global fund." An international fund will not invest in its home country or continent, whereas a global fund will. You may also find restrictions in the investment policies of different funds. The Templeton organization offers a good illustration; the Templeton Growth Fund may invest anywhere in the world whereas the Templeton International Stock Fund excludes North American shares from its portfolio. As a general rule, a well-managed global fund is the lowest-risk type of equity fund you can buy.

● **Large-cap funds.** These funds invest mainly in the shares of large corporations. The theory is that these blue-chip stocks are more stable and so this type of fund represents less risk to an investor. That may be true to a degree, but the reality is that if the market goes into a dive, these stocks will too. There is a specific fund category devoted to domestic versions of these funds called Canadian Large-Cap Equity.

● **Small to mid-cap funds.** At the other end of the spectrum, these funds focus on shares in smaller com-

HOW TO READ A MUTUAL-FUND PROSPECTUS

Once you've narrowed down the vast number of mutual funds available to a few top performers, send for the prospectus and annual report prepared by each. The prospectus is required to disclose any information that would be needed to make an informed decision regarding investment in the fund. The annual report must contain the financial reports on the fund, but may include other information as well.

Use these reports to determine how well each fund you have tentatively selected compares to your particular investment goals and preferences. The following checklist will guide you in covering a fund's most important characteristics.

● **Date of inception.** A fund that has existed less than one year is diffi-cult to judge since, techni-cally, it doesn't have a perfor-mance record. At times, it may be possible to rely on the record of the new fund's manager to gauge performance, but older funds are obviously going to give you more to go on.

● **Investment adviser's perfor-mance history.** The big question here is whose performance record is being relied on for the period being measured? Traditionally, a record belongs to the person or persons who are responsible for buying and selling securities during a particular period of time. Occasionally a fund will have an excellent long-term record in spite of changing advisers. In this case, the record may be credited to the per-

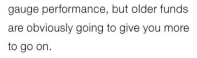

son(s) selecting the advisers.

A fund company should be willing to provide detailed information on all outside advisers if requested, as well as to provide bio-graphical information on in-house managers. You can also find capsule profiles on fund managers at Globefund.com.

● **External advisers.** Since advi-sory fees tend to be among the largest of a fund's expenses, any fund that hires outside advisers tends to have a higher expense ratio than those depending on in-house staff. However, if performance indicates that the fund has benefited from external advisers, the expense may be justified.

● **Expense ratio.** The average mutual-fund expense ratio will vary,

panies that are deemed to have above-average growth potential. The definition of a small-cap stock differs from one country to another, so the portfolio make-up can look quite different from one fund to another. Canadian investors can select from a wide range of small-cap stocks, some of which concentrate on this country, some of which invest mainly in U.S. compa-nies, and some of which are international in scope. These funds are generally regarded as higher risk than those which specialize in large-cap issues, but the rewards can be attractive. There are two official cate-gories for such funds: Canadian Small-to-Mid-Cap Equity and U.S. Small-to-Mid-Cap Equity. International and global small-cap funds are lumped in with the Global Equity and International Equity categories.

● **Venture capital funds.** These invest primarily in young companies that are usually not listed on any stock exchange. These may be start-up operations or companies in need of capital to expand their business. This type of fund is considered to be extremely high risk, and investors could face heavy losses. As a result, most of this activity is centered in the labor-sponsored funds, which offer significant tax breaks as an induce-ment to invest.

● **Sector funds.** These funds invest in a specific area of the economy. For many years, the only sector funds available in Canada were in the natural resource and precious metals sectors. But that changed in the 1990s with the launch of a wide range of sector funds in such fields as health care, telecommunications, financial services and technology. Some of these funds have experienced periods of tremendous growth, but they can be highly volatile as anyone who has invested in a technology fund will testify. Remember, when the

depending on the type of fund. Money market funds are the least expensive, with an average MER (management expense ratio) of about 1%. If the ratio is greater than 1%, try to determine the cause in order to make a judgment about whether the expense results in any added value. A good place to check for the cause is the management or advisory fee, since generally this is a mutual fund's largest expense.

For Canadian equity funds, the average MER is about 2.5%.

Foreign equity funds come in slightly higher, in the 2.75%–3.00% range. Here again, if the MER of the fund you're considering is greater, find out why.

● **Turnover ratio.** This figure indicates the level of trading in a fund's security holdings. If the ratio is greater than 75% to 100%, the fund's expense ratio and, ultimately, the shareholder's return may be adversely affected by high transaction expenses.

A high turnover ratio may be acceptable in one situation—specifically, a change in advisers. A new adviser will often sell many securities purchased before his or her appointment. This may be beneficial to a fund, particularly if poor performance prompted the change in advisers.

● **Fund's portfolio.** The prospectus will reveal what kinds of securities are being invested in and how diversified the portfolio is. Diversification usually reduces risk. So a sector fund, investing in securities in a single industry, will be riskier than a general stock fund.

● **Total assets under management.** Large fund groups can take advantage of certain economies of scale by spreading their costs over a larger asset base. On the other side of the coin, smaller funds—with less than $100 million in total assets—often find it easier to locate and purchase high-quality investments. Smaller funds can also change direction more quickly than the large funds if circumstances warrant it.

● **Other fees.** Many funds charge fees for processing certain kinds of shareholder transactions. This is especially true for RRSPs, where an annual administration fee may be applied. All charges should be explained in the fund's prospectus.

● **Shareholder services.** These vary considerably among funds. Some funds, particularly those that are part of a large fund group, offer almost every conceivable service from investment advisory and portfolio balancing services to telephone transactions. Other funds rely on brokers and financial planners to provide client service on their behalf.

Source: Elizabeth A. Watson, formerly assistant to the chairman and assistant treasurer, the Ivy Fund.

particular sector is hot, as technology stocks were in 1998–1999, the fund will do well. When the sector goes out of favor, unit values will fall.

● **Index funds.** These are passive funds, designed to track the performance of a specific stock index, such as the S&P/TSX Composite. They're designed for investors who want some exposure to the stock market, but don't want to take a lot of risk. Their track record in Canada is mediocre at best.

● **Dividend income funds.** Some dividend funds are really that in name only. Their portfolio composition actually makes them something else: balanced funds in some cases, large-cap funds in others. You'll have to look closely at the securities in the portfolio to determine where the specific fund fits.

In mid-2002, there were more than 2,400 equity funds of various types available to Canadian investors. So the selection process can be a difficult one, unless you have a sound strategy and stick to it. Here are some guidelines for choosing winning equity funds that may help you through the jungle.

Control your risk: Since equity funds represent the highest risk element in any mutual fund portfolio, it's essential to manage that risk effectively. This can be done in several ways.

1. Decide on an acceptable percentage of equity fund holdings. Conservative investors can reduce their risk in the equity area by limiting these funds to 25%–30% of the total portfolio. (Of course, you can eliminate them entirely but in doing so you lose all growth potential.) More aggressive investors may want to have their entire portfolio in equity funds, although that's not an approach we would recommend. The general rule is that the greater the total percentage of equity funds you own, the higher the risk factor in your mutual funds portfolio.

2. Select fund types that best fit your philosophy. You can limit your equity fund risk by concentrating on index funds and large-cap funds. Both will experience losses when markets drop, but they're likely to be less severe than with other types of funds. The highest risk categories of equity funds are small cap, venture capital, emerging markets and sector funds.

3. Diversify geographically. If you choose only equity funds that focus on a single market (e.g., Canada), your portfolio will be more vulnerable (and therefore higher risk) than if it is well diversified internationally. Adding some broadly based global funds to your mix will enhance stability.

> "The highest risk categories of equity funds are small cap, venture capital, emerging markets and sector funds."

4. Diversify by style. As a general rule, funds that use a value approach to stock selection are less risky than those that employ a growth style. A well-diversified portfolio will have room for both.

Invest in quality: There are a lot of equity funds out there, but only a few have demonstrated the rare combination of top-quality management and first-rate long-term performance. These funds may not always hold their preeminent positions, of course, but history indicates that they'll stay at or near the top for at least a decade.

Use special caution with RRSPs: It's all right to include equity funds in your RRSP, if that's the only investment portfolio you have. If you have enough investment money to build a non-registered portfolio as well, keep the equity funds outside the retirement plan. This reduces the RRSP risk and allows you to get the full benefit of the tax advantages that are associated with equity funds—the dividend tax credit and a reduced tax rate on capital gains.

If you buy equity funds for your RRSP, stick with the more conservative types. Don't speculate with your retirement savings. Small-cap funds, for example, really aren't appropriate for RRSPs because of the higher risk involved.

Spread your money around: Don't invest all the cash you've earmarked for equity funds in a single

fund or even with a single company, no matter how good its reputation. Overconcentration can lead to trouble. In the 1980s, for example, the Industrial funds of Mackenzie Financial were the darlings of the industry. Investors were attracted by their good returns and brokers loved to sell them because of the excellent commissions and special incentives (like exotic trips) they offered. But in the 1990s, they ran into trouble when the managers overcommitted all the equity portfolios to resource stocks. The funds languished and investors complained bitterly. Mackenzie learned an important lesson as a result; the firm now offers several distinct fund groups, each with its own separate managerial team. We suggest you spread your equity fund investments among three good fund companies, although you may choose one company for your core holdings.

One last comment on equity funds. Don't rush out and put a lot of money in them after an exceptionally good year. Chances are that, after a big run, the markets are due for a correction. Many people decided to get into equity funds for the first time after the spectacular success they enjoyed in 1998 to early 2000, when some funds more than doubled in value. Those same investors then watched in dismay as stock markets in most parts of the world hit rough water in the early spring of 2000, starting a decline that continued well into 2002 and caused most fund unit values to fall—in some cases dramatically.

The best approach to equity funds is to select carefully and take a long-range view. If the fund is well-managed, it will enjoy some very good years along the way, and you'll profit accordingly. An average annual return of 10%–12% over time is excellent; if you expect more, you are being unrealistic.

Source: Gordon Pape's Buyer's Guide to Mutual Funds, *by Gordon Pape and Eric Kirzner, published by Viking Canada.*

Mutual Fund Tips

There are a number of ways to increase the profit potential from your mutual fund investments. Here are a few tips.

● **Add foreign content.**
Ramping up foreign content
in your portfolio reduces
risk and adds profit potential through the magic of
diversification. However,
this can be a problem in
registered plans because
of the foreign content
rules. Here's a way around it.
Many Canadian equity funds
hold up to 30% of their portfolio
in U.S. and international equities.
These holdings do not count
against your personal foreign content limit if your fund
units are in an RRSP or other registered plan. So if you
want to increase the foreign holdings in a retirement
plan, choose Canadian funds that make maximum use
of this provision.

● **Look at iUnits.** A low-cost alternative to index
funds are the iUnits that trade on the Toronto Stock
Exchange. The original iUnits replicate shares in a basket of the stocks that make up the S&P/TSX 60 index,
a blue-chip index. They trade under the symbol XIU.
There are also several specialized iUnits, including
technology index units (XIT), mid-cap stock units
(XMD), energy units, (XEG) and S&P/TSE Capped 60
Index units (XIC). All can be bought through brokers,
just like stocks. You'll pay a sales commission, but the
annual management fee is lower than you'll find in a
typical index fund, so your return will more closely
mirror what the index itself does.

● **Steer clear of emerging markets funds.**
These are a subgroup of international funds. They
focus on developing economies throughout the world,
seeking to benefit from their higher growth potential.
These funds have proved to be very volatile, with big
swings in both directions. They're only for investors
who are prepared to accept above-average risk.
Certainly, they should not be held in a registered plan.

Source: Gordon Pape's Buyer's Guide to Mutual Funds, *by Gordon
Pape and Eric Kirzner, published by Viking Canada.*

Investing in Labor Funds
Many people are attracted to labor-sponsored venture capital funds because of the tax breaks they

Mutual-Fund Sales Charges
If you purchase mutual fund units on a deferred sales charge (DSC)
basis, find out in advance how the fee will be calculated if you decide
to cash out. In most cases, it will be based on the book value of
your units (your original purchase price). But some funds may base
the DSC on the market value at the time you sell. If the units have
appreciated significantly in value, that could add several hundred
dollars to your cost.

offer. But they can be very high risk. If you are considering investing in these funds, here are some of
the issues to look at.

● **See what tax credits the fund qualifies for.**
All funds get the federal credit but all won't necessarily get a provincial tax credit. Some provinces offer no
provincial tax credits at all. Others, such as Quebec,
Manitoba and British Columbia, restrict them to just
one or two provincially sponsored funds. Ask before
you invest.

● **Ask if the fund is eligible for direct RRSP
purchase.** Some investors have adopted a strategy of
buying labor-sponsored funds inside an RRSP, using
"old" money to generate a tax credit outside the plan.
This can be done with relative ease in some provinces.
But the rules are different across the country. If you're
interested in this approach, ask a sales rep whether it
is allowed where you live.

● **Remember that the credits can only reduce
your tax to zero.** The tax credits generated by labor-
sponsored funds aren't refundable. So if you don't owe
enough tax to make full use of them, you won't get the
maximum benefit from this strategy.

● **Recognize that the units are above-average
risk.** The mandate of all these funds is to invest in
small to medium-size companies that are usually not
publicly traded. Such companies may have above-
average growth potential—but they're also higher risk
than more established firms. Also, as a result of previous deals some funds may find themselves with a significant portion of their portfolio in publicly traded
shares. One way in which this occurs is when a
previously private company in which the fund has

invested goes public. Often under the terms of such an arrangement, the fund is required to retain part or all of its position for a certain amount of time. This is to ensure that a large block of shares is not dumped on the market, depressing the price of the fledgling company. Another source of public shares is the takeover of a private company in the portfolio by a company that is already public in a share-swap deal. Triax Growth is an example of a fund with a large percentage of publicly traded stock. As a result, it was especially vulnerable to the collapse of the high-tech market.

● **Don't forget that you can't get your money out.** All labor-sponsored funds have a minimum holding period of eight years. If you take your money out before then, you'll have to repay your tax credits—up to 30% of the value of your total investment! There are no exceptions to the eight-year rule. So these funds are not suitable for people who are likely to need access to their cash within eight years.

SHOULD YOU INVEST IN ART?

A rt should be purchased because it provides pleasure, not because it may appreciate. Historically, the art market has been unstable and, generally, unpredictable. *It progresses in cycles:* What is desirable today may be undesirable tomorrow. Due to the great number of variables involved in these cycles, it is best not to classify art as a sound financial investment.

Investment-Quality Art

For any work of art to become a good investment, it must be able to stand the test of time. The value of an item rarely appreciates overnight. Instead its value develops over a period of time, often after decades have elapsed.

Art that does appreciate is usually an outstanding example of a specific type of art. It becomes investment-quality because of its uniqueness and because it exemplifies the artist's style and period.

Trying to find these examples on today's art market is difficult. When they do appear, they are generally sought by museums, major institutions and established collectors.

Most contemporary art available for purchase has not met the test of time or uniqueness.

Be especially careful of purchasing prints as an investment. In general, contemporary art that is mass-produced does not appreciate. Most prints, whether they are designated lithographs, serigraphs, etchings, mezzotints or something else, are simply prints on pieces of paper containing an artist's signature.

There may be thousands of these prints available from a given work. Only a minute percentage of them will ever appreciate. Remember that an original is always more valuable than a mass-produced duplicate.

The Best Reasons for Acquisition

Art is an expression of a given artist. It is something that conveys a message, a thought or a feeling. If you are interested in acquiring art that may appreciate, ask yourself not only whether it has stood the test of time, but also whether it conveys anything to you.

Do not allow your judgment to be clouded because an item appears to be increasing in value. Disregard advice that says it is a good investment. Some dealers will tell you, "This is a great investment." Do not let them persuade you. If it is such a great investment, why is it still on the market, or why hasn't the dealer added it to his or her private collection?

Buy a work of art because it appeals to you and you feel that it will bring you pleasure. These should be your primary reasons for acquisition.

Source: Richard Friedman, president, auctioneer and appraiser, Chicago Art Galleries, Inc., 5039 Oakton Street, Skokie, IL 60077. He is a member of the Appraisers Association of America, the International Society of Appraisers and the American Arbitration Association, Panel of Arbitrators.

> **"Gold is an investor's best insurance against the changing value of money.... Gold tends to appreciate in value during inflationary periods, just like other tangibles such as collectibles and real estate."**

● **Look at the track record.** These funds have now been around long enough to establish an investment history and some are much more impressive than others. Big scores are always great, but it is best to focus on those funds that have shown the ability to produce above-average gains consistently, and importantly, with minimal risk.

A good strategy if you live in a province where several funds are available is to diversify. Ontario residents are especially blessed in this regard, as they have the widest range of funds available. There's no way of knowing which funds will perform best over the long term. So instead of putting all your money in just one, spread it around among three or four.

Source: Gordon Pape's Buyer's Guide to Mutual Funds, *by Gordon Pape and Eric Kirzner, published by Viking Canada.*

Gold vs. Inflation— Gold vs. Deflation

Gold is an investor's best insurance against the changing value of money. It's common knowledge that gold tends to appreciate in value during inflationary periods, just like other tangibles such as collectibles and real estate. *Little known:* The price of gold also rises in deflationary times.

Deflation usually occurs when people get themselves so deeply in debt that they must produce and sell increasing quantities of goods and services to raise the money to meet their interest payments. As more and more goods and services get dumped on the market, their prices fall and the real value of cash rises.

At first glance, it would seem that in this scenario the price of gold would go down. *Reason:* People with gold would sell it to raise cash to make interest payments. But this logic doesn't take into account the complexity of the financial system. The price of gold would actually rise. *How:* In a severe deflation, widespread default on bank debt would cause a rapid erosion of confidence in the bank system. Panicked investors would convert cash into gold, boosting the price of the metal. This buying would counter the selling of gold to raise cash to pay down debt.

To restore confidence in the financial system, as a last resort, central banks would have to raise the price of gold to such a high level that gold holders would finally be willing to sell it in exchange for paper money. This occurred in the deflation of the 1930s, when the U.S. government had to boost the price of gold by about 70%—to US$35 an ounce—to stabilize the financial system.

How to Buy Gold

● **Gold coins are the most convenient way for most people to buy gold.**

Best: The Mexican Gold Peso and Austrian Gold Crown, whose prices closely reflect their gold content. Collectors' coins, such as the American Eagle, carry a significant numismatic premium.

● **Gold-mining stock mutual funds.** Also Canadian Gold iUnits which trade on the Toronto Stock Exchange. They represent a basket of shares in the gold sub-index.

● **Gold-mining stocks.** The Canadian stock market offers a wide range of gold stocks, from junior companies with no production to giants like Barrick and Placer Dome. The bigger and more-established the company, the less the risk in the stock. But all gold stocks will reflect movements in the price of bullion to some degree.

Source: John Hathaway, principal, Hudson Capital Advisers, 3 E. 54 St., New York, NY 10022.

Why Rubies, Emeralds and Sapphires Are Safer Investments Than Diamonds

When prices of investment-grade diamonds plunged as much as 30%, colored gemstones magically held on to heady price gains. *Reason:* Scarcity. Only some US$200 million in rubies, emeralds and sapphires were sold in the United States in a recent year, a fraction of the amount of diamonds sold.

The areas where the finest stones come from: Cambodia, Thailand, Sri Lanka, Burma and parts of Africa. *Scarcity factor:* These areas are politically unstable and, therefore, are not reliable sources. *Note:* Canada has become a diamond producer, however the quality of its gems is not yet widely recognized by consumers.

● **Grading.** Although techniques in grading colored stones are less advanced than those for diamonds, tests under microscopes and refractometers allow gemologists to distinguish synthetic stones from real ones. They can often tell you the origin of the stone. Certain countries of origin command higher prices. *Example:* Burma rubies.

● **Flaws.** Although all stones have flaws, gross flaws ruin the stone.

● **Setting.** Determine whether the setting does justice to the stone. Does it overwhelm the stone?

● **Color.** It is the most important determinant of price once the stone is adjudged authentic. Never view a single stone. Compare it with several others. *Reason:* The clarity of the redness of a ruby, and the absence of orange, pink, purple or brown, is what makes it most valuable. The variation is best seen by looking at several stones.

A family-owned jewelry retailer with an excellent reputation is the best place to buy. It is willing to risk its own money investing in fine gems from around the world. Larger chains of jewelers can't afford to invest. They custom-order.

In small towns without direct access to a large selection of colored gemstones, go to reputable jewelers and commission them to find the kind of stone you like and can afford. Many fine jewelers have completed diploma courses offered by the Canadian Gemmological Association, which ensures they meet the highest professional standards. Ask the jeweler with whom you're dealing about his or her professional qualifications.

The best gems to buy are stones over one carat that are free of externally visible flaws. Buy one that will look good mounted in jewelry. That way, if the investment does not gain in value, at least you will have a remarkable piece of jewelry, not just a stone in a glass case.

Expect to keep a colored gem for at least five years, when buying for investment. Then evaluate what the stone would go for on the dealers' (wholesale) market. *Alternative:* Put stones up for auction at a house such as Sotheby's or Christie's. Although you cannot be sure of a definite sales price, you can put a minimum price on your item.

Bronze and Marble Sculpture

If you plan to buy a bronze sculpture strictly for decoration or sentiment, don't hesitate. If you plan to buy it as an investment—think twice. The bronze market is flooded with reproductions and prices have begun to fall, because the reproductions are almost indistinguishable from the originals.

On the other hand, if you plan to buy a bronze sculpture because you wish to own an original by a famous artist or artisan, make certain that you go to a reputable dealer or auction house. If you are not knowledgeable, always seek expert advice.

Old and New Bronze

An original will be accompanied by a history, or provenance. It will have been authenticated as an original work of the artist. *Be prepared:* Since old original bronze castings have all but disappeared from art market inventories, an original reproduction will probably also have a high price.

Because of the flood of reproductions into the marketplace, many serious collectors have turned away from the 18th-, 19th- and early-20th-century masters. They are now more interested in modern and contemporary masters. As a result, these works are bringing record auction prices.

To acquire the work of a modern master, watch the auction market carefully for artists' works that rise in value. Good sources of information are magazines such as *Art & Auction* and *Art & Antiques*. *Art News, ADEC Art Price Annual* and Mayer's *International Auction Records* are also valuable sources.

Marble and Alabaster

Unlike bronze sculptures, marble and alabaster sculptures are difficult to reproduce and relatively few copies have been made. Consequently, sculptures in these materials that appear on the market have increased in value.

Some marble and alabaster pieces of fine quality are available at less than exorbitant prices. Many late-18th- and early-20th-century works—good examples of the work of French, German, American and Italian artisans—can be obtained at estate sales.

Source: Richard Friedman, president, auctioneer and appraiser, Chicago Art Galleries, Inc., 5039 Oakton Street, Skokie, IL 60077. He is a member of the Appraisers Association of America, the International Society of Appraisers and the American Arbitration Association, Panel of Arbitrators.

Finding Good Sources and Honest Dealers for Collectibles

How do you locate the best dealer or source for collectibles? Whether you are interested in paintings, sculpture, silver or antique furniture, most major cities have a range of sources, including auction houses, dealers specializing in particular items, art galleries and wholesale/retail stores.

To find out which of these are good sources and honest dealers:

● **Make inquiries of persons** who have dealt with businesses in your area of interest.

● **Ask opinions of dealers in the trade.**

● **Check with the local Better Business Bureau** for information about business practices.

● **Study publications,** such as *Dun & Bradstreet,* which provide specific information on corporate conditions and credit ratings of individual firms.

Buying at Auction

Auction houses are excellent sources for collectibles, antiques and works of art. They usually have their own experts who can answer questions and advise you. Their auction catalogs give valuable information on the history, provenance and condition of the items that are for sale. *Note:* Conditions of sale will be published in the catalog. Read carefully—each auction house has its own conditions.

> " **Auction houses are excellent sources for collectibles, antiques and works of art. They usually have their own experts who can answer questions and advise you.** "

Trust officers of banks can be one of the best sources of information on the reliability of auction houses. Why? They are often called upon to liquidate estates through auction. Also, a variety of magazines and newspapers publish information on auctions. Among the more widely read magazines are *Art & Auction, Art & Antiques, Connoisseur* and *Antique Monthly.* Canadian publications of interest are *Antiques Showcase* and *Century Home.* There is lots of information about auctions available on the Internet. A good website for auction updates across Canada is http://www.canada.com/auctions.

At http://www.auctionsfind.com you can find details about upcoming auctions in Ontario. Another interesting site is http://www.antique-central.com/canada.html, which contains details about antique dealers and auction houses across the country.

Buying from a Dealer

If you don't have connections with the art world, magazines and newspapers are a good place to start when searching for a reputable dealer. The more prestigious magazines are selective in their choice of advertisers. You can expect that the dealers who are accepted as advertisers have been checked out and are generally reliable. Still, it is prudent to investigate them. Make inquiries to publishers, editors and critics of these publications.

Seek the opinions of those in the trade. Ask dealers their opinions about the reliability of other dealers. Look for dealers with connections to public and private institutions such as museums and banking establishments. Ask the curators of these institutions who they use for the acquisition of works of art for collections.

In addition to helping you locate the item you want, a reputable dealer will always try to answer questions. If an answer is not readily available, he or she will assist you in finding it.

Dealers sometimes allow you to purchase an item on approval. If, within a designated period of time, the item is not what you want, you may return it at no charge. Reputable dealers usually issue a certificate of authenticity for an item they sell. Some dealers also offer guarantees—others offer exchange privileges that hold for a particular period of time. Find out about the dealer's policy in these areas before making a purchase.

Source: Richard Friedman, president, auctioneer and appraiser, Chicago Art Galleries, Inc., 5039 Oakton Street, Skokie, IL 60077. He is a member of the Appraisers Association of America, the International Society of Appraisers and the American Arbitration Association, Panel of Arbitrators.

The New Rules on Hot Collectibles

It used to be that something had to be old to have collector value. That's still true for genuine antiques, of course. But these days collectors will pay hundreds of dollars for items less than two decades old. *Reason:* Many people got burned in the art boom of the 1980s. They spent a lot of money for things that shot up in value—and then lost it all when the market crashed.

Cheap collectibles are perfect for more cautious times. In a tight economy it doesn't cost much to get into as a hobby and the possibilities are endless.

Opportunity: Not everything in your closet today will be worth big bucks in a few years. But chances are that you do have some things stashed away that will be worth money.

(*Note:* Prices given below are in U.S. dollars, as of the late '90s. Check with a Canadian dealer for current prices in this country in Canadian dollars.)

Picks for the Future

Here are our guidelines for sorting through what you own—and finding items for which collectors will someday pay big. Generally, only consider things that can meet these five standards:

● **Possible to find,** but not so plentiful that it turns up at every rummage sale.

● **Well-known enough** that it will attract a number of collectors.

● **Priced low enough** that it will be affordable even to novice collectors.

● **Useful,** historic or visually appealing.

● **In the best possible condition.**

Our best bets for fairly common household items likely to increase in value—whose prices in some cases already are gaining:

● **Italian designers.** They are very hot right now and some pieces were made in limited quantities. *Example:* Gufram of Italy produced some plastic statues and six-foot-tall cacti. In 1975, those cacti sold for $250 each. By the late '90s, prices for those 25-year-old cacti ranged from $2,000 to $3,000.

● **1980s high-tech.** There is a lot of interest today in old handheld electronic games, teapots and actual usable high-tech items from the 1980s. *Also:* things like first-of-a-kind phones, answering machines, computers and other electronic equipment.

● **Almost anything with a "smiley" face on it.** Those smiley faces showed up everywhere in the early 1970s—on cups, T-shirts, mugs. We're just waiting for the first mug collectors to show up. We figure they'll pay $20 for them.

● **Kid stuff.** Good bet—children's dishes—done in plastic with cartoony drawings on the cup, saucer and plate. Some of the better designers of the 1980s also did doll dishes (the little bitsy size) that already are showing signs of popularity. Disney items of any kind are going to stay good.

● **Hard plastic bubble bath and shampoo bottles**—those shaped like popular Disney or other cartoon characters. These already are all over the antique stores. A Yogi Bear Bubble Club container with removable head from 1961 went for about $75 not long ago.

● **Political memorabilia.** It always has a following. Less than 15 years after the 1984 U.S. presidential election, a Reagan-Bush thimble fetched $4.

● **Cheap—often free—collectibles.** This category would include such things as sports programs, souvenirs, matchbook covers, swizzle sticks and Cracker Jack prizes. These are all enjoying a revival.

● **Sports stuff.** Anything from the days when the Dallas Cowboys were "America's Team" and winning all those championships is popular with collectors—especially those in Texas and Oklahoma. Keeping with the sports theme, Olympic stars are good future bets.

● **Costume jewelry.** It is fun to buy and wear, relatively inexpensive, and almost any piece that has a designer's mark is collectible. There is an especially active market for jewelry made by Marcel

Boucher, Hattie Carnegie, Chanel, Eisenberg, Kenneth Jay Lane and Trifari.

It does take time for things like toys, games and other collectibles from a particular era to gain a big following. *Example:* Baby boomers are buying all the stuff they remember from when they were kids in the 1950s. A set of 1959 Fleer bubblegum cards in mint condition went for $1,000 in the late '90s.

For your items from the 1980s to have value, you may have them for a while yet—when people who were kids in the 1980s can afford to buy back their childhoods. The above rule is not absolute. Fairly new items may already have value to someone who, for whatever reason, has decided to collect it.

Opportunity: Somewhere, there is someone collecting almost anything. In 1995, one of our newsletter readers wrote to us looking for a buyer for a collection of over 3,500 key chains from 60 different countries. We didn't know of one then, but by 1998 key-chain collecting had become a teenager fad.

You can also find collectors through newspapers, magazines, books and via the Internet; especially the online shopping malls and auctions. Authors of books about a particular field are often collectors or dealers themselves.

Flea markets and collector shows are great places to meet people who share your particular interest—and maybe pick up some bargains.

Warning: Beware of items that are in demand because of something in the news. Fame is fleeting. A hot collectible today can lose its value once the news event is past. *Example:* Everyone was hunting madly for an O. J. Simpson doll that was put out a few years ago. But the same thing happened to it that happened to a Pee Wee Herman doll that went way up when he was first caught in trouble—but then quickly went way down in value.

Source: *Ralph and Terry Kovel, editors of the newsletter* Kovels on Antiques and Collectibles. *They are also authors of* Kovels' Antiques & Collectibles Price List 2002, *Crown Publishing, and 75 other books.*

More on the Hot Collectibles Now

Many of the most popular items that seemed silly in the 1960s are worth big money now—if they survived years of rough handling and neglect.

CHOOSING AN APPRAISER

The qualifications of an appraiser are critically important to an appraisal's value. When you choose one, seek a professional rather than a local antique dealer who may have just opened last week and hung a sign in the window professing to be an appraiser.

Recommendations from people familiar with an appraiser's work are invaluable—attorneys, accountants and bank officers frequently utilize the services of appraisers. The local Chamber of Commerce and the local Better Business Bureau also may provide information regarding the business practices of appraisers. In certain instances, the opinions of other appraisers can be helpful as well.

Since the appraisal industry is not regulated, it is important that an appraiser belong to a recognized appraisal organization. These have developed strict requirements for membership and ensure that anyone carrying its credentials will know what he or she is doing. Some of the more highly esteemed organizations are the American Society of Appraisers, the Appraisers Association of America, the International Society of Appraisers and the Canadian Personal Property Appraisers Group. Most qualified appraisers belong to one of these organizations, and some belong to two or more.

Experience is important, too. An appraiser's years of experience give some indication of his or her knowledge and expertise. Do not expect to find an appraiser who knows everything. As in other professions, appraisers specialize in specific areas. Ask if the appraiser is qualified to appraise the items you have. Find out his or her areas of specialty.

Finally, check on the appraiser's fee in advance. It is a fairly accepted practice among appraisers to base their fees on the time they spend executing the appraisal, rather than on a percentage of the value of the appraisal.

Source: *Richard Friedman, president, auctioneer and appraiser, Chicago Art Galleries, Inc., 5039 Oakton Street, Skokie, IL 60077. He is a member of the Appraisers Association of America, the International Society of Appraisers and the American Arbitration Association, Panel of Arbitrators.*

Whether you're looking to sell what you own or want to recognize a bargain when you see one, here are the hottest collectibles of that decade.

Toys

● **Hot Wheels** are one of the most popular collectible toys from the era. The little metal cars introduced by Mattel in 1968—and still sold today—were designed to race on plastic tracks set up to take maximum advantage of gravity.

Hottest Hot Wheels. 1969 Volkswagen Beach Bomb, which had a surfboard sticking out through the rear window, was produced in small numbers and is hard to find today ($1,500); pink 1967 Custom Mustang ($200), the first car produced in the series; 1968 Custom Camaro ($250); Hot Heap ($55).

TEN GOLDEN RULES OF INVESTING

1. Don't be intimidated by the professionals. Small investors have been intimidated by the media into believing that they don't stand a chance of beating the market because it is dominated by professionals. *Reality:* The amateur investor actually has a better shot than ever of succeeding today. *Reason:* The professionals act like a mob. They all act the same and think the same, because they all went to the same few schools. How many are very wealthy? Very few.

The individual investor has the advantage of being able to think independently of the herd.

2. Look in your own backyard. My favorite source of investment ideas is a mall near my home. It provides a delightful atmosphere in which to study great stocks. As an investment strategy, hanging out at the mall is far superior to taking a stockbroker's advice on faith or combing the financial press for the latest tips. Many of the biggest investment gainers of all time come from the places that millions of consumers visit all the time.

An investment of $40,000 in 1986 divided equally among four popular retail stocks—Home Depot, The Limited, The Gap and Wal-Mart—and held for five years was worth more than $500,000 at the end of 1991.

Note: Your own backyard can often include the business or industry you work in.

3. Don't buy something you can't illustrate with a crayon. Buying stock in companies that make things you understand is a sophisticated strategy that many professionals have neglected. It would have kept you from losing a bundle in mysterious biotechnology and memory-module stocks.

On the other hand, you would have made out very well if you had bought stock in such easy-to-illustrate well-known companies as Walt Disney, Coca-Cola, McDonald's and Nike a while back.

4. Make sure you have the stomach for stocks. Market declines are as predictable as snow in Minnesota in January. Over the last 70 years, stocks have had average gains of 11% a year, while Treasury bills, bonds and certificates of deposit have returned less than half that amount.

But during this same 70 years, there have been 40 scary declines of 10% or more in the stock market. Of these declines, 13 have been drops of 25% or more, which puts them into the "terrifying decline" category.

A successful stock picker must be prepared to ride out these declines and seize them as opportunities to jump in and buy more of a favorite stock when its price goes down along with the rest. If you are susceptible to selling everything in a panic, you should avoid stocks and stock mutual funds altogether.

5. Avoid hot stocks in hot industries. A great industry that's growing fast, such as computers or medical technology, attracts too much attention and too many competitors.

When an industry gets too popular, nobody makes money there anymore. But great companies in cold, non-growth industries are consistent winners. In a lousy industry, the weak drop out and the survivors get a bigger share of the market. A company that can capture an ever-increasing share of a stagnant market is a lot better off than one that has to struggle to protect a dwindling share of an exciting market. *Example:* Shaw Industries, a Dalton, Georgia, carpet manufacturer. There hasn't been a worse industry in contemporary America, but Shaw has thrived as a low-cost producer. Since 1980, Shaw has managed to maintain its 20% annual growth rate. The stock price

● **Barbie dolls.** Among the most valuable Barbies are a mint-condition doll from 1959 that's still in its original box ($5,000), Bubble Cut Barbie—without the ponytail—from the early 1960s ($175 with its box/$100 without the box).

Note: The years are indicated on the dolls' bodies. *Also valuable*: Barbie's friends Ken ($400 in the box) and Skipper ($300 in the box) and accessories such as Barbie's 1964 Lavender Austin Healey ($450) and her Sophisticated Lady Outfit ($150 to $300).

● **Cartoon and TV characters.** These are in big demand right now—in particular, anything from the 1960s that depicts Rocky and Bullwinkle. *Reason:* Few items exist because the duo was never heavily marketed. *Examples:* Bullwinkle wristwatch ($800),

---

has followed dutifully and risen 50-fold.

6. Owning stocks is like having children. Don't get involved with more than you can handle. The individual investor probably has enough time to follow 8 to 12 companies. Your portfolio doesn't need to contain more than five companies at any one time. If you can't find any companies that are attractive, put your money in

the bank until you discover some.

7. Don't even try to predict the future. Nobody can predict interest rates, the future of the economy or the direction of the stock market, so dismiss all the forecasts. Instead, concentrate on what's actually happening to the companies in which you're invested. Their individual performance

is what's important—not the performance of the economy or the market or any of the indexes.

8. Avoid weekend worrying.

Beware: The weekends are prime time for dwelling on bad news and the consequences this news may have on stocks. Catching up on the news can be dangerous. It's no accident that Mondays historically are the biggest down days in stocks, and that Decembers (when tax-loss selling is combined with extended holidays during which people have extra time to consider the fate of the world) are the biggest down months. The key to making money in stocks is not to get scared out of them.

9. Never invest in a company without first understanding its finances. The biggest losses in stocks come from companies with poor balance sheets. *Example:* The U.S. Savings and Loan (S&L) industry, once an untouchable among equities. A while ago, there were two kinds of S&Ls—ones that were losing money

but had a good financial position— and ones that were losing money and had a bad financial position. The stock prices of the second type dropped to nothing, while the stock prices of the first type increased 5- or 10-fold.

10. Don't expect too much, too soon. My greatest stocks have turned in their best performances in the second, third and fourth years I've owned them, not the first week, the first month or the first year. The stock market is totally random over one or two years. If your horizon is that short and you need the money you're investing for something fairly immediate, like sending your kid to college next year, investing in the stock market is a bad idea. You should be in a money-market fund instead. But over 5, 10 or 20 years, the stock market will deliver fairly good results.

Remember, time is on your side. If you had waited 10 years after Wal-Mart went public, you could still have bought its shares for 90 cents. A share of Wal-Mart in mid-2002 was worth $55, and that's not even taking into account all the stock splits that have occurred in the interim.

Source: *Peter Lynch, the retired manager of Fidelity Investments' Magellan Fund, which soared in value during his tenure and beat the average equity fund every year he was at the helm. He is the author of* **Beating the Street,** *Simon & Schuster.*

Investing to Win

445

Bullwinkle target game ($250), Rocky and Friends coin bank ($250) and Bullwinkle coloring books ($15 to $40, if never used).

● **Flintstones** battery-operated Dino the Dinosaur, with Fred, Wilma, Barney and Betty riding on top ($500 and up), and 1960 Flintstones bowling-pin figures ($75 each).

● **Batman** board game ($165).

● **Addams Family's** "Thing" hand bank ($50 to $75).

● **Monkees**—for collectors, the second most popular rock group after the Beatles. The Monkees were extremely likable and had widespread TV exposure at the time. *Example:* Monkeemobile—a vehicle with the four group members riding inside ($500).

● **Soakies**—plastic figures that were filled with shampoo or bubble bath. They can be worth as much as $100 each.

Hottest Soakies: Superman ($100), Touché Turtle Bubble Club ($75), Yogi Bear ($72) and Casper ($37 at a recent auction, although the price will rise now that the movie was a hit).

Furniture

● **Heywood Wakefield Danish Modern pieces**—blond with rounded corners—command good prices. All post–World War II examples have a wood-burned stamp of the maker's name on the underside. *Examples:* A 34" x 44" sliding door cabinet with interior drawers ($1,100), a four-drawer dresser ($495).

● **Vinyl beanbag chairs**—labeled Sacco, which is the original by Gatti, Paolini & Teodoro—might be worth $500 to $1,000 each, if you can prove their age.

● **Rigid, colorful plastic furniture** from the period is hot and will likely get hotter because it's so useful and so brightly representative of the 1960s. Look for furniture items such as dressers with curved sliding drawers.

● **Plastic stack-of-cans storage units** made in the 1960s for kids are also rising in value. The cans stack up and have curved doors. They're great for storing toys, and their loud colors—usually bright orange, red and yellow—can add life to a room ($30

to $40 per unit). *Large:* 8½" high, 12½" diameter; *Small:* 9¼" high, 16½" diameter.

● **Nauga,** the pointy-headed creature that looks like an alien teddy bear was the spokescharacter for Naugahyde furniture ($100). These stuffed animals were given away as promotional items but never sold.

> "Georges Briard glassware is not hot yet, but hold onto it because it will be. Briard's set of eight highball glasses was a classic 1960's wedding gift."

The Beatles

One of the most popular items is a set of four six- to eight-inch-high Beatles dolls whose heads were attached to springs and bobbed up and down ($425 to $920 apiece). *Other hot collectibles:*

● **Set of four Yellow Submarine clothing hangers,** each depicting one of the Fab Four ($400).

● **Piece of Beatles wallpaper**—the size of a card table—depicting the Mop Tops playing instruments ($200).

Other Beatles collectibles: Guitar toys ($650), wigs ($100), clothing such as sweatshirts ($150), Halloween costumes ($50 to $125), lunch boxes ($350).

Beatles records usually fetch fairly low prices because collectors value good sound reproduction above everything else. *Exception:* Plastic 45-rpm records with the group's image on the vinyl. Collectors usually frame them as works of art. *Examples:* "All You Need Is Love" ($60 to $125), "A Hard Day's Night" ($100).

Clothing

● **Dresses made by Emilio Pucci** were—and still are—wildly colorful, psychedelic ($400 to $1,000). His fancy evening gowns command the best prices. Dresses should have labels reading *Emilio Pucci, Florence, Italy.* Most Pucci items have his signature on the front. Without the label or signature, you probably have a knockoff.

● **Any paper dress,** a quintessential 1960s fad ($75 to $100), if it is in decent condition.

● **Pierre Cardin's** navy blue wool dress, which has paddle-shaped flaps ($3,600).

● **Plastic mesh dress** by Paco Rabanne ($725).

Pez Dispensers

The first of these three-inch-high plastic candy dispensers were designed in Germany in 1948. They depict characters whose heads tilt back to eject tiny, brick-shaped candies.

The ones from the 1960s and early 1970s are in demand because of their nostalgic value.

Hottest dispensers: The Pineapple, from the Crazy Fruit collection ($700 to $900). The Pear ($650) and the Orange ($100) are also valuable.

Other hot dispensers: The baseball glove and ball ($299), Bullwinkle ($200), Green Hornet ($155 to $200).

Soon to Be Hot

● **The 1964 New York World's Fair** is not big yet—but it will be. Today, most collectors remain more concerned with the 1939 New York fair, which attracts Art Deco collectors. Others are nostalgic about the fair because it was their most pleasant memory before World War II.

● **Any item in vivid color.** For the collectible to be important, it has to virtually shout that it is originally from the 1960s.

● **Science-fiction crossover items.** While a television program such as *Star Trek* is still popular with collectors, other space-related shows are gaining strength, in part because the shows are being aired on TV again. Valuable collectibles are toys and lunch boxes depicting characters from *Lost in Space, The Jetsons* and *My Favorite Martian.*

● **Georges Briard glassware** is not hot yet, but hold onto it because it will be. Briard's set of eight highball glasses was a classic 1960's wedding gift. The distinctive glasses have gold geometric designs near the rim, and each piece is signed "Georges Briard." Briard's pebble-finished glass trays and chip-and-dip sets were also popular.

Not Worth Much

Not all 1960s icons have great value. *Examples:*

● **Original lava lamps** are not very valuable—in any condition. They were never great works of art, and there have been so many new ones produced recently that there is no longer any novelty to the old ones. An old one in good condition fetches $50 to $100. New ones go for around $50. *Exceptions:* Early examples such as prints on scarves ($100 or more), clocks ($200) and psychedelic tennis shoes ($400 to $500).

● **Pottery** without the maker's name.

● **Ashtrays** of any kind.

Source: Ralph and Terry Kovel, among the nation's top collecting experts. They are publishers of the newsletter Kovels on Antiques and Collectibles, *and authors of* Kovels' Antiques & Collectibles Price List 2002, *Crown Publishing, and 75 other books.*

How an Insider Buys at an Auction

Here's how you can bid like an insider at an auction.

● **Obtain an auction catalog.** Read the descriptions of the items for sale, noting their estimated selling prices (prices may not be included in the catalog).

● **Research the terminology** that will be used in the auction. A glossary is usually part of the catalog.

● **Attend the pre-auction exhibition** to scrutinize the items that most interest you. Leave no unsettled questions. (Once they are sold, items are the responsibility of the purchaser, so examine carefully for any chips, cracks, touch-ups, etc.)

● **Ask for estimates.** Decide what you are willing to spend and set your limits.

● **Arrive at the auction early** and select a location accessible to the vision and hearing of the auctioneer. Dealers generally sit or stand at the rear of the audience to gain an overview of the proceedings. They are interested in seeing who is bidding and how the bidding is progressing.

● **Take note of your competition.** Insiders, particularly dealers, are customarily discreet in their bidding. Occasionally, they will use a prearranged signal to alert the auctioneer. Most bidding is indicated by a wave of a hand, a catalog or a paddle.

● **To minimize the chance of error,** verbalize your bid if it varies from the increment established by the auctioneer.

Investing to Win

● **Do not exceed your preset limit** unless the item is rare and may not come on the market again. Do not be carried away by emotion.

● **You may bid against a known dealer.** If you bid after a dealer has stopped bidding, realize that you may buy the item and will probably pay far less for it than you would in the dealer's shop.

Intangibles Are Important

Act with assurance. Assume command of a situation when it is to your advantage and remain silent when it is not. Address people by their first names, especially the auctioneer. If you can, chat with the auctioneer before, during or after the auction. Conversely, you may choose to remain inconspicuous, sitting quietly, waiting for what you came to bid upon.

Insiders are astute and concise. They know when, where, how and how much to bid. Most important, they know when to stop bidding.

Source: *Richard Friedman, president, auctioneer and appraiser, Chicago Art Galleries, Inc., 5039 Oakton Street, Skokie, IL 60077. He is a member of the Appraisers Association of America, the International Society of Appraisers and the American Arbitration Association, Panel of Arbitrators.*

What You Should Know About Appraisals

When you need an appraisal for any type of collectible, certain information should always be included: the qualifications of the appraiser, the purpose(s) of the appraisal, a description of the object being appraised, its history or the provenance, the economic factors at the time of the appraisal, the

THE PRACTICAL VIRTUES OF JOINING AN INVESTMENT CLUB

The hard truth about investing is that you only learn when you risk actual money, and when you invest via an investment club, you risk little and learn a lot.

The 37,000 U.S. clubs that belong to the National Association of Investors Corporation (NAIC) have an average number of 17 members (there is no comparable national association currently active in Canada). Rarely do more than one or two of the 17 members have any investment experience when they join. After five years in the club, however, 13 or 14 of those people will have

individual investment accounts, investing three times as much as they do in the club—typically about US$40 a month.

Inside a Club

Each club runs like a business. There are regular meetings with agendas and officers.

The learning process starts when members are assigned individual stocks to research. They use practical guidelines from the NAIC, as well as from independent sources, to help them conduct their research. They are expected to write actual reports on the financial basics and the business outlook for the companies they research. Once completed, these

reports become the basis for detailed, in-depth discussions during club meetings.

After every member is satisfied that the stock has been discussed fully, a vote on whether or not to invest in the company is taken. No stock is purchased without majority approval.

Through the camaraderie of a club, members get the learning experience of studying the fundamentals of companies and discussing the pros and cons of a long-term investment.

More Learning Material

In addition to the research materials, the NAIC provides the names of stocks that have done well for other investment clubs.

It also provides a list of 150 U.S. companies offering dividend-reinvestment plans. Through these plans, the NAIC is able to purchase for the club one share of a desired company, which qualifies the club to continue to add to its position in the company without paying the brokerage com-

date and the appraiser's signature. Sometimes a photograph of the object is included.

The qualifications of the appraiser are of primary importance and should always be stated on the appraisal. They should encompass the appraiser's professional affiliations, his or her particular area of expertise, and the length of time appraising.

Appraisals may be done for several reasons: for insurance purposes (retail replacement value), tax purposes, donation purposes and "fair market value" purposes.

Note: Appraisals for tax purposes should be executed by members of recognized appraisal organizations, such as the Canadian Personal Property Appraisers Group. You can locate a qualified appraiser in your province through their website at http://www.cppag.com.

The description of the object should be well detailed. It should state what the object is, the material of which it is composed, its size, color, clarity, subject, rarity, age and uniqueness.

The item's history, or provenance, tells where the item originated, which galleries or dealers have sold it and for what prices, and gives an evaluation of its quality relative to others of its kind.

Source: *Richard Friedman, president, auctioneer and appraiser, Chicago Art Galleries, Inc., 5039 Oakton Street, Skokie, IL 60077.*

The Investment Mistakes That Too Many People Make

As an investment counselor, I've probably witnessed just about every possible investor mistake.

missions that have so discouraged individual investors in recent years.

In addition to the educational benefits of investment clubs, this advantage of inexpensive stock purchasing is a valuable aspect to being a club member.

Generally, the club has a bank and/or brokerage account and it receives monthly statements that are analyzed by the members to decide when to buy and sell stock positions. Again, all of this is very useful experience.

I belong to the Mutual Investment Club of Detroit, which has been in existence for 52 years. The 18 members have put in US$450,000—less than US$25,000 apiece. We make monthly investments of between US$10 and US$100 per member. Over the years, we've taken more than US$2 million out (to buy homes, finance college, etc.), and the club still has a net worth of more than US$4.5 million. That's an average annual compounded rate of return of 12%.

Our association's goal is to buy companies that can give a club a total return of 15% a year, including stock price appreciation and dividends. When that's achieved by a club's total portfolio (always some stocks will be losers), it will double its money in five years—not bad for any investor.

Lessons Learned

In these exciting years, club membership has given me many, many valuable insights into investing. If I had one piece of advice to investors, it would be to *start early.*

Most people don't even think of investing until they hit their 45th birthday. By starting earlier, you can take better advantage of the magic of compounding—that is, earning interest on your principal plus interest.

Once you accept this, the following three invaluable investment lessons will always serve you well:

● **Invest regularly.** One of the best lessons we've learned is that market swings can't be predicted.

Members who survive a market downturn and keep on buying in bear markets learn to become lifetime investors. Despite sometimes violent ups and downs, the long-term trend of the market is up. The U.S. economy doubles roughly every 23 years.

● **Reinvest earnings.** Insofar as possible, use dividend-reinvestment programs. When you sell a stock, quickly reinvest that money in another stock. The longer you compound your earnings, the better off you will be financially.

● **Pick value companies.** That means companies that can outperform the market over time. You can find them because their growth is better or, when lucky, you can find them at a bargain price because they're out of market favor for some reason unrelated to fundamentals.

Information on NAIC can be found at http://www.better-investing.org.

Source: *Kenneth S. Janke, president, National Association of Investors Corp., 711 W. Thirteenth Mile Road, Madison Heights, MI 48071.*

Here are the most common mistakes that investors tend to make on their own, before they finally seek professional advice:

● *Mistake:* **Chasing yield.** Many investors are particularly vulnerable to such behavior these days, with bank GICs paying very low rates. In their quest for higher rates, these investors are stretching out their maturities longer and longer.

Trap: When interest rates start to rise, the market value of these long-term investments will plummet. And their total return (rate of return plus appreciation—or depreciation) will fall as a result. Instead of focusing on current yield, you should structure your entire portfolio—which includes cash, plus stocks, bonds and mutual funds—so that it produces the total return you need.

● *Mistake:* **Failing to diversify your portfolio.** It's important to divide up your portfolio into different asset classes that move in opposite directions from each other. That way, if one or two of the asset classes in your portfolio move down, the chances are that the others are moving up.

In our firm, we work with 22 different asset classes, but the individual investor can diversify with just 5 or 10.

The most common asset classes are cash and cash-equivalents, such as money funds, bank GICs and Treasury bills, domestic and international stocks, domestic and international bonds, real estate and gold and foreign currency. You can further diversify in the stock area by dividing investments into large-capitalization, medium-cap and small-cap stocks. In the fixed-income area, you can divide investments into different maturities, ranging from short- to long-term, and along the quality spectrum ranging from government bonds to AAA-rated corporate bonds to junk bonds.

● *Mistake:* **Not understanding the trade-off between risk and return.** People now—as always—want to get something for nothing. But to get bigger returns on your investments, you have to be willing to assume more risk.

Problem: Most people don't quantify how much risk they're willing to accept. You should select a tolerable range of returns. *Example:* In 9 out of every 10 years, your rate of return on stocks—based on past performance of the Standard & Poor's index of 500 U.S. stocks—would have ranged from minus 15%/yr. to plus 37%/yr. If the performance of an individual stock falls within your allowable range, it's okay. Otherwise, bail out. Select a mutual fund or—better yet—buy an index fund. A properly diversified portfolio might be expected to earn between 5% per year and 14% per year in 9 out of 10 years. The performance of your overall portfolio, and whether it falls within your allowable range of return, is far, far more important than the performance of the individual securities or asset classes.

● *Mistake:* **Not using dollar-cost or value-averaging.** About 80% of individual investors are in cash or cash equivalents. And when they decide to venture into stocks, they either want to do it all at once, or to go much too slowly.

A much better approach is to dollar-cost average—invest a set amount of money on a regular basis, say once a month. This way, you smooth out market fluctuations and usually wind up purchasing at a lower cost per share than if you bought all at once.

Value-averaging is a variation in which you invest whatever amount is needed to make the value of your investments increase by some preset amount each period. If you've decided to try the stock market, I usually suggest averaging into the market over a period of 6 to 12 months, with a two-year investment period the outside maximum. *Example:* If your goal is to invest 24% of your entire $1 million portfolio in large-cap domestic stocks—that's $240,000. Buy $20,000/month over 12 months, or $10,000/month over 24 months.

● *Mistake:* **Giving too much to children through informal "in-trust" accounts.** A popular alternative to registered education savings plans for putting aside university money. The assets in the account automatically become your child's property when he or she reaches the age of majority.

If, at that point, the child wants to take the money and give it to a cult group or buy a Ferrari instead of going to university, the parents are powerless. But with a genuine trust, the parents remain in control.

When establishing the trust, parents can specify how and when to distribute interest and principal from the trust. Also, if a parent dies before the child reaches the age of majority, the assets in a properly drafted trust do not become part of the parent's taxable estate. Nor can trust assets be attached by creditors, or by a spouse in the event of divorce.

● *Mistake:* **Poor record keeping.** It always amazes me how often people will come into my office with their financial affairs in a state of total chaos.

I've had first-time clients who came in with huge portfolios—but were totally befuddled when I asked them how much they paid for each of their holdings. They didn't know the basis (tax cost) of the securities in their portfolios. This information is vital because it determines the profit (or loss) and, thus, the amount of capital gains tax you must pay to the CCRA if you sell.

> "The average investment club doubles the value of its portfolio every five years. There are few mutual funds that can claim such a prestigious record."

If you're in this predicament, you may have to hire an accountant to unravel the truth. Then resolve that you or your investment counselor will keep good records from here on out, especially if you are reinvesting dividends from stocks or mutual funds.

● *Mistake:* **Looking for the guru.** By concentrating on short-term performance results, you wind up choosing yesterday's guru. The probability is that that guru will wind up being tomorrow's average performer or—even worse—tomorrow's loser.

A much better approach, particularly with mutual funds, is to purchase index funds, which mirror a broad segment of the market. They are the lowest-expense, lowest-risk way to represent a particular asset class in your portfolio.

Sources: *Gordon Pape; and Gary Greenbaum, fee-only financial and investment counselor with Greenbaum and Associates, Inc., 496 Kinderkamack Road, Oradell, NJ 07649.*

Who Attends Investment Seminars?

Investment seminars attract two kinds of attendees: those who know too little and those who are already knowledgeable about investing. The novice investor can gain a broad, but possibly confusing, understanding of the investment field from these semi-nars, and the more experienced investor can gain access to the insights and techniques of respected professionals.

Caution: Remember, investment professionals' recommendations are aimed at a general audience and may or may not be suitable for your needs at that time. *Advantage:* These investment seminars allow you to identify people whom you feel you can trust and with whom you can schedule later consultation sessions.

Who Conducts Investment Seminars?

Investment seminars come in four basic flavors: (1) major exhibitions and national tours, (2) regional trade shows and local seminars, (3) investment advisers and (4) stock and insurance brokers. Most seminars are free of charge if you ask for tickets from an exhibitor or publisher.

In Canada, the largest national exhibition by far is the Financial Forum in Toronto, although smaller shows are staged in other cities including Vancouver, Calgary, Montreal and Ottawa. These shows, which usually take place during RRSP season, feature many speakers, newsletter writers and advisers who operate on a national scale. *Advantage:* National seminars provide many contrasting opinions rather than the single sales pitch typical of local seminars.

Regional trade shows tend to be run by newspapers or local entrepreneurs and often attract as exhibitors local offices of stockbrokers, mutual-fund families, banks and financial planners.

Local seminars are much smaller and conducted mainly by registered investment advisers (most are paid by managing your portfolio), and brokers and financial planners (most are selling commissioned financial products and services).

How to Get the Most Out of the Seminar

● **Get information in advance.** This allows you to decide which speakers will likely be of the greatest interest to you.

● **Find out if the experts publish a newsletter or have written a book.** This way you can visit the library and review their book or books to see if their advice suits you. Call them directly and get a free sample of their newsletter, which most offer (see number below for free sample copy of my newsletter).

● **Prepare a schedule of the speakers you want to hear in advance.** That way you can prepare questions you want to ask them.

● **Narrow the list of investments you want to learn about.** For example, focus on no-load mutual funds or small-company stocks. Be wary of options, penny stocks and get-rich-quick schemes.

● **Take a notepad or pocket tape recorder and take notes on the best ideas.** You may also want to pick up brochures or audiotapes of the presentations.

● **Attend the workshops of lesser-known speakers on your favorite subjects.** The contrasting opinions will help you put the best ideas in perspective and challenge superficial ideas.

● **Talk to as many people as possible.** Sometimes the best ideas—about speakers and investments—come from fellow attendees. Ask people their best and worst investing experiences.

● **Call some of your favorite advisers' offices** and talk with them about managing your money.

Caution: These investment seminars are designed to assist the advisers in selling their services. Even the most "educational" speakers are selling something. Remember that their presentations offer general advice for the masses. If you want to get a specific evaluation of your portfolio and your investment goals, call them after the seminar with a list of questions.

If an adviser does not ask you what your investment needs are before making a recommendation, and launches into a sales pitch, hang up. Ethical advisers are required to recommend only what is suitable to your needs.

Sources: William E. Donoghue, *publisher of* Bill Donoghue's Wealth-Letter, *Box 360, 100 Medway Road, Suite 401, Milford, MA 01757, 1-800-982-2455. Additional Canadian information by Gordon Pape.*

Investment Clubs

The average investment club doubles the value of its portfolio every five years. There are few mutual funds that can claim such a prestigious record. *The clubs top big mutual funds for several reasons:*

● **Funds** have to pay their managers.

● **Clubs can invest in small,** fast-growing stocks while the funds, because they are so large, must favor large companies.

● **Quarterly reporting requirements** force funds to do a lot of costly trading.

● **When the market is low and stocks are cheap,** funds are constrained by their unsophisticated individual investors, who tend to pull their money out just when it's time to buy.

Club Investing

Philosophy: Invest small amounts (on average $25–$40/month per member) on a regular basis—in up and down markets. Doing this reduces the average price paid per share of stock. *Example:* When a stock is trading at $4/share, $24 buys six shares—but if the stock rises to $6, the same sum will buy only four shares. You purchase more shares when a stock is cheaper—fewer when it's more expensive.

Clubs usually reinvest all dividends and select only stocks that they think have a good chance of doubling in value within five years. They also try to diversify their holdings, maintaining a portfolio of 12–20 different issues.

No matter how thorough a club's research, not all its picks will double—a few will even go down. But in most clubs' experience, there are always several big winners that pull up overall results.

Tried and true: If stocks are researched and selected carefully and a club invests on a regular basis, it will make money over the long term.

Trap: Going into an investment club to get rich quick—it won't happen. But within three to five years most clubs begin to realize a handsome payoff on their investment.

Forming a Club

The best way to get into an investment club is to form one yourself. Clubs have prearranged member limits, so unless you have a friend in a club, chances of getting in are slim. *Optimal number of members:* 10–15—a group that can meet at members' homes.

Look for prospective members in social or business groups to which you belong. Ask each interested person to bring a friend. Try to assemble a group that's not too homogeneous—in which each member contributes something different. *Example:* One member may be a computer whiz; another, someone with good intuition about trends; and another, a very sharp stock picker, etc.

Schedule monthly meetings on the same night each month—for example, the third Monday—so that everyone can plan ahead.

Big mistake: Starting out with substantial lump-sum investments of, say, $500 or $1,000. If the market happens to be topping when this first investment is made, losses and disappointment will ensue. *Better:* Set a regular sum of $25–$30—more if everyone is willing—and start investing those small amounts regularly. Later, members will be able to increase their participation, if desired.

Structure a Partnership

A partnership is a more favorable structure than a corporation because, unlike shareholders, partners don't pay tax on profits twice. Corporations pay corporate income tax, and then individual shareholders are liable for tax on dividends. But in a partnership untaxed earnings flow through to the partners directly and are taxed only once at the individual's level. *Extra tax benefit:* Potential losses are also passed through to partners, who can use them to offset gains for tax purposes.

Helpful: Check your province's registration requirements with an attorney.

You'll also need a lawyer to draw up a partnership agreement. This spells out the purpose of the club, its organizational structure, how accounts and book-keeping will be handled, and what happens if a member dies or wishes to withdraw funds. The partnership agreement should be signed by every member of the club.

Because money is involved, the agreement should also state what partners may *not* do. *Examples:* Obligate the partnership to any extent whatever—or use the partnership's name or property without proper authority.

At the first meeting the club members should elect a presiding partner to run meetings, a recording partner to keep minutes and a financial partner to keep records of receipts and disbursements, place buy and sell orders with the club's broker and prepare a statement of the liquidating value of the club's portfolio before each meeting is held.

The Broker

When the club's funds are still small, you may have trouble finding a broker willing to take your account. *Helpful:* Explain that you will add to the club's portfolio monthly.

Before each meeting, check with the broker for any comments on your holdings and any new ideas or recommendations on the two or three stocks that the club will be discussing that evening. (It's impossible for a broker to attend every meeting, but invite him or her at least once a year.)

Encourage your broker to provide annual and quarterly reports—and analysts' research. The relationship with the broker should be governed by a signed document in which both sides agree to their responsibilities. Securities can be kept in a "street name" with the broker, in the club's name or in the name of one or more nominated members.

Easiest: Keeping stocks in a "street name" at the broker's office.

Caution: If stock certificates are held by the club or its members, be sure to keep them in a very safe place. It's very difficult and expensive to replace lost certificates.

Broadening Horizons

The main function of membership is to learn about investments and how the economy works. *Best training:* Researching an individual company. *Great resource:* The broker's office, where you will find abundant research information that's available to the firm's customers.

Some clubs name one member their "economist." *Duties:* To follow economic indicators that could affect the club's holdings and report to the group on a regular basis.

You can find information on some of the investment clubs operating in Canada by going to http://www.investorlinks.com/directory/service-clubs-canada.html.

Sources: Thomas E. O'Hara, chairman, National Association of Investors Corporation, (NAIC), 711 W. Thirteenth Mile Rd. Madison Heights, MI 48071. Additional Canadian information provided by Gordon Pape.

Real Estate Strategies

13

Property Ownership That's Right for You

Property can be held in a variety of forms—as an individual, a corporation, a partnership, a trust or a syndicate, pool or joint venture. Within each general category there are further variations that affect your tax treatment and legal liability. The primary factors to consider when choosing among the different forms of ownership are the degree of economic protection and the tax incidence factor. Use the following list of general guidelines when deciding on the most appropriate form of ownership for you.

● **Individual ownership.** This is the simplest form of ownership, and the economic profits and tax benefits of property flow directly to you. Yet, it does have disadvantages. It exposes you to the greatest risk—your liability is unlimited. Ownership should therefore only be undertaken if the property in question does not unduly expose you to potentially excessive losses or legal claims from third parties. Also, for taxpayers in a high personal tax bracket, property that starts to produce operating profits may result in needlessly high taxation. Finally, individually owned property often becomes the center of disagreement during marital discord and divorce. (A spouse usually does have rights in such property.)

● **Partnership ownership.** Most frequently used for multiparty ownership, a partnership is not treated as a separate taxable entity—it merely acts as a conduit for gains and losses to pass to its members. A partnership facilitates the maximum use of tax-shelter deductions. As a partner, you can personally deduct losses to the extent of your capital contributions and loans to the partnership. In the case of real estate, you can also deduct losses to the extent of third-party nonrecourse loans to the partnership. A limited partnership, which has both general and limited partners, provides limited liability for the limited partners, while exposing the general partners to the greatest legal and economic risk.

● **Limited liability company ownership.** The creation of a limited liability company can provide its owners with the limited liability protection of corporate ownership and the favorable pass-through tax features of partnership ownership. This new type of entity is becoming the structure of choice for multiparty real-estate and commercial ventures.

● **Trust ownership.** A "land trust" operates solely as a title-holding vehicle—the trustee has no actual power over the property. Trust ownership of this type is treated not as a taxable entity, but merely as a conduit to the owners. It is important that the trustee not have "real" powers over the trust, or it will be considered a "business trust." In this event, unless very carefully structured and operated, the trust will be taxed as a corporation.

● **Real estate investment trusts (REITs)** are a special kind of trust whose treatment under the tax law is similar to that of mutual funds. To qualify as a REIT, the trust must meet strict ownership, income and asset tests and will usually distribute 85% to 95% of its taxable income. This kind of distributed income is taxed to the beneficiaries upon receipt rather than to the trust; however, the tax breaks associated with REITs will reduce the effective tax rate. Because REITs can only be effectively utilized for large, specialized ventures with numerous participants, this form of ownership has limited application.

● **Syndicate, pool or joint venture.** These are labels for individuals, partnerships, trusts or corporations that have joined together to acquire, hold and/or develop an interest in property. The distinction among the terms is not well defined, although for tax purposes each is generally treated as a partnership. Broadly defined, "joint venture" denotes a team effort on a single transaction; "syndicate" denotes the sharing of financial responsibilities; and "pool" emphasizes the joining of the participants' financial and management resources.

● **Joint tenants or tenants in common.** When real estate is purchased by more than one owner and is used as a principal residence, a decision must be made whether to take title as "joint tenants" or "tenants in common."

> " **Mortgage-backed securities, mortgage mutual funds, and REITs can produce real rates of return regardless of an inflationary environment. Programs such as these are appealing to income-oriented investors . . . "**

Joint tenancy means that each participant (very often spouses) owns the whole property together. If one joint tenant outlives the other, ownership passes automatically to the survivor. A joint tenant cannot will his interest in the property to anyone else. Transferring the title through joint tenancy has some estate planning benefits, such as the savings of probate tax.

But what if the co-owners in question aren't married, or even if they are, want to leave their share of the property to someone other than their spouse?

To solve this problem, co-owners can take title as tenants in common. In this case, each participant owns a separate, equal share in the property. If a tenant in common dies before another, their interest in the property is dealt with through their will.

It's wise to discuss each of these options with your lawyer before making a decision.

Source: Deborah Pape; and Richard J. Flaster, Esq., president, Flaster, Greenberg, Wallenstein, Roderick, Spigel, Zuckerman, Skinner & Kirchner, 5 Greentree Centre, Suite 200, Marlton, NJ 08053. In addition to working as a tax attorney, he has written several books and lectured widely on a range of tax subjects, including real estate taxation, divorce taxation and personal tax planning.

For the Income-Oriented Investor

Mortgage-backed securities (MBSs), mortgage mutual funds and REITs can produce real rates of return regardless of an inflationary environment. Programs such as these are appealing to income-oriented investors because they feature low-risk, high current return and capital growth potential.

Mortgage-Backed Securities

Many people aren't familiar with these but they are a useful investment for those who are looking for steady income with very little risk. An MBS certificate (they're also referred to by brokers as NHAs) represents a share in a pool of residential mortgages. These pools are put together by financial institutions, and vary in size. Each pool is self-contained, with its own coupon rate and payment schedule.

MBS units always are dated as of the first of the month and start paying returns on the fifteenth of the month following the issue. Most have five-year terms, although they can range from as little as six months to as long as 25 years. Minimum investment is usually $5,000, but that can vary depending on where you buy. They're eligible for registered plans. Here are some of their main features:

Safety: Residential first mortgages have always been low-risk investments. But these certificates are as close to no-risk as you can get. Canada Mortgage and Housing Corporation (CMHC) guarantees you'll receive full interest and principal payments on the due dates, even if there are defaults within the pool. Since the CMHC is a Crown corporation, your guarantee is backed by the government of Canada. And there's no limit on the guarantee (unlike deposit insurance, which covers only the first $60,000). You don't have to be concerned about the financial stability of the MBS issuer or of the mortgages within the pool. The government protects you both ways.

Competitive yield: The coupon rate in any given MBS pool is based on the mortgage-holders' interest rate, and must be at least a half point less than the lowest mortgage rate in the pool. If the lowest rate is 7%, the MBS coupon rate cannot exceed 6.5%. However, the coupon rate doesn't represent your actual return. MBSs, like bonds, are priced daily, and your yield will depend on the price you pay. According to brokers, these securities normally yield about 15 to 30 basis points (a basis point is 1/100 of a percent) more than five-year government of Canada bonds.

Liquidity: There's an active secondary market for MBSs. You can sell them through a broker before maturity if you wish, giving them a clear advantage over locked-in investments such as GICs. Although MBS prices tend to be more stable than those of government bonds, you could suffer a capital loss if interest rates rise after your purchase. If interest rates fall, on the other hand, you'll enjoy a capital gain, albeit not a large one.

Availability: MBS issues are available through major stockbrokers. If you don't have a broker or don't wish to open an account, you can buy them through some of the chartered banks.

Monthly pay: Very few securities offer monthly payments, especially combined with decent interest rates. That makes MBSs particularly appealing to retired people, either inside or outside an RRIF. But be aware that the monthly payment is not interest only—it's a blend of interest and principal. And it can vary, sometimes substantially, depending on the extent to which the mortgage-holders within the pool make early payments.

With blended principal and interest payments, you won't receive the full face value of the certificate at maturity. CMHC calculates that without prepayments, you'd receive about 6% of your original principal over a five-year term. At maturity you'd recover only about 94% of the original value of the certificate, or about $4,700 on each $5,000 certificate. Prepayments will reduce that even more. Remember to consider this in your calculations. If you don't like the uncertainty of prepayments, then consider a closed-mortgage pool. The closed MBS is the ideal income security. Payments will never vary over the term. No prepayments are allowed, so you know exactly what your monthly income will be. Yields on non-prepayable MBS certificates tend to be slightly lower for a comparable term.

When choosing an MBS, you might be wise to do a little shopping around, though. There may be slight variations (5 to 10 basis points) in the yields being offered by various brokers. A few phone calls will give you that information. If there's an edge, you might as well have it in your favor, especially if you're investing a substantial amount.

Source: 6 Steps to $1 Million: How to Achieve Your Financial Dreams, by Gordon Pape, published by Prentice-Hall Canada.

Mortgage Mutual Funds

Mutual funds that invest primarily in a pool of high-quality residential first mortgages are called mortgage mutual funds. Like mortgage-backed securities, they pay a return to investors based on the interest rates on the mortgages in the pool. Some of the investments in these funds are high-ratio mortgages backed by the Canada Mortgage and Housing Corporation or private mortgage insurance firms.

These mutual funds provide a fairly dependable rate of return, although the unit value will fluctuate with interest rates in general. They also provide steady though not spectacular growth, so the opportunities for capital gains are limited. They're relatively secure investments, since few people default on their mortgages. Also, some mortgage funds protect investors if any defaults do occur within the portfolio. For example, the Bank of Montreal will

purchase any defaulting mortgages from its BMO Mortgage Fund. This protection gives investors peace of mind.

You can purchase units in these mutual funds for as little as $500. Most of them are no-load, which means you pay no fee when you buy or sell your shares. However, before investors get anything, the managers of these funds take a management fee which usually runs to 1% to 2% of the fund's assets. They charge this fee in return for coordinating the interest rates and terms of mortgages in the pool with prevailing interest rates. When rates rise, for example, managers try to acquire long-term mortgages with high rates; when rates fall, they buy and sell short-term mortgages.

Mortgage mutual funds are available through banks, trust companies and credit unions, as well as through some independent firms such as Investors Group. They're eligible for inclusion in registered plans.

Source: The Canadian Mortgage Book: A Pape Starter's Guide, by Gordon Pape and Bruce McDougall, published by Prentice-Hall Canada.

Real Estate Investment Trusts (REITS)

Real estate investment trusts (REITs) are a special type of royalty trust. They specialize in any kind of property, from offices to health-care facilities.

For illiquid assets such as real estate, a closed-end fund like this makes the good sense. Open-ended or "mutual" real estate funds are subject to new-money and redemption problems that closed-end trusts avoid. In fact, the birth of REITs in Canada can be traced directly to the liquidity crisis with open-end real estate mutual funds in the 1991–92 real estate collapse. Faced with redemption demands from unit holders, the funds were presented with the unpalatable option of selling valuable properties into a distressed market to raise cash. Instead, they chose to close off redemptions and most of them eventually converted into REITs. Only a few open-ended real estate mutual funds continue to own property; most now invest in shares of real estate related companies.

The typical Canadian REIT usually distributes about 85% to 95% of its income (rental income from properties) to its shareholders, usually on a quarterly basis. This income gets a special tax break because the REIT shareholder is entitled to a deduction for the pro rata share of capital cost allowance (depreciation on the properties). As a result, a high percentage of the distributions is normally tax-deferred. However, the amount will vary from year to year and will differ depending on the REIT selected.

As with royalty trusts, the value of your tax-deferred income will reduce the adjusted cost base of your shares. If you buy 1,000 units of, for example, Riocan at $15.50 per unit, receive $3,000 ($3 per share) in aggregate tax-deferred distributions over time, and then sell the shares for $17.50 per share, you will have a capital gain of $5,000 [1,000 x ($17.50 – $15.50 + $3.00)] before adjustments for commissions. The gain will be subject to capital gain treatment so 50% of the gain, or $2,500, is included in income and taxed at your normal rate.

REITs are RRSP-eligible and are not considered foreign property as long as the real estate portfolio doesn't contain non-Canadian property in excess of the allowable limit.

REIT yields and the market price of units tend to be strongly influenced by interest-rate movements. As rates drop, REIT prices rise, and vice versa. When interest rates were pushed up in 2000 by the Bank of Canada and the U.S. Federal Reserve Board, the market price of the bellwether Riocan REIT fell to as low as $7.50. At that level, the units were yielding more than 14%. But by the autumn of 2001, with short-term rates dropping rapidly, the same units were trading in the $11 range, with a yield of less than 10%. Keep that relationship in mind if you're considering investing in these trusts. If interest rates appear poised to rise, you may want to defer any purchases. If you own units, you may wish to consider reducing your exposure and taking some profit.

Because REIT yields are much higher than the rates on preferred shares and other fixed-income securities, they may seem too good to be true. But remember, as the "no free lunch" theorem of investment finance tells us, anything that seems too good to be true probably is.

There are two catches with REITs. Since you are a unit holder rather than a shareholder, you are potentially jointly and severally liable with all other unit holders (plus the trust itself) in the case of insol-vency. Instead of limited liability, you are relying on the REIT management to have property, casualty and liability insurance, prudent lending policies and other safeguards in place. Nevertheless, there is the possibility of a problem—say, a catastrophic fire or a building collapse, something that isn't covered by insurance. That may have seemed like a very small risk prior to the attack on the World Trade Center in September 2001; now it is something that has to be taken seriously.

The second problem is less transparent. Real estate properties depreciate in value unless significant amounts of money are earmarked for maintenance and renewal of facilities. Since most or all of the REIT's income is being distributed and the capital cost allowance is being allocated to you, you are in a sense getting your own capital back. The book value of the real estate properties will be steadily depleting. Of course, if the properties are appreciating in value, this could offset the depreciation factor. The point is that the long-term income stream is quite variable, certainly more variable than some advisers would have you believe.

REITs have their place in a long-term investment portfolio, particularly for tax-advantaged income. But you need to understand their strengths and shortcomings. And don't buy them for capital-gains purposes unless you have a clear strategy for doing so—buying at an interest-rate peak and selling at the next interest-rate low.

Source: Secrets of Successful Investing, *by Gordon Pape and Eric Kirzner, published by Prentice Hall Canada.*

Real Estate Partnerships for Economic Returns

Real estate partnership investments should be made on the basis of true economic potential, which generally translates to a competitive cash-on-cash return. The following is a "back to basics" analysis of the economic potential of a real estate syndication.

Review the underlying properties of the investment. In most cases you will be looking at improved real estate, such as an apartment complex. For substantial investments, use someone with expertise to inspect the property for you. *Many factors affect the value of a property:*

● **Acquisition cost of the property,** including land and buildings, on a square-foot basis and capitalization-rate basis. Compare the cost with recent transactions on similar properties.

● **Type and quality of construction**—wood frame, brick, etc.; amenities—pool, fireplaces, landscaping; and the quality of heating, air conditioning, plumbing, wiring and insulation.

● **Age**—quality of the structure.

● **Occupancy** (present and projected).

● **Projected cost** for proposed improvements to the property, whether for maintenance, upgrade or rehabilitation.

● **Financing**—avoid short-term balloon payments (less than 10 years in most cases). Except in isolated instances, assume that you will hold a property for at least 10 years. Carefully examine interest rates and amortization periods, and conflicts, such as loans payable to the general partner or to the related parties.

● **Take into account all expenses,** i.e., fees, commissions and participation in sale and income proceeds.

Learn as much as you can about the sponsor. A partnership's sponsor can make or break the investment. *The first thing to look for:* Depth of real estate management and experience with the type of property and the area of your investment. You want a good, well-financed manager as general partner. If the investment is substantial, arrange to meet the general partner and key staff members in person. Look for hands-on long-term real estate acquisitions and in-house property-management experience.

● **Carefully analyze the sponsor's track record.** Remember, because of high appreciation rates, real estate investments covering the period of the late 1970s almost always look good, regardless of the sponsor's ability.

● **Find out if the sponsor plans to invest cash.** If so, is it really his or her own? Cash invested by the sponsor that has been taken out of the up-front fees charged by the sponsor is not a signal of good faith in the partnership.

Study estimated returns and objectives. Accurate projections are crucial to the success of a real estate investment. Therefore, make sure that the assumptions used in the sponsor's projections are conservative. Look closely at assumptions regarding rent

increases, operating budgets, refinancing terms and interest rates, inflation projections, sale price and terms, any other factors that affect the projected return. The projected increases in expenses should go up at the same rate as projected increases in rents. Don't be afraid to ask the sponsor to provide you with more conservative projections if you don't agree with them.

Look closely at the effect that projected tax losses (income), credits, tax preference items, investment interest expense and cash flow as a percentage of investment to date, will have on you. Make sure you can use projected tax losses in light of tax laws.

Compute the payback period (the time it takes to get your investment back through all projected benefits). Carefully consider the number of years in absolute dollars and the number of years in discounted present-value dollars.

Examine major tax-deductible items you can claim over the pay-in period. *Items to consider:*

● **"At risk" issues.**

● **Valuation issues. (Is there any appraisal to support the valuation?)**

● **Unusual tax structures.**

● **Accrual issues.**

● **Allocation issues.**

Find out whether a respected tax firm states unequivocally in its tax opinion that the tax treatments to be claimed by the partnership are correct. Also make sure a reputable CA firm is associated with the estimates of future operations and investor benefits.

Source: *Arnold G. Rudoff, J.D., CPA, former director, partnership analysis, Price Waterhouse, 555 California St., San Francisco, CA 94104. He assists clients in analyzing, structuring and financing real estate partnerships and direct investments.*

Investing in Rental Properties...the Right Way

With mortgage rates hovering near all-time lows, many investors are buying houses or apartments to rent out for extra income. While investing in rental property can be highly profitable, it's easy to make mistakes. *Here are the general rules:*

● **Consider properties that do not look good.** Few real estate properties are truly beyond repair.

A building that looks as if it's in bad shape may only need a fresh coat of paint and some light cleaning to get it back to fair market value and a potentially handsome immediate gain. *Strategy:* Before buying, hire a professional inspector to evaluate the condition of major items such as structural damage, the roof, plumbing, the furnace, termites, etc.

If problems are discovered, use them to negotiate a better price with the owner. Cosmetically distressed properties often have distressed owners, a potentially good combination for you, the buyer. *Rule:* If you can cover the cost of repairs and still make money, the property is a good investment. If you can't, it isn't.

● **The date of the closing is important.** When you buy *occupied* rental property, always arrange to take ownership on the third or fourth day of the month. Most rents are due on the first.

So if ownership transfers a few days after the rents are collected, you, the new owner, are entitled to receive a prorated share. And that prorated share can be applied against the down payment.

The same principle applies if you're buying a business. Some research on payables and receivables may reveal ways to generate more cash for the down payment.

● **You may not need to call in a company or professional to make every repair.** Contract with individuals rather than businesses to do any work you can't do yourself. A handyperson can replace washers in faucets a lot cheaper than a licensed plumber. He or she may also be able to do the bulk of your maintenance, too.

If you use a painting contractor, you will also be paying for the company's overhead and profit. Instead, find two or three people who can handle paintbrushes and put them to work.

● **Look for hidden costs and anticipate service needs.** For example, leaky faucets run up your water bill, and ill-fitting windows increase heating and cooling costs. Check with local governments or the utility company about the availability of grants to pay for any energy-conservation improvements.

Think about the basic services that your tenants will need, and try to accurately meet those needs. *Example:* If you provide a dumpster for trash collection, make sure the size is appropriate—not too small but also not too large—since an oversized one is costly.

● **Use as much of the space as possible to generate revenue.** Always try to create a *higher and better use* for the property. Look to turn unused space into a revenue source. Then maximize that revenue by upgrading the property cosmetically—a new paint job, some simple, attractive landscaping.

● **Don't assume that your taxes are correct.** Get copies of the tax bills for comparable properties in your area. This public information is easy to look up.

If your taxes are higher, file a protest with the tax collector's office. That's your right, and the tax collector's office can tell you how to do it.

● **Run the numbers.** Calculate your anticipated net profit without regard to any tax-shelter benefits for which you may be eligible. This is the money you have left after all of your expenses have been paid. *Formula:* Subtract all of your expenses (taxes, utilities, insurance, maintenance and mortgage payments) from the rent you receive. The result is your *net operating profit. Example:* If you have multiple tenants in a rooming house, you might want to build in a vacancy rate to be on the safe side. Your local realtor can give you data for your area.

Here's an example of how it's done:

Calculating Your Net Profits

Monthly gross rents (4 units at $500 each)	**$ 2,000**
Annual gross rents (12 x $2,000)	**$ 24,000**
Vacancy rate (at 10%, meaning that, on average, 90% of the units in your area are occupied) (0.9 x $24,000)	**$ 21,600**
Annual expenses	**$ 9,600**
Gross annual operating profit (minus annual expenses)	**$ 12,000**
Minus debt service (12 x $590, the monthly mortgage payment)	**$ 7,080**
Total net operating profit	**$ 4,920**

Rule: Never lose money on real estate just to get a tax break. With the right property, you can have positive cash flow and tax benefits, such as being able to deduct depreciation. Not all of your monthly mortgage payment goes toward the interest on the loan. Some principal is also repaid, resulting in a buildup of your equity over time.

Source: Russ Whitney, real estate and small-business entrepreneur in Cape Coral, FL. He is the author of Building Wealth: How Anyone Can Make a Personal Fortune Without Money, Credit or Luck, *Simon & Schuster.*

Five Simple and One Sophisticated Way to Analyze Rental Real Estate Investments

Even with the shrewdest real estate and tax experts at your side, it's essential for you to understand the basic economics of a rental real estate investment. While the combination of variables involved often makes it difficult for investors to compare the merits of different properties, there are five fairly simple formulas that can help.

The first step is to draw up a *pro forma* operating statement demonstrating the annual income, expenses and tax benefits expected from a proposed investment. Next, these figures and further information about the price of the property, type of financing, appreciation rates, etc., are evaluated according to several different criteria. The following definitions and explanations cover five of these criteria, along with the advantages and disadvantages of each, to help buyers make better investment decisions (and help sellers assess a property's worth better).

1. Gross Rent Multiplier (GRM)

GRM = sale price/gross annual rent.

The GRM (also known as the gross income multiplier) tells you the number of years of rent you would have to receive to equal the sale price of the property. The lower the GRM, the better.

Ideal for comparing a variety of separate yet similar properties, GRMs can vary widely depending upon the age, location, type of tenant and state of repair of the structures. The GRMs for very old buildings in poor repair with high tenant turnover may be quite low (sometimes less than 5); for new homes they may be above 12.

The GRM is simple to calculate, but does not make allowances for differences in investor objectives, financial terms, operating costs, changes in the annual income stream, tax considerations, appreciation or the time value of money. It can be misleading.

2. Debt Coverage Ratio (DCR)

DCR = net operating income/(annual mortgage principal payments + interest payments).

The DCR indicates the ability of a project to service its debt obligation without recourse to outside resources. Its most popular use is in comparing the merits of various financing arrangements rather than evaluating a project's profitability. The higher the ratio, the less risk there is of the project not being able to make its mortgage payments.

Lenders generally like a DCR to be at least 1.25. This means that net operating income will be at least 25% larger than the principal and interest payments. A ratio of less than 1.0 means that funds from outside the project will be required to meet annual mortgage payments.

The DCR is easy to use and is a meaningful indication of an investment's cash flow characteristics. However, it does not incorporate estimates of a property's potential for appreciation, the time value of money or the tax ramifications of the investment.

3. Overall Return on Total Capital (OAR)

OAR = net operating income/total investment.

The OAR measures the productivity of an investment. It is more reliable than the GRM because it accounts for operating expenses, vacancies and bad debts by using net rather than gross income. Generally, the higher the rate, the better. What is an acceptable minimum rate really depends on your particular investment needs and alternatives.

The OAR is a straightforward formula used to compare the returns from various rental properties. It does not, however, account for differing financial terms (most important, the degree of leverage involved in the investment), tax factors and the time value of money.

Real Estate Strategies

4. Cash-on-Cash Return (COC)

COC = cash flow before taxes/initial investment.

Many investors use the COC ratio as an indication of how productive their equity would be in a given project. Ratios a few percentage points above rates that are available on savings accounts at local banks and thrifts are frequently considered acceptable.

The COC ratio is suitable for investors who are primarily concerned about the cash flow of a project. The ratio assumes that all the benefits derived from an investment are in the form of cash flow—tax considerations and appreciation potential are ignored, as is the time value of money.

The COC is often negative, because many projects in today's market have a negative cash flow before taxes for the first few years. Thus a negative ratio can misrepresent the merits of a property—the investment may be very sound if tax advantages and appreciation factors are considered.

5. Equity Dividend After Taxes (EDAT)

EDAT = cash flow after taxes/equity investment.

The EDAT ratio shows how productive your investment would be on an after-tax basis, in contrast to the before-tax analysis of the COC. It is reasonable to expect the EDAT on your real estate investments to be in excess of 15%.

Most investors insist on a return that is at least equal to what they could earn on their best alternative investment, plus additional allowances for risk and the lack of liquidity associated with real estate. Although the EDAT will give you some idea of what the return would be, it fails to consider the time value of money.

6. Present Value (PV) Technique

The PV concept is a sophisticated technique for evaluating alternative investments in rental real estate. It has two major advantages over the more simple methods previously discussed. *First*, it provides dollar value for a specific property. This is in contrast to other criteria that help an investor choose among projects but do not indicate the precise dollar value of any particular project. *Second*, the PV recognizes all of the critical investment considerations, since it is based on the time value of money.

The time value of money is critical because a dollar received a year from now is worth less than a dollar received today, even ignoring inflation. The dollar in hand can be invested to earn interest for you—the dollar you haven't received yet cannot be. Therefore, you can only determine the value of future dollars by discounting them to reflect the interest you have forgone.

In real estate, the PV is defined as the current worth of a property's anticipated future costs and benefits, after the costs and benefits are discounted at a specific rate of return. The size of the discount depends on what rate the investor could have earned if the equity had been put to another use.

Example of PVs: The PV of a dollar to be earned in the future depends on both the discount rate and the length of time until that dollar is actually received. Thus the PV of a dollar to be received one year from today with a 6% discount is approximately 94¢ ($1.06 is what it would be worth in a year if it could be invested now at 6% interest = $0.9434). If that dollar is not to be received until two years from now, the PV drops to roughly 89¢ ($1/$1.12 = $0.8929). If the discount rate were 10%, the PV of a dollar to be received in one year would be about 91¢ ($1/$1.10 = $0.91).

The basic technique in calculating the PV of an investment property is to add the following three figures:

1. The present value of the property's cash flow after taxes for each year of the holding period.

2. The present value of the net equity reversion (selling price at the end of the holding period minus all selling expenses and mortgage retirements).

3. The initial amount of the mortgage balance. The total is the maximum amount an investor can pay for a property and still earn the specified rate of return on the cash investment. (The rate specified will be dependent on the investor's objectives and constraints.)

> "The time value of money is critical because a dollar received a year from now is worth less than a dollar received today."

This technique is far more comprehensive and accurate than other methods of evaluating rental real estate investments. The only limitation is that this technique requires reliable estimates of future revenues and expenses—the results are only as valid as the assumptions used.

Source: *Dr. Arthur L. Wright, economist, the Real Estate Center, Texas A&M University, as well as founder and CEO of Wright Properties. He is the author of more than 100 publications on various aspects of real estate and economics and has been active in both the local and the National Apartment Association.*

How Real Estate Investors Get Tricked

The urge to invest in real estate, which is still strong in most parts of the country, exposes buyers to sharp practices by sellers.

The most common distortion is a claim of high-paying tenants. If the rent roll of a commercial building shows that nine tenants pay $6–$8 per square foot and three pay $12, find out who the high-paying tenants are. One may be the building owner, and the other may be affiliated with the seller.

Any fudging of current and future income can cost an investor tens of thousands of dollars. In a small building, where the seller reports that 10 tenants pay $400 a month ($48,000 a year), if buildings in the area sell for six times gross, the market price would be $288,000. But suppose the owner had prepared to sell the building by raising the rents from $350 to $400 a month. That increase in the rent roll costs the buyer $36,000 (the difference between six times $48,000 in annual rents and six times $42,000).

Even worse would be the impact on future rent increases. If the rents in the building were close to market before the increase, the owner may well have offered tenants a free month's rent or a delayed increase. A delayed increase means that the buyer will not realize as much income as forecast. A free month's rent means that the actual increase in rents was only $17 an apartment, not $50. If the new owner tries to jump rents well above that, tenants may move.

> "If the building has not been assessed for several years, the new owner may have a ... tax bite on the next reassessment.... Ask the local assessment office for a tax card or listing sheet. It will show when [the building] was last assessed."

Other Seller Claims to Investigate

● **Low operating expenses.** Sellers may be operating the building themselves to avoid a management fee. If buyers cannot take care of the building personally, this fee must be added to real operating expenses. And if sellers do not factor it in, the bank will when it calculates the maximum supportable mortgage.

● **Reasonable property tax.** If the building has not been assessed for several years, the new owner may have a substantial tax bite on the next reassessment. Also, the seller may have made an addition to the building that has not yet been recorded with the tax assessor. As a precaution, ask the local assessment office for a tax card or listing sheet. It will show the building's assessment and when it was assessed. If it was assessed a year and a half ago and there has been no significant addition to the building, reassessment may not hurt the buyer. But if it has not been assessed for eight years, there could be a significant tax boost.

While checking the tax card or listing sheet, check the owner's property description against the one listed. If the owner says that 20,000 square feet are being sold but the tax card says 15,000 square feet, there has been some addition to the structure that has not been recorded and, therefore, has not been assessed. Or there may be an assessment error that, when finally corrected, will raise costs.

● **Low insurance premiums.** Is coverage in line with the structure's current value? What does the policy cover? Ask to see the policy. Ask an insurance adviser, if coverage is insufficient, how much more will proper coverage cost?

● **Energy efficient.** Verify the owner's claim with the local utility to determine actual energy costs.

Also check with regulatory commissions to see whether utility companies are scheduled to increase their tariffs.

● **A good buy.** Check the income statement with those of comparable buildings in the area.

Source: Thomas L. O'Dea, O'Dea & Co., Inc., 2150 Country Club Rd., Winston-Salem, NC 27103.

How to Successfully Manage Rental Housing

Do you really have the time and/or dedication to manage a rental property, maintain its physical structure and provide good service to your tenants? The problem with rental real estate as an investment is that once you own a property, you have to figure

KEY REQUIREMENTS FOR REAL ESTATE INVESTMENTS

Most people believe that the three key words in real estate are location, location, location. Wrong. In today's real estate market, the three key words are research, research, research. Only thorough research will enable you to determine if a property meets your economic requirements in the following key areas, whether you are looking at income-producing real estate or a primary residence.

● **Positive economic environment.** The most important factors here include the area's unemployment rate versus the national rate; the level of bank deposits compared with the national average; retail sales per capita; and migration and demographic patterns.

● **Location.** Location is the specific site you choose within a generally defined area. Ingredients that determine a good location include proximity to shopping and employment; convenient access to the property; availability of cultural activities; and minimum levels of noise and distraction.

● **Structural integrity.** In addition to being attractive, a building must be structurally sound. Before purchasing, make sure you have prospective real estate properties inspected by a qualified,

unaffiliated structural engineer. Remember, the replacement cost for one roof could wipe out your cash flow for an entire year.

● **Amenities.** The features that are unique to the property, such as recreational facilities, meeting rooms, parking spaces, and architecture, should match your personal or tenant profile. In the case of income-producing property, for example, if 90% of your tenants are married and over 65, a weight-lifting room may not be as attractive as a card room.

● **Capitalization ratio.** Your capitalization ratio—net operating income (operating revenues minus operating expenses) divided by the purchase price—is the purest form of analysis of your potential cash return from a real estate investment. Tax benefits and the availability of mortgage money are excluded from the analysis, giving you a better understanding of the actual amount of cash that will be generated by a project.

● **Mortgage.** Determining your capitalization ratio will enable you to design the most appropriate debt

service schedule for your needs. (All too often, investors do this in reverse—they figure out their mortgage first.) The most important issues when considering a mortgage are the term of the mortgage and the interest charged.

● **Leverage.** Leverage is the crucial link in a profitable real estate program. When used with discretion, borrowing can significantly expand your purchasing power.

Source: Allen Cymrot, president and CEO, Woodmont Realty Advisers, 1050 Ralston Ave., Belmont, CA 94002.

out a way to manage it. For owners of single homes or properties consisting of only a few units, the solution is usually easy—perform all the management activities themselves. For owners of larger units, however, delegating some or all of the manager's responsibilities to others is a much more practical solution.

Whether you manage a property yourself or turn over the responsibility to someone else, learn the essential elements of rental property management.

● **Marketing.** Renting apartments requires you to match the services of a unit (i.e., location, life-style, amenities and cost) to the needs of your prospective tenants. The first step is to develop and maintain a current rate schedule for the property by keeping abreast of market conditions for comparable rental units. Additionally, pay attention to the number of vacant units nearby and the concessions being granted by your competition.

The purpose of the market survey is to estimate the demand for particular types of rental units. Beyond knowing what your competition is up to, sound estimates of rental demand allow you to project the number of units that could be rented and the number left vacant at each of a series of different rental rates.

● **The value of vacancies.** Remember that "vacancy" is not a bad word. Apartments are like any other commodity—there are trade-offs between increasing rental rates and decreasing the occupancy rate. To achieve the greatest economic returns may mean less than 100% occupancy. Any property manager with 100% occupancy is probably charging too little for the apartments.

Rent reviews should coincide with changes in your area's economic activity and housing conditions. For example, to maximize profits in a rapidly growing economy with a shortage of housing, you should shorten the period between rent reviews. On the other hand, when supply and demand for housing change relatively infrequently, 12 months or more may be a sufficient interval between reviews.

● **Advertising.** You may want to maintain a certain degree of similarity among tenants in your rental units, e.g., single adults, young couples with children, retired couples, white-collar workers or students. The best advertising is usually geared to the individual traits of the group you've targeted. The three best forms of advertising are classified newspaper ads, word-of-mouth referrals and a sign in front of the property. As a general rule, if you have trouble renting a unit to at least one out of five eligible prospects, there is probably something wrong with the rental rate, advertising technique or condition of the property.

● **Leasing.** A successful marketing and advertising program will usually attract several prospective tenants. The next step is to carefully screen each applicant by using a lease application form and a required deposit. These have a double advantage: You should be able to screen out most of the nonserious prospects, and you will have additional information with which to evaluate your prospective tenant.

Four major criteria to use in evaluating a tenant:

● **Income level.** The household's monthly income should be approximately three times as large as the rent.

● **Employment record.** This indicates a tenant's employment stability, responsibility and willingness to cooperate with other people.

● **Credit references.**

● **References** from the tenant's previous landlords.

On the lease, directly state the attributes required of tenants living in the property. Be careful: As an owner, you must guard against any violation of a tenant's civil rights. It is fair to evaluate tenants on the basis of income level and household size. It's illegal to judge on the basis of race, color, religion, national origin or gender.

Don't try to rent an apartment without a written lease. Comprehensive leases address issues not specifically covered by the general body of law. The most important of these issues are delinquent rents, eviction procedures, property damage and repairs and abandoned personal property.

● **Repair and collection policies.** To protect your property against damages, use a "move-in, move-out condition agreement." New tenants should note all the major defects in an apartment (such as damaged or broken mirrors, appliances, etc.) in the agreement when they first move in. Refer to the same agreement, when the tenant moves out, to assess the condition of the unit and to determine who should bear the cost of repair. As an owner, expect to bear the cost of normal wear and tear—your tenants are liable for damages in excess of that amount.

A fair but firm collection policy reduces payment problems. For late rent payments, you may want to institute a progressive "late fee" for each delinquent day. Talk to the tenant immediately, send statements of overdue rent two days after the rental due date and follow the statement by a "final" notice shortly thereafter. If you don't get satisfactory payment, then begin eviction proceedings after more than two weeks. Municipal and provincial laws on this subject differ across the country. Check your local bylaws.

● **Tenant relations.** Sound tenant relations are crucial to the successful operation of a rental property. Poor communication between tenants and management can result in false expectations, misunderstandings and conflict.

> " **Poor communication between tenants and management can result in false expectations, misunderstandings and conflict. One study found that more than 70% of the lawsuits initiated by management were related to delinquent or nonpayment of rents; ... of tenant-initiated lawsuits, 62% concerned security deposit refunds.** "

One study found that more than 70% of the lawsuits initiated by management were related to delinquent or nonpayment of rents; 14% were due to destruction of property; and 11% were due to tenants moving out before the leases expired. Of tenant-initiated lawsuits, 62% concerned security deposit refunds; 33% were due to conflicts over maintenance and repair problems; and 5% involved charges of discrimination.

● **Personnel/Management.** If you have a large operation you can't manage by yourself, hire employees who have adequate technical skills and, almost as important, an ability to get along with you and the tenants. Before you hire, make sure that employees clearly understand their assigned duties and responsibilities, conditions of employment, working hours, vacation days and sick leave.

● **Physical care of the property.** Taking proper care of the premises prolongs its economic life and provides tenants with clean and secure facilities. The manager's responsibility is to authorize the amount, timing and type of operating and repair expenditures.

The best maintenance and repair arrangements will depend on the size of your operation. For large complexes, an on-site maintenance person is preferred. If there are fewer than 80 to 100 units, agreements with repair and maintenance firms should suffice.

● **Record keeping.** Any good record-keeping system includes a detailed account of all operating income and expenses relating to each property, as well as maintenance and repair records, employee activities and tenant information. Most small rental operations (fewer than 15 to 20 units) can use a simple journal of receipts and expenditures. Beyond that size, a simple-entry "pegboard" system works well. Computerized systems usually are not economically feasible until several dozen units are under management.

Source: Dr. Arthur L. Wright, economist, the Real Estate Center, Texas A&M University.

Real Estate Appraisers: Making the Right Choice

Today's prudent real estate owner can no longer rely on information from traditional sources such as friends or neighbors to determine the value of a piece of property. Brokers, while helpful, are still concerned with the marketing of real estate (that is, finding buyers), rather than tracking the sale of every single property in every single marketplace.

The best way to determine the value of a property is by using a professional appraiser. For a flat fee that ranges widely, depending on the type of real estate being appraised, an appraiser will compute the "fair market value" of a piece of property. There are many different types of appraisals available (examples include litigation, financial and relocation appraisals). Depending on which one you require, fees can range from $200 to $350 for a single-family home, condominium or town house. Appraisals for commercial or industrial properties are based on a percentage on the value of the property in question. Most appraisers rely on a study of comparable transactions in your particular geographic region to arrive at that value.

HOW TO PROTECT YOURSELF FROM YOUR BROKER

People who invest in real estate directly will find that a good relationship with a broker is probably the most important link to a potentially rewarding investment. For most busy investors, an experienced broker will serve as the primary source of leads and insights into a particular real estate market.

Here are a few general guidelines to follow to ensure a successful relationship with your broker:

● **Make sure that the communication** with the broker goes both ways. He or she should have a clear picture of your needs and objectives.

● **Be straight about your financial situation**—a good broker will always keep it in confidence. If a broker is misled about your investment ability, he or she will probably not be as willing to work for you.

● **Always be ready** to inspect a property at a moment's notice. In real estate, timing is often everything. Failure to investigate an opportunity when it presents itself can mean lost income for you and lead a broker to think you aren't serious about investing.

● **After you inspect a property,** communicate your reaction clearly—both positives and negatives. By the second inspection, everyone concerned with the buying decision should have seen the property and voiced their opinions.

● **Don't be afraid** to rely on the broker to guide you when making an offer. An initial offer that is too low can give owners a bad picture of your intentions and may cause them to dismiss you as a potential buyer. It's always wise to have a second offer ready, should the first one be rejected.

Remember: Try to keep the negotiations from stalling. Alternatively, if your price is accepted, be ready to move quickly to consummate the deal.

A knowledgeable broker will keep you up-to-date on market conditions and suggest the best times to sell a property for the greatest gain. He can also put you in touch with other investors who might be interested in structuring a partnership. Brokers should be able to help you get financing for additional purchases and provide guidance in such areas as tax considerations, property maintenance and zoning restrictions or variances.

How to Spot a Bad Broker

Tip-offs that indicate you're dealing with a bad broker:

● **The broker does not reveal** major defects or impediments of a property.

● **The broker does not bring to your attention** changes in price or terms.

● **The broker is slow** in conveying a seller's response to your offer. (You may lose the sale in the meantime.)

● **The broker wastes your time** by calling about properties he or she should know you have no interest in or are out of your price range.

● **The broker misleads you** by indicating there are other offers for a property—in effect pressuring you to make an offer when there is really no other immediate interest.

Source: *Austin K. Haldenstein, formerly a consultant to Douglas Elliman Gibbons & Ives, one of Manhattan's oldest and largest residential real estate firms.*

Finding an Appraiser

Financial institutions are a good place to start your search for an appraiser, since most standard real estate loan applications require a property's appraisal. This category of institutions includes commercial banks and mortgage brokers. Attorneys and real estate brokers are also excellent sources. Alternatively, you can go to the Appraisal Institute of Canada's website (www.aicanada.org) and click on "find an appraiser" to locate one in your city or province.

Like many other service occupations, the range in expertise and professionalism among appraisers varies enormously. Be careful in your selection—thousands of dollars can hinge on an appraiser's opinion of value. *The following should aid you in your choice:*

● **The type of property being appraised.** The first questions you ask a prospective appraiser should be about his or her experience, expertise and reputation for appraising the type of property in which you are interested. To check an appraiser's experience, begin with references. *Don't be satisfied with just a list of names:* Call the references, find out the types of property appraised and the ultimate accuracy of the appraisals.

● **The appraiser's credentials.** Founded in 1938, the Appraisal Institute of Canada (AIC) is the national society of professional real estate appraisers. Members of this association generally have a very high level of training that includes economics, product knowledge, financial matters and property law. The AIC grants the use of two separate designations: The CRA (Canadian Residential Appraiser) denotes members qualified in the appraisal and valuation of individual, undeveloped residential dwelling sites and dwellings containing not more than four self-contained family housing units. The AACI (Accredited Appraiser Canadian Institute) denotes fully accredited membership in the institute and may

Figures to Check Before a Real Estate Closing

● **Monthly payments.**
● **Per diem figures** for utilities, taxes and/or interest.
● **The broker's commission.**
● **The rent, security deposits** and/or interest on deposits that have not as yet been transferred.
● **A charge for utility bills already paid.**
● **A charge for loan fees already paid.**
● **A contractor, attorney, appraiser** or some other party to the contract who has not been paid.

be used by the holder for the appraisal of a full range of real property. Be sure to ask your appraiser in advance if they have either of these credentials.

● **The appraiser's database.** When interviewing an appraiser, find out about methodology: Where does he or she get sales information regarding comparable property? How does the appraiser make use of information regarding comparable transactions? What are the dates of the sales? What was the market climate during the time the comparable properties were available? What are the current trends in your particular marketplace? Is it a buyer's or a seller's market?

In today's real estate market, the difference between making a killing and taking a bath can depend on knowing what your real estate property is actually worth at the time you buy it and at the time you sell. Getting the right appraiser will help ensure that you don't make an expensive mistake.

Sources: *Sheldon F. Good, president, and Steven L. Good, vice president/general counsel, Sheldon F. Good & Company, 333 W. Wacker Dr., Chicago, IL 60606. One of Chicago's largest commercial, industrial and investment real estate brokerage firms, the company also has subsidiaries throughout North America, including in New York, Denver and Toronto.*

Reducing Real Estate Tax by Challenging Assessments

Effective real estate tax is tax rate multiplied by assessed value. There is not much an individual can do about tax rate, but assessment can often be challenged successfully. *Requirements:* The owner must show either that the property is overvalued or that the assessment is higher than on comparable property in the same area.

When to ask for reduction:

● **Just before making necessary repairs** of damages or deterioration that has lowered the value of the property.

● **Local tax records err** in description by overstating the size or income.

● **Net income drops** due to factors beyond the owner's control.

● **When the price paid** for the building in an arm's-length transaction is lower than the assessed value.

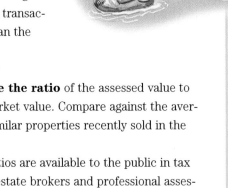

What to do:

● **Determine the ratio** of the assessed value to the present market value. Compare against the average ratios of similar properties recently sold in the same area.

Sources: Ratios are available to the public in tax districts. Real estate brokers and professional assessors can also be consulted.

● **Check tax records** for a description of the property and income.

● **Consult a lawyer** on the strength of the case, find out whether it can be handled by informal talk with an assessor, how much it will cost if a formal proceeding or if an appeal is necessary.

Read This 2X in Real Estate Contracts

● **"Mother Hubbard" clause.** It is important to have a true description of the property being conveyed. Sometimes there is more than one description of the property because it consists of several tracts of land. There may also be rights to travel over and use adjoining property. To cover the situation, a clause may be added to the effect that the seller is conveying any and all property rights owned at a particular location.

● **Certificate of occupancy.** The buyer may ask for a current certificate of occupancy to be sure that the buildings are in compliance with local laws.

● **Flood areas.** If there is any doubt—have the seller warrant that the property is not located in a flood-prone area. (If it is in a flood-prone area, don't buy the property.)

● **Brokerage fees.** It is not cast in stone that either party to a sale must pay the cost of brokerage. This sum can be a wide-open topic for negotiation, and the contract can specify any division of responsibility for payment.

● **Inspection clause.** The purchaser may obtain the right to inspect the property at specified times. Often, the purchaser will negotiate the right to inspect 48 (or fewer) hours before closing, to be sure all is in proper order as indicated in the contract of sale.

● **Condition precedent.** The purchaser or seller may want a specific event to occur before the obligation becomes fixed. For example, a purchaser may want the town to approve a building of a new road before the contract binds him to the purchase. Likewise, a seller may require that before the purchaser's rights become fixed, there must be a third-party guarantee of the purchaser's payments under the contract.

● **Authorization.** If the purchaser is a corporation, partnership or a representative, the seller may want proof of his or her authority to close the transaction. The form of such proof should be determined by counsel.

● **Survey.** An accurate survey can be very expensive, and either party can be forced to absorb this expense. It is a point of negotiation.

● **Building permits.** The seller may be asked to make the sale conditional on the purchaser's obtaining necessary building permits within a specified period of time. The buyer may also pay a predetermined sum to have the seller put the sale at risk during the period.

- **Guarantee.** The seller may ask the purchaser to obtain a guarantee of payment by a financially sound and acceptable third party.

- **Risk of loss.** Damage to the property after signing of the contract but prior to the closing can be borne by either party. The seller can be obligated to restore the property or may be able to subtract its loss of value from the purchase price.

- **Title report.** Who pays for the title report is another item that is open for negotiation. The name of the title company that performs the work is also a matter for discussion.

- **Assignment.** A buyer may want the contract of sale to be assignable. The seller will have to agree that such a substitution can be made.

- **"As is" clause.** The seller may allow the purchaser ample time to inspect the property to determine whether it meets his or her investment needs. At that point, the seller may wish an "as is" clause, stating that he or she is not making any representations or warranties of any kind.

- **Zoning.** The seller may be asked to warrant the zoning applicable to the property. Proof may be in the form of a letter from the local zoning board showing the present applicable classification.

- **Encumbrances.** The title report will examine all the encumbrances on the property, such as mortgages, leases, easements and restrictions of use. How these items affect value is a matter for negotiation.

- **Title insurance.** The cost of title insurance is often a major cash expense at closing. Who pays for this insurance is an appropriate item for bargaining.

- **Time of essence.** Unless the contract states that time is of the essence, delays of the closing date by the buyer or the seller may be excused. This clause removes all doubt that the closing must be held on a specified date.

- **Purchaser or seller action.** Where either party allows the contract to be contingent on something the seller or purchaser must perform, there should be a clause to ensure compliance. Such a clause appears where zoning must be changed, plans must be drawn, tests must be made, inspections must be done or some other matter affecting the property needs to be taken care of before both parties are satisfied. Sometimes such actions can be on a "best efforts" basis.

Real Estate Binders Explained

Real estate binders are not necessary to hold deals together and can cause confusion. If they are detailed enough, they can be interpreted as contracts rather than agreements to try to reach a contract. If you feel you must sign a binder, be sure it includes a statement that it is only a binder and is not binding until the parties and their attorneys have agreed to a definitive contract. This rule may vary from province to province. Check with your attorney.

Source: Lawrence Kobrin, real estate attorney, New York.

- **Mortgage assumption.** If the purchaser is assuming an assignable mortgage on the property, the specifics should be detailed. The seller may want more money because the purchaser is obtaining financing below the rates currently available in the marketplace.

Source: How to Make Money in Real Estate, *Steven James Lee, Boardroom Books.*

Buying & Selling a House, Condo or Co-Op

14

Mortgage Basics You Should Know

If mortgages didn't exist, we'd have to invent them, or there would be no active housing market. Just think about it. If you had to pay full price to buy your first home, how long would it take to scrape the money together? Years. Perhaps decades. Perhaps never. Meanwhile, you'd be forced to live in a rented house or apartment—there'd be no alternative.

Basically, a mortgage is simply a personal loan with some wrinkles attached. As with all loans, you promise to repay over a certain time, with interest. But mortgages usually involve substantial sums and the lender seldom knows the borrower personally.

In most cases, the lender will be a large financial institution. So most lenders want more than your word (good though that may be) that the loan will be repaid. To provide that level of comfort, you must offer the lender something as security with a value that's at least equivalent to the loan itself, in case you fail to repay the borrowed money. Usually this security takes the form of the real estate—a house, condominium, cottage or other property—that you intend to buy with the mortgage money.

If you default on the loan, the lender may take possession of the property or take other legal action to recover the loan. That usually involves a procedure known as foreclosing, and it can be messy. It's not something either you or the mortgage lender ever wants to happen, but it does occasionally happen, when people overextend themselves by buying too much house for their budget.

A mortgage consists of two legal documents: The note specifies the amount of the loan, the repayment terms and other conditions of the agreement; the mortgage itself gives the lender a claim on the property if you default. The mortgage also outlines the lender's rights relating to the property, if there is a default.

When a mortgage agreement is completed and signed, a copy is filed with the provincial land registry office. This creates an official record that enables the lender to claim the property if you default, and gives the lender priority over other creditors who might also try to recover money they've lent you. Normally, in any such unhappy situation, your mortgage lender will be first in line to collect (unless you also happen to owe the Canada Customs and Revenue Agency as well).

The lender is responsible for registering a mortgage, but you're responsible for removing the registration once the loan is repaid. So when you pay off your mortgage, make sure you receive a discharge certificate from the lender and that you or your lawyer records the discharge of the debt on the title.

Strictly speaking, the legal definition of a mortgage in Canada depends on several factors. A mortgage registered in a land registry office carries different rights and obligations than one registered in a land titles office. Also, a mortgage registered in Quebec carries different connotations than one registered in another province. For our purposes, though, we'll operate on the assumption that a mortgage provides security to a lender in return for money used to purchase real property.

So much for the basics. Let's move on to what everyone needs to know to successfully play the mortgage game. Here is a quick introduction to mortgage terminology.

● **Amortization.** The period over which you agree to repay the principal amount of the loan, plus interest. The longer the amortization period, the smaller your regular payments. Let's say you borrowed $100,000: Over a 25-year amortization period, you'd make 300 payments to repay the entire amount with interest; over a 10-year amortization, you'd make only 120 payments, but each payment would be much larger. The normal amortization period is 25 years, but you can choose a shorter time if you want to pay off the mortgage faster and save interest costs.

● **Term.** The duration of your current mortgage contract. The term of a mortgage covers only a portion of the amortization period and usually runs from six months to five years, although 7- and 10-year terms (and even longer in a few cases) are now available. Think of your mortgage as a travel itinerary: the amortization is the length of the entire trip; the term is the amount of time it takes to complete one leg of the journey.

● **Principal.** The amount you borrow is called the principal. As you repay the loan over time, the amount of the principal declines.

● **Interest.** This is the price you pay for the privilege of using someone else's money. The interest rate is adjusted at the beginning of each new term and is usually expressed as an annual percentage rate.

● **Mortgage payment.** The amount you pay at regular intervals (usually monthly) to the lender. The amount of each payment usually includes interest and a portion of the principal, and may also include property taxes, which the lender then pays on your behalf.

● **Open and closed mortgages.** An open mortgage allows a borrower to pay off part or all of the principal at any time without penalty. With a closed mortgage, you may not be allowed to make any extra payments during the term. If you can make payments, you'll likely be hit with a penalty.

● **Equity.** When you first acquire a property, your down payment represents your equity in it. The money you borrow to pay for the property represents your debt. Initially, most of your mortgage payments consist of interest, so your debt and equity don't change much during the early years. But as time passes, your payments will include more principal and less interest, and your equity increases accordingly (as long as property values remain stable). Your equity will change with the current market value of your property. If the real estate market falls, your equity will fall as well, but not your outstanding debt. A rising real estate market will give you more equity in your home.

HOW MUCH HOUSE CAN YOU AFFORD?

When buying a house, the critical question always is: How much can you afford? Many people answer this question using simple rules, such as 25% of your income should be spent on housing, but these rules can be confusing and are not applicable to all situations. If you overestimate your ability to pay back a mortgage, you may find yourself living a substantially lower day-to-day lifestyle than you expected.

Ultimately, the amount of house you can afford will depend on your personal needs, desires and financial capabilities. The best approach to take when determining actual amounts is to write up a household budget for the first five years of home ownership. This should give you an honest picture of how much you will have available for housing expenses.

Include a determination of the savings you will have available for a down payment and closing costs. Also, be sure to use a reasonable projection for inflation and to make reasonable allowances for purchases of major consumer durables (automobiles, home furnishings, appliances) and for education—especially if you will have children entering college. If you use consumer credit for some purchases, include an estimated monthly payment in your budget.

If you do not currently own a home or are moving to a new area, get help estimating your housing expenses. Most realtors and home builders can provide you with appropriate estimates, particularly for real estate taxes and utilities. Allowances for property maintenance and repairs should be 1% to 2% of the purchase price of the home, unless you intend to purchase an older unit needing substantial work. To determine your estimated principal and interest payments, you will have to get an initial estimate of mortgage amounts. Most personal computers have built-in software with amortization tables that can help you in this process. If you don't have a computer, you can consult your local bank or buy a book of mortgage amortization tables at any bookstore.

Write up your personal budget in conjunction with a mortgage loan qualification form. (See the accompanying mortgage worksheet for an example.) A realtor or builder can provide you with estimates of closing fees, such as settlement charges and tax escrow, to complete the form.

Source: Robert J. Sheehan, vice president and a partner of the management and economics consulting firm Regis J. Sheehan and Associates, 1606 Wrightson Drive, McLean, VA 22101. He is also the author of How to Acquire Land, *a contributor to professional journals and a management/economics newsletter, and is widely quoted in the media.*

WORKSHEET FOR MORTGAGE LOAN QUALIFICATIONS

Name _____

Cost of property	**$ 200,000**				
Down payment	**50,000**	Down payment is	**25%**	Loan/Value	**75%**
Mortgage loan	**150,000**	Interest rate	**7%**	for	**300** months

1. Monthly housing expense to income ratio (Maximum is 25%)

Income	Per month	Housing expense	Per month	Ratio	
Gross normal	**$ 3,600**	Principal & interest	**$1050.62**	Housing expense	
Co-borrower	**1,600**	Mortgage insurance	**N/A**	÷	
Dividends		Real estate tax	**208.33**	Income	
Interest		Homeowners insurance	**30.80**		
Rental (net)		Association fee	**N/A**	**1,289.75**	**24.8%**
Other		Total housing expense		**5,200.00** =	**Ratio**
Total	**$ 5,200**	(Ratio purpose)	**$1,289.75**	**QUALIFIES**	

2. Monthly debt repayment to income ratio (Maximum is 33%)

Installment debts (6 months or longer)	Per month	
Revolving accounts	**$ 60.00**	
XYZ Bank	**150.00**	
Auto loan	**165.00**	
Total	**$ 375.00**	

Total housing expense + total monthly debt

Total monthly gross income

$$\frac{1{,}289.75 \; + \; 375.00}{5{,}200.00} = 32\%$$

QUALIFIES

3. Cash required for settlement

Liquid assets		Cash needs	
Sales contract present house	**$**	Contract sales price	**$ 200,000**
Less _____ % commission		Estimated settlement charges	**+ 3,400**
Less mortgage & liens		R. E. tax escrow & adjustment	**+ 2,500**
Less payoff of debts		Partial association fee	**+ N/A**
Plus savings	**55,000**	Less deposit	**− 5,000**
Plus other		Less this mortgage loan	**− 150,000**
Total liquid assets	**$ 55,000**	Total cash needs	**$ 50,900**
Net surplus/deficit	**$ 4,100**	**QUALIFIES**	

- **Mortgagor, mortgagee.** In return for a loan, you, the borrower, are giving the lender the mortgage, so you're the mortgagor. The lender is receiving the mortgage from you as the title holder, so it is called the mortgagee.

- **Dower rights.** Even if a spouse does not put money into a home, the law gives him or her the right to live in and share the property. These rights, called "dower rights," come into effect on the death of one spouse or on the sale of the property. To eliminate dower rights and avoid the possibility that one spouse will remain in a house or condominium after the other spouse defaults on a mortgage, lenders usually require both spouses to consent to a mortgage in writing, with the advice of a lawyer, even if the mortgage document refers to only one.

Source: The Canadian Mortgage Book, *by Gordon Pape with Bruce McDougall, published by Prentice Hall Canada.*

Taxes and Home Ownership

In a low-inflation environment, buying or building a home for investment purposes is especially attractive. But the tax advantages of home ownership still remain. Here are the pros and cons, from a tax standpoint, of owning a home.

Tax-Sheltered Growth

Your home is a tax shelter—probably the best one you'll ever own. There are several ways in which you and your heirs can profit from this.

- The government won't tax the capital gain you realize when the house is sold, no matter how large it is or how big your profit. As long as the house is your "principal residence," any capital gain is yours to keep. However, if you rent the home for a period of time (perhaps you get a temporary foreign posting), it will lose its principal residence status for that period.

- When you die, the house passes tax-free to your spouse or, if you do not have, to your heirs. Most

Way to Pay for Your Dream House

Renting out a room or an apartment in your expensive house offsets monthly payments and provides tax breaks for maintenance/repairs and depreciation.
Result: More money available for more house.

Source: Jay G. Baris, New York City attorney.

assets in an estate are subject to tax on capital gains when they pass to the next generation but the principal residence retains its exemption.

- If you need income when you get older and don't want to sell the house, you can apply for a "reverse mortgage" on the property. Proceeds from such a mortgage can be used to purchase an annuity. Since the loan is used for investment purposes, interest is tax-deductible. That deduction will usually more than offset any taxes which might otherwise be due on the annuity income. So, in effect, you are generating tax-free income by this process.

The tax advantages are great incentive to invest in a home. In fact, many Canadians discover that their own home is the best investment they've ever made. However, the real reason for home ownership should always be for the lifestyle benefits it brings. The tax savings should be secondary.

Source: Gordon Pape, author of **6 Steps to $1 Million**, *published by Prentice Hall Canada.*

Making Your Mortgage Tax-Deductible

Residential mortgages in Canada are generally not tax-deductible; however, there is a way to make the mortgage deductible that generally works in certain circumstances. The idea is that if you borrow money to make money, then the interest on your borrowed money is tax-deductible.

According to the federal government: "You can claim the following carrying charges and interest you paid to earn income from investments: most interest you pay on money you borrow, but generally only as long as you use it to earn investment income, including interest and dividends. However, if the only earnings your investment can produce are capital gains, you cannot claim the interest you paid."

There is debate as to whether stocks or mutual funds qualify, but the general consensus is yes.

Inspection Checklist Before Buying a House

It's a good idea to have an engineer check a house for major defects before buying. But buyers should examine the structure so that they can direct the engineer to report on specific details.

✓ **Start in the basement,** where defects are the most obvious. Check walls for inward bulge, cracks or crumbling mortar, fresh patches and high-water marks. Check floor for signs of leaks, seepage or damp odor. Look for a sump pump, indicating frequent flooding.

✓ **Use a pocketknife to probe for termites or decay.** If the knife goes in easily, the wood is rotten. Other danger signs on joists: marks of water seepage from kitchen or bathroom above; pulling away from supporting masonry; notches more than one-third into the joist for pipes. If joists are propped up, find out why.

✓ **Check basement pipes for corrosion.** Hot-water pipes should be copper, preferably insulated. Cold-water lines should be copper or plastic.

✓ **Check fuse box for power adequacy** (16 to 20 circuits with circuit breakers needed for an 8- to 12-room house).

✓ **Study house from outside for sag,** alignment of walls, missing mortar, broken bricks, cracks in walls. One tip-off to trouble: extra-wide mortar joint on the stair steps may show house is shifting.

✓ **Siding: Aluminum is a plus.** If it's wooden, look for peeling that shows walls hold too much moisture. If windowsills are freshly painted and the rest of the house is not, paint may be covering rot.

✓ **Check roof for broken/missing shingles,** tar paper bubbles, broken patches. Check metal sheathing around chimney and ventilators. They should be watertight and made of nonrusting material. Look for leaks or breaks in gutters. If possible, check attic for watermarks on underside of roof.

To make your mortgage essentially tax-deductible involves an exchange of assets. Simply put, sell your investment assets and convert them to cash. Pay whatever tax is generated (there may be a capital gain or a capital loss) and use the available cash to either reduce the amount you owe on your mortgage or pay it off completely. Then, arrange a replacement or fresh mortgage and use that money to buy back the investment you previously held—or perhaps some new ones.

With this mechanism, you end up still having a mortgage on your house and still owning the investments. The difference, though, is that you have borrowed money to earn investment income, making the interest you pay deductible. There are things to be aware of, such as the aforementioned capital gains, as well as prepayment penalties that may exist on your mortgage. Check into those issues first.

Source: House Rich: Your Home As Your Best Investment, by Howard Turk, published by Prentice Hall Canada.

Deducting Moving Expenses

The federal government offers a break in the home-buying process by giving you the ability to deduct moving expenses. Basically, you can deduct moving expenses if you move at least 40 kilometers closer to your workplace or post-secondary school than you were before. (Before doing this, however, make sure you seek advice from an accountant.)

Source: Home-Free: Everything You Need to Know About Buying and Selling a Home, by Howard Turk, published by Prentice Hall Canada.

Home Buyers' Plan

In 1992, Finance Minister Don Mazankowski unveiled a program that allowed Canadians to borrow money interest-free from his or her RRSP for the purchase of a home. Although this was only supposed to be a one-year program to stimulate the economy, it has since become a permanent part of the RRSP landscape and has been immensely popular. According to the Canada Mortgage and Housing Corporation (CMHC), in 1999, more than 109,000 plan users borrowed over $1 billion under the Home Buyers' Plan.

To be eligible, you must be a Canadian resident with an RRSP, you or your spouse cannot have owned a home within the past five years and the loan must be for a principal residence in Canada. The maximum withdrawal is $20,000 per person (that translates to $40,000 for a couple with RRSPs). The loan is repaid at a minimum rate of one-fifteenth of the amount withdrawn annually, starting in the second year after you make the withdrawal (although you may repay more than the minimum amount at any time).

The application procedure is very simple. This program has a minimum of red tape attached, at least on the application side. Ask for Form T1036, *Applying to Withdraw an Amount Under the Home Buyers' Plan*, at your district taxation office.

Source: Gordon Pape's 2002 Buyer's Guide to RRSPs, *by Gordon Pape and David Tafler, published by Prentice Hall Canada.*

Refinancing Your Home

A common mistake by home-owners: Many buy a home, make all the payments over a period of years and never tap the potential cash value, or equity, a home has built up over those years. Yet, as a large asset, a home can serve as a substantial borrowing base.

By refinancing your mortgage, you can realize the cash value of your home without selling it. *Example:* You built a home for $85,000 in 1976. Your present mortgage balance is $22,000, and your home is worth $195,000. Your borrowing base is approximately 80% of your $173,000 in equity, or $138,400.

There are several reasons for refinancing: Payment for university education, starting a new business, major improvements to your home, or an investment that might yield more than the interest expense associated with the loan. *However, there is also a disadvantage:* Steeper loan payments.

Source: William J. Roll, CPA, partner in the CPA firm Herring & Roll, PC, 41 South Fifth St., Sunbury, PA 17801. He is the author of several tax articles.

Home Ownership As an Investment

If you are buying a home now, you will want to get every bit of appreciation you can from your investment. This certainly won't be as easy as it was in the days when average home inflation hovered between 15% and 20%, but there are some basic points you can cover to ensure that your home gives you the highest possible return over the long run.

What If the New House Is a Lemon

If you're concerned about serious defects in your new home's systems and appliances, consider a home warranty. Many Canadians are already aware that comprehensive warranties are available on newly built homes—in fact, in some provinces, such as Ontario and British Columbia, they're mandatory. It's less commonly known, however, that warranties are also available for resale homes across Canada through a variety of companies and some banks. Keeping in mind that prices and coverage may vary depending on the carrier and your province of residence, this is an attractive option for prospective home buyers looking for some added peace of mind on their upcoming purchase.

● **Economic outlook.** The prospects for the local economy should be strong. A steady and/or rising rate of employment and increased income are good signs, since employment gains usually precede increases in land values.

● **Home prices.** Make sure average home prices in the area are not excessively high. If prices have escalated too much, future appreciation gains will be limited.

● **Structure.** Buy the type of structure most favored in the area. For instance, a six-bedroom house in a three-bedroom community is out of place and can be difficult to sell. As a second example, some areas have a high concentration of ranch homes, while others favor colonials.

● **Turnover.** Areas with a high turnover of homes are better than those with a lower turnover. Realtors are comfortable showing these homes, and market prices are easier to estimate.

● **VRM mortgages.** Consider a variable-rate mortgage (VRM). VRMs can be up to 150 basis points (1½%) less than fixed mortgages, and are usually much better for families who think they will be moving in the near term or for young families who can benefit from lower mortgage payments initially.

● **Renegotiate.** If you prefer a fixed-rate mortgage, don't hesitate to renegotiate if market rates decline 250 basis points. This is an especially good idea for retirees, who usually find fixed-rate instruments more appropriate for their incomes.

● **Newly developed areas.** Existing homes located near higher-priced new developments of similar structures usually offer quick appreciation. Most older units offer a price advantage over the new homes.

● **Length of mortgage.** Carefully consider the choice between 15- and 25-year mortgages. The total interest savings that comes from shorter amortization is considerable, but carries the cost of lost investment opportunities. However, if you are a disciplined saver and/or investor, it is best to use a long-term mortgage and make alternative investments. Remember, you can always make additional payments to reduce your mortgage balance. If you are like most, and have trouble saving, the shorter-term mortgage may be the better choice.

HOW TO BUY A HOUSE WITH NO MONEY DOWN

As real estate prices skyrocket in many areas, the concern of most hopeful buyers is, "How are we going to scrape together the down payment?" As hard as it is to believe, however, it's not only possible to buy property with no money down, it's not even that hard to do—provided you have the right fundamental information.

Note: No money down doesn't mean the seller receives no down payment. It means the down payment doesn't come from your pocket.

● **Paying the real estate agent.** If a seller uses a real estate agent on the sale, he or she is obligated to pay the agent's commission. At the average commission of 6%, that can involve a substantial sum of money. The sale of a $100,000 home, for example, would return to the agent at least $6,000.

Strategy: You, the buyer, pay the commission, but not up front. You approach the agent and offer a deal. Instead of immediate payment, suggest that the agent lend you part of the commission. In return, you offer a personal note guaranteeing to pay the money at some future date, with interest. If you make it clear that the sale depends on such an arrangement,

the agent will probably go along with the plan. If the agent balks, be flexible. Negotiate a small monthly amount, perhaps with a balloon payment at the end. You then subtract the agent's commission from the expected down payment.

● **Assuming the seller's debts.** Let's say, as so often happens, that the seller is under financial pressure with overwhelming outstanding obligations. *Strategy:* With the seller's cooperation, contact all his or her creditors and explain that you, not the seller, are going to make good on the outstanding debts. In some cases, the relieved creditors will either extend the due dates, or, if you can come up with some cash, they'll likely agree to a discount. Deduct the face amount of the debts you'll be assuming, pocketing any discounts from the down payment.

● **Prepaid rent.** Sometimes you, the buyer, are in no rush to move in and the seller would like more time to find a new place to live—but you'd both like to close as soon as possible. Or, if it's a multi-apartment building and the seller lives there, he or she may want more time in the apartment. *Strategy:* Offer to let the seller remain

- **School system.** Look for areas with good school systems, even if you don't have young children. When it comes time to sell, your home will be more attractive to high-income households.
- **Bond issues.** If you do not have any children, avoid townships that are undergoing a rapid increase in the number of school-age children. Taxes will rise where there is a need for large bond issues for schools or other services.
- **Home equity.** Learn how to use your home as a source for short-term credit or long-term cash needs. Financial institutions have established loan programs that allow qualified individuals to borrow against the equity established in their homes. Another development is using the asset base of a house to provide retirement benefits.

Source: Richard E. Mount, formerly senior economist, Merrill Lynch Economics.

Best Time to Go House Hunting

Save your house hunting for the off-season. During an August heat wave or a snowy winter weekend, you may be the only prospect out there. *Result:* An anxious owner may offer a better deal.

in the house or apartment, setting a fixed date for vacating. Then, instead of the seller's paying the buyer a monthly rent, you subtract from the down payment the full amount of the rent for the entire time the seller will be living there.

- **Satisfying the seller's needs.** During conversations with the seller, you learn that he or she must buy some appliances and furniture for a home he or she is moving into. *Strategy:* Offer to buy those things—using credit cards or store credit to delay payment—and deduct the lump sum from the down payment.
- **Using rent and deposits.** If it's a multi-apartment building, you can use the rent from tenants to cover part of the down payment. *Strategy:* Generally, if you close on the first of the month, you are entitled to all rent normally due from tenants for that month. Therefore, you can collect the rent and apply the sum toward the down payment.
- **Using balloon down payments.** Arrange to give part of the down payment immediately and the rest in one or several balloon payments at later, fixed dates. *Strategy:* This technique gives

you breathing room to: (1) Search for the rest of the down payment and/or (2) improve the property and put it back on the market for a quick profit.

Caution: This move can be risky if you don't make sure you have a fall-back source of cash in the event that time runs out.

- **Using talent, not cash.** In some cases you may be able to trade some of your personal resources if you are in a business or have a hobby through which you can provide services useful to the seller in lieu of cash. *Strategy:* Trading services for cash is, among other things, very tax-wise. Many working people can provide services in exchange for down payment cash. *Most obvious:* Dentists, lawyers, accountants. *Less obvious:* Carpenters, artists, wholesalers, entertainers, gardeners. Note, however, that bartering produces taxable income, and taxes have to be paid on the value of such services.
- **Raising the price, lowering the terms.** Best applied when the seller is more interested in the price than in the terms of the deal. *Strategy:* By playing with the numbers, you might find that

you save a considerable sum of money if you agree to a higher price in return for a lower—or even no—down payment.

- **High monthly down payments.** If you have high cash flow, this could be a persuasive tactic to delay immediate payment. *Strategy:* A seller may be more interested in steady cash flow after the sale than in money up front. An anxious seller might bite at this offer because he or she can get the full amount from payments rather than negotiating the price, starting at the down payment. It also offers you the prospect of turning around and quickly selling the property—since you aren't tying up ready cash.
- **Splitting the property.** If the property contains a separate sellable element, plan to sell off that element and apply the proceeds to the down payment. *Strategy:* A portion of the land may be sold separately. Or there may be antiques that are sellable—the proceeds of which can be applied to the down payment.

Source: Robert G. Allen, real estate insider and author of the best-seller, **Nothing Down for the 90's**. He's also publisher of the monthly newsletter **The Real Estate Adviser**.

Buying & Selling a House, Condo or Co-op

Avoid Vacation Time-Sharing Traps

Some owners of time-shares in beach and ski-area condominiums are becoming disenchanted. They find that committing themselves to the same dates at the same resort every year is too restricting, or that they overpaid. *To avoid problems:*

● **Locate one of the companies** that act as brokers for swapping time-shares for owners of resort properties in different areas.

● **Don't pay more than 10 times** the going rate for a good hotel or apartment rental in the same area at the same time of year.

● **Get in early on a new complex.** Builders can usually sell the first few apartments for less.

● **Choose a one- or two-bedroom unit.** Smaller or larger ones are harder to swap or sell.

● **Deal with experienced developers** who have worked out maintenance and management problems.

● **Pick a time in the peak season.** It will be far more negotiable.

● **Look for properties** that are protected by zoning or geography.

● **Beware of resorts** that are hard to reach or are too far off the beaten track. Your time-share will be harder to rent, swap or sell.

What to Ask a Seller

● **Is the house built on a landfill?** If it is, it may be settling and may continue to sink, causing cracks in the plaster and creating more serious, recurrent structural problems.

● **Is the foundation's exterior** surface sealed and waterproofed?

● **What's the R factor** (the ability to resist heat flow) of the insulation? *Good ratings:* R 22 for ceilings, R 13 for exterior walls. *For colder climates:* R 19 and R 38.

● **Are windows insulated or double-glazed?**

● **Has the house been protected** against termites? Look or ask for written proof from a pest-control firm.

● **What is under the wall-to-wall carpeting?** Concrete, vinyl, another carpet?

● **If the house is in a rural area,** ask if the waste system is hooked up to a sewer system?

● **What is the inside diameter** of the water pipes? *Acceptable:* 1.2 centimeters for feeders, 1.9 centimeters for main runs.

● **Are major appliances and heating and cooling units** on separate electrical circuits?

The Worst Mistake That People Make When Buying a Home

The biggest mistake people make when buying a house (or any type of real estate) is securing the wrong kind of financing. This puts them in a very risky position and can end up costing thousands of extra dollars over the life of the mortgage.

Fixed vs. Variable Rates

Many people seeking a new mortgage choose a variable-rate mortgage (VRM). The interest on the loan fluctuates with the market, although overall monthly payments are fixed for the term of the mortgage.

Problem: Interest rates are bound to increase sometime over the life of the mortgage, so the interest portion of the payments also will rise. A VRM, therefore, puts all of the financial risk on the borrower. Fixed-rate loans, on the other hand, put the risk on the lender.

A VRM is fine if you plan to hold the property for four years or less—the interest rate probably will not vary too much in four years. But if you plan to own the home for a greater length of time, you may want to take out a fixed-rate mortgage (FRM). *Reason:* Although the interest rate on an FRM may start out higher, it does not change. You always know the interest and principal portion of your payment.

If you decide against an FRM initially, make sure that your VRM is convertible. This provision lets you change your VRM to an FRM within five years of the loan's inception (the time limits may vary depending on the lender, so check the details). Converting the loan puts the risk back on the lender.

Assumable Mortgages

An even better way to finance your home is to assume the seller's loan. *Benefits:*

● **A lower interest rate,** depending on the applicable rates when the mortgage was last renewed.

● **There is no credit qualification** necessary on most mortgages.

● **Shorter closing time**—only a few days, versus at least 60 to 90 days for conventional mortgages.

● **The loan will be assumable** when you decide to sell, making it more appealing to prospective buyers.

Problem: Some conventional mortgages contain a due-on-sale clause and are non-assumable. Those mortgages that are assumable may require a credit check and have additional fees.

Source: *Andrew James McLean, real estate investor and author of a number of real estate books, including* Investing in Real Estate, *John Wiley & Sons.*

Radon and Selling or Buying a House

Radon pollution has been found to be much more widespread than anyone previously believed. Its presence may affect home values and the pocketbook of any unwary homeowner. In many areas, a radon inspection—or proof that the house has been checked for radon—has become as commonplace as an ordinary prepurchase structural inspection.

Implications for Sellers

Take the initiative to have your home tested. If you discover unsafe radon concentrations, you can usually remedy the problem easily and cheaply. It is better for you to eliminate the headache before a prospective buyer discovers it during a structural examination—and either refuses to buy or gains a powerful bargaining chip.

The cost for an effective "do-it-yourself" kit is minimal—and it can be found in retail stores that sell building, hardware or health care products. Test kits consisting of charcoal canisters cost about $15–$30, including the analysis. Two canisters are used. One is placed in a living area, and the other is placed as close as possible to any suspected infiltration point in the lowest level of the structure. The canisters are exposed to the ambient air for a period of days and then forwarded to a laboratory

> " **Interest rates are bound to increase sometime over the life of the mortgage, so the interest portion of the payments also will rise. A VRM, therefore, puts all of the financial risk on the borrower.** "

for analysis. The cost of the analysis is included in the cost of the canisters.

There is no need for a professional to conduct the radon monitoring unless you need results immediately. Instant readout equipment is expensive, and you may pay a fairly stiff fee.

Buyers' Caution

Be cautious when buying a home in a high-risk area, or a home that was once found to have high levels of radon. Remember, the seller had control over the placement of the detectors. Tests using sophisticated equipment would probably be justified. Some warranty from the seller would be in order. Even if the problem was eliminated, it is a good idea to retest every two or three years.

Dealing With Radon

If you discover radon in significant concentrations, the problem is usually easily resolved. Radon is an invisible, odorless radioactive gas that seeps up through the ground and can enter a home through gaps in the walls and foundation slabs, or as a gas dissolved in seeping ground water. In modern, heavily insulated homes, the gas may be trapped and concentrated. Simply sealing the sources of infiltration—cracks in basement floors and walls, gaps around pipes, etc.—and waterproofing the basement may be all that's needed. In extreme cases, it may be necessary to install a ventilation system under the foundation slab to let the gas escape into the outside air.

Source: *John G. Rossi, president, John G. Rossi P.E., P.C., an engineering consulting firm specializing in home and building inspection services, Box 147, Canton, NY 13617.*

Finding the Perfect Mortgage

Getting the perfect mortgage for your home, co-op, condo, second home, ski lodge, etc., can be greatly simplified if you follow a few basic guidelines.

● **First, take the time** to find out about the wide variety of possible financing plans available to you (fixed rate, adjustable, graduated payment, balloon, etc.). Each type of loan is tailored to a specific set of personal needs and expectations. Carefully consider your long-range and short-range goals and your current financial status. It's better to have an idea of which type of mortgage you may be interested in before you start speaking to loan officers.

● **Next, shop the loan thoroughly.** Whether you do this through ads or word of mouth, your goal should be to come up with a list of the most competitive lending institutions. A possible alternative is to let a mortgage broker locate the best lending institution for your particular loan. Mortgage brokers track hundreds of different mortgage products from a variety of lending institutions. Some mortgage brokers charge a fee; others are paid by banks.

● **When shopping for the best loan,** contact each bank's main mortgage department first. Executives at branches are sometimes not as up-to-date on the latest mortgage information. Also, do your research quickly—mortgage components can change often. Ask for a simple statement that clarifies the details of any prospective financing package for both parties. Remember, it is required that all usual closing costs (title insurance, legal fees, appraisal fee, credit agency fee, etc.) be clearly spelled out before you receive a mortgage commitment. Your objective at this stage should be to avoid last-minute surprises.

Don't expect many concessions from a bank on your mortgage-financing package. Unless you are a customer who has substantial accounts with the bank, you will probably not be able to negotiate the terms of the loan.

● **Mortgage processing takes time.** If a full credit package is required by your lender, expect a delay of approximately three to four weeks to verify all of the information supplied in your application. You can speed up the process by providing the bank with accurate information as quickly as possible.

The problem with processing delays is that the competitive rate that attracted you in the first place to a particular bank may no longer be available. Ensure that your contract with the seller gives you ample time to have your mortgage application approved. Or you could face higher interest rates than you initially anticipated if your commitment for a mortgage expires before you are prepared to close.

As a rule, if a full credit package is required, you'll need a minimum of two to four weeks.

Source: Jane E. Greenstein, founder and president of Mortgage Clearing House, 1510 Jericho Turnpike, New Hyde Park, NY 11040, a division of The Seldin Organization, Inc.

Nonbanking Sources of Mortgage Financing

Most of us associate obtaining mortgage financing with commercial banks and trust companies. But these don't have to be your only source. There is a wide variety of alternatives you can turn to for help. *Here is a list of the best:*

● **Mortgage banking companies.** Mortgage banking companies originate mortgages and, in turn, sell them to institutional investors. In the past, mortgage bankers specialized in federal government-insured loans. However, as a result of the significant growth in the secondary market for all types of conventional mortgages, mortgage bankers have become very aggressive in the area of non-government-insured loans as well. Many mortgage bankers work directly with real estate agents, so that would probably be your best place to start your search. They are also listed in the Yellow Pages under mortgages or mortgage banking. A significant number of mortgage banking firms are actually subsidiaries of commercial banks.

● **Insurance companies.** Also increasing their involvement in the direct origination of residential mortgage loans, insurance companies were formerly a major force in the origination of single-family mortgages, but opted for secondary mortgage market instruments and other investments. For the time being, only the major insurance companies are likely to be a direct source of financing. Check with your insurance agent for prospects.

● **Credit unions.** Possibly your cheapest source of mortgage financing. There may be a credit union where you work—if not, you can usually join one with little difficulty. Credit unions are becoming more and more popular with a larger cross section of the population. They have spread beyond private firms and public agencies to include more broadly based social and fraternal organizations.

● **Home builders.** In many cases, home builders are a source of mortgage financing for the homes they are selling. Some of their sources are traditional lenders, such as banks. However, some of the larger builders have their own mortgage banking subsidiaries, while some large, medium and even small builders pool their mortgages and sell them directly into the secondary mortgage markets or through investment houses that have specific financing programs for builders. You can also find realtors that will participate in financing programs through investment houses and organizations that originate, sell and service mortgage loans.

● **Relatives and private individuals.** Relatives may not be able to provide you with the entire amount of the mortgage, but often can help with the down payment or a second mortgage to reduce the amount of your first mortgage. Relatives and people you know may accept lower rates of interest than an institution because the rate of return is still higher than many of the investments they can make otherwise.

Professionals such as doctors and lawyers often seek investment opportunities in mortgage financing, providing below-market interest rates as a way of deferring income. In return, they generally require a portion of the rights to the future appreciation of the home. If you pursue mortgage financing from an individual investor, it's smart to hire a lawyer.

● **Home sellers.** Cheap and readily available financing can be arranged with the seller of a home. Many will have an

QUALIFYING FOR A HOME LOAN WHEN YOU'RE SELF-EMPLOYED

If you are self-employed, qualifying for a home loan may be a little more difficult than if you were a salaried employee. Mortgage lenders generally require much more detailed income verifications, tax returns and company financial data (if you are a business owner). The specific requirements and documentation vary from lender to lender, but there are several basic criteria used by most in determining whether a self-employed individual can qualify for a loan.

The Requirements

Lenders usually require you to have been in business for at least two years. Self-employed individuals with less than two to three years of business operation do not have a long enough track record to convince lenders of their ability to pay off a mortgage.

Documentation is crucial. All lenders require the following documents: (1) copies of your notice of assessment from Canada Customs and Revenue for the past two years;

(2) a year-to-date financial statement signed by you or your accountant, plus a balance sheet; (3) if the business is a partnership—the partnership agreement and partnership tax returns for the last two years or, if a wholly owned corporation—the last two years' corporate tax returns; and (4) all information regarding your share in the business, major assets and debts.

The most important item to most lenders is your adjusted gross income figure as it appears on the business income portion of your tax return. But, don't worry if your gross income figure shows a loss. You may still qualify for a loan. Lenders usually allow certain items to be added back to that figure for purposes of evaluating a loan applicant, including RRSP contributions, pension or annuity, dividends and nontaxable deductions, plus some depletion and depreciation allowances, the non-taxed portion of some long-term gains, certain real estate depreciation and certain amortization.

Source: Ted L. Lyon, formerly a branch manager, Merrill Lynch Realty, 3115 W. Parker Rd., Suite 500, Plano, TX 75023. Recipient of the Merrill Lynch Society of Excellence Award and director of the Texas Association of Realtors, he has taught marketing and finance and has been a speaker for the Institute of Financial Education of Realtor/Lender Relations.

assumable mortgage with a lower interest rate than is currently available. The major problem with assumable mortgages is that they can require a large down payment if there is a substantial difference between the sales price and the remaining amount of the mortgage. You will also be required to contact the lender to determine if there are any special requirements or fees associated with assumption of the loan.

Home sellers may be willing to finance a prime mortgage or a second mortgage if you cannot obtain a large enough prime mortgage through a lender. Sellers most often interested in this type of arrangement are people who are anxious to sell; may be moving to a cheaper home and want to spread their profit over a long period of time; or, if they are older, may be seeking a steady stream of retirement income.

A seller may also provide a purchase-money mortgage. For example, the seller gives you a mortgage with a term to maturity of, say, 10 years. The monthly payments, however, are based on a 25-year loan. At the end of the loan term, you will be required to negotiate a new loan or find new financing.

> "Don't get caught up in processing delays. When interest rates are rising, a delay in the processing plan of a loan can cost you no matter who is at fault."

Source: *Robert J. Sheehan, vice president and partner, Regis J. Sheehan & Associates, management and economic consultants, 1606 Wrightson Dr., McLean, VA 22101. He has had over 25 years' experience in management and market research in construction and housing. He is a former staff vice president of National Association of Homebuilders.*

Hidden Mortgage Hazards

The increasing complexity of mortgages can leave a home buyer frustrated, confused and even angry about negotiations with a lending institution. Yet much of this emotional turmoil can be eliminated if the borrower avoids focusing on interest rates alone and instead looks at the full range of elements in a mortgage program.

Understanding Mortgage Programs

● **Two major insurers.** In Canada, only Canada Housing and Mortgage Corporation (CMHC) and General Electric Mortgage Insurance (GEMI) offer mortgage insurance programs. They insure a lender against a loss if a borrower defaults on the mortgage and the lender is forced to foreclose. For a down payment less than 25% of the total mortgage, the insurance is mandated by financial regulatory agencies.

● **Other fees.** Lenders may charge for document preparation, tax servicing, appraisal, credit reporting, overnight mailing, flood certification, attorney's fees and funding fees. There may also be a fee for locking in the interest rate.

● **When the interest rate is set.** Your interest rate can be set at the time of application, at the time of commitment or prior to settlement.

● **How long the rate is set.** The interest rate you are quoted during loan negotiations will be available only for a specified period, varying from 7 to 120 days. It is important that you keep the period in line with your closing date. For example, if your closing is scheduled for 60 days from the application date, an interest rate set for 45 days won't have an effect on the rate you actually receive. If rates suddenly turn up and your rate is not set, you could get stuck with much higher interest payments than first planned.

Don't get caught up in processing delays. When interest rates are rising, a delay in processing a loan can cost you no matter who is at fault. To avoid paying for delays, follow up continuously. Document phone calls, noting the date, time, content of the call and to whom you spoke. Make sure your employer sends the employee verification, ask the lender if the verification is acceptable, or what else is needed to submit the loan to the underwriter. Your loan processor will probably tell you that everything is fine. Do not accept this answer. Be specific. If everything is fine, ask when it will be submitted for approval.

The following checklist will help you track the nine common items that the lender will need to complete processing.

1. Employment verification.
2. Bank account balance verification.
3. Loan balance verification.
4. Credit report.
5. Appraisal.

6. Title report.

7. Wood infestation report.

8. Well water test certification.

9. With less than a 25% down payment, approval from a mortgage insurance company.

● **Amortization.** Monthly mortgage payments cover principal and interest—the amount of principal reduction is known as the amortization (positive amortization). A lender may offer a program with a lower than normal monthly payment in the first year or two. This loan may defer interest until a later time, resulting in the smaller monthly payment for the first year. The interest that is deferred is added to the balance of the principal and paid off gradually over the life of the loan. This is known as negative amortization.

Negative amortization can permit a borrower to obtain a loan and house he or she otherwise could not afford. But negative amortization is not recommended unless you expect your income to rise to cover the higher monthly payments in the second and subsequent years.

Variable Mortgage Loans

The foregoing elements are common to all loans. Variable mortgage loans (VMLs), however, require borrowers to look at even more complex factors.

● **The rate.** A VML is usually based on the bank rate set by the federal government. This leaves the rate out of the direct control of the lender. When choosing this type of mortgage loan, it's always a good idea to track the rate yourself (using the newspaper, Internet, etc.) to ensure that you know what you're paying in interest and principal.

● **The market's performance.** As the market moves, so does your mortgage interest rate—if the index goes up by 1.25%, your interest rate rises by the same percentage.

● **Margins.** Many mortgage interest rates are expressed as a percentage over and under the prime lending rate. For instance, if prime is at 8% and a lender has a margin of 2.5%, then the home buyer will receive a 10.5% interest rate.

● **Teaser rate.** A lender may offer a borrower a below-market (discounted) rate for the first year of a loan. The undiscounted rate is the sum of the current market rate plus or minus the margin. Confusion about the teaser rate can arise if the borrower

---

QUESTIONS TO ASK BEFORE SIGNING MORTGAGE PAPERS

Because it is such a long-term contract, conditions that may seem minor when signing a mortgage loan contract can end up costing a lot of money during the life of the agreement. *Some typical mortgage clauses to negotiate before signing:*

● **Prepayment penalties:** Sometimes as much as six months' interest or a percentage of the balance due on the principal at the time the loan is paid off. With mortgages running for 25 years, the chances of paying them off early are relatively high.

● **"Due on encumbrance" clause:** Makes the first mortgage immediately due in full if property is pledged as security on any other loan, including second mortgages. Not legal in some places and usually not enforced when it is legal. Request its deletion.

● **"Due on sale" clauses:** Require full payment of loan when the property is sold.

● **Escrow payment:** The popular practice of requiring a prorated share of local taxes with each monthly mortgage payment. The bank earns interest on the escrow funds throughout the year and only pays it out when taxes are due. Amounts to forced savings with no interest. Have your lawyer check the province's law to see if interest on escrow-account money is due to you. If not, try to eliminate escrow—pay taxes and insurance on your own.

Source: The Consumer's Guide to Banks, *by Gordon L. Weil, Stein & Day.*

does not understand that the rate is for one year only, and the rate the second year will be higher even if the market remains at the same level.

Your decision about a loan should be based on the undiscounted rate as well as the teaser. To calculate the actual rate, find out the current value of the market rate. Add or subtract the margin. If you are comparing two loan programs that give the same total, but one offers a teaser rate, you may decide to take advantage, even if it is only for one year.

● **Caps.** Some variable mortgage loans have "caps" or limits on increases and decreases. These protect borrowers if rates go through the roof. If you pick a program with a teaser rate, you should make sure that the cap applies to both the monthly payment rate (the starting discounted rate) and the note rate (for determining your future rates).

● **Convertibility.** In the event that interest rates come down, some VMLs are convertible into fixed-rate mortgages at specified times. This is an attractive option enabling you to lock in a future rate without extensive refinancing costs. Some convertibility options require some restrictions and additional fees.

Sources: Deborah Pape; and Charles A. Breinig, formerly a mortgage analyst, Mortgage Reporting Service, Inc., and now an associate broker with Weichert Realtors in Jenkintown, PA. Breinig is the author of, and lectures on, How to Comparison Shop for a Mortgage.

Variable-Rate Mortgage vs. Fixed-Rate Mortgage

Choosing between a variable-rate mortgage and a fixed-rate mortgage requires a risk/benefit decision by the individual borrower. Many elements involved affect each home buyer differently.

Affordability

Fixed-rate mortgages are more expensive than variable-rate mortgages, because the lender takes on the risk of a possible future increase in interest rates. With a variable-rate mortgage, on the other hand, the borrower assumes that risk in exchange for a lower initial interest rate.

By choosing a $5\frac{1}{2}\%$ variable-rate mortgage over a $7\frac{1}{2}\%$ fixed-rate mortgage, for example, you can increase your purchasing power by almost 20%. Assuming interest rates don't rise (making your variable-rate mortgage more costly over time), that could mean buying a $130,800 house versus a $110,000 house for the same monthly payments.

Alternatively, the advantage of a fixed-rate mortgage is that you know exactly how much you will have to pay in principal and interest over time. This can offer a sense of security to people who are concerned about future interest-rate hikes. In this case, the security of knowing exactly what your rate is outweighs the benefit of the potential savings of a variable-rate mortgage. However, the extra cost of a fixed-rate mortgage may force a buyer to settle for a smaller house or less desirable neighborhood.

Looking Forward

While your overall monthly mortgage payments remain the same with a variable-rate mortgage, the interest and principal amounts will rise and fall according to the market. If interest rates suddenly swing upward, the amortization of your mortgage could be longer than you planned for. Conversely, if rates drop drastically, you'll find yourself paying off the mortgage loan quicker than you anticipated. The end result in both cases means that it's impossible to plan exactly just how long you'll need to pay your mortgage off. If that doesn't sit well with you, you may want to consider a fixed-rate mortgage.

Keep in mind, however, that fixed-rate mortgages also require you to think about the future. Before you take on the mortgage, consider the costs involved in refinancing should interest rates drop and you want to get out of a mortgage that has become very expensive.

Do you plan on living in your home for a long or short period of time? Lenders charge a premium for fixed-rate mortgages because of the risk of increases in interest rates; the longer the term of the mortgage, the more difficult it is to predict interest rate fluctuations—and the greater the risk that interest rates will rise to the point where the loan is not producing an adequate return for the lender.

Don't pay a premium for the ability to keep a fixed-rate loan for a long term such as 10 or 20 years if you plan to sell your home in 3 to 5 years, either because of a job transfer or because the home is a "starter home." In this situation, a shorter term would be more appropriate. When making your decision, however, consider the following:

As a rule, a $150,000 mortgage (25-year amortization) at 7% interest requires your minimum earnings to be approximately $55,000* (combined family income). If you're thinking of opting for a fixed-rate mortgage with a shorter term, such as one year, how would you handle an increase in interest rates? If interest rates rose to 8% after that year, your monthly payments for principal and interest would increase to $1,144.82. At 9%, they would rise to $1,241.97.

*Calculation: (Allow 28% of income to pay for mortgage)

$55,000 ÷ 12 = $4,583		Monthly income
x 28%		Allowance
$ 1,283.24		
$1,050.62		*Principal & interest*
200.00		*Real estate taxes*
+ 30.00		*Insurance*
$ 1,280.62		*Monthly payment*

The Best Deal

After you've decided which type of loan is best for you, always shop around for the best rate. Rates between different lenders can vary widely. Rates on the same type of mortgage loan can differ by as much as two percentage points. Remember that even a small interest rate savings can mean a significant savings on your overall mortgage payments. For example, the difference between 8% and 7¼% (a ¾% reduction in the interest rate) on a 25-year, $100,000 mortgage would save you over $14,000 over the life of the mortgage.

Don't rely solely on your real estate agent for advice on the best rates. Real estate agents work with only a handful of mortgage solicitors who provide them with rate quotations on a weekly basis. You may be able to find a better bargain elsewhere. The real estate agent has been hired by the seller to sell a house and cannot be expected to spend his or her time finding you the best deal.

Sources: *Deborah Pape; and Charles A. Breinig, formerly a mortgage analyst, Mortgage Reporting Service, Inc., and now an associate broker with Weichert Realtors in Jenkintown, PA. He is the author of, and lectures on,* How to Comparison Shop for a Mortgage.

> " **After you've decided which type of loan is best for you, always shop around for the best rate.** "

When It Pays to Remortgage

If you bought your home in the past few years, you may now be able to save a bundle by refinancing your mortgage.

How Refinancing Works

If you have a $100,000 25-year mortgage at 10%, your monthly payment is $894.49. If you refinance at 7½%, your payment will plummet to $731.55. *Monthly saving:* $162.94.

Even if the drop in interest rates is smaller, you can still benefit. *Example:* If the same $100,000 loan dropped from 10% to 9%, you would still save $66.51 per month, which adds up to almost $35,000 over 25 years.

What to Choose

Best deal: Shorter mortgages. Many banks offer loans that can be paid off in as few as 15 years. Don't let the sound of that scare you. Monthly payments are not that much higher.

Installments on a $100,000 mortgage at 8% would look like this:

Mortgage length	Monthly payment
15 years	**$948.15**
20 years	**$828.36**
25 years	**$763.21**

Bottom line: The difference between payments on a 15-year and a 25-year mortgage is just $184.94/month, and you save nearly $58,000 over the life of the loan.

Source: *David Schechner, real estate lawyer, Schechner and Targan, 80 Main St., West Orange, NJ 07052.*

New Opportunities (and Traps) in Second Mortgages

Second mortgages are an increasingly flexible and attractive means of raising fairly large amounts of money.

Traditional second mortgages are exactly what they sound like: a second loan taken using your property as security while the first mortgage is still in place.

The sequence of a mortgage—first, second or third—depends on the date of its registration at the registry office. The first mortgage is the one that was registered first; the second mortgage, second; and so on. In case of default, the lender of the first mortgage has first claim on the proceeds from the sale of the property. If any money is left, it goes to the lender of the second mortgage. A lender assumes a greater risk in providing a second mortgage than a first mortgage and will usually charge a higher rate of interest to compensate for this additional risk.

You can get a second mortgage from a finance company, trust company or private investor. The mortgage will come with a short term of three years or less, and you can expect to pay an interest rate that's at least three percentage points higher than the prevailing rate on a first mortgage. Most lawyers, accountants and real estate professionals can introduce you to private investors interested in second mortgages. You can also find private investors through a mortgage broker. Before you commit to a second mortgage, you should always ask your lawyer to read the agreement.

In some cases, you may be required to submit your first-mortgage payments to the holder of the second mortgage. The second mortgagee then passes your payments along to the first mortgage holder. This reassures both lenders that you're keeping up with your payments. As an alternative, you may have to prove to the holder of the second mortgage that you've made your monthly payment to the first mortgage holder.

If the term of the second mortgage is longer than the term of the first mortgage, the second mortgage should include a paragraph called a postponement clause. This is a legal mechanism that lets you renew or replace your first mortgage without jeopardizing its position ahead of the second mortgage. It may

sound like a lot of technical mumbo-jumbo, but it's important. If you don't have a postponement clause in your second mortgage, you may have trouble renewing your first mortgage.

When you place a traditional second mortgage on your property, you receive a lump-sum cash payment for the amount of the loan. However, another varia-

Mortgage Scam

Fraud is increasing through phony notices of mortgage sales. Beware of notices from an unfamiliar bank or finance company saying that your bank has sold its mortgage—and requesting payments be sent to a new address. Send payments only if (1) your original bank also sends you a letter giving notice of the sale, the name of the new mortgage company, your outstanding balance and your account number; and (2) the new mortgage company confirms this information by sending you a book of payment slips with the same account number and the proper balance. *Helpful:* Call your old bank to double-check.

Source: *Real Estate Investment Digest.*

tion on the second mortgage concept has become more popular in recent years: The home equity line of credit.

Home Equity Credit Lines
When you use the equity in your home to secure a line of credit, you do not receive an up-front payment. Instead, you receive the ability to write cheques against the line of credit. That means you pay no interest until you actually tap into this resource.

Moreover, the interest rate on the credit line probably will be lower, possibly considerably lower, than it would be if the borrower had obtained an ordinary personal loan or a traditional second mortgage. Generally, the interest rate on a line of credit (because it is secured by residential real estate) is only slightly above the prime rate.

Second-Mortgage Risks
A borrower should be aware, however, of some of the dangers inherent in second mortgages. First of all,

the borrower is using his or her home to collateralize the loan. If for some reason the loan cannot be repaid as originally planned, there is the possibility that the house will be lost.

Considering this risk, a potential second-mortgage borrower should think carefully about what he or she plans to use the loan for. Is it prudent to put a lien on a home to take a vacation paid for by writing a cheque against a second-mortgage credit line?

When They Make Sense

Second mortgages have a very legitimate role to play and should be carefully considered, especially when large amounts of money are needed—paying for a child's education or an addition to a home, for example, or dealing with a large medical bill.

Potential second-mortgage borrowers should shop carefully. Different institutions offer substantially different kinds of second mortgages and a wide range of interest rates.

A critical element is the amount of money needed. Some lenders set relatively low limits, such as $20,000, while some will go several times higher.

Of course, the amount an individual can borrow under a second mortgage is limited by the equity he or she holds in the home. That is the appraised value of the property minus the amount owed under the first mortgage. The second mortgage allows the borrower to obtain cash for the increased value of his or her property and for the amount of principal already paid on the first mortgage. He or she thus can "unlock" the frozen cash equity in the home.

Some financial institutions will lend you up to 75% of the value of equity in your home, although most of them have a lower limit. Make inquiries.

Key Consideration

Is the loan fixed rate or variable rate? Usually, the initial interest rate on a fixed-rate traditional second mortgage is higher than it is on a variable-rate home equity line of credit. *Reason:* On a fixed-rate loan, the lender is assuming the risk of a rise in interest rates. Even if rates were to rise dramatically, the interest paid by a fixed-rate borrower remains unchanged. On a variable-rate mortgage, however, the borrower assumes this risk.

Therefore, an individual should consider the pur-

pose of the loan in deciding whether to opt for a rate that is fixed or variable. If the loan is for a long-term purpose, such as adding an extension to a home, it might be wise to take a fixed-rate loan through a conventional second mortgage, viewing the initial higher interest rate as a form of insurance against a sharp rise in interest rates in the future.

Warning: Check for prepayment penalties, and shop to see which lender's offer is least onerous.

Variable rates usually are better suited for loans that the borrower expects to pay off in a relatively short period. Loans used for investments could be expected to generate enough cash flow to at least keep up with sharply rising interest rates. Of course, interest payments on mortgage loans used for investment purposes are tax-deductible.

Beware of Balloons

Borrowers should also be careful about so-called "balloons." These are second mortgages that fall due within a few years, usually three to five. But the repayment schedule might have been calculated on a basis of up to 20 years. Thus, at the end of, say, five years, although very little might have been paid on the principal, the lender could demand immediate and full repayment. If that were to happen and the borrower could not raise the money, he or she might lose his or her home.

It is therefore essential that the contract have a clause requiring the borrower to renew the loan.

If your needs are special, many second-mortgage lenders will try to devise a program that is tailored to your requirements. For example, they might agree to postpone payments for a specified period of time.

Refinancing

An alternative to a second mortgage is refinancing a home. Conceivably, the holder of the first mortgage would be willing to write a new and bigger first mortgage on the home. The interest rate might be higher than that on the original mortgage, but the net cost might be lower.

In considering second mortgages, lines of credit, or refinancing an existing mortgage, look at all costs.

Sources: *Keith T. Gumbinger, HSH Associates, Butler, NJ 07405; www.hsh.com; and* The Canadian Mortgage Book, *by Gordon Pape with Bruce McDougall, published by Prentice Hall Canada.*

Home Renovations That Increase Value

Kitchens

Whether you plan a major kitchen renovation (incorporating an entirely new design) or a minor one (mostly cosmetic—refinishing cabinets, new countertops and a new appliance or two), the emphasis today is the same—new products and sophisticated design concepts. Energy-saving appliances and contemporary European styling are at the top of today's trend list. The following are other trends you may want to adopt in your renovation project.

● **Designer-look laminates** are very popular in many renovated kitchens, but wood is still holding its own as an accent element on counter edging, beams and trim treatments.

● **Colors** are an important selling factor. White, grays and light wood tones are the most popular. Dark woods and intense colors are losing favor.

● **Pay attention to lighting.** This is becoming an increasingly important factor in the appearance of a kitchen. Options range from high-tech fixtures that illuminate work areas to dimmer switches that provide a more subdued dining or entertaining atmosphere.

● **In great demand:** Open kitchens that are integrated into living areas. Some homeowners are taking walls out between kitchens and dining areas to achieve an open atmosphere.

In addition to providing energy savings, added convenience, style and enjoyment value, renovation can boost the resale value of your home. By completely remodeling the kitchen at a cost in the $6,700 to $22,000 range (with a typical cost of $15,000), you can expect to recover 50% to 80% of that expenditure in added value to your home if you sell it within five years.

Bathrooms

Most people have two choices when it comes to bathroom renovation—remodel an existing bathroom or add a new one. Additions often make the most economic sense, because houses with only a single bathroom are usually less salable. Adding a second bathroom at a cost of $4,400 to $10,000 (typically $6,000) can yield a cost recovery of 100% to 130% if you sell your home within five years.

If you decide to remodel an existing bathroom, use care. Total renovation is usually less costly than piecemeal replacement and repairs. But don't go overboard renovating a small or average bathroom— if you plan to sell your home shortly, it's probably not worth your while to spend a great deal of money. On the other hand, expanding an existing bathroom can add considerably to your home's market appeal, as can adding custom features. If your prime concern is resale, try using lighter, neutral colors and easy-care finishes when renovating.

In any case, don't compromise on quality. Brand names may be more expensive initially, but you are guaranteed that replacement parts will be available. Also, try to avoid major shifts in the location of the fixtures (sink, tub, toilet). This only adds unnecessarily large costs to your plumbing bill.

Windows, Doors and Skylights

Replace windows and doors that are not energy-efficient with ones that are. If you plan to keep your home awhile or want to sell at a higher price, make sure that your window and door replacements are attractive, too.

Important features to look for when replacing doors are richly carved wood doors with double locking devices, dead bolts and peepholes; windows should be double-glazed. Adding storm windows and doors are also a good investment.

Skylights are an increasingly popular source of natural lighting that can offer improved ventilation and a feeling of spaciousness. South-facing skylights are potential sources of passive solar heating. Almost any room with a roof directly over it is a candidate for at least one skylight.

Skylights are a great investment. Their short-term recovery rate is between 60% and 75%, and they are a strong selling point in both cold and warm climates. This is a household addition you shouldn't cut corners on, however. Top-quality units are easier to assemble and provide savings on installation and maintenance costs.

Fireplaces

Energy-efficient fireplaces are the remodeling project with the highest payback—sometimes offering homeowners up to a 130% return on their investment at the time they sell their home. The main reason for this is the low initial cost of fireplace renovation (normally less than $4,000) compared to other improvements. Another is the increased savings a homeowner enjoys with an energy-efficient unit compared to an open hearth.

Prefabricated units are attractive because of their space-saving features. The most popular models are only 90 centimeters wide and can be installed in corners to conserve on wall space. The current trend is toward top-quality models finished with floor-to-ceiling stonework, a mantel and a raised hearth. When you decide to buy, look at three or more different brands and types. And, of course, be sure to have whatever model you select properly installed.

Source: Henry F. Broesche, founder and president, Brighton Homes, Inc., 5450 NW Central Dr., Suite 250, Houston, TX 77092. He is a member and former president of the Home Owners Warranty Corp. and of the Greater Houston Builders Association.

Home-Improvement Mistakes to Avoid

Winter is a good time to turn dreams of adding a bedroom, kitchen or bath into reality. But that calls for shopping around, simple research and hard thinking before you convert your dream project into a contract to build.

The first rule in planning a home improvement is to make sure that you and your family will realize value from the project in convenience and pleasure right now—and that you can afford it right now.

First, shop around for the financing you might need. Tell your banker what you're thinking of doing, and ask for the rates and payment terms on second mortgages, home-equity loans or special home-renovation packages. And if you have a healthy business or personal account at the bank, see what kind of a rate you can get on a straight personal loan. Then, when you start talking with a contractor, you'll be able to compare any financing rates and terms he or she offers with those from other sources. Sometimes the contractor may do enough business with a bank to get lower rates than you can.

Follow the Rules

Once you and the contractor are in serious discussions, don't try to take shortcuts around local regulations. A qualified contractor will know local code standards and can obtain a building permit without delay and without hassle to you.

More and more local communities are licensing contractors. That gives you an opportunity to check them out. Call the local building inspector and ask whether he knows the contractor you're thinking of hiring and whether any complaints are pending. Chances are good that you'll get frank advice to look around further if the contractor has a record of faulty work.

Ask the contractor exactly how he plans to do the work. It's important that you have specific information on how long you will be without a working kitchen, or know how the contractor plans to protect your home if he or she has to open an outside wall. Let the contractor take you step by step through the method he or she will use so you'll know what preparations you will have to make—moving and storing furniture, making alternative living arrangements and the like.

Special precaution: When you're putting an addition on the house, be particularly careful about how the new plumbing lines are installed and protected. Contractors often fail to protect the lines from freezing temperatures. Once the walls and moldings are in place, leaks in these lines will be expensive to repair.

Make clear to the contractor that you expect the work site to be kept clean. Tell him or her that you expect workers to eat their meals in their cars or on trucks. ***Reason:*** Many homeowners find their homes infested with bugs and rodents after a major renovation because the workers dumped their leftover food in the wall spaces.

Good-Neighbor Policy

It usually pays to check your plans for a major renovation with your nearest neighbors before work starts. Put your project in the most positive light, but be alert to signs of opposition, and try to negotiate any differences. A compromise is very likely to be much cheaper than litigation.

Don't rush blindly into even simple projects such as widening a driveway or paving part of the backyard for a basketball court. Many communities restrict the number of cars that can be parked in the front yard, and most zoning codes have restrictions on covering more than a certain portion of the land, which includes the blacktop.

Be careful, too, about when you schedule the work. Most localities have rules about how early in the morning workers can start to use noisy equipment. Many resort communities prohibit major construction during the summer months.

Source: David Schechner, attorney and village counsel for South Orange, NJ, 80 Main St., West Orange, NJ 07052.

How to Hire the Best Home Contractor for You

Over the past 20 years, I have heard some horrible stories about unscrupulous contractors doing terrible things to homeowners.

As the number of home-improvement projects increases, some contractors find it easy to rip off people who have not had enough experience to know better.

A contractor is responsible for hiring others to install a new kitchen, add a new room or make major design changes. Here's how to hire the right one—and to make sure your interests are protected:

Sizing Up the Talent

● **Ask friends for recommendations.** Then get two to three references from each contractor.

Best: Visit at least one completed project as well as one project in progress. *Strategy:* Ask each contractor's former clients specific questions about his or her work and work style. *Key questions to ask:*

● **Was the job started on time?**

● **Did workers show up on time?**

● **Did they complete the job on time?**

● **Was the contractor always available?**

● **Did you get what you wanted?**

● **Were there any surprises?**

● **Was the contractor responsive** to problems after the job was completed?

● **What would you do differently** if you were hiring a contractor again?

Each of these questions is designed to yield critical information. Negative answers shouldn't necessarily rule out a contractor, but instead raise issues to discuss with him or her. *Example:* You may discover

that the contractor you like best isn't prompt about returning phone calls. By knowing this in advance, you can stress how important callbacks are to you and insist on a daily or weekly time to speak with him or her.

● **Interview the candidates you like in person.** Face-to-face meetings are always best, since you will be able to determine whether you are comfortable with the contractor. You don't want someone who looks impatient or seems reluctant to answer detailed questions.

Important: Before an interview with a contractor, put together a list of your general expected working rules. Give the list to the contractor so that he or she knows up front what you expect. *Example:* If you want to avoid having dirt tracked through your home, insist that the contractor bring his or her own portable toilet.

● **Ask each of the contractors you like for a bid on the project.** They should provide free job estimates that are typed, easy to understand and specific.

A good bid includes *start* and *completion* dates and pro-consumer clauses like daily working hours and promises to protect existing surfaces.

Important: Make sure there's no clause authorizing the substitution of materials without your written permission.

Making the Choice

If you find that all the contractors are great and all their bids are similarly priced, the answers to these questions may help you decide among them:

● **Does the contractor have a clean complaint record?** Call your local Better Business Bureau, which will provide a verbal or written report. More than one recent complaint is a red flag.

● **How many projects is the contractor working on right now?** If he or she is working on more than two or three projects at once, he or she may be hard to locate and is unlikely to spend much time at your job site.

● **Will the contractor give a warranty for the work for one year?** A written warranty should be part of the contract. All legitimate contractors will include one. A warranty is important because if something falls apart, it will usually happen within the first year. The warranty should state that the contractor will fix the problem within 10 days.

Before Signing the Contract

● **Ask for copies of all professional licenses and insurance documents**—including the contractor's driver's license, which confirms his identity. Without it, you can't be sure that the other licenses you request actually belong to that contractor.

Important: Make sure the contractor purchases a performance bond. It is bought through a surety company for about $100. A surety company provides a bond to the contractor for one year and pays the homeowner if the contractor skips out on the job. The performance bond covers the cost to complete the job if the contractor cannot for any reason.

Other important documents:

● **The contractor should have legible copies of the occupational license** from the city, as well as any other required licenses.

● **A subcontractor** should have the right licenses.

● **The contractor should have workers' compensation and liability insurance.** Request a certificate of insurance. If the contractor is a sole proprietor with no employees, confirm that he has personal insurance or workers' compensation.

PROTECTING YOURSELF IN HOME-IMPROVEMENT CONTRACTS

Improving a home has become more attractive than buying a new one for many people.

The key to protecting yourself when hiring a contractor for a major alteration is thoughtful contract negotiation. Even contractors with good reputations sometimes get in over their heads.

● **Try to do your own financing.** While some contractors get better rates from banks they deal with frequently, research the details. They may give the lender a second mortgage on your house—sometimes without your realizing it. That can leave you without leverage to force correction of bad workmanship.

● **Review the document from the contractor's insurance company** covering workers' compensation. A standard homeowners policy does not cover workers (except, in some provinces, an occasional baby-sitter).

● **Fix responsibility for repairing wind,** rain or fire damage, as well as possible vandalism at the work site.

● **Include a payment schedule in the contract.** Typically, a contractor gets 10% of the negotiated fee upon signing a contract, then partial payments at completion of each stage of succeeding work. You should withhold any payment until the contractor actually begins work. Then hold down succeeding payments as much as possible so that the contractor does not earn a profit until the work is completed.

● **Make sure the final payment** is contingent upon approval of the work by municipal inspectors.

● **Make the contractor responsible** for abiding by local building codes.

If you assume this responsibility, make the contract contingent on your ability to get all necessary building permits.

Be specific about what work you want done, how and with what materials.

● **Don't settle for normal contract language** about the project's being done in "a workmanlike manner," because homeowners' standards for work they want done is often higher than common trade practice.

● **To avoid misunderstandings,** refer in the contract to architect's drawings, where possible, and actual specifications.

● **Include a schedule** against which to measure the work's progress. Use calendar dates—for example, foundation and framing to be completed by March 1; roughing-in by April 1; sheetrock by May 1; woodwork and finish work by June 1.

● **Push for a penalty clause** if the work is completed unreasonably late—for example, all work to be completed by June 1. If, however, work is not completed by June 1, the contractor will pay the homeowner $100 a day thereafter.

If your contractor or the people he or she hires aren't properly insured, you're liable for any mishaps. Request a copy of the insurance documents, and call the agent to confirm coverage.

● **Set up a payment schedule.** A contractor is a businessperson; he or she will want as much in the form of a down payment as possible.

Ideal: You provide 10% of the project's total cost on the day work starts, not when the contract is signed. *Strategy:* Create a payment schedule pegged to specific work milestones. Be fair. But write the contract so that you withhold the final 10% to 15% until 20 days after the job is completed. That will give you time to see if everything was really done as you requested. Also, it will give the contractor an incentive to finish promptly. It's a bad sign if the contractor balks at this.

● **Make sure you're getting what you pay for.** Have the contract state that you'll have an opportunity to inspect all materials before they are used. *Example:* Consumers often get gouged on insulation jobs. Contractors frequently shortchange people on the amount of insulation that is required. *Solution:* Home-repair books or insulation packages can tell you how much you'll need based on the amount of space involved.

Important: Count the bags before the insulation is installed. Some contractors bring empty bags to fool people who count this way. If in doubt, ask the company to provide a density test.

Source: *Steve Gonzalez, a professional contractor in Fort Lauderdale, FL. He is the author of* Before You Hire a Contractor: A Construction Guidebook for Consumers, *Consumer Press.*

How Utility Meters Work

Both electric and gas meters operate on the same principle. Each has several dials with pointers that tell you how much of the utility you are using.

Electric meter:

● **It has five numbered dials** (older models have four). The pointers on three of the dials turn clockwise, while the two others go counterclockwise.

● **It is read from left to right.** The pointer always registers the number it has just passed. *Example:* If the pointer rests between three and four, read the number as three. This holds true even if the pointer is touching the four but has not gone past it.

● **The numbers** taken off each of the dials gives you the reading of the meter at that moment. When it is read again (usually in one- or two-month intervals), you know how many kilowatt-hours of electricity have been consumed.

● **Meters can be wrong.** Electric meters can wear out or be damaged during an electrical storm. A dramatic increase in your electric bill should signal a call to the utility company.

Gas meter:

● **It is read** exactly the same way as the electric meter. *Difference:* The gas meter has four dials. The pointers of two turn clockwise, while the two others go counterclockwise.

What You Should Know About Real Estate Agents

Knowing your legal rights and responsibilities when selling your home yourself or through a real estate broker can save you thousands of dollars—and a lot of worry and frustration over the possible wrong moves that you might make.

Selling your own home is not an easy task. You need to be able to provide buyers with information about zoning laws, community services and the condition of your home. Also, you have no security against intrusions by unqualified house hunters—curiosity seekers, potential thieves and the like.

If you decide to sell with a broker, shop around to find one who is knowledgeable about your community and with whom you feel comfortable.

The failure of sellers to read the legal documents pertaining to brokers' contracts is the cause of most misunderstandings.

Special points:

● **Commissions paid by the seller to the broker** are not established by any provincial or federal law agency or by any private trade association. The individual brokerages set their own fees. Some will negotiate a commission rate, others will not. The law does not require them to, however.

● **The listing agreement** is a legal document that outlines the understanding between you and the broker about how your home will be listed for sale. It includes your name, the broker's name, the address of the property, the asking price and other details about

Ways to List Your House

✔ **Open listing:** The owner reserves the right to sell the property him- or herself or to retain brokers.

✔ **Exclusive agency:** No other broker will be hired as long as the original broker is retained (usually for a specified period). It's up to the individual agent to market the property himself. Because this type of listing offers limited exposure of the home to potential buyers, it is very rarely used (usually less than 1% of the time).

✔ **Multiple listing:** Brokers combine to sell properties listed with any member of the brokers' pool. The listing broker offers to pay a portion of the commission to the selling broker.

　 This is the most common type of listing as it enables a home to receive the maximum exposure to potential buyers.

the home, as well as the amount of time you are giving the broker to find a buyer (30, 60 or 90 days is usual). This is a legal document, binding you to its provisions.

● **In an exclusive agency agreement,** the listing broker is authorized to market your property during the agreed-upon time period.

● **Buyers' cries of misrepresentation or fraud** are often heard these days. The seller has a duty to tell the broker about defects in the house that are known to the seller and that might affect a buyer's willingness to purchase the property. Knowing about such defects and not mentioning them invites a suit for misrepresentation or fraud. Honesty will save you fears and problems in the future.

● **Lawsuits against sellers and brokers** about other problems relating to a house and neighborhood are cropping up. Are you required or is your broker required to disclose that the land beneath the home was once a chemical waste dump, or that you were aware of plans for a sewage-treatment plant down the street? Those kinds of questions are still to be resolved by the courts, but the importance of full disclosure of what you do know is clear.

● **Signing a contract** and accepting a buyer's "earnest" money commit you to the sale—unless the buyer reneges and therefore forfeits the money, or some contingency to the sale negates the contract. If you've signed a contract and then refuse to follow through, you could face a lawsuit should the buyer want to initiate one. In any event, you may still be responsible for the broker's commission.

Source: *John R. Linton, former vice president, legal affairs, National Association of Realtors, and Laurie Janik, current general counsel for the NAR, 430 N. Michigan Ave., Chicago, IL 60611.*

Getting More for an Old House

An old house (built from 1920 to 1950) can be sold as easily as a new one. The right selling strategy and a few improvements may raise the selling price significantly. *Suggestions:*

● **Invest in a complete** cleaning, repainting or wallpapering. Recarpet or have the rugs and carpets professionally cleaned. *Approximate cost for a four-bedroom, three-bath house:* $2,500 to $3,000.

● **Get rid of cat and dog odors** that you may be used to but potential buyers will notice.

● **With the trend toward smaller families,** it may be desirable to convert and advertise a four-bedroom house as two bedrooms, library, and den.

● **The exterior of the house** is crucial. It's the first thing the buyer sees. Paint or replace shutters if necessary. Clean and repair the porch, and remove clutter. Repaint porch furniture.

● **Landscaping** makes a great difference and can sell (or un-sell) a house. Get expert advice on improving it. *Approximate cost:* $100 to $1,000.

● **Good real estate agents** are vital to a quick sale. There are one or two top people in every agency who will work hard to show houses and even arrange financing. Multiple listing lets these super salespeople from different agencies work for the seller.

Best Color to Paint a House?

In the United States, yellow houses sell faster than those of any other color. Most people associate yellow with optimism and warmth.

Source: *Leatrice Eiseman, color consultant and educator in Tarzana, CA*

Selling Your House in a Hot Real Estate Market

In a competitive real estate market, homeowners can get an edge over other home sellers with offers to finance the sale themselves. By offering financing, sellers may make their house so marketable that outside financing will be unnecessary. And the commission saving is substantial.

However, although financing the sale of a house is simple in principle, sellers should have the advice of a lawyer who specializes in real estate.

Two Types of Vendor Financing

● **Vendor-take-back mortgage.** Sometimes vendors will offer to help potential purchasers to buy their property by lending them a portion of the purchase price. This is called a vendor-take-back (VTB) mortgage, or purchase mortgage. Often, such a loan comes with favorable terms—after all, the seller is trying to sweeten the pot to encourage you to buy his or her piece of real estate. The loan may be open, for example, which means you can repay the principal at any time, without penalty. Or the lender may charge an interest rate lower than you'd pay the bank.

A VTB mortgage allows you to avoid a lot of red tape and administrative charges. For example, depending on the terms of the deal, you may not have to subject yourself to the kind of rigorous credit and income checks that a financial institution will demand before approving your mortgage.

Why would a vendor offer a loan to a purchaser? First, in a slow market, a VTB mortgage attracts potential buyers. On the other hand, if the property market is hot, you won't find many vendors who will offer to lend you money at favorable rates, unless their property is poorly located, derelict or shabby.

Buyers Who Back Out at the Last Minute

Selling a house can be a problem when the potential buyer makes the deal contingent on the sale of his or her own house. After months of waiting, your deal may fall through. *Solution:* Include a kick-out clause in the sales agreement. This enables the seller to keep the house on the market until the sale is completed. If another buyer makes an offer, the original buyer has 48 hours to decide whether he or she wants to buy the house or not.

Second, owners sometimes prefer the steady and consistent return of a mortgage secured by a familiar property to a riskier investment.

VTB mortgages can also be attractive to purchasers of investment properties. Normally, you can only get 60% to 70% mortgage on a rental property. But you may be able to work a deal in which the seller will finance the balance through a VTB mortgage, and then remain on in the house as a tenant. You get the house for little or nothing down, and you get a tenant who will likely take care of the place.

VTB mortgages take two forms:

● **First mortgage.** If you are trying to sell a $100,000 house that has no mortgage (a rarity), and the purchaser can afford only $40,000 cash down, then the purchaser simply gives you a first mortgage for $60,000, which is paid out over an agreed-upon period, at an agreed-upon interest rate. In case of default, you keep the cash and foreclose on the house.

● **Second mortgage.** If you are trying to sell the same $100,000 house with an existing $50,000 first mortgage, a second mortgage reduces the cash that a buyer would need. The purchaser assumes the first mortgage and gives you a $20,000 down payment. The purchaser then gives you a second mortgage for $30,000. Interest rate and maturity date are negotiable. But many existing first mortgages held by institutional lenders contain a due-on-sale clause, which prohibits the sale of the house without the consent of the lender. Typically, such consent is given only if the interest rate is increased.

If the VTB Mortgage Doesn't Fit the Need, Here's the Second Approach

● **Leasing with purchase option.** Lease payments may be applied to the purchase price, an amount agreed on when the deal is made. The best approach is to make the term as short as possible. Should another prospective buyer come along with ready cash, you won't be hindered by a long-term contract. And since you are still the owner, you can depreciate the house as a rental unit.

Source: *C. Gray Bethea, Jr., is a real estate lawyer in Atlanta, GA; and Gordon Pape and Bruce McDougall, authors of* The Canadian Mortgage Book, *published by Prentice Hall Canada.*

If the Seller Has a Change of Heart

Here's a scenario that took place in the United States: The seller of a house said he was canceling his contract to sell, and refunded the down payment. The buyer insisted the seller had no right to cancel. The seller argued that the buyer, by accepting and cashing the cheque, had agreed to cancellation of the sale. The court ruled for the buyer, and ordered the seller to perform the contract. The return of the down payment, the court said, had no legal effect. It was not a sum of money accepted in settlement of a dispute. It was the return of the buyer's money.

Source: *Merrill Lynch Realty v. Skinner, Ct. App., NY, 473 N.E. (2d) 229.*

Condos and Co-ops Defined

The terms *condominium* and *cooperative* are definitions of types of ownership.

● **In a condominium,** you actually own your unit—just as you do when you buy a house.

● **In a co-op,** you own stock in the building's corporation, which entitles you to the use of your unit.

In both types of residences, common areas such as lawns, gardens and pools are shared with other co-op residents.

Co-ops tend to be a bit more difficult to sell because of strong co-op boards that carefully scrutinize new buyers.

Condos and co-ops rarely compete for the same buyers in the same market. When they occasionally do, price differentials are most often determined by location, rather than by type of housing.

Source: *Robert Irwin, a Danville, CA, real-estate broker for more than 25 years. He is the author of more than 20 books about real estate.*

Condos vs. Co-ops

When you purchase a condominium, you own real property, just as when you buy a house. You arrange for your own mortgage with the bank, pay real estate taxes directly to the local government, pay water bills individually and have an individual deed.

When you buy a cooperative apartment, you are participating in a syndication. A corporation is formed, shares are issued and people subscribe to the shares. The corporation raises money, takes out a mortgage and owns the building.

Maintenance charges for a condominium can be anywhere from 30% to 50% of a cooperative's charges for an equivalent building. *Reason:* The maintenance on a condominium covers only the common area upkeep. *That includes:* labor, heating oil, repairs and maintenance of the playground, swimming pool and other community areas. Co-op maintenance fees cover those same items plus mortgage payments, local real estate taxes utility and water bills.

Capital improvements: If an extensive, major repair needs to be made (such as the replacement of a roof or boiler), the board of managers of a condo cannot borrow funds from a bank unless it receives the unanimous consent of the condo owners. *Problem:* If a dozen owners are content to live in a dilapidated building, improvements must be funded through maintenance cash flow, which may be very expensive. In a co-op, the board of directors can take out a second mortgage to fix a roof, plumbing or other major problem. Individual co-op shareholders cannot easily obstruct the board.

Exclusionary rights: Since a co-op is considered personal property, not real property, prospective tenants may be rejected by the co-op's board of directors for any reason whatsoever except race, creed, color, or national origin. *Reality:* As long as the co-op board members don't state the reason, anyone can be excluded for any cause. *Problem:* A tenant may have trouble subletting a co-op if the co-op board members don't approve of the new tenant. In a condominium, each owner has the right to sell or sublet to anyone the person wants, subject only to the condo's right of first refusal.

From the entrepreneur's point of view, a co-op can be more advantageous if the building at the time of the conversion date has a low-interest mortgage. *Reason:* When a building is converted into a condominium, it must be free and clear of all liens. In a co-op, the former financing can be kept intact.

Source: David Goldstick, former partner, Goldstick Weinberger, Feldman & Grossman, 261 Madison Ave., New York, NY 10016.

When Buying a New Condominium

Before signing any contract for a *new* condominium, which is harder to check out than an *established* condominium, buyers should study the prospectus for any of these pitfalls:

● **The prospectus includes** a plan of the unit you are buying, showing rooms of specific dimensions. But the plan omits closet space. *Result:* The living space you are buying is probably smaller than you think.

● **The prospectus includes this clause:** The interior design shall be substantially similar. *Result:* The developer is able to alter the size and the design of your unit.

● **The common charges** set forth in the prospectus are unrealistically low. Buyers should never rely on a developer's estimate of common charges. *Instead:* They should find out the charges at similarly functioning condominiums.

Common charges include: Electricity for hallways and outside areas, water, cleaning, garbage disposal, insurance for common areas, pool maintenance, groundskeeping, legal and accounting fees, reserves for future repairs.

● **Variation on the common-charge trap:** The developer is paying common charges on unsold units. But these charges are unrealistically low. *Reason:* The developer has either underinsured, underestimated the taxes due, omitted security expenses or failed to set up a reserve fund.

● **The prospectus includes this clause:** The seller will not be obligated to pay monthly charges for unsold units. *Result:* The owners of a partially occupied condominium have to pay for operating expenses.

● **The prospectus warns** about the seller's limited liability. But an unsuspecting buyer may still purchase a condominium unit on which back monthly charges are due, or even on which there's a lien for failure to pay back carrying charges.

● **The prospectus makes no mention** of parking spaces. *Result:* You must lease from the developer.

● **The prospectus is imprecise** about the total number of units to be built. *Result:* Facilities are inadequate for the number of residents.

● **The prospectus includes this clause:** Transfer of ownership (of the common property from the developer to the homeowners' association) will take place 60 days after the last unit is sold.

Trap: The developer deliberately does not sell one unit, continues to manage the condominium and awards sweetheart maintenance and operating contracts to his or her subcontractors.

● **The prospectus specifies** that the developer will become the property manager of the functioning condominium. But the language spelling out monthly common charges and management fees is imprecise. *Result:* The condo owners cannot control monthly charges and fees.

Source: Dorothy Tymon, author, The Condominium: A Guide for the Alert Buyer, *Golden-Lee Books.*

Your Financial Liability When You Sit on a Co-op or Condo Board

It's generally believed that you have "arrived" when you are asked to sit on a board of directors. This applies whether it is a corporation board, bank board, school board or condo or co-op board. However, along with the prestige goes a high level of responsibility and liability.

Whether you are on the board of directors for a profit-making corporation or a nonprofit organization, never underestimate your obligations. Many people who sit on nonprofit boards and who receive no compensation for their services have little understanding that their legal position is similar to that of someone on a corporate board. In fact, a nonprofit board member may even incur a higher degree of responsibility in the eyes of a court, because he or she is seen as holding a position of public trust.

The principles of corporate law are applied to most nonprofit boards. The would-be director of any nonprofit organization is therefore wise to check on the provincial or territorial law as to the category of directorship and the legal duties that accompany it.

The primary obligations of an individual on a co-op or condominium board are (1) to act within his or her authority, (2) to exercise "due care" and (3) to fulfill all fiduciary duties. A breach of any of these will result in the following kinds of liability of responsible directors, unless the law specifically exempts nonprofit corporations from statutory proceedings to enforce that liability.

1. If the directors of a co-op or condo do not act within the scope of their authority, a dissenting co-op member may be able to bring suit against the directors to enjoin them or set their action aside, or to render them liable for mismanagement.

2. By law, directors owe their co-op/condo associations a "duty of care." The legislative and judicial definition of this term is not clear as it applies to nonprofit boards. The definition for business corporations is that directors "discharge the duties of their respective positions in good faith and that degree of diligence and care and skill which ordinarily prudent men would exercise under similar circumstances in like positions." A duty of reasonable inquiry and reliance on information provided by others (corporate officers) is also encompassed by the corporate duty of care. The director is liable for dollar-for-dollar damages.

3. Failure to exercise one's fiduciary responsibilities can lead to suits in which a guilty director is liable for dollar-for-dollar damages.

As a fiduciary, a director may not disclose confidential information or use it for personal gain. If a director is ever in doubt about actions taken by management or the authenticity/accuracy of any or all information furnished, including financial, it is the director's obligation to make known his concern and receive appropriate documentation.

Apart from knowing the applicable law and performing well, what can co-op or condo board members do to protect themselves? Insist on coverage by directors and officers liability insurance.

Source: John M. Nash, president emeritus, National Association of Corporate Directors.

The Most Valuable Vacation Homes

For maximum resale value of a vacation home, purchase property on the water, with as much frontage as you can afford, a house that faces northwest (for best afternoon sunlight), mildly rolling terrain, a rustic exterior or a modern kitchen and bath.

Source: Money.

How You Can Save When Building Your Own Home

Much can be said for doing things right the first time, especially when it comes to building your own home. It may be financially helpful to cut corners, but make sure you cut the *right* corners. The very last thing you want is a shoddily constructed or designed home.

My advice is to treat the building of your home like any other business project. The two most important things you should do before building are to (1) hire a qualified general contractor, and (2) carefully plan your location, design and budget.

Using a General Contractor

Few people understand the actual number of day-to-day decisions that go into building a house—much less understand the local building rules and regulations. A good general contractor will procure the lowest-priced services, the desired quality, and guarantee the timely completion of your home. *Here are some criteria to use when you go about selecting a general contractor:*

- **Reputation and honesty.**
- **Financial capabilities.**
- **Communication skills.**
- **Business knowledge.**
- **Provision of a written warranty.**

Planning and Budgeting When You Decide to Build

The best way to ensure that your initial investment at least retains its value, but—more importantly—appreciates with time, is by selecting a good location and marketable design.

Buying & Selling a House, Condo or Co-op

501

WHEN IT'S TIME TO MOVE

Hiring a moving company should be approached the same way you would buy any other product or service—by becoming informed. A good way to start is by asking your friends which movers they've used. Contact the local Better Business Bureau and review all the literature provided to you by prospective moving companies.

If possible, try to select a mover six to eight weeks in advance of your ideal moving date to ensure availability. The peak season for movers is June, July, August and September. During these months, vans may be scarce and costs, higher. You can usually save money by moving between October 1 and April 30, when many movers offer lower, off-season prices.

It's a good idea to obtain estimates from at least two reputable movers. Determine all of their charges and the types of services they offer. Compare to see which mover best suits your needs and budget. Before reaching a final decision, pay a visit to the mover's place of business to get an indication of how professional the company is. Always look for (1) professional and business-like personnel, (2) clean and well-organized offices and warehouse and (3) equipment in good condition.

Getting Accurate Estimates

Unless you get binding estimates, most moving estimates are just educated guesses to help you anticipate your approximate moving expense. The final bill could be very different. To help movers calculate the most accurate estimate, show them every item to be moved. Try to reach a clear understanding about the amount of packing and other services you'll require—services that are not included in the estimate will be

added on to the final cost.

Moving costs are usually determined by the actual weight of your possessions or the amount of space they take up in the mover's van. Factored into this total is the distance your possessions are transported and the optional services provided.

Liability Options

Pay particular attention to the liability options. Moving companies usually offer a variety of liability plans:

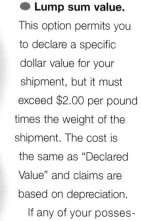

● **Released value plan.** You can seek recovery on an item at a specified rate of 60 cents per pound on long-distance moves, and 30 cents on local moves. The protection is minimal, but it costs nothing.

● **Declared value.** Under this option, the valuation of your shipment is based on the total weight times $2.00 per pound (although this amount may vary), and any damage or loss claim is settled based on depreciated value. Depending on the moving company, the cost can be anywhere from $4 to $7 for each $1,000 of liability.

● **Lump sum value.** This option permits you to declare a specific dollar value for your shipment, but it must exceed $2.00 per pound times the weight of the shipment. The cost is the same as "Declared Value" and claims are based on depreciation.

If any of your possessions are damaged or lost, it's always to your advantage to file a claim promptly—preferably in writing. The mover has 120 days after receipt of your letter to make an offer to settle the claim.

Try to plan your packing day one or two days before the actual loading of the van. To save on charges, you may want to pack part of your belongings yourself. Ask the moving company about its policy on liability for customer-packed cartons.

Source: Joseph M. Harrison, president, American Moving and Storage Association, 1611 Duke St., Alexandria, VA 22314, the trade association for the professional household-goods moving industry.

Although there are many decisions to consider, location should always be the first and foremost. *The main factors to consider:*

- **Travel time.**
- **Costs.**
- **Schools.**
- **Availability and accessibility of shopping in the immediate vicinity.**
- **Personal preference.**
- **Social and economic status of the neighborhood.**

The second most important decision that you will have to make concerns the design and the determination of the specific building requirements of that design. Carefully analyzing each room's size and utilization should help you eliminate or scale down little-used rooms or areas in the house, saving significant building and maintenance costs (e.g., heating and cooling).

Be sure to select a design that is marketable in the area you have chosen. In other words, avoid building a California-style home in Prince Edward Island. And remember, the design will have a large impact on the total cost of the house. *The major factors that you should consider:*

- **Two-story designs are the least expensive per square meter.**
- **Houses with one and a half stories are gaining in popularity,** especially those with first-floor master suites.
- **Ranches** (one-floor plans) are the most expensive per square meter, because the area between the foundation and the roof system is not maximized. It is always cheaper to build up than out.
- **Higher-pitched roofs are more expensive and more eye-appealing.**
- **Vaulted and cathedral ceilings are more expensive than flat ceilings.**

How to Choose Building Materials Wisely

Careful selection and specification of materials can save money without sacrificing quality. But be cautious—sometimes name brand choices can drive up costs and add only limited value. *Examples:* Name-brand plumbing fixtures are more expensive than contractor brands but usually no more effective.

High-fashion designs and colors increase costs and possibly date the home's appearance. Nationally advertised windows will add 25% to 30% more to window costs.

Pay attention to areas where short-term savings should be weighed against long-term operating and maintenance costs. *In particular, it is important to note the following:*

- **Energy-related items and equipment,** such as extra insulation, high-efficiency furnaces with less than a five-year payback, energy-efficient water-heating systems, add-on electric heat pumps for gas and oil heating systems.
- **Exterior siding selection:**

Material	Initial cost	Maintenance cost
brick	high	low
stone	high	low
wood	high	high
aluminum	low	low
stucco	low	low
hardboard	low	high

Lot Selection and Landscaping

A wooded lot can be very appealing as a place to live, but there are problems when it comes to building. The initial cost of a wooded lot is generally higher than for non-wooded lots.

Caution must be used to be sure that all of the trees on a wooded lot are not located where the house will be built. Clearing costs can run as high as several thousand dollars, and you can expect that construction equipment will lose some efficiency when operating in wooded lots, thereby adding more costs.

Landscaping expenses can be reduced by selecting small plants and trees that will grow rather than landscaping with fully grown stock, and by negotiating with the landscaping company on eliminating expensive guarantees for growth. This can reduce your total landscaping bill by as much as 25% to 35%. Also, if it is summer or early fall, seeding a lawn rather than sodding will reduce your lawn costs by 40% or more.

Source: Jim Sutliff, president and the owner of Sutliff Builders, Inc., a residential building company located at 3675 Africa Rd., Galena, OH 43201.